W4  /R

# Histories
## of the
# Hanged

# Histories
## of the
# Hanged

## The Dirty War in Kenya
## and the End of Empire

# David Anderson

W. W. NORTON & COMPANY
*New York • London*

Manufacturing by R. R. Donnelley, Harrisonburg Division

Library of Congress Cataloging-in-Publication Data

Anderson, David, 1957–
Histories of the hanged : the dirty war in Kenya and the end of
empire / David Anderson.— 1st American ed.
p. cm.—
Includes bibliographical references and index.
**ISBN 0-393-05986-3 (hardcover)**
1. Kenya—History—Mau Mau Emergency, 1952–1960. I. Title.
DT433.577.A53 2005
967.62'03—dc22
2004024804

W. W. Norton & Company, Inc.
500 Fifth Avenue, New York, N.Y. 10110
www.wwnorton.com

W. W. Norton & Company Ltd.
Castle House, 75/76 Wells Street, London W1T 3QT

1 2 3 4 5 6 7 8 9 0

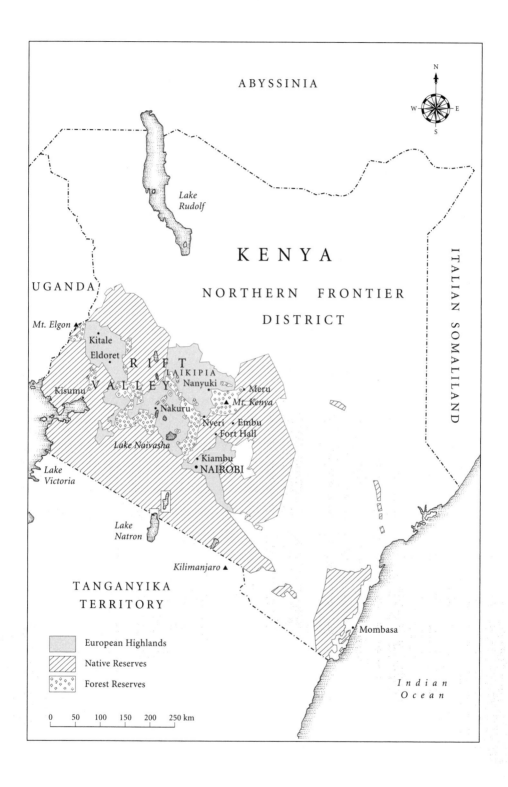

# Contents

# Maps and Tables

## Maps

## Tables

# Prologue
# The Hanged

Mau Mau. The very words conjure up memories of something evil lurking in history's dark shadows. Mau Mau was the great horror story of Britain's empire in the 1950s. The battle to suppress the revolt in Kenya was presented as a war between savagery and civilization, a rebellion made by men who could not cope with modernity, who reached back into a depraved, tribal past in an effort to stop the wheel of progress from turning. The principal chronicler of Kenya's white settler society, Elspeth Huxley, called Mau Mau 'the yell from the swamp';[1] and Robert Ruark, the American writer whose 1955 novel about the rebellion, *Something of Value*, remains the most widely read and best-known account of Mau Mau, warned his readers: 'To understand Africa you must understand a basic impulsive savagery that is greater than anything we civilized people have encountered in two centuries.'[2] His chilling adventure story was suffused with bloody, sadistic killing and seemingly senseless violence. For Ruark, as for many others since, 'impulsive savagery' was explanation enough.

It has always been easier to describe than to explain this seemingly aberrant revolt. Before Mau Mau, Kenya had an entirely different image. In the iconography of British imperial endeavour, it was the land of sunshine, gin slings and smiling, obedient servants, where the industrious white colonizer could enjoy a temperate life of peace and plenty in a tropical land. This was the 'white man's country', with its rolling, fertile highlands. Sturdy settler farmers had made their homes here, building a little piece of England in a foreign field. They brought order and prosperity. And they held a paternal view of the Africans whose land they had appropriated, and whose labour they depended upon. The bucolic romance of settler life in Kenya, portrayed most vividly by Karen Blixen, whose farm in Africa was set amid the Ngong hills, on the edge of Nairobi, was constructed around the myth of colonial racial harmony.[3] Blixen's Kenya was a place of benign white paternalism, and accepting black subservience. Mau Mau shattered this patronizing pretence in the most poignant, disturbing manner, as trusted servants turned on their masters and slaughtered them. It was 'a revolt of the domestic staff', wrote Graham Greene, 'it was as though Jeeves had taken to the jungle'.[4]

None of these colonial stereotypes of Kenya help much in understanding why the Mau Mau revolt happened when it did, and they are even less useful in explaining its peculiarly violent character. Yet they have dominated, in one way or another, all of the books written about the conflict over the last half-century.

This book tells the story in a different way, lacing the narrative of the war with the testimonies of those who fought on both sides. Using the court records of the hundreds of trials of captured rebels, it has been possible not only to portray the motives and violent actions of the Mau Mau fighters who made this rebellion, but also to map out the behaviour and deeds of the colonialists who so brutally, and at times so scandalously, suppressed it. It is a story of atrocity and excess on both sides, a dirty war from which no one emerged with much pride, and certainly no glory. It is an uncomfortable history, but it is a history that needs to be told.

On the face of it, armed rebellion seemed an unnecessary gamble in the endgame of empire. Kenya's explosion into struggle came just as the old European empires were running out of steam. By 1952, the year in which the Mau Mau 'emergency' began, the once mighty imperial powers were contracting. Britain had already given up India and Pakistan, and Palestine had been sacrificed for the establishment of the Jewish state. In South-east Asia, a guerrilla war was rumbling on against communist insurgents, but the British were already planning the hand-over of power, to a compliant, conservative Malay government, that would take place in 1956. Nationalism was on the march. Empires were in retreat. This was the new order of the post-war world.

In Africa, decolonization had been slower to get moving, to be sure, but Kwame Nkrumah had already become the first prime minister of the Gold Coast six months before Kenya's emergency began, and he would take his country proudly to independence in March 1957, long before the last of the Mau Mau fighters had surrendered. Sudan, Somalia, Sierra Leone and Nigeria would all achieve their freedom from British colonial rule, and the French even scuttled their empire in West Africa, while Kenyans still waited for political rights that would allow them to vote. Would not the 'winds of change blowing through Africa', so eloquently described to a disbelieving white South African audience in Cape Town by Prime Minister Harold Macmillan in March 1960, have swept Kenya towards freedom without a rebellion?

Those who took up arms against the British in Kenya didn't think so. They read the signs rather differently. Macmillan's famous Cape Town speech is usually remembered as heralding the new nations of Africa onto the world stage; but it was in fact intended as an attack on *apartheid*. South Africa's electorate had voted the National Party into power in 1948, instigating a programme of racialist social and economic policies that would entrench the supremacy of the white minority and condemn the black majority to a servile future of dispossession and inferiority. To the north, across the Limpopo river, white Rhodesians nurtured similar ambitions. The British had long ago given Europeans there a degree of self-government, and during 1951 it was agreed that settler-dominated Southern Rhodesia would be amalgamated into a federation with Northern Rhodesia and Nyasaland. Most African observers thought this nothing less than the creation of an enlarged white settler state. If African nationalism was on the march in Africa in the 1950s, so too was white power.

Kenya's white settlers cast envious glances towards Rhodesia and South Africa. They, too, hoped to promote an enlarged federation that would strengthen and steer the economies of the three East African territories – Kenya, Uganda and Tanganyika – with Europeans at the helm. And they worked hard to secure their own privileged political position, and, in the process, to suppress African advancement. In the years between 1945 and 1952, from the ending of the Second World War to the beginning of Kenya's rebellion against colonial rule, the white settlers vigorously campaigned against enhanced political representation for Africans, pushed themselves into key roles in the management of the colonial economy, and tightened their grip over local and municipal government. Some spoke admiringly of the achievements of the National Party in South Africa, of the security for all races to be found in 'separate development'. To African ears these were weasel words. The whites would take for themselves all the best land, and the other resources, and leave Africans the scraps.

That was how it had been in Kenya since 1902, when the first white settlers arrived, encouraged by a colonial governor, Sir Charles Eliot, who needed to find a way to pay for the railway that had been built from Mombasa to Lake Victoria. White capital, enterprise and energy would do the trick. Eliot thought that he did not have time to wait for Africans to come to commercial agriculture. White political and economic domination, the alienation of African lands, and the oppression of Africans as a poorly paid and exploited labouring class had all followed in short order. For fifty years the white minority ruled the roost in Kenya. Most of the white highlanders thought they would do so for another fifty years – and more, no doubt.

When it inevitably came, the rebellion began slowly, as rebellions often do, in a myriad of local struggles over the years following the

Second World War. It was not until October 1952 that the war properly got going, provoked by the British decision to declare a state of emergency and to move troops into the colony. When it finally came to an end, in January 1960, the revolt had lasted more than seven years. Three British prime ministers – first Churchill, then Eden, and finally Macmillan – had gnawed away at the problem, watching with growing concern as the measures adopted by the colonial government in Kenya became increasingly draconian and politically dangerous. Kenya's tragedy played itself out slowly and painfully, until, exasperated and embarrassed, Macmillan's government decided to wash its hands of the whole dirty business.

Contemporary accounts often cast it as a war against Kenya's white settlers, with the British government in the benevolent role of protector of the empire kith and kin. This misrepresents the character of the struggle. It was certainly a war fought against white power, but it never became the race war that some thought it to be. And there was nothing benevolent about Britain's ruthless prosecution of the war. Contrary to public perception, only thirty-two European settlers died in the rebellion, and there were fewer than two hundred casualties among the British regiments and police who served in Kenya over these years. Yet more than 1800 African civilians are known to have been murdered by Mau Mau, and many hundreds more to have disappeared, their bodies never found. Rebel losses were far greater than those suffered by the British security forces. The official figures set the total number of Mau Mau rebels killed in combat at 12,000, but the real figure is likely to have been more than 20,000.

Much of the struggle tore through the African communities themselves, an internecine war waged between rebels and so-called 'loyalists' – Africans who took the side of the government and opposed Mau Mau. This was partly brought about by the deliberate policy of the British to cultivate an African opposition, by arming vigilantes, styled as Home Guards, to protect villages from attack and to assist the police and military in operations against the Mau Mau fighters. But the opponents of Mau Mau were also those who did not share the values of the rebels, who rejected violence and armed struggle as a way forward, and who questioned the moral basis of the claims made by the rebels to rights in land and access to property. As the conflict went on, these divisions made it appear more and more like a civil war.

The intensity of the struggle was all the greater because it was largely confined to only one of Kenya's several ethnic groups, the Kikuyu. With a population of around 1.4 million in 1948, the Kikuyu occupied the rich highlands in the central region of the colony, close to Nairobi and adjacent to the main areas of white settlement. These energetic farmers worked the deep, red soil to good advantage. They were enterprising in business and, much as the advent of colonial rule had deprived them of lands and exploited their labour, many Kikuyu made the most of the opportunities afforded by the connections to an imperial economy. Those closest to Nairobi, in the district known as Kiambu, were best placed to reap the benefits. Commercial farming developed here far more rapidly than Charles Eliot had believed possible, and by the 1940s the district was renowned for the wealth of its farmers. To the north and east of Kiambu was the district of Murang'a, and further to the north again lay Nyeri. These three districts formed the Kikuyu heartlands, making up the Kikuyu Native Reserve. Further still to the north-east, far distant from Nairobi and the immediate influence of the colonial economy, were Meru and Embu, the last two Kikuyu-speaking districts. The Mau Mau war would range over all these locations, and into the white settler farms of the Rift Valley, where Kikuyu labourers worked the lands as tenants of the European owners.

The disruption wrought upon Kikuyu society by the emergency was almost unimaginable. Aside from the deaths of combatants, at the peak of the emergency the British held more than 70,000 Kikuyu supporters of Mau Mau in detention camps. The vast majority of these detainees were held without trial, simply on the order of the administration, on the basis of accusation or mere suspicion. In all, at least 150,000 Kikuyu, perhaps even more, spent some time behind the wire of a British detention camp during the course of the rebellion. In the midst of the war, draconian anti-terrorist laws were introduced suspending the human rights of suspects, imposing collective punishments, facilitating detention without trial, permitting the seizure of property of convicts, and vastly extending the death penalty to a wide range of offences. Between 1952 and 1956, when the fighting was at its worst, the Kikuyu districts of Kenya became a police state in the very fullest sense of that term.

This was not how empire was supposed to end. The British have liked to imagine that their retreat from imperial grandeur was dignified and orderly. Above all in Africa, the British tend to think they made a better job of it than anyone else.[5] Where the French lingered too long in West Africa and lost friends, where the Belgians were booted unceremoniously out of the Congo, and where the Portuguese made the grave mistake of fighting greatly prolonged guerrilla wars only to finally and humiliatingly capitulate, the British negotiated and bargained their way to peaceful and mutually beneficial settlements. Talks at Lancaster House, constitution-mongering, and deals struck in smoke-filled rooms were the stuff of British decolonisation.[6] This, at least, is the received wisdom. While this was surely true for some parts of Africa, it was not true for Kenya.

Nor was it true for those other places in Africa where white colonists had taken land and made their homes. Wars, of various kinds, were eventually fought in all the larger settler colonies – in Algeria, Angola and Mozambique, Zimbabwe, and even in the non-colony, South Africa.[7] Even by the degrading standards of other wars in the twentieth century, all these conflicts were unusually vicious and scarily brutal. It would be foolish to contest between them to find the worst, the one with the most atrocities, or the highest number of assassinations, mutilations or defilements: there is nothing to be gained from a league table that measures the order of barbarity; but there is something compellingly distinctive about the institutional bureaucratization of war in Kenya that sets it apart from the other examples, except perhaps for South Africa. The war against Mau Mau was fought not just by the military, or by the police, but by the civil administration, in a pervasive campaign that sought to strip the rebels and their sympathizers of every possible human right, while at the same time maintaining the appearance of account-ability, transparency, and justice. Nowhere was this more apparent than in the Mau Mau trials.

The Germans used to behead the convicts with a heavy axe, while the French preferred the neat, surgical precision of the guillotine. More recently, the American lust for artful technology, even in death, has drawn them toward the electric chair and the lethal injection.[8] In Britain, the execution of choice has long been the rope, the noose, and the drop. The British public has always liked a good hanging. They used to flock to the gallows at London's Tyburn in thousands to watch the bodies swing.[9] In Kenya during the 1950s, the white highlanders wanted to do likewise, clamouring for the public execution of convicted Mau Mau fighters, preferably immediately following the trial and without the right of appeal, so that Africans could witness for themselves the dreadful final rituals of British justice. This was not what Robert Ruark had meant by 'impulsive savagery', but it sounded very similar.

State execution is a mighty weapon, and in the colonial context it has generally been used sparingly. Not so in the Mau Mau emergency. Kenya's hanging judges were kept busy. Between April 1953 and Decem-ber 1956 the Special Emergency Assize Courts tried a total of 2609 Kikuyu on capital charges relating to Mau Mau offences in 1211 trials. Around 40 per cent of those accused were acquitted, but 1574 were convicted and sentenced to hang over this period. Others still had been convicted in the Supreme Court before the Special Emergency Assize Courts were created in April 1953, and there would be a smattering of further Mau Mau trials throughout 1957 and even into 1958. In total, approximately 3000 Kikuyu stood trial between 1952 and 1958 on capital charges relating to the Mau Mau movement.[10]

In all, over the course of the emergency, 1090 Kikuyu would go to the gallows for Mau Mau crimes. In no other place, and at no other time in the history of British imperialism, was state execution used on such a scale as this. This was more than double the number of executions carried out against convicted terrorists in Algeria, and many more than in all the other British colonial emergencies of the post-war period – in Palestine, Malaya, Cyprus and Aden. The research for this book was driven by a quest to uncover how this could have happened, in a colonial territory, at a time when the British parliament was contemplating the abolition of hanging.

It could have been even worse. More than 400 others were convicted but then reprieved, either because they were determined to have been under the age of eighteen at the time of the offence, or because it was decided to show clemency. Women convicts, of which there were fewer than thirty, were all reprieved and imprisoned for life. Even for those who were acquitted of these serious charges there was to be no freedom. As they walked from the court, virtually every one of the acquitted men was again arrested and detained on lesser charges. These usually required no further legal proceedings. They would spend the next several years in the notorious detention camps of the Kenyan gulag. British justice in 1950s Kenya was a blunt, brutal and unsophisticated instrument of oppression.

Yet, those same courts documented their proceedings in meticulous, voluminous detail. Much of the narrative of this book is structured around the courtroom testimonies of these trials, amounting to more than 800 capital cases that survive in the archives. Alongside the trial transcripts, witness statements, confessions and pleas for clemency are all documented. There are appeal papers, scribbled notes by advocates and judges about the proceedings and the accused, and sometimes letters about the background and history of the condemned. Here, too, are the names of the witnesses who gave evidence against Mau Mau suspects, as well as the details of African and European police officers who conducted interrogations and put together the prosecution papers. And, of course, here are the only available details of those persons taken for execution – the unnamed, and as yet unacknowledged martyrs of the rebel cause: the 1090 men who went to the gallows as convicted Mau Mau terrorists.

Mau Mau's war has until now been strangely anonymous. The names of Mau Mau generals have been known, and some of them have even been acclaimed as heroes – Dedan Kimathi, Stanley Mathenge and Waruhiu Itote are certainly the most widely known. But the subalterns of the movement, the food carriers, the couriers, the recruiting sergeants and oath administrators, the treasurers and fund-raisers, the assassins and enforcers, and, of course, the ordinary foot soldiers in the forest, have remained shadowy, and nameless. The records of the Mau Mau trials allow these people to be brought into the story. Their experiences bring us much closer to the violence, enabling us to discern its reasons more clearly.

It is grimly ironic that the Kenyan colonial state, so utterly dismissive of the rights and humanity of these Mau Mau fighters, should so meticulously have documented their lives as it processed them towards the final, highest punishment under the law. The requirements of Britain's highest court of appeal, the Privy Council, dictated that capital cases should be so systematically recorded. These first-hand stories of the Mau Mau struggle are extraordinary human dramas, but they gain even greater meaning when set within the historical context of the rebellion itself. To that end, the histories of the hanged have not been told here as biographical narratives; they have instead been placed in their social and cultural setting as part of a chronological narrative of the Mau Mau war. In this larger picture, we see not just the detail of the lives of the executed men, but their relationships to those whom they fought against – their struggles with African loyalists, with colonial police, with white settlers and their militias, with the barristers who prosecuted and defended them, and with the judges who ultimately presided over their fate.

There is nothing to glorify in this retelling of a tragic story, but there is much to be reckoned with, on both sides. This Mau Mau history is about the loss of an empire, and the making of a nation.

# 1

# The Hidden History of an
# Anti-Colonial Rebellion

In the years following the end of the Second World War, Kenya rapidly lurched into a crisis that was shaped by the racial complexion of its politics. Some 5 million Africans lived in the colony, yet they had failed to gain any meaningful form of political representation. In contrast, the 97,000-strong Asian immigrant community – which had arrived in the early part of the twentieth century – had done a little better: but most Asians 'believed that economic survival required political silence'.[1] Asian and African alike were dominated in the late 1940s by the political power of the 29,000 European settlers. Six years after the war's end, Kenya's constitution still served settler interests. Eleven elected white settlers sat in the Legislative Council alongside eleven representatives of the other races. Only four of these were African, and none were elected, all being hand-picked by government from a list of officially approved candidates. Had the European, Asian and African representatives ever combined, they could easily have outvoted the fifteen government officials on the Legislative Council.

These disparate groups never did combine. Kenya's politicians remained as they had always been, locked within the limits of a racial hierarchy that placed Europeans on top of Asians, and relegated the African majority very firmly to the bottom of the pile. Because Africans had no voice in selecting their representatives, those nominated to serve on the Legislative Council were all too easily dismissed as stooges and 'yes-men'. Those other creatures of colonial rule, the chiefs, were the only African group whose voice might be heard in government, but they, too, were compromised by their collaboration with the regime. This was no democracy, and there was certainly no space made for dissent.

Dissent found its expression all the same. Over the three decades leading up to the Mau Mau rebellion, Africans voiced plangent political concerns despite the obstruction of an unsympathetic colonial state. Four issues dominated African politics in central Kenya in these years. Two issues were paramount until the mid-1930s: the low level of African wages, kept so by Kenya's settlers eager to be competitive agricultural producers; and the abolition of the hated *kipande*, an identity card and passbook introduced after the First World War, without which no African could leave his home to look for work. European settlers frequently punished errant African workers by tearing up the *kipande*, thereby making it impossible for them to get another job, and it was the general practice on leaving employment for the employer to endorse the card and state the salary, making it extremely difficult for the worker to negotiate better wages in his next employment.

From the early 1930s, two other issues grew in importance. The first was the need to secure effective, elected African representation. This was a reaction to the attempts by the colonial government to manage politics through the nominated and salaried chiefs, and to use European missionaries as the conduit of African opinion. Many Kenyans rejected this as a system of compliance and subservience, and struggles developed over positions in local government and at the national level.

The second issue that came into focus from the early 1930s was land. The seizure of land by European settlers had been a bone of contention from the first days of colonial rule in Kenya. Settlers had first pegged out claims in 1902, in the fertile hills around Nairobi. By 1914 Kikuyu farmers throughout southern Kiambu and southern Murang'a found themselves increasingly hemmed in by the growing press of Europeans. Things were fluid at this stage, and there were no fences to impede movement. Kikuyu as yet had no real sense of the misery of dispossession and alienation that was to come; but from the 1930s the hardening of the boundaries between settler farms and African lands, combined with African population increase, brought the first real evidence of land hunger and emerging land-lessness in central Kenya. For the Kikuyu especially, the land question had by the 1930s become *the* crucial political grievance.

As these struggles took shape, there was a high degree of dispute within the African communities themselves. In the pioneering study of Mau Mau's origins, published in 1964, Carl Rosberg and John Nottingham presented these quarrels in simplistic terms, as conflicts between anti-colonial nationalists and colonial collaborators.[2] Many later writers, including Robert Edgerton and Wunyabari Maloba, have been inclined to follow their example, swallowing too readily the propaganda of the Mau Mau war that was intended to engrain this polar division in the public imagination.[3] The reality was more complicated. The divisions of Kikuyu politics were increasingly influenced by the redistributive powers of the state. Political leadership in central Kenya over the colonial years inevitably required the management of rapid social change, and it should not surprise us that Kikuyu disagreed with one another as to how this might be achieved. As East Africa's leading historian of political thought John Lonsdale has forcibly pointed out, this was the daily stuff of Kikuyu political life.[4]

By 1950 three political blocks had emerged from these debates, each reflecting a different group of interests. First there was the *conservative* block, represented by the chiefs, headmen and senior Christian elders of Kikuyu society, whose authority had been built up and greatly consolidated through association with the colonial project. This group was epitomized by Waruhiu wa Kungu and his family. Like all Kikuyu of his class and status, Waruhiu was both a prominent landowner and a businessman. His farmlands in Kiambu were productive and prosperous, and from their Nairobi offices his family ran various haulage, wholesaling and retailing businesses. A church elder since the 1920s, Waruhiu invested hugely in the education of his children. The chief was at the sharp end of Kenya's increasingly polemical politics, a struggle between 'the haves and the have-nots',[5] in which he proudly and vigorously represented the interests of the Kikuyu landed, Christian aristocracy. Such men as these were the gatekeepers of the colonial state, and they became used to wielding patronage under its auspices. Determined to hold on to their wealth and land, their conservatism deepened over time. This consolidated their personal wealth and power, but essentially amounted to a politics of exclusion. Over time, they inevitably made enemies.

Those enemies formed into our other two groups. The first, the *moderate nationalists*, were already in evidence by the early 1920s, having emerged from the first batch of educated 'mission boys'. Westernized in attitudes, often sporting European dress, and favouring urban, clerical work, these men saw the old conservative chiefs as a barrier to progress. Kenyatta epitomized this group, while Koinange wa Mbiyu moved into its orbit only in the 1930s. Though the two groups were essentially from the same class and background, typically coming from relatively prosperous families, they were separated by education and attitude. A materialist rivalry fuelled and intensified their political struggles. The moderates wanted to replace the conservatives in positions of political leadership, and although they frequently criticized the actions and motives of conservative chiefs, it is not at all clear that their own agenda of political leadership was really very different. However, by the 1940s, moderate nationalists were inclined towards national politics, and to the building of pan-ethnic political alliances, as a means to fostering greater credibility in the struggle for representation.

Koinange wa Mbiyu was a conservative chief of the 1920s who became a moderate nationalist in the 1930s. Koinange thoroughly deserves his reputation as Kenya's most distinguished chief of the colonial era.[6] He

came into government service in 1905, as a headman in Kiambu, swiftly
rising to chief in succession to his father. In 1930 he became Paramount
Chief of Kikuyuland, a role in which Waruhiu wa Kungu succeeded
him from 1949. By then the Koinange and Waruhiu families had become
political foes. It had not always been that way. In the early days of colonial
rule, both had been staunchly loyal to the government and to the
Christian churches. But from the mid-1930s, Koinange became disillusioned by the failure of the Kikuyu people to have lands returned to
them that had been taken by European settlers. Koinange had claims of
his own, and made an impassioned speech calling for the restoration of
his property before a colonial land commission in 1933. When the
colonial commissioners declined to restore the 'lost lands' to Koinange,
or to any other of the hundreds of Kikuyu claimants, his enthusiasm for
British justice waned. Through the later 1930s, Koinange gradually
shifted from the conservative Christian loyalism that had allied his family
with the Waruhius, to a position that was critical of the slowness of
African progress under British rule. He became active on behalf of the
Kikuyu Central Association, an organization he had vehemently opposed
in the 1920s. He gave land and financial support to the Kikuyu Independent Schools Association. During the 1930s, this movement for
independent education successfully challenged the mission monopoly of
primary schooling for African children.

When the British banned the KCA in 1940, Koinange was instrumental in the formation of a new party in 1945, the Kenya African
Union (KAU), a coalition of moderate nationalists. Koinange's persistent
carping now became an irritation to the colonial officials he had once
worked so closely alongside, prompting one to note wryly that 'even
when the end of the world comes, there will be Koinange making a
speech'. No longer compliant, and dangerously outspoken, his usefulness
as a colonial chief had diminished. He was eventually quietly removed
from his position in 1949, amid accusations of 'failing judgement', a
slight that the Koinange family would never forgive. By the end of his
life the pendulum had swung, and Koinange was dabbling in a more
militant brand of politics.

The *militant nationalists* among the Kikuyu first became visible in the
1930s. Their politics would give shape to Mau Mau by the early 1950s.
Their strategy was to mobilize cultural nationalism in defence of the
interests of those being excluded by social and economic changes within
Kikuyu society. Those interests coalesced around the question of growing
landlessness and the traditional obligations of Kikuyu elders to provide
for those without easy access to land. The leaders among militant Kikuyu
nationalists were often from less well-established families, with less land
and fewer resources. They used their limited Christian education first to

attack the conservatives, whom they characterized as corrupt betrayers of Kikuyu values and social norms, and then to attack the moderate nationalists whose programme of reform failed to address their basic concerns over the distribution of land and the level of African wages. The militant nationalists won strong support among Kikuyu evicted from European farms, among younger generations who by the 1940s found that land was no longer available for them in the Kikuyu reserves, and among urban workers and the unemployed.

Fred Kubai, Bildad Kaggia and James Beauttah were typical of the new breed of militant nationalists that had emerged to challenge the KCA by the end of the 1930s. These men would become involved in trade unionism, in rural protests against government-imposed agricultural schemes, and would assist Kikuyu in land cases. Their championing of the landless and the dispossessed made them unpopular with Kikuyu landowners who wished to retain the right to evict tenants or to develop their lands. Moving between the African estates of Nairobi and their rural homelands, they lived by their wits, sometimes on the fringes of criminal activity, sometimes in it up to their necks. They became increasingly hard-bitten and determined as their exclusion from the political circles favoured by the Kikuyu elders became apparent. These were the people who would take a lead in the Mau Mau movement.

As time went on, a growing number of more prosperous Kikuyu came also to sympathize with the cause of the militant nationalists. The struggles over power between these three groups were not entirely class-based, but were in large part framed in understandings of the character, essential qualities and values of Kikuyu life. At root, these were ideological debates about the kind of society in which Kikuyu would live.[7] Kikuyu politics under colonial rule was therefore a cockpit of complex internecine struggle long before it was reduced and polarized by the Mau Mau war. And these earlier struggles would play an important role in defining the positions people adopted in that war. The earlier history of grievance, and of political mobilization, therefore matters a great deal.

## Making a Rebellion

The seeds of rebellion were sown in three episodes of Kikuyu history between 1920 and 1940. The first tells the story of the efforts of well-meaning missionaries to manage African politics, which politics had been nurtured in the churches and schools established across the colony by the Christian missions from the earliest days of British rule. Anglicans of the Church Missionary Society, Scottish Presbyterians, the Methodist Gospel Mission, the fundamentalist African Inland Mission and the

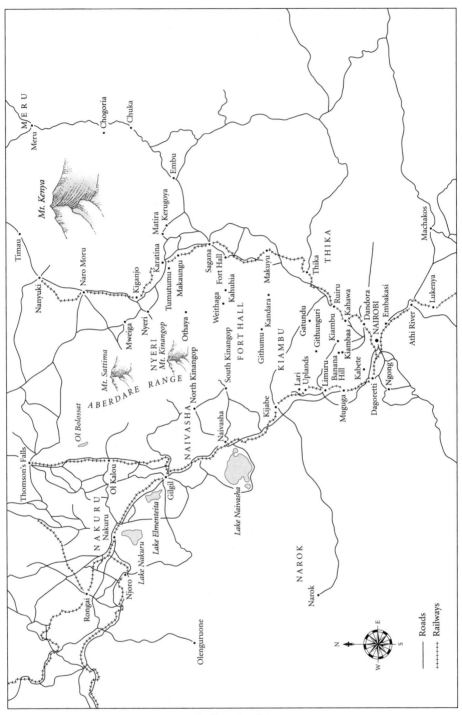

**Map 1.i Kikuyuland, c.1952**

Catholics of the Mill Hill order were all firmly established in Kenya by the eve of the 1914–18 war.

In an act of pious imperialism that echoed the partition of Africa among the great powers at the historic conference of Berlin in 1884, where Europe's leaders had haggled over who would have what bit of Africa, carving up the map like a slab of meat, these Churches divided the colony into religious 'spheres of influence'. This avoided too much unseemly competition for the saving of African souls. All these Churches had a foothold in the Kikuyu districts of central Kenya, but the Church Missionary Society (CMS) and the Presbyterian Church of Scotland Mission took the lion's share. The missions brought education. Basic primary schools were established at all mission stations. Demand for schooling was strong, and the missions soon extended their educational services. Glad to leave these things to the Churches, government retreated. Already by the early 1920s, then, the missions had nurtured their own literate Christian elite, a small but rapidly growing body of African men and (rather fewer) women, filled with ambition for 'progress and modernity'.

An engagement with politics was part of this message of modernity; but it was politics under the direction of mission patronage. The colonial government first invited European missionaries onto the Legislative Council to represent 'African interests'. The missions carried this paternalism into the structure of their own affairs, forming councils of African elders within the churches, and encouraging Christian Africans to represent themselves. By 1921 senior Kikuyu landholders and chiefs within the various missions had joined together in a single association, with the intention to lobby government over questions affecting the Kikuyu people, most obviously the issue of the return of lands taken by European settlers. Koinange became chairman of this dignified and lofty body, known as the Kikuyu Association, with senior representatives from the Presbyterian and Methodist missions filling the positions of treasurer and secretary. The 'four great pillars' of the Kikuyu Association were all chiefs: Koinange, Waruhiu, Josiah Njonjo and Philip James Karanja. With the help of prominent European missionaries, this Christian group sought to establish themselves as the representatives of African public opinion in central Kenya.[8] This was the first mobilization of conservative politics.

The rural and chiefly Kikuyu Association soon had a more radical rival. The East African Association was formed in Nairobi in 1921 to campaign for better pay and improved conditions for urban African workers. This association was multi-ethnic in composition, but it was naturally enough dominated by the Kikuyu, who filled the majority of the better-paid African jobs in Nairobi. Its leader and prime organizer was a Kikuyu named Harry Thuku, a product of the Methodist mission

school at Kambui, who by the early 1920s was employed as a telephonist
and clerk in the Treasury. Gauntly framed, with a clear complexion and
sharp eyes, Thuku was a charismatic and forceful personality. A skilled
orator, he knew how to win a Kikuyu crowd with a well-chosen phrase.
Like the chiefs and clan elders who held sway in the Kikuyu Association,
Thuku was from a prominent Kikuyu family, but his politics was cast in
opposition to traditional patterns of 'tribal authority'. Where the Kikuyu
Association accepted the leadership of the missions, and bowed to the
authority of government in its polite requests for reform, Thuku and his
followers rejected colonial rule and overtly questioned the legitimacy
of European domination. Among Kikuyu, a conservative politics of
gradualist reform was already in 1921 under challenge from those who
wanted constitutional change and elective representation.

Thuku was soon at loggerheads with the chiefs of the Kikuyu
Association, who baulked at his claims to speak for a wider African
constituency. Thuku stirred up trouble by touring the rural districts at
weekends, urging Africans to campaign against the *kipande*, and speaking
forcefully against the exploitation of African labourers, the levying of
hut tax, and against the laws that prevented Africans from purchasing
land. All of these issues had a strong popular appeal. Many of Thuku's
supporters in the rural areas were moderate, educated, younger Christian
men, who despaired at the conservatism of their elders. In Nyeri, the
least developed and most conservative of the Kikuyu districts, the chiefs
asked the government to deport Thuku, and in Murang'a district a
European missionary reported with some alarm that 'practically the
whole of the younger generation of native Christians were solid for
the agitator [Thuku]'.[9] Worried by Thuku's 'seditious' activities, the
Governor had him arrested and deported from Nairobi to the coastal
town of Kismayu, under the authority of the Natives Removal Ordinance
of 1909 – a catch-all piece of colonial legislation that gave powers to get
rid of any troublesome individual without recourse to a proper trial.

In a scene that would anticipate events thirty years later, Thuku was
taken into custody in Nairobi on 14 March 1922. The next day his
supporters protested at the police station. Some kept vigil there that
night. The next day the crowd swelled to between 7000 and 8000
Africans. The police, armed with rifles and with bayonets fixed, formed
a defensive line between the crowd and the jail. It is not entirely clear
how or why the shooting started. Some said that women in the crowd
had shamed and goaded the African police, until one finally fired his
rifle at them. Others said the crowd had thrown stones at the police line
and attempted to rush them. It was alleged, once the shooting had
started, that European settlers looking on from the veranda of the nearby
Norfolk Hotel had joined in the mayhem, firing randomly into the

panicking crowd. When the crowd dispersed from the scene, the official report on the incident reckoned that twenty-one Africans had been killed, including four women, and that another twenty-eight had been wounded.[10] Unofficial reports from African staff in the Nairobi mortuary put the dead at fifty-six.[11] Kenya had witnessed its first violent political protest. It would not be the last.

Thuku was banished from central Kenya for a few years, and by the time he returned politics had already passed him by. He remained as a marginal figure, sometimes wheeled out at political rallies as the symbol of righteous struggle; but as he got older, he became increasingly conservative. As Mau Mau emerged in the late 1940s, Thuku took a public stand against radicalism and violence. During the emergency he would stand tall with the loyalists. His value as a symbol of struggle had somewhat diminished.

Thuku moved on, but his ideas would germinate among a new generation of leaders. While the colonial government consolidated the authority of the chiefs through the formation of Local Native Councils, Harry Thuku's rural Kikuyu supporters in Murang'a formed a new political group in 1924, known as the Kikuyu Central Association. This party would nurture the ambitions of the moderate nationalists over the next fifteen years. A few KCA members first made it onto the Murang'a Local Native Council, and then they were successful in Nyeri in 1928. But the European district commissioners who took the chair at LNC meetings usually took steps to ensure that senior chiefs were not embarrassed or exposed by the slippery questions of 'agitators'. It was the chiefs, not the LNC, whom government relied upon to represent African opinion.

In 1927 the KCA opened a Nairobi office and began to broaden its membership and raise funds through subscription. There, in the commercial quarter of the town, the young African activists of the KCA mingled with Asian and European businessmen, whose offices sat above shops in the oddly assorted two-storey buildings that lined the main streets. Ox-wagons and rickshaws had been Nairobi's transport in the early days, but motor traffic now plied the dirt roads of the town, dodging the deep potholes that formed in the rainy season, and sending clouds of red dust swirling through the air when the weather was hot and dry. Nairobi was thriving and growing, but it still had the feel of a frontier town. It was a place where Europeans could buy things, take lunch in the hotels, or dance at the club reserved for whites only. If you had a black skin, Nairobi was a place of work, not leisure. Beyond the business district, the Asian and African residential areas were springing up in a muddle of small estates and irregular shanties. The workers who came to live here were urban residents but still rural men: for Africans, in Nairobi in the 1920s you made money, not a home.

Among those who joined the KCA in Nairobi during the 1920s was one Johnstone (later Jomo) Kenyatta, whose skills in written and spoken English soon saw him promoted as secretary of the organization.[12] A monthly newsletter was established under the title *Muigwithania* – 'The Reconciler' – with Kenyatta as its founding editor. Whether the name was chosen by Kenyatta or not is unclear, but it was a name that would be associated with him throughout his political career. In 1929 Kenyatta left for London, where he was to represent the KCA's views directly to the Colonial Office. He would return to Kenya briefly in September 1930, but London would be his home again from April 1931 until 1946. As Kikuyu anti-colonial politics took shape, with all of its divisions and rifts, Kenyatta would be a marginal figure.

By the end of the 1920s the KCA had a membership of nearly 4000. Its political manifesto was promoted through the pages of *Muigwithania*. The chiefs disliked the strident tone sometimes adopted in the news-sheet, but it was pretty tame stuff. Only when the KCA attacked the missions, and complained that the chiefs could not represent non-Christian Kikuyu, did the two parties really find things to fight about. It was around this question that the next political storm would break in our second episode of Kikuyu political struggle.

From the earliest days of colonial rule in Kenya, the Protestant missions had campaigned against those native customs they found morally repugnant. Just as the practices of suttee and infanticide had so enraged Christian sensibilities in nineteenth-century India, witchcraft, ancestor beliefs, modes of dress, African dances, polygamy and burial practices were all subjects that raised the ire of European clergy in East Africa. Among the many practices the missionaries found repugnant, it was female circumcision, properly termed clitoridectomy, that finally provoked massive resistance from the new Christian communities among the Kikuyu. Before the mid-1920s, each of the main Protestant missions had made efforts to prevent girls in their Christian families from being subjected to clitoridectomy. Missionaries argued that the practice was a danger to health, that it led to unnecessary complications in future childbirth, and that it was lewd and immoral to expose girls to so intimate an operation at so tender an age – the girls were typically between twelve and fourteen. Used to a more genteel morality, missionaries were also alarmed by what they heard of the explicit education in sexual matters that accompanied the rite.

The campaign against clitoridectomy split the African congregations. To accept mission direction on this was a bigger step than most Kikuyu Christians felt able to take, no matter how deep their faith. Kikuyu custom held that a woman could not marry until the operation and the rites associated with it had been properly carried out. Any woman who refused the operation would therefore not find a Kikuyu husband. Without clitoridectomy there would be no transfer of bridewealth – the exchange of livestock and goods given to the family of the bride by the family of the groom. In central Kenya this exchange was the glue that held social life together, binding families over the longer term in relations of obligation and reciprocity. The challenge to clitoridectomy therefore seemed, to many Kikuyu, to be a direct challenge to the reproduction of their society.

From the mid-1920s the missionaries provoked public debate over clitoridectomy by urging the Local Native Councils to pass legislation banning it. This placed the chiefs who sat on the LNCs in a tricky position. It was too good an opportunity for the KCA to miss. They took up the cause of Kikuyu culture, arguing that the practice of clitoridectomy was not a matter of Christian faith at all, but merely a matter of conflicting social morality. In the view of the KCA, it was quite possible to be both a good Christian and a good Kikuyu; clitoridectomy should be a matter for personal choice without the interference of the Churches, and it should certainly not be regulated by government edict. This was accompanied by an attack upon the authority of the chiefs to adjudicate over such a matter. The KCA's position was not, then, against the Church or against Christianity – most leaders of the party were themselves mission-educated and practising Christians – but it was against the chiefs and against the dominance of the missions in matters of politics, culture and education.

The debate rumbled on until March 1929, when a joint meeting of some forty of the senior African Christians of the leading Protestant Churches resolved that clitoridectomy was an 'evil practice' that should be 'suspended by the Churches everywhere'. The European missionaries observing the meeting now felt they had a sufficient mandate from their African congregations to institute a ban on clitoridectomy.[13] The missionaries first tried to use the laws passed by the Local Native Councils to have a circumciser convicted on a charge of 'grievous hurt', for having carried out the operation on a mission girl of fifteen, allegedly against her will. When the case failed, Dr John W. Arthur, of the Church of Scotland, wrote to the press and stirred up the Kikuyu Association to speak out in support of a ban. The KCA's president, Joseph Kang'ethe, responded with an open letter to all seventy-four Kikuyu chiefs, and followed this with another to the missionaries, pointedly asking whether the Kikuyu were to be declared heathens simply because of their customs?

Arthur then embarked upon an evangelical tour of central Kenya, preaching against clitoridectomy. At Weithega the congregation listened to him politely, but at Kahuhia there was open hostility. At Chogoria, Arthur was at his most forthright. He fulminated against the KCA, calling them agitators and despoilers of 'God's work'. Becoming agitated, he thumped the pulpit in anger, alarming even the other European missionaries who were present. His rage did more harm than good: 106 confirmed Christians left the church immediately, with only fourteen members remaining in the congregation.

The storm was gathering. By October 1929, the churches demanded that Christians sign a pledge against clitoridectomy. Church elders, catechists and teachers were dismissed from the missions if they refused. There were now massive defections from the Church of Scotland in Nyeri and southern Kiambu, and from the African Inland Mission and the Methodists. The Catholics stayed out of the conflict, and the Anglicans of the Church Missionary Society took a softer and less public line. Those who sided with the Protestant missions became known as the *Kirori* – a thumbprint – while those who supported the KCA were called *Karing'a* – the pure Kikuyu. As the crisis deepened, Kikuyu communities refused to send their children to the church schools, expelling the teachers and seizing back the land and the property. Dances were held near the mission stations and outside the homes of teachers and catechists, the crowds poking fun at the clergy and making up rude songs about them – some of which the government banned as seditious. As the congregations dwindled and Christians deserted the Churches in hundreds, the extent of the schism this had provoked became apparent.

Over this somewhat dubious act of faith, the missions had apparently sacrificed the work of twenty years. There were now bitter divisions among the European missionaries themselves over what had happened. To make their consciences suffer even more, on 3 January 1930 an elderly woman missionary at the Kijabe headquarters of the AIM was found murdered in her bed. She had been the victim of a forced circumcision in the night, and had died a horrible death in the struggle against her attacker.[14]

The murder brought the clitoridectomy crisis to a head. Shocked by the intensity of feeling they had stirred, the Churches now slowly retreated. The damage would have serious consequences. Some Christians returned to the missions after the crisis, but many more stayed away to establish their own independent churches. Having broken with the paternal care of their European spiritual masters, the new churches ran their own schools too, breaking the mission monopoly on education. These initiatives were funded by collections made in the communities. The more wealthy families gave land and substantial funds to set up the new churches and schools. From 1934, the Koinanges took a prominent role in this movement, supporting the main headquarters of the Kikuyu Independent Schools Association at Githunguri, in Kiambu. The Association, with strong support throughout central Kenya, and the Kikuyu Karing'a Schools, catering for former adherents of the Church of

Scotland Mission in southern Kiambu, fostered the development of independent education and religion in central Kenya over the next twenty years. They made rapid progress. By the mid-1930s government funds were being channelled to the independent schools through the budgets of the LNCs. Mission control had been irrevocably broken. The dissidents had found their voice in the independent churches and schools.

The clitoridectomy crisis had brought the KCA wide support and allowed it to secure membership and branches throughout central Kenya. Strengthened and emboldened, in the 1930s the KCA focused upon our third episode in Kikuyu political struggle: the land question. Among the many grievances of the Kikuyu, the loss of lands to Europeans was the deepest felt. Since the arrival of the first European settlers in 1902, land in Kenya had been divided by race, just as it was in South Africa. In 1915 the Crown Land Ordinance had recognized 'native rights' in lands reserved for their use, and in 1926 the British consolidated this division by creating African Reserves for each of Kenya's 'tribes', leaving the 'White Highlands' solely for Europeans. The White Highlands had absorbed large chunks of land in Kiambu and Murang'a, as well as areas further north, around Nyeri and Nanyuki, and great tracts of land in the Rift Valley, and far to the west on the plateaus beyond.

The legal designation of the White Highlands as being for European ownership prevented Africans from acquiring lands outside their own designated reserves, while it gave the existing European settlers far greater security of tenure. Many Africans, and especially those in the southern Kikuyu areas where there had been thick settlement of whites, still claimed land as their own that Europeans had seized. With the passage of time, and the steady increase in African population, pressure on the African reserves was already becoming apparent by the early 1930s.

The moderate nationalists of the KCA and the conservative chiefs differed little in their analysis of the land problem. When Chief Koinange headed an official delegation to London in 1931, he gave eloquent and forceful testimony on the pressing land questions facing his Kikuyu people. Thanks in part to Koinange's pleading, the British finally inaugurated an official enquiry into Kenya's land problems. The Kenya Land Commission visited the colony in 1932 to take evidence.[15] In the months before their arrival both the KCA and the chiefs were busy preparing their case. There was much common ground. The KCA organized the gathering of information on questionnaires, and many of the chiefs cooperated in their completion. Within the KCA a Kikuyu Land Board Association was formed to collate the land claims, gather evidence and identify witnesses who might give testimony to the Commission. The Kikuyu Association, by now recast and renamed the Loyal Kikuyu

Patriots – a name that would resonate into the Emergency of the 1950s – also prepared to make representations to the Commission.

The essential case was clear enough: the Kikuyu wanted the land that had been taken from them for European settlement to be returned, amounting by their own estimation to some 60,000 acres. When the Commission reported, in 1934, the Kikuyu were to be gravely disappointed. The Land Commission decided to confirm existing European title, and to give the Kikuyu extra land as compensation only in areas of lower fertility and less easy access – that is, places that were not wanted by Europeans; and the lands to be opened to Kikuyu settlement only amounted to a fraction of what had been lost.[16] Instead of righting the wrongs of earlier policies, as Kikuyu must have hoped, the Land Commission effectively extinguished all African claims to lands occupied by whites.

The Land Commission report was the stone upon which moderate African politics was broken. Koinange's response captured the deep sense of loss and betrayal. The Chief had held great hopes that the Commission would bring a fair settlement to Kikuyu grievances over land, and on a personal level he had hoped to regain lands belonging to his own family. In an emotional and dramatic episode during the Commission hearings in Kiambu, Koinange had been challenged on the veracity of his claims. To prove his case, Koinange took the commissioners onto the European farm in question, identified the site of his grandfather's grave, and had the bones exhumed in front of the disbelieving commissioners.[17] The incident impressed all who witnessed it as demonstrating the intensity of Kikuyu feeling over the land question, but it did not swing the commissioners' judgment in Koinange's favour. He was bitterly angered by the humiliation. In the wake of the Land Commission, Koinange ceased to be the government's loyal servant. Over the next few years he moved steadily into the camp of the KCA.[18]

If Europeans thought the Commission had settled the land question once and for all, for Kikuyu the real struggle over land had only just begun. Militant nationalism was conceived in Kikuyu reaction to the report of the Kenya Land Commission, and the embryo of rebellion then nurtured in the challenges mounted against every attempt by the colonial government to implement decisions contingent on the report. Kikuyu farmers obstructed their removal, raised protests against the suitability of the new lands, and increasingly contravened government regulations on land use and resettlement whenever the opportunity arose. Opposition to the Land Commission's findings fed militancy all the more over the next twenty years as the pressures upon land within the Kikuyu reserve became greater and the settler stranglehold on the political economy of the colony tightened. African rebellion finally exploded out of deepening grievance and frustration.

In these three episodes – the Thuku protest, the emergence of independent schools and churches, and the Land Commission findings – we can discern the origins of each of the three main factions of Kikuyu politics under colonial rule between 1920 and 1940. From 1940 to 1952 the militant faction would gain in strength as the legitimacy of the conservatives was undermined by the changing demands of colonialism, and as the moderates failed to deliver the constitutional advances their manifesto promised. Militancy grew around specific issues, each of which gradually came to be connected through political mobilization. These issues were the status of Kikuyu tenants who worked on European farms, the problem of land hunger within the Kikuyu reserves, and the poverty and disaffection of the teeming Kikuyu population of Nairobi's African quarters. The rise of militancy can be explored throughout a brief history of each.

### The expulsion of the tenants

By the 1940s one in every eight Kikuyu was a tenant on a European-owned farm. These tenants were known as 'squatters'. The term originated in the circumstances of European colonization. As European settlers arrived in Kenya from 1902, they claimed land in an ad hoc and irregular manner. Farms were pegged out on the ground and occupied by the settlers long before any proper survey could be completed, and before any formal title deed was issued. It took the colonial survey department nearly twenty years to catch up with the backlog of ratifying these claims. By and large, in areas legally opened for settlement, Europeans could claim the land they wanted. The law stated that the land should be unoccupied, but allowance was made to compensate any Africans who were dispossessed. European settlers paid little heed to these provisions, and hid behind the useful fiction that Africans had no notion of land ownership.

In the lands of southern Kiambu, where some of the first white settlers staked their claims, African residents watched, and frequently helped, their new European neighbours build houses and barns without realizing the full extent of the land they would subsequently claim, and without at first appreciating the permanence of the intrusion. Farms were seldom fenced, and most remained that way for many years. White settlers did not have sufficient capital to develop the farms fully, so no attempt was made to evict African residents in the early days. One thousand acres of Karen Blixen's farm at Ngong was given over to Kikuyu squatters and their *shambas* – the Swahili name given to the plots cultivated by each family.[19] The settlers needed labour, and offered work to those Africans living near them. Through this process, Africans became unwitting tenant labourers to their new European landlords. Only after 1912 or so, when coffee planting was greatly extended on the Kiambu farms and European owners found the need to move the squatters, did Kikuyu here come to realize they had been effectively usurped from their lands and become tenant labourers at the same time.[20]

There was a gradual movement of Africans away from the farms into the Kikuyu reserves by the First World War, but each European landlord still retained a number of squatters, who were now placed on formal labour contracts. A supply of those willing to take up squatter contracts was sustained by the tax demands of the colonial state. To the west, in the Rift Valley and on the Mau escarpment, European settlers sent labour recruiters back into the Kikuyu areas of central Kenya to bring tenants to their farms. This heralded a wave of Kikuyu migration that saw some 70,000 people move west between 1904 and 1920. The chroniclers of white settlement in Kenya describe these as the halcyon days of 'the pioneers', who carved their farms out of the African wilderness. 'Pioneering itself may be a sort of art', wrote Elspeth Huxley, 'in its own way as creative as the painting of a picture.'[21] This romantic vision meant nothing to the Africans whose sweated labour did the building and the land clearing. Squatter families were permitted to reside on the farms and use grazing, and also cultivate small areas for themselves. In return, they gave a limited amount of labour to the European farmers, up to 180 days each year, for which they were paid at the prescribed rate. For younger men keen to acquire livestock and capital the move west seemed attractive. The lack of good grazing in central Kenya enhanced the appeal of the Rift Valley farms in particular, and many Kikuyu families in Kiambu and Nyeri even encouraged younger members to move west in order to gain access to the resources available. But among those to leave for the Rift Valley were also many Kikuyu who had lost their land to white settlers in central Kenya.[22]

In material terms, the squatters who went west did pretty well. Incomes were relatively high, compared with those realized within the Kikuyu reserves, and as the links with their kin back in central Kenya weakened over the years, these pioneers found themselves freed from at least some of the obligations of customary life. They paid a price for this, however, as there was little mission activity on the farms, and therefore no easy access to schooling. Cut adrift from the main currents of social change, the farms were not the scene of 'progress and modernity' for African workers. It was a rough and ready world, where the European was very much lord and master.[23] By the end of the 1930s the Kikuyu squatter community numbered more than 150,000. They retained higher levels of illiteracy, and contained a lower proportion of Christians, yet were on the whole wealthier than their brethren in the Kikuyu reserves.[24]

There was an underlying tension between settlers and squatters that could not be easily resolved. It concerned the rights of the squatters to the land they occupied. From the very beginning there had been a grave misunderstanding on the farms of the Rift Valley. White settlers saw the recruited squatter labourers simply as hired hands, whose residence on the farm had no bearing upon their status. As they acquired greater capital, and looked to bring more of the land under crop, and eventually to mechanize their production, many white settlers sought to lessen their dependence on labour tenants and to move to wage labourers. The squatters' understanding of their rights on the farms held this to be impossible. They believed they had customary rights of ownership for their families and descendants, rights they termed *githaka*. In Kikuyu custom, *githaka* holders had full control over their land and could not normally be removed. Many of those who migrated west in the early days had not enjoyed *githaka* rights in the Kikuyu homelands; they moved believing that by doing so they would acquire such rights. Others claimed they had only sacrificed *githaka* rights in Kiambu because the same had been promised in the Rift Valley. The fact that they had usually cleared barren land for cultivation on the farms to which they were brought only served to strengthen their belief that they must therefore hold *githaka* rights.[25] Moreover, longevity of residence gave them confidence. Many squatter families were in their second or third generation of settlement in the Rift Valley by the end of the 1930s.

Though few squatters could have been aware of it at the time, a judgment handed down by Kenya's High Court in 1925 had, in effect, already sealed their fate. The ruling of Justice Barth established that resident labourers on European-owned farms were 'tenants at will' under the law, and could therefore by evicted on order of the landlord without the right of appeal.[26] This expunged any possibility of *githaka* rights being recognized, and meant that the landlord could freely set or adjust conditions of tenancy. Squatters were at the mercy of their white landlords.

The development of the European farming sector eventually heralded the end for the Rift Valley squatters by the eve of the Second World War. With the restructuring of white farming in response to the depression of the early 1930s, many more farmers now looked to the development of high-grade dairy and beef farming. Squatter-owned cattle presented a disease threat, and also took up grazing land that was now needed.[27] The European farming lobby succeeded by 1940 in pushing through legislation giving settler-controlled district councils in the White High-lands the authority to limit by law the number of cattle that could be held by each squatter.[28]

The outbreak of war delayed any immediate impact of this legislation, but in 1945 the first settler district in the Rift Valley began to impose limits on squatter livestock holdings. The war raised prices for Kenya's agricultural produce, and brought higher demand. Production expanded dramatically, allowing white farmers to make substantial financial gains. At last, thanks to the war, the white highlanders had the capital with which to develop the land. As the annual squatter contracts came up for renewal, the white highlanders now imposed the new limits on cultivation, restricting each squatter family to only one or two acres, and removing all their cattle. European prosperity triggered African misery. The effect on squatters' incomes was devastating, plunging them into economic despair. The annual family income fell from 1400 shillings in 1942, to 300 shillings in 1946. At the same time, wages increased from 8 shillings to only 12 shillings per month, this in no way compensating for the losses under the new contracts.[29]

The majority of the squatters simply refused to re-attest. Efforts were made to organize a strike and total boycott of the new contracts, and a meeting of squatters in November 1946 drew in representatives from more than 400 farms; but by early 1947 the strike had collapsed. Unless they wished to become landless urban workers, the squatters had little obvious alternative but to accept the new terms. Their dilemma was intensified by the decision taken by white settlers in some districts to be rid of squatters altogether.[30] By the early months of 1946, a steady trickle of families was to be seen on the escarpment road up to Kijabe, or herded like livestock into the third-class carriages of steam trains at Nakuru, Gilgil and Naivasha, bound for central Kenya. Between 1946 and 1952 the trickle would turn into a torrent, as more than 100,000 Kikuyu squatters were forcibly 'repatriated'. They carried their possessions with them in bundles and on carts; but they were not allowed to keep the livestock that was their store of wealth. Quarantine and veterinary restrictions prohibited the movement of live animals. Those leaving were compelled to sell their cattle and sheep, often at knock-down prices in a flooded market, sometimes even to the same European farmers whose decision was the cause of their impoverishment and misery.

The Kikuyu squatters who left were understandably bitter and angry. As their numbers grew, there was violent resistance. European cattle were maimed, and there were arson attacks on the property of white settlers. These were episodic, opportunistic and unorganized acts of vengeance.[31] For the most part, the dispersed squatter communities lacked the cohesion to cooperate on a larger scale; but at one place, squatters did succeed in organizing themselves to resist. That place was Olenguruone.

It was an unlikely setting for a revolt. Olenguruone was the name given to a government resettlement scheme in the Nakuru district, established in 1941 to accommodate some of the squatter families evicted from the Rift Valley.[32] On a high, scrubby piece of land on the edge of the bamboo forest above Nakuru, Olenguruone was a bleak unattractive land. It was intended as a test bed for resettlement, a model for schemes that might later be set up in other parts of Kenya. The government determined to establish firm agricultural rules on the scheme, dictating the crops to be grown, the type of cultivation, and the conservation and maintenance work required on the land. All of this was defended as 'best practice', but it provoked resistance among the Kikuyu resettled at Olenguruone.

On accepting resettlement in 1941, the squatters moving to Olenguruone believed they had been offered *githaka* rights. A high proportion of the 11,000 who came to Olenguruone were originally from southern Kiambu, where they had been forced out by European settlement in the early 1900s. They saw Olenguruone as the rightful restoration of their *githaka* lands. No one should tell them, as *githaka* holders, how to farm or what to do on the land. On this basis they rejected government authority and rebelled against the scheme. For nine long years the squatters at Olenguruone maintained a staunch resistance, engaging lawyers to fight their cause, and gaining support in central Kenya and Nairobi. The squatters' leader at Olenguruone, Samuel Koina Gitebi, was energetic in winning wider support for the struggle. He had strong links with the old KCA activists in Limuru, a crowded Kiambu town close to Nairobi, and had helped to bring the independent schools movement to the farms of Naivasha in the 1930s. He now encouraged his old friends to assist in the collection of money for the Olenguruone campaign. In 1946 he went to see Koinange, and even persuaded the new nationalist party, the Kenya African Union, to take up the case.

To cement greater political solidarity, the Olenguruone squatters first took an oath of unity in 1944, based upon the old KCA membership oath. By 1946 this traditional Kikuyu oath, usually taken only by male elders, had been widened at Olenguruone to include younger men, women and even children. Eventually, some of those at Olenguruone went a step further, and took a more militant oath, which threatened them with death if they broke ranks or refused to obey the orders of their leaders. This committed people to the possibility of direct violence in defence of Kikuyu community interests. It seems that this oath may have originated in the intensity of the Olenguruone struggle. It would quickly spread through the farms of the Rift Valley between 1946 and 1948, as other squatters facing eviction sought to build solidarity. Then, as evictions from Olenguruone began, the oath reached the Kikuyu of Nairobi and central Kenya. Here it was taken up and promoted by the leaders of the urban militants, a group who would later become known as the *Muhimu* (literally, 'important') and, later still, would form Mau Mau's central organizing committee (see below, pp. 37–9).

Eviction orders against the Olenguruone squatters were first issued in 1948. In the same year, far to the south, the election of the National Party in South Africa marked the beginnings of the apartheid era. Africans there would have to learn the arts of resistance just as in Kenya. At Olenguruone, the squatters fought the eviction order through the courts, and both Koinange and Kenyatta went to Nakuru to speak at the hearing, but without success. This was the limit of KAU support. The demolition of property on the scheme began in November 1949. Then the squatters' livestock was confiscated and sold. They were offered land on another government scheme, but few took it up. Between January and March 1950 the majority of the 11,000 made their own way back to the district they, their parents or grandparents, had left more than forty years before. The remainder were offered government transport for their repatriation to Kiambu. As the trucks came through Kijabe and Uplands to Limuru, the evicted squatters sang Kikuyu *nyimbo*, songs of resistance and defiance, to the cheers and encouragement of the Kikuyu they passed.

### Land hunger in the homelands

Despite their celebrity, it was not a happy homecoming for those from Olenguruone. Squatters arriving in central Kenya mostly found that they were not welcome in their 'homelands'. The families and clans they had left behind two or three generations previously simply had nowhere to put them. There were no jobs; there was no land; and there was precious little with which to feed them. The lucky ones found shelter with relatives, perhaps getting casual wage employment on the land of others. Those less fortunate joined the growing numbers of unemployed crowding into the illegal shacks springing up around towns like Limuru. Others found their way to the shanties of Nairobi. All depended upon the charity of others. This was a humbling experience for the once wealthy and proudly independent squatters.

As the Olenguruone martyrs were still straggling into Kiambu, their militancy posed challenges for the moderate leaders of Kikuyu politics. During the Second World War the government had seized the opportunity to be rid of the KCA, and banned it. Out of its ashes, at the end of the war, emerged a new, broader-based nationalist party called the Kenya African Union. With a core of old KCA activists, plus members from other ethnic groups, who were mostly urban workers in Nairobi, the KAU made a promising start.

The Koinange family were prime movers behind the new party. Old man Koinange now took a back seat, leaving much of the leg work to his sons, but his presence gave the KAU authority and status. Koinange's three sons shared a youthful radicalism that had done much in the 1930s to stimulate their father's political conversion to the nationalist cause. The American-educated and well-travelled Peter Mbiyu was a leading activist in the independent schools movement, and had first guided his father into the fold of the KCA. Peter had stood for election as the first African member of the Legislative Council in 1944, being only narrowly beaten by Kenya's first African Oxford graduate, Eluid Mathu. At this time it was a rare thing for a Kikuyu to be educated abroad, and both men enjoyed very high standing in the community.

Peter Mbiyu would travel to London in 1951 and remain there as the KAU's representative until 1959. In his absence, Peter's half-brother, John Westley Mbiyu, would be his father's constant companion, confidant and principal aid. The most determinedly nationalist of all the Koinanges, John Westley Mbiyu was by 1950 already in close association with the small group of Kikuyu men whose leadership the government would later come to believe had given inspiration to the emergence of Mau Mau. Known as the 'Kiambaa Parliament', this group comprised no more than a dozen activists who met regularly at the Koinanges' Kiambaa homestead, just to the north of Nairobi. A third Koinange son, Frederick Mbiyu, acted as the family secretary and clerk, recording the decisions reached at these meetings and organizing the necessary actions. All the participants in the Kiambaa Parliament were Kikuyu, most had been involved in the KCA in the 1930s, and all were by 1950 members of the KAU; but the group came to have a political life of its own. From 1947 this group encouraged the spreading of political oaths intended to bind Kikuyu people to political solidarity under the KAU. John Westley Mbiyu was an energetic administrator of these oaths. Despite what Special Branch would come to believe, the politicians who gathered around the Koinanges at Kiambaa were essentially moderate men who wanted constitutional reform, not revolution.

Into the Koinange family circle, in September 1946, had come another moderate nationalist, Jomo Kenyatta, on his return to Kenya after many years' exile in Europe. He assumed the presidency of the KAU some nine months later, on 1 June 1947. Kenyatta was then already a close friend of Peter Mbiyu Koinange, whom he had known in London, where Kenyatta had been sent in the inter-wars years as the representative of an earlier political party, the Kikuyu Central Association (KCA). Kenyatta enjoyed a fine reputation among Kikuyu as a trusted and responsible political leader. His return to Kenya had been eagerly awaited. The Koinanges guided Kenyatta back into the ways of Kikuyu politics, and also back into the established landed and educated elite of Kikuyu society. These links of friendship, culture and political affiliation were soon further cemented by marriage. Kenyatta already had an English wife, back in Sussex, and another Kikuyu wife, but political expediency demanded that he marry into a senior Kikuyu family. This was accomplished when Kenyatta took old Koinange's daughter, Grace Mutundu, as his third wife. Grace died in childbirth in 1948, but her daughter survived as the lasting embodiment of the alliance that bound the Koinanges to the Kenyattas.[33] The Koinanges, and now the Kenyattas too, were at the centre of Kikuyu politics and at the centre of the Kenya African Union.

This was all very well, but by the early months of 1950 the KAU was facing crisis. Kenyatta's leadership was not proving a success. The moderates who led the party had failed to win concessions from government, and had neglected to nurture a broader base of support. After an invigorating beginning in 1947, Kenyatta had shrunk away from public engagements and had done nothing to persuade the non-Kikuyu of the party's worth. The KAU's pan-ethnic credentials were in tatters by 1950, with only a few hardy politicians from the coast and Nyanza still standing up for the party, and this mostly in Nairobi. Despite a claim to 15,000 members, the party's finances were in a parlous state and its influence was rapidly waning.

The Kiambaa Parliament saw the need to capitalize upon the intensity of political feeling surrounding the fate of the Olenguruone squatters; but how should this be done? Since 1947 Kenyatta and the Kiambaa Parliament had been engaged in the slow process of seeking to build up support for the KAU among Kikuyu. This they did through the 'oathing' of carefully selected individuals, whose seniority, influence and authority would consolidate the position of the party. As the party's historian, John Spencer, explains: 'The oath was for the reliable, experienced, generally older men, not for the younger ones, the militants among the returning servicemen or among the urban unemployed.'[34] Kenyatta and Koinange feared the rowdiness of mass politics, and saw no need for it if the old guard of the KCA could be mobilized in the cause of moderate nationalism under the KAU banner. But the need for secrecy, the fee of more then 60 shillings that was demanded of oath-takers, and the simple reluctance of many Kikuyu to pledge support for the KAU made for slow progress.

At the same time, the dramatic events at Olenguruone had given rise to a different and more militant oath, which was not associated with the KAU or the Kiambaa Parliament but which rapidly gained adherents, especially among the squatters and the urban poor of Nairobi. The KAU was in fact being undermined and outflanked by a more militant, conspiratorial politics that held far greater appeal for the Kikuyu masses because it appeared to more directly address their grievances. The moderate Kenyatta was losing his grip.

By 1950 there were very good reasons why the people of the Kikuyu reserves had become more receptive to the militants. A growing agrarian crisis had enveloped the Kikuyu homelands of Kiambu, Murang'a and Nyeri from the mid-1930s. It was driven by mounting population pressure, declining soil fertility and land hunger. Quite simply, the land reserved for the Kikuyu was no longer sufficient for the needs of a population of more than 1.25 million. A colonial agricultural survey of south Nyeri, conducted in 1944, was a portent of doom for the Kikuyu reserves. Population density in south Nyeri had increased from a figure of 463 per square mile in 1931 to 542 in 1944, and the average size of landholdings had fallen over the same period from 8.09 to 6.71 acres. These trends were still accelerating, and it seemed likely that by 1955 average holdings would be reduced further to 5.22 acres. Food supply was reckoned to be adequate, but there was no longer, in 1944, any general surplus for export, and this had an adverse impact upon incomes. The livestock sector was also under threat, as there was a shortage of grazing provoked by increasing pressure for cultivable land. The prognosis was grim. There was little prospect of the Kikuyu of south Nyeri being able to maintain their standard of living, and yet this was already far below the minimum levels that were desirable for adequate diet and income. Whereas south Nyeri was, in 1944, home to some 29,000 Kikuyu families, it was reckoned that this number should be reduced to 15,000 if the population were to make a decent living from the land.[35]

A similar pattern of population pressure and declining income was apparent in other parts of central Kenya. In Kiambu, the most prosperous and intensively farmed of all the Kikuyu areas, land values increased tenfold between 1939 and 1952,[36] and throughout the Kikuyu reserves land litigation had exploded as people struggled to establish clear rights over what land they had in the face of the claims of the returning squatters. Court fees paid to the Native Tribunals in central Kenya from land cases alone climbed from £13,000 in 1949 to £25,000 in 1951.[37] The increase in litigation placed the chiefs who presided over the Native Tribunals in a powerful position, arbitrating the claims and counter-claims of their people. Some were thought to have abused their power for personal gain. In Nyeri, Chiefs Muhoya and Nderi had each acquired vast estates of more than 150 acres in extent, despite the general decline in average landholdings in their district (see table 1.i, p. 345, for a breakdown of Kenya's population by race).[38]

Land hunger provoked by population pressure and worsened by the return of squatters, increasing social differentiation and the acquisition of land by a relatively few powerful individuals were all part of the same problem. In tackling these issues, the colonial state was severely constrained by its past policies and its present alliances. The findings of the Land Commission of 1934 had foreclosed the option of giving the Kikuyu more land, and anyway the powerful political lobby of white settler interests would not countenance such a step. The growing individualism of Kikuyu, to be seen in the acquisition of private lands by

senior elders and chiefs, did not fit with colonial mythical ideals of the
egalitarian character of African society; but the power and patronage of
the chiefs could not be challenged without inflicting damage upon the
structures of colonial rule. Like conservative white settlers, conservative
Kikuyu chiefs were landlords. They, too, were seeking by the 1940s to
make greater commercial gains from their lands and to rid themselves of
the impediment of older obligations to their tenants. The returning
squatters quickly found that Kikuyu chiefs and landed elders were seldom
any more sympathetic to their plight than had been white settlers. The
colonial state was not prepared to challenge these prominent landed
interests, whether Kikuyu or European. The Kikuyu would simply have
to make better use of the land they had, while gradually being brought
to accept the fact that access to land was not an entitlement that every
Kikuyu could any longer expect. Greater social differentiation and landlessness were therefore to be among the consequences of colonial progress
and modernity.

To improve the productivity of Kikuyu lands so that they could accommodate a larger population, a campaign for conservation and improved
land husbandry was therefore launched in the 1940s. This was reinforced
by government propaganda that urged African farmers to adopt more
progressive and modern methods of farming, and to abandon traditional
practices that were harmful. The campaign was ambitious, though its
emphasis varied from place to place. Colonial estimations of the severity
of the problem of overcrowding, rapidly expanding erosion and declining
fertility intensified the resolve to push the campaign forward. There was
no time to prevaricate. Local byelaws were passed to give chiefs the power
to implement the necessary measures, and they were given authority to
prosecute those who declined to comply. The measures included the
building of terraces on sloping land, restrictions of cultivation along
streams, and the dipping of livestock to protect against disease. In Nyeri,
cattle dipping was made compulsory and fees were levied; in Murang'a,
terraces were constructed using communal labour forcibly recruited on
the orders of the chiefs; and in Kiambu, farmers were prosecuted for failure
to adhere to cultivation rules. Everywhere these interventions provoked
massive resistance. The chiefs, as the principal agents in implementing
these policies, bore the brunt of it. There was violent opposition in Nyeri
during 1946, where Chief Nderi was attacked by an angry mob of farmers.
In Kiambu, Waruhiu was harassed and threatened.[39] But by far the worst
disturbances were in Murang'a.

The Murang'a land husbandry campaign centred upon the construction of terracing, intended to protect sloping land from erosion
when cultivated. Building the terraces was heavy, unpleasant, very
unpopular work. The benefits brought by the terraces appeared to the

farmers to be negligible, and many of the walls washed away in the rains, necessitating that the work be started all over again in the next season. This seemed pointless effort. The work was carried out by the communal labour of women, under the direction of the chiefs. During 1945 some 3500 miles of terraces were constructed in Murang'a. The following year this figure doubled, as the district administration exhorted chiefs to compete to increase the extent of terracing in each location.

As the pressure mounted, some chiefs were not prepared to enforce the policy as vigorously as others. Older chiefs 'retired' from service because of their failure, while others resigned. They were replaced by new, younger men, who were enthusiastic 'modernizers' and more likely to get results. Although the work was based upon a traditional practice in the recruitment of communal labour, it was open to easy abuse by the more unscrupulous chiefs and their headmen. Among the new cadre of chiefs were many such men, keen to impress their colonial masters and to reap the dividends of their new positions. These men increasingly resorted to compulsion to force labour out, and they were not above victimizing the families of their political opponents and rivals in the process.[40]

The peasants of Murang'a finally revolted in July 1947. The unwitting catalyst was none other than Jomo Kenyatta, who visited the district on Sunday 20 July to give a speech in Murang'a town. A crowd of more than 10,000 streamed through the bustling market of this typical Kenyan trading centre, and passed the orderly stone-built offices of the district administration, down to the local showground. The tea shops emptied and the market stalls were deserted as everyone joined the throng. It was a noisy, disorderly gathering, stirred up by militants in the crowd intent on making trouble. Dressed casually, in a checked, open-neck shirt, and wearing his trade-mark leather jacket, Kenyatta cut a distinctive figure alongside the younger progressive chiefs in their khaki suits and plain ties, and the older chiefs, attired more traditionally in skins and cloth. When he took the microphone, Kenyatta weighed his words with care. A progressive and modernizing agriculturalist himself, he first praised colonial efforts to improve land husbandry; but, sensing that this praise did not suit the mood of his audience, many of whom booed and jeered, he went on to criticize the policy of using compulsory female labour as an abuse of Kikuyu custom, which it surely was.[41] It had been an adept performance. Kenyatta had kept the crowd with him, and he left the showground happy to have kept the militants at bay, and to have satisfied the bulk of his audience.

The next morning only a handful of women reported for work on the terraces, and within two weeks the government's campaign had come to a complete standstill across the district. Everyone blamed Kenyatta. The truth was that militants were already abroad in the Murang'a countryside, and it was they, not Kenyatta, who had stirred the local women to action. Feelings were strongest in areas where chiefs had been most vigorous in recruiting labour, but it was also apparent that militancy was high in north Murang'a, around the Church of Scotland missions at Kahuhia and Weithaga, where the KCA had built strongholds of support in the 1930s and where the independent schools and churches were now dominant. The militants were tapping into deep reservoirs of discontent.

The chiefs retaliated to the revolt by prosecuting over 600 people, but this only provoked violence: agricultural officers were now assaulted, terraces knocked down and destroyed, and the chiefs and their headmen subjected to public ridicule and harassment. In September 1947 Chief Ignatio was threatened at his home by a large crowd and one man was shot in the melee as guards sought to protect him. The resistance was still strong in May 1948, when women mobbed Chief Peterson Kariuki in Location 15, in response to the arrest of other protesters who had refused to come out for work. Order was only restored with the arrival of a force of truncheon-wielding police, who dispersed the crowd. In the face of such opposition, several more Murang'a chiefs now resigned or retired from government service.[42]

Making the chiefs the principal agents in the implementation of the land-husbandry campaign was a serious error of judgement. It too readily exposed them to their political opponents, making them easy targets in a popular protest at a time when militancy was anyway growing in response to the expulsion of the squatters. It seems likely that the attacks upon chiefs were coordinated and organized. The leading historian of this period, David Throup, has drawn attention to a smear campaign against prominent chiefs run in several of the leading African vernacular newspapers, and even taken up by the Asian press.[43] Ignatio in Murang'a, Muhoya in Nyeri, and Waruhiu in Kiambu faced the worst of these accusations. All three were conservative chiefs of the old school. They were devout Christians and active members of established Churches. All had opposed the rise of Kikuyu independent education in the 1930s, and none were sympathetic to the returning squatters in the 1940s. From around 1944, each of them was subjected to a string of well-publicised accusations about their corruption in land dealings, their preferment of family members and church associates, and their illegal arrest and harassment of rivals.

Several of these charges were brought to the courts. Waruhiu found himself before the magistrate on two charges. In an eerie foreshadowing of what was to happen during the years of the Emergency, the provincial administration worried about the loss of prestige that would be suffered if chiefs were dragged through the courts in this way. The Provincial Commissioner of Central Province, Wyn Harris, made a flagrant and quite shameless attempt to interfere with the prosecution. 'It is essential that Waruhiu's authority should be upheld,' he wrote, 'as these cases are beginning to break the hearts of our better chiefs as they feel they have not the support of government in keeping peace and good order in their districts.' The legal department was unimpressed by this 'special pleading', so Wyn Harris went directly to the Governor, alleging that the claim against Waruhiu was part of a carefully orchestrated plot by agitators to undermine the credibility of the senior chiefs. He was almost certainly correct, but there was also little doubt that even Waruhiu, admired for his devout Christianity and conservative fair-mindedness, overstepped the mark from time to time in exercise of his chiefly duties.

The district administration customarily turned a blind eye to such things. In the daily grind of life in the African locations, it was expected that a chief or headman might occasionally need 'to knock a few heads together', or 'bend the rules', in order to preserve control. Legal officers thought that chiefs 'should not behave like petty tyrants'; too many district administrators thought that tyranny in the name of order was no bad thing. Many other Kikuyu chiefs were more prone to excess than Waruhiu. His Kiambu neighbour in Lari location, Chief Makimei, a man well known for his temper and propensity to violence, had narrowly escaped conviction for manslaughter when he was still a headman. When he was once again brought before the courts on a charge of assault, Wyn Harris defended him as he had defended Waruhiu. When the magistrate found Makimei guilty of a 'grievous assault', Wyn Harris paid his £50 fine, and the £40 damages awarded to his victim.[44] Even before the declaration of the State of Emergency in October 1952, then, Kikuyu could be forgiven for believing that the colonial government condoned the use of gratuitous violence and the 'bending of the rules' by its public servants. During the Emergency, this culture of violence was to get far, far worse.

## Urban militancy

Through the 1940s, Nairobi became the undisputed centre of militant politics. Tucked onto a flat piece of land just below the hills, it was the gateway to the densely populated farming districts of Kikuyuland and the White Highlands. 'Nairobi was our town,' Karin Blixen had written in the early 1930s;[45] but the urban leisure of the white highlanders, concentrated in the colonial commercial centre of the town, was already even then being slowly surrounded and hemmed in by a sea of African urbanization. As the town grew, so its face changed. By the 1940s it was not the white highlanders, but the Kikuyu, who would say 'Nairobi was our town.'

Squalid, crowded and reeking of poverty, the African estates and shanties in the eastern part of the city sheltered more than 80,000 souls. Here were rich recruiting grounds for the militants. Among the vast army of the unemployed, there were many who drifted into crime, and who had time on their hands to become involved in low-level political activity. Over the war years, the trade-union movement established itself very firmly among many sectors of the African workforce. Unions became a base of mobilization for other kinds of political action, where the militants could win further support. For the moderates in the KAU, after its formation in 1945, the unions always seemed dangerously uncontrollable. In Nairobi the militants easily dominated the moderates.

It was a militancy closely intertwined with the urban criminal under-world. In 1945 and 1946, the town's European population became alarmed at the rising crime rate, with burglaries, street thefts and robberies all on the increase, though of course the usual victims of crime were not the wealthy European minority but the poor of the African estates. Large tracts of Eastlands, where all the African estates were located, were entirely ungoverned by the forces of law and order.[46] In the absence of the police, criminal gangs had grown up to control the estates, running everything from petty crime to smuggling and protection rackets. The criminal gangs reflected the ethnic segregation of the town. Kikuyu gangs dominated, and they tended to target non-Kikuyu traders, businesses and residents.

By 1947 the most powerful of these gangs was the *Anake a forti* – the 'Forty Group' – comprising a high proportion of Kikuyu ex-servicemen, most of whom were reputedly in the generation that had been initiated in 1940. Some 75,000 Kenyans had served in the British military during the Second World War.[47] Those among them who returned to Nairobi arrived with high expectations, and with accumulated remittances ready to invest in small businesses and trade. These ambitious men found their progress blocked by the conservatives who dominated African municipal government committees in Nairobi and who preferred to give the few licences available for new enterprises to their own clients. The ex-servicemen soon found themselves squeezed to the economic margins, where they took up a variety of irregular, unlicensed and often illegal activities. The town's Burma market was first established on a strip of wasteland near Shauri Moyo, as a meeting place for unlicensed traders, and named for the many ex-servicemen who gathered there. Traders built shacks here to store their wares, or kept their goods on barrows and carts, covered for the night with tarpaulin or sacking. Some slept by their stalls, whilst others employed guards to keep their possessions safe. By 1950 the Burma market was a renowned hub for criminal activity as well as militant politics.[48]

As their accumulated savings were frittered away in Nairobi's high-cost economy and their frustration mounted, the ex-servicemen of the Forty Group were first drawn into crime and then into political activities in which crime might play a part. The sociologist Frank Furedi has suggested that members of the Forty Group were from the outset motivated by a high level of political consciousness, perhaps inspired by their military experience.[49] Others have thought that their involvement in political activity was merely acquisitive – simply another means of making a living; and some have even suggested that the Forty Group was barely a group at all, but rather the collective name given to a cohort of criminals who operated largely independently of one another.[50] Whatever their inspiration or motivation – and it is likely that individuals had differing political perspectives – it is clear that the formal politics of the KAU held little appeal for the ex-servicemen. By 1947 the Forty Group was widely identified with militant politics. Some of their number had gone to Murang'a during the peasants' revolt there to support the protest, and they were also known to have supported the squatters at Olenguruone.[51] Mwangi Macharia and Stanley Mathenge were said to be among the members of the Forty Group, and union leaders and political activists including Fred Kubai, Eluid Mutonyi, Charles Wambaa and John Mungai were known to have links to the group.

It was these militant urban politicians, operating on the fringes of the murky, criminal world of Eastlands, who drew together the threads of African political protest, not the moderates of the KAU.[52] Though characterized by colonial officials as 'gangsters and spivs', their activities were far from being simply criminal. Kubai and Mutonyi, in particular, acted as intermediaries in forging links between the acquisitive skills of the Forty Group and the needs of political organizations, such as the unions and the Olenguruone squatters, for funding. Special Branch thought that the gang supplied money to politicians through protection rackets run on the African estates.[53] A militant political consciousness was therefore undoubtedly a feature of the Forty Group, and it had a wide support among the ordinary Kikuyu residents of Nairobi. As one of its members explained to Frank Furedi: 'We felt that the KAU was going too slow and that the only way to change things was through violence. This is why we started armed robberies. Most of the Africans in Nairobi were behind us and they would not inform the police on our activities.'[54] The Forty Group rose to prominence between 1945 and 1947, but by 1949 the gang had broken up, some of its former members finding employment in the casual trades of Eastlands, as barrow boys, hawkers and taxi drivers. From 1949 former gang members would play other roles in militant urban struggles, especially in the unions and in support of a group of like-mined radicals who became known as the *Muhimu*.[55]

The *Muhimu* comprised a small cell of militant activists who, by the end of the 1940s, were beginning to coordinate opposition to colonial rule on several fronts. *Muhimu* members were active in the Rift Valley, and in support of the squatters at Olenguruone, and in the slums of Eastlands, as well as on the committees of the KAU. They administered their own oath to people, and were gathering guns and ammunition in preparation for a violent struggle that they saw as inevitable if the Kikuyu were to free themselves from European domination.[56] Unlike the KAU's leader, Kenyatta, who thought politics was only for the elders, these militants sought to empower a younger and altogether more impetuous generation.[57]

Sometime between the end of 1948 and February 1950 members of the Kiambaa Parliament took the fateful decision to try to deal with the Nairobi militants of the *Muhimu*. Peter Mbiyu Koinange contacted two prominent union leaders in Nairobi, Fred Kubai and John Mungai. Both were then involved in the taxi drivers' union. He invited them to join the KAU and take its oath, and then to assist in the campaign to spread the movement. They eventually agreed, but only on condition that their supporters could administer the oath to any trustworthy Kikuyu without the payment of a large fixed fee, and that the oath itself should be made more militant.

This amounted to a dramatic transformation of the KAU's oathing campaign, in terms of both style and purpose. It is not entirely clear whether all the members of the Kiambaa Parliament, most importantly Kenyatta, fully appreciated the likely impact of this. It is certain that other leaders of the KAU, who were not members of the Parliament, did not know about this 'incorporation' of the militants. The potential gains for the nationalist cause from incorporating the militants were great, but the risks were high. The KAU might gain the mass support it had lacked; but would the KAU, or even the Kiambaa Parliament, be able to control and direct the militants and their followers?

This was to prove the fateful step on the road to rebellion. The militants wasted no time in seizing control of the political agenda, now using the name of Kenyatta to add legitimacy to their own oath and to their deeds. And Kenyatta was powerless to do anything about it. During 1949 Kubai and Mungai set about exploiting their opportunity by firstly oathing twenty-four key trade unionists, who would extend the campaign among their members. Next, they oathed a number of 'carefully selected criminals', who were asked to gather arms for later use against Europeans and the government. These weapons would be stored in the armoury at Kiambaa, amongst other stashes. Then, probably early in 1950, they extended the oath to Nairobi's Kikuyu taxi drivers, whose compliance was required in transporting the movement's members about their business.[58]

These were not the type of people Kenyatta had intended to draw into the fold of the KAU, and the decision to involve them would irrevocably change the pace and tone of the nationalist struggle. During

1950 the slow, selective oathing of Kikuyu elders gave way to mass meetings. It was around this time that the group of militants behind these developments first began to refer to themselves as the *Muhimu*. They now met more regularly, under the chairmanship of Mutonyi. He reported back to the Kiambaa parliament, and separately to Kenyatta – who, for reasons of security, no longer attended the meetings at Koinange's home. But what Mutonyi told them was only a carefully selected and very limited version of the *Muhimu's* full range of activites.[59] As another of the militants, Bildad Kaggia, recalls in his autobiography, the *Muhimu*, which had previously confined its activities to the Nairobi area, now despatched its own oath administrators throughout the Kikuyu reserves.[60] The moderates of the KAU had lost control, and they would never regain the initiative from the militants.

The growing power and influence of the militants were most clearly to be seen in the emergence of trade-union activism in Nairobi at this time. The KAU leaders had never given effective support to emergent trade unions in Kenya. Moderates, such as Mbotela and Kenyatta, frequently made public statements distancing themselves from direct actions taken by the unions.[61] Fred Kubai served as general secretary of the Transport and Allied Workers' Union, which had begun life as a union for Nairobi's taxi drivers, while Bildad Kaggia was a leader of the Clerks and Commercial Workers' Union. These two militants were instrumental, along with Makhan Singh, in the formation of the East African Trade Union Congress (EATUC) on May Day 1949. During its brief life, the EATUC was by far the most important 'militant vehicle for championing African aspirations' in Nairobi, a role epitomized in the drama of the general strike of May 1950.[62] They brought out more than 6000 workers in Nairobi across a variety of trades, even extending the action to other towns. Violence erupted very dramatically, with running battles through the streets of Pumwani and Shauri Moyo over several days. When the militants were finally persuaded to return to work, many who did so found their jobs filled by others. Of the Kikuyu workers in Nairobi who went on strike, some 2000 were dismissed from their employment *after* returning to work. This victimization of the strikers only added to the deepening pool of militancy in Nairobi.[63]

The rifts between moderates and militants in Nairobi had long been bitter. During the 1930s the KCA had established an energetic Nairobi branch. This went underground in 1940, when the party was banned as part of the wartime controls on African political activities. At this time the KCA could boast a membership of more than 7000, and an active support and influence that was far greater, most especially in Nairobi. However, within the city the party had never succeeded in building a solid base of support beyond the dominant Kikuyu community. Urban

politics remained stubbornly ethnic, a pattern sustained by the segregation of many of the estates and shanties and by the habits of employers
to select workers from a preferred ethnic group. When African political
parties were once again permitted at the end of the war, in 1945, and
the Kiambu elite opted to join a party that would draw in other ethnic
groups in a broader nationalist alliance (the KAU), there was little
enthusiasm among Nairobi's Kikuyu leaders. Where Nairobi had once
been a source of strength for the old KCA, for KAU after 1945 it
became a place of intrigue and internal squabbling, and from 1950, a
place of internecine violence.

In February 1951 two of the leading urban militants, Kubai and
Mutonyi, hatched a strategy to remove the moderates from control of
the KAU branch in Nairobi. They were assisted by other militant urban
leaders, many of them also trade unionists with 'little respect for the
KAU', including Kaggia, John Mungai, J. D. Kali, James Beauttah and
Paul Ngei.[64] When the KAU Nairobi branch held its elections for
office holders on 10 June 1951, the militants seized their chance. Their
supporters packed the Kaloleni Hall and, under the nose of a startled
Kenyatta, they swept the board, defeating the moderates in elections for
every key post. Kubai was elected chairman of the Nairobi branch, with
Mungai vice-chairman, Kaggia general secretary, and Ngei treasurer.

Kenyatta was shocked and horrified. Worse was to come. The militants
then used their control of the powerful Nairobi branch to summon a
national party conference later in the year, where they made further
gains, 'ousting the constitutional nationalists and gaining virtual control
of the national executive committee'.[65] It seemed that Kenyatta's authority had been irreparably damaged. The militants were no longer confined
to the secrecy of conspiratorial politics. They now held sway over the
KAU in Nairobi, and also over the national party structure.

Emboldened by these successes, the *Muhimu* now became more
aggressive within Nairobi and beyond, under the direction of no more
than a dozen urban militants, headed by Eliud Mutonyi and the ruthless
and increasingly strident Kubai. The main *Muhimu* committee in the
city was enlarged to bring in members from each of the Kikuyu districts,
including Embu and Meru, and also the Kamba district of Machakos.
Separate committees were then established within Nairobi to represent
each district. Only in the case of Kiambu did the *Muhimu* fail to fully
assert its authority, influence there remaining with the Koinanges and
the Kiambaa Parliament. The *Muhimu* district committees then set about
establishing a subordinate structure, connecting them to locations in the
Kikuyu countryside. Through this still covert network of committees,
each a small cell of committed activists linked to a wider cadre of militant
followers, oathing and the collection of funds spread rapidly over the

later part of 1951 and into 1952.[66] And as the strength and influence of the *Muhimu* grew, so too did the violence.

Kenyatta was not an impetuous man. These militants were his enemies, and he feared them. He spoke against the violence of Mau Mau during 1951 and 1952, principally because he saw it as uncontrolled and undisciplined, and therefore potentially dangerous to Kikuyu society itself.[67] But it is unlikely that Kenyatta was fully aware of how powerful the *Muhimu* had become until its leaders summoned him to Nairobi, early in 1952, to threaten him with death. It was Fred Kubai who was poised to carry out his assassination.[68]

## Emerging Violence

The official government history of the origins and growth of Mau Mau, written by a former colonial officer, F. D. Corfield, and published in 1960, gives a detailed account of the build-up of Kikuyu protest from 1945 to 1952. Corfield attributes everything to the plotting of the KAU under the control of Jomo Kenyatta. He portrays Mau Mau as a master plan against the colonial state, each step in the mounting conflict leading inexorably to the next, each fragment of information fitting together 'as neatly as pieces in a jigsaw puzzle'.[69] This interpretation reflected the white settler view of Kenyatta and the KAU. At the time, it all seemed to make a kind of sense – but only if you were prepared to believe that Kenyatta was an evil monster who had planned violence and mayhem from the point of his return to Kenya in 1946. Nothing could have been further from the truth. In convincing himself of Kenyatta's guilt, Corfield relied upon inference.

Though few Europeans had believed it at the time, Kenyatta's protestations that he had done all he could to thwart the militants were true. Peter Mbiyu Koinange's efforts to incorporate the Kikuyu militants into the Kiambaa Parliament and the KAU had succeeded from 1950 only in further marginalizing Kenyatta. With hindsight, it can be seen as a huge gamble that was doomed to failure from the start.

Why, then, did the Koinanges take such a risk? It was certainly clear by the end of the 1940s that the KAU had failed to engage a mass following through its strategy of recruiting senior Kikuyu patrons. The influence of the party had even faded among moderate nationalists. Between 1946 and 1950 the militants had successfully stolen the political thunder of the KAU on every front, stirring up direct action and winning widespread popular support. There can be little doubt that John Westley Mbiyu and Peter Mbiyu Koinange were frustrated by the failure of the Kiambaa Parliament to maintain Kikuyu unity, and they must have realized that the militants had seized the political agenda. There is some evidence to suggest that the Kiambaa Parliament itself at this time was already edging toward a riskier strategy of confrontation, although our information on this comes only from the memoirs of the militants. James Beauttah, for example, recalls that the meeting of the Parliament in February 1950 took the decision to horde arms, and discussed a proposal to begin a programme of assassinations. Kenyatta was by then no longer attending meetings of the Parliament, although it is difficult to imagine that he would not have been briefed on this. Whether the Parliament's remaining members were fully behind these moves, or whether it was only the younger Koinanges who opted to support a more radical approach, is not entirely clear. What *is* clear is that the Kiambaa Parliament was never in the vanguard of these developments, but merely followed along a trail already blazed by the likes of Mutonyi, Kubai, Kaggia, Beauttah and Mungai.[70] And that was the nub of the problem. The militants did not feel themselves to be bound by the authority of the Kiambaa Parliament, any more than they felt constrained by the policies of the KAU. They dealt with the Parliament, as they had with the KAU, only to use it and exploit it for their own purposes. They wished to tackle the popular grievances of the Kikuyu through direct action, by whatever means seemed most effective.

This conviction was immensely empowering, yet it also made their movement prone to indiscipline. Within the militant cadre were many criminal elements – 'a team of thieves', as Kubai would later call them.[71] As oathing was extended outside Nairobi from 1950 it became increasingly difficult to control such people. While the *Muhimu* was able to efficiently build up its network of support committees, raise funds through oathing fees, gather and stash arms, and target its enemies for assassination, the criminal elements who operated within the *Muhimu* were prone to independent and opportunistic actions, some even seeking simply to line their own pockets through the rapid and unguarded extension of oathing. This indiscipline held dangers. Extortion and bullying undermined the nationalist cause and built up resentments among the victims. Many respectable Kikuyu lived in fear of the *Muhimu*'s thugs, and paid their oath fees only to protect themselves and their families from harassment. These hooligans were deeply loathed by more respectable Kikuyu. They were illiterate, landless people who owned no property: men of no standing; and some of them were very young: youths of only seventeen or eighteen years. These were not the kind of people who should be administering oaths to their elders. Many people took the oath in fear, not in faith.

Indiscriminate and enforced oathing also made it more likely that some of those who were compelled to participate would eventually inform the colonial authorities of what had happened. In this way, the code of secrecy that had kept the militant leaders out of the gaze of colonial officials up to 1950 began to unravel thereafter. In the months leading up to the declaration of Emergency in October 1952, the emerging pattern of violence in the militants' campaign was therefore not the carefully orchestrated master plan of Corfield's imagination, but a grittier mix of organized political action, random opportunism, acts of vengeance and outright criminality.

## The militants' campaign

From the initial phase of the squatters' resistance on the farms of the Rift Valley, between 1946 and 1948, oathing had given rise to local skirmishes. Where militants demanded solidarity in opposition to the new labour contracts, Kikuyu squatters were pressured into taking the oath. In March 1948 trouble had erupted on a farm in Njoro, when two squatters refused to take the oath and were beaten. When the victims complained to the police, through their European employer, the investigation revealed a concerted campaign of oathing on all the farms in the area, with widespread intimidation and petty violence. The police identified George Ndegwa, an old KCA activist, as one of the principals behind the Njoro oathing. Ndegwa had in fact covertly maintained a KCA branch structure in the Rift Valley after the banning of the party in 1940, and had used this as a vehicle for organizing the squatters' resistance. In June 1948 Ndegwa was arrested and convicted of being a member of a proscribed society, the KCA, serving a sentence of one year's imprisonment.[72] Many old KCA radicals such as Ndegwa, who had never warmed to the pan-ethnic agenda of the KAU, would be recruited into the *Muhimu*'s cause over the next few years, especially in the Rift Valley and in Kiambu. They were men of conviction, but they were also impulsive and impatient.

The trouble at Njoro, and on other Rift Valley farms in 1948, was amplified and intensified from 1950 as the tempo of *Muhimu* oathing greatly increased throughout the Kikuyu countryside. As the oath administrators began their work in each location, moving out northwards from Nairobi, complaints filtered through to the colonial authorities. By March 1950 the District Commissioner in Kiambu had already encountered 'two or three instances of Africans being intimidated and forced to take an oath of secrecy' by 'political agitators'. Similar reports emanated from Murang'a in April and May, and Chief Nderi reported the first large-scale oath meetings in Nyeri during August. Information was speedily gathered on these illegal events, but attempts to prosecute the offenders proved difficult because the victims were 'exceedingly scared

and reluctant to make open accusations'. The first successful cases came
before the courts in June and July, one involving the prosecution of thirty-
nine Kikuyu who had attended an oathing ceremony on a Naivasha farm,
the other involving a known militant named Dedan Mugo, who was
convicted with twenty-five others of having been involved in an illegal
oathing ceremony in Kiambu. The key witness for the prosecution in
the first case was a farm worker who had been badly beaten for refusing
to take the oath, and in the second case it was a longstanding police
informer, Johanna Njuguna Kamau, who had been among those forcibly
given the oath in Kiambu.[73] Some white settlers believed the militants
were deliberately targeting them.

The Naivasha Farmers' Association wrote to the government at this
time complaining that the dissidents were 'ruining' their members,
packing farms with militant labourers who 'stirred up trouble', intimidating their workers and victimizing their foremen. Between September
1950 and January 1951 the police managed to bring five prosecutions
against militants for the violent intimidation of labourers on the Naivasha
farms. A similar pattern of events gradually became apparent in other
parts of the White Highlands, as the militants extended their oathing
campaign into the labour lines of farms in Nanyuki, Laikipia and the
Kinangop.[74] These were people the Kiambaa Parliament would never
have oathed before 1950 but that the indiscriminate campaigners of the
*Muhimu* were now sweeping up in their hundreds.

Alarmed by reports of the increasing scale of oathing, the government
had taken steps in August 1950 to ban 'the Mau Mau society' as an
unregistered, and therefore illegal organization. They did not yet have
any clear understanding of what comprised this society. It was hoped
that this would make it easier to bring cases against anyone believed to
be promoting the organization, but district officers continued to find
that people would not speak out.[75] Over the following months the focus
of militant activity shifted from the farms of the Rift Valley to the Kikuyu
reserves of Kiambu, Nyeri and Murang'a. Oathing here was usually
organized through KAU branches, which the militants had come to
dominate in many areas. South Nyeri and northern Murang'a were two
areas of notably belligerent militancy. In both areas the 'mob oratory'
of threats and intimidation at public meetings had begun to terrify
government servants and leading church elders, who feared physical
attack. The *Muhimu*'s oath administrators who visited these districts
made their mark on local politics. 'The hatred of the young men from
Nairobi is something that can be felt whenever one meets them in the
reserve,' commented the District Commissioner in Nyeri. 'A sullen,
subversive, anti-government, anti-European feeling can always be found
among a certain section of the Kikuyu,' commented another official,

who thought the majority of Kikuyu 'were being exploited' by these 'spivs and agitators' from Nairobi who wanted to make money by tapping into 'their genuinely felt grievances over land'.[76]

The sharp talk of the militants grew increasingly brazen. This prompted some district commissioners to ask for greater restrictions on freedom of speech, in order to better protect chiefs and headmen from threats and harassment, but the government's legal officers once again declined to support legislation that infringed what they considered to be basic liberties. By drawing attention to themselves, the militants were anyway now more liable to prosecution under existing laws.

The administration gained their first significant success in the courts towards the end of 1951, when James Beauttah was convicted of collecting money for Mau Mau. Around the same time, Beauttah and three other Murang'a activists were arrested for their role in a protest of 500 women against a government cattle-inoculation programme in the district. In February 1952 the four were convicted of causing malicious damage to government property – a number of cattle pens had been destroyed – and each was sentenced to two years' imprisonment with hard labour.[77] Beauttah and his comrades would spend the Emergency behind bars.

These prosecutions might be interpreted as a sign of the indiscipline and carelessness of the militants in exposing themselves so easily to government sanction. The prosecutions also reflected the fact that the emerging crisis was entering a new phase, with the chiefs, headmen and Kikuyu of a more moderate political persuasion now beginning to take a stand against the intimidating tactics of the militants. In January 1952 this escalated into open violence in Nyeri. Over six nights at the end of the month there were eleven cases of arson in the Aguthi and Thengenge locations. In each case the dwellings of persons linked in some way to the government were set alight. The next month, there was an outbreak of fifty-eight unexplained grass fires on the European farms in the nearby Nanyuki district, destroying several thousand acres of valuable grazing land.

This was followed by a second spate of attacks on the homes of Africans loyal to the government in Nyeri. The victims again included government headmen, those who worked in the local courts as clerks and interpreters, and persons who had given evidence in court cases or provided the police with information on Mau Mau activities. In all instances the victims managed to escape from their blazing homes, but the intent of their attackers was plain. The police were confronted by 'an impregnable wall of secrecy' when investigating these crimes, and it was reported that the events had so terrified the local chiefs, headmen and church leaders that they were no longer prepared to cooperate

with the government in any way. It was at this point that the District
Commissioner in Nyeri first suggested employing the Collective Punishments Ordinance in relation to Mau Mau cases. This law provided
for collective fines to be charged against communities who refused to
cooperate with police investigations, or whose members were thought
to be withholding information for the protection of guilty parties. There
was some debate as to the wisdom of punishing the innocent majority
'for the misdeeds of the few'. Against the obviously indiscriminate
character of the punishment, local officials argued strongly for the need
to show support for the victims, who had suffered because of their loyalty
to government, and to compensate them for their losses. The use of the
Collective Punishments Ordinance was approved on 4 April 1952, and
four days later the Governor authorised a fine of £2500 to be levied
against the population of Aguthi and Thengenge locations, this sum to
be distributed among those who had suffered losses in the attacks of
January and February.[78] The government would resort to this blunt legal
instrument with growing regularity as the Emergency deepened.

Corfield's official history of the rebellion suggests that central government was slow to respond to the worsening security situation in the
Kikuyu countryside at this time, and that the extent of the emerging
conflict was played down. The steps taken by government were certainly
localized, and they tended to place the onus upon African chiefs and
headmen to tackle the threat of Mau Mau themselves. From August
1950, when Mau Mau was first banned, loyal headmen and farm foremen
had been encouraged to hold meetings on the farms of the Rift Valley
to speak against Mau Mau and deter labourers from taking the oaths. A
CID officer had then been posted to Nakuru to work specifically on
the prosecution of Mau Mau cases, and a second was sent to Nyeri.
This helped in the gathering of better intelligence and confirmed the
information provided by moderates, such as Mbotela, that militant activities had made 'two divisions' of the Kikuyu.[79]

Then, from April 1952, at the suggestion of Louis Leakey, the government gave its backing to a wider 'counter-oathing' campaign, led by
the chiefs and elders, in which another Kikuyu oath was used to expunge
the effects of the Mau Mau oath. Louis Leakey was Kenya's 'white
African'.[80] The son of a missionary, and a Kikuyu-speaker, he was a self-
taught archaeologist and a renowned authority on African ethnography
and culture. His legendary skill in identifying the most productive
excavation sites led others to coin the phrase 'Leakey's luck' as he made
a string of important finds. By the 1940s he was established as a leading
archaeologist of Africa, and he earned the respect of the international
academic community; but his lore on the Kikuyu was not in the mould
of learned, academic knowledge: Louis Leakey presented himself as a

Kikuyu, as 'an insider', a white man who knew African culture because he had become part of it himself. In this guise he was the kind of self-made man that other white highlanders admired – the perfect antidote to the 'experts' who would be sent out from Britain to solve the problems of Kenya. As the Mau Mau struggle seized Kikuyuland, the politically conservative white African Louis Leakey would play a prominent role in the campaign to counter the rebellion.

The counter-oathing ceremonies were Leakey's first intervention against Mau Mau. The ritual required the use of a *githathi* stone and the participation of senior elders to 'cleanse' people. Chief Waruhiu, a close personal friend of Leakey, took a prominent role in this, leading six *githathi* ceremonies in Kiambu, each one attended by more than 600 people. Another Christian stalwart, Chief Njiri, then took charge of similar ceremonies in Murang'a. The *githathi* stone was believed to be powerful, and these activities seem to have posed the first real challenge to the authority of the militants in the Kikuyu countryside. In the wake of the *githathi* ceremonies, all the elders involved were threatened and their families harassed.[81] Leakey himself went in fear of attack. It was now that the killing began.

The first bodies were found floating in the Kirichwa river, in Nyeri, on 15 May 1952, at a remote spot away from any settlements. The two men had been shot and their bodies then mutilated. One was a headman. The other was identified as a police informer. The passer-by who had first seen the bodies tangled in the reeds, and reported to the police, was himself killed a few weeks later. By then, two more police informers had been murdered in Kiambu, and a chief's messenger in Murang'a had 'disappeared'. His body was later found, having been strangled and badly mutilated, and then tossed into a river. August saw further murders of police informers and Crown witnesses in Kiambu and Laikipia, the killings of three pro-government Kikuyu at Rumuruti for refusing to take the oath, eight murders in Murang'a, and a dramatic wave of killings and assaults in Nyeri, where a curfew was imposed upon Aguthi location and a detachment of police were sent out from Nairobi to try to stem the rising tide of violence.[82] By early September there had been a total of twenty-three known assassinations, and many other government servants, informers and witnesses were missing. Over these months, the police had to drop more than a hundred prosecutions relating to oath administration because their witnesses either 'turned hostile', or simply 'disappeared'.[83]

The stories of the desperate struggles that were taking place on the white farms and in the Kikuyu countryside at this time were later revealed in some of the cases that did come before the courts. One of the police informers murdered in the Kinangop area early in August was a Kikuyu squatter named Mbogo Karioki. Two months prior to his death, Karioki had given evidence in a case against other Kikuyu involved in administering oaths to the labourers on farms in north Kinangop. The prosecution was successful, and the accused were convicted and sentenced, but after giving evidence Karioki was threatened by Mau Mau supporters. Nothing more happened until Sunday 3 August, when Karioki walked the few miles from the farm where he worked to visit his brother, a trader at Geita market. After eating with his brother, Karioki set off for home. His assailants followed him from Geita, and attacked him on a secluded footpath. Karioki's shrieks were heard by a passer-by, who came nearer and saw two men running away from the scene and a third using a sword to hack at the neck of Karioki's prostrate body. It took this witness, a young girl named Waitherero, more than a week to pluck up the courage to tell her European employer what she had seen. He brought the police to interview her. She took them to the body, and they then gathered other evidence from witnesses in Geita. It was therefore ten days before Karioki's decomposed and decapitated body was exhumed from a shallow grave less than one mile from Geita. His partially decomposed head was found nearby, and was identified by several other squatters, and by the local European police inspector, who had known him well.

The case did not come before the court until April 1953, and over that period Waitherero had to be held in protective custody at the local police post. She had been able to pick out two men at a police identification parade, and the prosecution case rested largely on her evidence. In court, other witnesses who had made corroborative statements to the police in August 1952 mostly now retracted critical parts of their testimony. By April 1953 this had become a common experience in cases of this kind. It was the view of the police that these witnesses may have been intimidated, and it seems very likely that they were. Despite the lack of other corroborating evidence, Judge Henry Mayers found Kamau Ndirangu and Githuka Kagwe guilty of the murder of Karioki, and the convictions were upheld in the East African Court of Appeal. Both convicted men were unmarried and in their mid-twenties, the sons of squatter families who had originally come to the Kinangop from Murang'a. They were hanged together in Nairobi Prison during May 1953.[84]

This case was by no means unique in its essential characteristics. The difficulty for the police was one of obtaining reliable witnesses and of keeping them safe from harm or intimidation in the long gap between the crime and the trial. In many cases, the principal witnesses were themselves already known to the police as trusted informers. This gave the court glimpses of a murky and often complex underworld, in which the magistrates and judges frequently had to evaluate the nature of the witness's relationship to the police, as well as deciding whether the witness might not in fact be an accomplice to the crime. For example, in a further case of the killing of a police informer, from Njoro, in November 1952, four Kikuyu squatters were accused on the evidence of another informer, named Joram, who had been present when the murder took place. There was some suggestion that Joram might have been compelled to participate in the murder. His evidence against three of the accused was uncorroborated, and only the fourth, Kirogi Gathia, was finally hanged as a result of the prosecution.[85] In another case, arising from the murder of police informer Ngugi Mrefu in Kiambu, the court acquitted two men when key witnesses changed their statements. Mrefu had been executed on the orders of Mau Mau on 24 September, his strangled body then placed in a weighted sack and tossed in the Katimayu river below Kingida Falls.[86] In other cases, the sheer press of work on the police at this time led to mistakes and oversights in the presentation of evidence, and therefore to acquittals on legal technicalities.[87] The failure to secure a greater number of convictions, for whatever reason, was a matter of frustration for the police, and it greatly angered the white settlers.

In some cases the suggestion was made that police frustration spilled over into the violent treatment of suspects. In April 1953 Justice Cram heard a case relating to the murder of Gacheri Kabaya, during October 1952, in Thika. Kabaya had apparently refused to take the Mau Mau oath, and had been tied up and strangled in front of his neighbours as a lesson to others. His body was then disposed of in a river, from where it was recovered two weeks later. Among the men accused of his murder were Karaya Njonji and Gachoi Waithaka. They had both made extra-judicial statements to the police that amounted to confessions of guilt, and they had implicated others in the crime. At the trial the two men retracted these statements, claiming they were made as a result of prolonged beatings and systematic torture at the hands of their police interrogators. Justice Cram was shocked by these detailed accusations, describing them as 'unprecedented in my experience of five years on the bench in this colony'. The lapse of time between the alleged beatings and the trial meant that there was no medical evidence in support of the claims, and Cram therefore chose not to believe the accused. There was anyway sufficient evidence to convict Njonji and Waithaka without their confessions, forced or otherwise, and so both were sentenced to hang.[88] Claims of the kind made in this case were to become a commonplace of Mau Mau trials, and Justice Cram's incredulity was to wear thinner as the Emergency went on and it became apparent that not all such accusations were without foundation.

Two further cases must be mentioned here, as each illustrates important aspects in the emergence of Mau Mau violence. Both cases arise from the white farms in the Rumuruti area of the Rift Valley. The first concerns Mau Mau's ethnic dimension. Because Mau Mau at this time sought to administer the oaths only to Kikuyu, those of other ethnic groups who were resident on the white farms became a threat to the secrecy and solidarity of the movement. This was to be seen in the use of many non-Kikuyu witnesses in the prosecution of cases, and in the victimization of non-Kikuyu on the farms who were considered a danger to the militants. The murder of Mutuaro Onsoti, the Kisii foreman on a farm in Rumuruti, offers an example of the direst consequences of this ethnic conflict.[89] A former soldier, Onsoti had been recruited in 1951 by the farm's owner, James Kean, precisely in order to help combat the disruptive tendencies of his Kikuyu squatter labour. He became the farm headman in May 1952, and was soon at loggerheads with the squatters. Onsoti informed Kean of a plot among the labourers, apparently inspired by Mau Mau activists, to take over the farm. Kean took the threats seriously, and became so concerned for Onsoti's welfare that he insisted the headman always leave a note at his home about his whereabouts that day, and instructed him to be cautious in all his dealings with the labourers, whom the farmer considered to be 'truculent and non-co-operative'. Throughout June and July 1952, Onsoti was regularly 'threatened by various men of the younger Kikuyu on the farm, who on occasion menaced him with pangas'. On 25 August Onsoti was finally subjected to a brutal attack carried out by four Kikuyu squatters. His decapitated body was exhumed in a wood on the farm the day after his death, but the head had been carried off by one of his assailants and was never recovered. The publicity given to these events contributed to a massive expulsion of Kikuyu labour from the Rumuruti area in September and October 1952.

The last case we will describe from this pre-Emergency phase also made a significant impression on the Kenyan public at the time. The murder of Joseph Kibunja for his refusal to take a Mau Mau oath during a mass ceremony on another Rumuruti farm was in many ways unexceptional.[90] Kabunja and his wife had been among some 200 Kikuyu squatters rounded up by the Mau Mau oath administrators, who came to their farm on the night of 15 September 1952. When it came to their turn to be oathed, Kabunja and his wife refused. Kabunja 'was a man of God', and had taken a pledge with his church to reject Mau Mau. Kabunja was first beaten, as were many others who refused the oath that night. The others eventually gave in to their interrogators and took the oath, but Kabunja did not. A rope was placed around his neck, and he was slowly throttled in an effort to persuade him to comply. He still refused, and so died a slow and agonizing death inside the hut where the oathing was taking place. Kabunja's body was now taken outside and buried in a shallow grave nearby.

What happened next was to give the incident a more powerful resonance than any other case from this period. Fearing that the body might be discovered on the farm, the militant leaders among the labourers resolved that the body should be removed to a more distant spot. Some twelve days after the murder the already traumatized community, including women and children, were gathered up once again and made to participate in the exhumation of Kabunja's remains and their removal to a wood several miles from the farm. There, the friends and neighbours of the deceased were then each made to take a panga and hack the rotting corpse into pieces, 'to show they were not afraid to murder the enemies of Mau Mau'. One of the oath administrators then made each person touch the victim's bloodied flesh, and touch their hands to their lips. Mwangi Ngunju was among the squatters present that night, and he later told the court of his revulsion: 'After rubbing the rotting flesh to my lips and mouth and hands I was sick. Nearly everyone was sick. I heard people being sick all around me. And whenever I think of it now I still feel very sick.' Kabunja's putrefying body parts were then reburied in the wood, only to be exhumed for a second time a few days later, when a group of the deceased's terrified and remorseful neighbours led the police to the scene. This was a disturbing and utterly exceptional case, rumours of which fuelled anxieties among all African communities and added to the tales that circulated among white settlers of the perversion and horror of Mau Mau oathing.

The assassinations of informers and government retainers were planned by local militants in the Kikuyu districts, and often directed by the *Muhimu*'s representatives. The murder of unfortunate souls such as Onsoti and Kabunja was not planned by anybody, but emerged out of the dynamics of violence, fear and intimidation that surrounded the whole process of oathing and militant action. Both kinds of killing were part of what Mau Mau had become. Indiscipline and random violence were most widespread on the farms of the Rift Valley, where there were fewer police, no chiefs, and only a small number of church communities to place a brake on militant excess. Those taking the oath on the farms were often told that by doing so they would register their entitlement to land on the farm when the Europeans were thrown out of Kenya. They were staking a claim to a better future. Squatter anger was deeply felt, and *Muhimu* influence among them was only slight, and remote.

### Preparing for war

As the violence escalated in June 1952, Sir Philip Mitchell, Kenya's Governor since 1945, took his leave of the colony. Mitchell had promoted multi-racialism, but under his paternalist governorship white settlers had

consolidated their political position within government, while Africans
had not succeeded in making any significant headway in realizing their
ambitions for political representation. Mitchell had been a bitter disappointment. Perhaps the ill health that dogged the latter part of his time
in Nairobi had caused him to retreat from the fray. Whatever the reason,
his officials had found it very difficult to give him advice, or to tell him
things he did not want to hear; and he did not want to hear about Mau
Mau. Mitchell had ignored the signs of African frustration and had
certainly been guilty of complacency. He was convinced that the 'agitators' among the Kikuyu had no real political constituency, and did not
take the threat of disorder seriously.[91]

With his departure, there was to be an interregnum of three months
before Evelyn Baring came out to replace him. Baring had a sharp
intelligence, as his First in History from Oxford indicated, and African
experience. He had served in Southern Rhodesia in the early 1940s, and
then in other parts of southern Africa. Where Mitchell had been strong-
willed and opinionated, the worry with Baring was that he had no
opinion at all. The more strident figures among the administrative staff
looked forward to his arrival as an opportunity to get across their point
of view. The less strident worried that they might not be able to get a
hearing. Baring was certainly going to be offered plenty of advice.

Even in the three-month gap prior to Baring's arrival, the Kenya
administration responded more actively to the mounting crisis than had
been the case under Mitchell. Almost as soon as Mitchell had departed,
the Commissioner of Police, O'Rorke, produced a detailed report on
Mau Mau in which he expressed fears that 'a general revolt was afoot
among the Kikuyu'. He was the first official to say what Mitchell had
not dared to think. Among the many things he revealed was that mass
oathing was now widespread, although he reckoned that only around 10
per cent of the Kikuyu population had so far taken the most militant
oath, and that there had been a well-organized and systematic campaign
of oathing within the prisons: on their release from the gaols, ex-convicts
had become important and active participants in Mau Mau crimes.[92]

A flurry of meetings in Government House now followed, but little of
this anxiety was yet conveyed to London. The white settlers were by now
getting jumpy and, while they had not been able to railroad Mitchell into
precipitous action, they seized the opportunity to exploit the vulnerability
of the inexperienced acting governor, Henry Potter. Their leader, Michael
Blundell, provoked a debate on law and order in the Legislative Council,
and demanded the immediate banning of the KAU, the declaration of
an Emergency, and the reorganization of the legal department to separate
the role of the Attorney-General from that of the Member for Law and
Order – this last demand a thinly disguised attack on the Attorney-General,

John Whyatt, whom the settlers considered to be unsympathetic to their interests and too fond of legal rules for their more rough and ready methods. Blundell added malice to his demands by threatening a 'settler backlash' against Africans if the government did not act swiftly and resolutely to deal with the present crisis.[93]

It was not until 17 August 1952 that the acting governor finally informed London of the 'deteriorating situation', warning that 'drastic legislation' might be needed in order to regain control.[94] This salvo was the first clear intimation that London had received that Nairobi might require 'special measures' to tackle Mau Mau. On the advice of the Colonial Office, Whyatt now set about drafting the proposed legislation and plans were laid for him and Chief Native Commissioner Davies to visit London during September, to discuss the implications of the proposed measures. Their visit came as a surprise to staff in London, who had for too long listened to Mitchell's assurances that nothing was amiss. Feeling rather railroaded by the unusual suddenness of Kenya's predicament, officials in London were reluctant to give the Kenya government everything it now asked for, but a package was eventually agreed.[95] On 23 September, exactly one week before Baring's arrival, seven existing ordinances were amended. Among measures that allowed for the protection of witnesses by the police, restrictions on traffic movement at night and the control of printing presses, by far the most important change was to the rules of evidence. It was now permitted for a senior police officer to attest a prisoner's confession, and for this to be accepted as evidence before a court.[96]

This was to have a profound impact upon the conduct of Mau Mau trials as the emergency progressed. At the time these legislative changes were approved, a total of 412 people had already been convicted of offences relating to oath administration and membership of Mau Mau, but hundreds more awaited trial. The legal system was hardly coping, and the changes were justified as a necessary short-term palliative.[97]

The next day, 24 September, there was a further spate of Mau Mau activity on the European farms in the Timau area. The mass oathing of labourers was followed by a wave of arson attacks on farm buildings and the maiming and disembowelling of hundreds of settler-owned livestock. This event seemed to make a far deeper impact upon the minds of white settlers than had the murders of more than twenty Africans in government service over the preceding months.[98]

# 2

# Burying the Past

Governor Baring finally reached Nairobi on 30 September 1952. The mood in the city was sombre and impatient. In the previous week there had been further killings of Africans on farms in the White Highlands, and a policeman had been savagely murdered in Nairobi. The local newspapers carried reports every day of a rising tide of robberies, murder attempts and oathing ceremonies. The reports were not good, and Baring almost immediately began to form the view that he would need to act decisively if order was to be maintained.

A queue of officials waited to brief the new Governor, headed by Commissioner of Police O'Rorke, a quiet and highly professional officer but not really cut out for what was coming his way over the next few months, and Whyatt, the softly spoken, intelligent and somewhat pedantic Attorney-General. A lawyer's lawyer, Whyatt too was going to find the emergency a challenge to his strength of mind and his principles. Not far behind them was the settler leader Michael Blundell. An odd mixture of strident opinions and anxiety to please, Blundell's political resolve was too often undone by his keenness to be seen to be important. He liked nothing more than to place himself at the centre of events, to appear to be a man of firm resolve. The reality was rather different, as he usually played it both ways, telling the government that he was all that stood between them and a settler rising, and telling his white highlander colleagues that, but for his intervention, the government would have made some other damfool decision. It was characteristic of Kenya's white settlers that they always knew what was best for the country and for the Africans. Blundell called himself a liberal, but only in Kenya would that have any meaning. His views were firmly conservative. Baring would have to learn to rub along with them all. He had served in Southern Rhodesia and in South Africa, so he knew all about white settler society in Africa: but he had never held such a challenging post as this before.[1] It would not be easy. And before the Governor had time to take stock of his surroundings, things got considerably worse.

## Chief Waruhiu

By the time the police arrived at the Limuru road, in Nairobi's western outskirts, there was already a large crowd of onlookers gathered along the roadside, gawping at the vehicle. The doors of the dark-brown Hudson were open, and the body of the well-dressed passenger could be seen slouched across the back seat, his smart suit stained by the blood still oozing from the gunshot wounds to his neck and chest. The car's driver and two other passengers sat on the road beside the vehicle, dazed and in a state of shock. All were lucky still to be alive, and they knew it. Though the young European police officer who gingerly approached the scene did not at first recognize the dead passenger or his driver, those in the gathering crowd all knew the car and its principal occupant. Chief Waruhiu wa Kungu, of the Kiambu district, was the government's Paramount Chief for Central Province, and the senior African official under Kenya's colonial administration. The colonial government's 'tower of strength' was dead.[2] He had been the victim of a well-planned and carefully executed assassination, carried out on the orders of the leaders of Mau Mau.[3]

On that bright, clear morning of 7 October 1952 Waruhiu had left his home early to attend a Native Tribunal hearing close to Nairobi. Like other chiefs, he presided at such events as the Governor's representative, with powers equivalent to those of a magistrate. To the Africans of Kiambu his authority over their lives was certainly far more immediately potent than that of Evelyn Baring, Kenya's only recently arrived colonial Governor. Baring had already learned that land lay at the heart of the issues that motivated Mau Mau. The movement championed the cause of those Kikuyu who had been dispossessed by colonial changes to land tenure, and the cause of those evicted from European-owned farmlands, as modernization and mechanization took their toll upon older styles of labour tenancy. Some Kikuyu tenants had even been evicted by their African landlords, including Waruhiu himself. Grievances over land occupied much of Waruhiu's time at the Native Tribunal hearings, and dominated his morning's work on 7 October 1952. As a senior elder and a man of property, Waruhiu was bitterly opposed to the claims of Mau Mau that large landowners should be obliged to provide for the landless. None of this pleased the supporters of Mau Mau, and Waruhiu had long known that they wished him harm.

The worsening security situation in the colony was a matter that concerned Baring and Waruhiu in equal measure. But while the Governor could view Kenya's current problems from the cool heights of Government House, on the leafy hill overlooking Nairobi's city centre, the Chief's experience was amid the cut and thrust of acrimonious land disputes in his fertile Kiambu district, and in the hot, bustling African locations of Nairobi's Eastlands. A wealthy and conspicuous figure, his daily movements were widely known throughout Kiambu and Nairobi. It would have been impossible to disguise his plans, even if he had wanted to. Aware of his attendance at the tribunal on 7 October, Waruhiu's assassins simply lay in wait for him along his homeward route.

The killings of those who opposed Mau Mau had begun during 1951, though the government had been slow to grasp its extent and slower still to appreciate its significance. By the time of Baring's arrival, the pattern of attacks upon Kikuyu Africans in government service, and especially against those who spoke publicly to oppose Mau Mau, had become clear. Mau Mau invited all Kikuyu to take an oath of allegiance to the movement. Many did so willingly, especially those for whom lack of jobs and landlessness had greatly worsened their poverty by the early 1950s. Others did so because of intimidation, or out of fear. As word of the movement spread, it came to be realized that the oaths committed people to oppose the government through violence, if necessary, and to reject all things European. For Africans who worked as officials of the government – chiefs, headmen, councillors, clerks, teachers or policemen – the pressures to side with Mau Mau posed a very considerable personal dilemma. Once Mau Mau began to execute its opponents, that dilemma deepened. The Christian churches, in particular, saw in the movement an attack upon the commitment to 'progress and modernity' among their congregations, and many African clergymen were determinedly outspoken in denouncing Mau Mau.[4] Waruhiu was a chief and also a devout Christian, and in both capacities he had made clear his stand against the movement. His killing was only the latest in a lengthening list of political murders, but its impact reverberated across the colony. If the colonial state could not protect the Paramount Chief, who, then, was any longer safe from the gunmen of Mau Mau? This was one African murder that shocked and unnerved even the white highlanders.

As Waruhiu's Hudson headed along the Limuru road, his driver had become aware of a Ford Consul taxi following them. At a divide in the road, the taxi had sped past Waruhiu's car and come to an abrupt halt, blocking the way ahead. Only then did the Chief's chauffeur perceive that they might be in danger, but before he or Waruhiu had time to react, two men came toward the Hudson and opened the rear door. 'Yes, Chief Waruhiu,' one said, and drew a pistol from inside his jacket and began firing into the car. The first bullet from the Baretta ricocheted and hit the front tyre, and the second hit the chassis of the car, in which time the chauffeur managed to open his own door and roll out onto the road. For Waruhiu there was to be no escape. He was hit four times at close range, his blood splattering onto his two terrified fellow passengers, before the gunman fled back to his waiting taxi and sped away. On a busy main road, and in broad daylight, the murder of Kenya's senior African chief had been carried out in little more than one minute.

Waruhiu's eldest son, David, learned of the death of his father while in Caux, Switzerland, where he was attending an international meeting of the movement for Moral Re-armament (MRA). Like many other Christian Kikuyu of their class, the Waruhius were attracted to the MRA by its ready acceptance of the notion of racial equality. In the MRA David found a community of spirit that transcended the colour bar that still affected so many of the churches in Kenya. News of the death of Chief Waruhiu reached Caux by telegram, and it fell to an old friend of the family, Bremer Hofmeyr, to tell David of the murder. Hofmeyr was the husband of Agnes Leakey.[5] The Leakey family were amongst Kenya's most eminent European settlers. Agnes's father, Gray Leakey, farmed in the Nanyuki district of central Kenya, where she had been born and brought up. Her uncle, Louis Leakey, was by 1952 already a distinguished archaeologist, and would later play a prominent role in the British campaign against Mau Mau, firstly acting as the interpreter (from Kikuyu to English) at the trial of Jomo Kenyatta, then serving the government on several policy advisory committees on counter-insurgency measures, and also writing two books about the rebellion that had wide influence at the time. The Waruhius and the Leakeys were separated by race, but they shared close interests of class and of faith. Both families saw Mau Mau as an aberration that needed to be staunchly opposed, though their analyses of its causes were widely divergent. The Leakeys opposed Mau Mau because they thought it to be a backward and atavistic revival of ancient tribal practices in the face of the challenges of modernity and 'civilisation'.[6] Chief Waruhiu had opposed Mau Mau primarily because it challenged his authority as an elder and threatened to undermine his status as a landowner. The Waruhius had in October 1952 already paid the price of that opposition. For the Leakeys the reckoning would come later.

On returning to Kenya to bury his father, David Waruhiu, then in his early thirties, rallied to the cause for which Waruhiu had sacrificed his life, taking up the mantle as head of his clan and fighting hard to protect their interests throughout the years of the Emergency. But although the British tried to promote him to a more prominent political role, the young Christian lacked the *gravitas* to sway opinions of more traditional men in the increasingly embittered battle against Mau Mau. David

Waruhiu was eventually found a job in the Office of Information, from where he played an active role in organizing the Kikuyu loyalist opposition to Mau Mau and in the dissemination of government propaganda against the rebellion.[7]

In his pursuit for Mau Mau, David Waruhiu had good reason to be energetic and enthusiastic, and he and other loyalists were much encouraged by the rapid success of the Kenya Police in locating those suspected of his father's murder. The Paramount Chief's assassins had been swift, meticulous and calculating in their actions, but the driver and Waruhiu's two surviving colleagues, both of them government headmen, were to be crucial witnesses in the police investigation. Within one week of the murder, several suspects had been taken in for questioning. The driver of the Ford taxi, Wahinga Waweru Kamundia, was the first to be arrested, easily identified through the registration number of the car and the confirmation of the taxi's owner that he was indeed the driver in custody of the vehicle on the fateful day. Kamundia's testimony, which amounted to a confession, then implicated Gathugu Migwe, the gunman, who, after police interrogation, made a statement before a magistrate admitting his guilt and describing how the crime had been planned and carried out. In a pattern that would become all too familiar in subsequent Mau Mau cases before the Kenyan courts, Gathugu Migwe later sought to retract this statement, claiming that his confession had been extracted under duress and that the police had beaten him and tortured him. Without medical support for Migwe's claims, Justice Rudd dismissed his retraction and accepted his confessional statement as evidence. At the trial, witnesses confirmed Migwe's identification as the gunman, while other corroborating evidence established that both he and Kamundia had been seen in the vehicle before and after the crime. They were each found guilty of murder and sentenced to be hanged. They waited on death row in Nairobi Prison until their appeals were dismissed on 7 May 1953, and then went to the gallows.

Nothing that is known about either executed man marks him out as being anything other than ordinary. Migwe was twenty-seven at the time of his arrest, and Kamundia thirty-three years of age. Both men were married, each having two children, and both were from the Kiambu district. Neither man was prosperous, but each managed to make a reasonable living. Kamundia had been a taxi driver for several years, while Gathuga Migwe bought and sold second-hand clothes from a small shop he leased in the Kabete area of Nairobi. Gathuga was a Christian and a church-goer – he attended a service on the Sunday prior to Waruhiu's murder. No personal grievance with Chief Waruhiu came to light, both men claiming never to have met him prior to the murder. In all these respects, Migwe and Kamundia were typical of thousands of other Kikuyu caught up in the Mau Mau struggle between 1952 and 1960. Anonymity and ordinariness were pervasive characteristics of Mau Mau.

After Migwe and Kamundia had been convicted for the murder of Waruhiu, the British District Commissioner (DC) in Kiambu reported: 'both men and their families are said to have been well provided for by the instigators of the crime'.[8] Though he did not give names, the DC thought he knew who the 'instigators of the crime' were. Evidence on the matter had been revealed in the sworn statements of the two condemned men. Kamundia and Migwe both claimed that the Koinange family had planned the crime, and that the arrangements had been explained to them at the Koinanges' home, outside Nairobi, on the Sunday before the murder, when the assassins had been given the pistol with which Waruhiu was to be shot.

These were profoundly shocking revelations. Ex-Chief Koinange had been a respected colonial servant for many years, but it was widely known that he was now a member of the KAU, and that he supported many political causes among the Kikuyu. Koinange was a nationalist, but he was also understood to be a man of moderate political views. Most Africans in Kenya would certainly have thought him a very unlikely suspect in a murder enquiry. Others were not so sure.

By 1952 the British government in Kenya had come to the conclusion that Mau Mau and the KAU were one and the same thing. The evidence for this was not entirely well grounded. The Kenya Special Branch, short-staffed, inefficient and overwhelmed by the mounting crisis that was Mau Mau, had nevertheless managed to gather useful intelligence from within the KAU. Special Branch intelligence had begun to understand that divisions existed among African nationalists, that the KAU did not control all political activity, and that not all Kikuyu politicians favoured violence; but this nuanced analysis was not by then what the political staff of the colonial administration wanted to hear. The provincial administration in central Kenya preferred a simpler analysis. They had long nurtured deep suspicion of the politics of the Koinange family. The family's wealth was vast, and their influence seemingly pervaded every aspect of Kikuyu life. They were 'too clever by half' in the eyes of most Europeans. If there was mischief afoot, then the consensus was that the Koinanges must be behind it.

Where Special Branch saw divisions in the ranks of African politics, the political arm of the government made the fatal mistake of lumping all activists together and assuming that they all danced to the same tune – a tune they thought must be played by the Koinanges and Kenyatta. The prevailing opinion from Government House was that all senior members of the KAU must be, in some way or other, behind the Mau Mau

movement. Many African leaders, too, including Chief Waruhiu, shared
the perception that 'ex-Senior Chief Koinange and Jomo Kenyatta
were the actual ringleaders behind Mau Mau'.[9] Special Branch reports
suggested otherwise. Police informers had reported the covert activities
of militants who used the KAU to cloak their own oathing ceremonies
and fund-raising. These were dangerous radicals, to be sure and, according to Special Branch reports, they were not in the control of Kenyatta
or Koinange.

However, the analysis of Special Branch appeared to be seriously
compromised by the evidence gathered for the trial of those accused of
Chief Waruhiu's murder. In the statements made by Kamundia and
Migwe, the British were presented with evidence that seemed to implicate Koinange wa Mbiyu, John Westley Mbiyu Koinange and another
of his half-brothers, Noah Karuga. All three were held for questioning
in connection with Waruhiu's death. After the humiliation and ordeal
of arrest and interrogation, a committal hearing was held and the old
Chief was released for want of evidence against him. John Westley Mbiyu
was not so fortunate. He was charged as an accomplice to murder, and
on 30 March 1953 he stood trial for murder alongside Kamundia and
Migwe. With the help of the Labour MP Leslie Hale and Fenner
Brockway in London, the Koinanges were able to engage Dingle Foot
as counsel for the defence – another sign of the wealth and influence
that so offended Kenya's middle-class and low-brow white settlers. The
Liberal Foot took great delight in cocking a snook at these jumped-up
colonial types, and made the most of his moment in court to expose the
gross shortcomings of the police enquiry, doing little to disguise his
broad hints that there had been an attempt made to frame his client. As
there was no evidence against John Westley Mbiyu other than the
statements of his co-accused, and Eluid Mathu, the African Member in
Legislative Council, provided eloquent testimony in support of his alibi
anyway, Foot was able to demonstrate that there were insufficient grounds
for a conviction. Justice Rudd was persuaded, and while Kamundia and
Migwe were convicted to await the gallows, John Westley Mbiyu was
acquitted.[10]

Did John Westley Mbiyu Koinange really instruct the assassins and
supply them with the pistol with which Paramount Chief Waruhiu was
murdered? Was old Koinange privy to the crime? Or were the other
accused put up to say this by police officers, as Dingle Foot suggested to
the court? Perhaps the police were too keen to incriminate the Koinanges
in the murder? We may never know the answer to these questions. The
police rightly suspected that their Kiambaa house was a base for oathing
and the gathering of funds, but the family would with some justice claim
that these activities were on behalf of the KAU, not Mau Mau.

That said, they all knew more than they were prepared to admit at the trial of Waruhiu's murderers. From at least 1950, the KAU had been eclipsed by a more militant turn in the politics of central Kenya. In their endeavours to rebuild unity among Kikuyu and restore moderation, the Kiambaa Parliament had attempted to co-opt the militants. In doing so they had lost control of the politics of protest. Not all those who attended the Kiambaa Parliament from 1950 any longer shared a vision of a future in which constitutional change would be achieved through African unity, peaceful protest and negotiation. The militant men, among them Fred Kubai and Bildad Kaggia, actively promoted a more violent agenda of direct action. Old Koinange was aware of these things.[11] He may not have agreed with the politics of violence, but he was in no position to either silence or thwart its advocates. This was what the British misunderstood. The compromises and ambiguities of Kikuyu politics were obscured from British view by their own static model of a notional 'traditional tribal authority', which was in fact a creation of colonial rule itself. Old Koinange and Kenyatta were respected Kikuyu leaders, but they lacked the authority to control the men of violence. They could seek to lead by persuasion, but they could not direct. Mau Mau's militancy was born in the minds of those who were no longer prepared to accept leadership from the likes of Koinange and Kenyatta; and even within Koinange's own family there may have been some sons who no longer bowed to the authority of their father. By 1952 the pressures of colonial rule had splintered Kikuyu families as well as Kikuyu politics.

Had the police been more diligent in their search of the Koinange home, the old ex-Chief and his sons may not have been so fortunate in their treatment by the court. Concealed below their Kiambaa house was an excavated cellar, which served as an armoury. It contained guns that had been gathered and stored there between 1949 and 1952. Was it from this collection of weapons that Migwe was supplied with the handgun with which Waruhiu was shot? There can be little doubt that all the Koinanges knew of the existence of this armoury, for the cellar held a deeper secret: in that cellar was the grave of another of ex-Chief Koinange's sons, David Gathiomi, who, in March 1950, had accidentally shot and killed himself while cleaning a pistol from the weapons stash.[12] The family kept this painful secret to themselves throughout the years of the Mau Mau struggle, and for many more years after.

## Jock Scott and Judge Thacker

Governor Baring's first public function in Kenya was to attend Chief Waruhiu's funeral. It was a sobering experience. There he saw Kenyatta and other known associates of the Kiambaa Parliament, and also a gaggle of Kikuyu loyalist chiefs. The difficulty of discerning friend from foe amid the dignified crowd of African faces must have posed ominous questions in the Governor's mind. Among these Kikuyu faces, who was Mau Mau, and who was not?

By the day of the funeral, Baring had already taken the steps towards a declaration of war against Mau Mau: only two days after Waruhiu's killing, on 9 October 1952, Baring had cabled London to request that a State of Emergency be declared. If allowed, this would give the Governor powers to detain suspects under special emergency legislation, to impose other laws without reference to London, and to deploy the military in aid of the civil administration. It was not something that the Colonial Office was comfortable with in any British colony, but perhaps least of all in Kenya, where the volatile and often highly reactionary European community was known to be only too ready to take the law into their own hands. Baring made the case that firm and swift action would put a break on settler excess, that Chief Waruhiu's murder demanded a sharp response, and that the Emergency need not be prolonged if Mau Mau's leaders were quickly taken out of circulation. His argument seemed sincere enough, and there was certainly plenty of evidence to back it up. It was a difficult argument to refute from London.[13] He was thought to know how to handle settlers. On 14 October Oliver Lyttelton, Secretary of State for the Colonies in Churchill's Tory government, gave his consent to Baring's request and Kenya began to prepare for its State of Emergency.[14]

Baring's plan was simple enough. A tour of the Central Province had convinced him that those Africans who professed loyalty to the government lived in fear of 'Kenyatta and his henchmen'.[15] Their removal was deemed necessary to stiffen the resolve of the government's remaining African allies. A list of some 150 KAU activists and suspected Mau Mau organizers was compiled by Special Branch, and plans were laid for a mass round-up, code-named Operation Jock Scott, to take place from midnight on 20 October 1952. Kenyatta, the Koinanges, all known members of the Kiambaa Parliament and all senior officials of the KAU (many of whom had no connection at all with Mau Mau) headed the list.[16] It was thought this decapitation of Mau Mau would stop the movement in its tracks, and that the police, assisted by the military, could then regain control of the Kikuyu countryside and of Nairobi.[17] A show of strength was what was wanted. Three battalions of the King's African Rifles were recalled from Uganda, Tanganyika and Mauritius, giving the regiment five battalions in all in Kenya, amounting to more than 3000 African soldiers. To placate settler opinion, it was thought that British troops should also make a show. The 1st battalion of the Lancashire

Fusiliers could be diverted from their duties in the Egyptian canal zone, and hasty arrangements were made to fly them to Nairobi to arrive on the morning of 21 October.

By the time that the Lancashire Fusiliers had reached Nairobi and begun patrolling the city and the Kikuyu districts in their trucks, the British had succeeded in taking 106 suspects into custody. Many of those arrested appeared to have known what was coming. Some on the wanted list, including Stanley Mathenge and Dedan Kimathi, had managed to flee. These men would become the principal leaders of Mau Mau's forest armies. Kikuyu within the government – clerks and other officials in the police and military – had evidently leaked news of the planned arrests a few hours before Operation Jock Scott got under way. Kenya's government was not yet very good at keeping its secrets. While the real militants fled to the forests, the moderates awaited their fate. Kenyatta, for one, certainly knew they were coming for him. He made no attempt to escape and was taken in to custody.

The Koinanges were dealt a heavy blow by the arrests. John Westley Mbiyu, Frederick Mbiyu, Noah Karuga and James Njoroge were detained alongside their father, one of his wives and four of their sisters – ten of the family in all would remain in detention for the bulk of the Emergency. Under the Emergency Powers Act, all were charged and found guilty of being members of the banned Mau Mau organization. Their sentences ranged between five- and seven-year terms of imprisonment, with hard labour. Of the senior family members, only Peter Mbiyu, by then already in London, remained at liberty. Frederick Mbiyu was given a seven-year sentence. John Mbiyu Koinange spent the first part of his seven-year sentence with his father at Marsabit, in Kenya's remote and arid Northern Frontier Province, but they were then separated, old Koinange going to Kabernet and John Westley Mbiyu being sent to the camp for 'hard-core' Mau Mau on the Indian Ocean island of Lamu. While at Kabarnet, Koinange's health deteriorated.[18] He was only released when it became clear he was close to death. Koinange was hardly conscious when he reached his Kiambaa home, and died within a few weeks. He was then reckoned to be more than eighty years of age. His funeral was attended by the largest gathering of mourners ever to be seen in Kenya.[19] Governor Baring was not among them.

While the Koinanges and other accused were quickly and quietly disposed of in the magistrates' courts, under charges relating to membership of the banned Mau Mau movement, there was to be one show trial. Baring needed to demonstrate to London that his judgement in calling for Emergency powers had been sound. Jomo Kenyatta was to be the principal in this judicial spectacle, designed to placate settler opinion and to show the watching world how Kenya's colonial government proposed to deal with the menace of Mau Mau.

The show trial held risks, however. Would a conviction be secured? Though colonial legal officers appeared to be utterly convinced of Kenyatta's role as leader of Mau Mau, it was not an easy matter to assemble the evidence that would prove the case, or to gather witnesses prepared to testify. In his public pronouncements Kenyatta had never openly supported Mau Mau, and had indeed made a number of statements that he would claim at his trial were condemnatory of the violence and subversion carried out by the movement. And what witnesses would speak against him?

By November 1952, when the decision to go ahead with the show trial was made, Mau Mau's assassins already had a reputation for dealing summarily with those who gave evidence in court against their comrades. During the two months of September and October 1952, Mau Mau had murdered no fewer than twenty-seven Crown witnesses in other criminal trials. To ensure that fear would not compel his witnesses to retract their statements once the trial came upon them, Attorney-General Whyatt adopted some unconventional methods: witnesses would be given police protection, but if they did come to harm, then their home communities would be held responsible and subjected to collective fines; if witnesses refused to testify, then all protection would be immediately withdrawn – tantamount to a death sentence. It was a predicament none could have relished. If Kenyatta was a prisoner and a victim, then so too would be the witnesses who spoke against him. One week before the trial was due to commence, a group of some twenty Crown witnesses were taken into police protective custody. It was later claimed that they were well rehearsed in the evidence they would give; and the Crown would later pay them 'rewards' to a total value of over £10,000.[20]

The unconventional character of the trial did not stop there. Ostensibly to prevent Mau Mau interference with due legal process, it was decided to hold the trial in the remote northern town of Kapenguria. This had consequences other than easing colonial worries about security. Kapenguria was located in a closed district, and visitors from Nairobi or elsewhere would require a government permit in order to attend the hearing. This advice allowed the government to hamper the KAU in organizing Kenyatta's defence by refusing permits to certain lawyers and delaying the issuing of documents to witnesses for the defence. The removal of the trial from Nairobi also gave the government a far greater degree of control over how it would be reported and represented in the media. Many journalists sent to cover the trial never managed to get as far as Kapenguria, and received their reports at second hand, usually through the statements prepared by the Office of Information. The

Kenyatta show trial was therefore mostly reported from the settler town of Kitale, some 30 miles to the south of Kapenguria, or from the more congenial hotel bars of downtown Nairobi.

Baring could hardly contemplate the thought that there might not be sufficient evidence to convict Kenyatta, but it was whispered in Nairobi's legal circles that matters were not at all cut and dried. In the circumstances, the selection of a judge might be absolutely critical to the outcome. Though no jury was required and it was only necessary to appoint a suitably qualified magistrate – Kenya had plenty of those – the feeling in Nairobi was that a senior judge should sit so as to give the proceedings a greater air of authority. But in November 1952, with the trial due to commence the next month, it was widely rumoured that one senior judge had already declined the commission and that others were equally reluctant. A speedy solution was needed, and the one that was found was both elegant and shrewd. A retired High Court judge, Ransley Thacker, was reappointed as a First Class Magistrate and invited to hear the case. Thacker's credentials were impeccable. He had served the High Court of Kenya since 1938, and before that had been Attorney-General in Fiji. He had experience, judicial seniority, and the necessary *gravitas*. In retirement, he had opted to settle in Nairobi, where he augmented his annual pension of £474 with private legal practice. A man of renowned conservative persuasions, his appointment met with the warm approval of Kenya's white settlers. He was now, after all, one of their own.

Yet Thacker's appointment proved to be more complicated than was first anticipated. The retired judge was concerned for his personal safety in Kenya after hearing the case, where he would be as conspicuous a target for Mau Mau assassins as were the Kikuyu witnesses. He asked for 'special payments' to cover his likely expenses, and entered into negotiations with the government. Throughout the trial, which dragged on for more than three months, Thacker maintained a clandestine correspondence with Baring over the financial arrangements. In the view of Baring's biographer, Charles Douglas-Home, Thacker 'sought to capitalise on the situation', and Baring, 'acting with unusual cynicism and ruthlessness, saw that he could not afford to take any risk'.[21] The Governor eventually authorized a settlement, and Thacker was paid a sum of £20,000 for his troubles.[22] This was the price of British justice.

Even if the outcome of the trial was now a foregone conclusion, at Kapenguria justice had to be seen to be done. The colonial state gathered as much pomp and circumstance as it could muster in this dusty outpost of empire. The local jail was cleared to make way for Kenyatta and his five co-defendants, and the small, airless schoolhouse was spruced up for service as a courtroom. Rolls of barbed wire encircled the buildings and armoured cars patrolled outside. Smartly dressed African soldiers guarded the accused. These facilities exhausted Kapenguria's capacity for hospitality. With no other accommodation available, Thacker, his court officials and the prosecution counsel came up from Kitale, where they were settled in reasonable comfort in the local club and hotels, establishments exclusively reserved for the use of whites.

No such civility was afforded the defence counsel. The assorted African, Indian and West Indian lawyers who eventually gained permits to attend the trial, headed by Denis Pritt, QC, were a distinguished legal ensemble, with a decidedly imperial and radical flavour. Alongside the communist Pritt stood two accomplished and fiery local Kenyan-Asian lawyers, Fitz de Souza and Achroo Kapila; from India came Chaman Lall, an Oxford graduate who was a close associate of President Nehru; from Nigeria Chief Davies, a renowned advocate in West Africa who was well respected among colonial officials; and from Jamaica there was Dudley Thompson, a former Rhodes Scholar. Others, from Sudan, Egypt, India, Ireland and South Africa sought to join the team, but Baring's legal officers put paid to their ambitions. Friends of the KAU made arrangements to host the legal team, but their lodgings were far from palatial.[23] As the trial approached, the prosecution were well prepared and in good order, while the defence team was still gathering its collective wits, trying desperately to locate its witnesses, and grappling with the stifling inconvenience of the Kapenguria location. The scene was set for a ritual enactment of white colonial power.

In the end, the trial was a petulant and unedifying affair.[24] It began on 3 December 1952. Things got off to a bad start. Pritt's first step was to seek Thacker's removal from the case. The gambit failed, and did nothing to improve relations between the two men. Persistent and justified complaints about the location of the trial and the obstruction of the defence then resulted in Thacker threatening Pritt with a charge of contempt. The Supreme Court reviewed the charge and took Pritt's side, deepening Thacker's sense of irritation. As the trial progressed, the magistrate took less and less trouble to disguise his disdain for the accused and their defence counsel. Led by the Director of Public Prosecutions, Somerhaugh, a dour and unimaginative character, the Crown simply piled up 'the facts' on Kenyatta's links with Mau Mau. None of the evidence was strong, and little of it was coherent. When witnesses for the Crown seemed hesitant and unsure, Somerhaugh put it down to their anxiety and fear. Mau Mau's shadow darkened the proceedings even in Kapenguria, he argued. But for the most part, they recited their lines with reasonable assurance.

Pritt and his colleagues exploited every weakness as best they could, but their own witnesses were nervy and unsure and Pritt's unfamiliarity with Kenya and its politics meant that he missed many possible tricks. Kenyatta was accused of organizing Mau Mau through his leadership of the KAU, of having stimulated and led the oathing campaign, and even of having been present at an oathing ceremony, and of having preached the gospel of Mau Mau violence to his followers in several public meetings. The evidence was thin, the charges were untrue, and Kenyatta denied them all. But Somerhaugh need not have worried about the strength of his case: Thacker's mind was made up long before. He came to the trial with his attitudes already formed. When Kenyatta endeavoured to explain the nature of the grievances that lay behind Mau Mau, for example, Thacker expressed his exasperation and told the court: 'Grievances have nothing whatever to do with Mau Mau, and Mau Mau has nothing whatever to do with grievances.'[25] He found Kenyatta guilty as charged. The white settlers were satisfied with the outcome. So, too, was Governor Baring.

The Kenya government had got its man. Or so they thought. As Kenyatta began his seven-year sentence in the dusty, dry heat of the prison camp at Lodwar, with him were his five co-defendants. They were not a happy band of comrades. Among their number were two men who had indeed been behind the organization and management of militancy and violence, though the Kenyan police had no substantive information on their activities and nothing of consequence had come to light at the trial. Fred Kubai and Bildad Kaggia were leading militant politicians in the rough and tumble of urban Nairobi. They were members of the KAU, and they had occasionally attended meetings of the Kiambaa Parliament since 1950; but their radicalism was far more extreme than the constitutional nationalism of Kenyatta, and in stark opposition to the chiefly authority old Koinange had sought to maintain. The Kiambaa Parliament was an important forum of nationalist politics, but it was never quite the cockpit of revolution that the government believed it to be. This honour belonged to that secretive urban political cell based in Nairobi, known as the *Muhimu*, whose militant urban members, including Kubai, disparaged the moderates of the KAU even though many were themselves members of that party. This conspiratorial group had served as the central committee of Mau Mau.[26] While Kenyatta saw politics as the preserve of elders, the militants wanted to engage the energies of younger activists.[27]

The British had arrested the leader of the KAU, but he was not the leader of Mau Mau. He had supported the oathing of Kikuyu members within the KAU, but not the subversive and dangerous oathing of the *Muhimu*. Kenyatta had tried very hard to tell them this at his trial, but Thacker had not wanted to listen. By then Kenyatta knew that Kubai and Kaggia, standing beside him in the dock, were guiltier of the charge than he. But Kenyatta would not betray his fellow nationalists, even though they held widely different views on how the struggle against colonial rule should be conducted.[28] In lumping all these Kikuyu politicians together, the British misread the lessons of Kenya's recent history and misunderstood the critical internal dynamics of Kikuyu politics. Kikuyu grievances, to which Kenyatta had tried to refer at his trial and which ex-Judge Thacker had so lightly tossed aside, held the key to understanding the origins and factionalism of the rebel cause. This was the simple fact that neither the white highlanders nor the British administration in Kenya was prepared to acknowledge.

## Going to War

On 22 October, as the last of the suspects were being rounded up in Operation Jock Scott, another prominent colonial chief was killed. Nderi, a senior and long-standing chief, was hacked to pieces by an angry crowd as he tried to break up an oathing ceremony close to his own home. When the police arrived at the scene, accompanied by a platoon of the Lancashire Fusiliers, they were confronted by an 'uncooperative and hostile' mob. No one was prepared to give evidence of any kind. Though they had no legal authority to do so, the police confiscated livestock and moveable property, but still there was no information offered regarding the murder.[29] Nderi's rashness was perhaps provoked by his rage at such a flagrant disregard for his authority and the humiliation of seeing the militants of Mau Mau operating on his very doorstep, but he had long before lost the support of his people. The chiefs were not only impotent against Mau Mau, they were now its targets. Even if Mau Mau still remained mysterious and incomprehensible to the British, Kikuyu such as Nderi understood it only too well and recognized the very real threat it posed to them and their kind.

Waruhiu's assassination had been a carefully planned affair, Nderi's slaughter an opportunist act conducted in the heat of the moment. Together, they seemed to suggest a stronger purpose and direction than Mau Mau then possessed. For Mutonyi and Kubai, at the head of the *Muhimu*, the emergency had come at least one year too soon. They had plans to escalate the violence with a wave of high-profile assassinations, and had considered the implications of a guerrilla war; but they had not yet taken steps towards these goals. They had arms, but not enough. They had a strong network of support throughout the Kikuyu countryside, but no clear structure for supplying guerrilla bands; and they had no military command structure, no strategy, and no forest bases yet established.

The *Muhimu*'s committee structure, centred on Nairobi but connected to the districts, was the only thing that kept the movement alive after Operation Jock Scott. Other militants stepped forward into this structure to replace those arrested by the British. Many activists had fled when news broke of the arrests, although few at first went to the forests. It has been estimated that no more than a thousand militants took to the forests in the first month of the Emergency, most of these being ex-squatters who came straight from the Rift Valley farms. Of the men who would later lead the guerrilla bands, only Waruhiu Itote (General China) had entered the forest at this stage, having gone to Mount Kenya with a handful of followers in September 1952. As the Emergency began, though the murders of 'collaborators' gave the impression of strength, Mau Mau was barely a fighting force at all.

Over the next two months, British hesitancy over how to target the Mau Mau leadership, combined with heavy-handed repression against ordinary Kikuyu, allowed the *Muhimu* time to gather their wits and drove many of the wavering Kikuyu majority into the rebel camp. Military sweeps through Kiambu and Nyeri served no useful purpose other than to alarm the rural population, and the random screening of thousands of Kikuyu – nearly 60,000 would be held for interrogation between November and the end of February – led to some 17,000 prosecutions; but mostly these were to do with infringements of the pass laws and labour regulations, or failure to pay tax.[30] The pointlessness of this exercise struck some of those involved in it, as one of the more sober and reflective white highlanders observed:

> It is obviously illogical that any person of European extraction could, by looking at an African and examining his papers, know whether or not he has Mau Mau inclinations ... The methods adopted so far usually culminate in a parade of Kikuyu, and any that can produce a current hut-tax receipt and an employment card, or appear to be unaggressive, are released. Others who cannot produce these documents are frequently detained, and more often than not a proportion of these quite decent people are forced into close association with criminals and taken off to some detention camp. These decent people, or any of them who are in a state of indecision, immediately build up the utmost contempt for the methods of law and order, and are ripe for Mau Mau allegiance, either now or when released from detention.[31]

While the British busied themselves alienating 'decent people', the *Muhimu* immediately stepped up their campaign of assassinations, coordinated from Nairobi. In the week following Nderi's death, another seven murders were carried out, including the first European victim,[32] and throughout the next month the catalogue of killings steadily lengthened. By the end of 1952, 121 loyal Kikuyu had been murdered.[33]

There were no quick military successes for the British to set off against these serious political losses. The first 'major engagement' of the Emergency was a mixture of tragedy and farce. It occurred when police opened fire on a crowd of 2000 Kikuyu gathered at a market near Thika, on 22 November, apparently believing them to be a hostile Mau Mau gang gathering for an attack. The commanding European officer reported that some of the crowd at the market were armed with pangas – the heavy-bladed tool most Kikuyu farmers carried with them in their daily toil on the land. These were country folk who had come to the market about their business. A crowd had gathered around a young boy, who claimed to have been healed of dumbness by a miracle. The youth ranted and raged at his curious audience, prophesying that God would come to the market later that day and bring an end to the war. When the police moved in to arrest the youth, he called desperately upon the crowd to rescue him. People remonstrated with the police, some of the crowd surging forward. The commander panicked and ordered his men to fire. They killed sixteen, among them women and children, and wounded another seventeen.[34] The edginess of the security forces and the incomprehension of the Kikuyu crowd set the tone for much that would follow over the coming months.

Through to the early months of 1953 Baring would continue to express the view that the emergency would be over 'in a few weeks'; but there was much to suggest his analysis was far-fetched. For one thing, Baring's own government was getting twitchy. A further set of emergency measures was proposed in November. Several resident magistrates were elevated temporarily to the Supreme Court to try to deal with the enormous backlog of cases then awaiting trial. New powers were introduced allowing the compulsory seizure of property and the extension of collective punishment, effectively legalizing actions of the kind taken by the security forces after Nderi's murder. And sentences were increased for a wide range of offences: those convicted as members of the unlawful Mau Mau organization now faced fourteen years imprisonment, instead of seven; a person found guilty of maiming cattle would now serve fourteen years instead of two; and the death penalty was to be imposed for convicted oath administrators. Finally, a new tax rate was proposed only for the Kikuyu districts, doubling the annual payments for each adult male from 20 shillings to 40 shillings. District officers would have authority to exempt loyal Kikuyu from payment.[35] This last measure was both punitive and economic: Kikuyu were being punished for their insubordination, and they were being made to pay the costs of the emergency.

The Secretary of State for the Colonies, Lyttelton, was nervous about the harsh character of these measures. He had visited Nairobi earlier in the month, and had been keen to stress the need to offer carrots as well as waving sticks. London saw the danger of alienating local African support long before the Nairobi administration realized the effects of their actions. Churchill was not impressed by the 'special pleading' from Nairobi for this or that power: from the start, the Prime Minister emphasized the importance of negotiation.[36] Lyttelton, too, thought the latest proposals smacked of heavy-handedness, even of vengeance and retribution. The extension of collective punishments, of which the increase in tax was in reality but a new variation, troubled him especially. He wrote to Baring to remind him of the experience in Malaya, where such measures had been found to induce bitterness and hostility towards the government among innocent people, instead of what 'should be our primary purpose of persuading waverers to come to our side and above all volunteer information'.[37] But in an Emergency, it was considered of critical importance not to undermine the authority of the Governor. Having issued the warning, Lyttelton duly gave approval for all of the new powers Baring requested.

Two further measures also introduced at this time did not need London's approval, though both would have a very significant impact locally in Kenya. The first concerned squatters who remained on the white farms. With the Emergency, many farmers decided to sign off all their Kikuyu labour. This triggered an exodus of squatters, which began in the Thomson's Falls and Kinangop areas in mid-November, and then accelerated in December, when a new and more tightly controlled identification system for Kikuyu labour was announced. Settler belligerence towards squatters in the early weeks of the Emergency – some seemed to think that the new situation amounted to a kind of 'open season' on the Kikuyu – had led to an increase in beatings and harassment of 'suspects' on the farms.[38] Some squatters packed up and left voluntarily at this time, while others were forcibly evicted. Between November 1952 and March 1953, it is estimated that between 70,000 and 100,000 Kikuyu returned to Kiambu, Nyeri and Murang'a.[39] Among their number were many young men who would soon find their way to the Mau Mau armies by then taking shape in the forests of Mount Kenya and the Aberdares.

The second measure would also help to swell the ranks of the rebel forces at this time, when the government closed down thirty-four independent schools run by KISA and KKEA in the Kikuyu districts. It was believed that the schools were 'hot-houses of militancy', that teachers had been instrumental in oathing their pupils and in preaching revolution, and that many of the schools were little more than fronts for the collection of money for the rebels. The tradition of independence and resistance among the constituencies who supported the schools was deep and strong, and most were located in areas where there was known to be support for the militants. Among the teachers who were now unemployed, and the 7000 pupils who now had no school to attend, were many who would later take up arms in anger and frustration. The closures, and the seizures of school property that accompanied them, were bitterly resented by the communities who had invested so much of their own endeavour and money in building up these independent institutions. Far from diminishing local support for Mau Mau, the school closures only served to harden resistance in the areas affected.[40] And it was to trigger a violent reprisal that would mark the real beginning of the Mau Mau war.

## Christmas Eve in Nyeri

On 23 December 1952 a clandestine meeting was held at the homestead of Samson Gachura, in Aguthi location, south Nyeri. An elder of fifty-three years of age, Gachura was a leading militant activist in the area, and a lifelong supporter of the independent schools movement. The thirty or so people who crowded into his home that evening had already taken an oath administered by supporters of the *Muhimu*. The young men of the independent schools had been in the vanguard of oathing in Nyeri from 1950. At Mahiga, for example, they administered the oaths to small groups, immediately after Christian church services. A school-teacher there kept careful records of the oathing, 'promising that those whose names were written in the book would be entitled to grants of land after Africans got self-government'.[41] Gachura told those summoned to his home that evening that the time had come to act upon the oath. Their schools had been closed and their property forfeit. He pointed the finger of blame at those who had betrayed them by giving information to the government. Five Aguthi elders were mentioned by name. These men were all senior members of the Church of Scotland. All were said to have worked against the interests of the independent schools over many years past. It was known that they had refused the oath. The meeting resolved that all five should be killed. The next day, at a second meeting, leaders were assigned to lead the attack upon each of the victims. The group resolved to carry through their plot later that same night.[42]

With deliberate calculation the attacks took place just after sunset on Christmas Eve, when it was known that those good Christians would all be at home with their families. These rural dwellings were all in typical

Kikuyu settings, built on ridge tops, the mud-and-wattle thatched huts and barns shaded by trees, with the farm land falling away down the hillside. These were clean, respectable houses, furnished with neatly made wooden tables and chairs, adorned with tidy cushions and table-cloths. These were the homes of good Christian families, who valued cleanliness as they valued godliness, and who took pride and satisfaction from their families and friends. On Christmas Eve their loved ones were gathered around the table for the most significant celebration of the year.

Five homesteads were attacked simultaneously, at around 8p.m. The dozen or so men who went to the home of Richard Muhogo found him in conversation with a relative by the gate to his compound. They chased him inside his house, spearing him through the stomach, then hacking him on his bed. On leaving, they set upon his relative, Mbathia, and his daughter. Both were killed.[43] The same fate befell Kori Ruingi and his wife Wanjiro, who died together at the entrance to their family homestead.[44] Ndegwa Mugo was similarly murdered in his bedroom, and his wife slashed to death in their kitchen. One of their daughters escaped the assault and hid nearby, while another, aged nine, saw her parents perish before herself being grievously wounded and left for dead.[45] Douglas Kagorani and Stephen Ngahu were also victims of the attack.

The attacks threw the Christian communities of south Nyeri into panic. Fearing more slaughter, local headmen speedily recruited home-guard patrols to protect their communities, while the police took the remaining relatives of the deceased into protective custody. As accusation and counter-accusation swirled around between the opposed Christian communities, one Church of Scotland the other independent, those who had witnessed the attacks were at this stage too traumatized, and too afraid, to speak; but five days after the violence a young man finally came forward to give evidence. His name was Wamangi Wahome. He confessed to having participated in the attack upon Richard Muhogo, and named more than a dozen people who had attended the meetings at Samson Gachura's homestead, describing in considerable detail what had taken place.[46] Though several suspects were now taken in for questioning, and the police initiated a search for many more, in the weeks following the Christmas Eve attacks it proved impossible to glean any other relevant information that would assist a prosecution. People were simply too afraid to speak out.

It was not until May 1953 that the first capital trial relating to the Nyeri Christmas Eve murders came before the courts. No fewer than six further trials would follow, the last not completed until November 1955. As a consequence of these proceedings, thirteen Kikuyu were sentenced to hang. Ten of these men were executed, while the remaining three had their sentences commuted to imprisonment for life. The story of how these trials unfolded highlights many of the grave difficulties that confronted the British in their administration of justice over the course of Kenya's Emergency.

The problem facing the prosecution in each of these trials was to find corroborative evidence to support the statement of Wamangi Wahome. The court could not rely solely upon his evidence, as an accomplice to murder, to secure a conviction. In each of the trials, it was therefore necessary to bring forward other witnesses who could identify the attackers. In the first trial, during May 1953, wives of Richard Muhogo and his relative Mbathia gave evidence identifying two of their husbands' killers. Both men were sentenced to hang.[47]

At the second trial, in June 1953, four men were found guilty of the murder of Kori Ruingi, based principally upon the evidence of one of his surviving wives, Kio, and her daughter Waithumi. However, the Appeal Court overturned these convictions when it was realized that Kio and Waithumi had first made statements to the police in January explicitly stating that they could not identify any of the attackers. At the end of March the two women had made further statements, this time giving the names of the attackers. Both women were then able to pick out some of those named at police identification parades. The doubt in the minds of the three High Court judges who heard the appeal was not that the women should have recovered their memory so late in the day – it was accepted that fear might have prevented them giving a full testimony at an earlier date – but that the prosecution had not informed the judge of their earlier statements. In the opinion of the Appeal Court, Justice Cram should have been given the opportunity to weigh this matter in coming to a view on the evidence of Kio and Waithumi.[48] The convictions were therefore quashed, but the four men were not freed: the police immediately charged them with a second murder – that of Wanjiro, Kori Ruinge's wife.

They came before the court for a second time in April 1954, and this time the prosecution had strengthened their case. A further witness had been found. This witness, a woman named Chiriaka, lived in the homestead next to the Ruinges, and now gave evidence confirming the identify of the attackers. Fearing for her own life, Chiriaka had fled from Aguthi immediately after the attack, going first to another part of Nyeri, and then to Nairobi, where the police eventually tracked her down and persuaded her to return to make a statement. In another development, the headman in the village where the attacks had occurred, Robero, now gave evidence to the effect that Kio and Waithumi had in fact given the names of the attackers to him in January. He had written this down on a scrap of paper, but had mislaid that crucial document. He was now able to recall the details of his interview with Kio and Waithumi, and recounted it to the court. Robero was presented to the court as a loyal and stalwart government servant, the head of the local home guard and a man who had stood against Mau Mau at great personal risk. The judge decided that Robero was a credible witness, despite his inability to locate the crucial piece of paper. With his testimony, and Chiriaka's additional evidence, the four accused were again convicted; and this time their appeals were dismissed.[49]

In the meantime, another trial had taken place, in August 1953, this for the murder of Ndegwa Mugo. Among the four accused were two men whom the Crown prosecution believed to have been the principal instigators of the crime, Samson Gachura and Muhanya Kirisio. Both men were senior elders who had been with the Church of Scotland Mission before the clitoridectomy crisis and the breakaway of the independents in the early 1930s. Their complicity in organizing the murder plot was established through Wahome's evidence, and their role in the killing of Ndegwa Mugo was described in the evidence of his two surviving daughters, Elizabeth, aged fourteen at the time of the attack, and Mary, aged ten. Like the other female witnesses, Elizabeth and Mary had taken several months to give full statements to the police. Their testimony from the witness box was both emotional and compelling. Elizabeth had fled from the attackers and hidden in a woodpile, from where she had had a clear sight of the assailants. Mary had been with her mother in the kitchen when she was killed, and had herself suffered a serious wound to the head, from which she bore a severe scar. Acting Justice Salter had no hesitation in accepting the veracity of the evidence of these two young girls. All four of the accused were sentenced to hang (see table 2.i, p. 346, for conviction details for the Christmas Eve attacks).[50]

Two further cases came before the courts much later, one in June 1954, the other not until November 1955. The first of these brought Wahome, Elizabeth and Mary back to court to give further evidence against another two men identified as having been among the group that killed Ndegwa. These two accused had been in police custody since early in 1953. The pressures on the police had led to a muddle, the court was told. The two had escaped prosecution through simple bureaucratic oversight. Both were not convicted, although Justice Holmes suggested that their death sentences might be reduced to life imprisonment in recognition of the time they had spent on remand.[51] In the final trial from the Nyeri murders for which records have been located, another person said to have been involved in the murder of Ndegwa was convicted, once again on the evidence of Wahome, Elizabeth and Mary.[52]

This last trial was staged nearly three years after the crime.

The legal aftermath of the Christmas Eve killings reveals the many peculiarities of the Mau Mau trials. The difficulties in securing witness statements and the delays in processing evidence were features of the terror induced by Mau Mau attacks and the slender resources and limited competence of the police. Fear tied people's tongues. Investigations were too often haphazard and partial. Confessional statements and accomplice evidence were a commonplace resort for the police. In many of the most violent and significant cases it was the evidence of traumatized survivors, who were often young women, that carried the burden of the prosecution's case. Elizabeth and Mary were not the only young girls who found themselves giving evidence in several different capital cases. In the Nyeri trials, as in so many others, the judge had to decide whether or not to accept the evidence of these young and possibly impressionable people on capital charges. Without the statement of Wahome, a confessed accomplice to the crime, none of the thirteen Nyeri Christmas Eve convictions could have been secured. And then there was the question of the subsequent statements and the late 'discovery' of evidence. Were such things really credible, or did this imply that witnesses were being 'prepared' for the court? The circumstances surrounding headman Robero's evidence would surely raise questions in any reasonable mind, and the extent to which Wahome, Elizabeth and Mary had become almost professional witnesses by the time they testified in their fourth trial cannot be ignored. Samson Gachura, who would hang as a result of his conviction, certainly thought that Elizabeth and Mary had been induced to testify against him. When sentenced by the judge, he exploded in anger: 'The reason why the two girls have come here and given evidence against me', he told the court, 'is because they were living for months in the camp of the Home Guards, who told them what to say. They were taught to say this by people with whom I have cases about land. They are jealous because I have got some property.'[53] Headman Robero was the guardian of Elizabeth and Mary during their many months in protective custody: there was certainly the opportunity for collusion; and in locations such as Aguthi, where long-standing feuds separated people into opposed political camps, it was natural to assume that you knew your enemies. Were accusations perhaps too easily made on the basis of known disputes?

The events of Christmas Eve 1952 in Nyeri's Aguthi location were not to prove exceptional in Kenya's Mau Mau war. Nor was the pattern of legal cases arising from this night of violence. In many ways, the murders in Nyeri marked the real beginning of the Emergency. It was to be a very dirty war.

# 3

# 'Parasites in Paradise'
# Race, Violence and Mau Mau

When Henry Seaton arrived, in 1914, to take up a position as a district officer in the administration of British East Africa, as Kenya was then called, he knew little of the country or its peoples. His first impressions were to be formative and lasting. The government sent a European manager to meet Seaton at Nairobi railway station and to arrange for the onward transport of his luggage. This large, brusque man, carrying a coiled whip on his arm, greeted Seaton on the platform, barked orders to his African staff to deal with the assortment of trunks and bags, and took his charge to the station forecourt to find a rickshaw to carry him to his hotel. In the bustle and confusion at the station entrance the manager was accidentally knocked over by a mule cart driven by an African. What happened next would remain firmly etched in Seaton's mind for the next fifty years, then to be recounted in his published memoirs:

> He got up out of the dust in great pain and the hell of a rage, still clutching his stock-whip. This he uncoiled and with it lashed out in fury at the culprit. The native driver, with great presence of mind, shielded his face from the flying thong, got his mules going again and disappeared in a cloud of dust. The agent was quite undamaged. I thanked him warmly for his assistance and went off in a rickshaw wondering if this were anything unusual.[1]

As Seaton was soon to discover, the violent reaction of the European agent was not in the least unusual.

As a district officer and magistrate in Kenya's White Highlands, Seaton would encounter many examples of the violence meted out by European settlers to the Africans around them. Among white settlers there was always a tendency to take the law into their own hands. In 1907 a crowd of settlers flogged three African 'rickshaw boys' on the lawn outside the Nairobi courthouse for their alleged insolence toward two European women passengers.[2] If this was an exceptional case, with a political message for a colonial state then seen to be too sympathetic to 'African interests', on the remote farms, distant from the magistrates' courts, rough justice was the rule. Settlers punished their labourers and domestic staff with the *kiboko*, a whip made of rhinoceros hide. Floggings on the farms were part and parcel of the African workers' experience. By the early 1920s, the deaths of several African servants from beatings at the hands of their European masters earned Kenya's white settlers an unenviable reputation for brutality.[3]

The colonial state, too, through its legislation and the practices of its courts, deployed physical punishments as a means to retain order. Colonialism everywhere in Africa depended upon the threat of coercive power to sustain its authority, but in Kenya this had a particular sharpness. Kenya's settlers regulated their African labour through a version of the old English 'master and servants' laws, and defended their right under this legislation to administer corporal punishments to their domestic staff and farm labourers. Africans brought before Seaton, in his role as magistrate, were likely to be flogged if found guilty, regardless of the character of their offence. By the 1920s the vast majority of those Africans convicted by all Kenya's colonial courts were flogged, this in addition to other punishments handed down, such as imprisonment or fines. Flogging was a far commoner punishment for Africans in Kenya than in neighbouring Uganda or Tanganyika, where settler influence was absent. It is difficult to avoid the conclusion that Africans were flogged more in Kenya because Europeans believed they needed to be flogged.[4] Physical violence was an integral and characteristic part of European domination in Kenya from the very beginnings of colonial rule, and by the 1920s it was already engrained as part of Kenya's peculiar pattern of 'race relations'. Happy Valley, as some liked to call the White Highlands, was always a violent place if you were African.

Race was what set white settlers apart from the African masses, and from rival immigrants, the Hindus and Muslims from southern Asia. Race gave Kenya's white settlers a clear, visible superiority, and generated a solidarity that transcended differences in class and social attitudes. Whatever his background, and no matter whether he came to East Africa directly from Europe, or via the Natal or Transvaal, every white man who disembarked from the boat at Mombasa became an instant aristocrat. They exploited Kenya to attain a quality of life that few could have aspired to elsewhere. The privileges of a landed aristocracy, by the early 1900s already under severe attack in Britain, could be had by almost anyone with a white skin in Kenya. Land was bought for next to nothing, if it was bought at all; and there seemed to be plenty of it. In the coffee-growing regions, farms of 300 to 500 acres were the norm, and in the drier Rift Valley, where stock farming and cereals would be the mainstays of the settler economy, there were farms of 5000 acres. Kenya's Europeans were men of property, even though many of them remained as urban dwellers in Nairobi. Those who got in early, before 1914, including men such as Delamere and Grogan, then made money portioning out their estates, rural and urban, for sale to others as land values soared. Through such speculation, colonial Kenya turned some European paupers into imperial princes.[5] Yet the majority of the white settlers made only a modest living from their lands, benefiting principally through access to cheap African labour, its wages held down by a compliant colonial state. They were not wealthy: race alone was enough to elevate and preserve their social status. In her first journey through East Africa, in 1930, Margery Perham, Oxford University's expert in colonial administration, shrewdly observed the attractions of Kenya for these 'ordinary' white folk: 'I think I now understand the immigrant community,' she wrote in her diary. 'To own a bit of this virgin country; to make a house, and, still more, a garden in which you can mingle all the beauties of Western and tropical flowers; to have a part share in this thrilling sunlight; to have cheap, apparently reverential, impersonal labour; to feel the sense of singularity, of enhanced personality that comes from having a white skin among dark millions.'[6] This was a Mecca for the English middle classes. Kenya's most celebrated writer, Ngugi wa Thiong'o, would later call them the 'parasites in paradise'.[7]

## 'A sunny land for shady people'

Every white man in Nairobi is a politician; and most of them are leaders of parties.

Winston Churchill, *My African Journey* (1907)

From the earliest days of white settlement, Kenya established a reputation as a home for the English gentry, with a distinctly military orientation. Compared with Southern Rhodesia, Kenya's pioneers did indeed seem to be 'a cut above'. While Kenya attracted the officer class, Rhodesia made do with the rank and file. Retired captains, colonels and majors were prominent among the first settlers, and their numbers were greatly augmented by the Soldier Settlement Scheme in 1918, and again in the push for 'new blood' after 1945. On the eve of the Great War, there were 5438 Europeans settled in Kenya. Soldier settlers helped increase that number to 9651 by 1921. At that time, some 36 per cent of Kenya's white population was engaged in farming. Over the next two decades, that percentage would fall as the economy of the colony slowly diversified and greater numbers of the new European immigrants became involved in commerce and in the professions. There were more than 20,000 whites in Kenya by 1938. A decade later, a post-war campaign to encourage European immigration saw numbers climb to 30,000.[8] This last wave of settlement brought a new cadre of retired military men to the colony, including 400 'soldier settlers' who were subsidized by government support, many taking up small farms in the outlying parts of the White Highlands where land was less expensive. It also saw the balance shift away from farming and towards commerce as the mainstay of European economic interests. By the 1950s more white Kenyans lived in the towns than on the land, though this was not the image they would project to the world in their struggle against Mau Mau.

Kenya was a colony for gentlemen, not for artisans or the white working class. This was often explained as the consequence of government policy, with the exclusion of the poorer elements through rules demanding that new settlers should have some capital behind them. In reality, it was brought about by the historical accident that indentured labour from India had been used in the construction of the Uganda railway between 1897 and 1901. From the early 1900s through to the 1950s, Indian settlement in Kenya vastly outstripped European. By the 1920s there were already more than twice as many Asian immigrants as there were whites, and by the 1940s Indians would outnumber Europeans by three to one. Indians filled the artisan positions, dominating the construction industry, small-scale manufacturing (including textiles), and transport and haulage, as well as petty trading and local urban commerce. There was therefore little scope for European men of the artisan class in Kenya. In comparison with Southern Rhodesia, where Europeans did fill the artisan role, Kenya's earliest settlers contained a very high proportion of men who were the products of the English public schools and universities. Among them were many Old Etonians, including Delamere, Cranworth, Carnegie and Dennis Finch-Hatton. There were several titled aristocrats, although most of these had fallen on hard times – according to Kennedy, they tended to be 'the younger sons of peers, sons-in-law, nephews, lesser gentry and more distant members of the aristocratic network'.[9] In Kenya they could retain elements of the life of the English country squire, gaining greater respect and recognition among white society than might have been the case back home. Kenya's settlers were always predominantly drawn from British stock. A large contingent of Afrikaners had arrived before 1910, some 600 strong. They never mixed well with their British counterparts and did not share the same social aspirations. A visitor to the Uasin Gishu Plateau in 1913, where the majority of the Afrikaners had decamped, described the typical Boer farmhouse as 'a shanty infinitely less attractive than a Connemara shebeen'.[10] British snobbery did not encourage the integration of the Afrikaners. Later immigrants from the south were British in origin. By the 1930s South Africans (including both Briton and Boer) made up less than 18 per cent of the European population, and they lacked both political influence and economic clout. More than 55 per cent of the white highlanders were of British origin and, already by 1931, one in five settlers resident in Kenya had been born in the colony. This strong British element dominated the coffee farms of the central highlands and the larger ranches of the Rift Valley, and they took a leading role in the political life of the settler community.[11]

What did Kenya offer these immigrants? There were some immediate economic advantages to be seized. For the first settlers, good quality land came more cheaply here than anywhere else in the world, and long leases gave security of tenure. Whereas colonists in other territories, most obviously Australia, had to live or die by the labour of their own hands, those in Kenya could call upon the sweat of African peasants to push forward agricultural development. The legal procurement of that labour at rates of pay favourable to the colonists was the principal basis of settler domination, and this was supported by a colonial government that set wage rates and arranged a tax regime that drove African men into the labour market.[12] Alongside these economic benefits, social prejudice and ideological leaning played a part in shaping settler society. Many of the settlers who came to Kenya from Britain nurtured expectations of a gentlemanly lifestyle that was, by the end of the nineteenth century, being undermined 'back home' by the forces of industrialization, rising egalitarianism and the intensity of urban life. For people who did not welcome these social and economic transformations, Kenya held an obvious appeal. 'Here was a rural, hierarchical society', writes Kennedy, 'reminiscent of a past Britain more congenial to aristocratic sensibilities, sustained, so it must have seemed, by a semi-feudal relationship between European and African, with paternalism and deference the stable currency of interaction.' Fleeing from Britain, Kenya's white settlers found a new land 'free from the pollution of modernity'.[13]

These social and ideological gains compensated for the fact that, even with considerable levels of government subsidy and support, over the long haul, the economics of settler agriculture was always precarious. The 'pioneers' made more money from land speculation than they ever would from productive farming.[14] Land bought at less than 3 shillings an acre in 1908 was selling on the open market in the early 1920s at more than 70 shillings an acre.[15] At first, no one knew what crops would grow best. Nor did they have a clear vision of the export markets that could be most readily exploited. There were false starts with rubber and flax, and a brief boom in sisal before coffee and tea emerged as the front-runners. Plantings of coffee rapidly increased from 1914 onwards, but the brief boom enjoyed by the settlers during the 1920s was driven by high world prices, especially for cereals. Maize and wheat made money for white farmers in the 1920s, and they protected this income by keeping African producers, who were far more efficient, out of the export market.[16] The total area of European farmland under cultivation multiplied more then threefold during the 1920s. European farmers grew only 32,167 acres of maize in 1920: In 1929 that figure had climbed to 200,000 acres, from which over a million bags of maize were produced. This was the golden age of white farming in East Africa. It was short-lived. When the Great Depression came at the end of the 1920s, world prices plummeted, especially for cereals, and Kenya's export markets vanished. Exported maize had realized 13 Kenya shillings per bag before the slump, but by 1933 the price was less than 7 shillings, and well below the profit threshold. Sisal farmers needed £25 per ton to break even, and in the late 1920s had managed to achieve £39 per ton. By 1931, exported sisal fetched only £14 per ton. The fall in coffee was less precipitous, but equally damaging because it affected so many white producers. Coffee farmers, earning more than £6 per cwt in 1929, could barely make a profit when prices fell under £3 during 1930. The 2000 white settlers then in farming were hit hard. Without heavy government support the majority would never have survived. A government-sponsored Land Bank (providing restructuring loans to cashless farmers), the waiving of freight and storage charges, and the slashing of African wages, all helped to keep things ticking over. By the end of 1936 the Land Bank had assisted one in four of Kenya's white farmers, with loans totalling £631,260.[17]

Just as state assistance kept the white farmers afloat in the 1930s, it would launch their economic – and political – recovery in the 1940s. Kenya was marginal to the Allied war effort until February 1942, when the fall of Singapore put the agricultural wealth of South-East Asia into enemy hands. To foster greater production for the war effort, Kenya's farmers were asked to increase production, with the incentive that the government would guarantee the prices of their crops. The 1939–45 war therefore gave a huge boost to the settler economy. More of the White Highlands than ever before came under the plough, and capital flooded in to pay for mechanization. It was in the midst of this boom that settlers gained the confidence to contemplate the squatter evictions. The wartime economy also brought greater political power. Settlers were given a prominent role in the various government production boards, and for the first time had a voice in the administration of the agricultural sector. This was a gain they were reluctant to give up, and after 1945 Governor Mitchell was persuaded to retain the settler Cavendish-Bentinck as Member for Agriculture. Settler political influence within the colonial government had never been greater. Self-government for Kenya's white highlanders, on the model of Southern Rhodesia, was never seriously contemplated in London, but there had always been a flicker of hope among the white highlanders that it might be achieved. As plans were rolled out after 1945 to encourage new settlers to come to Kenya, the growing influence of the settler community over government policy seemed to be edging them closer to a political future that would secure their status and privilege. These trends did nothing to help African leaders, such as Kenyatta, to mount credible arguments in favour of a moderate, constitutional politics of African advancement.

By the eve of the emergency, Kenya's European population, numbering 40,000, was therefore reasonably confident of its future prosperity. There were by then still fewer than 2200 white farms, and those whites living on the land were greatly outnumbered by the European professionals in commerce and business; but this shift in the focus of the white community had done nothing to alter the pervading self-image of white society in Kenya. White highlanders still saw themselves as a robustly independent community, conservative in the best English sense of the term, and the things they valued remained the bucolic, paternalistic ideals of rural colonial life. Among their number were a few dissenting voices, who spoke up for 'African interests', and who warned of the dangers of anachronistic racial policies; but there were louder voices in favour of the status quo, and many more who looked with admiration at the 'progress' of South Africa under the Malan government from 1948. Even self-styled settler liberals, such as Blundell, who argued for a multi-racial future, saw this as a road toward 'power sharing', and not racial integration.[18] Among Kenya's white highlanders it would have been difficult to find any support in 1950 for rapid African political advance, for giving African workers parity with Europeans or, least of all, for permitting Africans to purchase land in the White Highlands. Even at the height of their powers, in the 1940s, this was a curiously anachronistic community.[19]

As time passed, the anachronism of settler privilege seemed all the more glaring. During the 1950s Kenya's white population was greatly swelled by a huge influx of government personnel. There was also a strong flow of whites into senior management positions in the service and business sectors. And, more surprisingly, the colony continued to attract new settlers almost to the very end, inevitably of a type who were determined to 'see off the threat of Mau Mau' and make the White Highlands a home for their children. The European population of 42,000 in 1953 had soared to 54,000 by 1956. Paradoxically, this most rapid period of growth in white immigration over the entire history of the colony precisely coincided with the height of the fighting in the emergency. By the end of the emergency, in 1960, there were 61,000 whites in Kenya, including 13,000 European children in Kenya's schools.[20] These new white immigrants were every bit as determined as Kenya's 'pioneer settlers' to preserve their privileged lifestyle.

When the emergency came, white highlanders had good reason to be fearful. Mau Mau aimed to restore the White Highlands to African ownership. The secret oathing of farm workers and the rumours of a planned rebellion tapped into a deep well of settler anxiety about their vulnerability amid a hostile African majority. White fears were quickly picked up in the coverage given to Kenya's emerging crisis in the British press. In reporting the Declaration of Emergency, the more popular papers inevitably emphasized the plight of Britain's 'kith and kin'. The *Daily Mail* described the arming of settler women, and a few days later the *Daily Mirror* carried a lurid report on the dangers then faced by the European community, under the headline: 'Suburbia in darkest Africa sits tight on dynamite'.[21] While the British papers never went as far as did the American press in openly suggesting that the Mau Mau rebellion was a 'race war', it was made clear that the white civilians, including women and children, were in the firing line.[22] This emphasis on the experience of the white minority dominated the press coverage throughout the war, and gave rise to the impression that the violence of Mau Mau was principally directed against Europeans. That may have been the intent of Mau Mau's leaders before the conflict began, but it was not in the event what happened. According to Corfield's *Historical Survey* of the rebellion, only thirty-two European civilians were killed in Kenya as a result of Mau Mau attacks, with another twenty-six being wounded. More European civilians would die in road traffic accidents between 1952 and 1960 than were killed by Mau Mau. These figures should be contrasted with the 1819 African civilians assassinated by Mau Mau, and another 916 African civilians wounded over the same period.[23] These latter figures do not include the many hundreds of Africans who 'disappeared', and whose bodies were never found. For Kenya's Africans, Mau Mau became a bitter civil war among the Kikuyu themselves, but it was never a race war.

While Mau Mau divided the Kikuyu, it united the white settlers as nothing had before. The threat posed by Mau Mau had begun to worry the settlers by 1951, but only because they feared that government was not taking sufficient steps to quell the unrest. They saw Mau Mau as 'a local difficulty' that required a firm hand. Despite their urgings, Governor Mitchell refused to act and the situation had been allowed to deteriorate. Kenya's many retired military men were full of views on how the mounting disorder should be handled, and there was no shortage of volunteers for militia service among younger and older white settlers alike. The colony already had its own military unit, the Kenya Regiment. Formed as a territorial force in 1936, members of the regiment saw service in parts of Africa, in Madagascar and in Burma between 1939 and 1945, as officers with the King's African Rifles. From 1950 Kenya's young white males were conscripted for national service into the regiment, undertaking training in Southern Rhodesia. As well as taking on operational duties as discrete military units, the three companies of the Kenya Regiment provided officers and NCOs to serve with other elements of the security forces throughout the Emergency. In this way, the 300 or so settlers of the Kenya Regiment played a very significant role in all aspects of the counter-insurgency campaign.[24]

A far larger number of white settlers were police reservists. The Kenya Police recruited more than 600 additional men from Britain on short-term contracts during the emergency, but the bulk of the additional manpower needed was found through a massive expansion of the Kenya Police Reserve (KPR). By the end of 1953 the KPR comprised 2000 full-time officers and another 4800 part-timers. Although there were some Asian recruits, especially in Nairobi, the vast majority were white settlers. As with the Kenya Regiment, the local knowledge of the KPR men made them indispensable to the security forces during the emergency, but their personal commitment to the struggle was not always seen as an asset. This white *gendarmerie* frequently took independent actions against Mau Mau 'suspects'. In Nairobi small groups of KPR formed their own 'strike squads'. Possessing their own weapons and ammunition, in the early months of the Emergency the regular police found it exceedingly difficult to control these renegade elements. It was rumoured that these groups carried out their own assassinations of Mau Mau. The military historian Anthony Clayton, for example, refers to the discovery of a decomposed body at the Meru police post as being one such victim of KPR 'excess'. 'There may well have been more Africans killed in this way,' speculates Clayton, 'as these groups represented a release of anger and frustration.'[25] As we shall see, other examples did indeed come to light. General Erskine, who arrived in Kenya in June 1953 to take command of the military, soon became wary of the tendency of KPR officers to extreme political views and their quick resort to physical force in the treatment of Africans. It was with the KPR in mind that Erskine first described Kenya to his wife as 'a sunny land for shady people'.[26]

The world in which the white highlanders lived was necessarily defined in terms of race. Race established the dominance of the European in Kenya. It established their legal access to land in the White Highlands, and denied rights of ownership to other races. It permitted them to elect their representatives to the Legislative Council by ballot, while Africans and Asians were denied any semblance of democratic choice. It allowed them to impose a colour bar in hotels and clubs, and at sporting events such as the Nairobi races. It secured for them better wages in supervisory and administrative jobs, which Africans might be well qualified for but could not obtain. It granted them licences to grow and export valuable crops, such as coffee, that were barred from African cultivation. And it gave them the right to be tried in court by a jury of their peers, a privilege denied to Kenya's other peoples. In all of these respects, the poorest, most ill-educated white person in Kenya enjoyed a higher social and political status than any person of African or Asian origin. Viewed from the perspective of white Kenyans, the Mau Mau rebellion was nothing less than an assault upon the racial supremacy that was the foundation of their society. They expected to be the target of Mau Mau violence; and Kenya's whites were never going to give up their privilege without a fight.

## Killing Bwana

The organized and concerted rising against whites that some commentators had feared once the Emergency was declared never materialized. The attacks upon settlers turned out to be sporadic and scattered. There was no apparent pattern by which one could identify those most likely to be singled out for attack. For those on isolated farms, and for the security forces that sought to protect them, this randomness only deepened the sense of vulnerability and uncertainty. The attacks in fact mirrored the chronology of the war itself, the majority coming in two main clusters at points of the struggle when the Mau Mau armies were on the offensive. Most of the attacks came in a cluster between October 1952 and July 1953, when the security forces remained in defensive positions but were spread too thinly to adequately protect all the farms, and when the newly formed Mau Mau units were mounting their first raids to acquire recruits, supplies and weapons and were seeking to set up secure communication links with their supporters in the Kikuyu reserve and in Nairobi. Amongst these attacks were some carried out in the same area over a few days, probably by the same individual Mau Mau units. Though the attacks lacked coordination, most were well planned and efficiently executed. They diminished after July 1953, when the British regiments went on the offensive along the forest fringes, keeping many Mau Mau units pinned in. The rapid growth of the Home Guard in the Kikuyu districts at this time also diminished the amount of oathing that was being carried out – as we shall see, many attacks on the farms were linked to the oathing of farm workers in an effort to secure lines of supply. A second, though far less intense, bout of attacks began in March 1954. These were, for the most part, less well planned than the earlier attacks. Some were highly opportunistic. Others indicated the desperation of Mau Mau units to replenish supplies, and perhaps also their frustration at being pinned back in the forests. In this phase the forest fighters found it increasingly difficult to move around on the farms without being detected, and so tended to stay away from areas where the majority of the African labourers had not already been oathed. This reflected the fact that the initiative was by now with the security forces, and that the forest fighters were becoming increasingly isolated and short of supplies. Rather than mount raids on farms that were not yet solid in their support for Mau Mau, which exposed local African workers to punitive sanctions and disrupted supply lines as security forces flooded the area in the aftermath of an attack, in this later phase the forest fighters covertly used the farms as sources of supply and support and mostly tried to avoid confrontation.

The first cluster of attacks, coming relatively early in the emergency, caused considerable alarm among settlers and played a large part in consolidating the image of Mau Mau's 'cold-blooded savagery'. The character of the violence horrified Europeans and Africans alike. Most victims died as the result of multiple blade wounds, the bodies being hacked and mutilated even after death. The severing of limbs, and the seemingly frenzied nature of the attacks, added to the terror induced by this violence. This was a messy, undignified and painful death. For Europeans, such brutal, physical violence recalled the killing of an earlier era and seemed very distant from the remoteness of modern violence inflicted by a bullet or a bomb. Here killer and victim were locked together, face to face. To kill in this way required commitment and determination. The European imagination found it difficult to under-stand how such attacks could be perpetrated unless the killers were in some way possessed or controlled by dreadful forces they could not defy. This interpretation was embraced by European settlers, who found it almost impossible to accept that the perpetrators of the violence might be their own farm workers or domestic servants – people whom they may have known well over several years, whom they may have felt a bond of friendship with, and whom they had trusted. In the majority of the attacks on white settlers, domestic servants and trusted farm workers were deeply implicated in the violence. This invasion of the domestic space – the murders usually took place in the homes of the European victims, and were carried out by people who had a legitimate place within the intimacy of family life – added another deeply disturbing psychological aspect to the violence: you knew your killer, and he knew you.

White highlanders could only 'understand' this gross breach of trust if their African staff were in some way deemed to be possessed, or in the control of other forces. This led many white settlers to take refuge in the interpretation of Mau Mau as a kind of illness, or even a disease. The mystification of the oath fed such anxieties: Kikuyu who had taken the oath were no longer in their right minds; they had been transformed and brutalized. The firm denial that Africans had any legitimate griev-ances against the way they had been treated by settlers closed the door to any materialist or social explanation. This all helped white settlers in their efforts to rationalize the behaviour of their trusted servants; but it did not, in fact, add up to a rational explanation. To see how this view took a grip of the troubled settler imagination, we must chart the sequence of events surrounding the first cluster of attacks, up to July 1953. Along the way, we will see that, viewed from the perspective of the forest fighters themselves, 'killing bwana' had a more prosaic and functional rationality.

Attacks on settlers began in the weeks leading up to the declaration of the Emergency. The Bindloss family were beaten up 'by thugs' on 5 October, and Mr Bindloss 'seriously wounded'. An elderly and infirm couple living in Thika, the Tullochs, were the victims of the next attack. They were also badly hurt, but survived.[27] Their ordeal was the first cause of European outrage against the callousness of Mau Mau attackers. The aged and the solitary were to be typical Mau Mau victims; but in neither of these first cases was it clear whether the assailants had mur-derous intentions, or whether robbery and the procurement of supplies and weapons was the principal purpose. There was similar doubt in the next attack, which took place on the evening of 27 October. The first European victim to be murdered by Mau Mau was the reclusive Eric Bowker, who had taken up his remote farm on the Kinangop, in the Rift Valley, as a retirement home.[28] Little known to his neighbours and seldom to be seen at the social functions held by the local white community, Bowker lived a solitary life, his two Kikuyu male house servants being his only regular company. Bowker made what little money he had not from the farm but from the rural store he ran there, selling clothing and other essential supplies to the African families who worked on the farms in the neighbourhood. This appears to have been the motive for the attack. The assailants entered the farmhouse just after sunset. They swiftly killed his two house servants, who could not have realized that the attack was imminent, then hacked Bowker to death as he lay in his bath. Many of Bowker's farm labourers fled after the attack, and it was suspected that some of them had been involved in the murder. Before leaving the scene the killers ransacked the farm store, taking all the clothing items and supplies with them. This was the first sign that those fleeing to the forests were preparing for the struggle ahead, but at this stage the conflict still seemed more like a crime wave than a war.

The gruesome photographs of Bowker's badly slashed, naked body were not printed in the local press, but news of the circumstances of his death sent a chill through the European community. The clamour for greater protection was now vociferous. Oliver Lyttelton, the Tory government's Secretary of State for the Colonies, visited Kenya a few days after Bowker's death and was immediately harangued by settler leaders to increase the penalties for Mau Mau offences and to 'beef up' the security forces. Many settlers were already keen 'to go after Mau Mau'. Lyttelton refused to be bullied, and followed Governor Baring's lead in pressing the settlers to be vigilant but to remain calm. Privately, the Bowker killing made a grave impression on his mind. On returning to London, he categorically denied to the House of Commons and the British press that Mau Mau was in any way 'the child of economic conditions', and instead stressed that it was merely 'a primitive, irrational attack against the forces of law and order'.[29]

It was an opinion that Lyttelton would hold to, despite the events of the next three years, and it would define his continued support for Baring. Political calculations invariably played a part in determining the approach taken by both men to the crisis. Lyttelton would never admit that the rebellion might be rooted in the failure of British policy, and the ponderous Baring would never be hurried into rash responses by the clamour of the settlers. Having stood firm in public against settler pressure, with typical calculation Baring then saw to it that the Lancashire Fusiliers were moved into the Rift Valley within the next fortnight, where they began regular, arduous and prolonged patrols of the farms. Companies and platoons of British soldiers were now dispersed in penny packets over a wide area of the White Highlands, where they were visible to the settlers.[30] This boosted morale, but had no effect in dampening Mau Mau activity. Reports of oathing campaigns, and of the dis-appearance of Africans to join the armies then forming in the Aberdares forest, often spurred by the continuing evictions of Kikuyu squatters from the farms, increased markedly in the Rift Valley over this period.

Mau Mau's next European victims were the Meiklejohns. Ian Meikle-john was a retired naval officer, his wife a doctor. Their small farm was in the Thomson's Falls district, not far from the border with the Kikuyu reserve. The attack again took place in the evening, after supper, when the Meiklejohns were reading in the sitting room of their farmhouse. Following the Bowker attack, instructions had been issued to settlers to arm themselves in their homes and both the Meiklejohns had handguns close to them as they read; but neither managed to get off a shot before their attackers were upon them. Mrs Meiklejohn's wrist was slashed as she reached for the gun from her handbag, and her husband was cut across the scalp and shoulder before he could rise from his seat. They were both further cut to the head and body, before being left for dead by their attackers, who then stole clothing and other supplies, and took the handguns and ammunition, before making their escape. Mrs Meiklejohn regained consciousness, and somehow managed to drive her car, warily and very slowly, along the track to the Thomson's Falls Police Station, some eight miles away. When the police reached the farm, now several hours after the attack, they found Ian Meiklejohn lying on the floor in an upstairs room, dazed and still trembling with shock, but trying to assemble a spare shotgun, which he had retrieved from its hiding place. He was almost unrecognizable owing to the extent of his injuries. They rushed him to the nearest hospital, in Nakuru, but he died the next day.[31]

In the week following the attack Baring imposed sterner collective punishment measures against African communities who assisted Mau Mau or withheld information from the police. At the same time the Lancashire Fusiliers launched a large-scale sweep through the neighbourhood of Thomson's Falls, removing 750 Kikuyu men and 2200 women and children from farms on suspicion of having taken Mau Mau oaths. The detained squatters were moved into hastily erected camps before being repatriated to the Kikuyu reserves. The troops seized 5000 head of cattle from these squatters, under the collective punishment laws, for their 'lack of cooperation' with the government.[32]

Amid these evictions, there were rumours of settlers, some of them in the KPR, dishing out their own retribution. There were random beatings of the squatters, identity cards and labour tickets were torn up, and wages remained unpaid. The journalist James Cameron, then a rising correspondent with the *Daily Mirror*, visited the White Highlands at this time. Cameron was bitingly critical of the heavy-handed and indiscriminate reaction of what he termed Kenya's 'trigger-happy settlers'. In an article styled as an 'open letter to Sir Evelyn Baring', and published in the *Daily Mirror* on 12 December 1952, Cameron appealed for reason and restraint. In settler excess he saw the death of colonial liberalism, and the loss of the moral order that gave empire its only possible justification. Cameron hit out against collective punishments, punitive sanctions against African workers, and the general repression of decent African people. The Kenya Police Reserve were little more than an undisciplined settler militia – vigilantes in uniform – who only made the ordinary work of the police and security forces more difficult by 'over-stepping the mark' in their methods. In doing such things, or in condoning them, white settlers should not believe that they represented 'British interests', he argued: rather, they sullied the good name of the British people.[33] Before most other commentators had yet focused upon the character of this rebellion and the response to it, Cameron had seen in Kenya's combustible mix of violence and racism the incipient danger of the settlers being 'let off the leash'.[34]

Cameron's 'left-wing' reporting was still being hotly disparaged by Kenya's white settlers when the New Year brought news of more attacks, again concentrated on the Rift Valley farms. The first victims were neighbours at Ol' Kalou, Charles Fergusson and Dick Bingley, who were murdered on the evening of New Year's Day 1953. They had taken to eating together each evening after work, for companionship and security. Both had bathed, and were in their dressing gowns when they sat down to the evening meal that night, at around nine o'clock. Fergusson's house servant was still dishing up the meal when Mau Mau attackers, perhaps as many as fifteen Kikuyu men, burst into the dining room and quickly overpowered both Europeans. Though they were armed, neither man had time to fire. Both men died still at the table, horribly hacked by their attackers. Both their houses were then looted before the gang fled.[35]

The next night a further attack against a settler farm, this time in Nyeri, was bravely fought off. The victims were two redoubtable elderly European women, Kitty Hesselberger and Raynes Simpson. They had followed the advice of the police in arming themselves and moving their table and chairs so that they had a good, clear view of the entrance to their sitting room. They were alerted to potential danger by the nervous behaviour of their house servant, and as the first member of the Mau Mau gang entered the room, Raynes Simpson shot him dead. She fired at another assailant, before Mrs Hesselberger let fly with her shotgun, forcing the attackers to retreat into the kitchen. The women then heard noises from the bathroom adjacent to their sitting room, and they fired repeatedly through the thin timber wall, killing two other Kikuyu. At this point, the attackers made their escape, leaving behind three dead.[36] Hesselberger and Simpson were the first settler heroines of the war. Their ordeal was reported in the Kenya press and their bravery received wide publicity. Mrs Hesselberger gave a robust interview to BBC radio, in which she never once flinched at the memory of the violence nor mentioned the fate of the three dead Kikuyu, but repeatedly lamented the death of her boxer dog, which had been accidentally shot in the general melee.[37] This was the fighting spirit that the settlers so admired and that they wanted the world to see.

Settler pride in the resolute bravery of Hesselberger and Raynes Simpson was to be short lived. Over the next six months Mau Mau attacked the farms with increasing regularity. In more than thirty attacks between January and July, another nine Europeans were murdered, with many farms being looted and burned. In these months the settlers were under siege. In February Anthony Gibson was killed in Nyeri. A British war veteran, who had been taken prisoner in the North Africa campaign, Gibson had only come out to Kenya as a farm manager in 1946.[38] The farm owner, Reginald Morice, was shot at by the attackers, but managed to fight them off.[39] In April an Italian woman, Mrs Meloncelli, and her two children were killed at the Chehe sawmill, in the forest fringe of Mount Kenya. The gang attacked on a Saturday, and may not have expected to find any Europeans at the sawmill. Mrs Meloncelli and her children had arrived in Kenya ten days previously, and had come up to Chehe only two days before their murder. The properties at the sawmills were looted, a variety of weapons and clothing stolen, and outbuildings set alight.[40]

Later that same month a settler in Kitale, far distant from the troubles of central Kenya, was found hacked to death in his farmhouse. The culprits were his two Kikuyu house servants. Although this was at first thought to indicate a dangerous extension of Mau Mau activity, it was later revealed that the murder was provoked by a dispute on the farm that was unrelated to the rebellion.[41] The murder none the less added to mounting tensions among settlers. Then, at the end of May, Hubert Rand-Overy was killed in crossfire on a farm close to Nairobi when security forces apprehended a Mau Mau unit.[42] The next month saw a spate of attacks on the Nyeri and Nanyuki farms, many of them carried out when the European owners were away. In the most serious incident, on the Bastard farm at Sweet Waters in Nanyuki, a Seychellois farm manager and his six children were killed by a gang who stole weapons and ammunition before burning the farmhouse to the ground. Some of the stolen property was recovered a few days later, when an army patrol encountered the Mau Mau unit involved, but not before the gang had raided three other farms.[43] Around the same time, an elderly Italian settler, Mrs Bighi, living alone on the Chania sisal estate in Thika, was attacked and made to hand over her .22 rifle and ammunition to three gangsters, and another Italian settler was robbed of his guns and cash in Nyeri.[44]

July saw a wave of activity on the Naivasha farms, three attacks being beaten back by the white farmers, but with considerable damage to barns and other buildings. Coinciding with these raids, several loyal African foremen were murdered on the Naivasha farms for refusing to be oathed. That same month, the seventy-three-year-old James MacDougall was murdered on his farm in Nanyuki. MacDougall had been among the earliest settlers to come to East Africa, arriving in 1906. He was the first 'Kenya Pioneer' to be killed by Mau Mau.[45] Although Mau Mau units continued to molest the labour lines on the farms throughout the remainder of the year, and some even sought to intimidate white farmers by issuing neatly typed 'eviction notices', left on the verandas of their homes,[46] after July 1953 the worst of the attacks was over.

The victims in the majority of Mau Mau attacks up to this point were elderly settlers, some of whom, such as MacDougall and Bowker, were not physically capable of defending themselves and yet had chosen to live in remote and inaccessible places. There was pity for the victims and their relatives, to be sure, and a sneering disapproval of Mau Mau cowardice, but it was widely recognized that such folk presented the rebels with easy targets. The plucky Mrs Hesselberger and Mrs Raynes Simpson had shown that wiser heads could do something to protect themselves from such vulnerability. As the months went by, settler security greatly improved, and by June and July 1953 it was increasingly common for Mau Mau units to raid farmhouses they believed to be unoccupied. The need to secure weapons and supplies was by then becoming greater than the desire to kill white settlers. The strongest emotional reaction among settlers was reserved for Mau Mau's killing of women and children; but the response to the murders of the Payet children on the Bastard farm, and the deaths of the Meloncelli family on Mount Kenya, was surprisingly muted. This was a matter of race. In Kenya's stratified social order, neither of these families, one Seychellois and the other Italian, could claim full membership of white highlander society. The full rage and fury of the settler community was reserved for the one incident of this period where the victims were an established, vigorous white family – a hard-working farmer of British stock, his attractive young wife, and their six-year-old son. The slaughter of the Ruck family, at their farm in Kinangop on 24 January 1953, was to be the definitive moment of the war for the white highlanders.

The Rucks represented everything that Kenya's Europeans held dear. Roger Ruck and his wife Esme were in their early thirties. Both were good-looking, sociable and popular, playing an active part in settler society. They were typical of 'the very best type of settler' that Kenya had hoped to attract in the post-war years. Ruck was a member of the Kenya Police Reserve, with a reputation as a man of 'strong views' – settler shorthand for conservative and outspoken. He was said to treat his African workers firmly but fairly. Aside from domestic staff, there were around thirty squatters living with their families on the Ruck farm, including Kipsigis and Maragoli workers as well as Kikuyu. The farm was in a remote part of Kinangop, not far from the homestead of Eric Bowker. It was some 30 miles to the nearest police post, and further still down to the small town of Naivasha on the Rift Valley floor. Europeans here tended to be hardy and self-sufficient. Esme Ruck had medical qualifications, and ran a clinic on the farm where she treated African squatters from all over the neighbourhood. Their son, Michael, aged six, spent his days on the farm amongst the children of the Kikuyu workers who lived in the labour lines below the Rucks' farmhouse. The family were well known locally, and well liked. It was in people like these that the future of white settler society was embodied. In the death of the Rucks, hope for that future seemed to dim.

The attack followed what was by now a familiar pattern.[47] There had been trouble in the area over the preceding week, and the local commander of the KPR, Tony Pape, had been shot at only the previous evening. Ruck and his neighbours were therefore aware that a Mau Mau unit was operating in the vicinity, and Roger Ruck had already taken the precaution of posting extra guards on his cattle and outbuildings. Unknown to Ruck, however, Mau Mau had already oathed his Kikuyu workers, and some of the forest fighters may even have been living with his labour over the previous few days. There had been much coming and going of labour on the Kinangop in these troubled days, with many Kikuyu returning to the reserves and others moving from farm to farm in an effort to secure better conditions. There had been a very high turnover among Ruck's labourers over the preceding year or more. Although there were strangers on the farm in January 1953, it seems that Ruck did not notice them.

It was to prove a costly oversight. These 'strangers' hatched the plot to attack the Ruck family, in collusion with some of the Kikuyu squatters resident on the farm. On that Saturday evening they waited until the family had eaten and their domestic staff left the house, and then, at around nine o'clock, they staged a ruse to lure Ruck onto the veranda. One of the farm workers called out to Ruck, pretending to have caught a Mau Mau suspect. Ruck emerged cautiously, armed with a Baretta pistol. He was grabbed from behind by one assailant, his arms pinned to his side so that he could not fire the weapon. Ruck struggled to free himself, but a second assailant then hacked at his legs with a heavy panga. As he fell onto the lawn in front of the house, further blows rained down on his head and back. Hearing his terrible screams, Esme then emerged into the darkness with a shotgun, poised to fire, but she too was swiftly overpowered and hacked down. A farm worker, Muthura Nagahu, who came running to assist the family, was killed too, his body left on the lawn where he fell, close to Roger and Esme.

The house was then ransacked and looted in the search for weapons, ammunition, money and clothing. The final horror came when Michael was found in his bed in an upstairs room. The attackers had to break through the lock on the door to get to him. He was viciously hacked where he lay. A photograph of Michael's blood-stained nursery, his toys scattered around the floor, had a profound impact upon settler emotions

when it was published in the local press.[48] The death of the Rucks and
their child – the breach of white trust, the invasion of domestic space,
and the murdering of innocence – seemed to the European community
to be the epitome of Mau Mau savagery.

## 'Them or us'

The settlers' political leader, Michael Blundell, heard of the Ruck
murders the next morning at Naivasha. He was then on his way to
Nairobi for a meeting of the elected members of the Legislative Council
with Governor Baring, to discuss the progress of the emergency. By the
time he reached Nairobi later that day, white settlers of a more extreme
persuasion had organized a mass march upon Government House to
protest at Baring's 'foot-dragging' and the timidity with which the
government appeared to be tackling the security situation.[49] The more
reactionary of the settlers wanted Kikuyu blood in revenge for the killing
of the Rucks.

   On Monday morning the Kenya Police Reserve were out in force on
the roads leading into Nairobi's commercial district, but their purpose
was not to deter Mau Mau: instead, they halted traffic to instruct
European motorists to attend the protest meeting later that day. By mid-
morning, several hundred whites had pushed their way past the startled
African policemen guarding the entrance to Government House, to
assemble on the lawn in front of the great main doors. When a line of
African police formed on the terrace, linking arms to prevent the mob
entering the building, the mood of the swelling crowd darkened. They
shouted for 'the nigger police' to be taken away, and called for the
governor to come out to see them. As they pushed up against the police
line, some pressed their lighted cigarettes onto the flesh of the African
constables in an effort to break through. At this point Baring was in
counsel with Blundell and other settler leaders in the Cabinet Room.
They could hear the crowd baying outside, but Baring did not permit
any reaction until one of his aides burst in to say that the situation was
becoming difficult. Baring retreated to the calm of his study, while
Blundell and his colleagues went out to placate the mob. By then, the
crowd was hammering against the ten-foot doors of Government House
as Baring's staff hurriedly pushed furniture into place to strengthen their
defences. Blundell later recalled the scene in his memoirs: 'As I emerged
round the corner, the crowd recognized me and there were shouts and
cries. I told the crowd to get right back on the grass below the terrace,
but they were worked up and refused to do so.' Only when Blundell
persuaded the commanding officer to dismiss his line of African police

did the crowd subside. Blundell then climbed onto a chair, and tried to gain the attention of the rabble, but as he did so the Sultan of Zanzibar, then a guest at Government House, emerged briefly on the balcony behind him:

> It was a nasty moment, hundreds of the crowd were armed, and they were in a highly emotional state ... Looking down over the scene, I saw in front of me a little woman dressed in brown who was, in normal times, the respected owner of an excellent shop in Nairobi. She was beside herself with fury and crying out in a series of unprintable words, 'There, there, they've given the house over to the fucking niggers, the bloody bastards' ... This was my first experience of men and women who had momentarily lost all control of themselves and had become merged together as an insensate unthinking mass. I can see now individual pictures of the scene – a man with a beard and a strong foreign accent clutching his pistol as he shouted and raved; another with a quiet scholarly intellectual face, whom I knew to be a musician and a scientist, was crouched down by the terrace, twitching all over and swirling with a cascade of remarkable and blistering words, while an occasional fleck of foam came from his mouth.[50]

It was only with the greatest of difficulty that Blundell and Humphrey Slade were eventually able to gain control and persuade the angry crowd to disperse. In doing so, the elected members assured their white settler constituents that Baring would indeed introduce sterner measures, and that there would be no need for them to take the law into their own hands.

Among the many settler complaints about the conduct of the emergency under Governor Baring's direction, the slowness of the legal process was the issue that raised their ire above all others. To put the matter bluntly, if Mau Mau murdered whites, then the settlers wanted to see the culprits hang. The mob gathered on Baring's lawn made this clear, belligerently threatening to lynch Mau Mau suspects themselves if the government had no stomach for the job. By the time of the Ruck murders, a huge backlog of Mau Mau cases remained unheard in the courts, and settlers were aware that the queue of cases included many serious and ghastly murders of African loyalists. How long would it be before those suspected of murdering whites could be brought to justice? Hangings had in fact already taken place arising from Mau Mau–related murders of Africans, for example in Thomson's Falls, on 13 December 1952, when four Kikuyu men, charged in two separate cases, went to the gallows. However, these offences pre-dated the Declaration of Emergency and the executions were not widely publicized.[51] Settlers had anticipated that the special powers conferred upon the Governor under emergency conditions would see an immediate acceleration in the pace of executions. Nothing of the kind happened. Historically, the Kenya judiciary had always been slow in processing capital cases, and the conditions of the emergency only served to make things worse. At the end of 1952, thirty-two Mau Mau murder cases had been committed to the Supreme Court and were waiting to be heard. There were too few judges on the roll to proceed with these cases rapidly, and it was anticipated that it would take three months or more to clear the backlog. Prisoners had to be held over this period, and Kenya's few secure prisons were already flooded with Mau Mau suspects. Even when a case had been heard and a verdict handed down by the Supreme court, the system still moved with excruciating slowness. It was not unusual in Kenya for convicts to spend several months on death row before their cases came before the East African Court of Appeal, and perhaps several months more still if there were deemed to be grounds for a further appeal before the Privy Council in London.[52] By January 1953 serious Mau Mau cases were still taking four months to come to court once the prosecution was ready, and then after sentence it was typically another six weeks before any appeal could be heard. For example, three Mau Mau cases heard before the Supreme Court in Nyeri early in December 1952, in which nine accused were convicted and sentenced to hang, did not get an appeal hearing until the week before the Ruck murders at the end of January. All these appeals were in the event dismissed, and the nine convicts were hanged in February.[53] In another case, heard at Naivasha on 22 December 1952, eleven men were convicted of a murder at an oathing ceremony. Their appeals were dismissed on 4 February, and they were hanged three weeks later.[54] These hangings, coming hard on the heels of the Ruck murders, gave the impression that Baring had indeed done something to speed up the process and they went some way towards placating settler opinion. However, the harsh truth was that the Kenya legal system was still understaffed and poorly resourced, and simply unable to cope with the dramatic increase in cases arising from the Emergency.

The powers granted to the Governor under the Emergency Powers Regulations included the right to alter the types of cases that could be heard by different levels of court, and to extend the range of offences for which a capital sentence could be handed down by those courts. Baring had already used these powers at the outset of the emergency, granting magistrates' courts greater sentencing powers, including the hearing of cases relating to those suspected of being Mau Mau oath administrators, for which the penalty could be life imprisonment. African courts – that is, those presided over by African chiefs – were also granted greater authority at this time. Another corner was cut for 'lesser offences' (i.e. being

suspected of having taken a Mau Mau oath), by greatly extending detention without trial through the issuing of 'Governor's Detention Orders'.
This was an effective, though extra-judicial means of getting rid of any
troublesome individual simply 'on suspicion'. Later in the Emergency, this
power would be released from its confines within the governor's office,
and extended to a system of 'District Detention Orders'.

The dangers of so radical an extension of extra-judicial authority to
detain suspects was readily open to gross abuse, and for that reason it had
not been supported by senior members of the judiciary. Blundell and his
colleagues were well aware that John Whyatt, the Attorney-General, had
vigorously opposed these developments, on the grounds that administrative officers (most magistrates were district commissioners or district
officers, and hence part of the political service of the government) would
be given unwarranted judicial powers. As a matter of general principle,
Whyatt saw no reason to tamper with 'due process', and was quick to
defend the legal rights of the accused. As the count of murdered settlers
mounted, Kenya's European community found this argument increasingly difficult to swallow. They wanted revenge, and they wanted it
speedily. The simple press of cases building up in the courts was persuasive
evidence that something had to be done – by December 1952, aside
from the murder cases, several hundred lesser Mau Mau cases awaited
hearings in the lower courts. In response to settler pressure after the
Ruck murders, even Whyatt had to concede that further special measures
might be necessary. Under Baring's direction, Whyatt and his staff
therefore began preparing further legal reforms. But, as ever, the Governor refused to be hurried.

Meanwhile, the legal officers saw to it that those accused of the
murders of white settlers now came before the courts at the earliest
opportunity. Over an eight-week period between mid-March and May
1953 trials were held relating to the murders of Meiklejohn, the Rucks,
Fergusson and Bingley, and Anthony Gibson. While settlers welcomed
this, the trials were to reveal as much about the violence and brutality of
the white response to Mau Mau as they were about the character of Mau
Mau violence itself. By January 1953 Blundell and Slade were already
only too well aware of the dangers of settler 'rough justice' against the
Kikuyu.[55] The Ruck murders greatly strengthened support for those
among the settlers who favoured direct action, 'the little group of fiery
men', as Blundell termed them, who 'were intent on going out and
shooting every Kikuyu whom they met on the streets of Nairobi'.[56] The
siege mentality that afflicted the settlers, especially among those living
in the most dangerous areas of Kinangop, Thomson's Falls, Nyeri and
Nanyuki, had already by early 1953 bred an attitude of 'them or us'.
There had been some violence in the evictions of squatters in November

and December 1952, and the Kenya Police Reserve had been widely criticized for its methods in administering collective punishments and questioning Kikuyu 'suspects' in the Rift Valley; and there was a great deal of private violence on the farms in the backlash to each of the settler killings. In the settler murder trials the full extent and severity of such excesses began to become clearer.[57]

In the first case to come to court three Kikuyu men were charged with the murder of Ian Meiklejohn.[58] The prosecution case hinged upon statements made by the accused in which they incriminated themselves, augmented by evidence from other squatters who lived on the Meiklejohn farm. Some of these statements were made to the European police officer handling the case, Assistant Inspector King, as a result of interrogations conducted over the forty-eight hours following the crime. Further statements were then recorded before a magistrate at Thomson's Falls, a Mr Louden, in preparation for the brief committal proceedings, which took place on 7 February 1953. Mrs Meiklejohn had recovered sufficiently from her ordeal to give evidence at the committal hearing, and to confirm identification of two of the accused, but she then returned to Britain and so did not appear in person at the trial.

The essential facts of the case were not contentious. All the farms around the Thomson's Falls area had been badly affected by squatter disputes and Mau Mau had strong support there. The Meiklejohns' squatter labour were known to be disaffected since Ian Meiklejohn had made them remove sheep from the farm and reduce their numbers of cattle a year earlier. It was suspected they had already been oathed before the Emergency. Early in November the local KPR raided the farm and removed some squatters on suspicion of their active participation in Mau Mau. Among those to give evidence at the murder trial were some squatters who had been evicted on that occasion, but whom Meiklejohn had subsequently allowed back onto the farm – like many farmers, he was struggling to obtain sufficient labour. One such squatter was a young man named Kamau Gatheru, of around eighteen years of age. He had been born on the Meiklejohn farm. He told the court about the organization of oathing on the farms in the area earlier during 1952, and described how he had been beaten by Mau Mau because of his reluctance to participate. Other witnesses explained that these same Mau Mau supporters had again come on to the farm on the day prior to the murder, saying that they wanted to steal the Meiklejohns' guns. In the evidence of Kamau Gatheru, and others among Meiklejohn's labourers, it is apparent that they believed that they had been chosen to join with the gang precisely because of their initial resistance to the oath; 'that is why they called me out', explained Kamau, who was made to act as a look-out while the gang entered the house.

The three accused were said to have been among perhaps as many as ten Mau Mau who visited the farm to carry out the attack. The first, Samuel Njehia Gachoka, had worked as a shopkeeper, carpenter and teacher in the area. He was identified by two of is former pupils, who were resident on the Meiklejohn farm. They had seen him in the labour lines on 22 November, carrying a weapon and helping to organize the attack. Gachoka admitted entering the house with the attackers and witnessing the murder, but stridently denied having struck any blows against the victims. This was of no relevance in law, as the confirmation of his presence with the murderers made him an accomplice. He was found guilty and sentenced to hang.

The second accused was Waweru Gitau. Described by Justice Paget Bourke as 'one of the most sinister-looking Kikuyus I have seen', Gitau was also identified by one of the young boys on the farm. He worked in Thomson's Falls as a barber, and so was known to many squatters in the area. Gitau was strongly suspected by the police of being an important organizer of Mau Mau oathing in the district. However, aside from the identification of a single young witness, there was nothing to link Gitau directly with the crime. 'Sinister-looking' or not, Justice Bourke was unwilling to convict on so slender a case, and acquitted Gitau of the charge.

The third accused was a house servant of the Meiklejohns, Watuso Githuri. Githuri had only been in the service of Ian Meiklejohn since August 1952. He had been in the kitchen when the attackers entered the house. The prosecution claimed he had assisted the attackers to enter undetected. Githuri said that he had acted under duress. He had taken a Mau Mau oath, and he believed he 'would be strangled' if he did not cooperate. This is what the gang had told him. Githuri named those members of the gang he knew, all of them Kikuyu squatters or ex-squatters living in the Thomson's Falls area, but these men had not been found by the police. On seeing the severely injured Mrs Meiklejohn struggling to her car after the attack, Githuri had burst into tears. He then ran to a neighbouring farm to raise the alarm. It was clear that Githuri had been a deeply reluctant participant in the events of 22 November, but it was not sufficient in law to support a defence of duress. On the weight of the evidence before him Justice Bourke had little option but to find Githuri guilty as an accomplice to the murder. He was sentenced to hang.

The appeals of Samuel Njehia Gachoka, shopkeeper, carpenter and former teacher, and Watuso Githuri, the house servant, were dismissed on 5 May 1953. They were hanged together on the gallows in Nairobi Prison. In some senses, Watuso Githuri was as much a victim as was Ian Meiklejohn. If we are to believe his own testimony, he took the Mau Mau oath only after being beaten. Then, by dint of his position as a house servant, he was singled out when the Mau Mau activists decided to raid the Meiklejohn farm. His claim that he would have been killed had he resisted their demands is almost certainly true. His status gave him a decent wage and reasonable working conditions. House servants were not subjected to the disruptions faced by the squatters, and by and large they enjoyed a comparatively favoured position among Africans living on the farms. Was this perhaps a reason why Githuri, and other domestic servants like him, were victimized along with the European masters they served?

When the police and neighbouring settlers got to the Meiklejohn farm after the murder, they were clearly shocked and enraged by what they found. The farm labourers and domestic staff were immediately suspected of complicity. At the trial the accused claimed that beatings had been administered to all those who were questioned, and that this was done repeatedly, and openly, in front of many witnesses. They further claimed that they had been instructed what to say in their statements, and that the statements had finally only been made under the most severe duress. Even those who appeared as prosecution witnesses made accusations of beatings in their statements. There was little serious effort made in court to deny the truth of this, and under medical examination two of the accused showed minor signs of physical abuse even four months after their interrogations. Justice Bourke did treat this matter with some degree of candour. He first exonerated Assistant Inspector King from any possible blame – Bourke was quite sure that a European officer of King's experience and calibre would not have allowed such things to happen – but he conceded that beatings had taken place. 'It may well be, such was the cold-blooded atrocity of the crime,' commented Bourke in his judgment on the case, 'that suspects were, through a not unnatural indignation and disgust, treated at the outset rather more roughly than gently.' This tacit admission might have led the judge to question the statements made to the police on the day following the murder, but as supplementary statements had later been made before a magistrate, Bourke felt comfortable with the finding that the extra-judicial evidence was not in fact undermined. So long as the beatings were not related directly to the extra-judicial statements, and so long as the judge showed that he had carefully explored this matter, there could be no grounds for appeal with regard to duress. In his judgment the experienced Justice Bourke left no room for doubt that the beatings had no bearing upon the evidence. Other judges would be less candid and less careful than Bourke in dealing with such matters, but they would almost invariably come to the same broad conclusions.

One final aspect of this case demands comment. The three Kikuyu assessors who heard the case with Justice Bourke declared their opinion that all of the accused were innocent. Bourke interpreted this as a consequence of the apparent fact that none of the three had administered any blows to the deceased, and that the assessors may not have full grasped the meaning under the law of being an accomplice to the crime. While that may indeed have been so, it is also possible that the assessors were more inclined to believe and appreciate the degree to which genuine fear for their own lives dictated the actions of Gachoka and Githuri.

Five days after delivering his verdict in the Meiklejohn case, Paget Bourke was back in the Supreme Court at Nakuru to sit in judgment over the Ruck murder trial.[59] This second settler murder case was to reveal a similar pattern to the first, with collusion between known Mau Mau activists in the locality and more reluctant participants among Ruck's own employees. Bourke would also once again be faced with the difficult task of deciding the status of extra-judicial statements that were crucial to the prosecution case but had subsequently been repudiated or retracted. In this trial, which was to last three weeks, the claims of beatings and intimidation of witnesses during the police investigation were especially serious.

Twelve Kikuyu stood in the dock together accused of the Ruck murders. All were employed on the Ruck farm, or on that of the Ruck's neighbour, Captain Nimmo. They included three juveniles. The story that unfolded in the courtroom revealed that Mau Mau was strongly supported among the labour on both these farms, and that a group of Mau Mau activists had been living in a hideout on the Nimmo farm for a week or more prior to the attack. It was these 'strangers' who had organized and planned the murders, and who had compelled the farm labourers to take part. However, there were no 'strangers' among those in the dock. The Mau Mau activists had apparently fled following the crime, leaving the farm labourers to bear the burden of the consequences.

The local KPR commander, Tony Pape, had been the first European to arrive at the Ruck farm following the murders. Pape told the court that he had known the Ruck family very well over the previous five years. He admitted that he was devastated and deeply shocked by what he had witnessed that night, especially when he had found the body of six-year-old Michael. The evidence as to how Pape behaved is highly contradictory. It is clear that his first act was to round up the farm labour and to begin questioning them. Pape claimed this was conducted in an orderly and calm manner. All of the Africans involved in this process had a different story to tell. They claimed that they were violently and repeatedly beaten with sticks, on Pape's orders. Such mistreatment apparently continued when they were held in police custody each night over the next week. There were further beatings each day on the farm as they waited in turn to be interrogated. Even key police witnesses, such as Chira Kiniaru, one of the Rucks' domestic staff, vividly described the beatings dished out to all the labourers, more than thirty of them, during the police investigation. These police witnesses had no reason to lie about the beatings. Indeed, logic would suggest that they might have seen good reason not to mention such things. That they did so freely, and moreover that virtually every witness repeated a broadly similar account, seems compelling evidence that beatings did in fact take place.

In court, however, Tony Pape persistently denied that there had been any mistreatment of suspects. The police officer who took over the enquiry from Pape, Steenkamp, was also adamant that no beatings had been allowed – though he knew that such things had happened 'in other investigations'. Steenkamp told the court that he had regularly enquired after the welfare of the suspects, making it clear to his African staff that they should not mistreat the prisoners. However, he was careful not to associate himself with anything that might have occurred in the first twelve hours of the investigation, when Pape was still in charge. The worst accusations of beatings related to this period, when it was claimed that the KPR, including Pape and other settlers, had watched while all the Ruck farm labourers were systematically beaten. Subsequent beatings allegedly took place in a stone outbuilding that same morning, where the suspects were held awaiting interrogation. All the witnesses claimed to have been repeatedly beaten on the legs with heavy sticks. Having been softened up in this way, they were then encouraged to make statements to Pape or Steenkamp. Those to be charged were then taken to Naivasha, where Mr Russell, the district officer and magistrate, recoded their statements. Some claimed they were told what to say in making these statements. Others claimed that they had been made to put their thumbprints to several blank sheets of paper before they made any statement to the magistrate. Others declared in court that the extra-judicial statements attributed to them were complete fabrications. And two of the accused, whose fingerprints had been found on items in the Ruck home, alleged that they had been blindfolded during part of their interrogation so that these items could be placed in their hands.

Justice Paget Bourke found these allegations 'astonishing'. He took the greatest of care to dismiss each and every one as being completely unfounded, principally on the basis of the repeated denials offered by Pape and Steenkamp, and the insistence of Russell that the prisoners bore no signs of ill-treatment at the time he recorded their statements. In delivering his judgment to the court, Bourke listed the allegations one by one, and then gave vent to his irritation:

> There is not a vestige of truth on the view I take of the evidence in
> any of these allegations. The investigation of the case was in charge of

British European senior Police Officers, in particular Supt. Steenkamp, who I am satisfied went out of his way again and again to ensure that the accused were decently treated. I am getting heartily sick of repeated allegations of wicked behaviour by persons in authority, which cannot stand the test of ventilation in a court of law for a moment. It is a duty, in my opinion, for responsible advocates appearing for a defence to question their clients searchingly and to scrutinize with the utmost care the evidence available to them in substantiation or otherwise before lending themselves to the putting forward of such allegations. In all my time upon this Bench I have happily not met with a case in the charge of a European Police Officer that was not investigated with considerable fairness to the accused. This case is no exception; the police have behaved decently and fairly and in all the revolting circumstances with a commendable restraint, though, to be sure, such is only to be expected from them.[60]

Justice Bourke's forthright comments in this case deserve close scrutiny. He acquitted two of the accused, and found the remaining ten guilty of murder. 'The bestial savagery of the murders beggars the power of words,' said Bourke. He accepted all of the extra-judicial statements as good evidence, and gave detailed explanations in each instance of how he reached that conclusion. In his letter to the Governor following the sentencing of the convicts, he left little room for doubt that he thought the law should take its course. In finding ten of the accused guilty, the judge placed himself in the somewhat uncomfortable position of accepting those parts of the evidence of the prosecution witnesses that assisted the conviction, but dismissing those parts that were in any way critical of the police investigation.

Anyone reading these trial papers now could not help but be struck by the absurdity of the judge's reasoning; but that reasoning was required firstly in order to allow the 'highly incriminating' extra-judicial statements made by the accused to stand as evidence, and secondly to exonerate the European officers involved. There was a great deal of other evidence in this case linking the accused to the crime, and the extra-judicial statements were not here as critical as they would be in other Mau Mau trials. The judge's determination to quash any accusation against the white officers involved in the investigation had as much to do with European image and reputation as with the need to obtain convictions. Bourke must have been well aware of the close attention given to this trial by Kenya's white public. The proceedings were reported in the daily newspapers, including the allegations against the police and KPR. In dismissing the allegations in such a forthright manner, Bourke was addressing a wider audience than was gathered in the Nakuru courthouse.

While the men convicted by Paget Bourke awaited the rope and the drop in Nairobi prison, the great and the good of the British Empire and Commonwealth gathered in London, on 2 June, to celebrate the coronation of Queen Elizabeth II. The young princess had been at Treetops, on the edge of the Aberdares forest, in February, when she learned of her father's death. The white highlanders imagined this built a special bond between themselves and the new monarch. On a personal level, it may have done, but in terms of international affairs, events in Kenya were increasingly an embarrassment to the British government. On the day after the coronation, as the prime ministers of the Commonwealth gathered for a summit meeting, Churchill was made uncomfortably aware of the difficulties of maintaining British mastery over this multi-racial and increasingly acrimonious club. Kenya, like apartheid South Africa, now divided Commonwealth opinion. India's Prime Minister, Jawaharlal Nehru, was the sternest critic. Two months earlier, on the anniversary of the Amritsar massacre, he had pledged his country's moral support for the Mau Mau freedom fighters. In London the British government had moved swiftly to condemn Nehru, and in Kenya the speech gave vent to a welter of allegations that the local Asian community was working on behalf of Mau Mau.[61]

Maybe these matters were in Paget Bourke's mind when he offered his criticism of the role of the defence lawyers for 'encouraging' allegations against the police as a device to besmirch the prosecution case. The targets of Bourke's criticism were two lawyers of Asian origin, Bhandari and de Souza, who had defended eight of the accused in the Ruck case. It was their probing of the police witnesses that brought out the full extent of the allegations of beatings and torture, and it was their clients who accused Russell of perjury and who described how they had been tricked into handling property from the Ruck house. Asian lawyers regularly appeared for Mau Mau accused. The better known among them were even sometimes requested by name by the accused. Many settlers believed that Asian lawyers took these cases because they were 'in sympathy' with the Mau Mau cause. The suspicion bred animosities that frequently surfaced in the Kenyan press as well as in the courtroom. Most European lawyers certainly did their best to avoid defence briefs in Mau Mau cases. This may well have been because they had no wish to be associated with such defendants. After all, most made their livings from private practice. Letters to the Kenya newspapers showed that some settlers were offended that any white lawyer could ever defend a Mau Mau suspect, while others thought it deplorable that they should be assigned a defence counsel of any description.

There were also financial considerations to be weighed. In most Mau Mau trials, the defendants had no resources with which to pay for counsel and so lawyers had to be assigned to them on what were termed 'pauper briefs'. This was, in effect, a form of legal aid, designed to ensure that all accused would have the opportunity to be properly represented. Pauper briefs did not pay well, and for lengthy trials such as the Ruck case the fixed fees were utterly derisory when compared with other kinds of legal work. Asian lawyers, most of whose practices were less lucrative than their European counterparts, were more willing to accept this – though even they regularly complained about the paltry fees. European lawyers generally only took such briefs when they were instructed to do so by the Chief Justice, whose task it was to see that unwanted pauper briefs were evenly distributed among the various available lawyers. Once instructed by the Chief Justice, a lawyer had to find a good reason not to take the brief, and was required to explain himself in writing. As there were never sufficient lawyers to go around, the assigning of pauper briefs became a delicate matter as the Emergency wore on, especially for cases heard in locations outside Nairobi, where there were even fewer locally based lawyers and to which Nairobi lawyers were reluctant to travel. Keen to retain the cooperation and support of white lawyers, the Chief Justice tended to assign briefs to the Asian lawyers who were anyway more willing to accept them.

This system required the cooperation of Kenya's lawyers, white and Asian alike. Statements of the kind made by Bourke, essentially accusing de Souza and Bhandari of unprofessional practice, exposed tensions that many senior members of the Bench generally did their best to conceal. When Bhandari and de Souza brought the consolidated appeals from the Ruck case before the East African Court of Appeal in June, the three appellate judges, Nihill, Jenkins and Keatinge, took the opportunity to show their disapproval of Bourke's outspoken criticism of their Asian colleagues. They praised the two Asian lawyers for the 'great assistance' they had rendered to the appeal court, stating that 'so far as these appellants are concerned nothing which could be said on their behalf has been overlooked'. This was only a thinly veiled swipe at Bourke's view that the defence counsel should not fully explore the allegations of the accused. Noting that de Souza and Bhandari had brought the appeal without a fee, the appellate judges also instructed that they be paid by the court.[62] This was a highly unusual intervention, sending out the clear message that not all the judiciary shared Bourke's views. Such disputes would become increasingly acrimonious.

Bourke had been reprimanded and de Souza and Bhandari rewarded, but the ten convicts did not win their appeal. Bourke's careful dissection of the allegations left the appeal judges no points of law on which to challenge his findings. Seven of the men were taken onto death row on 23 June, while the three juveniles began their detention.[63] The story took a further dramatic twist a few days before the scheduled executions, when four of the seven men who were to hang overpowered a prison guard and broke out of the condemned cells. They made it over the wire, only to be caught a few minutes later in a tremendous struggle with prison warders who had given chase. On 17 July 1953 the Kenya press reported that the four recaptured prisoners had been hanged the previous day, along with the three other convicts from the Ruck trial.[64] Kenya's white public took a grim satisfaction from the outcome.

One further piece of evidence in this case never came into the public glare at the time, but it has some bearing on Justice Bourke's robust defence of European reputation. When the seven men who were sentenced to hang arrived at Nairobi Prison, they were examined by the prison doctor, Anant Ram. On the medical record for each of these prisoners, Dr Ram recorded his observations: each man had serious leg scars from recently inflicted wounds. Ram thought it most likely that beatings were the cause of these unusual injuries. The revelation does not, of course, imply that the men were innocent of murder, but it does strongly suggest that the judge was wrong to have so readily dismissed their allegations of mistreatment simply on the basis of European denials.

By the time that the Ruck trial was drawing to a close, during the final week of April 1953, a third European murder case was already under way in the Supreme Court at Nairobi, before Justice Henry Mayers.[65] In this case, the court was told that a party of a dozen or more Mau Mau had arrived on the Fergusson farm at dusk on the day of the murders. Some of these men were squatters from neighbouring farms and were known to Fergusson's African workers. Others were strangers. The leader of the gang was a former tractor driver in Ol Kalou, and a well-known local personality. The police believed him to have been among the principal Mau Mau oath administrators in the area. It was allegedly he who had selected the Fergusson farm for attack, and he who had led the assault. After the murders and the ransacking of the farmhouses, the gang had returned to the fringes of the Aberdares forest, taking many local squatters with them. There, within one week of the attack, a patrol of the King's African Rifles had captured a group of forest fighters, some of whom were wearing articles of clothing belonging to Fergusson and Bingley. Among these captives were four men subsequently identified by witnesses as having been among the gang who had murdered Fergusson and Bingley. One was a former squatter from the Fergusson farm, and another had lived on a neighbouring farm. Both these men had fled with the gang after the attack. Two others had been

squatters in the Ol Kalou area until August 1952, when they had been
evicted. They had spent time hanging around Ol Kalou township until
the murders, when they, too, had disappeared. These four now stood
trial with a fifth accused, Thuku Muchire, Fergusson's house servant.
He was said to have assisted the gang to gain entry to both farmhouses.
A second-generation squatter, whose family had originally settled at
Eldama Ravine, Muchire was only twenty-two years old but had worked
on several farms in the Thomson's Falls area over the past six years and
had held his position with Fergusson for over two years.

As the trial unfolded it soon became clear that Justice Mayers, like
Justice Bourke before him, would have to confront allegations of gross
police brutality against the accused. The five men in the dock each
repudiated or retracted all the key elements of extra-judicial statements
they had made before the investigating European police officer, Espie,
and the magistrate, Mr Russell – the same Naivasha district officer who
had rejected the allegations of abuse in the Ruck case. The five Kikuyu
accused in this case alleged that beatings and torture had taken place to
induce their statements – one accused said that he had been hit with a
rifle butt and another said his testicles had been twisted in a pair of pliers
during his interrogation. After several days of questioning in police
custody, during which the men alleged they had been repeatedly beaten
'in very unpleasant ways', they conceded to the court that they had been
prepared to say anything, simply to bring the ordeal to an end. During
the interrogations it was claimed that Inspector Espie had told them
what to say, and had urged them to implicate Dedan Kimathi by name
as the gang leader – which some of them eventually did. This alleged
'leading of witnesses' was to become a very common feature of the
Mau Mau trials, with all the obvious advantages it brought for the
strengthening of the prosecution case. Justice Mayers was sufficiently
disturbed by the character of the allegations in this case and the condition
in court of one of the prisoners, Ngungire Njora, that he requested
medical examinations of the accused. This revealed that Njora, in particular, was indeed suffering from injuries corroborating his claims of
brutality, including broken ribs. Mayers concluded that Njora 'undoubtedly received a severe beating or beatings at the time of his arrest', and
he stated that this matter should be properly investigated. Like Justice
Bourke, however, Mayers felt unable to draw the inference that these
beatings had any influence upon Njora's extra-judicial statement made
before Mr Russell. The magistrate's evidence was critical: once again,
Mr Russell had failed to notice any signs on the prisoner of ill-treatment –
despite the fact that these signs were still apparent in the courtroom three
months later.

Though common sense must have suggested otherwise, having given consideration to the matter, Justice Mayers came to the view that he was justified in law in ruling that 'the beating was in no way connected to the giving of the statement to Mr Russell'. Any other conclusion would have implied that Mr Russell had committed perjury. The extra-judicial statements made by all five of the accused were therefore upheld as evidence, despite the admission of brutality and torture. Justice Mayers found all five men guilty on the charge of murder. Their appeals were dismissed on 18 June, and one month later Thuku Muchire, aged twenty-two, Wambogo Maina, aged twenty-four, Ngungire Njora, aged twenty-two, and Muchendu Mogo and Nderito Wambugo, who were both nineteen years of age, were hanged together in Nairobi Prison.[66]

In these first three trials arising from the murders of European settlers, twenty Africans had appeared in the dock, of whom seventeen had been sentenced to death and only three acquitted. This was a far higher rate of conviction than would become the norm in subsequent Mau Mau trials, in which the acquittal rate averaged above 40 per cent between 1952 and 1958. All the accused in these three trials were squatters or ex-squatters recently evicted from the farms, or domestic servants working in the employment of Europeans. All had known their victims, and most of the accused men knew one another intimately. The police interrogation of the suspects had exploited these relationships to draw out evidence implicating others in the crimes. The extra-judicial statement of one suspect often implicated two or three others, and in each of the three trials key witnesses appeared for the prosecution who might, in other circumstances, have been considered as accomplices – in the Fergusson and Bingley trial, for example, two other domestic servants provided the crucial identification evidence that placed the accused at the scene of the crime. Witnesses such as these had initially been suspects too and had been held in police custody over many weeks, sometimes in close proximity to those who would stand opposite them in the dock as they gave their evidence to the court. For all concerned, the intimate character of these trials made them all the more traumatic and intense.

The next European murder trial to come to court was a very different affair, but once again accomplice evidence played an important role.[67] When the police arrived on the Gibson farm in Naro Moru, Nyeri district, on 7 February 1953, they found that all the male farm labourers had fled the scene. Other than the Kipsigis watchman, and a Kikuyu child of twelve who worked in Gibson's house, the police had no witnesses of any consequence. They could do little more than compile a list of the names of those who had fled. Two weeks after the murder one of those named, a farm squatter, was arrested at his home village in Meru district. This man, M'Munyari M'Ntwali, told the police he had been forced to leave the farm after the murder, and that the Mau Mau gang had taken him, and all the other farm workers, into the forests on Mount Kenya. After several days he had managed to slip away from the gang, and make his way back to his home district to be reunited with his family, where he was quickly arrested by African loyalists. M'Ntwali might himself have been prosecuted had the police not enjoyed a considerable stroke of luck some four weeks later. A Kikuyu storekeeper in the Nyeri reserve, a Christian loyalist, became suspicious of an unkempt stranger who entered his shop to buy cigarettes and matches and decided to detain the man for questioning by the local chief. The man was found to have no papers or identity card and so was handed over to the police. After a few days of interrogation, they were able to use fingerprint evidence to confirm that the man was Gibson's nineteen-year-old servant, Augustino Kiiro Mwaniki. According to the statement of the Kipsigis watchman, Mwaniki had been seen leaving the farm wearing Gibson's KPR uniform and carrying a rifle and a panga. Furthermore, Mwaniki had even attacked the watchman, cutting him on the head with the panga. With this evidence in hand the police decided to prosecute Mwaniki and to present M'Ntwali as a witness. Life and death turned upon decisions such as this. While M'Ntwali told his tale to the court and left a free man, Mwaniki was convicted of murder. He was hanged on the morning of 16 July 1953, along with the five convicts from the Fergusson and Bingley trial.[68]

The extent to which farm labourers acted under compulsion in many of these cases was dramatically illustrated in the final trial we will consider from the first wave of Mau Mau assaults upon the settlers. The murder of the Kenya pioneer James McDougall had seemed the most callous of all these attacks. An elderly cripple, McDougall lived alone and was the easiest of targets. Settlers raged against the cowardice of such an act; but the circumstances of his death revealed far more about the character of the Mau Mau struggle than this.[69] Though McDougall was killed on 21 July 1953, the events leading up to his death began four months earlier, when a Mau Mau gang had attacked the farm of his neighbour, Payne Williams. The African labourers on the Williams and McDougall farms had for the most part resisted the overtures of the Mau Mau movement and were not trusted to collaborate in this attack. The Mau Mau gang therefore came under cover of darkness, at around 11p.m., and tied ropes around the huts of the workers, sealing them in, before mounting the assault upon the Williams' farmhouse. A gun battle ensued as the gang laid siege to the house, but one of the farm labourers, Kiahara Ndirangu, managed to break out of his hut and ran at considerable speed to the nearest police post and then to the home of a local KPR officer to summon assistance. As help arrived, the attackers were forced to retreat under heavy fire.

It was this same gang, numbering around sixteen men, who returned to the area in July. They sought out Ndirangu, and then selected other workers from the labour lines on the Williams and McDougall farms. These men were now to be punished for their actions during the earlier attack. Under threat of death, Ndirangu and his colleagues were roped and led to the McDougall house. There, they were given pangas and instructed to enter the house and carry out the murder, whilst the Mau Mau gang remained outside. Ndirangu was compelled to lead the way into McDougall's sitting room, to disarm the old man of his pistol and strike the first blow. This the terrified Ndirangu did, whilst his accomplices ransacked the house and retrieved other weapons and supplies for the gang. After the attack the gang disappeared into the night, leaving the hapless farm workers to their fate.

Justice Henry Mayers found five of the accused in this trial guilty of murder, but in doing so he recognized the predicament that had confronted them all, and most especially Ndirangu. The hero who had saved Williams was now the murderer of McDougall. Mayers wrote to the Governor at considerable length, explaining the background to the case: 'In my view', concluded Mayers, 'there is a strong case for considering whether the prerogative of mercy ought not to be exercised.'[70] Baring did not agree. After sitting on death row for nearly three months, Kiahara Ndirangu went to the gallows, along with four other convicts from this trial, on the morning of 13 February 1954. Five more names had been added to the growing list of executed 'Mau Mau terrorists' (see table 3.i, p. 347, for the sentences of the accused).

## Paradise Postponed

The cold dish of vengeance nurtured solidarity among the white highlanders, but by the end of 1953 it could not restore the robust self-confidence that had permeated the settler community in the days before the Emergency. With each European murder, settler doubts about their future grew, and were sustained by a nagging awareness that the defeat of Mau Mau would ultimately hinge upon the resolve of Baring's government. Baring did too little, and usually too late to assuage settler fears. The settlers wanted ever more draconian laws against Mau Mau, laws that Kenya's legal officers were very reluctant to implement. Michael Blundell found himself engaged in a constant battle with Baring, and sometimes directly with Lyttelton, to promote 'sterner measures'. In his desperation Blundell played upon British fears that the struggle might descend into a race war, with European vigilantes 'fighting fire with fire'. At the end of 1953 Blundell wrote to Godfrey Huggins, the

European leader of the Central African Federation, in typical style, lamenting the failure of the British government to tackle the situation effectively. Blundell described Mau Mau as 'a small atavistic outbreak by a tribe unable to stand up to the pressures of modern civilisation and their own nationalistic instincts'. It was British timidity that had turned Mau Mau into 'a test case for Black v. White in Africa'.[71] The lack of progress against the terrorists was a product of British weakness. If the government, and above all else its judiciary were really to throw their weight behind the settlers, then Kenya's 'local difficulty' could be resolved. This 'solution', according to Blundell's analysis, involved giving the settlers a greater role in the administration of the counter-insurgency campaign, as well as amending the law in ways that would make detention and conviction of suspects even easier than they already were. At no time, it seems, did Blundell consider that the worsening situation might be the consequence of settler intransigence and indiscriminate reaction.

Kenya's paradise had been irrevocably sullied by this increasingly acrimonious war, and for settlers it was the murders of their neighbours that stood apart as the key images of that struggle. The siege of the settler farms was brought to an end in July 1953, when a change of tactics by the security forces helped to contain the movement of the Mau Mau units in the farm areas, while the strengthening of Home Guard contingents among Kikuyu loyal to the government increased the supply of intelligence and made it more difficult for gangs to operate freely in the Kikuyu reserves. After this, attacks on the white highlanders became less frequent, and murders were more opportunistic in character.

On the farms, settlers had also become better at defending themselves and were now far more vigilant. In several notable engagements white farmers fought off their Mau Mau attackers. An attack on the Grimwood farm in Kinangop by a gang of over sixty heavily armed Mau Mau fighters, in January 1954, was beaten back by the farmer and his wife before the local KPR arrived. The Grimwoods shot four Kikuyu in the battle, but the labour lines on the farm had been destroyed and two workers killed. It seems likely that the Grimwood farm was targeted because their labourers were unsympathetic to Mau Mau.[72] In another attack on the Kinangop, in December 1954, on the Carnelly farm, the Mau Mau fighters left the settler woman and her young child unmolested, but took weapons and supplies from the farm before setting the farmhouse and barns alight. The rising smoke attracted attention, and there was a running battle as the police gave chase to the Mau Mau gang. By 1954 the distribution of small police posts among the more remote farms had greatly improved the response time of the security forces.[73] In addition, in some areas settlers had formed their own vigilante groups. One such 'commando', styling itself the Dobie Force, operated around

Nairobi, and another, the United Kenya Protection Association, made sorties into the Kikuyu reserves if a Mau Mau unit was sighted. Though the security forces officially refused to acknowledge such groups, they could in practice do very little about them,[74] and in the intelligence side of the security operations there is evidence to suggest close links between 'special operations' personnel and the leaders of these settler vigilantes.[75]

Settlers bared their teeth in defiance in the face of Mau Mau, but belligerence and their disregard for African rights would ultimately tarnish their own political ambitions by alienating liberal support 'back home' in Britain. As the war dragged on, there were no political gains that might boost the morale of settlers over their future in Kenya: the fragile self-confidence of the settler community was slowly but surely eroding away. After July 1953, murders of white civilians were less frequent, but the cumulative impact of each event chipped away at morale. The second, and more sporadic phase in Mau Mau's assault upon settler supremacy began towards the end of 1953, when a KPR officer, Lyall Shaw, was shot on his farm.[76] Then, in March 1954, a white woman was shot in a raid upon a dairy on the outskirts of Nairobi,[77] and in April a European child was killed while riding his tricycle on the driveway of his home.[78] In June 1954 a reclusive European spinster, Mrs Critchley, living alone in Nyeri township, was killed when General Rui's gang raided her house looking for supplies.[79] Then, in April 1955, two European teenage boys, Christopher Twohey and Geoffrey Danby, were killed by a Mau Mau gang in the Nairobi suburb of Ruaraka. Over the next day all the members of the gang were shot or captured. Twelve of them, including the gang leader, General Njeke, eventually hanged.[80] These random, unconnected and predominantly opportunistic murders indicated the gradually declining powers of the Mau Mau units.

Satisfaction over the convictions and executions of Kikuyu in the first European murder trials between March and July 1953 had been short-lived. By the early months of 1954 frustration with the legal limits imposed upon the response to Mau Mau again drew the settlers into conflict with the judiciary. For the majority of settlers the constraints imposed by the legal system seemed an impediment to the security forces: 'They had firmly fastened one of their hands behind their back with a cord of legal difficulties,' as Major Frank Kitson would later put it. The British would not admit that this was a war; they would not even formally concede that it was a rebellion, fearing that to do so might imply that the Mau Mau fighters had rights under international conventions governing the treatment of prisoners. Mau Mau was therefore treated as a civil disturbance. Rules of evidence, regulations governing the holding of suspects, the need for formal detention orders, and the codes of conduct applying to the questioning of prisoners were all requirements of the judicial system through which those suspected of Mau Mau offences were processed. Settlers found it difficult to accept that in this process the African accused had rights that must be respected. Members of the judiciary had at first expressed sympathy with settler frustrations. Early in 1953 Justice Bourke had considered the heavy-handed treatment of suspects by the KPR and the police to be 'understandable' in the aftermath of the horrific murder of the Rucks; but by 1954 many of his fellow Supreme Court judges had lost patience with the general disregard being shown for the law by the police, the KPR, the Kenya Regiment, and the European public in general.

The simmering anger within the judiciary finally boiled over in August 1954, when the appeal court considered the case of four Kikuyu sentenced to death for the murders of two elderly Europeans in Thika, Mr and Mrs Bruxnor-Randall.[81] The couple were killed on 14 March 1954. Their bodies were not discovered until some twenty-four hours later. The Bruxnor-Randalls' four domestic servants had by then disappeared from their quarters. Though they certainly knew what had happened, they had been too afraid to report to the police. The police soon found them hiding among the squatter labour lines on a neighbouring estate and took them in for questioning. Most settlers employed children or youths as house servants, but the Bruxnor-Randalls' domestic staff were all mature men. The cook, Mungai Kiarie, was forty-two years of age. Married, with children of his own, he had been with them many years. Their watchman, Ngotho Njuguna, in his forties, and their senior 'houseboy', Njuguna Kimani, aged thirty-five, were also both family men. The second 'houseboy' was a thirty-two-year-old Kamba named Mathumba Njau. He had a wife and family back in Machakos. These four men were the only suspects in the case. The police at Thika held them in custody for the next two months, during which time they were repeatedly questioned by Inspector Albrectson and by Dracup, the Thika CID officer. Several statements were taken from the men, but then, over a period of six days between 8 and 13 May, all four made lengthy confessions to the murder. These four 'inculpatory statements' were practically the only evidence in the prosecution case. Justice Holmes ruled that the statements had been made voluntarily, and on this basis the men were found guilty and sentenced to hang.

It is unlikely that the prosecution case would have been brought with so thin a thread of evidence in any circumstance other than the murder of Europeans. The Bruxnor-Randalls were popular and well liked among the settler community, and there was a great clamour for 'justice to be done'. Was Justice Holmes influenced by this wave of 'public opinion'? The three senior judges sitting in the appeal court certainly thought so. Justices Worley, Jenkins and Briggs seized the opportunity offered to mount a savage attack upon the security forces in general, and the police in particular, for their disregard of legal process. The arguments they mounted in overturning the convictions in this case in fact applied to the vast majority of Mau Mau investigations, though it was rare for the court proceedings to reveal so much about police processes. The three judges therefore used the case to express their deep dissatisfaction with many aspects of the operation of emergency powers. Their comments and complaints demand close scrutiny.[82]

The justices began by pointing out that when the four servants were initially brought in for questioning they were *not* suspects; they were at no time cautioned by the police, and were generally treated as potential police witnesses. It had become common practice for the security forces to round up everyone in the vicinity of a Mau Mau crime, and to hold them for questioning over indeterminate periods. Depriving people of their liberty in this way was justified on the basis that Mau Mau might otherwise interfere with potential witnesses. The police described this as 'protective custody'. Though the appeal judges understood that the police might find this necessary in order to 'keep hold of witnesses so that they are available for the trial', they trenchantly pointed out that 'this so-called protective custody is unlawful and amounts to a false imprisonment'. In short, without cautioning or charging those detained in this way, the police had no legal authority under which to hold them. The more sinister implication of this procedure was that it gave the investigating officers the opportunity to encourage witnesses to implicate one another in the crime. It was only on 31 March, after the four had been in custody for more than two weeks, that Dracup issued the first caution, to Njau, from whom he then recorded a statement. Kimani was cautioned the next day, and Kiarie on 11 April. However, several further statements were taken from the men before their 'confessions' were recorded early in May. Was this prolonged sequence of interrogations deliberately designed to 'soften up' the prisoners? Dracup admitted to the court that it was a matter 'of deliberate policy to hold the accused without charge, yet with the intention of charge'. The appeal judges pointed out the severe dangers of allowing an investigating police officer to legally attest a statement of confession in this way, and they expressed regret that under the Emergency Powers Regulations the Indian Evidence Act had been amended to allow this. This had removed an important safeguard for the accused, therefore it was all the more important that Justice Holmes should have taken greater care to satisfy himself that any such statement admitted in evidence had been voluntarily made.

Worley, Jenkins and Briggs made it clear that they felt their fellow judges were not always as thorough in this regard as they should be. In this case, as in virtually every other European murder case to come to court, the accused made allegations of ill-treatment, deprivation and torture, 'including subtle methods such as keeping awake, or standing to attention'. Justice Holmes had come to the view that all of these allegations were untrue, but the justices of the appeal court found that he had failed to direct himself 'properly and fully to this issue'. That the accused had been in custody since 16 March was 'an astonishing fact' that the judge should have pursued. All that time, they were locked up in the cells at Thika, under the control of the CID. There was a 'persistent course of questioning', far more than was formally admitted to in court, and none of it with cautions. Most of the interviews conducted over these months were not recorded. This 'highly improper' procedure was, in the opinion of the appeal court, designed to induce the accused 'to incriminate themselves'. The accused men each told consistent stories of this procedure, and each described serious ill-treatment immediately prior to their making the crucial confessional statements in May. Where the trial judge had dismissed these allegations, the appeal court judges believed them to be true. The judgment upholding all four appeals ended with a blast intended to stir their colleagues on the Bench, as much as the police and senior members of the colonial administration:

> It is a matter of grave concern if criminals go unpunished: It is a matter of equally great concern that the Court should administer justice according to law. The implications of this case are indeed grave, suggesting as they do the danger that the police force in Kenya is tending to become a law unto itself. The Courts will fail in their duty if they ignore or pretend not to see the danger when it is apparent on the evidence before them.

The conclusion to be drawn from these criticisms was that the police could no longer be trusted to present evidence impartially to the court, and that the judiciary were sometimes too compliant in accepting the statements of European witnesses as true and rejecting the allegations made by the African accused as false. This was an appeal to members of the Bench to keep the law, and not matters of race, to the fore in their deliberations.

The settlers dismissed such commentary merely as 'legal technicality'. If the *realpolitik* of combating the Mau Mau threat demanded measures that the judges of the Supreme Court could not stomach, then it was the law that must change. For every case of injustice highlighted by the appeal court, the settlers could point to another Mau Mau atrocity that enraged European sensibilities. Just two months after the appeal court judgment in the Bruxnor-Randall case, the settlers had an answer to the bleating from the Bench when the most disturbing Mau Mau European murder of all took place, an event that reinforced white opinion that Mau Mau 'was lost in the haunted wilderness of superstition'.[83] The murder was carried out under the direction of the infamous General Tanganyika. Like many other fighters who had by then been in the forests for nearly two years, Tanganyika had taken to consulting Kikuyu female prophets for guidance on the conduct of the campaign. One such prophet, known by the name Mama Mwangi, instructed that a European should be sacrificed in the manner of a Kikuyu leader who had died in British custody before the end of the nineteenth century. That leader, named Waiyaki, was popularly believed to have been buried alive by the British. Tanganyika selected a target and deputed a party under the command of General Kaleba to carry out this ritual act. The victim they chose was Gray Leakey, himself a Kikuyu-speaker and the cousin of Louis Leakey, who had acted as a translator in the trial of Jomo Kenyatta and who was, by 1954, a very active member of the government's various counter-insurgency committees. Kaleba and his small party of fighters broke into the Leakey farm in North Nyeri on the night of 13 October 1954. Mrs Mary Leakey was strangled, the family's Catholic Kikuyu cook hanged and disembowelled, and Gray Leakey taken captive. He was led into the forests of Mount Kenya, and high up on the mountain he was buried alive and upside down in the deep red soil.[84]

Two years earlier, Gray Leakey's daughter Agnes had been with David Waruhiu in Switzerland when he heard of the death of his father, Chief Waruhiu. In one of the many cruel ironies of this dirty war, David Waruhiu was now the person given responsibility in the Office of Information for contacting Agnes, then in North America, to tell her of the deaths of her parents.[85] The body might never have been found had not the young son of Leakey's cook followed Kaleba's party onto the mountain, where he witnessed the strange death of Gray Leakey. A few days after the abduction and murder the boy led police back to the grave. Gray Leakey was exhumed from this bleak and murderous resting place and reburied beside his wife Mary in the Anglican cemetery at Nyeri, just a few paces from the graves of the Baden Powells, other European residents of Nyeri who had met a more tranquil end.

The horror of this act stiffened settler resolve in the face of their critics; and they were soon to be provided with damning evidence of the dangers of adopting a gentler approach to Mau Mau, as advocated by some in the judiciary. Troops swarmed over the slopes of Mount Kenya on the Nyeri side following the Leakey murders, and on 24 October a patrol of the King's African Rifles trapped a small party of Mau Mau fighters in a cave. Four Mau Mau eventually surrendered, three men and one woman. The leader among them declared himself as General Kaleba. In the cave the soldiers found a large quantity of books and papers, and several items of property from the Leakey house. As was now usual in the aftermath of any European murder, General Kaleba was brought speedily to trial, the case coming before Justice de Lestang on 22 November 1954. There was insufficient evidence to charge Kaleba with murder, but he had been caught in possession of a Webly revolver and several rounds of ammunition, offences that anyway carried a capital charge. The settlers were keen to see him hang, whatever the charge. But the courtroom proceedings would reveal another unexpected drama: to the utter astonishment of the settler public, Kaleba told the court that he had in fact previously surrendered to the government in March 1954. He was then sent back into the forest to try to assist in the negotiation of a general surrender of Mau Mau fighters.[86] How could it be that the man who had so chillingly and pointlessly murdered Gray Leakey could have been considered a suitable ambassador to broker a peace settlement with other Mau Mau generals? If settlers needed any further evidence either of the government's folly or of Mau Mau's irredeemable wicked-ness, then this was surely it.

Each settler killing had an impact upon white consciousness in Kenya that far outweighed its actual significance in the context of the war. Each European murder stoked the fires of revenge and deepened hostility to the Kikuyu, raising an indiscriminate reaction that ultimately served only to undermine the anti-Mau Mau cause by tarnishing it with brutality and gross excess. In their anger and frustration, settlers too readily forgot that Africans were far more commonly the victims of Mau Mau violence than were whites, just as they also too readily overlooked the fact that it was Africans loyal to the government who would ultimately play the crucial role in the defeat of Mau Mau. European society in Kenya had been too long colour-blind to see it any other way. There was another war going on that settlers saw only in glimpses and could not properly appreciate: It was a war in the Kikuyu reserves, in the labour lines where African families resided on the farms, and in the squalid African estates of Nairobi; it was a war fought between and among Kikuyu communities; and it was a bitter and, as time went on, increasingly vengeful struggle in which the seemingly random violence had no pattern that Europeans could easily comprehend. Yet just as Mau Mau violence against Euro-peans had its reason and its logic, so too did the struggle among the Kikuyu themselves. Our story now takes us to one scene of this struggle, the home of a community loyal to the government, at Lari, in the northern part of Kiambu district, where, during one terrible hour of violence, in March 1953, more Africans would die then the total number of European civilians killed and wounded during the entire course of the Emergency.

# 4

# Death at Lari
# The Story of an African Massacre

The settlement of Lari, nestling in the shadows of the Aberdares forest in the northern part of Kiambu district, was to be the site of the greatest bloodletting of the entire Mau Mau war. Yet Lari appeared no different from many other rural Kikuyu communities in the early 1950s. The homesteads of local farmers were scattered along the ridge tops and clustered around the fringes of the high marshland. The mud-and-wattle buildings were mostly thatched, with the occasional corrugated-metal roof. Families gathered together in fenced compounds, each wife with her own hut, and buildings also for her sons. Water was plentiful in Lari, there was good grazing nearby and fuel wood could be gathered from the forest edge. Up here in the high country, at 7000 feet, soils were not as fertile as in the very best parts of Kiambu, but they were good enough. Vegetables were the mainstay of the local economy, grown as a cash crop for sale in the expanding market of urban Nairobi. Pyrethrum was also grown for cash, and everyone cultivated maize as a staple food. The hard-working and diligent farmer could earn a decent living at Lari. In 1952 this was a vibrant, energetic and economically thriving community.

An elaborate network of rural roads and tracks cut across Lari sub-location in every direction. These well-kept mud paths were the arteries that connected Lari's farms to the main highways of Limuru Road and Ruiru road, running along the ridges to the city of Nairobi to the south-east. Its economy was integrally linked to the urban commercial hub of the colony, less than two hours away by road. Many of Lari's peasant farmers had relatives in Nairobi and would make occasional journeys to the city by bus or by train. The great East African railway, from the Indian Ocean to Lake Victoria, ran through the area. At Uplands or Escarpment stations, its commercial farmers gained access to a wider world of market opportunities. In the fields round about, the day was regulated by the sound of the trains approaching and departing – a reminder of the passage of time, and of the proximity of a colonial economy.

Lari was a place of wealth, and of poverty. Amongst the leading commercial farmers were a few prosperous elders with large acreages under their control. They were in the vanguard of what the colonial state considered to be 'progressive' African farming. They had moved beyond the traditional constraints of family labour and the obligations of kin, developing their lands with commercial tenancies, waged casual labourers and more intensive farming methods. This wealthy minority were beneficiaries of the active market in land that had been stimulated in Kiambu by commercial success and growing land hunger. At the other end of the economic scale stood the majority of Lari's residents. Most made their livings as tenants on the land of others, producing a small surplus for themselves and supplementing their household incomes with casual work. Others were poorer still, having no access to land through ownership or rent. These were compelled to sell their labour to earn a living. Waged labour was already a fact of life in Lari. Many families included members among Nairobi's pool of migrant labour, and many others had connections with Kikuyu squatters in the Rift Valley, far to the west.

Commerce was vibrant in Lari. There were many businesses, of various types and sizes, owned and run by local Kikuyu. Those with money to invest did so in the trading centres of the location, where licences could be purchased to build and run small hotels and eating houses, or trading stores, known as *dukas*, selling groceries, second-hand clothes, farming implements and household goods. Transport services were also popular with African investors. Taxis ran from most of the trading centres in the area, and buses, lorries and carts could be hired to move produce and people from place to place. Some of the more adventurous and successful of Lari's entrepreneurs owned shops in the African locations in Nairobi, or ran wholesaling businesses there, bulking produce for delivery to the urban markets. The most prosperous entrepreneurs had wider business interests, especially in retailing and transportation, as far afield as Kampala, Mwanza and Arusha.

Artisans of every kind were to be found in Lari's trading centres – tailors, cobblers, carpenters, painters, basket makers, mechanics, and stonemasons. The latter were especially numerous, employed at the several quarries in the forest fringe, some working on road construction with the government, others hewing building blocks for Indian or Kikuyu contractors. Fathers sought apprenticeships for their sons to learn such trades and paid for the privilege. Tailors rented space on the verandas of the larger *dukas*, and trained their apprentices by turns on the one machine they could afford to maintain. Cobblers worked from small carts that could be easily moved from market to market, and carpenters set up their rough-hewn benches under spreading trees, making furniture to order. In the areas closest to the forest, many men worked as tree fellers, loggers and pit-sawyers. Much of this work was done under contract for Indian-owned firms, such as those run at Lari by Karjeet Singh and Musa Dad, whose Asian foremen and managers lived locally in the forest. Other Kikuyu worked on their own account in the same forests, gathering and cutting wood for charcoal burning. Every day the forest tracks were dotted with the filled grey sacks of charcoal, awaiting collection by the workers who would carry them into Lari trading centre for loading onto the donkey-carts bound for Nairobi. This was a rapidly growing and lucrative trade in the post-war years, as Nairobi's population expanded.

Lari also had its industrial labourers, mostly working at the Uplands Bacon Factory, in nearby Limuru. The factory horn bringing the day shift to an end also signalled the ending of the day for many of the farmers in the surrounding fields. Here, in 1930, Kenya had its first taste of trade-union protest, with the shooting of strikers by police and the imprisonment of the workers' leaders. Strikes and violence had again erupted at the factory in the late 1940s, stimulated by emergent trade unionism, and as recently as 1947 the local chief, Makimei, had assisted colonial officials in breaking a strike at the factory. Such radicalism had been driven by workplace concerns – poor conditions and low wages – rather than by political motives; but by the early 1950s the labour lines at Uplands were viewed with suspicion by colonial officials who thought that the factory was a seed-bed of radical, anti-government opinion. Lari's Kikuyu population saw the factory in simpler, material terms: jobs there were eagerly sought, especially by the landless. Work at the bacon factory brought a regular wage and the prospect of reasonable, if humble and overcrowded, housing. Other kinds of industrial work could be obtained through employment on the railway, either in the larger shunting yards at Limuru, or with the track-repair gangs that were assembled at Uplands or Escarpment stations. In the rainy seasons there was plenty of work of this kind, landslides being common along the precipitous incline of the escarpment, keeping the engineers and their labour gangs busy. Regular railway staff were properly housed by their employer, and although casual labour on gang work did not bring such benefits it was relatively stable employment; but it was heavy and unpleasant work, the kind of employment best suited for young, physically fit men.

Lari's women mainly worked within the domestic economy, tending their family farms. Every married Kikuyu woman whose husband owned or rented land would cultivate her own *shamba*, growing vegetables and maize for the kitchen. They would also hope to produce a surplus for sale at the daily markets at Kirenga, or Githunguri, or at the larger weekly markets at Escarpment and Limuru. Some would also make wicker baskets or sisal bags for sale. A visit to the market was a social occasion as well as a commercial opportunity, a chance to catch up with relatives and friends. Unlike women in other Kiambu locations, closer to Nairobi, few Lari women would venture as far as the city. Those who did so risked their reputations. Even in this fairly progressive part of Central Province, male householders still preferred to dominate domestic matters and to restrict women to the homestead. Lari was a male-dominated community, traditional in its support of Kikuyu patriarchy. The most senior elders and the largest landowners were all polygamous, and the wealthiest men had three or more wives. The payments of brideprice from one family to another on the arrangement of a marriage built ties of reciprocity and obligation between families, and these ties gave Lari a dense and complex network of linkages with the wider Kikuyu community within and beyond Kiambu. In making a good marriage, parents would endeavour to make a match for their children that would secure the wider interests of their family and clan. In this process of building alliances, the land-holding unit known as the *mbari* was of critical importance. Upon marriage, a woman gained entitlement to the use of land for herself and her children within the *mbari* of her husband. A landless or dispossessed man, indeed any man who did not have secure access to *mbari* lands, was therefore a very unwelcome suitor for any family that hoped to use marriage as a means of brokering future security and prosperity. Obligations, and their reciprocities, were built through marriages, and their proliferation was traditionally a sign of wealth and status. In the desperate times of the late 1940s and early 1950s, however, more and more men found themselves unable to secure *mbari* land. The evicted squatters who returned to Central Province found that their entitlement to *mbari* land had long ago been forfeited, while at the same time *mbari* elders increasingly saw little reason to allow dependents to use their lands when far greater gains could be made through commercial farming. In the midst of these socio-economic transitions, the character of Kikuyu domestic life was beginning to change along with the role and status of women within marriages.[1]

Landlessness was the key factor. Its emergence since the 1940s had fostered severe social divisions among this Kikuyu community. The fear of landlessness was the moving force of Kikuyu politics; and it lay, like a cold shadow, over the whole community of Lari. Lari was in fact a relatively new area of agricultural settlement. The farmers here were recent immigrants. The first of their number had arrived in 1939, the last some ten years later. They had come from Tigoni, in southern Kiambu, where they had been evicted at the instruction of the colonial government. Their removal and resettlement had been a fraught affair, resulting in the loss of land by many poorer families. These people were resentful about their fate. In the early 1950s, despite its appearance of tranquil prosperity, Lari was not a happy place.

Into this already combustible mix came others who were also landless. Lari lay near the escarpment edge, straddling the steep road from Kiambu down to the Rift Valley farms of Naivasha and Nakuru. The hundreds of evicted squatters who struggled up that road with what they could carry of their possessions drifted into Lari on their way 'home'. Soon learning that there would be no land for them, many remained in the Lari area, swelling the ranks of the landless and filling the bars and eating houses with an army of discontented souls. The nearby town of Limuru held a large concentration of such folk, some of whom had been evicted from the resettlement scheme at Olenguruone, in the Nakuru district, where the squatters had taken a stand against the implementation of government agricultural rules and where the Mau Mau oathing had begun. These migrants increased the local pool of casual labour, some finding irregular work with Lari's farmers and foresters and being sheltered by their kinsmen, others sleeping where they could among the shanties that fringed the larger trading centres and townships. With them came a new and far sharper politics of disillusionment.

Those ex-squatters who drifted into Lari tended to have had less formal education than the local people. Schools had not been easily accessible from many of the Rift Valley farms; nor had the work of the Christian mission churches made any sustained impact among the squatters, the majority of whom remained pagan. In Lari, churches had long been the source of literacy and remained the commonest marker of a political affiliation. The Anglicans of the Church Missionary Society were strongly represented in the area, and their schools had dominated the education of local Kikuyu until the 1930s. The African Inland Mission, from their base to the north at Kijabe, had a smaller and generally less well-educated following – the AIM established many fewer and much poorer schools; but some Lari residents would still make the two-hour walk to the AIM Hospital at Kijabe for the treatment of their ailments, whether professing Christians or not. In the wake of the clitoridectomy crisis the Kikuyu independent schools movement had made great strides in Lari and the surrounding locations from 1930 onwards, taking supporters away from the mission churches and schools. The resettlement of families from Tigoni brought several hundred Catholics into Lari during the 1940s, among them many wealthy families. No local church served them directly, but the devout among them made the journey every Sunday to the nearest Catholic church at Limuru. Although Christianity was popular in Lari, as elsewhere in Kiambu, even by the end of the 1940s probably less than half the local population professed the Christian faith.

Lari's relative prosperity obscured sharp socio-economic divisions within the community. Well integrated with the colonial economy, but with a large and growing number of landless people for whom wage labour was essential, Lari was an educationally progressive and increasingly Christian community. Hard work earned advancement in this meritocracy, mediated by the patronage of Kikuyu kin groups; but it was a community with a marked streak of dissent, with a history of strong support for the independent schools and independent churches, and with a tradition of protest and non-conformity. In so many ways, this was as quintessential a Kikuyu community as you could hope to find on the eve of the Emergency in October 1952, an intense microcosm of the rest of central Kenya.

The violence of the Emergency exposed the raw tensions amongst this volatile community. The high proportion of ex-squatters in Lari by 1952, along with numbers of other landless peasants, marked it as an area where Mau Mau support was known to be strong. The local chief, Makimei, had a reputation for toughness. His methods were often rough and ready, but colonial officials considered him a reliable and secure ally in these difficult times. Mau Mau despised him, and he received death threats even before the declaration of the Emergency. Not surprisingly, Makimei was among the first chiefs in Kiambu to organize a Kikuyu Home Guard unit, to defend Lari against Mau Mau incursion. Makimei's predecessor, ex-Chief Luka Wakahangare, privately sponsored the establishment of a second Home Guard post at Lari during the early weeks of the emergency.[2] If Lari was a nest of Mau Mau influence, then it was also a place where loyalists were prepared to make a stand. By the end of November 1952 there were 3000 Home Guard in Central Province, a kind of 'Dad's Army' gathered around those loyal Christian chiefs, like Makimei, who feared that they and their clients might be the target of Mau Mau attacks. Self-preservation and personal security were a necessary response of these respectable Christian Kikuyu to the lawlessness of Mau Mau's hooligans. When the British decided to give their blessing to the Home Guard and to encourage recruitment, from December 1952, numbers rapidly increased. The 'Dad's Army' now became a formal militia, given authority to act in assistance of the police and army. The Home Guard would be the force that would confront Mau Mau head to head in the struggle for the hearts and minds of the Kikuyu people. Lari would be the critical site in that struggle.

By the end of January 1953 there were reckoned to be 7600 Home Guard recruits, comprising 2333 in Nyeri, 1387 in Murang'a, 1083 in Meru, 1000 in Embu, and 1863 in Kiambu.[3] At Lari, the hundred or so men who had by then joined the Home Guard were mostly drawn from the landed elite gathered around Makimei and Luka Wakahangare, the wealthiest man in the location and the person whose influence had been behind the resettlement of those who had moved from Tigoni. Makimei and Luka had numbered the murdered chiefs Waruhiu and Nderi among their closest friends and allies. As the Mau Mau murder count mounted, they knew that their own lives were under threat. For men such as these, combating Mau Mau was quite literally a matter of life and death. The dogs of war finally caught up with them some five months into the emergency.

## Victims and Vengeance

*We are left alone with our day, and the time is short and*
*History to the defeated*
*May say Alas but cannot help or pardon.*
              from *Spain*, by W. H. Auden

Each night, at dusk, Lari's Home Guard unit gathered to begin their rounds, patrolling the main paths and principal properties in the location.[4] Just after 8p.m. on the evening of 26 March 1953 the Lari patrol was summoned to investigate the discovery of a body in the location of Headman Wainaini, three miles to the east on the Lari boundary. When they arrived at the scene, they found the mutilated remains of a local loyalist, nailed to a tree alongside a busy footpath. The body had evidently been left there deliberately, with the intention that it should be found. It had taken the patrol almost an hour to get to the spot. As they now looked back to the west, just after 9p.m., they began to notice fires breaking out in the direction of their own homes in Lari. They hurried along in the darkness, first reluctantly fearing the worst, and eventually running as they realized the terrible truth. They had been purposely lured to Wainaini's location, leaving Lari undefended. The Mau Mau attack they so dreaded had come at last.

While the Home Guard patrol had hurried to the scene of the murder earlier that evening, some several hundred attackers had gathered at pre-arranged meeting places throughout the Lari location. In five or six separate gangs, each numbering one hundred or more persons, the attackers descended upon their targets. Their heads swathed to disguise their identities, armed with pangas, swords, spears, knives and axes, and with some carrying burning torches, they swarmed over the unprotected homesteads. They carried with them ropes, which they tied around the huts to prevent the occupants from opening the doors before they set the thatch alight. As the occupants struggled to clamber through the windows to escape, they were savagely cut down. Most of those caught in the attack were women and children, but they were shown no mercy by the attackers, who seemed intent on killing every person in the homesteads. Shots rang out as some victims found their own weapons and made an effort to defend themselves and their families. But it was a hopeless cause. As the bodies were cut down and viciously hacked, the attackers threw them back into the blazing huts. The Home Guard patrol reached Lari just as the attack was coming to an end. They gave chase to some of the attackers, but they were too late to save the victims. By 10p.m. some 120 bodies lay dead or grievously injured in the smouldering ruins of fifteen homesteads. The killers had disappeared into the night. In their wake, there was chaos, terror, shock, anger and indescribable grief.

Kenyans read about the attack in their newspapers two days later. The report provided by the Office of Information appeared in English and Swahili versions, and gave a vivid account of what had happened:

> Armed terrorists stole upon the clustered huts of Lari, in the Kenya Highlands, in the dead of night. The sleeping Kikuyu people awoke to find flames roaring above them, as the Mau Mau fired the tinder-dry thatched roofs. Escape was impossible to most, for the doors had been securely fastened outside by the fanatical Mau Mau attackers. Men, women and children, forcing their way out of the windows, were caught and butchered. Some perished terribly in the flames; others were chopped and mutilated by the knives of their enemies – their own fellow tribesmen. Dawn revealed the macabre scene left behind by the bestial wave of Mau Mau; the mangled corpses, human remains literally chopped in pieces, all mingled with the smoking ashes of the burnt homesteads. The survivors, terror-stricken and helpless, told their pitiful stories to the police and government officials who rushed to Lari when the alarm was raised. They told of children being cut up with knives in the sight of their mothers; of others cut down as they tried to run to hide in tall maize, by terrorists insatiable for blood.[5]

These first press reports spread fear and horror throughout the Kikuyu communities of central Kenya. Where the events in Nyeri on Christmas Eve of 1952 had singled out leading male elders, the attack upon women and children at Lari was on a far larger scale and appeared less discriminate. No other attack during the emergency would have the tremendous impact on public opinion that came in the aftermath of Lari. The first reports stressed the murder of innocent Kikuyu civilians and stated that this was a 'loyalist community', but it was not explained that the homesteads attacked had in fact been very carefully chosen. The Lari attack may have seemed an indiscriminate slaughter of collaborators but was far from random in its violence. All of the victims were the families of local chiefs, ex-chiefs, headmen, councillors and prominent Home Guard. The male heads of these households were the leading members of Lari's loyalist community, and all were known as outspoken opponents of Mau Mau. Lesser members of the Home Guard, and those who were perceived as clients of wealthier men, were left alone. What shocked other Kikuyu most of all was that the vast majority of those killed were women and children. This was appalling to all, and even shocked many Mau Mau supporters, some of whom would subsequently try to excuse the attack as 'a mistake', or even try to blame it on the British. Assisted to some extent by government propaganda, Lari changed the way ordinary Africans thought about the conflict. If it was not recognized as such before, then at Lari the Mau Mau struggle had become a civil war − a struggle in which all Kikuyu feared for their survival. And in the hours, days and weeks following the massacre, the war sometimes appeared to be nothing less than a vendetta.

The principal victim in the attack at Lari was the loyalist community's senior statesman, Luka Wakahangare. At more than sixty years of age, Luka had continued to manage the affairs of his *mbari* after retiring from government office. An elder in the Catholic church, his extended family pursued a wide variety of business interests and dominated landholding on some of the most productive farms in Lari. As chief, and as the elder principally responsible for arranging the resettlement of the Tigoni people at Lari, Luka had profited from his association with the government. His murder was Mau Mau's punishment.[6] More than 200 attackers had descended upon his homestead, killing several of his wives, many of his grandchildren and other relatives. Luka, his younger brother, and one of his sons had fought bravely to defend the family. Armed with his shotgun, Luka had managed to break out of his hut to reach the cover of a lorry, parked in the compound. From there the old man had opened fire on his assailants, but had been quickly overpowered. Surviving members of his family would later describe how the gang, having recognized their victim, hacked repeatedly at his body, severing his head and detaching limbs, to carry them off in triumph. The torso was only identifiable after the attack by the distinctive clothing worn by the old man. Luka's youngest wife was the only adult survivor in the Wakahangare homestead, though she was horrendously slashed across the chest and head. As she fell to the ground with blood streaming down her face, the young woman saw both her children killed, one a toddler the other a baby.[7]

The attack on the homestead of Charles Ikenya's family was hardly less brutal. Ikenya was one of the five headmen who worked under Makimei's command. He had led the Home Guard patrol that had gone to Wainaini's location that evening. His breathless dash back to his homestead had been too late to save his wives and children. All bar four members of his entire extended family died in the attack.[8] A second, younger headman, named Paulo, also shared in the tragedy. Paulo returned to find the remains of his wife and all their children in the smouldering debris of his homestead. Samson Kariuki, another fellow elder in the Catholic church and a close business associate of ex-Chief Luka, was on Home Guard patrol when the attack began. Of the thirteen members of Samson's family at home that evening, nine perished, including a baby only a fortnight old who died in the flames and five other young children all of whom were hacked to death whilst running from the burning huts. The vivid testimony of one of Samson's wives, Mujiri, dominated the press reports in the days following the massacre, the young woman describing how she had watched one of her children being slashed, and then seen his murderers lick the blood from the blade that had decapitated the child.[9]

Several families of other prominent members of the Home Guard were also targeted. One of Lari's oldest and most respected elders, Kie Kirembe, was among the dead. Like Luka, he died trying to defend the women and children of his extended family. Four of Kie's sons were members of the Lari Home Guard.[10] The family of Machune Kiranga, another headman and Home Guard patrol commander, were also slaughtered.[11] The same fate befell the families of Arthur Waweru,[12] Nganga Njehia[13] and Mbogwa Mumya.[14] Aside from these men, who were directly linked to the Home Guard, prominent members of the African District Council were also among the victims. Councillor Isaka Kagoru[15] was killed with his family, as were Ndonga Karukoi and Kimani Wamboi.[16] All were substantial landowners, and each had business connections with Luka Wakahangare. From the fifteen homesteads attacked, spread over an area of some 30 square miles, the final death toll was seventy-four. Another fifty victims were wounded.[17]

There was nothing random about these attacks. The victims had been selected with care, their homesteads identified and singled out. The raid had been well planned, and its perpetrators were well equipped. Neighbours were left unmolested as the gangs went about their business, each attacking group moving systematically between the two or three homesteads for which it had been assigned responsibility. The motive in the choice of victims seemed all too obvious: the male head of each household attacked was a government servant. All were Christian, and all were from Catholic families who had come to Lari from Tigoni in 1939. In one way or another, they had all been clients of either Luka or

Makimei, or both. One reason for the attack might have been Makimei's own vigorous pursuit of Mau Mau, or his cold rejection of the claims of the evicted squatters who presented themselves in Lari hoping to revive kinship and find shelter and support. Lari was reputed to contain many Mau Mau supporters, and Makimei's Home Guard patrols were known to be deeply unpopular with a large section of the local population, 'treating the Rift Valley repatriates with disdain'.[18] About a month earlier Makimei had got wind of a plot to attack the loyalists at Lari and had brought this to the notice of the district officer.[19] He had warned Luka to build defences at his homestead, and Makimei had constructed a solid wooden fence around his own *boma*, with a stout gate that he bolted every night. On the night of the massacre this had surely saved the lives of his family. As the attackers battered at the gate of Makimei's homestead, the chief and his guards had opened fire on them. Over the next half-hour they had repulsed several attempts to scale the perimeter fence and torch the buildings. Others might have survived, too, had not the government made a fatal error of judgement only the day before the attack. Following rumours of the threat to Makimei and Luka, from 18 March a platoon of the KAR had been stationed at Lari to protect the loyalist community, patrolling the neighbourhood alongside the Home Guards; but on the morning of 25 March, this platoon had been withdrawn to other duties in Nairobi. The attack came almost as soon as they had gone. It was difficult to avoid the conclusion that the Mau Mau attackers had patiently awaited their opportunity. Once again, British intelligence had failed badly from a lack of coordination, exposing African allies to the worst possible consequences.[20] None of this was comforting to those other Kikuyu communities throughout Central Kenya whose members had taken a similar public stand against Mau Mau.

Loyalists at Lari at first sought vengeance, not comfort. They turned their anger and grief into violent reprisal. The Home Guard patrol returning from Wainaini's location saw members of the gangs making their escape and gave chase. Through the night there was sporadic shooting and skirmishing as the loyalists engaged what they thought to be groups of the attackers. Anyone abroad in Lari that night was taken as fair game. Other Home Guard from Lari, led by Makimei, were soon also in pursuit of the attackers. They were joined before midnight by Home Guard from neighbouring locations, by police from Uplands and Limuru, and by members of the KPR. The devastation and horror they witnessed on reaching the burned-out homesteads could not have been easy to take in. Samson Kariuki, Machune Kiranga and others among the survivors were there to give an account of what had happened. In their fear and anguish, the survivors were convinced that other Lari residents must have been among the attackers: how, otherwise, could hundreds have disappeared so rapidly into the night if they had not taken shelter in the homes of Mau Mau supporters within Lari itself? Makimei and his allies did not wait for corroboration of these suspicions, but set off immediately to seek out those they believed might have been responsible for the killings.

What followed between 10p.m. and dawn the next morning is not easy to describe precisely, for we have no detailed independent record of events, and there was never any official enquiry into the aftermath of the Lari attacks. We cannot therefore say with any certainty who did what to whom over the next few hours. All the same, there is no doubt that a second massacre took place at Lari that night. It was perpetrated by the Home Guard, later joined by other elements of the security services, who took revenge on any persons in the location they could lay their hands on whom they suspected of Mau Mau sympathies. There was anger, chaos and confusion; and there were beatings, shootings and brutal, cold-blooded killings. By the time the Lancashire Fusiliers arrived in Lari the next morning, to assist in the 'mopping-up operations', the Home Guard, police and KPR had exacted their bitter revenge. Some 200 bodies then awaited identification at the local mortuary – more than twice the number known to have been killed in the homesteads initially attacked. Many other bodies were left in the bush, and some would not be collected until four days later. The only contemporary European account of this second massacre, provided by the Irish lawyer Peter Evans, estimated the combined total dead from both massacres at more than 400.[21]

Evans's source for this estimate of the extent of the retaliation came from European settlers, including one notable individual of 'professional standing' (who may well have been a magistrate or judge). He described this informant as being 'as deeply shocked by the revelations of the reprisals as by the massacre'. According to Evans, most of the retaliation was carried out by Kikuyu Home Guard, but he had 'no doubt' that some of the killings were conducted under the supervision of European commanders.[22] His certainty was in part based upon first-hand accounts. A man of strongly anti-colonial views, Evans had been among the lawyers who had volunteered to assist Kenyatta's defence team. In the months following the Kapenguria show trial, he busied himself in Nairobi assisting supporters of the KAU. They provided Evans with a list of persons who were said to have 'witnessed' atrocities carried out by the security forces. Among those named was a resident of Lari, who told Evans how he had been rounded up with other suspects on the morning following the massacre. After spending the night in Uplands police station, this witness explained that he and two others had been bundled into a lorry by a European police officer and taken into the forest. There, the three Kikuyu prisoners had been ordered to walk away from the vehicle. As they walked, there was a burst of firing. While his two companions were killed, the witness miraculously survived unscathed. On the orders of the European officer, the assassins bundled their terrified prisoner back into the lorry, and returned him to Uplands police station, where he was instructed: 'Tell all your friends what happens to Mau Mau.' The witness to this atrocity was released from custody after two more days, and made his statement to Evans a month or so later.[23]

Even the partisan Evans conceded that this story was insufficient evidence, on its own, to condemn the European police officers who had been involved in the aftermath of the Lari massacre, but other sources confirm that killings such as these did indeed take place, even if their circumstances cannot be described in the same detail. Gladys Kiriga's account of events at Lari provides the best examples, being based on numerous interviews conducted among the Lari community. All of Kiriga's elderly informants, interviewed by her in 1989, made graphic references to the summary murders of suspects. Kiriga was told that there were several assassinations of the kind described to Evans, that there was 'indiscriminate shooting' of any men who were known to have taken a Mau Mau oath and that wounded suspects were left in the bush to die. Mwangi Gatari told Kiriga that the suspects at Lari even feared that the government had a 'plan to eliminate all of those who had been rounded up'.[24] No such plan existed, but those who determinedly claimed there to have been two massacres at Lari were surely correct.

Another first-hand account of events at Lari, authored by an African, was published in 1973. Karigo Muchai was a KAU supporter who, early in 1953, was instructed to investigate atrocity allegations in Kiambu. Muchai went to Lari on the morning following the attack and spent the day on a ridge above the settlement, looking down on the security forces as they scoured the area in search of suspects. A round-up of 'all male suspects' had begun at around 4a.m. on the orders of the local district officer, John Cumber, and was carried out by contingents of Home Guard under the direction of police and KPR.[25] Discreetly following the police and Home Guard patrols in the wake of these round-ups, Karigo Muchai walked amongst the smouldering *bomas* and saw the evidence of Lari's tragedy with his own eyes. There were still bodies left in the debris of the homesteads, and other corpses were scattered about in the surrounding fields and woodlands. These were not loyalist dead: they had by then been taken to the mortuary; but those suspected as Mau Mau had been left where they lay. Dogs roamed around, picking at the bodies, as if feeding on carrion.[26] Over the next three days, Muchai spoke with many people in Lari. He was told that the government counter-attack had been indiscriminate and severe, involving the murder

of women and children as well as the targeting of men known to have
Mau Mau sympathies. He came to the conclusion that most of the blood
spilt at Lari 'was on government hands'.[27] Other sources confirm this
view. The closest to an official reckoning of the extent of the killing
came in a brief government statement, reported in the *East African
Standard* on 5 April 1953, that 'the security forces had killed 150 people
alleged to have been involved in the massacre'.[28] Peter Evans's assertion
that the score for Mau Mau and the security forces at Lari was about
even therefore overstates the number of people finally acknowledged to
have been killed in Mau Mau's attack (74), and understates the number
officially reckoned to have been killed in retaliation (150). These figures
do not include those who were declared 'missing'. The real numbers of
dead may therefore have been a good deal higher. The grim truth was
that, for every person who died in Lari's first massacre, at least two more
were killed in retaliation in the second.

If the British were complacent about the character of the war against
Mau Mau before 26 March, the events that night finally extinguished
any lingering hope that the conflict might easily be snuffed out. The
scale of the attack at Lari surprised even the most professional officers
among the security forces, and its timing, after the withdrawal of soldiers
from the area, showed that Mau Mau was still far better at gathering and
making use of military intelligence than were the British. Moreover, at
around the same time as the attack on Lari another Mau Mau gang
had seriously embarrassed the security forces at Naivasha, where they
mounted a brave and well-planned assault upon the local police post.
The Naivasha raid was oganized by the thirty-three-year-old Mbaria wa
Kanui, a Mau Mau leader who operated mainly in the Kinangop.[29] The
purpose of the raid was to acquire weapons and ammunition from the
armoury at the police barracks. It was staggeringly successful. Using a
stolen truck to break down the gates of the post, Kanui's gang, some
seventy strong, stormed into the compound and opened fire on the
unsuspecting garrison. Armed with only a few precision weapons, but
including at least one Sten gun, the raiders killed one African policeman
and wounded several others. The remainder of the garrison fled in
terror. On breaching the armoury, the raiders seized eighteen automatic
weapons and twenty-nine rifles, and as much ammunition as they could
carry. Another contingent broke open the gates of the detention camp
adjacent to the barracks, liberating some 170 prisoners, among their
number several people being held for questioning in connection with
the murders of European settlers in the Kinangop area.

Naivasha lay on the floor of the Rift Valley, some 3000 feet below
Lari but less than 30 miles away. As the raiders fled northwards, with
four platoons of the Lancashire Fusiliers in hot pursuit, they climbed up

the escarpment and passed close to the still burning homesteads in Lari sub-location. The coincident timing of the two attacks, and their geographical proximity, added greatly to the confusion of the security forces on the night of 26 March. By the early hours of the morning, the British soldiers pursuing the Naivasha attackers were running into the Home Guard and police patrols from Lari, and there were several incidents of 'friendly fire'. Boastful Mau Mau commanders would later claim that this double blow had been purposefully coordinated to cause maximum impact. The evidence from Lari suggests that this could not have been so. The slaughter at Lari was entirely contingent upon local conditions, and would not have taken place at all on 26 March had the soldiers not been withdrawn from the vicinity the previous day. For once, the Mau Mau units had enjoyed a significant stroke of luck. The combined impact of the two events severely rocked British confidence, and the confidence of their African allies.[30]

Within a few days all of Kikuyuland knew the stories of what had happened at Lari and at Naivasha. The tales grew in the telling, with exaggerated claims of the scale of Mau Mau's Naivasha success and elaborate rumours of atrocity and barbarity on both sides at Lari. As the implications of these dreadful events dawned upon the population, the war became a more brutal and retaliatory affair than it had been before. After many months of murdering vulnerable white settlers and assassinating African collaborators in isolated but brutal moments of violence, Mau Mau had now shown itself to be a ruthless and coordinated military movement capable of operations on a far grander scale. The intensification of violence by the security forces now seemed more acceptable, as an angry but understandable response to the horror of Lari. The Home Guard, in particular, were encouraged to treat Mau Mau as Mau Mau had treated them. At this point, even the Kenya press briefly set aside its usual coyness in describing the circumstances in which Mau Mau suspects were killed, as if to emphasize the point that vengeance was merited and was being taken. The shooting of a gang of twenty-one terrorists by a Home Guard patrol in an area north of Lari – all killed and no prisoners taken – was reported in the *East African Standard*, on 3 April, for example, with the simple explanation: 'It is believed that the Home Guards' attack was a spontaneous act of retaliation against known suspects who have caused mischief in the district.'[31] The next night, twenty-seven more alleged Mau Mau were killed in similar circumstances, again reported as a simple matter of fact in the press.[32] These killings appeared to amount to little more than political assassinations, not dissimilar from those carried out by Mau Mau. The loyalists of the Home Guard had learned a lesson from Lari: they were no longer prepared to wait for Mau Mau to attack them; and in the dark mood of recrimination, no one was any longer taking prisoners. Nothing in central Kenya could ever be quite the same again.

For weeks after the attack, Lari was a place of intense conflict and bitter grievance. Seeing the pressing need to restore confidence among the Kikuyu loyalists, the colonial authorities were determined to bring prosecutions against those accused of participating in the massacre. This required the gathering of evidence, and especially the recording of witness testimonies from those who had survived the attacks, many of them grievously injured. It was a protracted and gruelling process. After the attacks the survivors had been directed to the police post at Uplands, where they were given shelter in the makeshift tented camp to the rear of the station and adjacent to the jail. The most seriously injured were moved to St George's Hospital in Kiambu township. Others were treated at Uplands. The medical staff were overwhelmed. One senior doctor, who had been in London during the Blitz, told reporters, 'This is just like the war.' No one in Kenya had been prepared for a disaster on this scale. While the doctors did the best they could to save the wounded, the dead were taken to the small, bleak mortuary at Uplands. When this was full to overflowing, other mortuaries, at Tigoni and Escarpment, had to be used. The mortuary buildings were primitive, to say the least, and even in the best of times there was little in the way of refinement or respect for the dead – and these were far from the best of times. The bodies reached the mortuaries on the backs of lorries and in cars, sometimes wrapped in blankets, sometimes heaped into gunny bags. Some had body parts missing, and very few of the corpses were labelled. If relatives accompanied the body, then identification could be established, but more often than not the corpse was given a number, not a name. Relatives who later came to seek the bodies of their loved ones must have found the scene difficult to bear. We have no first-hand description of the mortuary from these few horrific days, but the British military intelligence officer Frank Kitson did write about his visit to the Tigoni mortuary a few months after the Lari massacre, when conditions must have been a good deal better. His account is harrowing, all the same:

> From the outside the mortuary looked inoffensive, so I was not prepared for what I saw when I opened the door. The shambles inside was past all describing. There had been a number of actions recently and altogether there must have been eighteen bodies in a place the size of a small summer house ... Some of them had been there for five days and were partially decomposed. They were all lying around tangled up on the floor as there were no slabs in the Tigoni charnel house.[33]

There was to be no dignity in death for the Lari victims. It was not until four days after the massacres that the last of the bodies from Lari was finally collected and deposited at the mortuary in Uplands. By then, the dogs, hyenas, crows and vultures had all had their share.

In the aftermath of the attack, most of the survivors had fled to the police post at Uplands. There the families of Makimei, Samson Kariuki, Paulo and the other Home Guard commanders crowded into cramped temporary accommodation. Some of them would remain there for the next three years, living under constant police protection. The less seriously injured victims had their wounds treated here, and began to tell the stories of their ordeal. Next to the police compound, and within view of these shocked and still terrified survivors, a large enclosure had been hurriedly constructed from fence poles and barbed wire to hold the suspects rounded up in the hours following the massacre. By the evening of 27 March this enclosure already held 1500 men, and over the next few days the number rose to above 2000. Virtually every male resident of Lari sub-location who could be found, and who was not a member of the Home Guard or otherwise known to be an active loyalist, was taken into custody. Many of these men were badly beaten and abused by the Home Guard who arrested them, and this rough and ready treatment continued in the camp. Those arrested were not properly warned of their rights, and only a few were even questioned about their whereabouts at the time of the attack. Nor were the homes of these suspects searched for evidence – there was no collection of weapons, and no searches for blood-stained clothing or other clues, for example. This meant that the police were more or less compelled to rely upon a combination of identification evidence and confessional statements if they were to secure convictions. Before the police even began formal interrogations in the camp, on the second day after the massacre, Makimei and his senior headmen had already questioned some of the detained men, and had begun to compile their own lists of suspects from the evidence of the survivors. The figure of Chief Makimei loomed ominously over these proceedings, as he prowled the camp, at one moment seizing men for interrogation, at another moment pressing the survivors to recall the names of anyone they might have recognized. There were undoubtedly leading questions asked, and plenty of opportunities for collusion between the witnesses. As Makimei assembled his lists of names, it was often unclear who had first provided the name, or what exactly the person was to be accused of doing; but once a name was on the list, the interrogations began in earnest. Makimei's Home Guard began by beating the suspect, to encourage him to confess. Some of those in the camp would later claim that several suspects were beaten to death. The violence was unquestionably severe. When finally delivered into the hands of the police for 'formal' questioning, the suspects were already in a sorry state. For police officers professionally trained in the systematic collection of evidence, this was a chaotic shambles, in which the truth was obscured by a burning desire for vengeance and retribution.

The vast majority of the men caught in the round-up would spend a month or more in the ramshackle detention camp at Uplands, herded like cattle into the open compound, with no shelter, inadequate latrines and no proper food. Even as the police interrogations began, on 27 March, no one had thought to compile an inventory of the names of those held. They were simply referred to, anonymously and collectively, as 'suspects'. The police investigation was itself poorly organized, and in the early stages it was undoubtedly led very deliberately by the Home Guard, who essentially identified those for questioning and provided a catalogue of accusations. Inspector Aubrey was put in charge of the police operation, but at various times two other senior officers, Poppy and Baker, took command. As the police stumbled through the fog of confusion in the Uplands camp, it was inevitable that they would come to rely upon Makimei as their guiding influence. The officers who began the task of interviewing and recording statements faced a number of challenges. Few of the suspects spoke good English and some had no Swahili. Translators had to be found urgently. There were few volunteers. Kikuyu-speakers who had adequate levels of English or Swahili were dragooned as interpreters wherever they could be found – a local worker with the forestry department, a clerk from the Kirenga grocery store, any person who had mission education and was literate. Again, inevitably, such folk were mainly drawn from the friends and families of the Lari Home Guard. These people approached the task with their own prejudices and opinions, and they were inexperienced in the work and untrained. Mistakes were made; the results were sometimes dismal; and the queue of suspects waiting to be interviewed seemed never-ending.

In frustration, European officers quickly resorted to crude methods, taking the lists of suspects provided by Makimei and working through these people first, in the hope of getting clues to the identity of other attackers. The individuals Makimei selected were brought to the tents near the camp entrance, or into the offices of the adjacent police station for interrogation. Richmond Dauncey, a solicitor, joined the CID at Uplands on 11 April to take sworn statements from the accused as they were charged. He was far from comfortable with his duties. 'In the very early days I considered the witnesses from whom I took statements were bewildered and angry,' he would later tell the court. 'We had to take special care to avoid inaccuracies due to emotion. Later they improved and we did not have to probe things out of them ... When I arrived even on 11 April I sensed that their minds were still shocked, which was not the case, say, one month later.'[34]

To speed up the task, groups of suspects were loaded into lorries and taken to other police posts at Escarpment, Limuru and Kiambu. Others were taken further still. One group of prisoners who were suspected of deeper involvement in Mau Mau were sent to Kampi ya Simba, a notorious British interrogation centre on a farm in the Laikipia district. There, according to district officer Terence Gavaghan, they were 'severely mistreated by security forces'. The men were later briefly transferred into Gavaghan's care. Still outraged by events at Lari, Gavaghan later admitted that he 'made the mistake of having horrific published pictures of Mau Mau brutalities pinned inside the lorries carrying them', so that they could look at the results of their evil deeds.[35] That violence was used against those being questioned is undeniable, and was repeatedly acknowledged in the evidence given before the courts as the Lari accused came to trial. Acting Justice Cram was also brought to Uplands in the weeks following the massacre, in his capacity as magistrate, to attest the extra-judicial statements made by the suspects. Again and again Cram acknowledged in his reports that suspects had been beaten or mistreated whilst in custody. With his usual scrupulous honesty Cram did his level best to establish that the statements that he then attested were freely made. But it was a dirty business.

Over the weeks following the massacre, more than 300 suspects would eventually make extra-judicial statements that amounted to confessions of guilt. The investigating officers knew that such statements were unlikely to be sufficient on their own to satisfy the courts. Firm evidence of identification would be needed in corroboration if convictions were to be secured. The Lari survivors were the key witnesses and they became crucial in the construction of the prosecution case. Within a few days of the massacre the police had conducted interviews at St George's Hospital with those who were well enough to speak. The women survivors from Lari, including the wives of Luka and Samson Kariuki, and younger girls from other homesteads, were all placed in a ward together at St George's. There, still traumatized by what had happened to them, these women were interviewed repeatedly by police officers who were keen to establish the identity of the attackers. What did the women remember? Had they recognized anyone? If they had not seen the faces, then perhaps some had worn distinctive clothing? The interviews were conducted at the bedsides of the victims, in the open ward and in full hearing of the other patients. The process was difficult for the police and distressing for the survivors. One of the senior police officers involved, John Baker, later recalled the interview with Luka's wife, Mbura: 'She was not too well,' said Baker, 'She had been cut about. She needed a lot of prompting and appeared to be fed-up with it [the questioning] towards the end.' Mbura's bed was next to that of another of Luka's wives, Gacheri, who was also interviewed at this time. She, too, gave evidence only reluctantly at first; but eventually, and after much prompting and cajoling, both women provided a list of names of those they believed they had recognized during the attack. There was a strong congruence to the lists they provided. All those they named were residents of Lari, and neighbours of the massacre victims.[36]

As the injured women recovered sufficiently, they were brought back to Uplands to join their families and to take part in identification parades in the camp. These parades were unusual, to say the least. Hundreds of 'suspects' would be made to stand in lines within the camp, while the women were led slowly up and down the rows. In one such parade Mujiri, Samson Kariuki's wife, picked out more than twenty men whom she accused of having murdered her children. In another parade, Luka's wife Gacheri selected fifteen men from among more than a hundred who were about to be released, accusing them of having participated in the slaughter in her homestead on the night of 26 March.[37] Could these women really have had such a clear memory of the traumatic events of the massacre? Had the flames of the burning huts provided sufficient light to positively identify so many people among the attackers? Or had they sought vengeance by singling out their known enemies, and the known enemies of Luka and Makimei, for prosecution? The power of suggestion, collusion between witnesses, and the simple desire to punish might all have played a part in the identification of likely culprits. These would be questions for the courts to consider, but the combination of identification of this kind and a corroborating confessional statement would be all that was needed to send a man to the gallows.

By mid-April, after nearly three weeks of investigations, the police had compiled a picture of what they thought had happened at Lari. Their unpalatable conclusion was that the massacre had not been solely the work of a 'fanatical Mau Mau forest gang', but had been perpetrated in very large part by the neighbours of the victims. It seemed that part of Lari's population had fallen upon the other part. There was evidence that local Mau Mau supporters had been directed in the organization of the massacre by a small number of 'strangers'. These men may have been former squatters from the Rift Valley, but they came to Lari from the Aberdares forest, where they were active members of Mau Mau's forest gangs. These 'strangers' had infiltrated Lari in the weeks leading up to the attack, organizing meetings of Mau Mau supporters at which targets were identified and roles assigned. The assailants had then patiently waited for the departure of the soldiers of the KAR before launching their murderous attack. The slaughter had indeed been deliberate and well planned. The round-up of suspects immediately following the massacre had caught many people who were part of the gangs who had attacked the homesteads of the Home Guard that fateful night, but the handful of 'strangers' were not among those detained. They had already fled back to the sanctuary of the Aberdares forest. The very nature of the investigation of the massacre made it more likely that those apprehended and accused of the crime would be persons known to the victims. These were the people named on the lists compiled by Makimei and his headmen, and these were the people singled out in the identification parades. Over the next six months, some 400 of the suspects would face murder charges, in a total of nineteen capital trials.

Before we follow this disturbing story into the courtroom, it is necessary to ask the question why this should have happened at Lari? The answer lies in the history of Lari's settlement, and of land disputes involving the various families brought to the area from Tigoni. Other writers have suggested that this prior history marks Lari as an exceptional event, prompted not so much by the Mau Mau war as by other, more deeply rooted historical currents. Those historical currents undoubtedly flowed strongly at Lari, but to suggest they were unconnected to Mau Mau is entirely misleading. The Lari massacre had *everything* to do with the Mau Mau struggle, and it was the history of Lari's land dispute that made the place, and its factional politics, the focus of such an intense and bitter struggle. Like Olenguruone in the history of squatter militancy, Lari had long been symbolic of resistance for those in the Kikuyu Reserves who campaigned against the expropriation of lands by the wealthy and the evictions of the poor. The deeper history of Lari's tragedy therefore has a great deal to tell us about the character and motive of the Mau Mau war.

## A Deeper History

No doubt on platforms and in reports we declare we have no intention of depriving natives of their lands, but this has never prevented us from taking whatever land we want . . .
  Sir Charles Eliot, April 1904 (High Commissioner, British East Africa)

The deeper history of the massacre takes us some 20 miles to the south-east of Lari, to Tigoni, and back in time nearly half a century. Here, in April 1906, Italian Catholic missionaries took over a white farm and set up a church for local Africans. They occupied two plots, 1500 acres in extent, located in the midst of the White Highlands, surrounded on all sides by European-owned farms.[38] This part of Kiambu was already

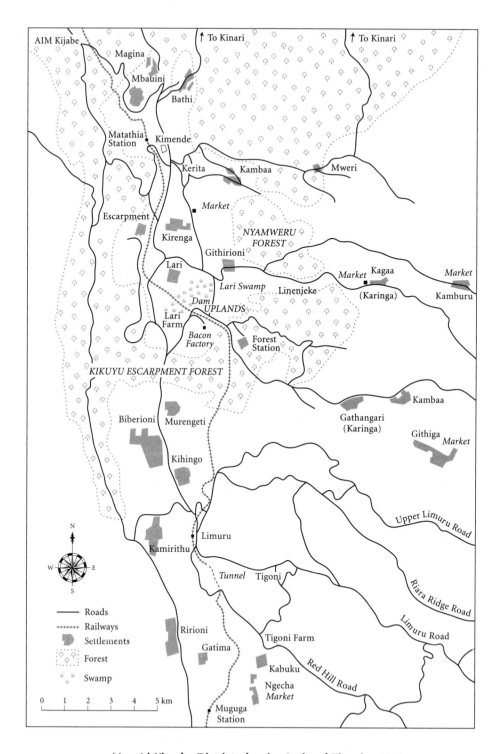

**Map 4.i Kiambu District, showing Lari and Tigoni, c.1952**

crowded with Kikuyu cultivators when the Europeans arrived to peg out their claims. Over time, these Kikuyu were gradually dispossessed, some retreating into what would become the Kikuyu 'Native Reserve' to the north, others becoming squatters and remaining on the land to work for the Europeans, others still migrating to the Rift Valley to work on European land there. Amid this prolonged turmoil, the land taken by the Catholic mission became a safe haven of relative stability and prosperity for its Kikuyu residents. The missionaries wanted Christian converts, not cheap labourers; and they seemed not to care how many Africans crowded onto the land belonging to their church.[39] By 1911 ten Kikuyu *mbaris* were living at Tigoni. The leading spokesman for this prosperous, industrious, conservative and largely Catholic Kikuyu community at Tigoni was Luka Wakahangare.

Signs of trouble ahead first became apparent in 1915, when the white settlers living around Tigoni asked the government to remove the Italian mission and evict the Africans living there. They wanted the plot to build a social club and other facilities for the local European community. The land was considered too valuable to be left 'in the hands of natives'.[40] Over the next ten years or so, the Tigoni Kikuyu slowly gathered political support against the threatened evictions. The Catholic fathers ensured that the claims of the ten *mbari* at Tigoni were included in a register of Kikuyu land claims in Kiambu compiled in 1921, and Luka publicized the fears of his people to the Kikuyu Association and the Kikuyu Central Association. By the mid-1920s Tigoni had become a symbol of resistance against further land alienation.

Faced with dissent, the government sought to placate its critics. In 1924, when the Chief Native Commissioner toured southern Kiambu, he reassured the 'loyal' Kikuyu at Tigoni that there would be no further alienations. But these were weasel words: only two years later, surveyors arrived at Tigoni armed with theodolites, pegs and tape measures, to prepare for the sale of commercial plots in the new Tigoni township. When the alarmed *mbari* heads demanded an explanation, they were curtly informed that Tigoni was not a *new* alienation at all, having been first surveyed as a farm in 1906: the statement of 1924 gave them no protection. The Tigoni Kikuyu were learning not to trust the government's words.

In the struggle to remain at Tigoni, the Kikuyu now found an unlikely ally. The Kiambu District Officer, Lydekker, had got to know the Tigoni people well. He considered them loyal, industrious and devout Christians. In January 1927 he set about encouraging the Tigoni Kikuyu in their own defence. Father Seraglio, the head of the Italian mission, organized a collection of sworn affidavits from the *mbari* heads, along with lists of the senior residents and their property. Other testimonies were found on the files. Once assembled, these were typed up in Lydekker's office, and copies forwarded to Nairobi.[41]

From these documents we learn a great deal about the people at Tigoni.[42] There were some 129 dwellings on the land in 1927, and though Lydekker guessed that only 20 per cent of the area was under cultivation, the rest of the land was given over to goat grazing. Settlement was dense, and the use of the land intensive. Each of the *mbari* heads explained that they had been living on the land before the Europeans came. Nganga Githanga was among those who was born at Tigoni 'before the 1898 famine'; he was able to describe negotiations with the first Italian missionaries.[43] Some complained that the Italians had taken land from them to establish the church.[44] Others told of how they had previously 'bought' the land from the forest-dwelling Nderobo people, giving details of the transactions.[45] Among the testimonies is one from the young Luka Wakahangare, who had been born at Tigoni. He made the statement on behalf of his elderly father. Luka was in effect already the family head, presiding over some fourteen separate households comprising the *mbari*.

Regardless of their respective size, each of the ten *mbaris* was adamant that their rights at Tigoni were recognized in Kikuyu law as *githaka*.[46] The distinction between *githaka*-holders and their tenants was to be crucial. Tigoni's residents numbered perhaps 600 by the late 1920s, around half being the direct descendants of the ten *mbaris* who claimed to have originally cleared and settled the land, and the other half being tenants. Under Kikuyu custom, the direct descendants of the original *mbaris* enjoyed the status of *githaka*. This meant they had inheritable rights that were unalienable. The tenants, on the other hand, who were collectively known as *muhoi*, did not enjoy these customary rights. Community consensus and social morality played an important role in protecting *muhoi*. 'None of us could sell any of this land without the consent of others,' stressed Wachuiri Kabatha, when commenting on the threatened evictions in 1926.[47] In the minds of the Kikuyu, *muhoi* were not a category whose rights could be collectively denied, but rather they were individuals who had negotiated their status and position within the *mbari*.

Kenya's colonial officials had no time to grapple with the labyrinthine network of relationships this implied. They sought to use the basic principles of Kikuyu custom to define who had rights in land and who did not. This led to a gross simplification of the position that worked to the grave disadvantage of the *muhoi* at Tigoni. The government thought that *githaka* holders had recognized rights that should be respected and compensated; *muhoi* had no such rights, and could be evicted at will and without compensation. At Tigoni, the 'protection of native rights' would therefore only apply to around half the residents.[48]

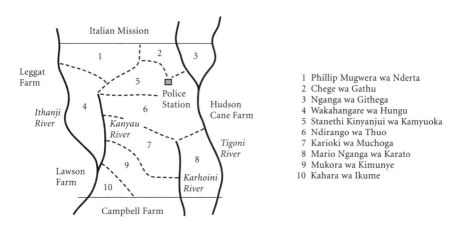

**Map 4.ii Tigoni Township Reserve, c.1929, showing Kikuyu *githakas***

The Kikuyu were aware of the implications of this. Some senior elders utterly rejected the idea. Others, led by Luka, took a more pragmatic view, fearing that resistance might ultimately jeopardize the rights of *githaka*-holders to compensation. If evictions were to happen, then all wanted the best possible outcome for themselves and their families. In October 1927 Lydekker reported that Luka was 'willing to consider an exchange of land, provided that the new land were equal in every respect, acreage, fertility and most especially water supply, to their *githakas* on Tigoni'. Given Tigoni's exceptionally favourable location, this would be a tall order, but a search was begun to find land to which the Tigoni people could be moved. In May 1928, Luka and other Tigoni elders made their first visit to Lari.[49]

It was Lydekker's successor as Kiambu's District Commissioner, the clever and determined Sidney Fazan, who finally brought matters to a head. A graduate of Christ Church, Oxford, Fazan was among the more academically inclined of Kenya's colonial officers. Diligent, serious and scholarly, he had little time for colleagues who refused to grabble with the complexities of African life. His copious reports on the social and political life of Kenya's African communities litter the archival record from the 1910s to the 1940s. At the time his influence upon government policy was probably greater than any other official. For Fazan, the devil was always in the detail; and he relished it all. His industry earned him an OBE in 1930, at the tender age of forty-two, awarded while he was stationed at Kiambu, still only a humble district commissioner.[50] In terms of colonial policy, Fazan was a conservative modernizer: though he was a keen protector of 'native interest', this meant pragmatic politics, not the preservation of bygone ways; and pragmatic politics in Kenya must necessarily incorporate the European settlers, whose rights in the White Highlands Fazan resolutely defended. On returning to Kenya after wartime service, in 1948, Sidney Fazan settled among those European farmers with his second wife. Ironically enough, he would choose to make his Kenyan home at Tigoni.

Fazan was to have a decisive influence over the fate of Luka and his followers. By the time he arrived at Kiambu, in 1929, Fazan was Kenya's acknowledged authority on African land tenure. In May 1929 Fazan produced his first report on Kikuyu land issues.[51] He was then nominated to serve on a committee on Kikuyu land tenure, under the chairmanship of G. V. Maxwell, the Chief Native Commissioner, and alongside Louis Leakey. Among the main recommendations of this enquiry was the recognition of *githaka* claims, the establishment of a register of claims, and the setting of limits to the rights of tenants within the *githaka* system.

In a minority report, Fazan went further, arguing for the recognition of title on small holdings – amounting to the beginnings of an economic land market within the African reserves. Maxwell and Leakey disapproved of this. Like most Europeans, they held firmly to the belief that Africans wanted no truck with private property, and that the tradition of communal ownership should be protected against those few individuals who might want to line their own pockets by acquiring rights to the disadvantage of their fellows.

Fazan had no time for this bucolic view of African society. Smallholdings were already being bought and sold among Kikuyu, Fazan claimed, and he cited examples. This was the product of demographic pressure and the closing of the frontier: Kikuyu practice was already modifying in response to the changed circumstances, most clearly in Kiambu. The trend towards individual tenure on holdings of decreasing size would inevitably mean that *githaka*-holders would become ever more reluctant to admit tenants, Fazan argued. Evictions were already being reported from some *githakas*. 'I am far from suggesting that these developments are bad in themselves,' wrote Fazan; 'they are the natural result of economic progress.'[52]

Fazan now put this thinking into practice in his handling of the Tigoni problem, with a typical piece of pragmatic politics. In May 1930 he summoned the representatives of each of the ten Tigoni *mbaris* to a meeting. There, he proposed that they be given 1.5 acres at Lari for every acre given up at Tigoni, plus compensation in cash for all dwelling huts, planted trees and fencing. It was a tempting offer, and the elders retired to consider their position. Some felt that they might get 2 acres if they bargained harder, but when they returned to make the counter-bid they found Fazan was unwilling to budge: 1.5 acres was a fair exchange, he argued, and they could expect nothing more. The implication was that the government had reached the end of the rope: it was Lari at 1.5 acres, or nothing. The elders retired again to chew things over. When they returned they were divided into two camps. Of the ten *mbaris*, a group of six, led by Luka, now expressed themselves willing to accept Fazan's offer, while the remaining four would not agree to the proposed move unless they received 2 acres for every one given up.[53]

Before Fazan could push ahead with the move, it was announced from London that there was to be a wider commission of enquiry into African land requirements over the whole colony. Everything came to a halt. When the commission came out to Kenya, in 1932, Fazan was appointed as its secretary. His views shaped the deliberations of the commission at every stage, from the writing of a precis on each 'problem area', to the drafting of conclusions and recommendations. The Land Commission did not bring the Kikuyu any satisfaction. Luka Wakahangare and other elders from Tigoni dutifully paraded before the commissioners. All made a passionate case for being allowed to remain at Tigoni, carefully setting out the history of their settlement and demonstrating the extent and character of their occupation. It was all to no avail.

The Land Commission was the great missed opportunity of Kenya's colonial history. It was clear by the early 1930s that Kenya's Africans needed more good land than they had been left by the alienation of the White Highlands. The land commissioners accepted this in principle, but saw the solution to lie in improved African land husbandry, not in the restoration of the lost lands. Aside from a few thousand acres awarded in order to resettle peoples such as those at Tigoni, Kenya's Africans would simply have to make the best of what they had. The commission confirmed white ownership of the Highlands as inviolate and insisted that Africans must adapt to their changed circumstances. Fazan's 'economic progress' demanded that they must, and forcing changes to African land tenure seemed as good a way as any of bringing about this 'progress' more rapidly. The commission decided that all the 'islands' of Kikuyu settlement within the Highlands, including Tigoni, should be evicted, and those displaced should be resettled on lands to be added to the Kikuyu Native Reserve on its fringes.[54] The Tigoni people were to move to Lari after all.

Kenya's colonial officials smugly thought that the Kikuyu would soon 'come to appreciate' the wisdom of the judgments that had been made by the land commissioners. They were wrong. While their political leaders sent petitions of protest to London, resistance to the evictions now became *the* political issue of the day. Complaints about the proposals flooded in. Previously compliant chiefs, including Koinange, now became uncooperative.[55] In May of 1936, the Central Province

Commissioner, La Fontaine, decided to tackle the grumbling head-on, and summoned a meeting. Old Koinange, Waruhiu and Luka were among those present. La Fontaine encouraged them 'to speak their thoughts and feelings freely'; and for over three hours they did just that. La Fontaine was taken aback by what he heard. In a long report written to the Chief Secretary in Nairobi the Provincial Commissioner began with humility: 'I am compelled to admit that the opinion which I held and expressed last year, that the settlement by the Land Commission had given general satisfaction to the Kikuyu and that any dissatisfaction expressed was merely the vagaries of individual agitators, requires considerable modification. It has not satisfied the Kikuyu of Kiambu district, and the dissatisfaction is deep and widespread.' Koinange and other leading chiefs felt the situation 'to be very serious'.[56] The 'compensation' offered by the Land Commission was 'woefully inadequate'; the land offered by the commission was of inferior quality; it was inaccessible and distant from markets. Kikuyu wanted title deeds, so that they could own land in the same way as Europeans.

If these views of the chiefly landed elite appeared to give sanction to Fazan's arguments for a market in African land, the concerns they expressed over what would be done with the tenants who would be rendered landless in the process got to the real nub of the problem. Fazan's vision of 'economic progress', endorsed by the Land Commission, was going to create a huge landless class. It was not clear to the chiefs how they would handle this, nor what its consequences might be. Their obvious anxiety alarmed La Fontaine, who now urged the government to look again at the problem, 'otherwise it might easily burst into a flame and have irrevocable results'.[57]

He was not the only official getting nervy. E. B. Hosking wrote at length to defend the Kikuyu's claims. Kikuyuland was overcrowded, stated Hosking, and there was nothing to blame but British land policy, 'or the lack of it'.

> I cannot stress too strongly the need for immediate action and for generous treatment of the Kikuyu [wrote Hosking], even if it entails the expenditure of a considerable sum of money. Apart from any question of justice, we cannot afford politically to leave a numerous and powerful tribe with a feeling of resentment and antipathy. We have not given the Kikuyu a square deal, and we are no longer in a position where we can retrieve all the mistakes we have made ... It is important to appreciate that it is no longer the Kikuyu agitators, who for political purposes or their own glorification are stirring up the natives, but that it is the responsible representatives of the tribe who are pressing for a settlement of the Kikuyu grievances.[58]

The only answer was to give the Kikuyu more land; and that meant restoring at least some of the lands taken by Europeans.

It was not a solution Fazan was prepared to entertain. The Kikuyu could not turn the clock back: they would be allowed a market in land, but *only* on the land assigned to them. In no circumstances could land be reallocated on the basis of historic claims. To do so would 'end not only in embitterment between groups ... but also in a clamour for more land'.[59] Both officials thus predicted future conflict – La Fontaine suggesting it was likely if outstanding claims were not acknowledged, Fazan arguing that it would occur only if they were. The salient difference was that La Fontaine saw the pressing needs of the Kikuyu landless, whose dissent might ultimately undermine the authority of the chiefs, while Fazan trusted in the chiefs to win the argument and contain the problem. Events would prove La Fontaine the wiser.

Luka Wakahangare had been amongst the more outspoken elders gathered in La Fontaine's office.[60] Like Koinange, Waruhiu and other Kiambu elders, Luka was aware of his responsibilities to those *muhoi* under his patronage. But he also knew that his first duty lay with his *githaka*; and if it came to a choice between the two, then it would be the *muhoi* who would suffer.[61] In fact, by the time of the meeting at La Fontaine's office, Luka had already grasped this nettle. In defiance of those Tigoni *mbaris* who still opposed the move, he had visited Lari in November 1935, with Koinange and two British officials, to mark out the boundaries of the land to be resettled.[62] It was an act of capitulation and betrayal for which some Kikuyu would never forgive him. The Tigoni people were now split right down the middle. The seeds of the Lari massacre had been sown.

It would be another five years before the move to Lari finally began, in 1940. Delays ensued as efforts were made to persuade the four recalcitrant *mbaris* to belatedly accept the offer. One *mbari*, that of Kararu Ikumo, comprising five households, managed to negotiate compensatory land at Muguga, and moved there instead. Though one or two families capitulated and accepted land at Lari, the bulk of the households in the Kimotho, Muchuga and Waikanya *mbaris* held firm. These forty or so families 'passively resisted all the orders of government' at Tigoni over the next few years, and swore an oath against ever settling at Lari.[63] While these families held out, Luka and his followers began to move to Lari, selecting the best of the available land for themselves. As time went by, the dissenters faced an increasingly unattractive choice. Resentment against Luka deepened. Finally, in 1949, eviction orders were issued against those remaining at Tigoni. A few now agreed to accept the Lari offer, and their possessions were taken north. Those remaining – some thirty-five families – were removed from their land by a contingent of armed police, and then watched as their Tigoni homes were put to the torch.[64]

The struggle of the dissenting *mbaris* told only part of the story of dispossession at Tigoni. Within those *mbaris* who agreed to the move there were many tenants who were not given land at Lari. Some of these people moved away from Tigoni to seek land elsewhere, often with other kin. Many more drifted into the wage-labour market around Limuru and Uplands. Others reluctantly went to Lari with Luka and his followers, where they settled in the trading centres or in the compounds of friends. They would have no land, but they would work for others as casual labourers. Their loss of status was a humiliation that became a lasting grievance.

If this pool of bitterness were not deep enough, there was further disquiet, even among those who had willingly gone to Lari, over the manner in which the land at the new resettlement area was allocated. Following the publication of the report of the Land Commission, a sub-committee of the Kiambu Local Native Council (LNC) had been formed in October 1935 to oversee all land allocations connected with resettlement.[65] Koinange served on this sub-committee, in his capacity as ex-paramount chief, alongside Divisional Chiefs Waruhiu and Josiah Njonjo, and Locational Chiefs Kioi and Luka. The job of this little group was to adjudicate upon which family should get which plot of land. This was a tricky business, in which European officers were disinclined to become embroiled. It was decided that 'custom should prevail'. The sub-committee was therefore left to its own devices, taking decisions as best it could, visiting the resettlement sites to hear the claims of various parties, and pacing out plots on the ground. They had no surveyor to assist them, but instead relied upon the limited plane-tabling skills of the LNC clerk, John Ngotho, to mark out and map the plots. For such an important matter, these were haphazard arrangements, to say the least. Disputes were inevitable, and every resettlement area was soon the subject of rancorous quarrels, amid accusations of the sub-committee's incompetence and rumours of favouritism, bias and corruption.[66]

Among the many letters in the archival files from this period alleging 'shady' dealings over resettlement, one of the earliest is of particular interest. It dates from January 1935, just a few months after the publication of the Land Commission report, and its author was none other than Chief Philip James Karanja, who would later that year become clerk to the Kiambu land allocations sub-committee. A senior elder of the Church of Scotland and a chief of the 'old guard', the Presbyterian Karanja was a man of high principle. He wrote to the government to appeal that land should be given to *muhoi* about to be evicted from a European farm. To emphasize the plight of such people, Karanja raised the case of Ndeiya, an area designated for resettlement by the Land Commission. 'The state and conditions of Ndeiya are not yet laid down properly,' wrote Karanja in his rather halting English, 'for these reasons':

> The rich people who have large areas of land in the Reserve have also better *shambas* [farms] there [at Ndeiya]. This is to prevent the poor people who got no land in the Reserve from getting place to live there. If it is possible the owners of lands in reserve should not get *shambas* at Ndeiya. This will give a chance to the poor to get *shambas* and live without trouble in the future. There are some who have already fenced very large areas and kept them for their own reserves. This is also another way of preventing others from getting *shambas*. I know that if those who got large *shambas* at Ndeiya hear of what I am talking about would be very angry on me, but I would not mind that. It is better to help the poor rather than to help the rich men.[67]

Karanja was telling the District Commissioner that wealthy and influential Kikuyu *githaka* holders were already involved in a land-grab, carving up the resettlement areas among themselves in an effort to block the claims of others.

Though British officials were aware of these dangers from as early as 1935, they left it to the chiefs.[68] The members of the committee became brokers, portioning out responsibilities between themselves, visiting resettlement schemes on an ad hoc basis and adjudicating disputes 'on the hoof'. Luka was therefore allowed oversight of decisions at Lari with little, if any, interference from his colleagues on the committee. The effect of this was to lessen the overall influence of Koinange and Karanja, who had fewer of their own people to resettle, and to expose Waruhiu, Josiah Njonjo, Kioi and Luka to the intense pressures of the multitudes for whom they were responsible. It was a system designed to fall prey to vested interests.

No colonial officer got around to looking closely at the process of land allocations until October 1943, when Wally Coutts finally became so irritated by the persistent complaints reaching his Kiambu office that he resolved to spend a few days at Ndeiya to see things for himself. When he got there he could scarcely find words to describe 'the scandalous state of affairs' that prevailed. Coutts discovered that only one in six of those settled at Ndeiya had a legitimate claim to land in the resettlement area. Around half the land was cultivated by people who did not live at Ndeiya at all, and a further 20 per cent was owned by only four *githaka*-holders, who included Chief Kioi himself. His clients and supporters, augmented by others from Josiah Njonjo's following, cultivated much of what remained of the Ndeiya land. As Karanja had warned, the allocations at

Ndeiya had been dominated by the rich and powerful, to the exclusion of the displaced Kikuyu for whom it was intended. Coutts did not mince his words in condemning the members of the allocations sub-committee for this state of affairs. When confronted by him they made no effort to disguise their activities. The means of acquiring a plot at Ndeiya 'was the offering of a fat bribe to the apportioners'. 'This was admitted freely by the members of the committee,' reported Coutts, 'and jokes were made about it.' One member of the committee unashamedly told Coutts that 'Ndeiya had been sold to the highest bidder'.[69]

Each Kiambu resettlement area was subject to the deliberations of this same group of chiefs. Petitions, complaints and claims flooded into the district offices from every resettlement area.[70] Lari was no exception. No report on the allocation of lands at Lari survives in the archive, so we cannot be sure; but the catalogue of complaints strongly suggests that Luka exploited the situation to enhance the interests of his own *mbari*.

John Mbugwa, of the *mbari ya* Kimothi, and Marius Ng'ang'a Karatu, of the *mbari ya* Muchogu, were Luka's sternest and most persistent critics at this time, both making claims that the chief had taken an excessive portion of land for himself and his clients.[71] Mbugwa was the most vociferous supporter of the rights of *muhoi*, his own *mbari* having very large numbers of these dependents. He stayed at Tigoni until he was forcibly evicted. Even after his dispossession Mbugwa continued to send petitions to the government, demanding answers to an endless string of questions about the procedures surrounding land allocations at Lari. It was Mbugwa who won the admission from a somewhat ruffled District Commissioner that no record had ever been kept of the acreages allocated at Lari, as this was entirely in the hands of Luka.[72] Karatu's motivation was to be found in the long-running dispute between his *mbari* and the Italian mission. He saw Luka as having dishonestly undermined his claims.[73] Luka had other critics besides. George Kimingi, an ex-squatter of the *mbari ya* Waikanya, who returned to Lari in 1948, was among many who alleged that Luka was guilty of having 'sold' land at Lari and allocated it to those who paid the highest price.[74] There was little doubt that old Chief Luka 'had done very well' out of the move to Lari.[75]

None of the allegations made against Luka was ever investigated. None the less, it was widely accepted that his forced retirement from the chieftaincy, in June 1949, was intended as a gesture of reconciliation towards the many people who had lost faith in his leadership.[76] At this point Luka's duties at Lari were transferred to Makimei Kuria, chief of the neighbouring location of Uplands. Once free from the burden of office, Luka became more outspoken against his opponents and critics – to the embarrassment of the British administration. In September 1949 he wrote angrily to the District Commissioner in protest at the suggestion that a few remaining plots at Lari might be given to landless Kikuyu from elsewhere. Luka insisted that land should be given only to those who had come *with him* from Tigoni. The ex-chief blustered that no other solution would satisfy his people. He did not get his way. The District Commissioner wrote to tell him that his followers had 'already received their fair share of compensation'.[77] Many in Kiambu thought they had received far more than that.

Somewhere in the midst of these struggles it came to be widely believed that the land at Lari was cursed. Rumours of this began to circulate in the early 1940s, after Luka and the first families had relocated to their new farms at Lari. It was alleged that the land was claimed by other *mbaris*, and that their elders had placed a traditional and powerful curse upon anyone who took up residence there. In the later 1940s John Mbugwa cited the curse in defence of his own reluctance to go to Lari, stating that the curse would kill anyone who disobeyed.

In the Mau Mau war, those who had been involved in the corrupt distribution of lands in Kiambu would be called to account. The murder of Luka Wakahangare and his followers illustrated only too clearly how those who supported Mau Mau 'read' the deeper history of the Kikuyu people. Lari's tragedy was emblematic of the historic pattern of land alienation and dispossession that had driven the Kikuyu people into the Mau Mau revolt. The slaughter of women and children had its reason: it signified the denial of inheritance, a determination that those who had rejected their obligations toward dependents and subverted custom to claim land as property for themselves should not be allowed to benefit. It was a powerful message. And there could have been few in Kikuyuland who did not know precisely why ex-Chief Luka had been singled out.

## Courtroom Dramas

Oliver Lyttelton visited Kenya again in May 1953 and was taken to see Lari for himself. There he met survivors and spoke with Chief Makimei and other Home Guards. Lyttelton must surely have grasped the grim desperation of the struggle in these rural communities. He would later recall that he had never before 'felt the forces of evil to be so near and so strong as in Mau Mau'.[78] Back in the calm sanctuary of Government House, Lyttelton discussed the need for further legislative measures with Baring. Loyal Africans needed protection and if something were not done, Baring argued, Lari might dramatically lower morale among the government's African allies. Those wavering needed reassurance. Baring wanted to bring the Lari culprits speedily before the courts, see them convicted and take them to the gallows. Better justice through due process than the retribution and vengeance of vendetta killings.

Some steps had already been taken. Within two weeks of Lari, and before Lyttelton's visit, the range of capital offences had been greatly extended. Kenya's judiciary had stubbornly resisted settler pressures to extend the death penalty, but in the wake of Lari even Whyatt gave way. Enactments issued between April and June 1953 made it a capital offence to administer or freely participate in the taking of a Mau Mau oath; to be known to be a member of a Mau Mau gang likely to carry out acts prejudicial to public order; to be in possession of any item of explosives, arms or ammunition; to consort with those likely to carry out acts prejudicial to public order; or to consort with persons whom it was reasonable to know were carrying arms or ammunition. The provisions to convict those 'consorting' had far-reaching implications. Anyone identified as having been with any Mau Mau group might now be hanged. Lyttelton had backed Baring's judgement. However, the new capital offences would hugely increase the number of cases coming before the Supreme Court, at a time when there was already a backlog of several hundred cases waiting to be heard. Officials in London had been very wary of the suggestion that Kenya should set up special courts, and before arriving in Nairobi Lyttelton had warned Baring that he would need to make a strong case if the legal changes were to get through.

Draft proposals for the creation of new Special Emergency Assize Courts had reached London in mid-April. The courts would have authority to hear only cases relating to Emergency Powers, clearing all Mau Mau cases out of the High Court. There would be no preliminary hearing – Mau Mau capital offences would come straight to the Special Assizes, removing them from the magistrates' courts altogether. The special courts would sit in Nairobi, Nakuru, Githunguri (in Kiambu), Thika, Nyeri, Nakuru and (latterly) Meru and Embu, so that cases could be heard in the localities where the offences had been committed. To staff these special assizes, several of Kenya's most experienced magistrates would be declared special acting judges, and given the full powers of a Supreme Court judge. Other judges might also be recruited from outside the colony. (In the event, two retired judges were brought in from London.) Special sittings of the appeal court would also be arranged, to prevent a build-up on death row. These changes were presented in neutral terms, with no suggestion that the accused would be in anyway disadvantaged.

Though Baring brusquely defended the proposals as a necessary 'gesture to public opinion', officials in London thought that any local advantage would be vastly outweighed by adverse response in Britain and internationally. There was a strong and growing lobby in Britain in favour of the abolition of the death penalty, and there were sure to be questions asked in parliament about the nature of the Kenyan legislation. With this in mind, Lyttelton wrote on 28 April with instructions *not* to announce changes to legal procedures until London had agreed. After further pressure from Baring, Lyttelton wrote again on 7 May saying that he would support the proposals in principle, despite a number of serious worries. The threat of settler violence and Home Guard reprisals loomed large, with Baring giving the impression that Kenya was rushing towards mob rule. The colony's legal officers also stressed the tremendous strain on the legal system caused by the Lari massacre. Barclay Nihill, one of Kenya's most respected Supreme Court judges, warned that the whole legal system would collapse if there were to be another massacre on this scale. Baring reinforced the point by reporting rumours that other attacks were planned. This calculated brinkmanship nibbled away at the resolve of the anxious Lyttelton, who was reluctant to spike the guns of his Governor at a moment of real crisis.[79]

Baring played upon the fact that the white highlanders were liable to take the law into their own hands. Officials in London were even alarmed by the 'liberal' settler leader Michael Blundell. When news of Lari broke, Blundell was in London and went at once to the Colonial Office. He demanded that the legal process be dramatically accelerated to get the culprits to the gallows as swiftly as possible. This could be achieved, he asserted, only if magistrates were given powers over emergency capital cases, if the appeal process was removed completely, and if the Governor reviewed the death penalty without reference to advice. Blundell presented these as the views of liberal, fair-minded settlers.[80] Meanwhile, his settler colleagues back in Nairobi had asked Baring for executions without appeal and within twenty-four hours of conviction.[81] Roberts-Wray, the senior legal adviser to the Colonial Office, was outraged. Blundell argued that these measures would 'result in expeditious justice'; Roberts-Wray thought it more likely to lead to 'expeditious injustice'. 'He [Blundell] thinks in the present circumstances it would be better to hang an innocent African occasionally then to tolerate protracted legal proceedings,' commented Roberts-Wray. 'I cannot agree. I must adhere to the principle upon which I have been brought up, that it is better for 10 guilty men to go free than for one innocent man to be condemned.'[82]

The worst of the settler demands would be resisted by London. It was more difficult to dismiss the considered views of the Governor. Blundell's 'liberal' belligerence was echoed in Baring's dire warnings of settler reaction. On 11 May, just prior to Lyttelton's departure for Nairobi, Baring had written again to prepare him for the burden of their discussions over the need for legal reform:

You should know that the question of summary justice is still the most
burning issue here, not only among Europeans, but amongst loyal
chiefs, headmen, Home Guard, and loyal Africans generally, who are
quite unable to understand why it should take weeks and months to
complete criminal proceedings against the terrorists after arrest.
Recent Mau Mau gangs have been operating in far greater force than
ever before, and fighting has become far more fierce. The result is,
that in the very near future, we shall certainly be faced by so great a
number of capital cases that it will become more urgent than ever to
devise a means to administer criminal justice more speedily than is
practicable at present.[83]

Faced with pressure of this kind, officials in London had little room for
manoeuvre. By the time that Lyttelton left for Nairobi, the consensus
had emerged that Baring's proposals should be reluctantly accepted *so
long as* the Governor was able to give assurances about the appeals process.
At his meeting with Baring at Government House, on 17 May Lyttelton
therefore gave his verbal consent to the establishment of the special
assizes.[84]

On returning to London Lyttelton had now to explain the background
of the scheme to his Cabinet colleagues. The strain upon the existing
legal system as the crucial issue, he contended, telling the Cabinet that
more than 200 people might be hanged as a result of the Lari incident
alone. The point struck home, but the implications greatly alarmed the
Prime Minister. Churchill reacted strongly to the suggestion that there
might be anything resembling 'mass executions' in Kenya. To execute
such large numbers was not in the PM's view either 'necessary or
desirable'. Thrown onto the defensive, Lyttelton reassured the Cabinet:
'We should not wake up and find that large numbers had been hanged,
since the accused had the right of appeal.' After the Cabinet meeting,
Lyttelton sent an urgent telegram to Baring: 'All of this is likely to be a
troublesome question,' he wrote, 'and I wanted to give you the earliest
warning of the PM's attitude.' But Baring was undaunted by Churchill's
political anxieties. He reminded Lyttelton: 'The main pressure for executions comes from the Kikuyu and not the Europeans.'[85] After Lari,
Governor Baring now had the bit firmly between his teeth.

Regulations for the new Emergency Assize Courts were approved in
Kenya on 12 June 1953, though London had not scrutinized the details.[86]
It was an oversight the Colonial Office would come to regret. Over the
next six months the courts caused growing concern. It was not until
July, in response to questions from MPs, that Roberts-Wray came to
appreciate that the removal of committal proceedings had, in effect,
denied the accused the opportunity to know the nature of the evidence

that would be brought before the court. Too late, Roberts-Wray declared this to be 'a cause for serious concern'.[87] 'It needs no argument to demonstrate,' he now declared, 'that any accused person will be grossly hindered in his defence if he comes to his trial knowing nothing of the evidence to be given against him.' Attempts to alter the regulations brought a cool response from Baring, who pointed out that backsliding would be 'politically very difficult'.[88] Concessions were eventually made to allow the defence counsel to see witness statements for the prosecution in court, but in practice these were presented too late to be of much use.

Having allowed Baring to have his way, London could not now easily retract. Baring ruthlessly exploited the advantage. In August he pushed through a measure to allow summary dismissal of appeals if no obvious legal ground could be established, a measure the Colonial Office had earlier refused.[89] Lyttelton's promises to Churchill were already beginning to ring hollow. The Kenya situation was slipping out of London's control. While Lyttelton still backed Baring in public, his officials were increasingly anxious in private. As the Special Emergency Assizes began their work, other worries would surface, among them the inexperience of the acting judges brought onto the Bench to serve in these courts, and the indignity shown to the accused in mass trials, where more than fifty persons stood in the dock together. The Lari trials would feature very prominently in these criticisms.

Baring did not wait for the new regulations but pushed the first few Lari trials through the courts under the old system. As early as 7 April he had told London that up to 500 of the 2000 suspects then held 'in cages at Uplands' would face murder charges.[90] Before the end of the next week, on 13 April, the committal proceedings for the first Lari trial had begun. It was staged in converted buildings at the Githunguri Teachers' Training College, a few miles to the east of Lari. The college had been founded by Mbiyu Koinange, in January 1939, after his return from the United States. The Koinange family were the main benefactors of the college, but its running costs were raised from voluntary public contributions. Jomo Kenyatta had joined Mbiyu at Githunguri on his return to Kenya in 1946. Kenya's Europeans believed that the college was a front for raising funds for the Mau Mau cause. The government had closed the college, but it still stood as a symbol of Kikuyu resistance. Here, in the Kikuyu heartland of central Kiambu, two courthouses were set out for the Lari trials, with holding pens for the prisoners; and beside them, behind a high fence, a pair of gallows was constructed.[91] The intentions of the colonial government were clear for all to see.

Though the shadow of the gallows darkened the Lari courtrooms, Attorney-General Whyatt did his best to see that the rudiments of justice were adhered to. Finding defence barristers proved tricky. A handful of the wealthier among the accused were able to engage lawyers. For the others, counsel was assigned through the system of paupers' briefs. The administrative staff in Kiambu went out of their way to make life as difficult as possible for the barristers who came to Githunguri for the trials. Kenya's only African lawyer, Chiedo Argwings-Kodhek, was singled out for special attention. Argwings-Kodhek had been called to the Bar at Lincoln's Inn in 1951, returning to Kenya with his Irish-born wife a year later. Offered a job in the Department of the Attorney-General, but at a third of the salary of his white peers, he had turned his back on government service and gone into private practice. He was a close associate of many KAU members, and at the outbreak of the Emergency he willingly took briefs to defend those accused of Mau Mau offences. By 1953 many of those who came before the courts charged with Mau Mau crimes requested that he defend them, even though they had no means to pay his fees. Much of the work Argwings-Kodhek did in the Mau Mau trials was therefore at the paltry rates of paupers' briefs – fees that barely covered his costs. So many of these did Argwings-Kodhek take that Kenya's white settlers called him 'the Mau Mau lawyer'.[92]

At Githunguri he fought a running battle with officialdom. As an African, he required a special pass to visit any area affected by the Emergency, and this provided opportunities for repeated harassment by police officers and KPR demanding to 'see his papers'. In the worst example of interference, Argwings-Kodhek was arrested at Uplands on the grounds that he did not possess the relevant pass permitting him to visit Kiambu. When he presented instead his letter of authorization from the Registrar to the Supreme Court, it was brushed aside. The local magistrate, Mr Baxter, declined to acknowledge the letter from the Registrar, and promptly found Argwings-Kodhek guilty, fining him 50 shillings.[93] This was wilful obstruction, designed to humiliate and dispirit Argwings-Kodhek. Many of his Asian colleagues, including Ajeet Singh, A. R. Kapila and Fitz de Souza, also accepted paupers' briefs in Mau Mau cases. They were all roundly criticized for doing so, and all were subjected to the spiteful petty interference of police and European district officers; but it was Argwings-Kodhek who was most frequently the victim of the indignities imposed by a callous and disregarding administration.

Contempt for the rights of the Mau Mau accused was expressed in other, less subtle ways. In the midst of the Lari trials, Blundell tried to have the paupers' briefs withdrawn for all Mau Mau cases. He objected to the array of lawyers that sometimes gathered in the mass trials, with as many as seven or eight barristers defending groups of accused. Blundell argued that this was too costly, and that a limit should be set. He also wanted means-testing introduced, so that those accused might pay for their own defence.[94] It was not justice the settlers wanted: it was retribution; and they didn't much care how they got it.

The lust for retribution acted as a powerful force throughout the nineteen Lari capital trials. From April until December 1953 Lari dominated Kenya's courts. In the largest trial, eighty-three accused persons stood together, numbers draped around their necks to ease identification. Defence counsel took briefs for groups of defendants; the courtroom was crowded with barristers, jostling to challenge the prosecution and cross-examine the witnesses. Several senior investigating officers spent practically the entire five months in court, moving from one case to the next in rapid succession. Key witnesses found themselves in the dock for days on end. Many African witnesses appeared in several different trials. The larger trials all lasted for more than a month.

For the single judge presiding, the complexities of proceedings so large and prolonged demanded keen attention. It was exhausting. In the mass trials, each individual accused had to be disposed of in turn, so the judge needed to be diligent in keeping notes and tracking the precise evidence against each. The unfamiliarity of Kikuyu names often bamboozled the Bench. The evidence hinged upon simple questions of identification. The Crown relied upon the evidence of survivors. Among them were leading loyalists, men such as Makimei and Headman Paulo, who had fought for their lives on 26 March; but most witnesses were women, and many were children and teenagers. All had named their attackers, then picked them out in the many identification parades. Their eyewitness accounts of the death and destruction were the only real evidence. The people they had accused were well known to them – neighbours, old acquaintances, former workmates, people known on a casual, social basis, sometimes even members of their own extended families. For the victims and the accused alike, the trials were arcane and unfamiliar proceedings, but they were also intensely intimate and emotional. A whole community was drawn into the courtroom, and the scars of its past laid bare.

In the nineteen trials, 309 people stood accused of murders. Another 300 or so of Lari's residents appeared as witnesses, mostly for the prosecution. The stories revealed glimpses of Kikuyu daily life and the intricacies of relationships. Many defendants recounted the past quarrels that fuelled animosity and suspicions, citing land disputes and unfulfilled marriage arrangements. Others said they were accused because they had refused to join the Home Guard: in the intensity of Lari's politics, this implied Mau Mau sympathies. But alongside those who robustly defended themselves were others who appeared to accept their fate. They stood expressionless in the dock, refusing to speak, their dull eyes revealing fear, sadness and resignation. In the yard behind the Githunguri courthouse the gallows awaited. For the most part, the court proceedings were sombre and deeply depressing.

In sharp contrast to the settler-murder cases, where confessions were the lynchpin of the prosecution case, extra-judicial statements rarely featured in the Lari trials. The reasons were pragmatic: the excesses of the Lari investigations were widely known and were at least in part acknowledged by many prosecution witnesses. To lead with confessional statements made before police officers in an investigation where beating and the ill-treatment of suspects were known to have taken place would open the door to criticism, and might result in easy acquittals. The prosecution only offered confessional evidence attested by the magistrate who had assisted in the Lari enquiry, Arthur Cram.

Waittitu Kanini was among the few who were convicted on this basis, from a statement made before Cram and corroborated in court by two Home Guards, both of whom were neighbours of Kanini and 'knew him well'.[95] Kanini was typical of those caught up in Lari's violence. 'On the Thursday night of the trouble I was called by Mwangi Njuna and Nduati,' Kanini told the magistrate. 'They asked me to go with them. We went to the house of Nganga Ngara.' There, Kanini took a Mau Mau oath, and then went with his accomplices to the homestead of the Waweru family. Kanini's account of what happened next is recorded in sparse, halting prose:

> A woman inside the house opened the door and came out and began to run. She was Wangui Nganga. She was carrying a child. They killed her with pangas. I had no panga. The other men had pangas. They also killed the child. When I saw that I ran away. I was chased by Githito [a Home Guard] but he did not catch me and I got away and went home ... I heard of the rest of the killings next morning. This was a bad affair.[96]

In Kanini's own mind, and indeed in the minds of other Africans in the court, he was not guilty of murder: he had accompanied the killers to the Waweru homestead, but he had struck no blow. African assessors sat in each trial to assist the judge, and in this case they declared their opinion that Kanini should be acquitted as 'he had not killed anyone'. It was a distinction that the law did not acknowledge. As an accomplice to the crime, on his own admission, Kanini was as guilty as those who had severed in half the body of Wangui's child.

Ndutumi Nganga was another who went to the Githunguri gallows on the basis of an extra-judicial statement attested by Cram. Nganga was charged with the murder of Mbogwa Mumya, whose eleven-year-old daughter identified him in court as the man who had slashed her father. The statement from Nganga, as recorded by Cram, unquestionably implicated him in the murders. Nganga told Cram how plans for the Lari attack had been laid one week before, on 19 March, when he was summoned to a meeting 'in the bush'. He went on to admit his part in the violence.[97] Cram attested to this statement having been freely made, but he added his own commentary to the text before making his signature. Cram's 'explanatory note' was not read to the court. What it revealed was undoubtedly more than the prosecution wanted the court to hear:

> The deponent [Nganga] was covered with dust and stated he had been beaten by the Home Guard and a European after being hunted and brought into camp. He was sick, vomited twice and had difficulty in moving his limbs. His lips were bleeding. I questioned him most carefully if he had been threatened to make a statement but he denied this firmly and said what he wanted to say was of his own free will. He spoke quite clearly and apparently lucidly and coherently. My impression is that he had some rough treatment on capture but none of this had been directed to making him come before me, at least that is what he says himself.[98]

Cram took many such statements in similar circumstances. His carefully chosen words show him to have been a man struggling to do an honest job in trying conditions.

Another confession was made by Muranja Iguru, who stood trial for the murders of Samson Kariuki's family. In court, Iguru retracted his statement, and told of his interrogation at the hands of three European police officers, who he claimed were drunk. One of these men asked for a whip to be brought. 'When the European brought the whip he hit me with it on the back', Iguru said. 'He then told me that I was one of the people who drank the blood of children and he would shoot me with his pistol. Another European knocked me down and kicked me ... Then two of them beat me severely ... [one of the officers] came with two knives and said that if I did not say everything about the crime he would remove my testicles.'[99]

Others told very similar stories. It must be doubted whether any statement made in the wake of Lari could really be said to have been 'free' from the taint of threat and coercion.

The prosecution built the cases against the Lari suspects primarily on the basis of the eyewitness evidence of survivors. This was powerful and often compelling evidence, but it needed to be grounded in secure identifications. The details of the police identification parades held at

Uplands were crucial. The details of these parades were earnestly disputed in the courtroom. Though the court never explored this issue, it became apparent that Makimei's Home Guard had conducted their own identification parades, usually working with members of the KPR. Josephine Becker, of the CID, referred to these as 'screening' exercises, by which she meant that Makimei was looking for people who were Mau Mau sympathizers.

In reality Makimei was doing rather more than this. He was selecting suspects and then carrying out his own interrogations. Many were beaten by the Home Guard in the Uplands camp. While it was admitted there had been 'rough handling' of prisoners – in the light of the comments of the magistrate, Cram, it could hardly have been denied – European witnesses told the court that they had no knowledge of systematic ill-treatment. This denial was utterly implausible. The geography of the camp at Uplands, and of the police post, meant that all of these activities were conducted in close proximity. Moreover, alongside the police investigation at Lari, intelligence officers, with a special operations role, were free to haul out suspects for questioning, and even to remove these suspects from police custody and take them to other places for interrogation. Among these officers was a Kikuyu-speaking member of the KPR, Dennis Kearney, who directed Home Guard interrogations and consulted with Makimei over suspects. Kearney was widely known by his nickname of *Twatwa*. The nearest English equivalent to this Kikuyu colloquialism is the word 'thwack', representing the sound of people being beaten on the legs by a flexible switch.[100] *Twatwa* was deeply involved in the Lari interrogations.[101] Despite what European officers claimed, the excesses and irregularities of the investigation were by no means confined to the actions of African Home Guard.

The problem of identification plagued the Lari trials from start to finish. When they are viewed as separate, individual cases, it might seem that the many mistakes and uncertainties over the recognition of the accused were simply the product of genuine confusion amid the events of 26 March. It is hardly surprising that traumatized and grief-stricken witnesses, some of them children, should have had difficulty in recalling the precise details of what happened. The defence counsel also did their best to expose inconsistencies in evidence, and there is no doubt they succeeded at times in bamboozling otherwise honourable witnesses who were not used to the adversarial interrogations of the courtroom. Defence counsel such as Ajeet Singh, A. R. Kapila and Argwings-Kohdek all energetically pursued weaknesses in the Crown case, often gaining acquittals as a result. In the face of this hostile questioning the prosecution's case against some of the accused simply fell apart. When these nineteen trials are viewed as a group of related proceedings, however, the individual mistakes, errors and uncertainties take on a more sinister meaning. How thorough was the prosecution in collecting and collating evidence? Did they verify and corroborate the evidence of witnesses? Were the identifications reliable? And were witnesses to be trusted? At best, the Crown was sloppy and hasty in preparing its evidence – there was immense political pressure to bring these cases swiftly to court. At worst, the accumulation of evidence from the courtroom suggests a random, scattergun character of the accusations, a tendency to assumptions of 'guilt by association', and, in the worst examples, strong suspicions of collusion among prosecution witnesses to fabricate evidence. To illustrate these aspects, we will now turn to the stories of the attacks on three of the Lari homesteads – those of Charles Ikenya, Machune Kiranga and Luka Wakahangare, as told in the dramas of the courtroom.

Charles Ikenya was one of the Makimei's staunchest headmen in Lari. Four trials arose from the attack upon his family. In these trials, we see the prominent role played by key witnesses in framing accusations and the grave inconsistencies of the legal system in evaluating these crucial testimonies.

The first Ikenya trial, heard before Acting Justice Salter, saw twenty-six accused in the dock, charged with the murder of Penina, the wife of Headman Charles.[102] The evidence hinged upon the identification of the accused by Charles's surviving wife (Mathae) and daughter (Lois Wanjiru), four of his Home Guard patrol who had tried to fight off the attackers and the mother of his deceased wife. These witnesses gave powerful descriptions of the killing of their relatives and friends. It was a grim and emotionally charged story. But the witnesses were far from consistent. The evidence of Lois Wanjiru, Charles's daughter, was highly suspect. She had picked out several of the accused at parades at Uplands. She made detailed allegations against each man, describing what she claimed to have seen him do. This was dramatic and compelling evidence; but her testimony was immediately undermined: one of the accused could not have been present with the attackers, as she described, because there was 'unassailable and unchallenged evidence that he had been in police custody at the material time'.[103] The man was swiftly discharged.

Lois Wanjiru continued to give evidence against other accused. Salter noted further inconsistencies in her evidence, but on the whole considered her a 'credible witness'. Salter found seventeen men guilty of the murder of Penina. When the convictions came before the appellate court three weeks later, the evidence of Mathae and Lois Wanjiru was called into serious question. As a consequence, five of the men were freed – all of them having been convicted on the evidence of these two women.

Within a week of the first Ikenya trial finishing, Lois Wanjiru and

Mathea were back in the Githunguri courtroom again. This time they received a frosty reception. Judge Mayers was deeply disturbed by the character of Lois Wanjiru's evidence. He catalogued her principal sins: she had misidentified one of the accused in court, despite having claimed to know the man well; she then admitted, under cross-examination, that she had 'been informed by certain other people (including Mathae) of the presence at the scene of the crime of certain persons whose names she then specified'; and she persisted in altering her evidence in court, usually to the disadvantage of the accused. Mayers concluded that he regarded her evidence 'with such suspicion that I can place no reliance upon it at all and do not consider that it can even be treated as slight corroboration of the evidence given by other witnesses for the Crown'.[104]

Clive Salter would preside over two more trials relating to the Ikenya family. In each a single accused would stand in the dock, and in each Lois Wanjiro and Mathea would again be the principal prosecution witnesses. The first of these trials came before Salter on 3 July. It was to be a most extraordinary case. The accused man was Gatenjua Kinyanjui. A senior elder of fifty years of age, Kinyanjui was a prosperous man in the Lari area, with three wives and several children. He was not an associate of Makimei or of Luka, and the Home Guard at Lari suspected him of involvement in the administration of Mau Mau oaths. Kinyanjui was charged with the murder of a male child in the homestead of Charles Ikenya. Lois Wanjiru and Mathea told the court that they had seen him hacking at the body of the young boy, both again giving powerful eyewitness testimony. Salter praised the witnesses, stating that he had no reservations in accepting their account of events and in dismissing the alibi offered by Kinyanjui.

It was an alibi of a most unusual kind. Kinyanjui told the court that he had been arrested by Home Guard on 6 February 1953 and taken to Uplands police post, where he had remained in custody up until the time of the massacre. This was not disputed by the prosecution, who instead alleged that Kinyanjui must have escaped from police custody sometime during the day of 26 March, in time for him to take part in the massacre. They could not say how he had escaped; nor could they explain why no one appeared to have noticed that he was missing. They were only able to confirm that Kinyanjui was back in police custody a few hours after the massacre, taken in during the round-up of suspects.

This, then, was the second man to be accused by Lois Wanjiru who would seem to have been in police custody at the very time he was supposed to have participated in the Lari massacre. In the previous case Salter had immediately discharged the falsely accused man. This time the prosecution's extraordinary claims were corroborated by three Lari Home Guards. These men swore to having seen Kinyanjui at liberty on the afternoon of 26 March. Their statements, combined with the evidence of Lois Wanjiru and Mathae, were the only basis of the prosecution case. Incredibly, Salter chose to disbelieve all the evidence offered by the defence and to accept the evidence offered by the prosecution, despite its many oddities. Kinyanjui was found guilty as charged and sentenced to hang.

The case did not come to appeal until 14 September. The judges sitting on the Appellate Bench could hardly disguise their contempt for Salter's findings. Reviewing the case papers, they found that the evidence as to the identity of Kinyanjui 'was certainly unsound', that the evidence of the Home Guards who claimed to have seen Kinyanjui at liberty was 'at least in part elaborated' and 'may even have been concocted', and that the claim of his escape from custody was 'utterly implausible'. Salter was sternly reprimanded for having neglected to give sufficient weight to the evidence put forward by the defence counsel, and the conviction quashed.[105]

In the last of the Ikenya trials, one week after Kinyanjui's conviction, Salter, Lois Wanjiru and Mathea were back in court yet again. This time, the two women gave 'emphatic' evidence that they had witnessed Njehia Njuguna hack at the body of Charles Ikenya's wife Penina with an axe. Neither woman had named nor identified the accused until one month after the attack. Njehia was yet another 'enemy' of Makimei, who had refused to join the Home Guard and who had long been suspected of Mau Mau sympathies. Njehia spoke eloquently in his own defence, denying the charges and giving the court a detailed account of his activities on the day of the massacre. He admitted that he knew many people who had been involved in the murders, and made no secret of the animosities that had driven the community to this awful night of violence; but he strenuously denied his own complicity. He called a neighbour as a corroborating witness and this man was able to confirm everything Njehia had said. Salter was unmoved: Njehia's witness had been accused in another of the Lari trials, and although he was acquitted of the charge of murder, Salter thought this damaged the defence. In his summing-up the judge stated his opinion that both the accused and his witness were 'unconvincing and did not impress me as being truthful'. Stung by earlier criticisms from the appellate judges, Salter was now determined to defend his findings more categorically and thus reduce the likelihood of his verdict being overturned. This time he took greater care to deal with the inconsistencies in the prosecution evidence, quizzing Lois Wanjiru and Mathea and addressing any remaining ambiguities in his summing-up. Having carefully explained his reasoning in accepting the testimony of Lois Wanjiru, Salter declared her to be 'a most convincing witness. Her demeanour was quiet and straight-forward and her evidence unexaggerated.'[106] This left little scope for the appeal judges to challenge the findings of the court. Njehia's appeal was dismissed on 9 September, and Salter's conviction confirmed.

In this woeful process, covering four separate trials over a period of two months, judges sparred with one another but the law did not learn from its own experience. The key prosecution witness, Lois Wanjiru, was dismissed by one judge as unreliable and deceitful, but praised by another as convincing and truthful. Her testimony, along with that of her close friend Mathea, had brought fifty-four men to trial, eighteen of whom went to the gallows. Traumatized by their ordeal, and fearful of further recriminations, the two women had spent the weeks after the massacre cooped up in the camp at Uplands police post. There they saw the processions of suspects being taken for interrogation, and watched the endless identification parades. They talked with other survivors and sat into the night with Makimei and his Home Guards. Their accusations had slowly emerged out of these interactions with survivors and other Kikuyu loyalists. Collusion, manipulation and suggestion may have been purposeful and deliberate, but it may also have merged imperceptibly into false memory, fuelled by anxiety, trauma, stress, grief and fear. Lois Wanjiru and Mathea were victims as well as accusers. In the evidence of these young women, the fine line between guilt and innocence was obscured in a fog of collusion, deceit, and past animosity.

The second example we shall consider focuses upon the single trial of fifty-two suspects charged with the attack upon the family of the Home Guard Machune Kiranga. This case opened before Acting Justice Harley on 29 June 1953, and was not completed until 18 September, when forty-eight of the accused were convicted and sentenced to death – more convictions than in any other Lari trial. This case reveals the many ways by which vengeance influenced the trials, the finger of accusation being pointed at all those who were suspected of rebel sympathies. For Machune Kiranga and his Home Guards the search for the Lari culprits became a kind of witch-hunt. In this they were supported by colonial officers and by the police, though, as we shall see, not by the senior judiciary, for, in a dramatic and defiant gesture, the appeal judges over-turned all forty-eight of Acting Justice Harley's convictions in this case.

The attack on the Kirangas had been widely reported in the press coverage of the massacre back in March. Machune Kiranga's wife Wanjiru survived the assault; but her tragedy had been the slaughter of her two young children, one a baby, the other a boy of two years. In court, she told her story with a cold, quiet detachment. Her misery was palpable. Wanjiru's husband Machune was an entirely different witness. His fury still burned red-hot.[107] A large and strong man of around fifty, Machune was Chief Makimei's senior headman. A staunch Christian and loyalist, he proudly told the court that he had been a Home Guard 'since the beginning of the Emergency', describing the many troubles with Mau Mau supporters, who were in the majority among Lari's residents. He told the court that he knew of his danger, and had even dug a pit with a trapdoor under his bed, so that he might hide 'if Mau Mau came to kill me'. It was the pit that had saved Wanjiro and three of the children. They had managed to clamber down into the hole and pull the trapdoor shut before the attackers broke into their hut. But the pit was too small to hold all the family, and the other children had perished.

Unlike Wanjiro, Machune was talkative and animated, responding in a rush of words to the probing of the prosecution, but too easily goaded into anger by the five defence lawyers who lined up to quiz him. His story was filled with detail. Machune had been out with his Home Guard patrol on the night of the attack, visiting the homes of suspected Mau Mau supporters. As he spoke, he pointed to several of the accused in the dock, asserting they had been absent that night. The implication of their guilt was clear; and Machune had evidence to support his assertions: in each of the houses the Headman had taken a thumbprint or a signature from the wife of the missing man. Asked whether this was usual, Machune explained: 'No, there was no procedure in that respect, but what happened was that after visiting five houses and finding no man in the house I suspected there was something unusual and I began this procedure of taking thumbprints of all those who were absent.'

When Machune had seen flames rising from Luka's place, he had realized that an attack was indeed under way and rushed back to his homestead. He had arrived just before an army of some 200 attackers swarmed over his farm. Terrified, Machune and his Home Guard patrol had not rushed to the defence of the Kiranga family, but instead had scattered and fled. Only one man, Nganga Ngara, had hesitated as the attackers came through the gate. He had been caught not ten yards from the hiding place Machune had taken, in a thick hedge on the perimeter of the property, and mercilessly hacked down as his headman looked on. Machune was no hero. As he had cowered in the hedge he had watched the many atrocities committed against his family by persons he recognized as fellow Lari residents. When he could stand it no more, he had turned away and run to the Uplands police station.

Over seven days in the witness box, Machune's accusations poured out in a torrent. He named fifty men, and described the part that each took in the attack. Some were accused of murdering Ngara, others of slaughtering the children as they ran from a hut, others of setting light to the thatch, others of simply being in the compound. All of this he claimed to have witnessed over the few minutes he had crouched in the hedge, watching the carnage in his compound.

It seemed implausible that he could have seen so much and remembered it so well. The defence counsel tried to unpick his evidence, but they were keener to undermine his character. It was not difficult. Machune was a man with an interesting past. He had a fiery temper and was inclined to acts of violence. He had been prosecuted for assault on several occasions. Though most of these cases had resulted in acquittal, he had once been fined and in another case sentenced to five months' imprisonment. Several of the accused claimed that he had abused them; some said he had victimized them because of past disputes over land, others that he had tried to extort bribes from them in return for not reporting minor misdemeanours, such as illegal trading in liquor – an activity in which Machune himself allegedly participated. Many claimed they had been beaten by Home Guards under Machune's direction. As this catalogue of accusations was put to Machune in cross-examination, he finally lost his temper. 'I came here to testify about my children and my family,' he exploded. 'The Indian advocates [the defence counsel] have advised their clients to come here and speak ill against me. The Indians are the people who are promoting Mau Mau in this country.' Acting Justice Harley told him to calm down, but the proceedings continued in an intense atmosphere of bitterness and distrust.

Of all the defendants, Duncan Mahinda produced the strongest alibi against Machune's accusations. Animosity between the two was acknowledged – Machune admitting to a long-running land feud that had been decided in favour of Mahinda's father. A well-educated and prosperous businessman, Duncan claimed that Machune had continued to persecute his family in revenge for this decision. On hearing that he was wanted in connection with the Lari massacre, Duncan had gone to a lawyer in Nairobi and made a voluntary statement. Duncan was the owner of the Nairobi General Provisions Store, in the city's Pumwani location. He produced invoices and stock books to show that he had been at the store all day on 26 March. Seven witnesses were brought forward to support his claim that he had eaten there at 8p.m. that evening, among them an Asian businessman, an Arab trader and a Luo friend from Nairobi.[108] Yet Machune said he had seen Duncan Mahinda directing the attackers and himself slashing at the victims. Machune had picked Duncan out at an identification parade on 11 April at Uplands.[109] The defence counsel put it to the court that this parade had been a farce, the final act in what amounted to a deliberate plot to frame Duncan – a plot in which even Chief Makimei was implicated, for he gave evidence to the court to contradict Duncan's alibi, claiming that he had seen the accused in Lari on the afternoon before the massacre. Acting Justice Harley preferred to believe the evidence of the loyal Chief, and so dismissed the claims of Duncan's seven witnesses as an elaborate concoction.

Among the other accused men were several who, like Duncan, were in business on their own account. All owned shops or eating-houses in the Lari area, or dealt in supplying vegetables to Nairobi or other more distant markets. These retailers and wholesale traders had been subjected to investigation by Makimei and Machune earlier in the year, when their account books had been seized in an effort to identify those who might be acting as treasurers or fund-raisers for Mau Mau. None had been charged with any offence. In court these men now suggested that Machune had continued to harass and intimidate them. One or two made thinly veiled hints at extortion.

Among these accused was Mwangi, a business partner of Duncan Mahinda, to whom the prosecution paid close attention. The account books taken from Mwangi after the Lari massacre seemed to show 'deposits' made at his shop, without the apparent purchase of goods. 'Were you collecting subscriptions in the shop?' the prosecution asked Mwangi. He explained that he gave credit to regular customers, and acted as banker for others, who then received discounts. Mwangi was the local banker and moneylender.[110] The prosecution thought he was collecting money for Mau Mau.

In no other Lari trial was the evidence so hotly contested. As accusations and counter-accusations swirled around the courtroom, Acting Justice Harley showed signs of losing track of events. He frequently interrupted both prosecution and defence counsel to ask additional questions and to seek clarification; but clarity was elusive – especially when it came to the crucial evidence of the principal witness, Machune. Harley plainly admitted as much in his summing-up. He conceded that it contained 'obvious and frequent discrepancies', that reports of his statements and the identifications of suspects 'did not tally', and that there were frequent 'contradictions and omissions'; but were these inconsistencies 'the result of normal human fallibility, or the product of deliberate dishonesty?' the judge asked. Harley gave Machune the benefit of doubt, finding forty-eight of the fifty-two accused guilty as charged.[111]

The appeals were heard on 1 December 1953. The appeal judges were deeply alarmed when they reviewed the trial papers. Harley had openly and categorically contradicted himself, in highlighting the discrepancies in Machune's evidence in his detailed summing-up but then declaring his complete faith in the same evidence in his judgment. No fewer than twenty-nine of the forty-eight convicted men had been accused and identified by Machune and Machune alone. In all the remaining convictions Machune's evidence was a significant element in the prosecution's case against the accused. It had surely been incumbent upon the judge to address the evidence against each individual accused man, but Harley had not done so. On this point alone the sentences were quashed.

*The Times* carried a full report of the verdict of the appeal court on 2 December, highlighting the doubts cast upon Machune's evidence and the criticism of Harley.[112] Inevitably, Lyttelton was confronted by questions in parliament.[113] This was the kind of scandal the Secretary of State had feared all along, and he now wrote to Baring asking for the figures on the other Lari trials. The reply was sparse, but reassuring: there had been no other case of this kind, and in the Lari trials to date acquittals greatly outnumbered convictions. A relieved Lyttelton was able to report that the appeal court had made no criticism of mass trials *per se*, and that in this case the outcome was due to errors of a technical nature, committed by a judge who had limited experience.[114] As would become their habit over the next two years, Nairobi's senior officials had chosen to place the blame upon the wayward actions of an individual, rather than on the wayward character of the system over which they presided.

The fuss died down in London a good deal quicker than in Nairobi. A storm of settler protests blamed the government for having failed to adopt measures that would see justice done. Whyatt was again the butt of criticism, though he thought Harley's spectacular disgrace had long been an accident waiting to happen. The two had known one another as law students in London. Harley then left legal practice to join the International Brigade in Spain, their paths crossing again upon Whyatt's arrival in Kenya in 1951, where Harley had settled and become a magistrate. Only a few months before the Emergency, the Chief Justice had elevated him to Acting Judge – much to Whyatt's dismay: 'He has always been difficult and troublesome,' Whyatt wrote to Roberts-Wray after the appeal court ruling, 'but it is difficult to take any steps in regard to matters of this kind until the Judge concerned commits a grievous judicial error which calls down upon him the criticism of the Court of Appeal.' To keep him out of harm's way, Harley was now assigned work only on civil cases.[115]

In all of this, the principal witness, Machune Kiranga, was quietly forgotten. Was his evidence against the accused men truthful? Or had he conspired with others of his family, and other Home Guards, to make accusations against those they suspected of being Mau Mau supporters? If he did so, as the defence counsel claimed, then he was guilty of perjury; but we should not imagine that all of those accused by Machune were innocent. Among their number is at least one man who has, in recent years, privately confessed to the part he played in the attack upon Machune's family.[116] The sad truth was that in the Lari trials many of the innocent were hanged alongside the guilty, while many others among the guilty walked free. It was little wonder that Kikuyu thought British justice to be a haphazard and random affair.

Our final example features the trial of those charged with the murders in Luka Wakahangare's homestead. This momentous trial began on 3 September, before Acting Justice Clive Salter. Judgment would not be delivered until three days before Christmas, on 22 December. It was a gruelling trial. The survivors from Luka's homestead had been more reluctant than most to speak after the massacre. Many of them had been severely wounded. Their evidence, with the accusations it contained, was only slowly pieced together. The parades at which the accused were picked out were among the last held at Uplands, on 19 and 25 April. The lateness of these parades, and the role of Makimei, Machune and other Home Guards in the compilation of lists of named suspects for the attack on Luka's *boma*, gave rise to suspicions that the Wakahangare family members might have had the opportunity for collusion in shaping their evidence. From this trial we gain a clear sense of the deep fear and bitter retribution that masked everything at Lari in the wake of the massacre.

Among the principal witnesses in this case was Luka's younger brother and driver, Benson Njenga. He identified twenty-nine of the accused brought to the court. Benson named some people immediately after the attack, but he did not give other names until several weeks later. Similar delays were apparent in the evidence given by other key witnesses. Luka's wife Kahuria eventually identified twenty-two accused, and she, too, did so over several weeks. Another wife, Gacheri, was another who took time to recall the names of her assailants. Gacheri had been savagely slashed in the attack, losing an arm, and her children killed. She was interviewed in hospital after the massacre, but she had been reluctant to say very much. She returned to Uplands early in May, to live in the police compound with other members of her family. A special identification parade was hurriedly arranged for Gacheri on 15 May, when she announced that she was willing to identify her attackers. At that moment a group of several hundred suspects were about to be released from the Uplands prison camp because there was no evidence against them. Instead of being released the men were lined up and prepared for the parade. Despite still suffering the effects of her wounds, and being barely able to walk, Gacheri spent four hours that afternoon, moving slowly up and down the rows of suspects. *Tiwatwa* – Dennis Kearney – accompanied Gacheri, translating her Kikuyu accusations into English, and recording the details against the name of each man she picked out. At this hastily arranged and prolonged parade Gacheri accused twenty-five men.

The defence counsel were especially concerned about the circumstances in which Gacheri had picked out the accused, and the role of Makimei. In cross-examination it was put to Makimei several times that he had influenced other witnesses in making accusations. The Chief bluntly denied all such suggestions. Hurst, for the prosecution, upheld Makimei's integrity, and instead explained that fear and trauma were reason enough for the initial reluctance of the Wakahangare family to speak out. Only as they slowly recovered from their ordeal did they gain the courage to speak and to name their assailants, she contended. As the trial proceeded, this line of argument came to be known as 'the fear hypothesis'. For the prosecution, this useful catch-all explanation glossed over many otherwise puzzling aspects in the evidence – not least the peculiar timing of Gacheri's decision to speak out and accuse her attackers after many weeks of silence.

In his summing-up, Salter decided to accept the 'fear hypothesis'. It was a crucial decision. Benson Njenga and Gacheri were the only witnesses to name many of the accused, and Salter was able to deploy the 'fear hypothesis' to explain the delays and contradictions in their evidence. The appeal judges took the same view, stating that 'the witnesses were frightened to say very much at first because of the terrifying ordeal they had been through, and through fear perhaps that if they gave names, further punishment might overtake them'.[117] 'So far as women witnesses are concerned,' the appeal judgment continued, 'we regard this "fear hypothesis", as it has been termed during the hearing of this appeal, not only as reasonable but as highly likely.'

The 'fear hypothesis' applied to the evidence of Benson Njenga in a rather different sense. He had avoided serious injury in the attack – although he narrowly escaped death when an attacker shot at him, the bullet grazing his ear – and had taken an active role in the investigation of the crime, assisting Makimei and the Home Guard in rounding up suspects; but Benson's initial enthusiasm for this task later waned. He became less talkative, and he mysteriously 'lost' the list of suspects' names he had earlier compiled. In court Benson's hesitant and nervous evidence betrayed a man who had lost his nerve. Reading the case papers, one cannot escape the thought that Benson's reluctance was prompted by intimidation and threat – that he had perhaps been warned against assisting in the prosecution.

Benson had reason enough to be fearful. During May, after the evidence against the Lukas' attackers had been compiled, one of the key interpreters who had assisted in recording the evidence of the family was found murdered. Then, in the midst of the trial, another interpreter from Lari was found dead. Venasio Wakahangare was Luka's eldest son, and stood to inherit a large portion of his father's estate. Well educated, literate and with good spoken English, Venasio had come to Lari after the massacre to be with his family. He spent the following weeks working as an interpreter with the police at Uplands. He assisted in the interviews of many of his distressed relatives, compiling the lists of names of those who would be accused of the attack upon Luka's homestead.[118] At the end of April, Venasio returned to Nairobi to resume his employment as a clerk and driver with a European businessman. Among his duties, Venasio drove a haulage van, supplying catering to the staff at Nairobi's Eastleigh Aerodrome. The van was well known in the commercial areas of Nairobi's Eastlands. On the afternoon of 22 October 1953, exactly one year after the declaration of the Emergency in Kenya and while the prosecution evidence was still being heard in the Luka trial at Githunguri, the Nairobi police were informed that Venasio's van had been abandoned beside a petrol station, on the edge of the Ziwani estate. Trussed up in a gunny sack in the back of the vehicle was Venasio's mutilated body.

Venasio had been warned to take greater care, but the police had not offered him protection. He was an easy target. On the day of his death he was seen by his employer before noon, and sent to Eastlands to collect goods for the aerodrome. The goods were never collected. Venasio died sometime that afternoon. He had been badly beaten, with multiple injuries to his ribs, to his internal organs and to his head. Having lost consciousness from the beating he would almost certainly have died from the blows, but his murderers finally put their victim out of his misery by strangulation.[119] Venasio had been purposefully lured to his death, his murder the result of a well-planned scheme.[120] Mau Mau's assassins had been waiting for the right moment, and the coincidence of the anniversary of the declaration of the Emergency and the process of the Lari trial was too good an opportunity to miss. The British might build gallows at Githunguri, but Mau Mau also knew how to instil fear.

As the Luka trial drew towards a conclusion, in late November 1953, Attorney-General Whyatt found himself seated next to Clive Salter over dinner at a Nairobi function. The two men had a respectful professional relationship, but they were not close. Salter, a Kenya settler and magistrate who had been elevated to the Special Emergency Assize Courts to meet the pressing need of the moment, was a man of robustly conservative views. He was just the kind of settler who was impatient with Whyatt's reluctance to institute special measures to deal with Mau Mau, and had been among those calling for the Attorney-General's head in the wake of the Ruck murders. On his appointment as an acting judge, London officials had worried lest these political attitudes be championed from the Bench.[121] Salter's handling of the Lari trials gave substance to these anxieties, but he now surprised Whyatt by expressing grave misgivings about the conduct of mass trials such as the Luka case. Salter warned

Whyatt that his judgment in the case, soon to be delivered, would contain critical comments about the procedures of the Special Emergency Assize Courts. At seventy-two days' duration, the trial was then the longest legal proceedings in Kenya's history. Salter had found it exhausting, stressful and unmanageably complex. He thought that both defence and prosecution counsel 'had found it difficult to recall the demeanour of witnesses in so large a trial'.[122] With no fewer than ten different defence counsel representing the accused, the interruptions and cross-examinations had seemed interminable, repetitive and confusing.[123] Salter thought there were very real dangers of a miscarriage of justice in these very difficult circumstances.

This was music to Whyatt's ears. The next morning he wrote privately to Roberts-Wray at the Colonial Office to warn of the possibility of adverse publicity. Though he did not say so, Kenya's Attorney-General must have been quietly satisfied that his own objections to the Special Courts were about to be echoed by one of the Colony's most conservative judges.

Whyatt was in for an unpleasant surprise. When Salter delivered his judgment in the Luka trial, on 21 December, he only briefly alluded to the technical difficulties of the trial that Whyatt had thought would be the target of his attack. Instead, Salter pronounced a guilty verdict against twenty-seven of the accused, and then gave vent to his irritation that fifty-six of those charged had *not* been convicted.[124]

> I do not hesitate to say [Salter declared to the court], that the evidence in most, if not all of those cases, gave rise to the strongest suspicion that the accused concerned was in Luka's boma as a member of that evil gang during that attack, and they may well count themselves lucky that justice in our courts is of a standard where suspicion, however strong, is insufficient to support a conviction ... I have reason to suppose that these men will not be allowed, at any rate for a period of time, to have their freedom, but they will be well advised to remember for the rest of their lives that they owe their acquittal in this case to the standards of justice which Our sovereign Lady the Queen commands shall be preserved throughout her Realms.

The hindrance to justice in these mass trials was not, in Salter's view, the danger of wrongful conviction, but the tendency to wrongful acquittal.

Fifteen of the twenty-seven men sentenced to death by Salter were condemned on the identification of a single prosecution witness. Salter, once again, placed complete faith in the evidence of the witnesses for the Crown. His final address to the convicted men in the Githunguri courtroom was typically forthright:

Each of you have been convicted of a foul murder. Not only did you take part in the brutal and savage killing of an ex-chief of your own tribe – Luka – but you took an active part in the butchering in the most bestial manner of women and children of your own tribe whilst they were asleep. That is a massacre which will always go down in history as a disgrace to the members of your tribe who took part in it. I do not deceive myself that any words of mine will have the slightest effect upon you; but let those who share your views realise that you cannot achieve your aims by resorting to unlawful and savage violence, and those who do so will sooner or later themselves be destroyed. There is only one sentence which the law permits me to pass upon you for this offence – and it is a merciful one compared with what you did to your victims. The sentence upon you ... is that you will be hanged by the neck until you are dead.[125]

Learning from Harley's humiliation, Salter took enormous care to explore every possible inconsistency in evidence when delivering his judgment. Two of these twenty-seven men would die in custody before their appeals could be heard, and three others were determined upon medical examination to have been under the age of eighteen at the time of the offence, and so were spared the noose, to be detained 'at the governor's pleasure' instead. The appeals of the remaining twenty-two men were dismissed on 3 March. They would wait another three and a half months on death row before their executions.

## Executions

After the trials, it was time to see the bodies swing. In the old British tradition, Baring's Emergency Committee had discussed the beneficial impact of public executions at Githunguri, to show the Kikuyu the full might of British justice. Though the idea had support, it would never have met with London's approval and no request was made; but Baring had skilfully used the spectre of lynch-law after Lari in forcing Lyttelton's hand to gain consent for the extension of capital offences and the introduction of the Special Assizes. Better the sanitized, procedural niceties of state execution than the vengeance of the mob, he had argued.

Yet even with the new laws on the statute book and the courts in place, getting the guilty men to the gallows proved tricky. By the end of September 1953, six months after the massacre, not a single person convicted of murder at Lari had yet been executed. On 8 October Blundell introduced a Legislative Council debate on the Emergency legal machinery with a scathing attack on Whyatt for the failure to hang the Lari convicts. Blundell once again asked for an acceleration of procedures and the shortening of the right of appeal, while other white highlanders thought that Kenya would do better to adopt martial law, immediately shooting convicts by firing squad on the passing of sentence.[126] Whyatt defended the principles of British justice with his usual firm dignity. Though his speech received prolonged applause, it was the aggressive determination of the white highlander lobby that impressed Baring. The legal department were instructed to speed up the executions.

The problem lay in the East Africa Court of Appeal. By September 1953 it was still usual for there to be a gap of more than three months between conviction and the hearing of an appeal, and a month more might then lapse before the execution was finally carried out. An additional appeal to the Privy Council might add another three months' delay, though such cases were few in number owing to the expense involved (even Argwings-Kodhek charged a minimum of 50 guineas for each appeal to the Privy Council, a fee that might rise to 80 or even 100 guineas if the documents were bulky).[127] Though Whyatt could influence the order in which cases were heard in the Special Assize Courts, it was not so easy to press political considerations upon the judges of the East African Appeal Court, who vigorously defended their independence. It was fortunate for Baring, who was now keen to assuage settler opinion by seeing the Lari convicts hang as speedily as possible, that the appeal court had heard several Lari cases only in September.

Within one week of Blundell's tirade in the Legislative Council, the gallows at Githunguri despatched their first victim. In the bitter cold of the early morning of 15 October, in the hour of grey darkness just before dawn, twelve Lari convicts were hanged at Githunguri. They had waited on death row for five months since Clive Salter had sentenced them to death. The Githunguri gallows was shielded from public gaze, though the contraptions were visible behind the main buildings of the teachers' college. The hangman came up from Nairobi prison the day before to make the arrangements, measuring the drop and testing the mechanism with the grim, methodical precision of his trade. The prison doctor and the Kiambu District Officer were there with the hangman to witness the executions, conducted one after the other at fifteen-minute intervals – long enough to allow the body to be taken down and the gallows reset for the next victim. Once the sombre procession was over, the bodies were bundled into a lorry and removed to Nairobi's Kamiti Prison for burial in unmarked graves.

To publicize the execution of the twelve men, notices were printed in Swaili and Kikuyu and distributed widely throughout the colony that same morning. The condemned men were each named, and it was stated that their crime had been the murder of Penina, the wife of Headman

Charles Ikenya, part of the infamous Lari massacre.[128] The Githunguri gallows would be used on fourteen more occasions before the end of the month, and another fourteen Lari convicts would be executed there during November. The final Lari convicts, the twenty-two men convicted of the murders in Luka Wakahangare's compound, would not come to the gallows until June 1954.[129]

The hangings brought satisfaction to Blundell and his supporters, but they were not at all pleased with the overall outcome of the Lari trials. Given Baring's original estimates to London of how many persons might be hanged for Lari, the number of acquittals arising from the trials seemed very high indeed. From 309 accused persons, only 136 had been convicted, and of these only seventy-one men were finally executed. In the course of the nineteen trials, 120 men had been acquitted, and a further fifty-six were discharged. Fewer than one in four of those accused of murder at Lari had been hanged.

Baring was embarrassed by these figures, and did his best to avoid publicizing them for fear of renewed criticism in Kenya.[130] He had hoped for more hangings, and seemed disappointed that the legal machinery had not managed to achieve better results. Indeed, Baring seems to have shared Salter's view that the accused persons had escaped conviction owing to legal difficulties, rather than because they were innocent of the charges (see table 4.i, p. 349, for a list of the Lari hanged).

Like those who hanged for the murders of European settlers in their farmhouses, those executed for crimes at Lari did not conform to the received image of the heroic Mau Mau freedom fighters. This was no well-drilled army of young disciplined fighters. Lari's violence had been communal, enveloping a wide variety of people. Those who organized the slaughter had come in to Lari from the Aberdares forest, but they were not among the convicts because no one had recognized them. As on the farms, there were doubtless some willing participants among Lari's residents, including those who had been very active in oathing and in collecting funds for Mau Mau. Many others only reluctantly, and with great remorse, joined the mobs that swarmed over the homesteads of the loyalists on the night of 26 March 1953. The proceedings of the Lari trials do not allow us to differentiate easily between these categories of people: The law merely needed to establish to the satisfaction of the judge that the people accused were present at the scene of the crime.

It is difficult to generalize about the social status and background of the seventy-one men that hanged. Only one was a stranger to Lari, though several were men who had returned to the area from the Rift Valley over recent years. The majority were relatively poor, many being landless labourers and casual workers, and most of these men had but little education. These poorer men were generally young, mostly in their twenties. They included men who had worked at the bacon factory in Uplands, and others who sometimes worked in Nairobi. These were precisely the kind of people we might expect to have been supporters of the Mau Mau cause, those marginalized and dispossessed by the resettlement at Lari and the natural enemies of the acquisitive and self-serving ex-Chief Luka; but one in seven of those executed were much wealthier men, mostly of an older generation. These included land-holding farmers, and businessmen of various kinds, most of whom were better educated than their fellows. They represented Lari's 'respectable classes', but they, too, were people at odds with the heavy-handed and extractive behaviour of the Kikuyu chiefs and headmen who ruled over Lari as agents of the colonial state. It was these wealthier men who most often protested that they had been falsely accused on the basis of past disputes over land or commercial rivalries. All of these men had refused to join the Home Guard or identify themselves with the loyalist side. This alone made them suspects in the eyes of Makimei and his followers.

Were the convicted men guilty? This is a dangerous question to ask, but surely an essential one. The investigation of the Lari crimes was deeply flawed, and the court proceedings stripped down to a simple question of fact: was this person present on the night in question? A nagging doubt was present at the time, and has lingered since, that those outsiders who planned and motivated the attack were not amongst the accused. By the nature of the way in which evidence was collected and suspects identified, those prosecuted were inevitably going to be persons *known* to the survivors. Again and again in these nineteen trials the Kikuyu assessors asked for the acquittal of men who were known to have been present at the massacre but who did not use weapons against the victims. Among the local community there was certainly a strong sense that many of those present at the killings were not guilty of murder, and there are many indications that even the assessors thought that Makimei, Machune, Samson Kariuki and their kind had manufactured evidence against their known enemies. The trial transcripts by no means reveal everything there was to know. Lari still holds its secrets.

Whether a man was guilty or innocent, all of those accused of the Lari crimes were punished in one form or another. Those released by the court – the 120 men who were acquitted, the fifty-six who were discharged, and the fifty-eight who had convictions quashed on appeal – did not go free. On their release from custody all were immediately re-arrested and issued with detention orders. These orders allowed the State to detain them without trial under suspicion of Mau Mau activities. Some would be detained in the Emergency prison camps for only a few months; others would be incarcerated for the next five years. While in detention, the property of these men was often seized by their loyalist neighbours. Many returned home to find their lands had been distributed to others, that their wives had been subjected to gross abuses, and that their children had fled to the forests to avoid persecution and exploitation. The harassment of the families of the accused, and of their witnesses, began even as the trials were in process, and drew stern complaints of interference and intimidation from the defence counsel. But the court could do nothing to prevent this victimization.[131]

The State did what it could to protect and restore the lives of those who had been the victims of Mau Mau violence at Lari. An appeal fund was established by the Kenya Red Cross to raise money for the survivors, and by October 1953 £2220 had been collected. This money was spent on 'social work' at Lari among the survivors in the months following the attack, caring for the women and children, and eventually building new houses and providing furnishings and basic household utensils. The government provided pensions for Lari's widows, and paid the school fees of the numerous orphans of the massacre, many of whom were taken in by loyalist Christian families in other parts of Kiambu.[132]

## Colonial Consequences

The Lari massacre became the crucial turning point in the Mau Mau war. On a national scale it changed the character of the military campaign; at a local level it greatly intensified the conflict within the Kikuyu communities. Before Lari the majority of Kikuyu had done their level best to avoid taking sides. After Lari that became increasingly difficult. The fate of the Wakahangare family and their clients stood as a lesson to all; and the violence, having been unleashed on so terrifying a scale on both sides, would now be difficult to restrain. Fear and vengeance marked every aspect of the struggle.

Lari was the war's iconographic moment. The propaganda value of the horror was 'squeezed out to the last drop', in lurid press releases, accompanied, of course, by the gruesome photographs. Headlines around the world told the tale of Kikuyu 'primitive barbarism' and 'blood lust', and it was these images of charred, twisted corpses that provoked Robert Ruark to declaim Mau Mau's 'impulsive savagery'. At Lari, Mau Mau became something evil, to be despised and detested. This was how Mau Mau would for ever be remembered.

As the British propaganda machine exploited the opportunity to the full, the rebels were painted as pitiless souls who had lost any vestige of human dignity. They would now be hunted like animals, and this was no more than they deserved. But while the story of sickening brutality was hashed and rehashed, the state's counter-terror in the aftermath of the attack was only vaguely hinted at, and then most often in terms that gloried in the idea of righteous vengeance against the culprits. The Lari trials revealed plenty of evidence about the mistreatment of suspects in the aftermath of the attack, but at no time was the implicit accusation of systematic state counter-terror explored. Lari's second massacre, conducted in the hot swell of grief and anger, was to be forgotten; British propaganda would see to that.

There were two principal targets for British propaganda over Lari. First, the attack was used to convince public opinion back in Britain of Mau Mau barbarity. Blundell always held the view that if the British public truly understood the character of Mau Mau, then they would better appreciate the need for 'stern measures' and 'appropriate reprisals'. The images of Lari seemed to make the point. Someone in the Office of Information made multiple copies of the prints and circulated them far and wide. It was hoped that the copies sent to Britain would have the greatest impact on the opinions of Kenya's critics, including Marjory Perham, Leslie Hale and Barbara Castle.

The second target for propaganda was Kenya's African population. Luka and his followers were presented as typical of the loyal Kikuyu who were now all potential targets of Mau Mau savagery. The Christian faith of the victims was emphasized (though their Catholicism was not). There were numerous articles in the local-language press, and for weeks after the attack the letters columns still carried commentary on the Lari events and their implications. In their largest venture to date, the Office of Information produced a sixteen-page pamphlet, entitled 'Mau Mau!', printed with a lurid red cover, giving an account in Swahili of Lari, and reproducing several disturbing photographs. The images of Lari were a cold reminder of vulnerability. After Lari no Kikuyu could feel safe.

Lari also had consequences for the colonial government's conduct of the war. The events at Lari and Naivasha shook London out of lingering complacency about the situation in Kenya, and brought about the first really significant changes in the command structure of the security forces. Both reversals were blamed upon a high degree of incompetence. The decision to withdraw British troops from the Lari area the day before the attack, and despite the protests of Chief Makimei, had cruelly exposed British allies to the failings of intelligence. At Naivasha the poor discipline of the police and the disregard for camp security appeared farcical. The ridiculing of the Mau Mau as 'Mickey Mouse', popular among both settlers and the security forces, now suggested an arrogance and complacency that seemed increasingly inappropriate.

A more professional approach was required in both the military and the police. Decisions were therefore taken, during April and May 1953, to change the overall command structure in Kenya and to put in place a new military Commander-in-Chief and a new Commissioner of Police. Each would be required to direct operations effectively *and* possess the moral strength of character to tackle Nairobi's more extreme elements among the Europeans. By now London had realized that those elements were by no means confined to the settler community. Among the senior colonial administrators in Kenya were several hawks, keen to see a more draconian regime imposed under the Emergency regulations. These officials, typified by the likes of Windley and Johnson, lobbied against those doves who took a more cautious line. The Attorney-General, Whyatt, was a favourite target. Never popular with the settlers anyway, Whyatt was bitterly attacked by the hawks after Lari over his reluctance to support the extension of capital offences and new laws imposing increased communal punishments. In the clamour for new powers and sterner punishments, liberal doves such as Whyatt were in danger of being silenced altogether. These disputes added to the Governor's burdens as he looked around him for advice. Baring was notoriously slow in coming to any decision, and the deep divisions among his senior advisers hardly helped. He was anyway not in good health and, after Lari, Lyttelton even wondered whether Baring any longer had the stomach for the fight.[133]

Lyttelton had already come to the conclusion that Police Commissioner O'Rorke certainly did not. O'Rorke was made the scapegoat for the Naivasha debacle, but the truth was that London had already recognized the dangers of an excessive and ill-disciplined police presence and wished to get to grips with the situation. A police commander in an older colonial style, O'Rorke was too ready to defend his men against all criticism and too slow to investigate allegations of excess. His stance reflected a long tradition of coercive methods within the Kenya Police, which London had been made aware of on several occasions in the past but had not, until now, considered to be sufficiently serious to merit interference. O'Rorke now had to go. To sugar the pill of the major shake-up that was required, a visiting Police Commission was appointed to report on the Kenya force and to make the necessary recommendations.[134]

Changes on the military side were more rapidly achieved. 'Loony' Hinde had outlived his usefulness as director of military operations. Having been instructed on coming out to Kenya to 'jolly things along', Major General Hinde took his brief rather too literally. He made no secret of his sympathy for the 'hard-liners' among the settlers, and on his frequent tours of the White Highlands he energetically socialized among them. Once the uprising assumed significant proportions, he was out of his depth both militarily and diplomatically. His cavalier, pro-settler *bonhomie*, coupled with some extravagant use of language, finally landed Hinde in hot water, when a remark made at a private function – 'that 100,000 Kikuyu should be put to work in a vast swill-tub' – was quoted too widely and became the subject of an embarrassing parliamentary question. The British Commander-in-Chief, Middle East, visited Nairobi in May 1953, only a few weeks after Lari, and informed the hapless Hinde that he was to be replaced.[135]

The new appointee was General George Erskine. Having argued his corner before accepting the posting, Erskine began from a stronger position than Hinde had ever achieved. As Commander-in-Chief, Erskine assumed full command of all military units but only took operational control of police and all reservists, including the Home Guard. He had wanted more than this. He asked to be given powers of martial law in the districts affected by the Emergency, which would give him sole authority over the conduct of the campaign without reference to Baring.

For the Colonial Office, this looked too much like an admission of defeat, and they opposed the suggestion. Others in the British government were increasingly nervous in the weeks after Lari that the Kenya situation was slipping out of control, and there was growing support for the idea of a military administration, such as that successfully run by General Templer in Malaya. The Prime Minister had all along been uncomfortable with the approach and methods of the Kenya administration. Having allowed draconian legislation through after Lari, against his own better judgement, Churchill now saw Erskine's efficient calm and pragmatism as a foil to the excitable hawks surrounding Baring. Churchill took a hand in Erskine's appointment and saw to it that he was provided with a letter authorizing the assumption of martial powers, should the situation demand it. It was to be the ailing Prime Minister's only meaningful intervention in Kenya's sad story before giving way to Anthony Eden in April 1955.

Churchill's letter would be like the sword of Damocles dangling above Baring's head. On arriving in Kenya in June 1953 the wily Erskine let it slip that such a document existed, and that he kept it 'nice and handy' in his spectacle case. As he sat in meetings at Government House, he would snap the case open and shut as a useful device for concentrating minds.[136] This did not endear him to those colonial officials and settlers with whom he had to work, but Erskine usually got his way.[137] The new commander would fight many battles in Kenya, political as well as military, and he would win them all. Though the white highlanders did not at the time realize it, Erskine's arrival marked the beginning of the end of their dominance in Kenya.

# 5

# Struggles in the City
# Mau Mau in Nairobi

When, in 1950, Nairobi was declared a city by order of King George VI, the white highlanders celebrated with a parade through the commercial district and a grand reception at the newly renamed 'City Hall'; but as the proud councillors sipped cocktails in the mayoral chambers, in the industrial area to the east Nairobi's African workers downed tools and went on strike. Over the next eight days they brought the empire's newest city to a standstill. Each morning strikers 'streamed like safari ants' to the public meeting grounds.[1] Pickets moved through the industrial estates to consolidate the strike, and scabs had their heads shaved and were made to clean the public toilets. The strikers lit fires in the streets as the police circled in armoured vehicles, firing tear-gas and mounting baton charges to arrest the ringleaders. The thousands in the African crowds wheeled and fled 'like little birds' at the smallest police gesture, only to regroup and gather again to listen to their leaders 'cry for immediate self-government, cheaper maize, or higher wages'.[2] For the underpaid wage-workers and the miserable unemployed alike, the royal charter was nothing more than a symbol of their oppression. The strike was a brief, belligerent show of defiance, deliberately timed to prick the bubble of white self-congratulation. In this 'city in the sun', European achievement and African dissatisfaction were two sides of the same coin. Nairobi was a place of deep contrasts and sharp conflicts.

The visitor from Europe, arriving as Oliver Lyttelton had done at Eastleigh Aerodrome, at once encountered this disconcerting turmoil. The journey from the aerodrome to Government Hill first took the visitor past the Asian residences, 'small, painted stone-block houses with wooden verandas carved in Indian scrollwork'. This comforting order soon disappeared as the road plunged into the dense, turbulent 'native quarter', where African housing intermingled with the 'squirming bazaars' in a jumble of stone, tin, wood, cardboard and sacking. This was Eastlands. The place was teeming with life. The tiny, flyblown shops that lined the road were shabby and poorly stocked. Most were Asian-owned, but some displayed proud signs indicating that a Kariuki or a Kamau had 'come to commerce'. This higgledy-piggledy world was revealed in glimpses of 'shops enclosed by crazy-slanting walls of mud and thatch, or old packing boxes, with lumpy earthen walls and smoke-crusted interiors'.[3]

Along the kerbside the terrific press of humanity scurried about its business, loading barrows and donkey-carts and removing goods from battered old lorries. Behind the rows of small shops that took prime position along the main thoroughfare, narrow lanes and alleys led to a warren of ramshackle houses, shrouded in an umbrella of thin, grey smoke from a thousand cooking stoves. The poverty of the buildings was mirrored in the poverty of the people, poorly dressed in blankets or hanging cloth, or adorned in cast-off clothes of European style, ragged and worn out by use. The vigorous but careworn bustle of the native location only subsided as the traveller reached the edge of the city centre, coming along Delamere Avenue and Government Road. This looked more familiar to the eye of the European visitor. Older colonial-style stone buildings, with pillars and porches, stood alongside newer, modern, multi-storeyed constructions of concrete and glass. The shoppers here were mostly white-skinned, browsing through stores owned by Asians, who stood behind the counter and the till watching their African serving staff with an eagle eye of stern paternalism. In Nairobi the racial hierarchy was always visible. Crossing the railway line and climbing up to Government Hill, the visitor could look back at a fine view of this essentially Europeanized commercial district. The hill had long been the preserve of government officials, who lived in comfortable large houses, set in the midst of flowered gardens but only a short distance from their place of work. On top of the hill, where the cooling breeze rippled through the trees of the Arboretum, was the Governor's residence, and beyond it, to the west, the slowly extending suburbs, where the white highlanders had built their homes.

If the visitor found Nairobi's native location unfamiliar, so too did most of the city's European residents. They knew of it only by repute; and what they knew they did not care for. Unless taken there by the needs of work, few Europeans would ever enter the eastern areas of the city. Squalid and crime-infested, Eastlands was for Africans. It had been this way since the early 1900s. Africans were not welcome in other parts of the town, except as labour. They were not permitted in the bars or cafes of central Nairobi, and the vigilant Asian shop-owner in the business district would seldom allow an African to linger at the window,

Jomo Kenyatta, photographed at the Pan-African Congress meeting in
Manchester, 1945.

The co-defendants at the Kapenguria trial; Paul Ngei, Fred Kubai, Jomo Kenyatta, Achieng Oneko, Kungu Karumba and Bildad Kaggia wait to enter the courtroom.

Kikuyu woman preparing
to assist the security forces
in a sweep through the
forest in search of Mau
Mau, November 1952.

A scene from Chief
Waruhiu's funeral,
Kiambu, October 1952.

Cattle confiscated from the Kikuyu of Nyeri under the collective punishment laws, because they had failed to co-operate in operations against Mau Mau, November 1952.

A scene from the white highlanders' protest at Government House following the Ruck murders, January 1953.

*Above* Defendants in the courtroom during one of the Lari mass trials, each identified by a number draped around their neck.

Defendants in the Lari trials, waiting to go into the courtroom at Githunguri, 1953.

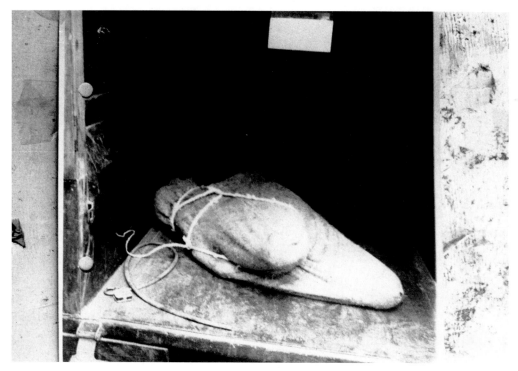

Venasio Wakahangare's body, trussed up in a sack, and left in the back of his delivery van parked on a Nairobi street corner, October 1953.

Evelyn Baring and Oliver Lyttelton at Nairobi airport, April 1953.

'The redoubtable Chief Njiri'; an image of the foremost Loyalist chief, proudly wearing his government medals.

Michael Blundell in 1959.

General China in the courtroom at Nyeri, flanked by armed policemen and still wearing his hospital gown.

never mind enter the store. In deed, if not in law, Kenya's colour bar was vigorously policed in the colony's capital. Black and white rarely mixed in colonial Nairobi, any more than they did in Johannesburg, Durban or Harare, except in the roles of master and servant. And that was how the white highlanders liked it.

As Nairobi celebrated the granting of its city charter in 1950, the future did indeed seem bright for its European citizens. The war years of the 1940s had brought unprecedented growth to the Kenyan economy, with high agricultural prices acting as the catalyst to increased investment. Nairobi began to emerge as the commercial and business centre for the wider region of East Africa. Corporate investors were encouraged by the enhanced capital expenditure of government during these years. A major programme of urban development had begun in the 1940s, funded by colonial grants and by loans raised on the London money markets. Economic growth stoked the fires of European political ambition. Settler leaders began to speak of Nairobi as the flagship capital for a new white dominion in East Africa.[4]

This visionary scheme was encapsulated in the 1948 *Master Plan for a Colonial Capital*, which set out a design for the development of the urban infrastructure of Nairobi for the next twenty-five years.[5] The ostentatious plan featured new administrative buildings set in landscaped public spaces, a modern commercial centre, a greatly enlarged industrial area to attract investment and a vastly improved transport system. There were even to be 'model' housing estates for the better class of African white-collar worker who would be needed to staff this commercial expansion. In 1950, as new African estates were built and Nairobi's business district remodelled in this grand scheme, *National Geographic Magazine* trumpeted the city's arrival as an international destination of note: 'Today Nairobi is popping at the seams with newcomers. Hotels are packed, housing shortage is acute and building costs are high.' Nairobi was booming.[6]

Three years later, economic progress had dampened. Commodity prices fell on international markets, and Kenya's trade suffered. The postwar era of European optimism and African aspiration crumbled away as the municipal authority saw its debt burden mounting faster than its income. Enhanced earnings from rates and municipal services had failed to materialize. The housing schemes that had been the proud symbol of a new colonial commitment to urban welfare could not in fact be made to pay at sub-economic rents. Construction had failed to keep pace with African demand, and even in Kenya's low-wage economy, building standards had been pared back to keep costs down.[7] The grand design for a better future had been built upon fragile economic foundations. The *Master Plan* was expensive, and money was now tight. As the

Emergency took hold, commerce contracted further. No one was spending, and trade was anyway blighted by African boycotts of Asian shops and European services throughout the city. Armed police and troops patrolled the streets, barbed wire encircled the main public buildings and roadblocks halted the traffic along every major highway leading into the business district. The African estates of Eastlands were more remote and more threatening than ever. In the alleyways of dirt streets of the shanties, and even in the new model estates, Mau May held sway. Nairobi was a city at war.

## African Life in Eastlands

The racially segregated pattern of residence in colonial Nairobi took shape between the wars. Low-density European housing was located on the higher ground to the west and north of the central business area, in leafy settings and on large plots. The poorer elements of the city's Asian population crowded into the residential areas across the Nairobi river from the bazaar and the commercial zone, whilst those who could afford it moved into the Parklands area just to the north. African housing, all of it in high-density estates, was to be found in Nairobi's Eastlands, running from the railway station along the Doonholm Road, bisected by the tracks and shunting yards, and with the industrial zone to the south and the Mathare river to the north.

When Nairobi began to grow in the 1940s, it was this eastern area that mushroomed. The urban population more than doubled between 1938 and 1952. The city was then home to 11,000 Europeans, 34,000 Asians and more than 85,000 Africans. In the crush of Eastlands African life was a constant struggle for employment, for housing and for respectability. Those who came to Nairobi to take up clerical working or teaching, or to run businesses in transport or trade, had ambitions and aspirations to better themselves. In Eastlands self-improvement was never easy. The great majority of the African population of the estates and shanties were illiterate labourers and unskilled men. Africans aspiring to middle-class respectability struggled to find social space among the rougher labouring classes and the armies of the unemployed. In this struggle for respectability the colonial government did little to help.

By the 1940s commerce had grown to dominate the agricultural sector in Kenya, and the town was increasingly a place for business and the professions; but the character of African urban employment changed little. The male migrant wage-earners who came into Nairobi from the surrounding Kikuyu districts, or from Kamba or the more distant Luo regions of Nyanza, were all essentially rural men. They never lost their ties to the countryside. These workers numbered nearly 10,000 by 1906, and 28,000 by 1936. Then came Nairobi's wartime boom, and by 1946 there were more than 65,000 African job-seekers in the town.[8] Workers were split fairly evenly between employment in the public sector, with government departments, and in the private sector, predominantly with Asian and European-owned businesses. Most of the work given to Africans was unskilled or, at best, semi-skilled. In 1954 17,500 workers (56 per cent) employed in Nairobi's private sector were unskilled labourers, while another 1500 were watchmen or guards. The remainder had skills of a kind – there were 2000 drivers, 1500 clerks and cashiers, and among the artisans were 400 African carpenters, 400 motor mechanics, 800 masons, 400 painters, 100 printers, 700 tailors and 200 cooks and bakers.[9]

These city workers were ostensibly protected by a statutory minimum wage, but the huge pool of unemployed men kept wages down. For many years the minimum wage was the only wage. Even so, a city job was an attractive option. That began to change in the boom of the 1940s. As inflation took a grip, the retail price index rose much faster than wages. The cost of basic foodstuffs soared. A bag of maize meal, the staple of the labouring man, known locally as *posho*, sold in Nairobi at 29 shillings in December 1948; in 1939 it had cost only 5 shillings. Over the same period, vegetables and milk increased in price by 50 per cent. Inflation turned even the more mundane pleasures of life into luxuries. By the early 1950s a bottle of European beer cost 1 shilling 65 cents in Nairobi, and cigarettes 3 shillings 65 cents a packet. When the urban worker took account of housing, of transport, of clothing and the occasional purchase of soap, cooking oil, charcoal or other necessities, and of the tax that was due to government, he was unlikely to be able to make ends meet. Nairobi had become a poverty trap.

In 1949 African wages were worth less in real terms than they had been twenty years earlier.[10] The average African monthly wage in Nairobi was 51 shillings 68 cents, 23 per cent above the statutory minimum. Four years later this had climbed to 77 shillings, 29.4 per cent above the minimum. A government enquiry, the Carpenter Report, revealed that these real wage levels were still grossly inadequate even for the needs of a bachelor worker.[11] A powerful case was made for increasing the minimum wage to meet the needs of a working man *and* his family. An immediate 30 per cent increase of African wages in Nairobi was recommended, followed by steady improvements at 15 per cent per annum over the next decade. The report was accepted in principle, but there was never enough cash in the government's coffers to implement the recommendations. They tinkered, slowly increasing the minimum wage, and the African worker was left to make the best of it. By 1956 the monthly average wage was 111 shillings, only 11 per cent above the statutory minimum.[12]

Housing was the real bane of the urban workers' life. Nairobi had long been a city of shanties. Already, by 1921, more than 12,000 Africans occupied the eight largest shanties in the vicinity of the town.[13] The four lying to the west were demolished as European suburbs swallowed them up, while the four to the east eventually formed the heart of Eastlands. The largest was Pangani, alongside the Mathare river. Pangani served as a camp on the trading road from the coast in the 1890s.[14] Europeans thought it to be nothing but a haven for crime, vagrancy and African mischief. This was where the most urbanized of Nairobi's Africans lived. In March 1931 Pangani comprised 312 houses, occupied by 3177 inhabitants, 947 of them women. No less than 146 of Pangani's resident 'families' had then lived in the location for ten years or more, and some 233 residents earned their living as 'lodging house keepers'. Among the family heads of households, 105 were Kikuyu. These were respectable people, for whom urban property had meaning and value. Pangani was finally demolished in 1938, and the bulk of its remaining residents forcibly relocated to a new estate, Shauri Moyo. Though the South African authors of Nairobi's *Master Plan* were later to proclaim that Pangani's residents had received 'liberal compensation', the few pounds awarded by government was far from satisfactory settlement against their loss.[15]

Shauri Moyo was a typical government housing estate, with accommodation for 3042 Africans in 174 cement-block buildings. Constructed by the council at a cost of only £46,000, it was grimly utilitarian, dirty, crowded and uncomfortable. There was little to take pride in here. Those moved in from Pangani hated it, and many soon left. Shauri Moyo supplemented earlier public housing at Kariokor, on Quarry Road, and at Starehe, where two-roomed block houses were built. The stark and cold Starehe rooms were soon full to bursting, but even among the most desperate the Kariokor dormitories, reminiscent of barrack rooms, were never popular. At Pumwani also, the oldest and largest of Eastland's estates, African residents had little liking for the style of housing offered by government. Here, new plots were laid out in 1919, with communal running water and sewage provided by the town authorities.[16] By 1929 only 317 houses had been built in the 'serviced' area of Pumwani, while around the edges new shanties of unregulated settlement had again sprung up. Eastland's residents built what they could afford, greatly preferring this to costly serviced sites or the grim dormitories that the government favoured as 'cheap and suitable'.[17] Respectable people

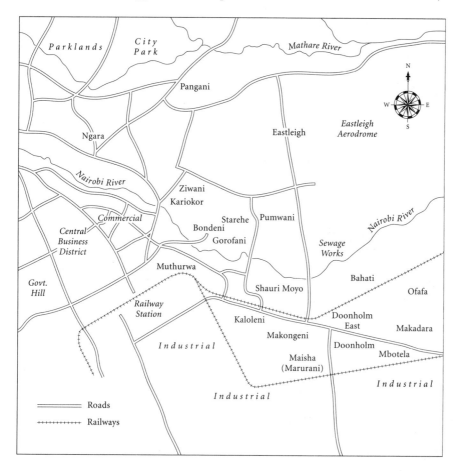

**Map 5.i Nairobi's Eastlands in the 1950s**

wanted privacy, and a home to call their own, at a price they could afford.

The white highlanders on Nairobi's municipal council were never keen on putting much money into African housing, but in the early 1940s two important changes occurred allowing the council to borrow on the money markets. The first step was the passing of the Colonial Development and Welfare Act (CDWA) in 1940, creating the opportunity to raise finance for housing investment from London. With encouragement from the Colonial Office, a scheme was drawn up to provide low-cost housing in Ziwani, for around 6000 workers at a cost of £150,000. The project was begun in 1942. Then, in 1943, Kenya passed a new Housing Bill, establishing a Central Housing Board to provide grants and loans to the local authority for construction projects.[18] With these innovations it at last seemed as if it might be possible to construct better homes for a more respectable urban African community.

Ziwani was Nairobi's pioneering 'municipal housing experiment'.[19] It was soon augmented, as the city council oversaw the construction of 12,000 housing units in Nairobi between 1945 and 1952, mostly on Ziwani's 'neighbourhood model'.[20] On these estates provision was made for shops (to be let only to African traders), schools, social centres and sports facilities. Profits from the municipal brewery and from the butcheries on the estates went towards the costs of welfare provision.[21] There were other municipal schemes at Bondeni, Bahati and Gorofani. Employers also provided better housing. At Makongeni the most privileged railway workers shared communal kitchens, but the estate boasted 'welfare clinics, a club, a library and reading room, a dance hall and tea room, football grounds and even tennis courts'.[22] By 1950 up to 15,000 Africans occupied these new estates, paying subsidized rents. The neighbourhood schemes, literally and metaphorically, were a breath of fresh air.

They could not put them up fast enough, however. Nairobi's housing shortage greatly worsened in the early 1950s. Between 1946 and 1957 30,000 bed-spaces were created in the estates of Eastlands, but even this was 22,000 short of what was required; and the gap was getting wider. The city's population was growing at the rate of above 7 per cent per annum. Over these years, the respectable middle classes were swamped by the great wave of the unemployed who saw the city as a refuge from other kinds of tribulation.[23]

Keeping urban order amid this swelling population was not easy. On the eve of the emergency, the Municipal African Affairs Office had executive authority for the administration of all the Eastlands estates, guided by an African advisory committee, with a European superintendent appointed to manage each estate. It was a condition of tenancy that applicants for accommodation should have a job in the town.[24] But control of the estates was weak. Tenants regularly sub-let to others, or shared rooms far beyond the regulation capacity. It was common to find fifteen men or more occupying a single room in some of the older Nairobi estates. The pass laws, which were supposed to control the flow of job-seekers into the city, had virtually broken down by 1950s, as the police retreated from the enforcement of social offences to concentrate on the rise in serious crime. For all of Nairobi there was only one policeman to every 1000 inhabitants in 1950, and for all of Eastlands there was only one African inspector with five constables. The police protected Europeans and, to a lesser extent, Asians. The African poor were left to fend for themselves.

The scale of petty theft and illegal trading in Eastlands, never mind the more serious organized crime and violence, had simply overwhelmed the police during the 1940s. The housing estates were a law unto themselves, and the shanties were worse. The shebeens were filled day and night by the hordes of jobless men, where women found work brewing native beer and running 'lodgings' for male workers who could afford to pay for some of the 'comforts of home'.[25] A lively black market in stolen goods allowed the multitude of hawkers to make a cent or two, and in the shanties the more enterprising set up small kiosks from which they sold whatever they could lay their hands on. Criminal gangs operated everywhere, the Forty Group among them, fleecing traders and retailers with their protection rackets and scams.[26]

In this outcast Nairobi, class and ethnicity meshed together to deepen social and cultural divisions. Eastlands' estates gradually succumbed to their own form of segregation, defined by ethnic origin. Access to the scarce resources of Eastlands depended upon kinship and affinity. The Kikuyu had long been the largest group among Nairobi's African population; by the early 1950s they became a dominant majority. Moreover, the labouring classes and the unemployed consisted almost exclusively of Kikuyu. Respectable Kikuyu simply had less reason to make Nairobi their home. They could continue to maintain the family farm in nearby Kiambu or southern Murang'a, keeping in touch with friends and kin through regular visits. In contrast, those Africans coming to Nairobi from the coast or from distant Nyanza could return to their family less easily and did so less frequently. Nairobi's most urbanized Africans were therefore not to be found among the Kikuyu but among the Swahili and Luo residents; and such men were more likely to travel to the city only for better-paid skilled work, rather than as labourers. This was to be seen in the dominance of non-Kikuyu among Nairobi's African middle class, and was reflected in their disproportionate representation on Nairobi's African Advisory Council. Immediately after the war 46.3 per cent of Nairobi's African workers were Kikuyu, yet among the dozen or so senior officials on the city's African Advisory Council there were only two Kikuyu: Dedan Githegi and Muchohi Gikonyo. The most influential members of the Advisory Council were all from the coast: Francis Khamisi, Tom Mbotela and Jimmy Jeremiah. These leaders of African opinion were 'isolated by both class and ethnicity from the mass of illiterate and unskilled Kikuyu', who formed by far the largest element of Eastlands' population.[27]

Between 1948 and 1952 the isolation of the respectable middle classes worsened. The displacement and 'repatriation' of squatter labour from the European farms, coupled with increasing land-hunger within Central Province, provoked a new influx of Kikuyu into Eastlands. Official estimates suggested that there were some 30,000 African male workers in the city in 1948, among whom 17,000 (or 56 per cent) were Kikuyu. By 1952, the total workforce had doubled to 60,000, but Kikuyu males now accounted for 45,000 (or 75 per cent) of this total.[28] Nairobi was by then overwhelmingly dominated by displaced Kikuyu, including many destitute women and children, the vast majority of whom were unemployed and living in gross poverty and overcrowded discomfort. In the months after the declaration of the Emergency, the flow of migrants continued as refugees flooded into the city 'to evade the uncomfortable and trying conditions' prevailing in the Central Province. According to Nairobi's District Commissioner, these people were 'virtually war refugees', and they included 'thousands of women', most of whom flooded into Pumwani and the least regulated estates such as Bahati.[29] 'Every nook and cranny of the city was occupied by these invaders, living under the most deplorable and unsanitary conditions', wrote the Municipal Affairs Officer: 'By sheer weight of numbers they dominated the other tribes and were in a position to gradually extend their baneful influence into every facet of Nairobi life.'[30] By then, Mau Mau had long been a powerful force in all the estates and shanties of Eastlands.

The radicals who organized Mau Mau oathing in Nairobi from 1950 had taken their message to the mass of unskilled and illiterate Kikuyu. They appealed to ethnic solidarity, but also to the embryonic class-consciousness of the unemployed, the disadvantaged and the dispossessed. In the clamour of Eastlands this was a potent mix. As radical politics took hold, the respectable middle classes were firstly bypassed and, then, in their vulnerability, attacked. Those who worked in government employment, as clerks, cashiers or office assistants, were singled out as collaborators. In European-style jackets and trousers, with polished shoes and neckties neatly fastened, these men were highly visible as they walked along Doonholm Road each morning towards the commercial district and the offices on Government Hill. Mau Mau had a name for them, ridiculing their dress and mocking their subservience to European masters: they called them the *tai-tai*.

## Terrorizing the Tai-tai

Nairobi's number one *tai-tai* was Tom Mbotela. As a member of the executive committee of the KAU and as a senior official on Nairobi's African Advisory Council, Mbotela had watched the rise of radical politics in Eastlands with growing unease from 1945 onwards. A nationalist, but also a conservative, he feared both the ethnic particularism of Kikuyu radicalism and its disregard for status and authority. The subversive intent of the radical *Muhimu* leadership was clear to him, and he had bitterly opposed Peter Mbiyu Koinange's efforts to incorporate the Nairobi militants within the KAU. Koinange had hoped to broaden the party's popular appeal; instead, he had given the gloss of legitimacy to men who preached violence. Radical leaders such as Eluid Mutonyi and Fred Kubai could certainly harness mass support, but Mbotela knew from his long experience in Eastlands that they would bring nothing but trouble.

Mbotela fought hard to thwart the influence of these dangerous radicals. When they organized the general strike in 1950, Mbotela opposed it. When they called for a boycott of the celebrations to mark Nairobi's achievement of city status, Mbotela refused to comply. The next week there had been an attempt made upon his life. His moderate colleague, Muchohi Gikonyo, was fortunate to survive another murderous assault just a few days later. It was Kubai, along with an accomplice, whom the police eventually charged with Gikonyo's attempted murder. Though his friend was convicted, after having spent nine months on remand Kubai was acquitted of the charge. In releasing Kubai the judge did little to disguise his sense that the case against him had been 'one of the gravest suspicion'.[31]

After this, Mbotela resigned from the KAU and spoke out against the militants with increased vigour, telling his African audiences that oaths of all kinds were divisive to the nationalist cause and that Mau Mau was an evil and illegitimate movement that they should oppose.[32] He eventually paid for his principles with his life. One month into the Emergency, on the evening of 26 November, Mbotela was stabbed and hacked down in a Nairobi street as he walked home from a mayoral reception. His body lay in the gutter, close to a busy thoroughfare in Shauri Moyo, for nearly twelve hours before a European motorist, passing the scene on his way to work, noticed the corpse and stopped.[33] No African had dared go near the body. It was an undignified end for a brave and resolute nationalist. More than any other African politician of his generation, Mbotela had stood firm for constitutional methods and moderate views. He had opposed violence and publicly condemned those who supported Mau Mau. His murder was symbolic of the death of moderation in African politics. It sent a chill through other middle-class urban Africans, whom the colonial state was so keen to nurture but whom they could do so little to protect.

By the time of Mbotela's killing, the forces of Mau Mau already held Eastlands in their grip. Oathing ceremonies organized by the *Muhimu* had begun slowly and selectively in 1950, gradually spreading through the estates and slums, block by block. By June 1952, the *Muhimu* were confident enough to hold mass ceremonies for groups

of up to 800 Kikuyu in Pumwani. A policeman who stumbled upon
one such gathering was brutally slaughtered. His body, 'almost hacked
to pieces', was later found some ten miles from Nairobi. No Kikuyu
politician dared any longer to oppose Mau Mau; in the gritty reality
of daily life in Eastlands, it was easier to accept the oath than to refuse
it. The oathing campaign served the dual purpose of raising money
and of winning acquiescence: everyone who took the oath paid a fee
to the movement, and though the majority would never be expected
to act on behalf of the struggle, their complicity in the actions of
others was essential. The oath built solidarity and silence as well as
bringing much needed cash.

Between June and October 1952 oathing had been gathering pace in
Eastlands, but with the declaration of the Emergency the *Muhimu* were
thrown off balance. Some leaders were rounded up in Operation Jock
Scott. Others fled from the city. The committee structure that had been
initiated by the *Muhimu* in 1950 remained in place, however, and new
officers now took over the organization of Mau Mau activities, each
group of city activists working in liaison with supporters in their home
district to gather the weapons and supplies that the guerrilla bands by
then forming in the forests to the north would need. By the turn of the
year oathing regained momentum in Eastlands again, but now more
cautiously than before. Many Kikuyu now took the oath despite their
anxieties about its meaning and purpose. By the year's end it was
estimated that virtually all the Kikuyu in Eastlands had taken one oath,
and many had taken two. Workers from the most northerly Kikuyu-
speaking areas of Meru and Embu had now been pulled into the movement, and in Kariokor and Bahati oath administrators had even begun
to induct Kamba workers.[34]

The police were by then on the ground in numbers, but although
Special Branch knew in outline how Mau Mau was organized in the
city, they could yet do little to prevent it.[35] Pairs of police patrolled all
the estates in daylight hours, and night patrols began in March. Roadblocks were regularly mounted on all the main thoroughfares, and
armoured cars prowled slowly through the streets of Pumwani and Shauri
Moyo. An additional 300 police reservists had been drafted from among
the city's European and Asian populations in October 1952, and by
January Home Guard units were established among all the non-Kikuyu
communities of Eastlands, including the Muslim coastal Swahili. But
sheer weight of numbers could not compensate for lack of intelligence,
nor overcome the fear that silenced the *tai-tai*. Indiscriminate and heavy-
handed policing hardly helped either. The burning-down of Burma
Market, in Shauri Moyo, on the morning after Mbotela's body was
discovered nearby, was typical of the retaliatory approach of the police.

Mau Mau supporters lost property in the fire, but so too did many others.

Such actions drove people to the rebel cause. Cordon and search operations, begun on the estates in November 1952, became a regular feature of daily life by the middle of 1953. Highly disruptive and in-discriminate, these searches were deeply unpopular. 'Operation Rat Catcher', in July 1953, for example, involved the questioning of 17,000 Africans, resulting in the arrest of twenty or so Mau Mau organizers, including the then chairman of Nairobi's *Muhimu* committee, Hirwan Kamau.[36] The searches were stepped up again in October 1953, when the Royal Inniskilling Fusiliers were moved into Eastlands to try to dampen down Mau Mau activities. When the shanties adjacent to Pumwani were cleared, dozens of bodies were found in shallow graves, the victims of execution after sentencing by Mau Mau courts. The slums were flattened and barbed-wire fences were erected around the most troublesome Kikuyu estates, with armed guards at the now permanent checkpoints. All Kikuyu were prohibited from entering the Eastleigh district of the city. Eastlands increasingly resembled a vast, sprawling prison camp.

In the October operations 1700 Mau Mau suspects were arrested, 100 of these for 'serious offences'. They included another member of the *Muhimu*'s central committee, Harrison Njeroge, as well as fourteen members of the various Mau Mau district committees in the city.[37] Bahati and Kariokor were made exclusively Kikuyu estates, and those Kikuyu settled in the better neighbourhood housing at Ziwani and Kaloleni were forced to move out in October 1953.[38] The creation of exclusively Kikuyu estates was intended to make surveillance easier, but it was a clumsy and ill-considered measure that effectively punished the Kikuyu *tai-tai* and threw them into the arms of Mau Mau. The colonial state might need the support of a Kikuyu middle class, but the security forces treated all Kikuyu the same way: from March 1953 all Kikuyu in the city had to obtain a special permit, without which they were liable to arrest and detention. Later that month police mounted their largest raid to date in Pumwani, screening more than 8000 residents. Over the next four months further large-scale raids were mounted in Kariokor, Shauri Moyo, Pumwani and the railway *lhandies*.

More than a thousand Kikuyu were being expelled from the city each month because they did not have the necessary passes, or because they were 'tainted by Mau Mau'. All this was time-consuming and expensive, yet there was little evidence that the government's measures were really hampering the rebels.[39] The government's intelligence adviser, Mac-Donald, expressed his exasperation to the Colony's Emergency Committee in January 1954:

The Nairobi thugs and gunmen have proven to be one of the most intractable problems. The destruction of the shanty towns of Kariob-angi, Buruburu and Mapirani in the Mathare Valley, the breaking up of the Mau Mau courts and the liquidation [of the central *Muhimu* committee] ... and its subordinate committees brought some relief, but as soon as the pressure has had to be relaxed, the situation again deteriorates and new organisations are formed to control and direct the activities of the gunmen and the criminal elements. The proximity of the city to the most crowded of the Kikuyu reserves presents an almost insoluble problem and despite all efforts we have been unable to effect any *permanent* improvement in the situation.[40]

In Eastlands, the Kikuyu *tai-tai*, once the symbol of progress and modernity, were now viewed with the gravest suspicion. Traders and shop-owners came in for the closest scrutiny. The police knew that such people often acted as treasurers to the Mau Mau committees, collecting the money and keeping records of who had paid oathing fees. Kikuyu business premises, and especially shops, were therefore regularly raided by the police. When residents were moved from one estate to another, after October 1953, the government reviewed all licences, denying renewal to Kikuyu traders whose loyalty might be suspect. They were replaced with 'loyal Kikuyu', or, more usually, with Luo or Kamba. Then, in January 1954, new photographic identity cards were issued to all traders and hawkers in Eastlands, including 800 market traders, 50 veranda traders, 250 authorised shop-owners and 500 licensed hawkers.[41] This closer surveillance of traders bred deep resentment among Kikuyu who were not Mau Mau supporters. Many thought that the government was using tribalism as an economic weapon against them.

The government's use of emergency legislation was also indis-criminate. Under the collective punishments ordinance, the police had the authority to close shops in an area if the population failed to cooperate in the investigation of a crime. This was used repeatedly in Eastlands, damaging the businesses of allies as well as enemies. Other measures specifically targeted the Kikuyu. In September 1953 an ordinance was issued banning car drivers from carrying more than one Kikuyu passenger at a time, and all taxi owners were ordered to paint a yellow band on their vehicles for ease of identification.

In retaliation against this harassment of Kikuyu business, Mau Mau announced a series of boycotts. The first, called in September, was a highly successful boycott of the municipal bus service. Africans walked to work as Nairobi's buses an empty for the next eight months, denying the municipal authorities the revenue from fares. A further boycott was declared on the smoking of European cigarettes, and Mau Mau also instructed Africans not to buy goods from any Asian-owned shops in Eastlands, to eat in establishments that were not African-owned, or to drink European bottled beer. The government responded to this on 26 October 1953 by temporarily closing all Kikuyu-owned retail premises in Eastlands as a punishment 'for the failure of the traders to cooperate' in the battle against Mau Mau. Kikuyu shop-owners were trapped. Those under suspicion risked having their licences taken way by the authorities, while those who refused to assist Mau Mau were likely to be either victimized or robbed. Shops owned by known loyalists were blacklisted by Mau Mau, with thugs stationed in the street outside to discourage anyone from going inside.

General levels of crime in Eastlands increased during 1953, despite the presence of the security forces. In the poorest quarters of Bahati there were reports of criminal and subversive activities at a rate of more than five incidents a day by November 1953,[42] and in the city as a whole the police reckoned there were 950 serious crimes per month.[43] Many more crimes now involved guns. The *Muhimu* in Nairobi had been purposefully preparing for an armed struggle since 1950, and some radicals had been gathering arms even before this. Thefts of weapons and ammunition from police and military depots had begun in earnest in 1949. The carelessness of the security forces in the pre-Emergency period beggared belief. Up until April 1949 the Command Ammunition Depot at Gilgil, holding 12,000 tons of ammunition, was protected only by a flimsy fence 'of poles and a few strands of barbed wire', which afforded no protection whatsoever, especially after dark. In April 1949 the army finally admitted to the loss of more than 130,000 rounds from the depot. In Nairobi, rifles and automatic weapons regularly 'went missing' from military stores. Soldiers and African police were liable to carelessness, some accepting bribes as an inducement to 'mislay' their weapons. The leakage of civilian arms to Mau Mau was even greater. Between 1948 and 1952 a total of 504 private firearms were reported missing by owners in Kenya, only eighty-seven of which were recovered. Gun dealers, too, were lax. A prominent firm of Nairobi arms dealers admitted to the loss of thirty-four pistols from their warehouse between January and April 1953. In 1953 a grand total of 674 firearms were lost or stolen in Kenya. In 1954 the figure was 497.[44] Most of these weapons would eventually be recovered from killed or captured Mau Mau fighters.

Many of these weapons passed through Nairobi and they were inevitably used in acts of urban crime promoted on Mau Mau's behalf. Robberies had been common enough in Eastlands before 1952, although the use of guns had been rare. From the early months of 1953 the incidence of armed robberies increased very dramatically as Mau Mau sought to raise cash and further increase its supply of weapons. Baring explained to Lyttelton that Nairobi's problems were worsened by 'hot-headed young fanatics', whose activities were not under the control of the leaders of the rebel movement.[45] Crime merged imperceptibly with rebellion. A raid upon the Government Medical Research Department on the morning of 29 September 1953, just as the office clerks were putting the staff wages in their envelopes, was typical. All went well, until a European official unexpectedly entered the office and raised the alarm. The gang fled, stuffing bank notes into their pockets and down the front of their shirts as they ran. Two were caught, but a third escaped, carrying about half the total wages for the department.[46]

In another carefully timed operation a gang of four Africans raided Thackar's dairy just as the week's takings were being counted. When the gang threatened to shoot the Asian proprietor, Omparkash Thackar, he drew his own pistol and fired. The four robbers fled into the road, where there was a brief gun battle before one of the gang was caught.[47] Other robberies were more opportunistic, such as the raid upon Som-chand's Post Office, on River Road, when four men came into the small trading store at lunchtime and seized the petty cash – only 450 shillings. When passers-by tried to stop the men from escaping, one of them drew a pistol and fired three shots before the raiders jumped into a waiting taxi and sped away.[48] Incidents such as this had become a daily occurrence in Eastlands by the middle of 1953.

Business premises were targeted for money, while policemen were attacked to steal their weapons. Police Sergeant Kaliki was murdered with a bullet from his own Baretta pistol after being set upon as he left a beer hall, and Sergeant Major Korir was jumped by a group of five men as he left the police headquarters carrying a Sten gun and two magazines of ammunition.[49] European and Asians, many of whom were members of the Nairobi KPR, usually kept weapons in their homes, making them obvious targets for burglary. Burglaries were usually conducted in broad daylight, when only the servants were present in the house. If the servants tried to protect the property, the consequences could be dire. In a ghastly incident over the New Year holiday in January 1954 a Kamba watchman, his wife and four children were all murdered when robbers broke into a European home in Kileleshwa looking for weapons.[50] More usually, the servants made a hasty escape, or were locked up in their own quarters by the raiders. In many of these burglaries the raiders took no precautions to disguise themselves, the culprits escaping through the streets, brandishing their weapons as they ran. After convicting one armed burglar to hang, Judge Holmes commented upon the bravado of so many of Nairobi's 'young gangsters': 'Under present conditions', he wrote, 'with personal prestige in the youthful society of Africans in Nairobi, so much depends upon having and using a firearm, and breaking the laws, that many are ready to run any risk to attain it.'[51] These were the hooligans whom the respectable middle classes so feared.

The increased patrolling of Eastlands by the security forces, and the setting up of checkpoints on footpaths and bicycle tracks, led to the interception of many Mau Mau couriers. These were usually young men, who had been given a pistol or a few rounds of ammunition for delivery to another Mau Mau activist. It was a simple enough chore, but to be convicted of possession of either a weapon or ammunition after April 1953 brought a death sentence. There was no suggestion that men such as Ndungu Kamau, caught in possession of a Baretta pistol in Pumwani, or Wakianda Gachunga, found with two rounds of ammunition at Kariokor market, were intent on armed crime themselves, but under the Emergency regulations their convictions carried an automatic death sentence.[52] The same fate befell Karanja Hinga, who stole thirteen rounds of ammunition and unwittingly handed these over to a police informer for sale.[53] None of these men was pardoned, nor were many others like them. All would hang. Baring's government determined to make an example of such men so that others would be deterred from assisting Mau Mau.

It did not seem to have much effect. The loss of weapons when couriers were captured had become costly by the end of 1953, but there was no let-up in the steady rate of assassinations carried out by Mau Mau in Eastlands. The capacity of the movement to conduct cold-blooded, calculated killings was well established. The most chilling case was surely that of Chief Hinga, who had been severely injured in a Mau Mau attack in his location at the beginning of November 1952. Hinga was taken to the King George VI Hospital. There, as he lay in his private room, a Mau Mau assassin gained entry disguised as a hospital orderly and shot the Chief through the head. The man convicted of Hinga's murder was Zakayo Mwaura Maina, a Presbyterian, whose father and brothers were Home Guards. Maina was an ex-soldier who had served in Burma, gaining skill as a mechanic. After demobilization he had worked as a Nairobi taxi driver. There is no evidence that Maina had been convicted of any previous criminal offence, but it is quite likely that he had been linked with the Forty Group after 1945. In many ways, Maina fitted the profile of the classic Mau Mau activist in Nairobi.[54] Mau Mau's ranks contained many such people. Throughout 1953 they continued the assassinations of loyalists, policemen and informers without respite. In Eastlands, hardly a day passed without a murder attempt.

Among the targets were many *tai-tai*. Philip Makume was typical of the chosen victims. A teacher at Pumwani African School, he joined the Home Guard early in 1953. He was shot and badly wounded in Starehe, where he went to visit his brother, who ran a tea kiosk. Makume knew his attacker: it was often a Mau Mau ploy to choose an assassin who could get close to the victim without being suspected.[55] Wilson Mwiruri, the Anglican verger of Pumwani, was shot dead coming out of his church early in 1953,[56] and Mohamed Mudhikiri, chairman of the Pumwani village committee, was severely wounded. In November Ambrose Ofafa, a city councillor, was gunned down on the Doonholm Road as he was being driven home from his shop.[57] In December Sheikh Omari, the headman of the Muslim Home Guard, was wounded on a busy street when two assailants fired at him.[58]

Those Kikuyu serving as assessors in the special emergency courts were especially vulnerable to the assassins. Three court assessors sat in each trial, drawn from the same ethnic group as the accused. Though they had no powers over the outcome of a case, the judge was required to ask them for their verdicts and to take these views into account. As cases were often reported in the press, and with others sitting in the courtroom to listen and watch, the pronouncements of Kikuyu assessors easily became widely known. Attacks on assessors began in earnest in Nairobi in July 1953. Many of the loyalist elders, who had until then volunteered for this work, took heed and speedily withdrew. New assessors had to be found. The government first turned to younger *tai-tai*, but they proved exceedingly reluctant to declare any accused Kikuyu to be guilty, regardless of the evidence. The case of Chege Mwangi was an example. Mwangi was caught in Pumwani on the afternoon of 17 October 1953. He resisted arrest and then fought hard to escape. He was carrying a loaded revolver and twenty-eight rounds of ammunition. When the case came to court, Justice Holmes found the evidence against Mwangi to be overwhelming and was convinced that the man was an ardent Mau Mau supporter; yet the three assessors each declared him not guilty.[59] Again, in the trial of Njehia Kimani, the assessors refused to find the accused man guilty despite the fact that he had been seen with a weapon in his hand by several witnesses and was then shot by a policeman while still holding his gun.[60] 'I find the attitude of the Assessors in this case and other cases difficult to understand', commented Justice Law, 'unless they are actuated by the fear of reprisals.'[61] Elders from Kiambu and Thika were then brought to serve as assessors in Nairobi trials, but they, too, were liable to interference and intimidation. By 1954 the judges generally ignored the assessors. The system in the Nairobi courts had become a farce.

What successes Special Branch had in gathering intelligence in Eastlands over the first eighteen months of the Emergency came through informers who were not Kikuyu. Early in December 1953 a tip-off from a Tanganyikan informer sparked a police raid on a massive oathing ceremony in Pumwani's Majengo shanty. Several Mau Mau activists were arrested, and substantial funds seized – the 200 people who had participated in the ceremony that night, including Kamba as well as Kikuyu, had each paid 80 shillings. The two leading organizers, both from Meru, were later brought to trial and convicted. They both hanged.[62] By the latter part of 1953, the police had informers in Kariokor and Shauri Moyo, and in the shanties of Pumwani along the Mathare river. They began to learn of the Mau Mau courts that tried and executed those who refused to carry out orders, and gathered information about the houses used to stash arms. A number of successful police raids followed.[63] Informers were also used in a more deliberate ways to entrap suspects. One, known by the name 'Karkar the half-caste', was responsible for the arrest of several Mau Mau rebels. Karkar's ploy was to offer a pistol for sale, and then lure the buyer into a trap after he had taken possession of the weapon. One of the men convicted on Karkar's evidence told the court, 'They are after him in the tea-shops of the city.'[64] In December 1953 they caught him: Karkar's body was left in Eastleigh for the police to find, his tongue cut out and his throat slit.[65]

For such dangerous work, money talked. The most reliable informers were well paid for their regular reports. One such man was Hussein Mohamed, a small-time criminal and ex-convict living in Pumwani. Paid a handsome retainer of up to 100 shillings each month, Mohamed received additional rewards for specific information leading to the recovery of weapons or the arrest of any 'wanted' rebel.[66] Hussein Mohamed had many successes to his credit, but his best would be his last. He was the man responsible, in January 1954, for the arrest of Kariithi Muthumo, known as 'General No. 6', one of Mau Mau's chief activists in the city. Special Branch had long been aware of his involvement in organized assassinations, oathing and recruitment. Thanks to information provided by Mohamed, Muthumo was caught in a police roadblock just after having collected a pistol with which he was to carry out an assassination. In court, Muthumo admitted to having command of ninety-five Mau Mau fighters in Bahati, and boasted that he was 'well know to the people of Eastlands'. There was little doubt that Muthumo saw himself as a popular hero. When sentenced to hang, he warned the court that his confederates in the town would avenge him.

They already had. The previous day the informer Hussein Mohamed had been gunned down. The assassin was a man who had previously served a gaol sentence with Mohamed, and had greeted him warmly in the street, as an old friend would, before drawing a pistol, pressing it to his victim's chest, and gently squeezing the trigger.[67] Passers-by left him bleeding in the gutter, until a European police officer arrived at the scene. Hussein Mohamed died a traitor's death, despised and ignored; but Kariithi Muthumo saw dignity in his own demise. 'I am dying for my land,' Muthumo declared to Judge Holmes, 'and I'm not afraid to die for that.'[68]

Muthumo's bold defiance told its own story of Mau Mau's strength in Nairobi. The number and severity of daylight attacks was still on the increase by January 1954.[69] While there may have been as few as 300 active Mau Mau fighters among Nairobi's residents,[70] a majority of the city's African population were passive supporters of the movement. This urban population played a major role in supplying and supporting the forest fighters, as well as harbouring active 'terrorists' who launched attacks upon targets within the city and in the neighbouring locations of Kiambu district.[71] Nairobi was Mau Mau's beating heart.

At the beginning of 1954 the commander of the British military in Kenya, General Erskine, decided it was time to confront Mau Mau's domination of the city. He had experience of urban terrorism, having served in Palestine at the time of the Jewish insurgency. There, the small, tightly knit terrorist cells had been able to operate with relative impunity, the local population either too afraid or too compliant to provide useful intelligence to the British administration.[72] Erskine saw the similarities with Nairobi and resolved to crack the problem in the same way. His scheme was brutally simple: to mount a massive, sudden strike at the heart of the movement's organization in the city, if necessary removing every single Kikuyu from Eastlands. Over the next few months, a joint steering committee of police and military met in secret with senior administrative officers to piece together the plan.[73] Operation Anvil would be the largest urban cordon and search action ever mounted.

## Operation Anvil

When dawn broke on the morning of 24 April 1954, Nairobi's citizens woke to find their city under siege. British troops and Home Guard units had ringed the suburbs. By 4.30a.m. every road, track and path was sealed, and no African was allowed to leave or enter. As those who made the daily trek into the city reached the roadblocks on the outskirts, they were turned back. Buses and trains leaving Nairobi were cancelled and African taxis were taken off the roads. By 6a.m. Eastlands swarmed with police, KPR and soldiers. Their trucks and armoured cars blocked the main junctions. Alongside each estate, barbed-wire enclosures were hastily erected. Machine-gunners took positions on rooftops, their ghostly silhouettes just visible in the early-morning gloom. As the first rays of the tropical sun penetrated Nairobi's grey smog, Africans emerging to yawn and stretch on their verandas saw the first signs that this would be no ordinary day. White settlers of the KPR stood about in huddles, poised and energetic, as ever keen to get on with it; while the fresh-faced British squaddies, many of them conscripts of eighteen and nineteen years of age, sat in their trucks, smoking and talking, edgily nervous of what might happen next. No African would leave Bahati, Pumwani or Kariokor that morning, except in the back of a caged lorry. Operation Anvil had begun.[74]

Nairobi would remain a 'closed district' for the next month. Five British battalions and one battalion of the King's African Rifles worked alongside more than 300 police and several hundred Home Guards, with a host of KPR staff to assist with interrogations – a total force of around 20,000 men. The military had gone to great lengths to keep Operation Anvil a secret: even the officers involved in the action had little idea of what was planned until taking up their positions. Rumours of an imminent 'clean-up' of the city had inevitably leaked out all the same, although the worst that the African residents expected was the usual lower-key focus upon one of the more troublesome estates. A few Mau Mau activists had taken the precaution of moving to hideouts in the urban fringes,[75] but for the most part Erskine had managed to maintain the element of surprise.

Over the previous four months an elaborate scheme had been worked out to systematically search the city and to 'screen' every African. Those estates and shanties where Mau Mau was firmly entrenched were prioritized. Bahati's 12,000 Kikuyu residents would be the most difficult to tackle, but the warrens of Pumwani, home to perhaps 8000 Kikuyu, and the Kariokor dormitories, where 4000 more lived, were also targeted on the first day. The industrial estates, particularly the railway *lhandies* area came next, along with the African-owned commercial properties along the main thoroughfares of River Road, Grogan Road and Racecourse Road. In later days the searches extended to other estates, into the commercial district, and then to the Asian-dominated residential areas of Eastleigh and Parklands. Finally, African labour quarters in the European areas were checked.

Four investigating teams were put in place as the estates were cordoned and searched. These 'screening teams' were each led by three European district officers, three labour officers and nine European members of the KPR. The intention was firstly to identify all those who were illegally resident in the city. Africans were hustled out of their houses and herded into the barbed-wire compounds, where they waited for the cogs of colonial bureaucracy to turn. Each Kikuyu male resident was required to carry five separate documents: an employment registration card; a card setting out his history of employment; an identity card; a poll-tax receipt; and a Kikuyu Special Tax receipt. Failure to produce any one of these documents was grounds for suspicion. Men with missing or faulty documents were held for questioning at a holding camp outside the city, as were men who could not establish a place of residence in the city or whose papers revealed 'suspiciously frequent' changes of employment. The security forces also detained anyone whom they suspected of being a Mau Mau supporter. To identify the more important suspects, the screening teams were assisted by *gikunia* – the dreaded hooded informants – who sat quietly watching the multitudes being shepherded past them, from time to time leaning to whisper into the ear of a European officer, giving the name and alleged offence of any Mau Mau activist they noticed. The *gikunia* were loyalists and informants, mostly residents of the estates. Their silent and anonymous testimonies would condemn many men to the detention camps.

The capricious nature of this operation gave little room for the benefit of doubt. As the screening team sifted through the hundreds of Africans waiting behind the wire, they employed only the crudest of distinctions. The first step was to check the identity cards (*kipande*) of each person, and separate the Kikuyu (including the Kikuyu-speaking groups from Embu and Meru) from the other Africans. The union leader and political activist Tom Mboya, a Luo and a resident of one of the better non-Kikuyu estates, was caught up in Anvil when the soldiers entered the commercial district:

> Leaving several colleagues in my office on the first floor of the Kundi Building, I went down to the street. Within a few seconds, I was challenged by a soldier pointing a gun at me. I raised my hands above my head as ordered and walked to him. He gave me a shove with the butt of his gun and ordered me to walk on. I was taken to a street island where other Africans were already sitting, and ordered to squat down ... For hours we waited until we were ordered into a lorry and driven to a reception camp which was cordoned by barbed wire. Here we again squatted for hours. Then we were lined up and European police officers asked each of us his tribe and separated us accordingly. Those of us who were non-Kikuyu ... were free to go home ...[76]

The Kikuyu were not so fortunate. Though the instructions to the screening teams had made clear the undesirability of mistreating 'decent members of society', the routine of the process and the overwhelming numbers of people involved, combined with a strong disinclination to trust any Kikuyu, rapidly undermined the good intentions of the planning committee.[77] There were soon many more Kikuyu on their way to the transit camp than the 12,000 or so that preliminary estimates had suggested might be detained.

New prison camps had been constructed before Anvil at Langata,

Mackinnon Road and Manyani. Even as the operation got under way, the camps were barely ready to welcome their inmates. It was reckoned that the new camps would house 20,000 prisoners in total. Langata was intended only as a transit camp, where suspects could be interrogated and properly classified. All Kikuyu suspects were taken here first. At Langata, the *gikunia* went to work again, and more detailed notes were taken of the background and activities of individuals. Those who were implicated in Mau Mau were then transferred to the other, more permanent detention camps at Mackinnon Road and Manyani.[78] At these camps, teams of loyalist Africans from the reserves worked with the security forces to build up a dossier on each man, identifying which of them might be released and who among them should be committed for trial because they were believed to have participated in a known crime.[79]

A crude grading system was put in place, categorizing suspects by their supposed degree of commitment to the Mau Mau cause. Borrowing from the experience of the Allies in Germany at the end of the Second World War, Africans screened in Anvil were classified as 'white', 'grey' or 'black' – the black colour used to connote that which was most negative or dangerous. 'Whites' were not considered a threat to security, and were usually repatriated to the reserve, or allowed to return to their employment in the city; but 'greys', who were suspected of being passive supporters of Mau Mau, and 'blacks', who were thought to be active terrorists, later to be termed 'hard-core', were taken to the camps for further interrogation. In practice, the only Kikuyu initially classified as 'white' were those whom the security forces knew to be members of the Home Guard, tribal police and police reservists, or those in other trusted government posts. Anyone whom the *gikunia* picked out, or who was named on the Special Branch 'wanted list' was graded 'black'. Everyone else – the bulk of people for whom there was no immediate evidence of loyalty or misdemeanour – was labelled 'grey'. This was hardly sophisticated, but the system would soon be modified and extended throughout all of Kenya's emergency detention camps.

The power of the screening teams was absolute. Under the emergency laws, suspects could be detained without trial on the basis of a Delegated Detention Order, signed by any official of the rank of district officer or above. These sparse documents set down the detainee's name, pass number, and location of origin, with a brief comment on the reason for the order. Nothing more was needed to condemn a man to incarceration for two years, or more. Suspicion that a man had taken an oath, or even that he was thought to be in sympathy with the aims of Mau Mau, was sufficient for detention without trial. Accusations made by others, such as the hooded informants used at Langata, needed no corroboration. The use of elders brought from the reserve in the screening of men at

MacKinnon Road and Manyani was intended to act as a check against any possible victimization, but it was impossible to prevent score-settling or personal vendettas. More serious offenders, who might be likely to come to trial later if evidence could be gathered for a prosecution, were subject to a Governor's Detention Order, signed by Baring. Later in the Emergency, all those persons who had been issued with Governor's Detention Orders would lose their rights to land, and their families would forfeit whatever property they had. In the chaos and confusion of Anvil, there were many, many cases of mistaken identity. Once labelled, it was exceeding difficult for a man to challenge any detention order. During Anvil, Nairobi's district officers signed more than 20,000 detention orders.

Aside from the detained men, around 2150 women and 4000 children – the families of some of the detained men – were 'forcibly repatriated' to the reserves. A further 1050 women and 2000 children had gone back to Central Province 'at their own request'. These were 'either unattached women, who could not properly be described as dependants, or were families who earlier this year had sought refuge in the city from the more seriously disturbed areas of Fort Hall, Nyeri and Embu'.[80] These women may have expressed the wish to get out of Nairobi, but they did not accept their displacement passively. None of the women did. The Europeans and Asians who volunteered, through the East African Women's League, to help serve tea and bread to the African women as they were loaded onto buses and trains, found that their charity was not wanted. The Kikuyu women loudly sang protest songs, snarled abuse, or sat in silent, sullen resentment. The tea and bread were refused and thrown back in the faces of the welfare workers. The Kikuyu women displayed their own brand of defiance, and retained their dignity; they would not be patronized by the white highlanders or their Asian allies.

Nairobi's vagrant children posed a different kind of problem. Despite the 'repatriation' of thousands of Kikuyu juveniles to the reserves during Anvil, Eastlands was again swarming with vagrant juveniles only a few weeks later. It was a process that would continue over the next decade and beyond. Almost as quickly as they were removed to the rural areas, these youngsters seemed to return again. Some of the Kikuyu juveniles coming to the city were war orphans, others the children of parents who had been detained. The Mau Mau war marked the real beginnings of Nairobi's 'street-children' phenomenon. By 1955 youth camps were established on the city's fringes to accommodate these youngsters and attempt their 'rehabilitation'; but this limited welfare provision simply could not cope with the numbers involved. Aside from those admitted to the youth camps, in 1956 some 3547 vagrant juveniles were officially 'repatriated' from Nairobi back to the countryside.[81] This was yet another indication of the massive scale of social dislocation among the Kikuyu communities caused by the war.

In the morass of Operation Anvil, bureaucratic procedure had taken over from common sense: with these numbers, what did it matter if one more Kikuyu was detained? And if in any doubt, it was surely better to detain the man than let him go? Anvil epitomized an attitude of mind that pervaded the security forces. The Kikuyu had come to be seen as a kind of sub-species, a group that could only make claims to an inferior kind of humanity. Over the following months of 1954 the Kikuyu population in Kenya's detention camps would swell to more than 70,000.

Anvil set the trend. In the first forty-eight hours of the operation, 11,600 Kikuyu taken from Bahati, Pumwani and Kariokor were screened, of whom 8300 were detained for further questioning, and another 1250 dependants and juveniles were returned to their home areas in Central Province. In that period alone, the police reckoned that they had identified 206 active Mau Mau terrorists, including two oath administrators, four intelligence officers, nine treasurers, one courier, twenty cash collectors, nine 'other officials', and 129 guards and gunmen.[82] By 26 May, when Anvil finally came to an end, the numbers screened had climbed above 50,000. Of these, 24,100 Kikuyu males had been detained. It was a simply astonishing number: nearly half the total number of Kikuyu in the city had been imprisoned without trial.

Of those detained, Special Branch reckoned that 700 were 'hard-core' Mau Mau, who had been involved in criminal activities on behalf of the movement. They considered this a great achievement; but the fact that this represented less than 3 per cent of the total number of people detained told a rather different story. Senior military officers acknowledged that the evidence against most of them was pretty slight, but no one seemed much concerned.[83] The Kikuyu population had been reduced to only one-quarter of Nairobi's workforce.[84] In its pervasive, all-encompassing magnitude, Operation Anvil had been both a bureaucratic triumph and a political disaster. The British had pilloried friend and foe alike.

When Lyttelton asked for a preliminary assessment, he was told that Operation Anvil had been 'thoroughly satisfactory'. Hooliganism had all but ceased in the city, and there had been a spectacular fall in crimes of violence. Eastlands was quiet, and 'law-abiding Africans [were] once again able to go about their day's work without fear of attack of intimidation'. The Mau Mau boycotts had been broken; buses were again running through the African estates, although even on the busiest routes use was still at less then 50 per cent of the pre-Emergency level; Africans were again to be seen smoking cigarettes in public; while the reassuring collection of empty bottles surrounding the beer shop in Pumwani indicated that the *tai-tai* again felt able to purchase their drink of choice – European bottled beer was an icon of modernity for the African office worker.[85] Most important of all, every one of the dozen or so Mau Mau organizing committees in the city had been broken up. Without the impetus and direction given by these small cells of activists – it was reckoned there were no more than ten men on each committee – it was difficult to see how the movement would be able to mobilize its urban support again. For Erskine, this was as good an outcome as he could possibly have hoped for. It seemed that Mau Mau had been caught in the trap, and broken. Nairobi officials assured Lyttelton that the respectable African community had welcomed Anvil; indeed, it was claimed that 'the chief African criticism of Anvil [was] that it was neither wide enough nor tough enough'.[86]

While Baring's government congratulated itself for having conducted Operation Anvil with such restraint, others took a less sanguine view. The loudest complaints were first heard from some of the larger employers in the city, who found their workforce decimated overnight. With the Kikuyu population of the city reduced by 50 per cent, the pool of unemployed job-seekers had been taken away. By reducing Nairobi's 'surplus labour', Anvil did more to raise African wages in the city than had two years of negotiation with employers. The stricter controls now placed upon the administration of passbooks, including the insistence that workers should have proper accommodation within the city, also increased the pressure upon employers to provide adequately for their staff.[87] All of this was costly, and deeply unpopular with European and Asian employers. They had no choice but to employ the new job-seekers who flooded into Nairobi from the Kamba areas, and from western Kenya, even though these workers were less experienced, less efficient and often far less reliable than the Kikuyu whom they replaced (see table 5.i, p. 352, for a breakdown of the African population in Nairobi).[88]

While the government had surely expected a backlash of complaint from employers, they were less well prepared for the criticism that poured down upon them from the leaders of Kenya's main churches. The churches had led the fight against Mau Mau even before the start of the emergency, and in Nairobi African Christians had been subjected to gross intimidation and violence. These were people who might have welcomed Anvil, but they were far from happy with what had happened. Late in June, Morrison, the General Secretary of the Christian Council of Kenya – representing all the larger Protestant churches in the colony – wrote to the deputy governor, Sir Frederick Crawford, about more than sixty Kikuyu Christians who had been rounded up in Operation Anvil. These were all persons for whom the churches vouched in unconditional terms: many were senior church elders, including several who had very publicly opposed Mau Mau and some who had been victims of attempted assassination. The loyalty of these men was above question; yet it appeared they had been swept away into the detention camps as Mau Mau suspects. Other African Christians had gone to look for them, but found it impossible to penetrate the confusion of Langata, Mackinnon Road and Manyani. 'We are informed either that persons cannot be traced, or that they must be re-screened, or that they cannot return to Nairobi because they were self-employed, or some other reason is given which prevents or delays release,' wrote Morrison, barely able to conceal his frustration. 'Every time we raise the issue, we are informed that the security forces insist on this or that ... The effect on the churches and on the loyal Kikuyu is most depressing,' he continued. The government was in danger of alienating the one group among the Kikuyu on whose support they must ultimately rely as a nucleus for influencing the rest.[89]

Crawford saw the dangers clearly enough. He gave instructions that the camp authorities should locate the named men, and wherever possible release them. His directive had little impact. Over the next month only a handful of the men emerged from the screening camps. Many more remained inside, and it soon became apparent that several had been classified as 'grey' or even 'black'. Archdeacon Peter Bostock, of the Anglican church, visited Langata in person twice during June in an effort to identify the 'missing' men. He was shocked and disturbed by the experience. The wire pens in which the men were held appeared grossly overcrowded and the Europeans in charge seemed to be only barely in control. There were no complete lists of names, and even when a man's dossier could be found, he could not. Allowed to wander through the pens on his own – a privilege he only exacted after a huge quarrel – Bostock eventually found eight members of his church, but could not persuade the camp authorities to release any of them. The officer in charge, Ellis, ignored the Archdeacon's pleas, and showed no interest whatsoever in the letters of recommendation he brought in support of each of the incarcerated men, nor in the directive from Crawford. It seemed that the camps were a law unto themselves, regardless of the Deputy Governor's instructions.

Angered by the rebuttal, Bostock got to work. Over the next nine months, he tirelessly pursued the matter at every possible opportunity, writing repeatedly to officials at all levels, and providing copious detail on the backgrounds of the men concerned. The Anvil detainees included evangelical Christians such as Rowland Kariuki, renowned for his opposition to Mau Mau in the slums of Kariobangi and the nearby sisal estates of Dandora; Peter Muceke, who had provided information against Mau Mau activists in Bahati; and Leonard Njeroge, the respected headmaster of an Anglican church school. Dedan Kihato was typical of the well-educated, enterprising *tai-tai* Christians caught up in Anvil. A resident and shopkeeper in Bahati, he was known to be a wealthy man, and had been generous to his church, buying bibles and furniture, and giving money to assist the poor. Bostock considered it 'quite impossible' that Kihato could be a Mau Mau supporter. The screening team at Manyani agreed. Dedan Kihato was classified as 'white', but when he applied to be allowed to return to his shop in Bahati he was refused. Self-employed Kikuyu like Kihato were thought too vulnerable to Mau Mau influence, and were no longer welcome in Nairobi. Kihato's licence was revoked, and his shop given to another, non-Kikuyu trader. There is no record that Kihato was compensated for his loss of stock. An urban man through and through, Dedan Kihato had no land back in the reserve; in Operation Anvil this Christian loyalist lost everything he had built up in a life's work. Worse still, he was not released from custody at Manyani, but sent instead to the Fort Hall Works Camp, where he languished for the next year.[90] His experience was by no means unusual.

The other churches, too, now came forward with their own lists. Among those sought by the Church of Scotland were several revivalists, who appeared to have been classified as 'black' merely because they professed complete ignorance of Mau Mau. There was Leonard Waru-ingi, a deacon and Sunday-school teacher who had refused to allow his daughters to be circumcised and who had risked his life several times in opposition to Mau Mau; and Jonathan Kariuki, another school teacher and revivalist, whose wife had been molested by Mau Mau supporters. Waruingi was classified 'black', and held at Mackinnon Road; Kariuki had been graded only as 'grey', but it still took several months to extract him from Manyani.[91] In September, Archbishop McCarthy, of Kenya's Roman Catholic Missions, joined the queue of plaintiffs, presenting his own list directly to Governor Baring. The Anglican Baring ordered that these cases be 'looked at immediately', but in his hesitant, almost apologetic tone, even the Governor appeared to be aware that this might be easier said than done.[92] Baring already knew that Kenya's bureaucratic machinery had become unwieldy and uncontrollable. In practice, the camp commanders and their staff did much as they pleased.

Church leaders had been mildly critical of the government throughout the emergency; Anvil turned this into a unified chorus of dissent. For the most part, the criticism was measured and polite, only expressed in the privacy of meetings with senior officials. The missions did not want to be seen as giving succour to Mau Mau. Yet as their frustration mounted, the churchmen became increasingly outspoken. In January 1955 the Church of Scotland moderator in Kenya, David Steele, startled his Presbyterian congregation with an impassioned attack from the pulpit against the arbitrary callousness of government policies, taking Operation

Anvil as his principal case. Steele described how the government had alienated Christian support through its heavy-handedness, summarily throwing the innocent into detention, where they were contaminated by the wicked, and failing to protect decent people from the abuse of those whom the government armed as their protectors, the Home Guard.[93] Carelessness, and an utter disregard for the rights of Africans had resulted in many honest, law-abiding citizens being incarcerated during Anvil.[94]

Steele also knew, however, that there were more sinister forces at work. False accusations had removed many people to the detention camps, and this had sometimes been deliberate and calculated. In the chaotic turmoil of Anvil it was obvious that this had happened more frequently than the security forces were prepared to concede. What the clergy knew only too well, but were usually too cautious to say outright, was that the system of informants run by the security forces was far from infallible, and that the Home Guard units who policed the Nairobi estates were hopelessly corrupt.

Home Guard units had been established on all of the estates of Eastlands in the early months of the Emergency with the direct support of the churches. Recruiting Kikuyu had not proved easy. People feared retribution. The missions did their best to foster a stronger Christian community against Mau Mau, holding confessional prayer meetings every Sunday, where those who had been compelled to take the oath were encouraged to recant. They did so at their peril. Mau Mau targeted the leading Christians in Eastlands, and especially those Kikuyu who joined the Home Guard. A typical example was Boniface Waweru, who survived several attacks before becoming head of the Bahati Home Guard in 1954. Without Waweru and his like it would have been impossible after Anvil to organize any Home Guard activity in those estates that were predominantly Kikuyu; but for every Waweru there were many more Christian Kikuyu in Pumwani, Bahati and Kariokor who were too afraid to take a public stand against Mau Mau.

Elsewhere in Eastlands the Home Guard comprised non-Kikuyu. There was a large Muslim Home Guard contingent in Pumwani, and in Kaloleni the Luo *tai-tai* had been recruited. Though notionally overseen by European officers, the city's Home Guard were left pretty much to themselves, under the authority of the chiefs and headmen appointed on the estates. After Anvil, with the establishment of closer administration in the city as a whole, the numbers of non-Kikuyu Home Guards greatly increased; and so, too, did their boldness. With Mau Mau's organization in disarray, Home Guard confidence grew. Many of them sought to exploit the opportunity to full advantage.

Home Guard corruption in Nairobi was hardly a secret. 'Most people are aware of the system of bribes employed by the Chiefs and Home Guards,' commented one of Nairobi's European residents, observing that extortion 'to avoid arrest' and subsequent detention was 'rife in the African Home Guard'. The usual fee was 20 shillings, but if the victim was thought to be in better-paid employment, then larger sums might be demanded.[95] Even during Anvil, the Kikuyu relatives of men swept up and taken to the camps tried to bribe Home Guards and the police to effect releases. When the Nairobi District Commissioner resolved to send a small party of African Home Guards from Pumwani to Mackinnon Road to assist with screening, within two days of information about their posting being released the men 'received bribes amounting to £600 from the dependants and hangers-on of various wealthy shopkeepers arrested in Anvil'. On this occasion, the corruption came to light, but in other cases the classification of suspects in the Anvil camps was 'a matter of who ha[d] paid the most momey'.[96] In late colonial Kenya, justice was too often an expensive luxury.

The *tai-tai*, along with other Kikuyu business people remaining in Eastlands after Anvil, were at the mercy of the Home Guard, as European officials were well aware. '[T]here are many Africans, irrespective of their status of government servant, Home Guard, or civilian, who are only too pleased to kick the Kikuyu, Embu and Meru when they are down,' wrote Nairobi's District Commissioner, 'especially if they can squeeze some financial gain out of it at the same time.'[97] Respectable people had more money, and wealthy Kikuyu made for especially easy pickings. The experience of a Kikuyu trader named Kabura was typical of many. Kabura was a prosperous vegetable vendor. She had been licensed to trade at the municipal market since 1948, and lived in one of the best houses Eastlands had to offer on the Gorofani estate. She was among the few Kikuyu who retained a licence to trade at the market after Anvil. One evening in June 1954, when Kabura was relaxing on the veranda of her home, four Home Guards burst in and demanded that she hand over the cloth bag in which she kept her earnings. Kabura refused. One of the Home Guard then seized the bag, and Kabura shouted for help. The neighbours who came running to her aid soon melted back into the night when they saw the Home Guard. No one dared intervene. By then, the leader of the group had removed the money from Kabura's bag, a sum of 1010 shillings. Waving the bundle of cash for all to see, he declared that Kabura 'must be a Mau Mau treasurer'. Kabura protested her innocence, and was told that their silence would be costly. When she indignantly refused to pay any bribe, she was arrested.

Kabura was detained at the Pumwani Home Guard post overnight. The next morning she was taken before the African court, where she was charged with being out on the road after the curfew. Despite her protests, the Chief convicted her without hearing any evidence. Kabura paid her fine and left the court. She never saw her bag again, nor her week's earnings of 1010 shillings. Over the next month Kabura was repeatedly menaced by the same Home Guards, who stole further belongings from her home. Complaints to the Chief brought no action. Finally, run ragged by intimidation, Kabura gave up her home and went to live with a friend in another part of Eastlands.[98] It was an all too familiar story.

Justice had a hard struggle for mastery in Nairobi's turmoil. Though Nairobi's European administrators regularly issued directives warning the chiefs, headmen and Home Guard commanders 'not to alienate Africans who were sympathetic to the government', harassment, bribery and corruption were indiscriminate and widespread. Anvil only made matters worse. It seemed that no one among the *tai-tai* was immune: even City Councillor Musa Amalemba complained of harassment 'by drunken Home Guards' at his home in Kaloleni in May.[99] Government staff living in Starehe reported that the Pumwani Home Guard stole property from their houses during searches, and regularly took any money they found in the pockets of people they searched. A Home Guard headman had told one resident: 'You people of Starehe know English very well, and consider yourselves to be very high people, and for this reason we are going to beat you.'[100] The Pumwani Home Guards were reputedly the worst offenders, making nightly rounds of houses occupied by Kikuyu and demanding 5 shillings from each to leave them in peace. Those who refused to pay were hauled before the African court the next morning – just as Kabura had been – where a fine would be summarily issued.[101]

Some employers were moved to register complaints on behalf of their workers. The traffic superintendent of Kenya Bus Service complained bitterly that his staff from Kariokor and Ziwani were being intimidated by the Home Guard, who said 'ammunition [would] be put in their rooms' unless they paid bribes. His workers were 'very frightened' that they would be framed. They knew only too well that the penalty for possession of ammunition was execution.[102] The security officer of Block Hotels also wrote to complain of Home Guard intimidation of workers who were taken home by private bus after midnight. Home Guard in Bahati had formed the habit of waiting for the bus each night and harassing the workers for bribes once they were deposited at their homes. The management of the hotel had first written to the police at Shauri Moyo, but got no reply. They then wrote to the District Commissioner, who redirected them to the European in charge of the Bahati Home Guard, a Mr Purves. He refused to acknowledge the complaint. Finally, they contacted the district officer, Rylands, who lamely confessed that he was not empowered to take any action. This was typical of the maze of bureaucracy and official indifference that shielded the Home Guard from accountability.[103]

Anvil broke the back of Mau Mau's organization in Nairobi, but at what cost? For the respectable Kikuyu middle classes, many of whom lived in fear and dread of Mau Mau intimidation, Anvil had been nothing less than a betrayal. Already threatened by Mau Mau, they had now been the victims of a state-sponsored raid. They had lost their livelihoods and their property. Those rounded up had been asked to clear their homes, labelling all of their belongings – tables, chairs, wooden beds and mattresses, cooking utensils, clocks, bicycles, ornaments and framed photographs, even their clothes. Their possessions had then been heaped onto lorries and transported to two huge military storehouses at Langata – but not before the Home Guard and police had taken a few things for themselves. At Langata the store was poorly guarded and was continually burgled. Though this was reported, no one seemed to care very much.[104] Those Kikuyu who did return to collect their things after release from the camps were left to rummage through the remnants to recover what they could. At the end of 1957 the stores still held what was left of the treasure of mundane artefacts – a vast, disorderly museum to the urban lives destroyed by Operation Anvil.

## Fighting Back

In the months after Anvil, Mau Mau fighters found it increasingly dangerous to operate permanently within the urban area. Movement in and out of the city was closely monitored through to the end of October and Mau Mau activists were constantly harried. By the end of June several remaining groups of fighters had already decamped from the city, forming into new gangs in the peri-urban fringe of Nairobi. The fightback was about to begin.

Among the leaders of these new gangs were David (Mohamed) Mathu, Mwangi Toto and Karioki Chotara.[105] These young, impetuous firebrands seized the initiative to mount their own counter-attack in the Nairobi area between June and December 1954. They were not controlled by any committee, nor did they liaise much with elders in Nairobi or Kiambu, who were slowly attempting to reconstruct the movement's organizational structure in the wake of Anvil. Mathu, Toto and Chotara were too impatient to wait for this: they cut loose on their own. Some Kikuyu thought of them as *komerera* – bandits or renegades – who were taking advantage of the rebellion for their own gain and glory, and who behaved irresponsibly, endangering local Kikuyu communities with their recklessness. At whatever cost, they seemed determined to ensure that Mau Mau in Nairobi would not go down without a fight.

Throughout July, Mwangi Toto's gang carried out numerous attacks against police and loyalists in the settled area of Kiambu,[106] and by early September other gangs had joined in what appeared to be a renewed Mau Mau offensive around Nairobi. Through September and October there was a spate of attacks to the north and south of the city, and in neighbouring locations of Kiambu. The Mau Mau fighters had their moments of triumph in this offensive, but it was ultimately to prove a costly final fling. On 1 September European farmers were attacked at Limuru, on the borders of the city; but three days later, six Mau Mau fighters were shot in a running battle with security forces to the north of the city. A further attack was launched against a Home Guard patrol in Kiambu on 25 September, in which Mohamed Mathu claims that six Home Guards were killed.[107] But on the same day the security forces uncovered and destroyed a Mau Mau hospital and substantial food stocks, all well hidden on the edge of the city.[108] This discovery was a sure sign of continued Mau Mau activity, but its destruction indicated that it was the security forces that now had the upper hand.

In the midst of this flurry of activity came the most spectacular event of all: a daring raid upon Lukenya Prison, to the south-east of Nairobi. This attack was one of the great successes of the war for the Mau Mau fighters. A band of twenty, under the command of Mathu, made their way from Kiambu to Lukenya – a distance of more than 20 miles – skirting the northern and eastern fringes of the city, via the labour lines near the Tusker Brewery and Embakasi Airport, where supporters provided them with food and shelter. At Lukenya they launched the attack under cover of darkness. Some 296 Mau Mau detainees were freed from the prison, a guard being killed and others wounded; but the attackers failed to find the armoury: 'To our disappointment,' Mathu later wrote, 'we found only three rifles, two shot guns, a revolver and about 300 rounds of ammunition.'[109] This aside, the raid was a huge propaganda success, and tied down the security forces in efforts to recapture the escaped prisoners over the next week.[110]

But the success at Lukenya brought an intensification of security operations in the vicinity of Nairobi that would see the capture of many of the leading fighters before the end of the year. Moreover, although the adventures of Mwangi Toto, Chotara and Mathu over this period can be presented as acts of glorious resistance, their activities served only to divert funds and supplies away from the increasingly beleaguered forest fighters in the Aberdares and Mount Kenya. By October 1954 many of the forest gangs were already splintered, isolated and in desperate need

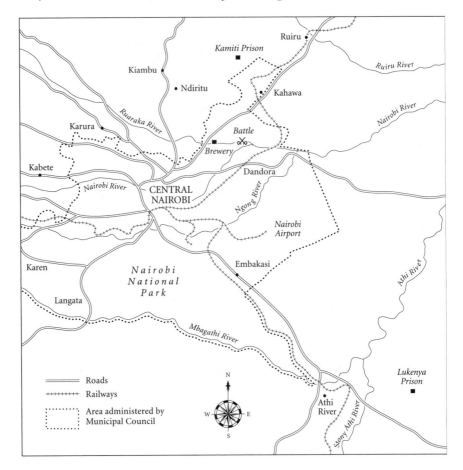

**Map 5.ii Nairobi and its environs, c.1954**

of supplies and new recruits. Operation Anvil had achieved far more than the disruption of Mau Mau in Nairobi: it marked the turning point in the British campaign against the rebels.

The now fragile vulnerability of Mau Mau's Nairobi-based recruit-ment and supply networks was vividly exposed five months after Anvil, in the battle of Dandora swamp. On the afternoon of 25 October 1954 security forces on the north-eastern edge of the city received information that armed terrorists were on a nearby sisal plantation. The informant was a young Luo migrant worker. As dusk fell, a platoon surrounded the spot, in an uncultivated part of the plantation in Dandora, near the swampy junction of two rivers.[111] The gang were camped at the base of a spreading thorn tree. All around was thick papyrus, in which avenues had been cut leading to sleeping places. This was clearly a regular Mau

Mau base, a link in the supply chain that connected Nairobi to the forests. Amid the papyrus, the members of a Mau Mau unit could be seen, huddled together in groups of three or four.[112] As darkness fell, the platoon tightened their encirclement. As they did so, those resting in the papyrus became aware of their peril. When the attack began, just after 9p.m., the Mau Mau fighters were ready and returned fire with a ferocity that surprised the European commander. Now realizing that his adversaries were well armed and determined, he pulled his men back to take cover and summoned reinforcements. Later that night officers of the Kenya Regiment arrived with members of the local Kikuyu Home Guard, shortly followed by CID officers and police from Thika. Then came a platoon of the Royal Northumberland Fusiliers, who took up positions for an assault on the swamp. Before dawn the Mau Mau fighters were invited to surrender; but none did. The Mau Mau camp was then heavily mortar-bombed for over an hour, this being answered by constant sniping from the guerrillas holed up in the papyrus beds.

In the clear light of mid-morning, the Northumberland Fusiliers finally entered the swamp, whilst the other security forces maintained the cordon. The British soldiers moved slowly, cautiously searching amid the papyrus. The skirmishing in the swamp lasted most of the day, as small groups of Mau Mau were flushed out. When discovered, some stood their ground and died with their weapons in their hands – several shotguns, home-made pipe-guns, pistols, bottle-bombs and pangas. In the confusion, part of the gang slipped through the cordon, escaping to the north along the course of the Kamiti river, past the startled and ill-disciplined Home Guard. Others lost their nerve and ran from their hiding places, throwing away their weapons and ammunition as they ran, only to be shot by the Kenya Regiment officers or caught by the Home Guards stationed in the cordon. Some emerged from the papyrus with their hands aloft, and quickly surrendered to the British soldiers. Among them were a few women and young children.[113]

When the final sweep through the swamp was completed that afternoon, around fifty prisoners had been taken, some of them seriously wounded. More than thirty guerrillas lay dead, many having perished in the mortar attack before dawn. Among the prisoners was the gang leader, Captain Nyagi Nyaga, who defiantly proclaimed his authority. His accomplices included several fighters whom the security forces immediately identified by their appearance and attitude as 'hard-core' Mau Mau; poorly nourished, dressed in tattered remnants of military and police uniforms, and with their hair matted and uncut, they carried the signs of having spent a considerable time living rough in the forests.

In a campaign where the enemy usually melted into the bush and major engagements were a rarity, the defeat of Captain Nyagi Nyaga's army at Dundora was heralded as a notable success for the security forces.[114]

The interrogations of Captain Nyaga and his followers lasted more than three weeks.[115] When the evidence was gathered, forty-one of those arrested at Dandora came before the Special Emergency Assize Courts in seven trials. The thirty-seven men and four women who stood in the dock can be broadly grouped into three categories. The first comprised seasoned Mau Mau fighters, who had been in the Aberdares forest for many months. There were only five such fighters among the Dandora captives brought before the court: Kaburuki M'amamja, a married man of around twenty-two years of age from Meru; Irongo Mwangi, a former tailor from Ndegba in Fort Hall, who had been educated to Form II at a Church Mission Society (CMS) primary school; Jacob Maina Gituru, in his early twenties, another CMS affiliate, who had been employed as a clerk in Nairobi prior to the Emergency; Kirongochu Nyaga, a young man of twenty years, from Kirioniri, in Embu, who freely admitted his activities with the forest fighters in the Aberdares; and their leader, Nyagi Nyaga. It is striking that so few of this large gang fell into this category. Several other experienced forest fighters were certainly among those killed at Dandora, and we know that others were among the few who slipped through the cordon on the morning of 25 October; but there had been only around a dozen experienced Mau Mau fighters at Dandora.

The court heard that the 'talkative' Nyaga had been cooperative under interrogation. Carrying the insignia of a British army captain on his tattered, improvised military uniform, Nyaga made no effort to conceal his role as a freedom fighter. A married man in his early twenties, from Meru, with a little Anglican education, he had joined General Simba on Mount Kenya at the outbreak of the Emergency in October 1952, later coming under the command of General Kassam. He had come to Nairobi at Kassam's instigation in September 1954 with a small band of a dozen or so fighters, to secure supplies and to gather new recruits for the movement.[116] Nyaga told the CID of his life as a forest fighter, and gave general information on the activities of the Mau Mau gangs. During his interrogation, Nyaga had been promised 'that nothing bad [would] happen' if he provided useful information: 'If I make a true statement of my activities in the forest,' he later told the court, 'then I would be one of the members of the police.'[117]

He was even taken into Nairobi to be interviewed by Special Branch on his more recent adventures in and around the city. It was here, in Kileleshwa gaol, that Nyaga encountered Mohamed Mathu. The two men had first met a fortnight earlier, when Nyaga had gone to visit Mathu and Mwangi Toto at their camp on the city's southern fringe. Captain Nyagi Nyaga impressed Mathu as 'a friendly, talkative man', telling 'many stories about Kimathi, Mathenge and the fight in the Aberdares forests'. Nyaga explained that he had come to Nairobi from the Aberdares because his forest battalion 'were urgently in need of arms, ammunition and other supplies'. Mathu gave Nyaga seven shotguns, a quantity of ammunition, clothing and some cash, and provided him with an escort to take him safely back to his followers camped at Dandora. The two comrades now exchanged news of the circumstances that had brought each of them to Kileleshwa. Mathu had been wounded and captured on 12 October, just after his first meeting with Nyaga. Six Mau Mau comrades met their deaths that day, including Mwangi Toto.[118]

Nyaga evidently believed that cooperation would save him from execution. Bargaining of this kind was effective in other cases, but it did not save Nyaga. He was sentenced to hang, along with the four other seasoned fighters amongst the Dandora accused.

The second element identifiable among Nyaga's army was former inmates of Lukenya Prison, who had escaped to their freedom in September as a consequences of the raid by Mohamed Mathu and his comrades. Prisoners at Lukenya were committed to detention for having taken a Mau Mau oath, for being in possession of false identity papers, or on suspicion of rebel sympathies; none were 'high risk'.[119] On their unexpected release, these men found themselves in a predicament: having consorted with a Mau Mau gang in the escape, they were now liable to prosecution for what was a capital offence. Without pass papers, labour documents or certificates of release they could not return home; nor could they safely remain in Nairobi. These fugitives had little option but to go to the forests. Five Lukenya escapees now appeared in court with Captain Nyaga. All five were found guilty of consorting with terrorists and sentenced to hang, though two were reprieved because they were found to be only seventeen years of age.

The third category among Nyaga's followers was by far the largest. Of those before the court, twenty-nine professed themselves to be new recruits to the Mau Mau cause. Many claimed to have been taken by force from their homes and jobs in Nairobi. They told the court of their 'capture' by Mau Mau in Kariokor, Pumwani, Kasarani, Shauri Moyo or Mathare, of oathing ceremonies, and of being forced to move to the Dandora hideout. They included many who had been 'gathered up' by the men of General Mwairuthi, then Mau Mau's chief recruiting agent in the city. Others had been recruited directly by Nyaga and his men, as they administered oaths in the vicinity of Kahawa and Dandora during

October 1954.[120] They employment records of several of the accused supported their claims, showing they had worked for local employers up to a few days before their arrest.

Among them were all varieties of people. Wanjiru Mugo was one of four women arrested at Dandora. Originally from Embu, she worked in Nairobi as a street vendor, at a kiosk close to the railway station. Unmarried, but with one child, she had been 'taken by Mau Mau' to Mathare to be oathed. M'Anambio M'Itara, a Catholic from Meru, worked at a city hotel before his capture, while Edwin Waiyaki Thoroba was a clerk with Express Transport. Kariuki Kimotho was the oldest amongst those arrested at Dandora. A twenty-eight-year-old Catholic, originating from Nyeri and married with a child, Kimotho worked at Ruaraka before being press-ganged.[121] Karanja Kihara was a sixteen-year-old student at the Remington Business College, on Government Road in central Nairobi. Kihara told the court, 'Mau Mau abducted me by pretending to be policemen.'[122] Maina Gatembu had worked in the main railway stockyards until 18 October. Literate and articulate, having been educated up to Standard III at a Church Missionary Society in Embu, Gatembe told the court that Mau Mau agents had seized him near his home in Kariokor. M'Minati M'Igiria also lived in Kariokor, working as a labourer and lorry turn-boy until 23 October.

As Kikuyu workers in Nairobi, all these men and women had been screened during Operation Anvil in April and May 1954. The fact that all had retained their employment indicated that the security forces had then considered them to be free from Mau Mau influence.

The remarkable courtroom testimony of another of the accused also supported the claims of Mau Mau coercion and press-ganging. A confessed Mau Mau forest fighter, Kirongochi told the court that he had been in the Aberdares for many months before coming to Nairobi to gather new recruits. He described how he had gone from place to place and 'arrested people'. Starting out from Shauri Moyo, where Captain Nyaga made contact with Mau Mau leaders in the city, they had split into two recruitment patrols. His had gone first to Majengo, then to Kariokor, then near to the Khoja mosque, and finally to Kasarani. 'We had over thirty prisoners' by the time Dandora was reached, Kirongochi told the court.[123] He described how three of his fellow accused, Ngugi Njaguna, Marete Kilela and Gatuthu Gecha, were all in fact captives, and explained that he had personally been assigned 'to guard them'. His evidence was detailed and fitted well with the statements made by his co-accused; but it did not help any of them escape conviction. Justice Rudd declared that he 'did not believe Kirongochi's statement', as there 'was nothing else to support the contention'.[124] Nothing, that is, except the statements of his fellow co-accused in the dock. Kirongocha, and the three reluctant recruits he had guarded, all hanged together in Nairobi gaol on 3 January 1955.

Justice Rudd saw no reason to show mercy to Kirongochi, but he did have doubts about some of the other convictions. He confided to Governor Baring that many of the gang 'were obviously new recruits'.[125] 'I think it possible', he wrote, 'that none of the accused in this case have done much, or any, actual fighting.'[126] And Rudd was palpably disturbed by the last of the Dandora cases, on 18 December 1954. In this trial five accused stood in the dock together, four males in their early twenties and a young, local Dandora girl of only twelve years of age, Njoki Macharia, who had become embroiled in the battle having brought food to the hideout. After questioning the prosecution counsel, Rudd speedily acquitted her.[127] Njoki Macharia was spared the ordeal of the trial, but her very presence in the courtroom exposed the haphazard and callous procedures of arrest, interrogation and prosecution that marked the Mau Mau war.

What does the battle of Dandora swamp tell us about the conduct of the Mau Mau war? In a campaign where sustained contact with the enemy was rare, the entrapment of so large a gang was certainly a notable event. The battle was hardly the glorious success that the security forces claimed, however, given the comparative youth and lowly status in the movement of the majority of those captured. From a gang of more than eighty strong, forty-one persons were brought to trial and thirty-eight were found guilty, no less than fourteen being juveniles. A total of seventeen convicts from the Dandora trials went to the gallows, all being hanged in Nairobi gaol between 3 January and 20 March 1955, and their bodies taken to Kamiti for burial in unmarked graves.[128] Acting Justice Rudd, who presided over six of the seven trials, accepted that only five of these executed men were in fact Mau Mau fighters. Under the law he had no choice but to find them all guilty as charged: all were undoubtedly 'consorting with terrorists'. The inability – or unwillingness – of the colonial government to distinguish between active Mau Mau fighters and those swept into the net by dint of fear and vulnerability fundamentally weakened the counter-insurgency campaign, and undermined the rule of law.

The Dandora trials also revealed a great deal about the impact that the success of Anvil was having upon the Mau Mau units beyond Nairobi. The fighters who had opened up a second front against the security forces around Nairobi in the weeks after Operation Anvil were speedily run to ground. By the end of January 1955 both Mathu and Chotara had been captured, and Mwangi Toto killed. Operation Anvil had successfully 'pinched off supplies to the forest bands and made it much more difficult for the passive wing to help the guerrillas'.[129] Recruitment of fighters from within the city became increasingly difficult, and this explains the high proportion among Captain Nyaga's army who were coerced into service. Those taken into the gangs after May 1954 were generally younger than those who had gone to the forests earlier in the emergency. This was symptomatic not so much of the radicalism of the young but of the growing desperation of Mau Mau's city-based recruiting officers.

Within the city the months following Anvil were relatively peaceful, with only sporadic signs of Mau Mau activity.[130] Eastlands was then one of the most closely administered parts of British Africa, with its own District Commissioner, two district officers, and four European Home Guard commanders. No fewer than eleven chiefs reported to these officers, with thirty headmen and 300 tribal police working through the chiefs.[131] For the first time since 1951 Kikuyu opposed to Mau Mau began to breathe a little easier; and as a consequence Special Branch was able to recruit a substantial number of Kikuyu informants. The flood of good intelligence this brought utterly transformed the war in Eastlands.[132]

Mau Mau influence had been squeezed out of the urban economy. Virtually all hawkers' licences held by Kikuyu were cancelled after Anvil. Those few Kikuyu running tea kiosks, charcoal stalls, or shoe-repair carts after June 1954 were loyalists. Other than in the Kikuyu estates of Bahati and Kariokor, the majority of shops were transferred to non-Kikuyu. The business interests of the Kikuyu were worst hit in Pumwani, where some 150 shop-owners were forced out. Pumwani was no longer in the control of Mau Mau, but the security fence built around the estate would not be taken down until 1957 (see table 5.ii, p. 352, for a breakdown of shop closures in Pumwani).[133]

Mau Mau was on the back foot in the city after June 1954, but its influence had by no means been entirely expunged. Armed men still went about the town on the movement's business, many of them persons who had been screened during Anvil and found to be 'untainted by Mau Mau'. In mid-June, for example, a Kikuyu loyalist in Gorofani was shot by a man who had just been released from the Anvil screening camps; and in the first week of July, an armed man arrested near River Road was found to have been in Nairobi with forged identity documents since long before Anvil, but somehow had escaped screening altogether.[134] Nyaga and his recruitment parties had been able to operate throughout Eastlands without being apprehended in September and October. These incidents indicated that the struggle was far from over.

The war in Eastlands had moved into a new, more covert phase, as Mau Mau's supporters and Special Branch's army of informants gingerly circled one another in an elaborate game of cat and mouse.[135] As the informers grew more confident, they targeted the gunmen and the 'enforcers', of whom they had previously lived in fear; and increasingly, and inevitably, the energies of the Mau Mau urban fighters turned inwards, as they sought to 'weed out' the informers in their midst. It was a grim and dirty business, sapping the morale and deepening the distrust among Nairobi's Kikuyu communities.

The murders of informers began even as the soldiers were departing from Eastlands. One of the first victims was a Kamba, Mule Ntheimi, who was strangled and stabbed near Dandora on 25 May 1954. His assassin, a butcher named Njeroge Muhoro, may have thought Ntheimi was the informant who, during Anvil, had directed police to a property in Dandora that was being used as a Mau Mau safe house.[136] Muhoro was convicted on the eyewitness evidence of Ntheimi's wife. He hanged at Nairobi gaol on 5 July.[137] From the same area, one week after Ntheimi's murder, other informants led police to the home of Kiiru Gauma, who was found to be in possession of ammunition. Gauma was convicted, and hanged in August.[138] This sequence of events was not unconnected.

The game of tit-for-tat went on all over Eastlands. There were many examples of Mau Mau fighters who had long remained unmolested in the city now being picked out by the informers. One such was Kinga Migui, a powerfully built man from Embu and a leading personality among the municipal sweepers employed by the city council. He was arrested in August and prosecuted for possession of ammunition. Judge Holmes thought him 'a natural bully and a dangerous criminal'. Proud of his contribution to the anti-colonial cause, Migui showed no respect for the court or its justice. He was taken for execution on 4 October 1954. Nganga Kimani, another hardened Mau Mau rebel, was first arrested at the end of July after an informant gave away his hiding place in the roof of a Duke Street shop. Kimani then escaped from custody, and was only re-arrested two months later. He had remained in Nairobi all this time, using several different identity cards, all forged. The twenty-year-old son of a squatter, born in Laikipia, Kimani had come to the city as a teenager before the Emergency, when his family had been evicted from the white farm where they had lived. He was convicted and sentenced to hang. Another committed rebel, Gitau Kamau, was caught after being wounded in a running gun battle with police through the railway workers' quarters at Muthurwa. Kamau was identified after police received a tip-off from an informer. When confronted amid the houses at Muthurwa, he resisted arrest and fired his Smith & Wesson revolver repeatedly at the Home Guards and police chasing him. Kamau, a father of three from Murang'a district, was convicted in a brief trial on 20 September, and executed at Nairobi gaol on 12 November 1954. British justice in Kenya was speeding up. By then, more than 700 Mau Mau convicts had gone to the gallows.

The housing estate at Muthurwa, known as the railway *lhandies*, where Kamau had been cornered, was a key site in the struggle for ascendancy in Nairobi after Anvil. The railways had been allowed to retain a higher proportion of Kikuyu workers than had other employers following the purge of the city's African labour, and the police suspected that Mau Mau sympathizers were still very prominent among the residents at Muthurwa. From August 1954, Special Branch infiltrated the railway *lhandies* with informants. As the supply of useful intelligence began to flow, the first raids began; it soon became obvious that the police had inside knowledge. As suspicions rose among the workers, the atmosphere on the estate became incredibly tense. Kamau's arrest in the *lhandies*, late in October, further deepened animosities among the residents. The cloak-and-danger game played out between the informants and their suspects finally exploded, on the evening of 13 September 1954, in one of the most dramatic and intense acts of public violence of the entire Emergency.

The housing blocks occupied by the railway workers at Muthurwa were long, single-storey buildings. The doors of the living quarters opened onto a veranda running the length of each building and connecting to communal kitchens directly opposite. These facilities were basic and squalid, but there were tables and benches where meals could be taken in relative comfort. Latrines were located at the ends of the blocks. This was rudimentary, strictly functional housing, typical of the kind thought appropriate in Kenya for single, young male migrant workers. But the community occupying the railway *lhandies* by 1954 also included many women, the wives and daughters of workers. During Anvil, these women went through screening in order to be issued with a pass to remain in the city. The vast majority had been refused a pass and expelled from the city, and those who now remained were the family members of men who were loyalists or Home Guard. As tensions mounted in the *lhandies*, suspicion naturally fell upon the women residents. Among these were three girls, two sisters, Hannah and Wairimu, aged seventeen and eighteen, and their foster-sister, Ndururu, who was only fifteen, but looked even younger. Their father, Japhet, was an elderly and trusted railway employee who had long lived at Muthurwa.

On the evening of 13 September the three girls came to cook a meal at their father's home, Room 10 in Block H1 of the *lhandies*. As they sat preparing the food by the light of an oil lamp, two men they knew came and stood by the door, talking casually. Japhet, who was sitting in the kitchen gossiping with some friends, suddenly became aware of other men approaching, carrying pangas and knives. When he made as if to move, they signalled to him to keep still. Japhet froze, his elderly mind in a panic of terror. He heard the men accuse his daughters of being 'friends of the Home Guard', before they lunged into the room. When the attack on his daughters began, Japhet fled to the police post to seek help. As he ran, he could hear the pitiful screams.

The twelve men who burst in upon Hannah, Wairimu and Ndururu hacked them to pieces. Hannah suffered twenty-two stab wounds and cuts, and Wairimu only slightly fewer. Both had struggled against their attackers. Hannah died outside the door of the room, Wairimu on the bed. When Inspector Mathews of the CID arrived at the scene twenty minutes after the attack, the doorway and veranda were swimming in blood. Some of that blood was Ndururu's. She had also been slashed several times, the worst wound being a deep and savage panga cut across her abdomen, whereupon she had fallen to the ground. Presuming all three to be dead, the attackers retreated from the scene, leaving the girls where they lay. Ndururu, miraculously still alive, somehow found the strength to pick herself up and, gathering her own entrails in her arms, made her way down the street, screaming and wailing as she went. A young Luo railway worker, Petro Ouma, came to her aid and helped her to a neighbour's house. Later, on her way to hospital, Ndururu provided the police with the names of those among the attackers whom she had recognized.

The terrified screams of the three young women had been heard by Kikuyu, Luo and Kamba workers in housing blocks up to 300 yards away from where the murders took place, yet the police could obtain no witness statements from any person living in the houses close to the scene of the crime. Many residents were evidently traumatized and appalled by what had happened, but none felt able to speak. The only witnesses of any use at all were the elderly Japhet and his foster-daughter Ndururu. When the case finally came to court, in December, it was Ndururu, barely recovered from her dreadful injuries, and visibly displaying the many scars from her ordeal, who was the crucial witness. Her evidence, coolly and intelligently delivered, led to the conviction of seven men. All but one of the convicts were railway workers, and the seventh was a student who was also resident at Muthurwa. This was a very 'local' affair. The bitterness of relationships among the community of the *lhandies* was apparent in the courtroom. The convicted men were content with what they had done. Judge Holmes thought that one of the convicts, Douglas Kinene, 'even seemed to glory in his part in the murder, and never tried to conceal it'. Kinene, only seventeen, had known his victims well. He and another two of the convicts, also under eighteen years of age, had their death sentences commuted. Their four co-conspirators were hanged at Nairobi gaol on 4 March 1955.

The troubles in the railway *lhandies* did not end there. Only a month after the conviction of Hannah and Wairimu's murderers, Special Branch received further information of Mau Mau activity. They sprang a trap later that night and cornered a Mau Mau gunman in a lavatory at the end of one of the housing blocks. He refused to give himself up. When a tear-gas grenade was lobbed into the latrine, he burst out, wildly firing his revolver. A European inspector was hit in the leg, but after a chase through the *lhandies* the gunman was wounded and caught. His name was Gathuku Kinyanjui. He had come into Nairobi from Kiambu, where Special Branch believed he had been working with a Mau Mau gang. An informer had seen him entering the *lhandies* on the morning of his capture, with a revolver tucked into his waistband. He was convicted in February and hanged one month later.[139] Kinyanjui's arrest was the second big success the police had enjoyed in the *lhandies* that week. Two days earlier, only a short distance away, Mau Mau's General Mwairuthi had been captured. An informer had first spotted him in the late morning, walking close to Muthurwa. As a gust of wind blew his coat open, she had caught a glimpse of the butt of a pistol. She had followed him discreetly, taking careful note of the people he talked with and the number of the house he finally entered, before she rushed to the police post with her valuable intelligence. The police who arrested General Mwairuthi one hour later were full of praise for the young informer's calm professionalism. It was another good day's work for Ndururu.[140] Her vengeance was costing Mau Mau dear.

## Corruption at City Hall

The Emergency was more intensely fought in the alleyways of Eastlands than in any other part of central Kenya. Even after Anvil had broken the back of Mau Mau's organization in the city, those Africans who refused to be oathed, who opposed violence or who were loyal to the government still went in fear for their lives. It was not until the latter months of 1955, by which time the forest war, too, was nearly over, that the killing stopped in Eastlands.

No one could pretend that the city had been governed in a 'normal' manner during the fight against Mau Mau. The harassment of African citizens in pursuit of Mau Mau suspects had been relentless, and many innocent souls had been caught up in the indiscriminate sweeps through the estates and the repeated 'cordon and search' operations. The ending of the rent subsidies in 1953 had brought greater hardship to all African tenants,[141] and even as Operation Anvil had begun, in April 1954, the City Council announced yet another round of rent increases.[142] The economics of urban life threatened what fragile support the government had gained in Eastlands. African allies had come to expect rewards for their loyalty. The government gave proven loyalists remission from tax payments, and in some cases reinstated their housing subsidies. All hawking licences and retail tenancies were reserved to loyalists, and after Anvil the allocation of accommodation in all the government estates was subject to the 'screening' of applicants to weed out potential Mau Mau supporters.

At the higher levels, the colonial government was aware of the pressing need to reward its Kikuyu friends; but this was not a view that the white highlanders who still dominated Nairobi's City Council necessarily shared. When, at the beginning of 1953, the council had come to debate a further programme of house building on the African estates, there was massive opposition. The more vociferous European elected councillors saw no good reason to reward Africans with anything, least of all at a time when the colony's economy was on the slide. Governor Baring did his best to persuade them otherwise, working hard through officials in London to secure a grant from the Colonial Development Corporation. Several councillors were not easily convinced: Kenya's white settlers could always be relied upon to be parsimonious when it came to expenditure on African welfare. When the council finally put the new housing development to the vote, it was a close-run thing: the decision to accept the grant was taken by a margin of only one vote, 14 against 13. This was hardly a ringing endorsement for what was to be the largest housing development ever planned in British colonial Africa, with an investment of £2 million over five years, for the construction of 13,000 new bed-spaces each year.[143] As the project got under way, the government made no effort to disguise the symbolic and material place of housing provision in the struggle for 'hearts and minds', naming the new estates after the African city councillors who had been murdered by Mau Mau, Tom Mbotela and Ambrose Ofafa.

It was never going to be easy to manage a project as vast as this in the midst of the Emergency. The City Council was understaffed, and there were doubts that the local construction industry had the capacity for the task. The industry was dominated by a dozen larger European- and Asian-owned firms. These firms had little need to work on African housing projects, where budgets were tight and margins narrow, pre-ferring corporate contracts or private work for Europeans. The remaining contractors were smaller firms, perhaps numbering thirty, nearly all of which were Asian. These were 'one-job-at-a-time operations', with only the most basic capital equipment, no workshops and a tendency to rely upon cheaper casual labour even for skilled work.[144] When the City Council put the first stage of the Mbotela and Ofafa developments out to tender, all the most competitive bids came from these smaller Asian firms, and they were duly contracted to take on the work. Construction had got under way in the early months of 1954, only a few weeks before the commencement of Operation Anvil.

The scandal broke only a few months later, when, in June, the Nairobi CID informed the City Council auditors that allegations of corruption had been made against senior council staff. The whistle-blower was not named, but it was most likely someone fairly senior in the circles of the municipal government, perhaps a European member of staff in the accounts office. The tendering for and administration of the building contracts on the new housing developments at Ofafa and Mbotela estates featured prominently in the police investigation. A flurry of rumours now swirled around the city, suggesting that massive fraud had been discovered. The European councillors at first tried to play this down, rejecting calls for a public enquiry. As they struggled to keep the lid on things, colonial officials in London got wind of the brewing scandal; if the grant from the Colonial Development Corporation had been misused in any way, then Nairobi was told it would be imperative to hold a full public enquiry. In August the City Council reluctantly accepted the appointment of Sir Alan Rose to head a three-man commission, with a brief to examine accusations of corruption and malpractice in every aspect of the affairs of the Nairobi City Council. The implications were deeply alarming.

Never had a commission of enquiry been less welcome in Kenya than was that led by Sir Alan Rose. A distinguished barrister of the Inner Temple, and a confirmed bachelor with a reputation for probity, austerity and sternly conservative values, Rose was hardly the kind of man likely to find many kindred spirits among the robust, hard-drinking and womanizing white highlanders. He arrived in Nairobi during December to a frosty welcome. The commissioners declined the suggestion that their deliberations should wait until after the holiday, and began hearing evidence in the week before Christmas. It was a wise decision. They were immediately overwhelmed with petitioners. The commission was unable to finish its business until the end of March.[145]

The scale of corruption unearthed by the Rose Commission surprised even Kenya's most cynical observers. The operation of the City Architect's office, and its supervision of the Ofafa and Mbotela contracts in particular, came in for savage criticism. At Ofafa the work was split into three contracts. The first, valued at £80,722, went to Chanan Singh. His company had no experience of large-scale contract work, and was badly under-capitalized. Local architects' reports on the tender were highly unfavourable, yet these were ignored. In June 1955 the Council had finally evicted the contractor from the site, the work still incomplete.

On inspection, numerous contraventions of the building specifications came to light – shallow excavation of footings, under-strength concreting in floors and lintels, substandard joinery, the use of cheaper, weaker materials throughout, and generally poor standards of workmanship. Yet, throughout the contract this work had apparently been inspected and approved by City Council officers. The cost of setting these matters right was £60,000. A similar sorry story was revealed on the second Ofafa contract, awarded to the firm of Ata-Ul-Haq at £85,475. Here again, the Council had only independently investigated the quality of work once the corruption investigation was under way, and had then swiftly moved to evict the contractor. It was estimated that a sum in excess of £60,000 would be required to make good the work on the Ata-Ul-Haq contract. On the third part of the Ofafa development, another Asian firm, the Colonial Construction Company, had undertaken a smaller contract of £60,568. Here the quality of workmanship was better, but the same deliberate shortfalls in specifications were discovered, and again all work had been inspected and passed fit by Council officials. The picture was very much the same on the Mbotela estate.[146]

The implications of these revelations soon became clear. European officials had accepted 'gifts' from building contractors before and during the Ofafa and Mbotela contracts, entering false specifications and logging inspection reports when no inspections had taken place. Malpractice was found to be widespread in every aspect of the tendering and management of the Council's building contracts, and had evidently been so for many years. Among the senior officials named in the enquiry was the City Engineer, Harold Whipp. He was found to be implicated in fraudulent construction work going back to 1949, when he first came to East Africa from Bombay. The sums involved were considerable, running to thousands of pounds in some years. In Nairobi, Whipp lived in one of the smartest new suburbs of the city, enjoying a lifestyle that belied his relatively humble salary. On 13 February 1956, in the midst of the Rose Commission's deliberations and just after he was warned of the likelihood of prosecution, Harold Whipp's body was found on the railway line near to Nairobi. He had committed suicide.[147]

If Whipp was the most notorious official to be exposed in this scandal, he was by no means the only person to have his reputation tarnished. Following the example of Governor Baring, Nairobi's councillors protested that what failings there were lay only with 'a few rogues' on the city payroll – the kind of people who had found their way to East Africa only in the difficult conditions of the Emergency. It was a poor excuse.

The Rose Commission anyway came to a quite different view. It wasn't just African Home Guards who had cultivated a culture of bribery and extortion in colonial Kenya. The examples Rose listed covered

virtually every aspect of municipal government. Two European contractors, for example, were found to have conspired with city officials in
a fraud costing the Council £16,154 in payments made for goods never
delivered. The whiff of corruption also tainted the reputations of the
highest aldermen of the Council: the Mayor of Nairobi, Israel Somen,
and the former Deputy Mayor, Dobbs Johnson, were heavily criticized
for having failed to declare their substantial interests in companies supplying goods to the Council. Somen was also accused of using council
workers for his own enterprises, including the construction of his private
swimming pool. Even in the City Fire Brigade, a group of senior
European officers were involved in a longstanding scam to 'sell' city
property, and then have it bought back at a margin. The profits earned
were placed in a bank account by the group, for their personal use. At
the city market, corruption was rife in the allocation of licences and
plots, the senior African clerk taking bribes as a matter of course from
all the traders, and the European Market Manager, Mr Burton, abusing
his position to secure unpaid labour from the stallholders to work his
own farm on the outskirts of the city.[148] Sir Alan Rose reached the
unequivocal conclusion that bribery and corruption were 'by no means
uncommon' among city office holders at 'all levels and in all departments'; that the scale of cash inducements involved to secure services or
preference from the Council was often significant; and that such behaviour was accepted as the norm and widely tolerated.[149]

The exploitation of traders at the city market was typical of a wide
range of petty corruption that marred the daily life of Nairobi. Its victims,
the stallholders and wholesalers who operated the market, were not the
hardline supporters of Mau Mau but members of the aspirant African
middle classes. These were the kind of people for whom the new houses
on the Ofafa and Mbotela estates had been built. Their loyalty had been
tested in Operation Anvil. They had won the right to retain their trading
licences and urban work permits, and had remained in Nairobi despite
the intimidation of Mau Mau threats. Like the office workers who staffed
the government departments throughout the emergency years, they had
been forced to make difficult choices. They might be applauded by
Europeans on political platforms, and have eulogies written to their
bravery in the government's propaganda pamphlets, but very few of
Kenya's white highlanders would ever treat them with genuine respect.
Their new 'model' homes had ill-fitting windows, doors that warped in
the damp, and drains that flooded when it rained, and were built to
standards that no European would have tolerated; and in their working
lives, they were subjected to the abuse and exploitation of anyone who
had authority over them. Europeans were as guilty of corruption and
malpractice in colonial Nairobi as anyone else, and Africans, at the

bottom of the colonial racial hierarchy, were most often its victims, regardless of their politics.

This was the experience of the vast majority of those who stood on the loyalist side of Kenya's anti-colonial war in Nairobi. These people did not *like* colonialism. In taking a stand, these so-called loyalists were in fact motivated by more prosaic and personal concerns: by the interests of their families; by the need to protect their property; by their sense of social status; and by their own values. These people were not fools; and if they had ever been naive, then the harsh realities of African life in Nairobi in the 1950s had surely brought a sharper awareness. During the emergency, even the most ambitious *tai-tai* came to realize that they could never be the equal of the white man in Nairobi's rotten borough.

# 6

# General China's War
# Freedom Fighters in the Forests

Of all the Mau Mau fighters, the British were perhaps most eager to capture Waruhiu Itote. He had been among the first rebels to take to the forests in 1952. Known by his military name of General China, he directed the formation of the fighting units on Mount Kenya, securing supplies and weapons, and bringing recruits into the mountain camps. Like Dedan Kimathi and Stanley Mathenge, the two senior commanders in the Aberdares forest, there was a price on China's head, dead or alive.

Most Mau Mau generals would die fighting, or be captured and go to the gallows. Not General China. He had a good war, and lived to tell the tale. After the war was over and the British retreated from Kenya, the General reverted to a civilian identity and, as Waruhiu Itote, became a political personality of importance. In Jomo Kenyatta's first government he was appointed section commander of the National Youth Service, rising to Deputy Director. Itote was responsible for training programmes and welfare work, and he organized the youth wing of the party, the Kenya African National Union. As a former forest fighter, Waruhiu Itote represented the heritage of the nationalist struggle for land and freedom. In independent Kenya he became a hero.

Born into a prosperous farming family in the South Tetu division of Nyeri, Itote gained only a little education at the local Church of Scotland mission. His father had no faith in the teachings of the white man, and instead encouraged his son in farming. Impatient for a more adventurous lifestyle, the teenage Itote left his rural home for the urban lure of Nairobi. There, at the age of twenty, he enlisted with the King's African Rifles. It was 1942, and Itote would join other Kenyans in the fight against the Japanese.[1] Strongly built and physically fit, he adapted well to military life, enjoying the camaraderie and the discipline, and seizing the opportunities to learn new skills, working his way up to the rank of signals corporal in his regiment. The gregarious Itote made friends easily as he moved through Asia with the army. In Calcutta an African-American soldier named Stephenson told him about the liberation of Haiti, and he met Indian nationalists who asked him why Africans were not pushing off the yoke of colonial rule. For Itote, travel certainly did broaden the mind.

Returning to Kenya, and demobilization, he quickly became aware of the lack of opportunities for men of his generation who had fought in the war. First, he earned a crust selling charcoal, before finding better-paid work in Nairobi's railway yards as a fireman. There he drifted into urban politics, joining the KAU in 1946 and then becoming a member of the Transport and Allied Workers' Union, where he was inspired, as were other itinerant veterans, by the radicalism of union organizers Fred Kubai and Bildad Kaggia. In the company of former army comrades, he dabbled in the criminal underworld of Nairobi's Forty Group, augmenting his fireman's wages with 'night work' in Eastlands. He took his first Mau Mau oath in 1950, though he claimed that he had no political awareness of what the movement was. Within a few months he was heavily involved in the activities directed by the *Muhimu*, working through the Nyeri committee in Nairobi. He organized oathing, and was an executioner of 'traitors'. By now, Itote 'knew that our people could never win their independence solely by peaceful means'.[2] As the killings began in earnest, Itote was in the thick of it.

In 1952 he went north to Nyeri, to assist in oathing there. Itote believed in oathing the community *en masse*, even forcing the reluctant into compliance. 'Afterwards we explained what was expected of them,' he later wrote; 'the British had taken our land, we said, and we had dedicated ourselves to the fight for our liberty – those who had taken the oath must now help us in every possible way.'[3] Itote would never apologize for the intimidation of reluctant supplicants, or for the murders. 'This was not wholesale, indiscriminate murder as the British government tried to say,' he would later write. 'Only a real two-faced traitor, and there is nothing worse in the world, would be sentenced to death. Our courts were much fairer than those of the government with their summary justice, their framed evidence, their perjuring, bought witnesses.'[4] These words would be thrown back in his face, but in building solidarity, Itote was prepared to do what must be done.

In August of 1952, as the police clamped down on *Muhimu* in Nyeri, Itote moved into the Mount Kenya forest with a rag-tag band of perhaps thirty followers. The numbers soon grew. When the emergency was declared in October, Itote had established his forest camp and adopted his Mau Mau name. His military experience, gained in the Burma campaign against the Japanese, served him well. The rudiments of a command structure were quickly established among his men. General China maintained discipline and drilled his recruits; and he was careful to liaise with elders in the reserve, whose support he depended upon for supplies and munitions. The Christmas Eve attacks heralded the beginning of hostilities in Nyeri. Soon after this, General China's notoriety was established, as the British gathered the first intelligence on his activities.[5]

From January 1953 the wave of attacks on European farms in Nyeri and Nanyuki was directed by China, in connection with the oathing of farm labourers and the recruitment of forest fighters. China's gang was well armed, and through these raids they acquired several more good precision weapons. He gained a reputation as a skilled commander, with ability to organize. On the night of 20 June 1953, for example, China was responsible for simultaneous attacks on three Home Guard posts in northern Murang'a. His men also targeted loyalists in nearby villages, destroying road bridges to disrupt their pursuers. The next month China coordinated attacks on mission schools in north Nyeri, razing buildings in retaliation for church support of the Home Guard; and it was General China's men, on a mission to steal arms and supplies, who murdered the Italian settler Mrs Meloncelli and her children at the Chehe sawmill at the end of April 1953.

China's glories came to an end on 15 January 1954. With a stroke of luck, the security forces intercepted a Mau Mau group, reckoned to be more than a hundred strong, as they crossed the reserve at Karatina, between Mount Kenya and the Aberdares. General China was among them. In a sporadic battle, China's men were pinned down in a valley, with soldiers and Home Guard on the ridges above. Scrambling up toward the neck of the valley, seeking a gap in the encirclement, China was caught in crossfire and struck twice, once in the throat and once through the chin. He fell back down the hill into thick undergrowth, injuring his leg and briefly losing consciousness. Later that afternoon, having lost a great deal of blood and believing that he would soon die of his wounds, General China limped into a KAR camp and gave himself up.

China's capture caused great euphoria amongst the British, who were starved of positive news. This was the first senior general who had fallen into British hands. Here was an opportunity for good publicity in a campaign that had too few real successes, and Special Branch was keen to make the most of any intelligence that might be gleaned. China's interrogation was to be more revealing, and to have greater consequence, than anyone could have imagined.

The man brought to deal with the General was Assistant Superintendent Ian Henderson, the son of a pioneer settler and a white highlander through and through. Henderson had grown up on a farm in Nyeri, among Kikuyu children, and spoke the language with vernacular fluency.[6] Expecting to be tortured, the nervous General China had impressed upon his captors that he was a former British soldier, and that he held high Mau Mau rank. No one had beaten him. Instead, he was taken to hospital to have his wounds treated. He was too valuable a catch to be thrown into the hands of a vengeful Home Guard, as other captives might have been. General China was an asset to be exploited.

It came as a great surprise to China to be interviewed in his own language, and courteously addressed, by a white man who was his own age yet showed him respect. In physique the interrogator and his prisoner were remarkably similar: both short but of wiry, strong build, both keen and furtive in their movements, both with an aura of command and control over those around them. They were wary of one another. Henderson thought China seemed resigned to his fate, knowing that, whatever might happen, he would die. It was not so much a conversation at first, more an exercise in stalking. Henderson kept his distance, but from time to time rushed forward to provoke a reaction. The strategy began to work.

Proud of his role in Mau Mau's leadership, China was keen to correct misapprehensions about the movement's discipline or organization. As Henderson probed, China blurted out his answers. The tirade of assertion and description quite took Henderson's breath away.[7] When the process was over, after many hours, Henderson had forty-four pages of closely typed script. For the first time the British had glimpsed life within the forest gangs.[8] China had been careful not to divulge information that would place his forest comrades in danger, but he gave detailed description of the military formations on Mount Kenya, including the names and deployment of the 'regiments' and a sense of the size of the rebel forces – China's own command had grown from thirty to a force 4000 strong.

In a further stroke of luck, the British were able to consolidate and corroborate parts of this picture. Unknown to China, a senior officer in his Hika Hika Company, Karani Karanja, had also been captured. A brigadier by Mau Mau rank, and one of China's scribes, Karanja was in possession of documents on the organization and supply of the Mount Kenya forces. Between them, China and Karanja gave away a great deal more about the connections with the reserve than Special Branch had previously understood. This was the first intelligence breakthrough of the war. The British thought it a major triumph.

General China came before Judge MacDuff at Nyeri on 1 February 1954, charged with possession of ammunition and consorting with armed persons.[9] He appeared clean-shaven and sharp-eyed, his thin gaunt face set below a mat of plaited hair. He was wearing a white hospital shirt, and looked in far better shape than most of the other Mau Mau suspects who had stood in that courthouse. China was flanked by African constables, who towered over him, one holding a Sten gun at the ready. In front of him were two more policemen, with pistols in their belts. Others patrolled outside. The British were taking no chances on China escaping, or Mau Mau mounting a rescue bid.

In contrast to most other legal proceedings, this trial was mercifully short. Itote's defence counsel, Kapila, built a stout defence that the two rounds of ammunition found in China's pocket had been planted. They were British army issue, so it seemed a reasonable plea. But there was nothing the young lawyer could do about the detailed statement describing China's role in the forest, extracts of which were read to the court. Kapila's task was not helped when his client declined to refute the statements: China was not going to deny his rank or status. Justice MacDuff lost little time in finding China guilty of consorting with terrorists, and sentenced him to hang. It seemed that he would take his pride to the gallows.

What happened next would cast a shadow over General China's war. As China waited in the crowded cells on death row in Nairobi gaol, he had an unexpected visitor. Ian Henderson had persuaded his bosses in Special Branch to let him take a gamble and offer China terms to cooperate with the government. It was a controversial suggestion for many officials in Nairobi, but negotiation with the rebels was what London, and especially Prime Minister Churchill, wanted. With London's backing, Henderson interviewed China again, and put it to the Mau Mau leader that he might save his own skin if he cooperated. Would China help to offer a surrender deal to the Mount Kenya armies? The Governor would pardon China if he agreed, and even if the surrender came to nought, he would be allowed to live, albeit as a prisoner. Henderson made the case persuasively, and China agreed to write letters to instigate a process of negotiation. Work on the surrender deal started immediately, and Henderson prepared to take China back into the forest. On 4 March 1954 Baring announced to a startled Kenyan public that General China had been pardoned.

As China and Henderson were hatching the surrender strategy, Karani Karanja, China's brigadier, came before the courts. The articulate Karanja made a clean breast of his Mau Mau activities. Armed with information from China's interrogation, Special Branch were able to probe Karanja and draw him out. It was an indication of the benefits to flow from China's 'cooperation'. Karanja cooperated too, but it wouldn't save him: he was sentenced and went to the gallows on 21 April 1954.[10] By then, China had returned to the forest.

The story of the surrender deal and the critical role played by China reveals how Mau Mau's forest command imploded as the tide of the conflict turned against them from January 1954. But before we come to the surrenders, we need to get a flavour of what forest life was like in central Kenya for those who bravely took up arms in the fight to be free from colonial rule.

## Flight to the Forests

The forest covered the deeply ridged slopes of Mount Kenya and the Aberdares hills in a thick, green blanket that spread over the land like a shroud. The image of the whole conflict was made in this damp, dark environment, where you could hardly see more than a few yards in front of you, and where it always, always seemed to be raining.

The forest was cold, too, as its paths were sheltered from the heat of the tropical sun by the canopy of branches from the tallest trees. Moving over the thick swell of ground foliage was made worse by the need to cross the many streams and rivers. The water ran noisily in stone-cold torrents down the valleys between the sharp ridges. Many were deep and fast-flowing. No sortie into the forest would happen without the British soldiers having to wade across half a dozen such streams, holding their rifles high above their heads and praying they wouldn't slip. It was a wet, cold, miserable experience.

The sheer size of the area covered by the forest is difficult to grasp. The Aberdares marked the north-eastern edge of the Kikuyu reserves. Covering about fifteen miles in width, before dropping into the farms of the Rift Valley to the west, these hills were forested over their entire length, forty miles from north to south. Another forty miles to the east, across the Nyeri Settled District and the Kikuyu reserve, lay the Mount Kenya forests. The sea of trees here went on for mile after mile, up the slopes towards the mountain peaks, and to the east, then the north, across the shoulder of the mountain and into Embu and Meru districts. With only the forty miles or so of inhabited European farmland and cultivated African reserve in between, this gave the Mau Mau armies a vast playground over which to roam. It was no wonder that the British had such trouble finding them.

Looking up at the forest from the farmland below, it could appear as one dense mass of green foliage. In fact, the character of the forest changes dramatically with altitude. The farmlands in Nyeri climb to 7000 feet before you can even enter the forest. The tree line begins, with podo and cedar trees of varying sizes, with frequent clearings and glades. There are game tracks here, taken by Kikuyu entering the forest to gather honey, collect firewood, or to hunt. In the dry season livestock comes to these glades. After a few miles the slope is steeper and the forest thickens. The trees are bigger here – sixty and eighty feet high. They tower above, blotting out the sun. Game paths are fewer, too, and it is often necessary to cut a path laboriously through the thick undergrowth, dominated by creepers and twines.

A few miles more brings you to 8000 feet or thereabouts, where the bamboo begins. The terrain here is treacherous. The bamboo poses a seemingly impenetrable barrier of between three and eight miles wide. Beyond it, above 10,000 feet, the forest suddenly breaks open into moorland. The sun shines here, but the wind blows hard and steady; and when the winds drops, the mists come down, thick and icy cold. Looked at from the air, these moors appear enticing to the keen walker, but on the ground is a morass of peat, tall heather and thick, springy gorse. Above the moorland is only the craggy stone of the mountain tops – Sattima and Kinangop in the Aberdares, at 13,000 feet, and the peaks of the majestic Mount Kenya itself, some 4000 feet higher still. It is an awe-inspiring landscape.

As the war proceeded, Europeans would nurture the myth that the Kikuyu were 'at one' with this landscape; that here, in this primordial forest, their primitive instincts came surging to the fore. This was the stereotype of the Kikuyu 'forest psychology'.[11] The thought no doubt helped to console British troops as they spent day after day trudging through the damp undergrowth without ever catching sight of their quarry; but there was little truth in the notion. Though many Kikuyu lived by the forest edge, the distant high forests were no more welcoming to those who fled there in the early days of the emergency than to the troops who would eventually trundle off in heavy-booted pursuit. Kikuyu were farmers, not men of the trees: a forest was a thing to be cut down and cleared, to make way for cultivation, livestock, and settlement. Kikuyu had domesticated their land by the sweat of honest labour with axe and hoe; the forest was wild, uncivilized and unruly. Men who, as boys, had taken animals to the glades, or collected firewood or honey in the forest fringe, may have been more at home here; but for the majority the higher forest, especially the bamboo, was a strange and unfamiliar place. They would learn about life in the forest as they would learn to be guerrilla fighters.

Who followed Waruhiu Itote into the forest? They were by no means an army-in-waiting. The emergency had come too soon for the *Muhimu*. Given more time, they might have been better prepared for what lay ahead. As early as 1951 the *Muhimu* had appointed Stanley Mathenge to oversee military operations, but his activities had got little further than establishing caches of arms. The British declaration of war precipitated the conflict when the *Muhimu* still lacked a coherent plan. In the first few days of the emergency, some thousand Kikuyu fled into the Aberdares forest, perhaps rather fewer to Mount Kenya. These were fugitives, not an army. Over the next few weeks they formed into bands, each in isolation, but gradually coming together into larger formations. It was unstructured at first, but a semblance of order did emerge.

The first to come to the forest were mostly *Muhimu* activists, taking to their heels to avoid arrest, or ex-squatters evicted from the European farms of the Rift Valley. Landless, jobless and rejected by the elders in Central Province, who had nowhere to put them and no desire to honour what claim to land they may once have had, the ex-squatters were desperate and disillusioned. Some were hardened by earlier struggles – at Olenguruone, or on the farms of Nakuru and Thomson's Falls, where their tenancies had been cancelled. Those who gathered in the first forest camps were mostly young, between twenty and thirty years of age. Few of them had yet married. Some had a little education, but on the whole they were illiterate, rural men.[12] At this stage the forest was no place for boys or elders. This vanguard would become the backbone of the Land and Freedom Armies: men with something to fight for, and reason enough to think they had little alternative. First to come into the forest, these men would be among the last to come out.

A second wave of recruits joined the forest armies from late November. These were people many of whom had been victimized in their home areas, either because it was known they had willingly taken a Mau Mau oath or because they had refused to join the Home Guard. Between November and February the British boasted that they had subjected 58,000 Kikuyu to 'screening', mostly in the Rift Valley and the 'hot-spots' in the reserve where Mau Mau support was strongest.[13] For many people, this was evidence that the government really had declared war on the Kikuyu. Faced with the choice of remaining to be interrogated and arrested, or leaving to join the Mau Mau armies, many younger men elected to take their chance in the forest. Such people had taken a Mau Mau oath, but they would not have come to the forest without the spur of harassment. This second wave of recruits swelled and rebel ranks to around 10,000.

From April 1953, in the wake of the Lari massacre, the steady flow of willing recruits turned into a torrent of fearful refugees as people fled from persecution. Violence and intimidation exploded in the reserves, Home Guards and police rampaging against those suspected of rebel sympathies. This rapidly changed the character of the forest units. Men who would not otherwise have taken to the forests were now thrown into the rebel militia, many of them older, and married with families. There were also boys, among them teenagers of fourteen and fifteen years. Some of these new recruits, young and old, came because of idealism, with zeal for the struggle; but many others came because their relatives had been killed or detained, or because they had themselves been beaten and threatened. Muchange Macharia was typical of this third wave of recruits, fleeing to the forest from Nanyuki after severe beatings at the hands of the Home Guard. A farm labourer in his thirties, Macharia went to the Aberdares forest in June 1953. He was caught two years later, and hanged.[14] Wambuga Wandura's experience was similar. He, too, fled in June 1953 after beatings by the Home Guard in Nyeri. A welder by trade, his skills in repairing weapons had been useful in the forest. Wandura hanged in April 1956. Njau Thorongo would be more fortunate. His mother died in 1948, and then his father and elder brother were killed by Home Guards. Thorongo took to the forest in June 1953 and made his own gun 'to shoot any Home Guard who might attempt to shoot me'. Judge Hooper, impressed by Thorongo's integrity, sentenced him to hang but made a plea to the Governor for clemency. Earlier in the Emergency, the judge would not have believed Thorongo's story; by the end of 1954 it was all too familiar. The sentence was commuted to life imprisonment, with hard labour.[15]

The sharp increase in the number of men arrested in the reserves and sent into detention without trial from April 1953 also sparked a new exodus of women and children into the forests. Though the total number of such people was not high – it seems that many more women and children moved to Nairobi or into the other towns of Central Province rather than into the forests – those who came presented the Mau Mau commanders with a dilemma. These camp followers could be employed in menial chores servicing the fighters, but as the security forces stepped up their operations, such people too easily became a liability. These later recruits would be among the first to surrender to the security forces, or return to the reserves, as the war in the forests intensified.

While the fighters in the forests prepared for war, the British were not sure what to prepare for. They certainly did not want to call it a war: to do so had implications. In a war, combatants had rights under international conventions and were protected from criminal prosecution. That wouldn't do at all, least of all in a British colony. If not a war, could Kenya's trouble be called a rebellion? This word, too, was unhelpful. In other places, and at other times, the British deprived rebels of all their rights – they were traitors to the Crown, liable to forfeiture of property and summary execution. With Kenya's trigger-happy, gibbet-loving white highlanders lurking in the wings, Lyttelton had the word 'rebellion' expunged from all declarations on Mau Mau, anxious not to inspire any 'regrettable actions'. War and rebellion were too loaded, too dangerously suggestive of something gone badly wrong, for the sensibilities of British politicians: instead, they called Mau Mau a 'civil disturbance'.

The ambiguity of language paralysed the military. The first British regiment to arrive, the Lancashire Fusiliers, took up defensive positions 'in aid of the police', and waited for something to happen. When it did, as in the raid on Naivasha or the murder of Chief Nderi, they were caught napping. The Lancashire Fusiliers contained more than their share of conscript soldiers – getting on for 70 per cent of the soldiers who served with the British battalions in Kenya were conscripts. These raw, barely trained, reluctant young soldiers were untried. Their presence in Kenya was at first intended as a show of force, not the beginnings of a major campaign. Kenya's civil disturbance was therefore placed in the hands of the police, their allies the KPR, and the Kenya Regiment. These auxiliary units, dominated by Kenya's young white highlanders, made powerful claims to 'local knowledge'. In the first months these units set the pace and the tone. There is no evidence to suggest that Baring or his military commanders thought this in any way a gamble. The British army was already badly overstretched by simultaneous operations in several outposts of empire – Malaya was the most demanding, where British troops faced well-trained communist guerrillas, but there were also the Middle East and, from 1954, Cyprus to contend with, in addition to British support for the war in Korea. British commanders were glad to leave Kenya's Emergency to the locals. Better-trained and more experienced regiments could then be deployed to other, 'hotter' struggles. For the first eight months the British military stood back and let the white highlanders, the police and – increasingly – the Home Guard get on with it.

The Kikuyu Home Guard was, without question, the most important factor in determining recruitment to the forest gangs. In short, Home Guard aggression sent recruits flowing to the forest. They were the internal resistance to Mau Mau – the government's African army, stoutly defending the loyalist, Christian Kikuyu, who lived in dread of Mau Mau. The British put them to good propaganda uses, but the Home Guard were also a potent weapon. Corfield, author of the official report on the Emergency, described them as 'the deciding factor in the long fight against Mau Mau in the Kikuyu reserve'. Corfield praised their bravery and resolve.[16] Elsewhere, the Home Guard have had a less good press, lampooned as self-seeking scoundrels, collaborators and quislings. In the eyes of nationalists, Home Guards were 'stumps', whose obstinate resistance obstructed the rebellion. Mau Mau memoirs recall Home Guard violence as a pernicious betrayal; 'It was as if they had turned into beasts,' wrote Joram Wamweya.[17] Similar images haunt the novels of Ngugi wa Thiong'o, whose evil, money-grabbing counter-hero in *Petals of Blood*, Kimeria, was a former Home Guard.[18] Ngugi derided Home Guards as 'the running dogs' of British imperialism.

The creation of the Kikuyu Home Guard turned the 'civil disturbance' into a civil war. We have already seen the signs of this in the tragedy at Lari, and on the grim streets of Eastlands. In the reserves, too, the bitterness of local division became the focal point of the war, as Kikuyu turned against Kikuyu. For the forest gangs, the Home Guard and the 'stumps' became their principal targets. By the middle of 1953 Home Guards would be caught in a maelstrom of violence, both as victims and as perpetrators. We need to understand something of the background to this.

Kikuyu resistance to Mau Mau first emerged during 1951, promoted by churches and their senior Christian chiefs and headmen. Vigilante groups were formed to protect church communities from the night-time activities of Mau Mau, and a few brave souls even found the courage to make public confessions to oath-taking. Among Catholic Kikuyu, Bishop John McCarthy threatened excommunication upon those who did not confess to having taken a Mau Mau oath,[19] and in the Rift Valley town of Nakuru, the Christian Kikuyu formed the Torchbearer's Association, as a rallying point against Mau Mau influence.[20] In Central Province, African clergy banded together as 'The Army of Christ', to sign a pledge against the oath.[21] There were even attempts to deploy traditional Kikuyu practices of counter-oathing and cleansing to purge those who had 'been smitten by Mau Mau'. Supported by their friend Louis Leakey, Chief Waruhiu and his son David took a lead in organizing anti-Mau Mau ceremonies in rural Kiambu, as did Chief Nderi. Both chiefs had received death threats. Mau Mau's leaders recognized the danger that internal resistance posed.

The suggestion that resistance groups might be mobilized as a militia was first discussed at Government House in November 1952. By then, there were 580 persons enrolled in church-led groups in Murang'a, and another 817 in Nyeri.[22] This was a small beginning, but it might be developed into a proper vigilante movement. Baring saw the potential: an official Kikuyu militia to fight Mau Mau would break through the notion that this was a race war that pitted African against European. Drawing parallels with wartime Britain's, the name 'Home Guard' was mooted. Discussion swung to the practicalities. Senior officers in Central Province were sceptical, warning that this would 'have to be most carefully handled': Mau Mau supporters might easily infiltrate the units, or, more likely still, the general population would simply dismiss the militia 'as a government-engineered organization'. The consensus emerged that it would be far better to make it seem that the militia was a purely Kikuyu initiative.[23] The first steps had been taken in the making of civil war in central Kenya.

The idea was speedily put into effect. To encourage things along the right lines, chiefs and headmen were granted an honorarium for leading a Home Guard unit, initially 15 shillings per month. They would be issued with a shotgun, a welcome protection in these troubled times, and they and their recruits would be granted exemption from poll tax. These incentives spurred recruitment over December 1952. By the end of the year units had formed in all the main towns throughout the White Highlands, and in the chieftaincies within the Kikuyu reserves. Not all chiefs welcomed this initiative, but as the momentum built up, it became difficult to resist without drawing suspicion. The loyalty of a chief who failed to gather an impressive militia might be called into question, but in places where Mau Mau influence was strongest allowances had to be made.

Kiambu emerged as a difficult area. Passive support for Mau Mau was strong in Kiambu, and people were well aware that to join the Home Guard would place them in the firing line of the assassins. Efforts to set up the Home Guard therefore met bitter opposition. With some justification, elders complained that creation of militias would deepen divisions. For European officers who wanted to expose Mau Mau sympathizers this was, of course, precisely the point. The British forced the issue, pressing chiefs and headman to 'encourage' recruitment, and by the end of 1952 some 1618 men had joined the Kiambu Home Guard. Of the nine chiefs in the district, it was Makimei, at Uplands, who had fared worst, managing to muster a force of only twenty-seven men.[24] Over the next two months he would draw upon loyalists at Lari to bolster his Home Guard contingent, but not without stirring up a great deal of animosity. 'The district is now tending to divide into two camps, whereas formerly the entire population was sitting firmly on the fence,' it was noted in the Kiambu intelligence report for December 1952: 'Now that there are targets for the attacks of the thugs in the shape of the Home Guard, incidents of violence are likely to increase, but this is a more healthy atmosphere than the uneasy quiet which has hung over our district for so long.'[25] The British were forcing the Kikuyu to take sides. Kiambu would see the most bitter of all the cycles of reprisal between Home Guard and Mau Mau as the war unfolded.

Home Guard recruitment is a ticklish subject to unravel. By March 1954 there were 25,600 Kikuyu Home Guards, 14,800 full-time and 10,800 part-time, a total that exceeded the strength of the rebel armies in the forest.[26] But we should not interpret this to mean that loyalism was a popular cause, or that those who joined the Home Guard necessarily opposed the broader aims of the Mau Mau movement. Nothing in this dirty colonial war could ever be so simple. For the most part, recruitment to the Home Guard was left solely in the hands of the chiefs and their headmen. Here lay the problem: some cajoled and persuaded; others bullied and threatened; some tested the political views of their recruits, others dragooned their enemies. The Kikuyu Home Guard was a rag-bag army, whose membership had little to do with matters of conscience but everything to do with circumstance.

Bethwell Alan Ogot, one of the few Kenya-born historians brave enough to write about the loyalists and the Home Guard, identified four categories of recruit: the constitutionalists, the traditionalists, the opportunists and the Christians. The *constitutionalists* were men who saw Mau Mau's violence as illegitimate in political terms, subverting authority and threatening stability. These men included the 'landed gentry' of the Kikuyu – property-owning heads of extended families, whose values were essentially bourgeois and conservative. The *traditionalists*, Ogot's second category, shared these values but were driven into opposition to Mau Mau on the principle of the movement's subversion of Kikuyu cultural practice, to be seen in the misuse of the oath for violent ends and its administration to adolescents and young men who had no moral responsibility. Ogot's next category, the *opportunists*, comprised people who used the emergency for primitive accumulation, gaining wealth and property at the expense of those who had been unwise enough to side with the rebels. This category grew in size as government policy increasingly punished the rebels while showering the Home Guard with the gifts of victory, including land titles. The last category, the *Christians*, was probably the most numerous. A rich literature emerged during the emergency in celebration of the commitment and resolve of these African Christians, and for that reason their role has come to be seen as crucial.[27] But by no means all Kikuyu of Christian faith opposed Mau Mau. Their opposition was organized through their church affiliation, and many members of the Christian congregations in fact chose to 'face both ways', taking the Mau Mau oath but remaining within the church.

Just as the composition of the forest gangs altered over time, so did recruitment to the Home Guard. Motive might be complex and far from transparent. In the first months of the war those who declared themselves as loyalist and joined the Home Guard were mostly prosperous, Christian men of moderate political views. They were followed, slowly and with great reluctance, by their clients. Then, as the process of war deepened old enmities through acts of violence and retaliation, vertical divisions emerged between lineages and between churches, driving whole groups to the rebels or to the Home Guard. The war made it necessary to consolidate affiliations, if only for the sake of protection.

For those who had hoped to avoid taking sides in this struggle, at least in public, the push for Home Guard recruits presented an unwelcome dilemma. Chiefs might consider a refusal to join the Home Guard as a tacit admission of Mau Mau sympathy. By the middle of 1953, suspicion of such sympathies could easily see a man detained without trial. Many joined the Home Guard simply to avoid any taint of suspicion. Elsewhere, chiefs were accused of compelling all their own clients to join the Home Guard, regardless of whether they had any known association with Mau Mau. Rather like the servants of British officers in the Crimean War who found themselves sent to the front to fight in place of their masters, the clients of Kikuyu patrons were not allowed to plead neutrality. The Home Guard thus included many a hapless, poor peasant who was there only because of circumstance, and who may very well have taken more than one Mau Mau oath. Such people were not loyalists in any meaningful sense, yet they found themselves as militiamen opposing Mau Mau.

Having created this militia, the government protected and reinforced them. To strengthen their authority, Kikuyu Home Guard units were confined within their own locations. Local knowledge was the key to their success, but it also gave vent to no small degree of private feuding and score-settling. This worsened as the Emergency wore on. After Lari, more firearms were issued to the militiamen; they became proactive and belligerent. Having been left to their own devices until this point, later in 1953 European officers were assigned to act in a supervisory role. By then each Home Guard unit had its own fortified post, with spiked ditches, barbed-wire fencing and a drawbridge to keep Mau Mau at bay. Inside the barricades were barrack rooms and lock-ups, where prisoners could be interrogated and held. Tall watchtowers enabled a constant lookout over the countryside. Proud Kikuyu militiamen were photographed manning the ramparts, their spears at the ready. By day the whole scene inspired confidence in the might of empire. The image made excellent propaganda back home in Britain, showing how Africans were rallying to the flag in the fight against the rebels; but as darkness fell, confidence in the might of empire ebbed away, and apprehensive Home Guards retreated to their fortified stockades, seeking refuge from the Mau Mau attack that all feared.

A kind of order emerged in the forest that oddly mirrored that of the Home Guard. On Mount Kenya, China had made contact with several other groups, establishing a command structure. In the Aberdares, Stanley Mathenge and Dedan Kimathi were the principal leaders, Mathenge carrying the authority of his seniority among the *Muhimu*, and the ruthless Kimathi with a fearsome reputation as an oath administrator in south Nyeri. Both men reached the forest by early December. Their command structure in the Aberdares took longer to consolidate, and was always looser, with tensions and animosity between the two leaders. Other gangs, operating on the fringes of Kiambu and Thika, and in the Rift Valley, remained outside these structures, and would continue to operate independently. Though it would take the British over a year to realize it, the bands in each forest area had little contact with one another.

The links they developed were back to the reserves, and to Nairobi, where their supporting committees organized supplies of food, weapons and ammunition, and raised recruits. Units often took on a 'local' character, with a majority of recruits from one area, in the older style of the British regional regiments. This brought organizational advantages, and helped foster an *esprit de corps*, though it also bred an independence of mind within each unit and a latent mistrust of other fighters.[28] Mau Mau was a significant fighting force by the middle of 1953, but it would never be a unified guerrilla army.

The make-up of the Mau Mau units changed as the war progressed and the character of forest life altered. We can break this down into three broad phases:

- In the first, from October 1952 to June 1953, the camps were located in the lower forest, and recruitment, organization and training dominated. This was an optimistic phase for the fighters. They began to launch attacks into the reserves, and onto the farms, mostly against carefully selected targets. Numbers reached maybe 12,000 in this first phase.
- The second phase began in July 1953, with the early camps being disbanded as the fighters moved deeper into the forest to avoid detection by the army. This response to the first offensive mounted against the forest gangs by the British brought a harsher regime to the Mau Mau armies. As the camps were moved into the bamboo belt and the high forest, launching attacks and raids became more difficult and the daily logistics of survival increasingly time-consuming. Home Guard aggression and the tightening of police control in the reserves fuelled the supply of recruits. The numbers would peak toward the end of 1953, at a figure somewhere between 18,000 and 24,000.
- The third phase came following Operation Anvil, from May 1954. Recruitment now virtually ceased, and supplies became difficult to procure. The police and Home Guard laid siege to the reserves, hampering the committees and disrupting Mau Mau's passive support, while the army penetrated into the forest, forcing the gangs to move frequently and to remain vigilant. It was a slow but steady process of attrition. The fighters were on the defensive and in decline. By the beginning of 1955, as the bands became more isolated, and their numbers decreased, the war had become not so much a glorious rebellion as a grim struggle for survival.

In the beginning, forest life had not been so bad, and may even have seemed alluring and exciting to many young men. Mau Mau were in close touch with the reserves, and fighters could move relatively freely between the two areas. Men made regular visits back to their homes.

Camp life was organized and disciplined, and had a sense of purpose. Weapons were properly cared for, and records were kept of membership and the assignment of ranks, tasks and weaponry to each fighter. Food was regularly procured from the neighbouring reserves, brought in by parties of younger women. Their arrival brought news, entertainment and companionship. At this stage, Mau Mau commanders could be choosy about who remained permanently in the camps. Rules were enforced and punishments issued.

In these early days in the forest there were meetings and debates about strategy and tactics. These are documented in Karari Njama's memoirs of the struggle, and even Itote recalls a discussion in July 1953, not long after Lari, about the morality and advisability of killing women and children.[29] Mau Mau's fighters saw themselves as connected with the elders back home, linked to the moral codes that mediated Kikuyu social life. The Kikuyu name they took for themselves – *itungati* – implied subordination to the discipline of elderhood. China acknowledged this in his interrogation, surprising Ian Henderson, who had imagined that the forest armies did as they pleased without recourse to any other authority. Over time, with isolation, growing disillusion and creeping, constant fear, each band would indeed move closer to the image of unruly brigandage that Henderson had in mind.

Mau Mau forest camps varied greatly in size, getting smaller and more scattered with the passage of time. The largest Aberdares camp, at Karia-ini, was home to between 4000 and 5000 fighters at its peak. The first camps in the forest fringes each held only a few hundred at the most. Karia-ini was much higher, up in the forest's bamboo zone. These larger camps were well organized and neatly arranged, with areas for stores and supplies, hospitals, kitchens and mess areas – Karia-ini needed three kitchens – as well as workshops for gun repair and manufacture. Accommodation was set out by rank, senior commanders enjoying the driest and warmest bivouacs. To protect each camp, sentries were posted on the forest paths. British commanders came to respect the efficiency of these lookouts as, time after time, soldiers burst into a rebel camp only to find it deserted.[30]

From the memoirs of Njama and China we can gain insights on the daily routines of forest life. A breakfast of maize porridge, taken at dawn, was followed by prayers. Then the day's rosters were issued, with drilling, training and fitness, watches to be set and food parties sent out to forage, to check the game traps, or to collect supplies from the reserve. The rebels did not eat again until evening, when a thin meat stew was served, with the ubiquitous maize meal and vegetables (gathered wild from the forest floor). Prayers were again said as the fighters settled down for the evening, the men talking, chewing tobacco and smoking bhang, if they

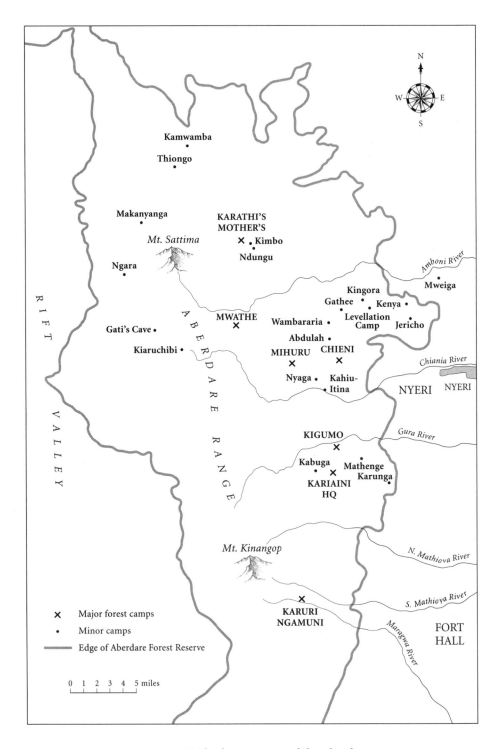

**Map 6.i The forest camps of the Aberdares**

had it, before turning in. High up in the bamboo, the sleeping quarters were dry and snug, cut out of the forest floor with a canopy above giving shelter.[31]

Camp discipline was maintained in the traditional style of the British army, with floggings, punishment tasks, and food deprivation. The worst infractions of discipline led to execution. Miscreants were tried in front of an assembly of *itungati*, presided over by the camp's judge. Some commanders became notorious for the execution of their followers, especially in the last phase of the war, when the gangs greatly feared the infiltration of spies and turncoats. Alphonse Nganga, who served as a camp judge in the Aberdares, blithely told police during his interrogation in January 1955 that he had sentenced a hundred of his comrades to be executed.[32] This tale may have grown in the telling – it was avidly publicized as a sign of Mau Mau's ruthlessness – but all the memoirs of forest life are clear that discipline in the camps was harsh.

Mimicking the British army, Mau Mau fighters adopted military ranks. The forest bristled with generals, brigadiers, colonels and captains. Everyone, it seemed, had a rank. Promotions were frequent. Elaborate titles and fanciful forest names were ridiculed by the British, but they had purpose in giving structure and authority to the bands of raw, inexperienced recruits. They were not seriously intended to impose Mau Mau's legitimacy, as some writers have laboured too hard to argue.[33] The adoption of pseudonyms – the forest names that were given to each fighter – gave new identities that submerged the differences in age, status and authority between the men. In the forest they entered a new order, and the pseudonyms made this easier.

In the camps were many non-combatants – perhaps more than one in five of those in the forests. These include male cooks and foragers, who would not be expected to go to battle, but also women. The numbers of women in the camps varied greatly, but was far greater in the Aberdares than on Mount Kenya. Kirari Njama reports that the largest of Kimathi's camps had a staff of nearly 400 women, including the chosen concubines of the leading officers. A handful of these are reported to have joined the men in military training and taken part in raids. The presence of women in the forests were a bone of contention.[34] Njama thought it a bad thing, as too many squabbles were sparked over the winning of women's favours.[35] As the campaign wore on and the rebels were forced to retreat deeper into the forest, the number of camp followers, and especially women, dwindled. It was easier for women to quietly return to their homes in the reserve after a few months' absence, without catching the attention of the Home Guard, than it was for fighters to do the same. By the beginning of 1955 there were few women left among the forest gangs.

Religion and faith played a large part in forest life. The prayers to
the Kikuyu god Ngai, always said when facing towards Mount Kenya –
Kirinyaga, as Kikuyu more poetically named it – were reinforced by consultation with prophets and seers. These mantic figures accompanied the
fighters to the forest, being consulted on whether a planned attack or
proposal was auspicious.[36] The extension of these practices of Kikuyu
warfare from an earlier age was one of the few parallels that can be drawn
between the behaviour of the Mau Mau armies and their Kikuyu warrior
counterparts of a half-century before. In Kikuyu terms, the forest battalions of the Land and Freedom Army were remarkably modern. The
activities of the prophets became more important as the war turned against
Mau Mau, and the forest leaders increasingly isolated and desperate.

Though the forest fighters came to be known as the Land and Freedom
Army, there never was a single Mau Mau army. Each leader did pretty
much as the fancy took him. Kimathi, Mathenge and China each tried
to impose a more rigorous structure of command, but none succeeded
in exerting authority over the bands in the forests. China and the other
Mount Kenya commanders, Generals Tanganyika and Kaleba, managed
not to fall out with one another; the Aberdares leaderships was deeply
divided. Kimathi and Mathenge had collaborated in May 1953 to form
a council comprising Mau Mau commanders of fighters from Nyeri,
who were dominant among the Aberdares units. The Ituma Ndemi
Trinity Council, as it was called, met several times over the next few
weeks. An attempt was made to organize a coordinated attack on
numerous targets throughout Central Province at the end of June, but
the majority of the units involved failed to act upon the instructions.
After this the council held no further meetings.[37]
    On Mount Kenya, China did rather better. He managed to meet his
commanders regularly and kept in closer touch with the committees in
the reserves, frequently using the intelligence they supplied to identify
targets. Better organization and good communications allowed China to
retain firmer control, even after Special Branch arrested members of the
passive wing committees in the Mount Kenya area during July and August
1953. In the Aberdares the situation had become chaotic around this time
after two major military sweeps along the reserve boundary. With no
properly working command structure and each unit acting independently,
the Mau Mau fighters here were unable to respond to this first British push,
and fled in disorder.[38] It was a sign of trouble ahead.
    During August, Dedan Kimathi tried again to restructure the
command of the Aberdares units, calling a meeting at Mwathe, high in
the moorlands. As many as 4000 fighters attended, but not every unit
was represented. Stanley Mathenge was among the most notable absen-

tees, and there were no fighters from the cadres operating in the Rift Valley and the reserves. Kimathi's own supporters were in the majority and he was easily able to get their agreement by acclamation to a command structure that recognized himself as supreme commander, with eight separate armies each under the control of a named general. This sensible proposal recognized the leadership of Mathenge, China, Macharia Kimemia, General Kimbo and General Waruingi, among others, and imposed a structure that could have allowed greater consultation in deciding strategy and selecting targets; but this was never to materialize. Much of it was wishful thinking. Not all of the leaders Kimathi honoured in his command structure recognized his authority, and many would remain ignorant of his intentions for many months to come. Mathenge opposed the proposals when he was told of them, and a deep rift developed between him and Kimathi. The command council formed at Mwathe never again met, although Kimathi increasingly behaved as if he were supreme commander, issuing instructions without consultation.[39] This failure, with the internal dissent it bred, was to prove fatal to the Mau Mau cause.

The quarrel between Kimathi and Mathenge has become the stuff of Mau Mau legend. Memoirs of the war written by survivors who knew the two and were privy to the dispute have contested different points of view. Karari Njama first provided an account favouring Kimathi. Njama had been an official scribe to Mathenge and Kimathi, writing letters and organizing communications. Njama attended tactical meetings in the forest and makes strong claims to authenticity. Kimathi's obsession for having everything recorded and written down was endorsed by Njama, one of the few in the forest who had a secondary education.[40] On the other hand, the bureaucratic authority of the written word offended illiterate commanders, who found it alienating. Literacy was a pervasive symbol of colonial domination, a device that some fighters wished to reject as threatening and divisive and others wanted to embrace as a weapon of their own.[41]

Mathenge accepted the importance of good communication but stood up for uneducated forest fighters, those with perhaps less interest in ideology, political structure and negotiation, and with a stronger yearning for complete victory and the re-establishment of their property and their dignity. His champion was Wachanga, whose memoir challenged Njama's account, presenting a critical view of Kimathi as capricious and dangerously volatile, treating his men with authoritarian disdain and enforcing an unnecessarily rigorous discipline. Mathenge, in contrast, is seen sympathetically, as a steady rock in a stormy sea, unmoved by the crashing noise around him and unbending in the struggle.[42]

Wachanga's romanticism overlooks the superstition and conservatism that sometimes clouded Mathenge's view. The unpredictable and increasingly reclusive Kimathi was almost certainly the wrong man to put in charge, yet his instincts were surely right. With Mathenge's opposition entrenched and Kimathi intransigent, the moment of high command, so nearly grasped on the Aberdares in the middle of 1953, was gone before the end of the year and would never be recovered. Ironically, China was the one senior commander who might have drawn together the loose strands into a meaningful confederacy. Without it Mau Mau's military potential would not be realized. The falling out between these two Aberdares leaders stood alongside the capture of China as events that would hasten Mau Mau's military defeat.

One of the crucial effects of this failure of command was the weakening of relationships between the passive supporters in the reserves and the forest gangs. As the security forces put greater pressure on the passive wing of Mau Mau, there was a need for the fighters to be more cautious in selecting targets. Unwise choices, or poor timing, might place Mau Mau supporters at risk from reprisals. The most dangerous fighters in this respect were known as *komerera* – bandits. Smaller Mau Mau units of this kind sprang up in Kiambu repeatedly, as local young bucks settled scores and made mayhem against loyalists, often in league with renegade elements returning from the forest in search of action. These desperados were a law unto themselves. They undoubtedly placed Kikuyu communities at risk, but they caused serious difficulties for the British, taking up the fight at a time when other Mau Mau leaders were on the defensive. It was fighters such as these who joined Mwangi Toto and Chotara on the outskirts of Nairobi in the months following Operation Anvil, and in the Kiambu area General Wairuingi harnessed them into an effective fighting unit during 1954. The most successful of the renegades was surely General Kago, who fought a long and successful offensive campaign along the forest edge of Murang'a. He defied Kimathi's authority in launching attacks within the reserve, but it is certain that Kago's shrewd choice of targets and his skilful tactics did far more damage to the security forces than Kimathi himself ever managed.[43]

In Mau Mau's struggle it was the likes of Kago and the lesser-known commanders who more often led the charge into battle. When the forest fighters made raids into the reserve, their targets were the police stations and Home Guard posts that served as the rallying points of opposition within their own Kikuyu communities. Even for the forest armies the Mau Mau war was not a single strategic campaign; it was instead an intricate series of local struggles. As the battle lines were drawn and the offensives began, Kenya's Emergency quickly descended from rebellion into civil war. In the battles to come, the tried and trusted tactics of divide and rule defined Kenya's liberation struggle just as it had defined the country's conquest half a century earlier.

# Bugles and Battles

Loyalists in the Embu district, to the north-east of Nairobi, came to dread the harsh cry of the Mau Mau bugle. As violence exploded in the district from July 1953, rebels led by General Gatunga terrorized the local Christians who had refused the Mau Mau oath. When his men were ready to attack the homesteads and schools where the dissenters were gathered, Gatunga's bugler would sound the charge. His chosen victims then knew that death was coming. Among them was Ephantus Kanji, a teacher at the Catholic Mission School in Kivote. A stalwart of the Embu Home Guard, Kanji was a known target and had been issued with a pistol by the police so as better to protect himself. It didn't do much good. When Kanji heard the fateful bugle call on 25 January 1954, he was in his car on the road into Embu town. The ambush was carried out swiftly and without mercy. With no opportunity to defend himself, Ephantus Kanji was hacked to pieces. His mutilated remains were later recovered from the shell of his burnt-out car.

Six weeks after Kanji's murder, General Gatunga was caught by a Home Guard patrol in Embu. He suffered bullet and shotgun wounds as he fought to escape, but this did nothing to deter his captors from administering a savage beating once they had disarmed him. So bad were his injuries that his trial had to be delayed for several months to allow sufficient time for his recovery. When he was finally brought before the court, in July 1954, the police had removed his hat decorated with a medal ribbon captured from a soldier of the KAR, and the three full medals he had proudly worn on his coat, also taken from his victims. Judge Holmes thought Gatunga to be one of the most determined terrorists he had yet encountered. In Holmes's eyes Gatunga was all the more dangerous because he was not an ignorant, illiterate peasant, but a well-educated man of some sophistication. General Gatunga was, in fact, Joshua Douglas, who, before taking to the forest, had been known throughout Embu as the gifted and charismatic Christian teacher at one of the district's best independent Kikuyu schools. Each of the attacks conducted by his gang had been meticulously recorded in five notebooks that Gatunga kept over his months in active service for Mau Mau. Alongside the detail of Kanji's slaughter the serial number of the pistol that had been taken from his body was recorded, along with the name of the member of Gatunga's gang to whom the weapon had then been issued. As Gatunga's notebooks revealed, many of his victims had been well known to him as fellow Christians – including Kanji – and, in some cases, former classmates.[44] Mau Mau's battles were often as chillingly intimate as they were bloody.

Mau Mau's violence was seldom random, which contrasted sharply with many Western perceptions at the time. Even when forest gangs made sorties into the reserve, targets were carefully chosen and precautions were taken to protect the movement's supporters. When the renegades of the *komerera* groups behaved recklessly, or when Mau Mau units made mistakes, they were admonished. Those in the forest knew that they depended upon the support of those in the Kikuyu reserves. For the most part, attacks within the reserve were organized in conjunction with local people. The rebel force commanded by General Gatunga in Embu comprised a band of forest fighters, who operated in conjunction with a larger number of supporters who remained living in the villages. The group would rendezvous before an attack, to identify and locate their target, those resident to the area acting as guides. Even when local advice of this kind was not easily available, rebel commanders would select fighters who knew the area to be attacked – often men who came from that very location. The intimacy of the struggle derived from this local focus of violence: rebels often had some personal knowledge of their victims, and hence the witnesses to an attack often recognized many people among the attackers.

This very intimate, personal brand of violence was to carry right through to the war's end, when Mau Mau turncoats hunted down their former comrades in the forests. That came in the final phase of the fighting, in the months following Operation Anvil. Prior to that the forest fighters had enjoyed an initial period of domination, up to June 1953, followed by a period of twelve months when the fighting was at its most intense. Our discussion of the forest fighter's war will follow these three phases in chronological sequence.

The attack upon loyalists in Nyeri on Christmas Eve 1952 had marked the real beginning of the war for the forest fighters. Before that, there had been a number of sorties into the reserve to assassinate informers and government lackeys. The murder of Chief Nderi had been one such incident. The gangs also raided European farms in the Rift Valley and along the border of the reserve in Kiambu and Thika, with the primary intention of securing supplies and capturing weapons. After the Christmas Eve attack the rebels, their forces growing in strength and now better organized, took the fight into the reserve with increasing regularity. Their main target was the Home Guard, the units of which were only then being drawn together around the chiefs and headmen.

No sooner were men recruited to the Home Guard than Mau Mau passive wing members identified them as targets. The most aggressive loyalists were singled out for assassination, while plans were laid to infiltrate the Home Guard posts by oathing some of the less prominent recruits.

In February 1953 Home Guards in Murang'a were systematically victimized, with several murders.[45] A similar wave of attacks swept through Embu in July 1953.[46] On the farms, too, those Kikuyu who helped to organize either Home Guard units or farm watches were vulnerable. In the Naivasha and Nakuru districts, during May 1953, loyalists were attacked on the farms. One of the victims was Benson Kagori, who was shot and his body placed in a sack, like an African version of a Verdi plot come true, and then thrown into the river. No one had the courage to report the incident, and his disappearance might never have been explained had not the sack caught in a reed bed and his decomposed, maggot-infested body been recovered from the river two weeks later. Those convicted of his murder were Mau Mau supporters, resident on a neighbouring farm, who regularly supplied a gang from Kinangop with food.[47] Benson had taken charge of the Home Guard then being formed on the farms in the area. The murder was typical of many others, carried out with collusion between the forest fighters and their friends on the farm.

The attacks had a dramatic effect on the Home Guard. It was rumoured that some loyalists had received letters warning them not to assist the government in recruitment. As intimidation mounted, morale among recruits dissipated. By February, in the parts of northern Murang'a and Nyeri closest to the forests where Mau Mau support was especially strong, the loyalists were effectively under siege, patrolling in groups by day but unable to leave the sanctuary of their fortified posts as evening approached. Police units and army platoons were more regularly assigned duties in conjunction with the Home Guard to stiffen their resolve, and the government looked for ways to encourage those who remained loyal. A fund was set aside from which to reward Home Guards for especially noteworthy service at the end of each month. Any success against the rebels, however small, got its reward and was loudly trumpeted in the propaganda war, as Baring's government did its level best to hold the Kikuyu Home Guard on the front line in the war against Mau Mau.[48]

Besides these bonuses, loyalists received other economic advantages. The colonial government raised taxes on the Kikuyu above the level paid by other Africans, but Home Guards were given exemptions. Communal labour orders were issued in the wake of Mau Mau attacks, to repair bridges and roads or to restore the damaged property of loyalists. Again, the families of Home Guards were spared the indignity of this forced labour. Communal labour was also deployed in the construction and subsequent reinforcement of Home Guard posts, police stations and other government camps. Pass laws were now more rigorously policed within the reserve, and only Home Guards and known loyalists were given authority to move out of their own locations. In the most troublesome areas curfews were issued from dusk to dawn. Collective punishments were levied against communities who were accused of harbouring terrorists, or withholding information from the security forces. In Nyeri this involved seizures of livestock. During 1953 the government confiscated 6000 cattle and 22,000 sheep and goats from Mau Mau suspects, along with over a hundred bicycles. By the time the collective punishments stopped, in May 1956, those totals had more than doubled. Aside from these official confiscations, a great quantity of moveable property was simply seized by the Home Guard as war booty.[49] Markets were also prohibited in areas where Mau Mau was active, and shop licences withdrawn from traders who were suspected or rebel sympathies. Loyalists, often members of the Home Guard, were granted licences instead. Between November 1952 and June 1953 these measures made it clear that the government would direct its patronage only at those who declared themselves loyal, taking a public stand against Mau Mau. This drew many 'opportunists' towards the Home Guard.

Legal notices were issued delimiting Kikuyu movement and giving the security forces authority to act against suspects. The forests of the Aberdares and Mount Kenya were declared prohibited areas. Any person found within these zones could be shot on sight. The Kikuyu reserves, including Embu and Meru, were declared a 'Special Area', within which the security forces could shoot at anyone who failed to halt when challenged. In one of the first instances of this kind, a young Kikuyu man was shot in the back when riding his bicycle away from an army roadblock. The KAR officer who fired the shot claimed that he had called the man to halt, but that he had continued. No weapon, or anything else of suspicion, was found on the dead man's body. The soldier who fired the shot was, ironically, one Idi Dada Amin, serving in Kenya with the Ugandan regiment of the KAR. Nineteen years later this same soldier would seize power in his native Uganda in a British-backed military coup.

Incidents such as this were a common feature of the first phase of the Emergency in the reserves, usually passing without comment or investigation. These were the events that led the Mau Mau fighters to view the government's violence, not their own violence, as random and uncontrolled. Even the attack upon Lari, in the view of rebel commanders, was strategic and specific. If they came to regret any aspect of this infamous raid, it was not that a community of Home Guards and loyalists had been punished, but that so many women and children had been among the dead. It was this that rebounded to the movement's disadvantage, giving the British a propaganda opportunity and terrorizing many Kikuyu into taking a firmer stand against the rebels. Though the Lari raid was extraordinary in its scale, with its origins in such a deep-rooted history of land conflicts, it fits neatly into the type of attacks being mounted by Mau Mau in the first phase of the emergency, which began with the murders of the Nyeri Christians on Christmas Eve 1952. These attacks were all designed to isolate and punish loyalists and Home Guard, the 'stumps' who blocked the path of rebellion.

The frequency of attacks intensified in the weeks following Lari. Rebels from the Aberdares raided into Nyeri and Murang'a several times during April and May 1953, targeting the police as well as loyalists. There were many successes. The Home Guard post at Kairuthi was overrun and routed, and at Gatumbiro the attackers set fire to the buildings and the watchtower. But at Othaya police station, in north Nyeri, the rebels suffered a setback. The attackers had hoped to free the thirty or so Mau Mau suspects held in the lock-up at Othaya, and seize weapons and ammunition from the police armoury. As the rebel force took up position for the attack on a wet and cold night, police sentries opened fire on them. With the rain pouring down, the Mau Mau bugler rallied the attackers for a second attempt to cut through the barbed-wire fencing. As they did so, grenades were lobbed onto them from the watchtower and they were showered with machine-gun fire. With comrades falling all around them, the attackers panicked and fled, running downhill towards the Thuti river. The police gave chase, and several more Mau Mau were shot trying to cross the river, which was in spate. Of the forty attackers, sixteen were killed, and sixteen more required their wounds to be treated when returning to the forest camp at Karia-ini. After searching the bodies of the dead, and taking their fingerprints, the police unceremoniously buried the Mau Mau fighters in a mass grave, in a hollow below the police post.[50]

The contrast between the successes against the Home Guard posts and the failure to penetrate the defences of the Othaya police station set a pattern that would become clearer over the following months. Though Home Guards might rule their locations by day, when darkness fell the rebels had the advantage. Even if the Home Guards stood their ground to defend the post, the rebels knew that they would be unlikely to venture beyond the barricades to pursue their attackers. The police were better disciplined and posed a more formidable problem. For this reason, the Home Guards posts became sitting ducks for any rebel group – an easy target that could be attacked with relative impunity.

Even before Lari, this had led to problems of retaliation. Unable to grapple with the gangs from the forests, Home Guards took their vengeance on those they believed to be members of Mau Mau's passive wing. Intimidation, victimization, rough handling and beatings were already the norm by February 1953, but would get far worse after Lari at the end of March. A fortnight before the Lari attack the government learned that several Nairobi advocates were engaged in private prosecutions in cases of alleged assault by Home Guards in Kiambu and Nyeri. This exposed the fact that the Home Guard lacked authority for their actions – there was in fact no legislation permitting their formation, nor any legal document outlining their powers. To protect them, Whyatt now moved swiftly to place them under the Tribal Police Ordinance. This thwarted the initial attempts to prosecute Home Guards for their violence, but it was an issue that would return to trouble Baring's government at a later stage.

Whyatt's legal department had at first hesitated in defining the legal authority of the Home Guard because of doubts about the motives and character of many of the recruits. As early as January 1953 it had been found necessary to purge many Home Guard units in Nyeri of 'Mau Mau elements'. In Murang'a, too, infiltration of the Home Guard by rebels had been common, and in one case an entire unit had been found to be in league with a rebel gang from the nearby forest. The government's own estimates suggested that more than half the men recruited into the Home Guard by the end of 1954 had taken a Mau Mau oath. As Sorrenson summed it up, Kikuyu had little choice but to 'accept the facts of power': they were 'loyal to the government in the day-time' and 'loyal to the rebels at night'.[51] No one was naive about the Home Guard. The risks had been clear to Baring's government from the start, but as the fight increasingly turned in upon the Kikuyu communities after Lari, in a spiral of violence and counter-violence between Mau Mau and the Home Guard, the gamble seemed to be paying off. By June 1953 the Kikuyu rebellion was already slowly but surely defeating itself in a flurry of local, intimate, internecine violence.

The exacerbation of the violence carried out following Lari can be illustrated from a single incident that took place less than a fortnight later, at Marige, in Kiambu.[52] There, a Mau Mau unit made up predominantly of local men attacked loyalists, killing women and children but failing to seize upon the 'stump' who was their principal target. The screams of the victims were heard at the Marige Home Guard post, and the militiamen emerged in time to see the culprits making their escape. The chase rampaged amid the homesteads of Marige, with the Home Guard catching some rebels in the fields and dragging others out of the huts where they had taken refuge. They treated them with all the savagery of bitter, fearful vengeance. Eleven were summarily shot, and one man was tortured to death. The Home Guards were joined by a police contingent, who took charge of other prisoners. A Christian pastor from Marige, Wanyoike, would later write about what happened next:

... residents began to feel intensely the terrible consequences of the Emergency when they witnesses mass executions without trial of all those who were arrested in connection with the killings. While it was yet dark, all the suspected culprits were driven into the school playground where they were made to stand in a circle as if to be taught a new game. The police stood well behind them, surrounding the victims, while in the centre of the circle fire was opened up from an automatic weapon, killing them all instantly.[53]

No attempt was made to disguise what had occurred. In the wake of Lari, attitudes hardened. Kiambu's District Commissioner, Swann, was full of praise for the robust actions of the Marige Home Guard: 'They went straight in and killed the terrorists, before the gangsters knew what had hit them,' he proudly told the press.[54] Five members of a loyalist family had been killed, and four others badly wounded. Only three men remained alive to stand trial for the crime, out of twenty-five or more who were caught in the hot pursuit. They were convicted by Judge Nageon de Lestang, and hanged at Nairobi on 11 February 1954.[55]

By April 1953 the determination of the administration to inculcate 'an aggressive spirit' in the Kikuyu Home Guard needed little encouragement. Following Lari, each district was given fifty rifles for distribution to the Home Guard.[56] The issue of arms was soon justified, as the Lari and Marige incidents were followed by a series of further raids on Home Guard posts. The most spectacular success for the rebels came on 9 May 1953, when a gang of sixty fighters overran the guard post at Iriaini. Chief Eluid managed to escape along with thirty-seven of his men, who fled in terror. Two men and four women were killed, and the rebels seized weapons and liberated more than a hundred persons detained at the post for 'screening'.[57] In response to this wave of attacks, the Kikuyu militia were then let off the leash. Home Guard indiscipline and excess became the key feature of the emergency in the Kikuyu areas of central Kenya over the next year.[58] The government was determined to be as ruthless as Mau Mau; but nothing could have contributed more to reinforcing the ranks of the rebel army than did the harassment of the general population by the Home Guards. In May, the district officer in Meru candidly described his two Kikuyu militias as nothing more 'than an armed rabble'.[59] All over central Kenya other Home Guard units were behaving just the same. The war was entering its most violent phase.

General 'Bobbie' Erskine arrived in June 1953 to take command of the military. Whatever previous politicos might have wanted to call the crisis, Erskine knew this was a rebellion; and he knew that unless it was fought as professionally as any other campaign then it would not be defeated.

Counter-insurgency tactics were required, and there would have to be political concessions as well as military successes. Brisk and to the point in everything he said and did, with no time at all for the bleating of the white highlanders, one could almost see the British regiments snap collectively to attention as Erskine sized up the situation.

Erskine was indeed deeply shocked by what he found. A culture of intimidation and gratuitous physical abuse of Kikuyu suspects had been in the air from the beginning of the emergency, but since the Lari massacre many elements in the security forces had been allowed to get dangerously out of control. Though Kenya's administrative officers invariably blamed the excesses on the Home Guard and African police, it was quickly apparent to Erskine that the problems ran much deeper. Among the KPR and Kenya Regiment, the bully-boys, thugs and racists were having a field day, unconstrained and ill-disciplined. They had become brash and proud in their excess, disregarding possible consequences. Even the European-owned Swahili-language newspaper *Baraza* felt the need to carry an editorial on 11 April that was bitingly critical of the KPR: '... amongst this organisation are groups of men of whom undisciplined sadists is not an unfair description. Young men in the KPR can often be heard boasting of the way they have beaten up prisoners.'[60] The Kenya security forces had too many men of this calibre.

Even among the British regiments, as well as within the KAR, Erskine was shocked to learn of 'indiscriminate shooting', of alleged atrocities and of cavalier and inappropriate behaviour.[61] One regiment, the Devons, kept a scoreboard of kills at their camp, and soldiers received 'bonus' payments for each rebel accounted for. To 'prove' kills, and ostensibly to aid the identification of rebels by fingerprinting, soldiers had formed the habit of cutting off the hands of Mau Mau victims, bringing their trophies back to the mess. And among some platoons of the KAR discipline appeared to have broken down completely, with the ill-treatment and shooting of prisoners. The enraged Erskine put an immediate stop to these practices and despatched the brigade commander of the KAR back to Britain in disgrace.

Erskine then issued a public letter to all officers of the army and police. In it he made no explicit reference to atrocities, but it was clear enough that Erskine saw the problem to be incipient racism, and that he was determined to stamp it out:

> ... I will not tolerate breaches of discipline leading to unfair treatment of anybody. We have a very difficult task and I have no intention of tying the hands of the security forces by orders and rules which make it impossible for them to carry out their duty – I am practical soldier enough to know that mistakes can be made and nobody need fear my

lack of support if the mistake is committed in good faith.

But I most strongly disapprove of 'beating up' the inhabitants of this country just because they are the inhabitants. I hope this has not happened in the past and will not happen in the future. Any indiscipline of this kind would do great damage to the reputation of the Security forces and make our task in settling Mau Mau much more difficult. I therefore order that every officer in the Police and the Army should stamp at once on any conduct which he would be ashamed to see used against his own people. I want to stand up for the honour of the Security forces with a clear conscience – I can only do that if I have absolute loyal support and rely on you to provide it.[62]

The message concluded by warning that all allegations made against the police or the army would be properly investigated.

Erskine could not enforce these threats against the police, as he was not responsible for their command. The problems there would inevitably continue. But he could, and did, bring about a sharp improvement in the behaviour of the army regiments. The dismissal of the KAR brigade commander was followed by the court martial of a KAR officer, Captain G. S. L. Griffiths. A veteran of the Second World War and a Kenya resident, Griffiths had re-enlisted for the Emergency. A brutal sadist, he was accused of murdering two Kikuyu prisoners with heavy Sten gun fire at close range, severing one man's body in half. Before the murders Griffiths and his platoon had subjected the men to tortures and humiliations, including cutting off an ear.

Erskine intended to make an example of Griffiths, but to the General's intense fury he was acquitted of the murder charge on the technicality that the prosecution could not establish the victim's identity.[63] Griffiths was charged a second time, this time accused of torture. In the second trial it became clear that two of Griffiths' fellow officers had perjured themselves in the earlier proceedings. This time they gave fuller evidence. Griffiths was convicted. He was returned to Britain and locked up in a London gaol to serve five years as a common criminal.[64]

The Griffiths case demonstrated Erskine's resolve, but it took six months to get a conviction. Very few officials in the Kenya administration supported the prosecution, which they felt 'undermined morale'. Erskine also had to endure the bad publicity that the case attracted. The acquittal caused a furore in the British newspapers,[65] and Griffiths' eventual conviction prompted a heated debate in the House of Commons, with the opposition leader, Clem Attlee, demanding a full enquiry into the conduct of the British military in Kenya.[66] Erskine took great pains to ensure that the enquiry did *not* delve into matters prior to June 1953. To his relief, the report, produced in January 1954, revealed no further examples of atrocity in the six-month period of his command.[67]

Erskine was aware that abuse in the military was relatively minor compared with other arms of the security forces. Back in February 1953 a flood of complaints about the security forces had provoked Baring to issue his own directive. This rather lame pronouncement, known as 'The Governor's Directive on Beating Up', made no charges and threatened no prosecutions, but emphasized the need to avoid alienating 'lawful Kikuyu'. It was widely ridiculed and universally ignored.[68] Police use of violence had become so routine by this time that some British soldiers were reluctant to hand over prisoners. British platoons let some prisoners go rather than commit them to the 'care' of especially notorious officers of the KPR or Kenya Regiment. Many young British conscripts, in particular, found the violence appallingly shocking. 'The police just treated the prisoners like animals,' recalled one conscript who served with the Devons. 'As soon as you handed them over, the kicks and slaps began. Goodness knows what they did to the poor buggers when they got them behind closed doors.'[69]

In private, Erskine must have wondered much the same. In public, he maintained a firm and positive line. His first political report to London after his arrival was warmly generous to his new colleagues, and up-beat about the military campaign.[70] It was a report calculated to reassure, and to smooth relations with the many-headed Hydra that was the British administration in Kenya. Erskine knew only too well that he had a tricky task on his hands. He had nothing but contempt for Kenya's white highlanders, whom he considered indolent, arrogant and reactionary in the extreme. As his tour of duty went on, greater familiarity with the settlers only deepened his loathing: 'I hate the guts of them all,' he told Lady Erskine; 'they are all middle-class sluts.'[71] These were not the type of people Erskine thought were fitted to rule over others, and the jumped-up settler representatives on the Legislative Council irritated him above all others. But he was no happier with the officials. Within a few days of arriving in the colony Erskine declared that Kenya's troubles were largely due to 'rotten administration'. 'In my opinion,' he told his wife, 'they want a new set of civil servants and some decent police.'[72] It became his habit to remind anyone who cared to listen, that Kenya's predicament demanded political reforms, not only military actions, and that the grievances of the Kikuyu were real and needed to be addressed. With the notable exception of John Whyatt, the General at no time placed his full trust in any of the senior political officers of the Kenya administration. To Erskine, they were part of the problem.

As the General took a grip, the Governor seemed to wilt. The two men were never comfortable colleagues – how could they have been when one carried with him a letter that so categorically undermined the authority of the other? While Erskine wanted to stamp his energetic authority on the war, Sir Evelyn Baring was already tiring of the whole interminable business. Erskine's robust determination to be a new broom threatened Baring's own diplomat's view of the need for 'a steady hand'. The squabbling between the hawks and doves had worn Baring down, and he must have realized that Erskine's outspoken style would only fan the flames. Erskine's very presence made Baring seem ineffectual and limp. Friends explained that the 'strain of overwork' had begun to tell. Others were less well disposed towards Baring's intellectual, hesitant manner, to his tendency to look always for a middle way before, later, capitulating to one side or the other. These people said that he could not cope, that ill-health was the result, and that he now spent more time deep in contemplation in his private chapel at Government House than he did dealing with matters of state.[73]

Baring increasingly gave way to his new deputy, Sir Frederick Crawford. The siege mentality of Nairobi came as a shock to Crawford, who had come from the tranquillity of the Seychelles in June 1953. He knew Nairobi well, having served there in the 1940s. Tough and resolute, Crawford was direct and businesslike. Blundell and the white highlanders were not sure if they liked him or not. He was honest and straight, but less biddable than Baring, and unmoved by settler bluster. There was a cold, ruthless streak: Crawford wanted Mau Mau defeated, and quickly. He was another hawk to add to the gathering flocks. His arrival weakened Whyatt, the dove whose respect for due process thwarted settler ambition.[74] Whyatt and Crawford had been contemporaries at Balliol College, Oxford, a connection that middle-class white highlanders viewed with grave suspicion. The empire of the 1950s was still a very small world, but Crawford and Whyatt were men of quite different temperaments. Ironically, the moral lawyer Whyatt found he had much more in common with the principled soldier, Erskine.

Having marked the cards of the political officers, Erskine turned to the military campaign. He was keen to make a fresh beginning, though the intelligence available remained poor. In August 1953 Special Branch reckoned there to be 2500 to 3000 forest fighters, among whom only 600 were 'hard core'.[75] This was a gross underestimate. On Mount Kenya alone the camps under General China held more than 5000 Kikuyu in a dozen separate units, with another 6000 in the Aberdares, and more men still operating independently in the Rift Valley and along the edges of the reserves.[76] At this point, the forest units were still growing. The availability of weapons and the security of supplies were all that kept a ceiling on numbers. China reckoned that one in four of his men was armed with a precision weapon, and that he had another 600 men on standby to come to the forest from Nyeri and Murang'a if he needed them. Erskine remained ignorant of all this until after the end of the year.

His first attempts to grapple with Mau Mau proved frustrating. He opted to go on the offensive, sending troops into the forest fringes, augmented by police and Home Guard. Operations Buttercup and Carnation swept through the Aberdares boundary with Murang'a and Nyeri during July 1953, and in August Operation Primrose penetrated further into the forest in the same region. Other similar actions followed on the slopes of Mount Kenya. Although Buttercup resulted in the killing and capture of more than 200 rebels, the later sweeps were far less successful as Mau Mau learned how to cope and melted into the trees. At no time in these two months did Erskine's troops achieve sustained contact with the enemy.[77] A few hideouts and camps were located, but by the time the troops got to them, the enemy had fled. In July 1953, for example, the Devon regiment overran Karia-ini, forcing Dedan Kimathi and his followers to retreat deeper into the high forest.[78] As British platoons blundered into the forests on these sorties, they followed routes and routines that were all too easy to predict. Mau Mau learned to disperse by day, and to return to their camps in the evening, when the British had gone. Erskine was bitterly disappointed by the failure to engage the enemy.

He was also taken aback by the strength of support for the rebels. Like the Vietnamese and the Algerians in their struggles against the French, and the Greek Cypriots and the Jews of Palestine who fought insurrectionist wars against the British, Mau Mau's rebels were deeply embedded in local communities. Erskine described the Kikuyu locations of western Murang'a, along the forest edge, as 'nothing more than Mau Mau republics'.[79] This was not a problem the military could easily deal with. By the end of July Erskine had already formulated a plan that would leave the messy business of controlling the passive wing in the reserve to the police and Home Guard, allowing the army to concentrate on the forest. 'I have a much clearer picture now,' he wrote to London. 'These gangs are determined and well organized, well protected and in hide outs deep in the forest and difficult to reach.'[80]

Erskine now requested reinforcements and decided not to mount any further major offensive until they had arrived. The Black Watch regiment replaced the Lancashire Fusiliers, and in September two further British battalions arrived, the Royal Northumberland Fusiliers and the Inniskillings. This brought the total of British regiments to five. In addition, a further battalion of the KAR returned from Malaya at the end of August. While these forces were acclimatizing, Erskine saw to it that the police were greatly strengthened in the Kikuyu reserves, with additional recruitment from Britain.[81]

During August, Kikuyu detainee labour cut five wide tracks deep into the Aberdares. Twenty more tracks were cut before the end of the year. These highways allowed the army to move speedily into the forest, from where they were better positioned to mount offensive operations. At the end of each track, the army built a formidable base camp. The efficiency of army sweeps immediately improved, and the rebels were once again forced deeper into the forest and higher up the mountains. This stretched their lines of supply, and made it more difficult to raid into the reserves. Bombing of the forest by the RAF now got under way in earnest, with ten Harvard bombers and four heavy Lincoln bombers being used. This may not have accounted for many rebel casualties, but in conjunction with ground operations bombing was often effective in driving the forest fighters towards the army positions.

At the end of September Erskine went on the attack again. Through October there were constant army operations within the Aberdares, driving many rebels back into Nyeri and others west, into the Rift Valley. In November similar actions on Mount Kenya forced rebel groups into South Nyeri and Embu, while some retreated north-east, towards Meru. The army often pursued the rebels into the reserve, where Home Guards joined in the running battles across the ridges.

While the British groped towards a strategy, Mau Mau's fighters sustained their offensive against the Home Guard and other 'stumps' in the reserves. If we examine these offensive actions through 1953 and into the first quarter of 1954, the sheer number of incidents suggests strength and purpose on the part of the rebels. British military tactics did begin to undermine the rebels, however, increasingly harrying the gangs that left the sanctuary of the forest, whilst in the reserves the gradually tightening authority of the police and Home Guard made liaison with the passive wing more difficult. As we can see from a closer examination of the prosecution of the war in one Kikuyu district, Murang'a, towards the end of 1953, the initiative was already swinging toward the British.

Some of the worst fighting of the war took place in Murang'a over the twelve months from April 1953 to March 1954. The first major attack on a Home Guard post here came on 28 April, at Ruathia, where a gang of fifty rebels broke through the fencing and looted the post, killing six Home Guards. Headman William, the principal target in the raid, was fortunate to escape. Four days later the same rebel unit ambushed William in his car, killing him and a Kenya Regiment officer. One week later the shops at the Kanderendu trading centre, a loyalist stronghold, were raided. The large gang then ambushed a KAR patrol from the shelter of the buildings. As the gang escaped, the soldiers gave chase and called up reinforcements. Harvard aircraft, directed by the ground forces, bombed the forest as the rebels retreated. The security forces reckoned to have killed forty Mau Mau in this engagement. Another attack six days later, on the shop of a renowned loyalist, Samuel Githu, led to a prolonged battle as the store was ransacked and the gang set fire to loyalist huts in the area. The Mau Mau leader of this raid, Maiori Kambo, was killed near Kiganjo School on 25 May by a party of Home Guard and police led by Samuel Githu.[82]

The next month saw no let-up. Ichichi and Nyakianga posts were attacked on 2 and 3 June, the rebels being beaten back. Three weeks later a coordinated raid on three posts on the forest fringe at Chomo, led by China, was far more successful. At the largest post, a Mau Mau supporter among the Home Guard opened the gate to let the attackers in. At another of the posts the homes of 160 loyalists were set alight, shops were raided and supplies loaded into three lorries that were driven to the forest, where the vehicles were overturned and torched. More than 200 rebels took part in this swift and devastating raid.[83]

At the end of June, Headman Thigiru, the son of tough old Chief Njiri, Murang'a's leading loyalist, met his death in a carefully laid Mau Mau ambush. When Njiri was brought the news, he was thrown into a grief-ridden rage. Later that day Njiri's Home Guard took remorseless vengeance on 'suspects' whom they had rounded up close to where the ambush had taken place.[84] Killings such as these never featured in the official returns of Emergency casualties, but they were part and parcel of the war in the reserves.

In July three more posts were completely overrun in Murang'a, and Home Guards killed in each of the attacks. By this stage, morale among loyalists in the district was low. When Headman Kiarie's post was attacked at the end of the month, most of the Home Guard threw down their arms and fled. The murder of Chief James Kiru and Jerome Kihori in yet another ambush showed that the government could not protect even its most important allies – Kihori was the principal organizer of Mau Mau confessions in Murang'a, from which Special Branch gathered much of their intelligence on Mau Mau activities.[85] Hardly a night went by without a Mau Mau attack somewhere in the district. By August 1953 Mau Mau was winning the war in Murang'a.

At this point the disruption to the Mau Mau units brought about by the activities of the army began to be felt and attacks on the posts slackened. The police were reinforced throughout the reserves and communal labour was used to greatly strengthen the fortifications at many of the Home Guard posts. By October the Home Guard, now better protected, better armed, and becoming hardened to their circumstances, were having greater success in beating back rebel attacks. The main rebel gangs operating in the district, led by General Matenjagwa and

General Kago, made frequent raids to obtain supplies, and this exposed them to counter-attack. The security forces were now receiving better intelligence on the movements of the main gangs, and Home Guard regularly joined police and KAR patrols in tracking down rebels. Towards the end of December Matenjagwa was killed in a fight with one such patrol.[86] The tide was turning.

As the security forces gained greater success against the gangs, more and more rebels from the forest were brought before the Special Emergency Assize Courts. Until this point the majority of those put on trial were not forest fighters at all but Mau Mau activists who had remained in the reserve. The forest fighters presented the court with an altogether different view of Mau Mau. As opposed to the hapless farm workers caught up in the murders of European settlers, who were so evidently filled with remorse and hopelessness in the dock, these men were often aggressive and outspoken, seeking to make political statements, or continually interrupting the prosecution. Some refused to address the judge. Others would not stand when told to do so and had to be dragged to their feet by their guards. Some declined the services of the counsel appointed on their behalf, insisting that Argwings-Kohdek, Kapila or Jaswat Singh be brought to defend them. The exasperated judges found them 'insolent', 'truculent' and 'uncooperative'. For these men the war continued in the courtroom.

Two examples from the battles in Murang'a revealed the stubborn determination of this resistance. The first concerns captives from the battle of Manungu Ridge, fought on 7 and 8 October 1953. The story began a few days earlier, when a well-armed gang from the forest, more than seventy strong, entered Murang'a to find food. They went to Gatara, where loyalist families refused to help them. As a consequence, the gang attacked two homesteads, murdering the men and abducting the women. KAR and Home Guard then swamped the area, in search of the women. A sweep through the forest fringe on 7 October revealed the gang's temporary hideout, and a very substantial battle ensued. When it was over, sixteen rebels were dead, and another twenty captured. At the rebel camp the security forces found the bodies of the two women, raped and then strangled.[87]

The twenty captives were brought to court in March 1954. Fourteen were under twenty-one years of age, and seven of those were juveniles of sixteen and seventeen years. Three more were in their early twenties, two were around thirty, and the last accused was reckoned to be fifty years of age. All were originally from Murang'a, and several had been born very close to the area where they were captured. Six of their number admitted to church affiliations, and each of these six had some degree of education, though none of them professed to be literate. A few had been in the forests since the beginning of 1953, but most had only left Murang'a three to four months earlier, fleeing as the Home Guard campaign against the passive wing was cranked up.

They behaved sullenly in court, refusing to obey instructions and demanding that Jaswat Singh be brought to defend them. When other lawyers were brought, they refused to utter a word and stood mutely before the bench. The judge contacted Singh and asked him to take the case, but he refused. His patience at an end, Justice de Lestang determined to hear the case without defence counsel. The prosecution witnesses were brought, all Home Guard, police and soldiers, who gave evidence as to the circumstances of the capture of each of the accused. The judge found every one of them guilty of consorting with terrorists, sentencing the seven juveniles to be detained at the Governor's pleasure, and the thirteen others to be executed. They were taken to death row at Nairobi gaol, and there, in the small hours of 8 May 1954, they were hanged, one after the other, at twenty-minute intervals.

The procedure in a trial of this kind was rudimentary, to say the least. Matters of fact and of identity were rarely contested when the accused were captives from a forest gang. The same was true in the trial of three other gang members captured in Murang'a in December 1953. These men were part of a rebel unit that laid an ambush for the security forces. The senior among them was Mwangi Marige. A twenty-seven-year-old tailor from Murang'a, Marige had attended an Anglican primary school to Standard 3. His accomplices were both from Embu. Neither had any education. Kiambati Murithe was a carpenter by trade. Mwangi Macharia was only seventeen, and described himself as 'a herdboy'. All three refused to cooperate in court, declining the counsel offered and refusing to acknowledge the judge. De Lestang convicted all three of consorting, sending the older two men to the gallows.[88]

The pattern of behaviour in these two trials was repeated in many others involving forest fighters. The similarities strongly suggest that conduct in court was discussed amongst the fighters in the forest, and the names of lawyers put forward. It is also apparent that these men were resigned to their fate. None mounted any serious defence, nor did they say anything that might assist the security forces or hinder their fellows. Even in court their resolve and determination were disciplined and purposeful. As they went to the gallows, as they knew they surely would, they did not bow before the British.

As Murang'a's rebel captives waited their turn to be tried in the Thika courtroom, more and more of their comrades were being run to ground. As the year's end approached, Kago remained the most important Murang'a rebel still at large. It was not until the end of March that he was at last killed. A small contingent of Kago's unit had presented themselves at headman Kire's guard post, dressed in police and tribal police uniforms. They tried to persuade the Home Guards there to accompany them in pursuit of a gang. Suspicions were aroused when one of Kago's men was recognized, and a bloody battle erupted, fought at close quarters by the gate to the Home Guard post. The gang swarmed over the post, throwing grenades and spraying the defenders with machine-gun fire. Only two of the ten Home Guards survived, and Kire was also killed. The gang were still ransacking the post when police reinforcements arrived. Over the next two days Kago and his men fought a sporadic battle with the Home Guard, the police and the Royal Inniskilling Fusiliers, through the farms and across the ridge tops of southern Murang'a. The rebels lost twenty-three men on the first day, and on the second day, 30 March 1954, Kago himself was among the casualties, shot by a tribal policeman.[89]

After twelve months of bitter local fighting between the rebels and the Home Guard, the government side had the initiative in Murang'a. The story was not so different in the other Kikuyu districts of Kiambu, Nyeri, Embu and Meru. In Nyeri, the fighting was as intense and protracted as in Murang'a, but the loyalists more quickly adapted to withstand rebel attacks. In Kiambu, raids on Home Guard posts were many fewer, but the assassinations of the 'stumps' went on without respite in a sinister and intensely localized struggle. Here, Mau Mau never seemed to lose the capacity to target its victims. In Embu the war heated up rather later, with the worst violence coming only after August 1953, as Erskine's military operations pushed the Mount Kenya rebels away from Nyeri and into the remoter and less densely settled areas to the east. Even as the embers of Mau Mau's offensive were dying out, violence flared in Embu. The Home Guard post of Headman Charles, at Ngariami, was attacked in January 1954, for example, by a gang all of whom were said to be 'strangers' to the district.[90]

As many of the forest gangs retreated northwards in both the Aberdares and Mount Kenya, attacks also took place with increasing regularity in the remoter European farmlands north of Nyeri, between the two vast forests. Our final example from this period, an attack upon guards on a farm in Nanyuki, underscores that not all the violence was between Kikuyu: others who stood against the rebels were also targeted by forest fighters.[91] In this case a European farmer named Bastard had brought Turkana to the farm as a deterrent against rebel incursion. The Turkana replaced Kikuyu labourers, and for that reason alone might have been singled out; but they were also very effective in hindering Mau Mau activities throughout the area.

On the night of 6 May 1954, while Operation Anvil was already in full swing far to the south in Nairobi, a large rebel force of more than a hundred fighters descended upon the Bastard farm and made straight for the Turkana encampment, in a remote spot two miles distant from the farmhouse. With bugles blaring, they fell upon the homesteads at 2a.m., scattering the occupants with volley after volley of rifle-shot. More than 140 spent cartridges were found at the scene. Nine Turkana were killed, and another dozen seriously injured. Though the firing was heard for miles around, none of the white highlanders came to investigate, and it took the local police five hours to get to the scene. The contrast with the intensity of the security presence in Murang'a, and the speed of their likely response to an incident of this kind at this stage of the Emergency, could hardly be greater.

By May 1954 the Mau Mau offensive was over. Matenjagwa and Kago, who had taken the fight into the reserves, were gone. Other commanders still remained, but they had more cautiously led their followers deeper into the forests. The rebels were on the defensive throughout central Kenya, each gang increasingly focused on supplies and survival. After Operation Anvil, their predicament would get worse.

Operation Anvil sealed the fate of the forest fighters. Supplies from Nairobi no longer reached the camps, and the stream of recruits dried up. Between China's arrest in January and the completion of the Anvil interrogations in July 1954, the government had made vast strides in intelligence gathering. Special Branch now understood how the passive wing operated, and systematically disrupted the committees in the reserves. More and more passive wing organizers were removed into detention, and the links between the forest and the population in the reserves dwindled. And all the time, the Home Guard and police took a firmer grip.

The isolation of the forest was made more complete by the construction of deep ditches along the reserve boundaries in Nyeri and Embu. Dug by forced communal labour, these huge excavations were overlooked by Home Guard posts and watchtowers. Spiked poles filled the ditch, making this a difficult barrier for the rebels to cross coming to and from the forest. In February a policy of closer settlement was imposed in areas of the reserve adjacent to the forest. Where Mau Mau sympathies were strongest, villagization was rigorously enforced, with curfews limiting the number of hours that people could leave the village to tend their crops and animals. The new villages were fortified camps, the serried rows of huts neatly aligned behind the barricades. Everyone was under close scrutiny. The villages had a dramatic affect in denying food to the rebels, but it was a bleak, brutal place for the inhabitants. It was not entirely clear whether the fortifications were there to keep Mau Mau out, or to keep the Kikuyu in.

With these measures coming into place and Nairobi neutralized,

Erskine was able to concentrate upon the forest. Reorganization of political decision taking greatly enhanced his authority at this time. Up to the early part of 1954 the Colony Emergency Committee had taken executive authority for the conduct of the conflict. This large and ponderous body met only once a fortnight. Erskine found it impossible to get quick decisions; the committee was unable to properly coordinate the arms of government, and lacked clear reporting lines. From mid-March, at Erskine's urging and with Lyttelton's strong support, a slimmed-down War Council was formed, comprising Baring, Crawford, Blundell and Erskine himself. This group met twice a week, with its own dedicated secretariat to see that decisions were acted upon. The new structure gave Erskine control: military policy could be coordinated with the police and other arms of the security forces on his terms.[92] This also marginalized the white highlanders, whose nominated representative, Blundell, could exert little influence on the War Council.[93]

In the weeks after Anvil, Erskine prepared for the next phase in his push against the forest gangs. From August 1954 his battalions tackled the remaining problems in and around Nairobi, and scoured the Aberdares border with South Nyeri and Nanyuki and the Mount Kenya zone bordering Embu and Meru. The objective was to ensure that the gangs were completely isolated in the sanctuary of the forests.[94] Casualty rates inflicted upon the forest units now climbed steadily. By October the rebels were losing more than 600 fighters each month. With recruitment falling sharply, this was unsustainable. The killing and capture of gang leaders had also eaten away at morale. Only thirteen Mau Mau leaders had been captured or killed up to April 1954, but between then and September another fourteen more were accounted for.[95] By December 1954 Erskine's best guess was that there were fewer than 4000 Mau Mau fighters left in total.

From mid-December Erskine took the fight into the high forests. Operation Hammer would sweep the Aberdares moorlands, flushing the gangs back down into the bamboo and the lower areas, where they would be engaged by stop lines set along the forest fringe. Patrolling increased over the next few weeks, and by early February 1955 the army was in the high forest in force, keeping the rebel gangs constantly on the move. Though the basic method appeared to work, the results were meagre and expensive – fewer than 200 rebels killed or captured, at a cost of £10,000 each.[96] However, Erskine now had a much better idea of how many men were left in the Aberdares (he reckoned around 1700).[97] Operation First Flute adopted similar tactics on Mount Kenya from late February 1955. This netted nearly 300 rebels, but intelligence suggested a further 2800 insurgents remained at large.[98] This was slow but steady progress. By May 1955, when Erskine's tour of duty came to end, the forest war had essentially been won. His successor, General Lathbury, would oversee the mopping-up operations, picking off the remaining rebels.

If the forest war was moving towards a conclusion, it also seemed that the government had re-established its authority in the reserves in the months after Anvil. Home Guards and other loyalists now ruled the reserves with an iron fist, smashing down upon their opponents. The process of interrogation and screening of Mau Mau suspects led to a flood of 'confessions' as people admitted to having taken Mau Mau oaths. No one was any longer able to openly support Mau Mau. Loyalists felt more secure than they had done for two years past.

The violence still erupted from time to time, though; and it could do so almost anywhere, even in areas the security forces thought to have under their firm control. In Kiambu and around the Nairobi outskirts incidents continued after Anvil all the way through 1955. Oathing was still conducted among the labourers on some of the larger estates, and Mau Mau supporters were still capable of targeting the 'stumps'. Kikuyu loyalists on the Githembe estate were attacked in August 1954, for example, by *komerera* elements under the command of Muchiri Mwehe. The gang murdered ten labourers. Though two of the attackers were caught shortly after committing the crime, and both were convicted and sentenced to hang, Mwehe escaped detection until May 1955, when he was arrested in the Pangani area of Nairobi.[99] In another Kiambu case, on the Kassarini estate in January 1955, a loyal headman who refused the oath was executed and, in an incident reminiscent of an earlier stage of the Emergency, the other labourers gathered on the estate were made to hack at the dead man's body with a panga. Three men hanged for this murder, but the man who organized the killing was never caught. If the British had begun to think the war was won by early in 1955, there were many Mau Mau supporters who had not yet given up the fight.

Mau Mau was directing its violence entirely against Kikuyu loyalists. Though they preferred not to think too deeply about it, Kenya's British administrators knew that the Home Guard, despised by a large section of the population, had come to exert a draconian power over the Kikuyu reserves. As he prepared to depart at the end of March 1954, Kenya's retiring Commissioner of Police, O'Rorke, allowed himself a rare moment of candour in reflecting upon the part played by the Kikuyu militiamen:

> The maintenance of the Kikuyu Home Guard for much longer is a matter I regard with serious apprehension. It is true that a number of its units are active and ruthless in exterminating terrorists, but their quarrel is with the terrorists and their own private enemies and not

generally with Mau Mau and what it stands for. The sooner, therefore, it can be disarmed, dispensed with and its strongholds removed after the main threat of Mau Mau violence is dealt with, the sooner can there be law and order enforced in Kikuyu country.[100]

O'Rorke's fears for the future were well founded. Once let loose, could the chauvinistic authority of the Home Guard now be reined back in? As the war entered its final phase, the benefits dished out to the Home Guard in particular, and loyalists in general, served only to entrench their position and deepen the resentment of their rivals.

The decision was taken in September 1954 to start running down Home Guard numbers from the end of the year. There were by then more than 20,000 Kikuyu militiamen, manning 550 fortified posts. Each unit had an African ex-KAR soldier in their midst to stiffen the ranks, and there was a European district officer to command every dozen units. This astonishing militarization of the countryside needed careful dismantling. After January 1955 some 800 Home Guards were gradually transferred to the Tribal Police, bringing the strength of this force up to 1800. A further 6400 Home Guards were kept on the payroll by being made into a Tribal Police Reserve, albeit at a lower salary. The remaining 14,000 Home Guards were not immediately disbanded, but employment was found for many of them in the detention camps and with the screening teams over the next few months, until, by the end of 1955, the vast majority had been discharged.[101]

Favouritism to loyalists, and denial of the rebels, seeped through every facet of social life in Central Province. By 1954 even the bursaries paid to schoolboys attending the Alliance High School, Kenya's top African secondary school, were only awarded to the sons of Home Guards. Despite the complaint of the school's headmaster that 'several very good students' had been seriously disadvantaged, the government was not prepared to interfere with the choice of the African committee who had made the decisions.[102] In Kenya the British did nothing to prevent their allies reaping the rewards of this dirty war; indeed, they encouraged it, and in the process they legitimated expropriation and exploitation.

The expropriation of land was at the heart of Mau Mau's message, and the same issue would now become a weapon in the endgame of the struggle in the reserves. From an early stage in the emergency, the white highlanders had wanted to confiscate the lands of convicted rebels. A Forfeiture of Lands Bill was brought before the Kenya Legislature in December 1953, and passed by a large majority: the African members all voted against it, but everybody else seemed to think it was a jolly good idea. The regulations were tightly framed: land could only be taken from named individuals whose property was undisputed and not shared with others. The land concerned would also have to be surveyed. These technicalities limited the likely use of the act, and so the Colonial Office gave its approval and the bill became law in March 1954.

The act was used sparingly, and up to June 1955 only 269.62 acres was confiscated, all from imprisoned Mau Mau 'leaders', or named gang commanders still at large. Kenyatta, for example, lost 31.42 acres of land, from four plots in Kiambu. Kihonge Kingara, a wealthy rebel leader from Murang'a, lost 116 acres, while Kimathi's family was evicted from their 11.26 acre farm, and Mathenge's relatives from the paltry 1.4 acres that they held in Nyeri. In all, twenty-three persons lost their lands through this ordinance.[103]

Then, in June 1955, with the fighting war all but over and Baring's government looking towards the future, the bill was amended to allow the confiscation of lands jointly held as part of an *mbari*. The amendment was made effective from 11 July 1955, to tie in with the expiry of the government's final surrender offer to the rebels, as an incentive: those who remained in the forest after 11 July would surely lose whatever property they had. A blanket order could now be issued against named individuals, and it would be left to local African committees to ascertain the extent of confiscation. Decisions were confirmed by local land boards, endorsed by the provincial commissioner. This was but a formality: the power lay with the committee, and the committee of course consisted entirely of local loyalists. In the Legislative Council, European members chided the government for not having adopted so forceful a measure much earlier.[104]

Within a week, the loyalist land grab had started. Orders were issued against 406 persons from Kiambu, 868 from Murang'a, 1700 from Nyeri, and 447 from Embu. Over the next year, confiscations were enforced against these 3471 named rebels. Many were men who had been detained without trial on the suspicion of their Mau Mau beliefs: they had never been convicted of a crime, but they were now to sacrifice their landholding on the evidence of a committee of loyalist elders, probably the same men who had sent them into detention in the first place.

No clear record exists of the exact totals of land confiscated, or of the process involved. In some places, acquisitive loyalists are said to have made substantial gains, but for the most part the holdings involved were small. Sorrenson, who made an analysis of the records that were available in the mid-1960s, reckoned that the majority held less than 2 acres, and that perhaps one in four were deemed to have no land to confiscate.[105] If it was the intention of government to reward its allies, then the measure was less successful than might have been hoped; but the confiscations stood as a telling evidence of where power lay as the war drew towards an end. The victors would take all.

# Surrenders

The white highlanders had never much liked the idea of surrender. When Erskine had first suggested that a surrender offer be made to the rebels, back in July 1953, their reaction had been savage. He'd pushed ahead, despite the criticism; but the 'Green Branch' offer, implemented from August 1953, had not been a success. Up to February 1954 only 159 rebels had surrendered to the security forces.[106]

When Special Branch came up with the idea of a second surrender ploy, this time involving General China, Governor Baring's reaction was understandably cool. Nervous of raising the bile of the white highlanders yet again, he consulted London for advice. Lyttelton, supported by Churchill and the Cabinet, insisted that it was a gamble worth taking. So the plan to use General China to initiate a mass surrender of forest fighters was given official blessing.

Once China's cooperation was secured, early in February, Erskine suspended Operation Anvil to allow time to get the surrender talks under way. All of this was controversial, and had to be kept secret. Publicity might sabotage the whole scheme, especially if settler opposition was stoked up. Blundell was kept in the dark. Baring left Crawford to handle the details. On 14 February Henderson and China flew up to Nyeri to set up the Special Branch operational headquarters. Someone with a lame sense of humour decided to call the project Operation Wedgwood.[107]

At Nyeri, China wrote twenty-six letters, each addressed to a Mau Mau commander. These were delivered via passive wing elements in the reserves. As the letters reached their intended recipients over the next week, word of China's capitulation and the possibility of surrender swept through the forest like a wildfire. Karari Njama was with Kimathi at the time. The letter, as described by Njama, was simple and to the point, asking that representatives of the Aberdares and Mount Kenya armies be sent to meet with China and members of the government to discuss terms for a settlement and surrender. Kimathi called a meeting of forest leaders to discuss the proposal. According to Njama, there was a willingness to enter negotiations, and it was agreed that representatives would be sent to meet with the government. A reply was sent back to China.[108]

The reply was never received by Special Branch, leaving Dedan Kimathi to think that his response had been ignored. Kimathi then learned that another senior Mount Kenya fighter, General Tanganyika, had given himself up, on 6 March, in order to participate in the surrender talks. Tanganyika met with China in Nyeri, and returned to the forest with a second set of letters for the Mount Kenya commanders.[109] Kimathi's paranoia now got the better of him. Fearing that he was being deliberately excluded from negotiations leading to a unilateral surrender of the Mount Kenya armies, Kimathi denounced Tanganyika at a second forest meeting, rejecting the surrender plan. Many forest fighters were now convinced that China and Tanganyika were traitors, leading them into a government trap.[110]

By this time, rumours of the surrender offer were being whispered in Nairobi. Worried that a leak would embarrass him yet again, on 4 March Baring opted to make a public announcement about China and the surrender talks. Blundell, humiliated by his exclusion, ranted as never before, castigating Baring for duplicity and accusing him of being 'party to brutality, filthy oaths and murder'.[111] He was not alone in his anger. There was little support for the surrender plan among administrative officers. In Nyeri the hostility was acute. Henderson's Special Branch team found local administrators uncooperative and even obstructive. This was more than a nuisance: it posed real dangers. In order to maintain communications with Tanganyika and other forest leaders, Henderson needed to clear security forces out of designated areas. Despite explicit orders, they repeatedly found Home Guard and tribal police swarming all over these areas at times when they should have been clear. There was clear evidence that Special Branch instructions were being regularly, and quite deliberately ignored. This 'sabotage by non-compliance' threatened to destroy the entire operation.[112]

Failures in communication appeared to have placed the negotiations in jeopardy as March drew to a close, but then a third senior Mount Kenya commander emerged from the forest. On 27 March General Kaleba boldly presented himself to a KAR officer, declared his identity and insisted on being taken to see China.[113] Kaleba's intervention revived hopes that things might yet turn out well. The forest gangs were deeply divided over the surrender, he told Henderson, but some were certainly prepared to negotiate. Their fear of Home Guard retribution and anxiety about how long they might spend in prison seemed to be the two greatest barriers. On the understanding that he would bring others to continue the negotiations, Kaleba was allowed to return to the forest the next day.

When Kaleba re-emerged to meet Henderson on the forest edge three days later, he was accompanied by five comrades. The men clambered into the Land Rover, and set off for Nyeri. With typical guile, Henderson gave his loaded gun to one of the rebels to hold as the vehicle bumped along the forest tracks. That afternoon, forty miles to the south, the battle that would bring General Kago's death was raging across the ridges of southern Murang'a, as twelve men crowded into the provincial commissioner's dreary office in Nyeri to begin the surrender nego- tiations. It must have seemed more than a little surreal. Alongside Kaleba and his five nameless comrades sat Tanganyika and China. Windley, the Member for African Affairs, was there to represent Baring, Colonel Heyman for the army, and Gribble and Henderson for Special Branch. The rebels spoke in Kikuyu and Henderson interpreted for everyone. The room was bugged. Transcripts of what was said later appeared in correspondence between Nairobi and London.[114]

The meeting lasted three hours. Once the initial political posturing was done with, the key issues on the Mau Mau side became clear. They were keen to come out of the forest and then negotiate a political settlement, but they did not trust the government not to shoot them; if they were not shot, they expected to be ill-treated. They also wanted to know whether the government would prosecute them for their previous crimes – if so, they could all be hanged. Undertakings were given on all of these issues, but it was stressed that each person who surrendered would be detained 'for an indefinite period'. They were not happy with this, but the government team would go no further and so the point was grudgingly accepted.

To give the rebels time to consult in the forests, and to marshal those who wished to surrender, the security forces would respect a ceasefire in the Mount Kenya forest area, and on the Aberdares fringe north of the Murang'a boundary, until 10 April. On that day, those willing to surrender would rendezvous near Konyu, in Nyeri, at the south-west corner of the Mount Kenya forest. The meeting broke up, and Kaleba and Tanganyika were driven back to the forest edge with the other five rebels. Before departing, they were given clothing and food. Special Branch officers would not see any of them again for a very long time.

The negotiators returned to find a heated debate raging among their forest comrades. Another Mau Mau commander, General Gatamuki, now openly accused them of leading the rebel forces into a trap. There were rancorous exchanges, culminating when those who had been in Nyeri were disarmed by Gatamuki. The division among the forest fighters was deep. Kimathi now opposed the negotiations, threatening violence against rebels taking part in the surrender; but on Mount Kenya opinion swung the other way. In the end, each man was left to decide for himself.

The first groups of fighters, about a thousand, were already camped in the Konyu area by 6 April, and another 600 were on their way with Kaleba from Meru and Embu. Among those gathering was Gatamuki, with his band of a hundred followers. They were spotted by a KAR reconnaissance patrol, camped just inside the boundary of the reserve. Though they were in the vicinity of Konyu, and it was obvious by their behaviour that they were waiting for the rendezvous and did not feel themselves to be in danger of attack, they were in fact *outside* the forest area designated in the ceasefire agreement. The next day, 7 April, the KAR swept along the forest boundary and attacked them. Caught unawares, twenty-five rebels were killed and seven captured, including the furious Gatamuki. The noise of the battle echoed through the valley and up the forested slopes. Other rebel bands waiting to surrender took fright and fled.

Brigadier John Reginald Orr of the 7th Battalion of the King's African Rifles robustly defended his actions in opening fire on Gatamuki's gang. 'I regard the action with nothing but satisfaction,' he told Nairobi's eager press pack.[115] Though some thought Orr's action deliberate sabotage, others countered this by suggesting that Gatamuki's intentions were to disrupt the surrender.[116] Erskine, intensely frustrated, but never one to criticize his own soldiers, put it down to 'bad luck'. Among the forest fighters there was only one interpretation: the surrender had been nothing but an elaborate government trap designed to kill them all.

For Special Branch, the disappointment of failure was softened by the knowledge that they had driven a sharp wedge through the command structure of the forest gangs, dividing one general against another, and by the many intelligence gains that had been made along the way. General China had proved to be the most potent weapon of the war.

Among his many victims was the young Miano Ngemwe. Captured just two weeks after China was taken into custody, Ngemwe was told of China's revelations and encouraged to 'save himself' from the hangman's noose by following suit. The trick worked. Ngemwe agreed to return to the forest on 'operational duties' with the British. Over a three-week period he led his captors to several forest camps and provided an intelligence bonanza that contributed to the killing and capture of more than a dozen other Mau Mau fighters. When he was eventually brought to court, two months later, Ngemwe expected to be treated with leniency. In the dock he was confident, even cheerful, answering questions with direct honesty, and giving full answers about his life with the forest fighters. As the trial came to a close, Ngemwe reeled back in shock when Justice Law sentenced him to hang. When asked if he wished to address the court, Ngemwe's desperation and distress was clear. He struggled for words, choking back his emotion as he spoke: 'I am faced with a difficulty,' he began: 'I have already helped the security forces by pointing out Mau Mau hiding places and food supplies.' He paused, his mind in a panic. What else could he do to save his skin? He turned to the Judge, and pleaded with him: 'What about General China and General Tanganyika? Has either of these two given the names of a medicine man? If someone is to die, then he can do something important before he dies. I want to help the authorities. I have betrayed Mau Mau, and would be killed by them. I will point out the medicine man who advises Mau Mau where and when to attack.'[117] Ngemwe was led from the dock, still desperately bargaining for his life. He had been promised salvation, but he now knew that the British did not keep such promises. Ngemwe was hanged.

General China had been allowed to live simply because of his usefulness. After the failure of the surrender negotiations at Konyu, China made two further visits to the forest with Henderson, but he no longer had the trust of his former comrades. At the end of 1954 China was spirited away to the detention camp at Lokitaung, in the hot, arid far north of Kenya. He would remain there for nearly nine years, not being released until the British had packed their bags ready to leave Kenya. At Lokitaung, China fell in with the camp's most distinguished inmate, Jomo Kenyatta. They made an odd couple: Kenyatta, the constitutional nationalist who had opposed the violence of the Mau Mau hooligans, and China, the rebel 'enforcer' whose murders had helped to instil the discipline and fear that gave the movement its strength, but whose defection had helped to swing the war the way of the British.

Thinner and quieter than when China had last seen him, at a KAU meeting in early August 1952, Kenyatta tucked the new arrival under his paternal wing.[118] Always respectful of his elders, and viewing him as the national leader, China bore Kenyatta none of the animosity that was felt by Kubai and other more radical men incarcerated at Lokitaung. Kubai had once menaced Kenyatta with the threat of death. Did these radicals view the captured and pardoned Mau Mau general as a traitor? At first, perhaps. Relations between the prisoners at Lokitaung were strained, and Kenyatta had even been physically attacked; but the shared endurance of incarceration built bonds. Kenyatta and China, on the face of it a most unlikely pairing, now found solace in one another's company. Kenyatta taught China to speak and write in English, and the tough Mau Mau general loyally protected his leader. Their friendship grew strong in confinement. After independence, Waruhiu Itote would again serve Kenyatta well.

The saga of the surrender talks had a deeper significance for British policy in Kenya. All along it had been Churchill's opinion that the Kenya government should make a settlement with the Kikuyu. In a meeting with Michael Blundell, in 1954, Churchill 'kept returning again and again to the need for negotiation'. In Churchill's view, the Kikuyu 'were not the primitive cowardly people which many imagined them to be, but people of considerable fibre, ability and steel'. When Blundell protested that they could only make a settlement once the military campaign was won, the Prime Minister simply raised his voice to repeat the question 'Why can't you come to terms with the Kikuyu?' For Churchill, the 'highly individualistic and difficult' white highlanders were as much the problem as any rebel army.[119] Erskine held much the same opinion, and it was he, against stern opposition from Blundell and within the Kenya administration, who promoted the surrender talks as a useful tactic in the war. It was a strategy that had only lukewarm support from Baring, and none at all among Nairobi's hawks.

Because of the opposition to negotiation among senior administrative officers in Nairobi, Operation Wedgwood might easily have stalled long before the unfortunate battle at Konyu had it not been for some powerful and timely interventions. General Sir John Harding, Chief of the Imperial General Staff, was in Nairobi from 20 February 1954 to consult with Erskine, just as Henderson was moving the plan along. With Erskine's encouragement, Harding threw his weight behind the scheme. This appears to have calmed the anxious Baring, who was more concerned about the settler backlash should anything go wrong. Then, more important still, Oliver Lyttelton arrived in Nairobi on 28 February. He seized upon the opportunity to draw Baring towards negotiations, even taking part in discussions with Crawford and Special Branch over the surrender scheme.[120] Without the presence of Harding and Lyttelton, it is doubtful that Henderson's careful plans would have got as far as they did.

The intransigence of Baring's government had begun to alienate London's support by the closing months of 1953. The Conservative Party held only a thin majority in parliament and the embarrassments of the Kenya campaign posed an increasing political threat. On the one hand, Lyttelton could not risk retreating from his public support of Baring, for that might have caused dissent among the right wing of his party; but on the other hand, it was clear that Baring had no real idea how to break out of the impasse. Within the Colonial Office plans were moving ahead at pace for constitutional changes in all of Britain's African colonies that would bring about electoral government and, eventually, self-government – by June 1954 Kwame Nkrumah formed the interim government that would take the Gold Coast to independence from Britain. Despite the war against Mau Mau, Kenya could not remain immune from these trends. In the Colonial Office it was argued that constitutional changes in Kenya might help to bring a speedier end to the conflict, by showing British willingness to reward its loyal allies with political gains. Lyttelton arrived in Nairobi in February 1954, in the midst of the surrender talks, clutching plans for a new constitution.

London had decided that Kenya would have a multi-racial government, whether the white highlanders liked it or not. Faith in Baring was on the wane. He had too often bowed before the hawks, and London

The portrait of himself that Dedan Kimathi sent to the British security forces on learning that they did not possess a photograph of Kenya's most-wanted Mau Mau leader.

Kenya's War Council, 1954: Deputy Governor Frederick Crawford,
Governor Evelyn Baring, General George Erskine and Michael Blundell.

A fortified Home Guard post, at Kiajogu in Nyeri District, with watchtower and staked moat.

*Left* A fortified Home Guard post in Murang'a, late 1953.

Police examine a dead Mau Mau fighter killed in the attack on Othaya Police Post.

Local Kikuyu residents leaving Kamiritho Home Guard Post, having gathered there overnight for protection against Mau Mau attack.

KAMIRITHO

General Erskine (centre) relaxing with Chief Njiri (far left) and members of the district administration, late 1954.

A street scene from Nairobi at the time of the Jubilee. The city's white high-landers put up bunting, but the African population staged a strike and a boycott of the municipal bus services. Only a few women and children are gathered at the normally busy bus stop, and the streets are unusually quiet.

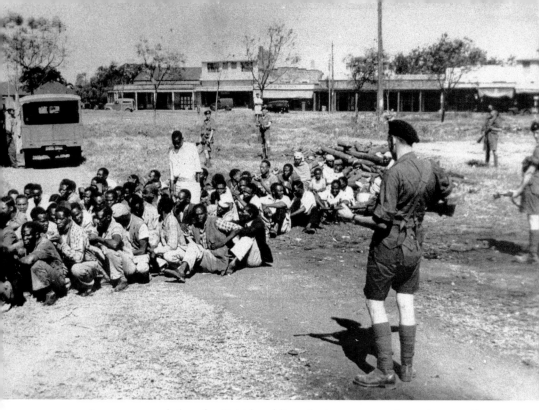

Suspects rounded up by British soldiers during a sweep through part of Nairobi's Eastlands, 1953.

Kikuyu suspects rounded up during Operation Anvil are marched into the interrogation camp at Langata.

*Left* Kikuyu suspects, rounded up in Nairobi during Operation Anvil, 23 April 1954. The caged trucks took the suspects to the Langata Screening Camp for interrogation.

The hooded informants, *gikunia*, used to identify Mau Mau activists during Operation Anvil.

Kikuyu detainees being released from Aguthi Camp in 1959.

officials had too often heard the plaintive call that this or that action could not be taken because of settler opinion. The new constitution was not a matter for negotiation, and although Lyttelton took the time to discuss the proposals in Nairobi, he was not prepared to change anything. On 10 March, Lyttelton announced that Kenya would have a new constitution establishing a multi-racial Council of Ministers, to include two Asian members and one African member. It was a sharp reminder to the settler community that London would determine their political future, regardless of how the Emergency turned out. No one in Kenya much liked the proposals, African, Asian or European; but Lyttelton stood firm.[121] For those who wanted greater African representation, the new constitution was too small a step. To the white highlanders it looked like another kind of surrender.

## Psycho Docs and Pseudo Ops

Before Mau Mau, no one had ever suggested the Kikuyu to be a brutal people. Europeans in Africa were fond of racial stereotypes, and those they applied to the Kikuyu were almost wholly positive: They were industrious and progressive, the kind of Africans who seized upon the benefits of European civilization and made the best of it; they embraced education; they took to Christianity; they were happy to accept wages for their labour; and they were entrepreneurial. Their politics sometimes became assertive and disputatious, but on the whole Kikuyu were compliant. Most Europeans in central Kenya employed Kikuyu house servants, who washed their clothes, cleaned, cooked their food and looked after their children. Trust was there, even if it was paternalistic, patronizing and muted by a heavy sense of racial superiority.

The emergence of Mau Mau altered the image irreparably. Suddenly, overnight, the smiling servant had become the murderous savage, enveloped in 'a wild, red rolling madness', like Ruark's Mau Mau anti-hero Kimani, who returned to the farm of his childhood to murder the white man who had once slapped him across the face: '[H]e struck with the panga, struck again and again, slashing away the slap in the face.'[122] Kikuyu interest in Europeans was now 'couched in hatred'. Instead of looking after their children, they possessed 'a wild desire to carve them up with machetes'.[123]

The explanation for this dramatic change, for the reversion to chilling violence, was to be found in Kikuyu psychology. Michael Blundell summed it up in one pithy remark: Mau Mau, he said, was a 'mind destroying disease'.[124] Kikuyu vulnerability to this mental illness was a product of their eagerness for progress. They had rushed too quickly towards the glare of civilization and been blinded and frightened by its brightness. They could not cope and had now shrunk back into the darker recesses of their past, seeking security and comfort in barbaric superstition. The wicked perversion of the Mau Mau oath was evidence enough of this atavistic reversion. In their trauma, the Kikuyu had been easily led to violence by men who had all along rejected civilization, wanting to re-establish the pre-colonial order of things. By this reasoning, Mau Mau was not provoked by the denial of things to the Kikuyu but by their own inability to grapple with the challenges of modernity.

It was a theme that very quickly came to dominate the official government analysis of Kenya's dreadful troubles. There were no grievances or justifiable claims to be aired by the Kikuyu; only an illness, a mental disease. The Kikuyu were sick. Kenya's government built its whole anti-Mau-Mau strategy around this interpretation. It was a neat argument: if Mau Mau was a mental illness, innate to the African in transition, then British colonialism could not be blamed. Similarly, the white highlanders, whatever their politics might be, found it comforting because it exonerated them too: the terrible violence was not then *their* fault; it was not the consequence of things *they* had done. Their once trusted Kikuyu servants were only to be pitied for the feebleness that had brought them to this miserable condition.

These views pervaded every nook and cranny of European opinion on the matter. Even in the highest political circles, Mau Mau continued to be explained in these terms as the Emergency was coming to an end. Alan Lennox Boyd, who succeeded Oliver Lyttelton as British Secretary of State for the Colonies at the end of 1954, gave his parliamentary colleagues a succinct account during a debate on Kenya: 'Mau Mau is a conspiracy based on the total perversion of the human spirit by means of the power of the oath and by witchcraft and intimidation, all of which combined to place its followers mentally almost in another world, in which the pursuit of their twisted aims was the only important thing.' That the 'twisted aims' of the movement included the return of their stolen lands, improvement in their wages and standards of living, and political equality with whites and Asians was not explained. The definition of Mau Mau's evil depended upon the denial that such material or political grievances had any legitimacy. Mau Mau's adherents had moved beyond the pale of legitimate politics, into a dark void. Lennox Boyd went on to remind parliament about 'the bestiality' of Mau Mau's oaths:

Originally the oath differed little from the normal Kikuyu oath used in tribal ceremonies [he explained] ... but as the terrorists grew more brutalised, their moral degradation was reflected in the characteristics of the Mau Mau oath. This developed sexual and sadistic aberrations which, in the higher form of the oath, included murder and cannibalism. All this ritual played its part in building up the Mau Mau mind, and the activities to which they were driving themselves tied them more and more to it. ... What is clear ... is that the taking of the oaths had such a tremendous effect on the Kikuyu mind as to turn quite intelligent young Africans into entirely different human beings, into sub-human creatures without hope and with death as their only deliverance.

This was why so many Europeans objected to the very idea of surrender negotiations. If Mau Mau were 'sub-humans', then what was the point of negotiation? It no longer mattered how you treated them. Death was 'their only deliverance'.[125]

How had this interpretation of Mau Mau come about? Elements of it were surely already floating in the pool of prejudice about African adaptability to social change long before the Emergency. Kenya had been home to an unusually vociferous eugenicist lobby in the inter-war years; and even the more reforming enlightened thinking of colonial policy makers emanating from London after 1945 had not easily penetrated Kenya. Conservative views were in the great majority among the colony's administrators as well as with the white highlanders. When the Emergency came, Kenya rejected any suggestion that outside 'experts' might help solve the problem and instead looked inward, to its own home-grown intellectuals.

What gave the 'disease theory' of Mau Mau substance was the work of a small group of men who were brought together on a government committee in the early phase of the Emergency. The 'Committee to Enquire into the Sociological Causes and Remedies for Mau Mau' was formed, with the urging of officials in London, in an effort to find some positive ways of tackling Mau Mau.[126] The Colonial Office staff promoting it had issues of social welfare and improvement in mind. The men appointed to this committee by Baring steered things in a quite different direction.

The committee was a strange fusion. Each of its principals brought a perspective that in some way helped to frame the overall interpretation that would emerge. In the chair was the earnest do-gooder Tom Askwith. Liberal, pro-African, an evangelical believer in social welfare and self-improvement, Askwith ran the colony's community development programme and had been intimately involved in the improved housing schemes for Africans in Eastlands. He did not believe that Mau Mau was 'irredeemable', but instead sought a 'cure' for its evils in re-education and what came to be termed 'rehabilitation'. Two other officials on the committee, H. E. Lambert and Sidney Fazan, had special knowledge of

Kikuyu customs. Lambert would publish his ethnography of the Kikuyu during the Emergency.[127] He had been a district officer in Kikuyuland over many years, and believed strongly that counter-oathing and traditional Kikuyu cleansing rituals could be adapted to reverse Mau Mau's taint. Sidney Fazan was not so sure about that. His interests lay in defending the government's land policy, which he had played such a prominent role in implementing over the previous thirty years. Fazan did not believe that Kikuyu claims to land could be accepted as legitimate, and said so whenever the chance arose.

The two leading Kikuyu representatives on the committee took a more equivocal view on the land question, but they were equally vehement in their rejection of Mau Mau's legitimacy. One was David Waruhiu, the son of the murdered Chief Waruhiu and a crusading Christian with the movement for Moral Rearmament. He wanted to assert the role of religion in defeating Mau Mau, seeing salvation in a rejection of the pagan practices of Mau Mau adherents. The other was Harry Thuku. He had led the first protest against colonial rule in Kenya back in the 1920s, and been imprisoned for his pains. After 1945 he had first been happy to parade as a figurehead for the new African nationalists, but as the Kikuyu hooligans took the initiative, he had walked out in disgust. Now a committed loyalist, he had spoken out against Mau Mau on many occasions. His presence on the committee was useful in propaganda terms. Both these men found Mau Mau oaths abhorrent, though for different reasons: Waruhiu was outraged by the rejection of Christian faith they implied; Thuku fumed at the subversion of Kikuyu custom – the angry young men of Mau Mau had no right to administer oaths of any kind to anyone.

By far the most influential members of the committee were its two European intellectuals, Louis Leakey and Dr J. C. Carothers. Between them they would quite literally write the prescription for Mau Mau's cure, though how it would be administered to the patients was taken out of their hands.

Leakey was colonial Kenya's resident expert on all things Kikuyu.[128] He had grown up among devoutly Christian Kikuyu. He spoke the language, and had even been initiated into a traditional Kikuyu male age-set. He liked to describe himself as 'a white African', and his friends suggested that he 'thought like a Kikuyu'. These things gave him an authority none could rival, and his connections to senior Kikuyu Christians, such as the Waruhius, brought him close to conservative African opinion. Before the emergency began, Leakey, with the Waruhius, had been behind the counter-oathing ceremonies. He was convinced of the evil influence of the Koinanges and Kenyatta, and had served the government as a translator at Kenyatta's show trial in Kapenguria. Once the Emergency was under way, he wrote two short books on Mau Mau, in which he elaborated his ideas about the powerful psychological effect of the oaths, and about the need to strengthen other aspects of Kikuyu custom in order to defeat the evil.[129] In describing the oaths Leakey never laid stress on bestiality or perversion; those who wished to show the Kikuyu as morally degraded would amplify this theme. For Leakey, the important thing was to understand the basis of the oath's authority and how it could be challenged. On the committee it was Leakey who agued that 'confessions' were essential if the curse inflicted by having taken the oath was to be lifted. Though couched in scientific terms, his analysis was heavily influenced by his Christian faith.

Though Leakey was undoubtedly the committee's moving force, Dr J. C. Carothers brought the weight of medical opinion to the table.[130] Carothers had been the director and principal psychiatrist at Nairobi's Mathare Hospital, Kenya's only institution for the care of the mentally ill. Previously employed as a general medical officer, he had had no qualifications in psychiatry when taking up the position in August 1938, but the previous incumbent had left under a cloud and there was some urgency to find a replacement. Carothers stayed at Mathare for eleven years. A six-month course in psychiatry, at the Maudsley Hospital in London during 1946, was the sum total of his professional training.

Colin Carothers made the best of what little expertise he had. On returning from his brief course at the Maudsley, he published his first articles on 'the African mind'. After he left Kenya to return to a psychiatric practice in England, in 1949, Carothers would draw his ideas together in a book published in 1953, *The African Mind in Health and Disease*. Written before Kenya's Emergency began, it became a leading work in the then emerging field of ethno-psychiatry. Carothers did not believe that African and European minds were radically different, or that they were necessarily predisposed to different mental problems. The key factor was social context. Traditional social systems sustained African mental health, he claimed. If you removed the African from the rural setting and placed him in the colonial city, where he would be subjected to the social forces of 'detribalisation', then he was more susceptible to mental illness. Lacking the cultural and spiritual cocoon of tradition, the 'African in transition' was vulnerable.

It was Askwith who got Carothers back to Kenya to advise on the 'rehabilitation' of Mau Mau. By then, the key elements of the 'cure' had already been identified through the practical necessity of combating the movement. Mau Mau detainees were assumed to be possessed by evil, and this might be cleansed 'by public confession as performed in Kikuyu law'. Manual labour (the gospel of work), literacy classes and Christian witness were also deployed in the fight to obtain the all-important 'confessions'. Carothers brought the theory that would legitimate this approach, giving justification and authority. He moulded his ideas of the vulnerability of the 'African in transition' to the circumstances of Mau Mau, providing the government with a report on *The Psychology of Mau Mau* (Nairobi, 1954).[131] This was the authoritative account the government wanted.

The deliberations of Leakey, Carothers, Askwith and their committee colleagues combined to give the government an explanation of Mau Mau and, more importantly, endorsed a programme for tackling it. As the ideas escaped from the confines of the committee's discussions and the precision of the written word on the page out into the public sphere of the daily fight to defeat Mau Mau, some of the subtleties would disappear. The authoritarian streak in Kenya's colonial administration would see to that. But the psycho docs had provided the analysis and the fix that quickly became everybody's 'received wisdom' as to what this strange rebellion was all about.

The logic of the psycho docs became the mantra of rehabilitation, the process by which Mau Mau adherents were treated for their sickness in the many detention camps. Not until the very end, in 1959, would this process, and the thinking behind it, be scrutinized and challenged. By then, at least 70,000 Kikuyu had been subjected to rehabilitation. Yet in the forests and reserves, where the final phase of the battle against Mau Mau was being fought from late 1954 onwards, the absurdity of the logic of rehabilitation was being demonstrated every day.

As 'Bobbie' Erskine was preparing to leave Kenya, in May 1955, the large army sweeps through the forest areas to flush out the remaining rebels were proving less and less effective. There were perhaps 2000 fighters left. Many of these men had now been in the forest for two and a half years. They were familiar with forest life and had become skilled at avoiding contact with the security forces. They no longer posed a serious military threat, but for the war to be properly concluded, and the Emergency brought to an end, they needed to be flushed out. It was a tricky military problem.

Erskine's successor, General Lathbury, decided that the regiments could be taken out of the forest. In September 1955 two British battalions were withdrawn from Kenya, and one KAR battalion returned to Uganda. The endgame of this war required a more imaginative approach. Lathbury decided to give his full backing to the use of special operations teams known as 'pseudo-gangs'.

The pseudo-gangs have become central to the European myth of how Mau Mau was defeated. This myth, popularized in magazine articles and a few colourfully presented television documentaries, tells the daring tale of a handful of white highlanders, all of them Kikuyu-speakers, who 'blacked-up' their faces, put on ragged clothes and stinking, plaited, dread-locked wigs, and strode into the forest to hunt down the last Mau Mau. The bravery and ingenuity of the canny white highlanders gives the tale its glamour and excitement, while the credulity of the Mau Mau fighters is only to be marvelled at.

It is a good story, but it is not quite true. The pseudo-gang idea of sending security forces into the forest disguised as rebels was not unique to Kenya. The technique was used by the British in Palestine and Malaya. The method had been applied in Kenya during 1953. The handful of European officers involved in these first operations were all men from the Kenya Regiment, and the pseudo-gangs they formed were in fact made up of loyal Kikuyu who 'impersonated' Mau Mau, sometimes but not always accompanied by a disguised white highlander. Special Branch took up the idea in the early months of 1954, using captured rebels instead of loyalists. This was far more effective, as the turncoats could locate forest gangs or infiltrate passive wing committees without being suspected, so long as news of their capture had not got out. The important feature of the pseudo-gangs was not the blacking up of white faces, but the use of Mau Mau rebels who had come around to the other side.[132]

A military intelligence officer named Frank Kitson played a major role in developing the pseudo-gang technique in Kenya. He built up small teams of 'pseudos' and deployed them to contact rebel gangs and gather intelligence. Once he had a team he could trust, offensive operations were mounted to target Mau Mau gangs. Kitson only very rarely went on the pseudo operations, but the younger intelligence officers under his command did so more often. By June 1954 these techniques were producing remarkable results in the Kiambu and Thika areas, and played a part in the running down of Mau Mau activists in the period following Operation Anvil. Kitson later established a training course for other officers, where he taught the techniques of 'turning' and then making operational use of former rebels.[133] Through to the end of the war, the pseudo-gangs proved to be the most potent weapon in tracking down Mau Mau.

Kitson's carefully refined methods were not replicated in every situation. Others did things in a more rough and ready manner. Peter Hewitt's colourful account of the Emergency – he offers advice on 'how to eliminate elusive Micks', as well as giving a very detailed account of his life as a Kenya police officer – contains the story of a turned rebel he calls Mwangi. Having been with a Mau Mau gang on the Kinangop, Mwangi surrendered and was immediately handed over to Hewitt to see if he might be of any 'operational use'. Within a day of his surrender Mwangi had led Hewitt's team to the forest hideout of his former

comrades and watched while they were killed. All the time he was in
Hewitt's custody Mwangi provided 'a torrent of information' on Mau
Mau's organization and activities. Hewitt admits that he was never sure
whether Mwangi and his like were 'just stoically facing up to it all', or
whether they really had come to loathe their forest comrades and all
they stood for; but Mwangi was left in no doubt that if he had ever tried
to escape, Hewitt would have killed him.[134]

White officers involved in the turning of captured rebels shared a
sense of surprise at the ease of the process. Frank Kitson ensconced
the man with his Kikuyu team, and left it to them to talk things over
and encourage the captive. It usually took no more than a few days
to gain the trust and cooperation of the former rebel. Within a couple
of weeks, sometimes sooner, the captive might be returning to the
forest on his first anti-Mau-Mau operation. Was this the wonder of
'Mau Mau's baleful influence' being lifted from the captive's shoulders?
Kitson didn't think so. He realized that there were more immediate
and prosaic issues looming, issues that his Kikuyu team spoke about
as they cajoled and persuaded. If the captive did not cooperate, then
he would go to court to be charged on a capital offence and would
certainly hang. Faced with this choice, and contrary to the wisdom
of Alan Lennox-Boyd, captives did not generally see death 'as their
salvation', but instead chose to cooperate, and to live at least a little
longer.

Those in the security forces who ran the pseudo-gangs, and who
deployed turned rebels in tracking operations, knew that the 'disease'
theories of the psycho docs were bunk. The grievances of the Kikuyu
were real enough, no matter how hard the white highlanders and British
administrators tried to deny them. This had given the rebellion its start;
and if Mau Mau had come to have a hold over people, then the reasons
were not hard to find. You did not need theories of mental disease, social
collapse or the 'crisis of transition' to understand fear and intimidation.
Kenya was not the first conflict where allegiance and action were primarily determined by those who were most prepared to use violence,
and it would not be the last.

By the early part of 1956 the pseudo-gangs had accounted for most of
the known rebel leaders, but the biggest catch of all still eluded them.
Dedan Kimathi was still at large, somewhere in the Aberdares forest
above Nyeri. Where China's leadership was grounded in respect for his
Kikuyu elders, Kimathi respected nothing but the movement's cause.
He is not an easy character to describe. Kimathi's actions in the forest
are steeped in controversy. Kenya's own nationalist writers, among them
some of his closest comrades from their days in the forests, cannot agree

whether Kimathi should be lauded as a noble, brave and unswerving leader who inspired others, or pilloried as a brutal, hard-bitten, ruthless thug who became increasingly psychotic as the fearful isolation of the forest ate into his soul. What we know of his life is difficult to disentangle from the propaganda: the British did all they could to besmirch his reputation and, in reaction, his Kenyan biographers have tended to gloss over anything that might compromise his heroic status. Kimathi's myth remains potent in Kenya today; his name, more than anyone else's, is synonymous with the struggle for freedom. He is unquestionably the heroic figure of the Mau Mau rebellion.[135]

Kimathi is a very uncomfortable character to have as a national hero, however. Peeling away both the negative propaganda and the nationalist hagiography, we are left with a portrait of a deeply troubled and violent man. Even dismissing British accusations about callous murders and the consummate slaughter of his camp followers in a string of pointless executions, the evidence of Kimathi's excesses is overwhelming.

He was born in Nyeri district, probably in 1920 or thereabouts, not far from the family farm of Waruhiu Itote. Kimathi's father, unlike Itote's, saw some value in education, and sent young Dedan to school. The boy did well, being praised for his skills in writing and as an orator; but there was a nasty, bullying side to his character that even came out when he was amongst his age-mates. Fiercely competitive, Kimathi baulked at any discipline or control, and was always in trouble with his teachers. He drifted in and out of education, never fulfilling the potential of a bright academic career. In the late 1930s he made the journey to Nairobi, just as Itote would do a couple of years later. Kimathi, too, took the King's shilling, signing up for service with the British army during 1940. He didn't last long. After one month he was discharged, for drunkenness and persistent violence against his fellow recruits.

He drifted from job to job, moving back and forth between Nairobi and Nyeri over the next few years. He did a little bit of everything, from primary-school teaching, for which he was dismissed after accusations of violence against his pupils, to work as a swineherd on a farm in Ol Kalou. It was here, in 1947 or 1948, that he took an oath. Ol Kalou was one of the areas most seriously disrupted by the cancellation of squatter contracts, and the old KCA activists had been busy organizing resistance here before the KAU came onto the scene after the Second World War. These militant squatters drew Kimathi into politics.

By 1950 he was secretary to the KAU branch at Ol Kalou, a branch controlled by militant supporters of the *Muhimu*. Kimathi presided over oath taking. Again like Itote, he believed in compulsion to bring solidarity of purpose. He administered beatings and carried a double-barrelled shotgun. When the Emergency began, in Ol Kalou the white highlanders very quickly turned out their remaining Kikuyu labour, in a violent and vindictive show of force. During one of the many 'screenings' of farm labourers in the area Kimathi was arrested. The statement of another worker had implicated him in the murder of a farm headman on a neighbouring property. He was handcuffed and taken to the police cells in the small settler town of Thomson's Falls. There, the resourceful Kimathi bribed the warder to let him escape and he disappeared into the night, heading for the forests of the Aberdares.

Strangely, it is the account of the man who would finally hunt Kimathi down, Ian Henderson, that gives the most balanced and textured account of the rebel leader in the forest.[136] There is no doubting Henderson's loathing for the things he believed Kimathi had done – the murders and mutilations, the senseless executions of his own men – but there is also admiration for the rebel leader's dedication, resoluteness and sheer grit. Henderson acknowledges the power of the man to command respect in others, to engage his following, to inspire and lead; and that, of course, was what made him so dangerous to the British. Maybe Henderson also glimpsed parts of his own stubborn, adrenaline-dependent character in Kimathi's determined, restless, single-minded focus on sustaining the struggle. The white highlander, who worked for Special Branch in the shady world of intelligence gathering, double-dealing and informers, knew only too well that there was a very fine line between acceptable force and excessive violence. He saw evidence of this every day in Kenya's dirty war. In their final duel in the forests above Nyeri, like the truly mad, both Henderson and Kimathi had nothing left but their reason.

Henderson describes the story of his obsessive hunt for Kimathi in a book first published in 1958. Having isolated the area of forest in which Kimathi was hiding, Henderson set out to capture and recruit rebels who might have had recent contact with Mau Mau's increasingly reclusive commander. Over several months he built up a team of more than a dozen turncoats, gradually laying siege to the several hideouts that Kimathi had been using, and steadily restricting his area of movement in the forest. Finally, in the very early hours of the morning, on 21 October 1956, four years to the day since the start of the Emergency, they cornered Kimathi and moved in for the kill. But the trap did not quite work, and Kimathi broke out of his hiding place, racing through the forest ahead of Henderson and his pseudo-gang. He made for the forest edge and the Nyeri reserve, and there he ran into the stop line set by Henderson. At 9.30a.m. he was shot and captured by a tribal policeman. The forest war was over.

# 7

# Crimes of Punishment
# Law and Disorder in Kikuyuland

Dedan Kimathi's wound was treated, and he was placed in a cold, concrete-block cell at Nyeri prison. He had escaped from a colonial jail once before by bribing an African warder. This time a British soldier was placed in the cell with him, and another stood outside the door. The priest from the Nyeri Catholic Mission, Father Marino, visited him many times over the next three weeks while he awaited trial. Father Marino spoke Kikuyu well, and he and the rebel leader spent many hours in conversation.

Kimathi took great interest in the priest. Marino brought in books for the prisoner to read, all of them religious in theme. He steered away from politics. They discussed religion, Kimathi's family, and his education and life. Kimathi told the priest that, as a very young boy, he had first attended the Catholic out-school at Wamagana, close to Tetu Catholic Mission. He fondly remembered the African teacher there. But he had moved to another school, nearer to his home at Ihururu, where he had been baptized into the Anglican Church. It was education that determined Kikuyu church affiliations.

The trial was held at Nyeri Special Assizes, on 27 November 1956, before Justice O'Connor. Kimathi was charged with possessing arms and ammunition. He made no attempt to dispute this. He needed the weapons to defend himself in the forest, he explained. Kimathi's defence, as with so many other rebels who were captured at the forest edge, was that he had been coming to surrender, in accordance with the instructions given in the leaflets dropped by the government's aircraft. The judge rejected this, on the grounds that Kimathi had run away from the tribal policemen when they confronted him. Dedan Kimathi was convicted and sentenced to hang.

The next day he was taken, under heavy escort, from Nyeri to Nairobi prison, to await the outcome of his appeal. Kimathi spent nearly three months on death row. During that time he was visited almost every day by Father Whelan, the priest with responsibility for the many prisoners crowded on death row at Nairobi gaol. The East African Court of Appeal summarily dismissed Kimathi's case on 27 December, but there was a further appeal to the Privy Council. The papers were prepared in London by Dingle Foot. There was no repeat of his success in saving the Koinanges from the gallows. Kimathi's conviction was confirmed.[1]

On the eve of execution, alone in the condemned cell, he found sleep would not come. At 1a.m. he took paper and pencil: 'I am so busy and happy preparing for heaven tomorrow,' Kimathi wrote to Father Marino. He thanked the Catholic Fathers for the books they had given him, 'which have set a burning light through my way to paradise'. But some matters were troubling him as the end drew near:

> Only the question of getting my son to school. He is far from any of your schools, but I trust that something must be done to see that he starts earlier under your care.
>
> Do not fail from seeing my mother who is very old and to comfort her even though that she is so much sorrowful.
>
> My wife is here. She is detained at Kamiti Prison and I suggest that she will be released after some time. I would like her to be consulted by sisters e.g. Sister Modester etc, for she too feels very lonely. And if by any possibility, she can be near the mission as near Mathari so that she may be so close to the sisters and to the Church.
>
> I conclude by telling you only to do me a favour by getting education to my son.

Kimathi signed himself, 'with good hope and best wishes, I remain dear father, your loving and departing convert'. The Anglican schoolboy, who had prayed to the Kikuyu god Ngai and listened to the advice of seers in the forest, went to his death as a Catholic on the morning of 18 February 1957.[2]

Kimathi was among the last of Mau Mau's rebels to be hanged by the British. By 1957 the pseudo-gangs in the forests were eliminating the rebels, not taking prisoners. The number of cases dwindled away through 1957. Those who came before the courts were convicted in the usual cursory manner, but the Governor now granted clemency to those charged with consorting or possession of arms and ammunition. Only the convicted murderers still went to the gallows.

Throughout the whole grisly business of the Mau Mau trials the British determined not to allow politics to enter the courtroom. The accused were not to be treated as political prisoners. The movement they belonged to and the cause they fought for were ignored. This avoided show trials. It prevented discussion of political motives, rights or grievances. At Kimathi's trial in Nyeri no mention was made of his leadership of the rebellion, or of his known part in many killings. The words 'Mau Mau' were not even mentioned.

Between October 1952 and March 1958, when the very last Mau Mau offender was executed, Kenya's courts sentenced 1499 Kikuyu to death. Of these convicts, 160 lodged successful appeals – forty-eight of these in one Lari trial alone – and another 240, including all the women convicts, had their sentences commuted. The hangman was at his busiest between April 1953 and June 1955. Over these months the Nairobi prison was bursting with convicts waiting on death row. At the height of the hangings, more than 170 condemned men were held in the prison. In the final tally, the British hanged 1090 Kikuyu men for Mau Mau offences.

Convicted murderers among this total numbered 346. All the other executed men had been convicted of offences specially defined as capital charges under the Emergency Powers Regulations: 472 were found to have been in possession of arms or ammunition; sixty-two men were found guilty of having participated in the administration of oaths; and 210 were convicted of consorting with terrorists.

Over the same period, Kenya's courts convicted 247 persons on capital charges unconnected with the emergency. All of these were murderers. Among them, thirty-six had their appeals allowed, while five convicts were certified insane. The governor commuted the sentences in no less than 106 cases. By comparison, only twenty-seven persons convicted of murder in relation to Mau Mau offences had their sentences commuted (see tables 7.i, 7.ii and 7.iii, pp. 353–4, for breakdowns of the convictions and the monthly returns of the Special Emergency Assize Courts).

The figures are eloquent testimony to the state's morality. Mau Mau offenders were more harshly treated than others. State judicial execution, the highest form of institutional violence available under the rule of law, was ruthlessly deployed in the suppression of the rebellion. Back in 1910 Winston Churchill had written: 'The mood and temper of the public with regard to the treatment of crime and criminals is one of the most unfailing tests of the civilization of any country.' In 1953 it was his government that gave assent to the massive extension of capital punishment in Kenya. Was this a reflection of the 'mood and temper' of Britain? Or only of Kenya's white highlanders?

It would be easy to blame the white highlanders, but public opinion was hardly liberal in 1950s Britain. Some European nations – Belgium, Holland and Portugal among them – had abolished the death penalty in the nineteenth century. Others had then followed: Norway in 1905,

Sweden in 1921, Denmark in 1930, Italy in 1948 and West Germany in 1949. England had a Select Committee to look into the abolition of hanging in 1929, but rejected the idea. A Royal Commission took it up again in 1949. It was again rejected. When the matter was once more under discussion by the British parliament, over 1956 and 1957, the death penalty in Britain was held in abeyance for eighteen months. It was precisely in this period, when convicted murderers in Britain were being spared immediate execution, that Dedan Kimathi went to the gallows in Kenya.

In February 1956 Sydney Silverman's all-party bill for the abolition of hanging was debated by the British parliament. The elected members in the House of Commons eventually passed the bill, but it was over-turned in the House of Lords and the law remained unchanged. In the Lords debate, even the Archbishop of York declared that 'retribution was a necessity in our penal code', while his fellow clergyman the Archbishop of Canterbury reassured parliament that the death penalty was not 'always un-Christian or wrong'. The Church of England would change its views by 1962, but by then it was too late to save any of Kenya's hanged.[3] This was Britain's public morality. There was virtue in the desire for vengeance.

Kenya's exceptionality in the use of judicial execution in the Emergency is remarkable even when compared with other colonial experiences. Hanging was available in the suppression of the communist insurgency in Malaya, in the terrorist war in Palestine, and in the fight against EOKA in Cyprus, but was used far more sparingly in each case. Other colonial powers, too, had less resort to state judicial execution: neither the Dutch in the East Indies nor the French in Algeria came anywhere near to Britain's tally of the hanged in Kenya.[4]

It is clear, however, that institutionalized violence in all its forms, from hangings to gratuitous beatings, was viewed differently in its colonial context than back home in the seat of empire. The French war in Algeria, fought between 1954 and 1962, offers the most meaningful parallel with Kenya. Not only were the two conflicts substantially con-temporaneous, they also involved politically dominant settler popu-lations, and the co-option of large 'loyalist' militias from among the indigenous population who were pushed into the frontline of the struggle against the rebels. In both cases, colonial governments studiously avoided declaring the conflicts to be wars – historians have termed the Algerian conflict 'the war with no name'.[5]

It is in the area of extra-judicial punishment that the parallel between Algeria and Kenya becomes most intriguing. The Algerian war was just as notoriously dirty as the British campaign in Kenya, with several allegations of state torture and atrocity being published at the time and never seriously disputed; but whereas in Britain allegations of this kind have been left to slip into the forgotten litter of history, in France memories were revived in 2000 when two leading French military commanders from the Algerian war simultaneously made public confessions to the institutional use of torture by the security forces of the state.[6] The revelations have sparked a re-examination of the French experience in Algeria, and a national reckoning.[7]

The British have always been coy about torture, and with good reason. Torture is a dangerously double-edged and self-destructive weapon in any war: 'It soils the honour of the army and the country,' as Alistair Horne has written of French use of torture in Algeria.[8] There was torture in Kenya during the Mau Mau emergency, institutionalized and systematic, and also casual and haphazard. Given the attitudes of the time, it would have been surprising if there had not been. The political scientist Bruce Berman has coined the elegant phrase 'incumbent violence' to describe the commitment of Kenya's political administration to a firm, military solution to Mau Mau.[9] 'Incumbent violence' was in every sense as vicious and barbaric as anything the rebels could dish up. In Kenya as in Algeria, its memory has lingered to soil reputations. In Kenya's dirty war there were many crimes of punishment.

## Carrots and Sticks

Almost on his first day in Kenya, 'Bobbie' Erskine had brusquely told the white highlanders that they would need to win the hearts and minds of the Kikuyu as well as suppressing them militarily. Over his time as chief of staff, and especially after the formation of the small War Council in March 1954, Erskine pushed forward any scheme that would give the Kikuyu an incentive to be loyal.

Punitive measures taken against those who were disloyal were one side of this. Collective punishments were readily dished out against communities thought to be in league with Mau Mau, normally taking the form of livestock seizures or market closures. These simply required an order from the local colonial officer. In addition, illegal seizures of property were common. Loyalists often simply took what they wanted and defied the victims to challenge them. When complaints were brought to the district office, it was very unlikely to result in any serious investigation. Castro and Ettenger's study of these events in Embu gives just a smattering of examples from one small area of Central Province[10] (see table 7.iv, p. 355, for details of collective punishments in Kirinyaga). The same process of predation backed by official acquiescence was repeated throughout Kikuyuland.

The most punitive measure of all was surely villagization. In June 1954 the War Council took the decision to enforce villagization throughout Kikuyuland – the compulsory resettlement of people from their scattered, ridge-top farms, into centralized, regulated villages, situated at key points along the busier roads. The historian of this process, Sorrenson, says that it bore 'a striking resemblance' to the British campaign in South Africa during the Boer War to control Afrikaner women and children, although its more immediate model was colonial Malaya. It was this forced villagization and not Operation Anvil, according to Sorrenson, that was 'the master stroke' in defeating Mau Mau.[11]

The colonial authorities made no effort to disguise the punitive character of this massive dislocation of the rural population. Some villages were principally intended for the protection of loyalists, but most were little more than concentration camps to punish Mau Mau sympathizers. The speed of implementation was astonishing. Between June 1954 and October 1955, a period of only fifteen months, 1,077,500 Kikuyu were resettled in 854 villages.[12] With the villages in place, punishments and rewards could be applied to greater effect. Villages that did not cooperate sufficiently would have curfews imposed, while those that did would receive benefits – agricultural services, the reopening of shops, and the lifting of curfews to allow night-time activities. More than anything else, villagization allowed the government to stamp its authority on the countryside, destroying the last elements of passive wing support for the forest fighters.

There were other effects that the government considered to be more generally beneficial. To reward loyal Kikuyu, an agricultural development programme had been embarked upon in 1954, known as the Swynnerton Plan. Under this programme, commercial agriculture was encouraged in Central Province, alongside a process of land consolidation. Villagization hugely assisted, by removing people from their land so that government could more easily go ahead with the adjudication of claims and the surveying and setting-out of new plots. Consolidation was initially seen 'as just one more reward for the loyalists', but as the security situation improved, the government's optimism about the wide economic benefits of the programme grew markedly. All the same, it was indeed the loyalists who were the principal beneficiaries, as convicted Mau Mau rebels were usually excluded from land re-allocations and many others were unfairly treated in the distribution of holdings decided by the local land committees.[13] The repercussions of these decisions would wrangle on for many, many years after Kenya's independence.

The herding of Kikuyu into enclosed, guarded settlements had other side effects that were relevant to the prosecution of the war. By the time villagization began, in the middle of 1954, the efforts to get Mau Mau passive wing supporters to confess to their 'sins' had become a central part of the struggle in the reserves. People brought in for questioning by the police or Home Guard were likely to be subjected to an interrogation designed to make them 'confess'. In scenes reminiscent of witch-hunts in early modern Europe, suspects would be goaded and chided to 'unburden themselves' and release the 'evil that lay within'. Though it was never the intention of the psycho docs who recommended confessional methods that they should be violent, interviews were often deliberately intimidating and sometimes far worse. Some 'screening teams', based at Home Guard posts, were renowned for physical violence to extract confessions, and in some places this certainly amounted to institutionalized torture.

Though such methods were conducted behind closed doors, the villagization programme led to the development of what were termed 'confessional *barazas*'. At these public meetings, villagers would be gathered together to listen to the confession of one of their number. Others would then be encouraged to follow suit. Sometimes names were called out, and individuals were challenged to say what they knew about a specific person or a certain crime. When people did speak, they would later be subjected to a deeper interview, in private, at the hands of the 'screening teams'. Such teams usually comprised Special Branch officers, African police, and Home Guards.

The success of 'screening' and confessional *barazas* depended upon the ability of the security forces to collate intelligence, and act upon it effectively. Many cases coming to court from the later part of 1954 onwards show that this was happening more regularly. Kangethe Kangau and Gibson Mwangi, for example, had been forest fighters for over one year when they decided to return quietly to their home area of Thika in March 1954. They managed to obtain forged identity documents, and to gain employment on a local European-owned estate, where they worked undetected for several months. Then, when local labourers were being screened, the past of the two men was revealed. Confronted by Special Branch, the two agreed to return to participate in pseudo operations around Thika, helping the security forces 'a great deal'. The two men were rather surprised to be tried and convicted, in September 1954, when Special Branch had finished with them. Baring commuted their sentences, and both went to prison.[14]

The prosecution of Karioki Kungu, alias General Korea, in May 1955, illustrated the uses to which confessional *barazas* could be put in clearing up unsolved murders. Kungu was a major gang leader in the Rift Valley, and in a number of confessional *barazas* the security forces had built up a lengthy catalogue of crimes for which they had evidence implicating him. These included no less than fifteen murders, conducted between

December 1953 and February 1955. Kungu was convicted and sentenced to hang.[15]

The prosecution of the murderers of Police Constable Wambua Mbithi was a more typical case using evidence of this kind. The six men were accused of killing Mbithi during January 1954, in Kiambu, when he interrupted an oathing ceremony. The evidence against the men only came to light when a young woman, who had been present to be oathed, confessed and told her story at a *baraza* conducted by Chief Josiah. She subsequently made a full statement to the police. Other statements were then acquired, corroborating the woman's claims. On this basis a search was made through the camps and prisons for the men who had been named, and six were identified. They were brought to court in September 1955 and convicted. All six hanged.[16]

Public confessions sometimes led to the discovery of the bodies of missing persons, and then to a trial. Njaria Muthanya, a loyalist from Embu, was murdered in December 1953. His body was only unearthed in June 1955, and one month later a man was convicted of his murder.[17] Kariuki Kiuni, believed by Mau Mau to be an informer, disappeared in July 1954. Information gathered at confessional *barazas* in Thika, and then followed up in the screening of other witnesses, led to the discovery of his remains. A man was convicted of his murder twenty-one months after the crime, in March 1956, and hanged.[18]

In all such cases, Home Guards, African police and Kikuyu loyalists played a crucial role in extracting and recording information. The methods they used were seldom revealed in any detail, although there were frequent allegations of beatings and worse. In November 1954 a case came before Judge Goudie, at Nakuru, in which the details of the treatment of suspects in 'screening' was revealed in all its grisly detail. Mwangi Mweru's statement, presented to the court at his trial, described his experience, when interrogated along with Githinji Njaguna:

I was taken into an office where there was a clerk and two askari (policemen) armed with rifles. They put a rope around my neck, and the other end they put around the neck of Githinji. They said, 'If you don't say what we ask you, you will die.' Before being questioned we were beaten and the rope tightened. We were very frightened. I said we had killed nobody. We were beaten again, and they put to us that we had killed two persons. We denied this. . . . We were beaten up again. The askaris beat us with open palms and with the butts of their rifles on my head and body. . . . We stayed two days in the Screening Camp. . . . What I told them first was true. Then I was beaten again and I said whatever they wanted me to say.

At no point did the prosecution make any effort to challenge these allegations of ill-treatment, treating it all as a matter of course before finding the two men who had been so abused guilty.

When the papers came to the Appeal Court, in December 1954, the judges confirmed the convictions of the two men but seized upon the opportunity to pass comment on the 'screening teams'. They saw 'no good reason to doubt that the appellants' allegations of ill-treatment were substantially true', but they questioned the legal authority under which the 'screening team' had been given custody of the accused men. The appeal judges assumed that the function of such a team 'was to sift the good Kikuyu from the bad', but to do this it appeared that people were 'subjected to a softening up process, with the object of obtaining information'. In point of law, the Attorney-General was in no way responsible for screening teams; nor were the police. Rather, they were entirely under the authority of the district administration. That being the case, Justices Worley, Jenkins and Briggs continued, 'it is difficult for us to believe that these teams could continue to use methods of unlawful violence without the knowledge and confirmation of that authority. Such methods are the negation of the rule of law which it is the duty of the courts to uphold.' They concluded by insisting on a full enquiry of all such cases.[19]

This was a challenge to the district administration to put its house in order. As they delivered this judgment, in another court just such an enquiry was taking place, albeit not entirely intentionally.

## Ruthagathi: Kenya's Belsen

The trial of Muriu Wamai and five others was no ordinary case.[20] Wamai was a Kikuyu headman and loyalist. Working under Chief Joshua in the southern part of Nyeri district, he commanded the Home Guard post at Ruthagathi. This was an area of intensive Mau Mau activity, where the majority of the community were passive supporters of the movement. Mau Mau attacks were frequent. Many local loyalists had been brutally murdered. Muriu Wamai was a member of the Home Guard from its initiation, early in 1953. He became a headman in January 1954. He was well regarded by British officials, who saw him as a stalwart ally. Wamai liked to boast that Mau Mau generals from Nyeri identified him as one of their principal targets. He was a tough man.

Muriu Wamai's fall from grace began on 18 July 1954. That evening an incident occurred in the vicinity of the Ruthagathi Home Guard post, and a series of shots was heard. When the European police officer and district officer arrived together to investigate, they found Wamai and his men waiting by the gate to the Ruthagathi post. They described how they had detected a Mau Mau gang nearby and gone out to attack them. In an exchange of fire, two Mau Mau had been killed, the rest then taking flight into the night. Wamai showed the British officers where two bodies lay in the bush, both dead from gunshot wounds. The dead men were not apparently known to the Home Guards. The deaths were simply recorded as two more anonymous Mau Mau kills, and Wamai and his men were congratulated for yet another job well done.

There matters might have remained, had it not been for a series of unsigned letters sent to another white police officer over the next month. These letters claimed that the dead men were not strangers at all, but well-known local Kikuyu farmers. The headmaster of the school near Ruthagathi then called at the police post and specifically requested to see the same officer. He made a lengthy statement, in which he explained that the deceased men had been arrested and detained at Ruthagathi, by Muriu Wamai, several days before their deaths. No one had seen them since that time. In a remarkably strong piece of corroboratory evidence the headmaster also revealed that he, too, had been 'screened' by Wamai at this time. He claimed that he had been beaten and tortured in the Ruthagathi Home Guard post, and that he had heard the two deceased men being treated in the same fashion in the neighbouring cell.

Kamwagira, the wife of one of the deceased, Mathenge Wanjua, was now found. Frightened and deeply distressed, she had to be persuaded to make a statement. What she said corroborated the evidence already assembled, adding weight to the growing suspicion that there had never been any battle with a Mau Mau gang at Ruthagathi on the night of 18 July. By now the case had been put into the hands of the CID, who were responsible for the investigation of all allegations made against members of the security forces. If the evidence offered by these witnesses was correct, then Muriu Wamai and his fellow Home Guards had murdered the two men, though in what circumstances remained to be revealed.

Accusations of this kind were not unusual by 1954. The Kenya police were normally unwilling to pursue such cases against Home Guards, if they could avoid it. Most accusations were brushed aside as Mau Mau plots designed to discredit the loyalists. On other occasions the police were persuaded to drop prosecutions on the grounds that a court case against a trusted loyalist ally would 'lower morale' in the fight against Mau Mau. In this way, excesses were condoned if not actively encouraged.

The Wamai case, however, came to light at a time when the head of the CID, Donald MacPherson, was personally engaged in pursuit of a number of allegations against police and Home Guard, with the intention of initiating legal proceedings. This had been prompted by the arrival in the colony, in March 1954, of Kenya's new Commissioner of Police, Arthur Young. The decision to retire the previous man, O'Rorke, had been taken in principle after the Naivasha debacle, in April 1953, but it had not proved easy to find a suitable replacement. Baring eventually got a man who could hardly have been better qualified for the position. Young was Commissioner of the City of London Police. A highly respected and experienced officer, he was an outspoken advocate of consensual and community-based policing. He had served with distinction in an advisory capacity in Malaya, where his methods had played an important part in consolidating the role of the police in the counter-insurgency campaign. And he had then participated in a review of the Kenya Police, so he took up his second colonial appointment fully aware of the problems that might lie ahead. An intelligent and highly principled man, Young had clear views on the standards of professionalism required in a modern police force; and, as his Malayan experience showed, he did not believe that those standards should be any different in a colonial context than at home. This was widely known in London, and no doubt influenced the Colonial Office in pressing for his selection. It was no secret that the Kenya police needed 'sorting out'.[21]

Though reluctant when first approached, the ambitious Young eventually agreed to take the Kenya job on secondment from Britain, but for a contract of only two years' duration. This would give him time to knock the Kenya Police into shape, but would not condemn him to a further career in the colonies. Commitments in London prevented Young from getting out to Kenya until March 1954. By then, the problems of ill-discipline in the police force, the district administration, and the Home Guard had reached a level that Young found difficult to comprehend.

Just as Erskine had moved swiftly to tackle indiscipline in the military, Young endeavoured to do the same in regard to the police and auxiliary services. It proved a much tougher task. The culture of impunity was deeply embedded: police and Home Guard did just as they pleased because they had no fear of having to face consequences. The openness with which brutality and violence were spoken about showed how far standards of discipline and professionalism had sunk. Robert Edgerton, who was in Kenya in the final years of colonial rule and later wrote a book about the Emergency, found it astonishingly easy to get white police officers and members of the KPR to talk about atrocities. The example of one officer, who told Edgerton about the arrest of three suspects – 'Mickeys', as the officer called them – underlines the problem faced by Young only too graphically:

... while we were waiting for the sub-inspector to come back I decided to question the Mickeys. They wouldn't say a thing, of course, and one of them, a tall coal-black bastard, kept grinning at me, real insolent. I slapped him hard, but he kept right on grinning at me, so I kicked him in the balls as hard as I could. He went down in a heap but when he finally got up on his feet he grinned at me again and I snapped, I really did. I stuck my revolver right in his grinning mouth and I said something, I don't remember exactly what, and I pulled the trigger. His brains went all over the side of the police station. The other two Mickeys were standing there looking blank. I said to them that if they didn't tell me where to find the rest of the gang I'd kill them too. They didn't say a word so I shot them both. One wasn't dead so I shot him in the ear. When the sub-inspector drove up, I told him that the Mickey's tried to escape. He didn't believe me but all he said was 'bury them and see the wall is cleaned up'.[22]

To crack down on incidents such as this, Young faced intense opposition from the hawks. Investigations needed to be mounted and prosecutions taken out before the courts; but it would not be easy. To start the ball rolling, the CID was separated from the other arms of the security forces, so as to maintain its impartiality, and placed under the authority of Whyatt. Even before MacPherson began his investigation, the political opposition had taken guard.

MacPherson decided to concentrate on Nyeri, where there were known to be deeply rooted problems of indiscipline. By the end of the year he had a dossier of some sixteen serious cases, each arising from incidents over the period between April and December 1954. He made it known that he intended to initiate criminal proceedings in all these cases, and opened a CID prosecution file for each one. The enquiries met with concerted and well-organized obstruction. This came from all levels of the administration, up to and including the Central Province Commissioner, C. M. Johnson, and the Member for African Affairs, Windley. There is nothing to suggest that these senior officials denied that beatings, torture and murders had been carried out by members of the police, KPR and Home Guard, only that they thought such matters should not be brought before the courts. It was more important to protect the reputation of the security forces, and especially to nurture the fragile morale of the Kikuyu Home Guard, than to bring people to justice. What they feared above all else was an avalanche of cases that would utterly destroy the Home Guard. This was not just about individual cases: it was a struggle over the methods to be employed in combating Mau Mau. Young wanted discipline and the rule of law; his opponents, including senior officers in Baring's administration such as Johnson saw a degree of 'counter-terror' as a necessary weapon.[23] The degree of state complicity in Berman's 'incumbent violence' was being exposed through Young's insistence upon prosecutions.

The prosecution of Muriu Wamai and five co-defendants for the murder of two Kikuyu farmers was the first case that MacPherson and Young managed to bring before the courts. Over the opening days of the trial, in late November 1954, the prosecution presented a detailed account of the circumstances in which it was claimed the two deceased had been murdered. Acting Justice Cram had been selected to hear the case. Meticulous, moral, and less inclined than many of Kenya's judges to be swayed by race in assessing the veracity of evidence, Cram had been the magistrate at Lari after the massacre. Over the following year and more he had presided over a score of Mau Mau capital trials. By the end of 1954 he was well aware that the methods used by the security forces did not always conform with the rule of law. As the fascinating, and disturbing story of Ruthagathi unfolded in the courtroom, Cram listened attentively and took copious notes. There was much for the judge to reflect upon.

The prosecution explained that the two Kikuyu farmers, Marathe and Mathenge, having first been rounded up on suspicion of Mau Mau activities, were severely beaten and tortured in the Ruthagathi Home Guard post. Evidence was produced by the Crown to show that Ruthagathi was no ordinary post: it was an interrogation centre, to which suspects were routinely taken for 'screening' from a wide surrounding area. Beatings and torture were allegedly part of this routine. Several witnesses were produced, all of them local Kikuyu, who had at various times over recent months been victims of what Acting Judge Cram was later to describe as Muriu Wamai's 'reign of terror' over the local community of Ruthagathi.

It was revealed that suspects who confessed to Mau Mau crimes under torture in Ruthagathi would then be taken before the local African court, where Chief Joshua would preside over the administration of fines or detention orders. Fines were the norm. Muriu Wamai kept a log of the 'confessions' of his suspects, and presented this log before Chief Joshua's court as 'evidence' against the accused. The court took enormous sums from people in fines, and it was noted that wealthier members of the community found themselves hauled in for this treatment with greater regularity. Judge Cram saw this as little more than an elaborate 'extortion racket', and asked how it was that a lower court be allowed to proceed in such a manner without supervision or oversight. The prosecution's answer was that British officers simply left the Chief and his headmen to get on with it.

The court was nudging towards a rare and disarmingly frank insight as to the real methods by which the security forces dealt with Mau

Mau; but then the European witnesses were brought forward to give evidence – district officers attached to the Home Guard, the District Commissioner, Hughes, and several police officers. None would admit culpability in any of the actions described by the prosecution; and they all staunchly defended Wamai. The evidence of these officers supported Wamai's story in many important respects. The police officers all confirmed Wamai's assessment of the battle that had taken place, as did the district officer, John Garbutt, who described hearing 200 to 300 shots fired – many more than a number of rounds issued to the Home Guard patrol. Logbooks were produced from Ruthagathi, and from the police post, to show the signing in and release of prisoners. This showed that the deceased men had not been in custody on the night in question. The evidence was utterly consistent from one witness to the next. All told the same story – of the killing of two Mau Mau who had attacked the brave Ruthagathi Home Guards, and the shameful attempt by local Mau Mau sympathizers to frame one of Nyeri district's staunchest loyalists.

The prosecution case appeared to be floundering as Wamai took the stand on 3 December 1954. At first none of this appeared to bother the unflappable Muriu Wamai. Tall, strong and proud, he resolutely deflected the accusations against him. He had done as he was ordered at Ruthagathi. Chief Joshua knew about what went on there. So did the district officers, Garbutt and Richmond. They screened suspects, yes, but no one was beaten. British officers knew what was happening: they brought suspects to Ruthagathi for interrogation, and often remained there while the screening took place. Wamai kept this up, under stern examination, for two whole days.

There was considerable drama to come, however. On his third day in the dock Wamai was questioned closely about the entries in the Ruthagathi logbook, specifically about the suggestion that several entries, all of them to do with the two deceased men, might have been added subsequently. As this line of questioning persisted, Wamai was twice directly accused of having murdered the two men. As he was pressed again, he broke down. Cram called a recess.

When the court reconvened, Wamai's defence counsel instructed it that his client wished to change his plea. The previously calm and seemingly nerveless Muriu Wamai now deluged the court in fast-flowing narrative, giving full answers to every question. He made a full confession to the murders. He admitted that the two deceased were local men who had been brought in for questioning, under suspicion of having taken an oath. Both had refused to confess, despite interrogations and torture. They had been held for three days. On Sunday 18 July, Wamai and his accomplices had taken the two men outside the Ruthagathi Home

Guard post and led them into the bush. There, Wamai had himself shot them both at close range and in cold blood. He had then instructed his patrol to fire into the air to simulate the fighting off of a Mau Mau attack.

This would have been drama enough, but it was followed by further highly incriminatory revelations. Wamai provided the court with a detailed account of what went on at Ruthagathi. It was a special inter-rogation centre. Prisoners were taken there to be beaten and tortured. The chief and the British officers all knew this. Wamai had merely done what he was told. Moreover, the screening of prisoners from the Ruthagathi location was a deliberate policy to wage 'economic war' against Mau Mau's passive wing in the area. Wamai did not know who had decided this policy, but he knew that it was a systematic practice to fine these people.

There was worse to come. Muriu Wamai also told the court that he had at first wanted to confess to what he had done, and that he had frankly told Chief Joshua and the local district officer, Richmond, what had happened. Both had advised him to cover it up and to lie. Richmond and Chief Joshua had even gone so far as to obtain the Home Guard post record book, showing the log of prisoners received and dismissed, so that alterations could be made to disguise the detention of the two murdered men. Wamai had followed their instructions in forging entries in the log in his own hand. Richmond and the Chief had assisted in the concoction of sworn statements from the other five accused supporting the defence. John Garbutt had also lied to the court about the supposed battle, presumably elaborating his story to strengthen Wamai's defence. Wamai said that he had made a confession of the murder to the Karatina police in August, when MacPherson's team had exhumed the bodies of Mwathe and Mathenge for examination. If this was indeed true, then two police officers, Stevenson and Woodgate, had committed perjury, and a third, Besant, had given false evidence in a statement presented to the court. According to the evidence now presented, one African chief and five British officers were complicit in this conspiracy to cover up Wamai's crime. For Cram, this had been an unusually interesting day in court.

In a judgment running to thirty-two closely typed pages, delivered on 10 December 1954, Cram let rip. His anger leapt from every page in the barbs and thrusts he aimed at the corruption, dishonesty and flagrant perjury of all those connected with Wamai's defence. The language was intemperate – Cram suffered from a florid style at the best of times – but he was forthright. Three extracts from his judgment illustrate the most salient points.

On the 'extortion' in Chief Joshua's court:

I find almost complete corroboration that the court sat and operated as part of a vast conspiracy to pervert justice to the means and ends of war. The armed bravados of the first accused [Wamai] swept all and sundry into the net. Any whisper, any suggestion that a man had anything to do with Mau Mau, or if the first accused were jealous, or conceived a dislike for him, was enough. The man either confessed in fear at once, or was aided in his confession by unrestricted violence or a sojourn in the unpleasant dens of Ruthagathi.

... When there were sufficient victims in the net, the accused took his prisoners under armed guard to the African Appeal court at Karatina, where out of hearing of the prisoners he informed the elders (who were to be judges) of his evidence ... The obdurate were given a chance to think matters over. There was ample to influence their minds. Against them were the accused and his armed bands of bravoes, and a hostile bench primed with lies, and the shadow of the cells, flaying whips, and threats ... Throughout the whole year there were hundreds and hundreds of pleas of guilt and convictions on the one charge ... From the patent injustice of this court flowed fines at the rate of very often £300 a sitting ... Thousands of pounds in the year were paid to the South Nyeri district administration ... But one would have thought that the steep incline upwards of fine money would have attracted attention at district headquarters ...

On the complicity of the members of the colonial administration, and their counter-allegation that Wamai had been the victim of a Mau Mau plot to frame him:

In my view whoever else was involved in this plot – and the accused alleges Chief Joshua and Mr Richmond, and the evidence casts a shadow on Mr Garbutt – the only plots revealed by their evidence is a plot to execute innocent prisoners, and then a plot to defeat the ends of justice, and to maintain the barbarous tortures of Ruthagathi ... They were a prey on the countryside ...

And on the character of the Home Guard who carried out Ruthagathi's tortures:

If the first accused must be regarded as the counterpart to a Gestapo man, then so must the second accused ... They not only knew of the shocking floggings that went on in this Kenya Nordhausen, or Mauthausen, but must be taken to be the men who were said to have carried them out. From the brutalizing of flogging it is only a step to taking life without qualm.

Cram convicted all the accused, sentencing Wamai to be hanged and the others to prison terms with hard labour; and he demanded that the African Court at Karatina be immediately suspended, pending a full enquiry into its affairs.

Baring was horrified by the damage that might be done by Cram's outspoken criticisms. An embargo was placed upon the judgment in an effort to stop it circulating; but a copy was leaked from the Legal Department in Nairobi in January, and word quickly spread. A London-based group called the Federal Independence Party made copies of the judgment, with a cover sheet headed 'Kenya's Belsen?'.

The Cram judgment brought the simmering conflict between the judiciary and the administration over the rule of law to the boil. Cram had, in effect, accused the administration of being complicit in illegal detentions, torture and extortion. The evidence was indeed compelling, but the hawks were not likely to concede these points without a fight. Three things happened as a consequence of Cram's judgment, all of which were part of the struggle within the government. The first was that Young tendered his resignation to Baring on 14 December.[24] Everything about the Ruthagathi case had confirmed Young's belief that the Kikuyu reserves were run by a 'rule of fear', and that the highest officials in the land, including Baring himself, condoned this. The conspiracy at Ruthagathi and the continued obstruction of MacPherson's investigations indicated as much. Young wanted further prosecutions; Baring wanted all the cases then under investigation to be halted. It was too much for Young. He wrote to London, clearly stating that his resignation was prompted by 'malpractices committed against Mau Mau suspects' that were 'condoned by officers of the Provincial Administration'. He further asserted that 'the Governor of Kenya had attempted to interfere with the police investigation into one such incident'. This was too explosive to be made public, and Young was persuaded to agree to a tamer letter of resignation, in which he expressed his concern about 'indiscipline' in more muted terms, and in relation to his differences of opinion with Baring over the future of the Kenya Police.

Whyatt and Erskine were sorry to see him go, but both understood the reasons only too well. Erskine wrote to London himself later in December, warning that the friction between the administration and CID in Nyeri had reached dangerous levels and was a threat to the smooth running of the campaign against Mau Mau.[25] A few months later, after the fuss had died down, Young admitted the reasons for his resignation to the Labour Party's Barbara Castle, and gave her assistance in trying to pursue other cases of gross abuse; but in public Young kept his silence, and therefore spared the Secretary of State, Lennox-Boyd, from a worse scandal. MacPherson left Kenya a year or so after Young, after having been ostracized and hounded by his colleagues. He applied for a job in Fiji but was turned down, and so took a position managing a construction project in Australia. His side of the story never reached a wider public. Whatever Alan Lennox-Boyd may have thought about all of this in private, coming only a few weeks after he took over from Lyttelton – and he certainly did know, as the matter was carefully documented[26] – it seemed never to shake his conviction, often expressed in public, 'that the British ruling class, both at home and abroad, could do no wrong'.[27]

Next, the decision was taken to issue another surrender offer. Erskine had wanted this for some time, but the Ruthagathi trial was the catalyst to Baring's agreement. Cram's judgment had not gone down well with the Home Guards. There were rumours of disaffection, and even fears of large-scale defections if members of the Home Guard came to believe that there would be a spate of similar prosecutions. 'Depression and despair are setting in and morale is dropping,' Erskine wrote early in January.[28] The War Council discussed the possibility of offering surrender terms alongside an amnesty, which would apply to members of the security forces as well as the rebels. This would give the rebels amnesty from prosecution for all past crimes, including murders, and it would wipe the slate clean for the Home Guard, halting all of the other investigations by CID that had not yet reached the courts.[29] Baring had no trouble getting approval from Lennox-Boyd.[30] The Governor made his public announcement of the amnesty at a gathering of Home Guard and tribal police in Nyeri on 18 January.[31]

When the appeal court confirmed Wamai's conviction, Baring used the excuse of the amnesty to issue a pardon for the murderer. When the Colonial Office expressed some surprise at this action, Baring trotted out his now well-worn defence that it was necessary to maintain morale and solidarity among the African elements of the security services.

Finally, Baring announced that there would be an enquiry into the African Court at Karatina, and that it would also be extended to look at the administration of similar courts in other parts of Kikuyuland. This would not have happened without a hefty nudge from the appeal court judges, who explicitly directed their attention to the need for such an enquiry in their comment on the Ruthagathi case. The enquiry inevitably became another round in the battle between the hawks and the doves. The person chosen to head the enquiry was Judge Holmes. Sober, conservative and of hawkish tendencies, Holmes steered a careful path that was designed to placate loyalist sensibilities. His findings on the Karatina court were deeply critical of Cram, whom he accused of having grossly exaggerated the problems; but his general findings on other courts suggested many ways of improving procedures and ensuring that abuses could not happen. It was a neat balancing act.

The battle was not over quite yet, however. Windley, the Member for African Affairs, immediately insisted that the section on Karatina be published, to exonerate the administration from Cram's 'ill-judged criticisms'. The Colonial Office stalled, not wanting to publish any part of a report that washed dirty linen in public. Kenya's judiciary came to their aid. Nihill, the senior judge in the appellate division, and O'Connor, the Chief Secretary, jumped to Cram's defence. They felt that Holmes had not given weight to the illegal detention of suspects and the complicity of administrative officers in the practices described, and threatened to raise the matter in public, and with London, if Baring opted to publish only selective parts of the report. Their complaints successfully thwarted Windley's efforts to clear the name of the administration.[32]

The Ruthagathi case exposed the 'reign of terror' in Kikuyuland to public scrutiny, but the urgency to hush up the real reasons for Young's resignation, and Young's own reluctance to discuss the matter, dampened the fires of criticism. Cram's intemperate language made it too easy for the dissemblers to dismiss his comments as 'emotional' and 'ill-advised'. Young, too, was subjected to a 'quasi-sympathetic character assassination' by Lennox-Boyd, who implied that he had 'succumbed to an outburst of emotionalism'.[33] But in Kenya the Ruthagathi case exposed and widened the breach between the hawks and the doves in Baring's increasingly troubled administration; and things were not going to get any better.

## Excessive Force

The memory can play tricks on old men – especially, it seems, old men who try to recall colonial service in Kenya during the 1950s. In his sepia-tinted memoir of Kenya's district administration, Charles Chevenix-Trench tentatively admits that the Mau Mau rebellion in Kenya led to 'some abuses' by the security forces; but, he grandly assures his readers, 'never by a nod or a wink did the administration connive at them'.[34] It is a view that even Oliver Lyttelton endorses, recalling in his auto-biography that there may have been 'one or two isolated incidents of atrocities' during Kenya's Emergency, but no more.[35] Reading them against the massive documentary record of abuse, excessive force and violence, it is difficult to accept these statements as a fair reflection of reality.

Apologists for the colonial regime, of whom there were many, tossed off Ruthagathi as an aberration of war – the kind of thing that might happen now and again in any conflict. This was general line adopted in the first, and certainly most widely read, full study of the Mau Mau war to be published (in 1962), Fred Majdalany's *State of Emergency*. A crusty, right-wing journalist and film critic, with a fondness for writing adventure yarns about Allied 'derring-do' in the Second World War, Majdalany saw the Mau Mau struggle in black and white. All the whites, and their co-opted African allies, were heroes who could do no wrong; and all the Mau Mau fighters were either evil depraved monsters, or child-like animals of the forest, for whom human values had no meaning.

Majdalany told his readers that the excesses in Kenya were fewer than imagined, and that those that did occur were best explained by the 'passionate impulses' of the white highlanders, whose 'commitment' was understandable. In his view, most accusations against the security forces were deliberate attempts by Mau Mau to frame the best officers, and no right-minded person should believe this nonsense. The people who publicized these complaints deserved nothing but his contempt: former security service personnel, renegades who had left under a cloud and were motivated by malice and resentment; inexperienced and gullible missionaries, who had no stomach for the fight, and no place in Kenya anyway; do-gooders out to make trouble 'back home'; or barrack-room lawyers – that 'tiny disloyal minority of articulate misfits' among the conscript soldiers in the British regiments.

A war-time veteran of the North Africa campaign, where he was awarded the Military Cross, Majdalany's hatred for those among the military who betrayed their comrades drew him into ranting extremes: among these men there were 'hard cases', he wrote, 'who had learned that a chip on the shoulder and a grudge against the commanding officer could conveniently be exorcized by writing a scandal-provoking letter of complaint to a member of parliament or a newspaper'.[36] He dismissed them all as worthless troublemakers. Majdalany's was the best-selling account of the Emergency, and his views probably represented what the British public came to think about the conflict.

There were other voices of dissent, however, and they made themselves heard very early on. Fenner Brockway, the veteran socialist campaigner, led the charge. At a packed meeting in London's Holborn Town Hall, on 29 November 1952, he called for the withdrawal of troops from Kenya, the ending of the Emergency, and the restoration of proper civilian government. He said that the Africans should be given back their lands and white settlement brought to an end. This was radical stuff in the England of the 1950s, and even though a growing number of people viewed empire with a degree of scepticism, there was still more sympathy for the plight of white families who had made Kenya their home than there ever was for African rights.[37]

The Movement for Colonial Freedom in London acted as a rallying point for the critics of British policy in Kenya, and a number of Labour Party MPs were energetic in publicizing the abuses, Barbara Castle, Leslie Hale and John Stonehouse among them. Baring was merely irritated by the constant sniping from the left in London; the white highlanders hated it. Ione Leigh, author of a rabidly anti-African account of the early stages of the Emergency, approvingly quoted Harry Thuku's comments on the critics of empire. Thuku wondered why so many whites came from England 'just to find fault': 'Why is it that when loyal Africans are killed by Mau Mau, there are no questions in the House of Commons?' he asked. 'But if a Mau Mau is killed, they make a horrible noise. We don't understand the reason.'[38]

Kenya's many critics made sure that the excesses of the security forces were well publicized whenever they came to light. Indeed, what is astonishing about Kenya's dirty war is not that it remained secret at the time but that it was so well known and so thoroughly documented. These things were not hidden. They were openly talked about in Kenya. They were reported to London on many, many occasions; and numerous individuals and pressure groups lobbied and campaigned, from as early as January 1953, to highlight the extent of the atrocities and abuses that were taking place. Officials at all levels, from the Prime Minister down to the lowly district officer, had these abuses brought to their attention. No one in authority could claim they didn't know. Their reaction, like that of Majdalany, was to deflect and deny, disparaging the accusers or making light of the accusation. Most abuses were blamed on the actions of 'misguided' individuals; at no time did Baring's government ever accept responsibility.

Ruthagathi was not an isolated case. In February 1955 Chief Mundai was acquitted in a murder case that was remarkably similar. Once again, officers of the administration would appear to have done their best to sabotage the prosecution, the district officer telling the police 'a pack of lies' to try to protect the chief. In the same month African members of another screening team were in court to face rape charges.[39]

Throughout the course of the war, many other examples of beatings, torture and murder by the security forces came to light. In December 1952 it was acknowledged that forty-five prisoners had been 'badly beaten' at a temporary detention camp in Rumuruti, 'with the object of extorting information or confessions'. According to Baring's deputy, members of the KPR 'were probably involved'.[40] The next month Baring was embarrassed to receive a letter from Canon Bewes, providing a long list of alleged tortures carried out by whites in the security forces against African members of his church.[41] Bewes would later publish an account of visiting the people injured in these assaults: 'I saw a hospital ward of inoffensive, yet badly injured men; had they been beaten up by Mau Mau? No, they had been "questioned" by the police.'[42]

The day following Bewes's complaint to Baring, Elijah Njeru was killed in Embu, beaten to death by two KPR officers, named Reuben and Keates. The case came before a magistrate, but he decided that it would not be in the public interest to pursue the matter, though they were later properly charged and fined – though only after Bewes had again raised a stink.[43] It was as a consequence of this case that Baring issued his 'Governor's Directive on Beating up', on 11 February 1953. Peter Evans, the Irish lawyer who stayed on in Kenya after initially coming out to assist in the Kenyatta trial, worked with African friends in the KAU during 1953 to try to follow up on a number of alleged atrocity cases. His book, published in 1956, documents some of these, including a case of the cold-blooded assassination of suspects by a European officer. Evans's relentless pursuit of this case led to the Kenya government deporting him. In the process, they seized his papers and thus confiscated his evidence.[44]

Throughout 1953 and into 1954 many more cases of excess came to public notice. Another KPR officer, Brian Hayward, was convicted for burning a suspect's eardrums with lighted cigarettes. He was fined and sentenced to three months' hard labour (but in fact never served this sentence). His brother was fined £25 at the same time for pouring paraffin over a suspect, and another officer was fined in the same case. In one of the more gruesome cases KPR officers Pharazyn and Sawyer were convicted of torturing a prisoner over a fire. Their colleague Hvass was fined £50 for administering floggings to prisoners, and Horsfall and Searle were given prison sentences on review for committing perjury to secure the conviction of a suspect. Torture was also the reason for the convictions of four police officers – Fuller, Waters, Coppen and Bosch. Their victim died. As Antony Clayton commented in surveying this list, it was but 'the tip of the iceberg of unrecorded but widespread roughing up'.[45]

The archive record confirms Clayton's assertion that there were many more examples. Among the hundreds of Mau Mau trials there is clear evidence of regular and systematic violence against suspects in more than 80 per cent of cases. While some of the accusations made by prisoners may certainly be fabricated, there are many other cases where beatings and torture were confirmed by the court. Although examples of abuse of suspects can be found in all areas, the severity of cases in Nyeri in the middle months of 1954 – just as MacPherson was beginning his investigations – was particularly bad. Justice Law, who tried far more Mau Mau cases than any other member of the Bench, became so exasperated by the procession of injured suspects being brought before him at the Nyeri assizes at this time that he wrote to the Chief Secretary to complain.[46] It made no difference. By then the abuse and mistreatment of suspects had become the norm. 'Incumbent violence' had been thoroughly institutionalized as a system of control in the reserves by 1954; but it was in the detention camps and prisons that the crimes of punishment were most obviously part of an authoritarian system of control.

## The Gulag

The dirt road leading to the detention camp all but petered out a few hundred yards before the tall gate came into view, festooned in barbed wire. The journey out from Nairobi had not taken long. The traveller and his guide, a white Rhodesian employed in the colony's prison service, had come to pay a visit to the closest Mau Mau prison camp to the city. The traveller was the writer Anthony Smith, who was then, in 1959, having an adventure – journeying from Cape Town to Cairo on the back of a motorbike. A visit to the camp seemed a good way to kill time on a dull Nairobi Saturday, while his bike was being repaired. The rainy season had begun. It was grey, cold and miserable. The weather suited the setting.

They drove up to the gate, the car splashing through the potholes. Staring out from the wire mesh stood a burly African sentry in a heavy army greatcoat, a Lee Enfield rifle slung over his shoulder, his hands thrust deep into its pockets and his head tilted against the drizzling, misty rain. The Rhodesian spoke at length in Swahili, and the sentry turned and walked fifty yards to a second wire-mesh gate, where another guard stood. Between these inner and outer fences of mesh and coiled barbed wire was a ditch, fifty feet deep, lined at the bottom with neat, symmetrical rows of white, sharply pointed wooden stakes. Looking to left and to right, the fences, the ditch and the camp beyond were dominated by looming watchtowers. Smith thought it looked just like all the *stalags* and *oflags* of war-time Germany.

The sentry returned, and questioned the Rhodesian further. They were suspicious of his companion. Guests of this kind were not welcome. The government did not want any more bad publicity about the detention camps. The guards were nervy. After more talking, the sentry went to his guardhouse, picked up the heavy bakelite phone, and called up the camp commandant. He asked to speak with the Rhodesian, then with Smith. Only after this interrogation were the two visitors allowed through the first gate, past the ditch of spikes, and through the second gate. After thirty minutes of haggling, the two white men had made it into the camp.

Ahead of them were more fencing and barbed wire, separating the several compounds, each filled with row upon row of oblong wooden huts, set out at regular intervals. The commandant came briskly towards the visitors, dressed in a military-style uniform of boots, leggings and breeches, and with an army cap on his head. The tour began, starting with 'the facilities' – kitchens, latrines, communal areas – all basic and functional. Then came the prisoners. The warders were in the midst of a roll call and the inmates were gathered in the exercise yard, all squatting on the ground in neat, silent, orderly lines. 'They had been arranged like platoons of infantrymen,' Smith would later write in the published account of his epic journey:

> . . . every man was wearing an identical uniform. This was just a short-sleeved white shirt and a pair of shorts. Their hair had been shaved . . . but . . . the only thing I really saw and remembered about these men . . . was their eyes. They were like nails, every one of them; sharp and pointed, and fixed with a deadly accuracy upon us. Not one of them had expression, not one differed from the other. They existed as row upon row of pointed, featureless, hateful spots in a sea of shirts, shorts and jet-black skin. The eyes of them all were fixed unerringly upon us; they stared at us almost as if there was the power and authority of a weapon behind each pair of their eyes. I have never before been confronted with such a profusion of dull and expressionless loathing.

African warders walked between the rows, counting audibly as they went. Among the squatting prisoners, hardly a muscle moved. The tension was palpable.

As the commandant kept up his tour guide's banter for the benefit of his visitors, the warders became agitated. The head count did not tally. The commandant broke off and went to the warders, snatching the paper from the hands of the senior warder to add up the figures for himself. There was a man missing. Several warders scurried out, and a search of the huts began. 'He must have escaped from the working party,' explained the commandant. 'They all go down to the quarry every afternoon and it's the devil's own job seeing they don't slip away. If I had my way, they'd never leave the camp. Not for any damned reason.' The visitors were told they would have to leave. 'As soon as he's outside he'll just take off his clothes and run like hell,' the commandant concluded. All this while, the rows of squatting prisoners remained motionless and silent, their eyes staring blankly ahead.[47] This was a typical scene from daily life in Kenya's gulag.

★

Nowhere in the British empire was confinement ever used as extensively as in colonial Kenya. In December 1954 the daily average number of Mau Mau detainees and convicts held in the colony reached a peak figure of 71,346, among them some 8000 women. They were interned in a variety of prisons, detention camps, work camps and district camps. More than 98 per cent of these detainees came from the Kikuyu-speaking peoples of Kenya's central highlands, with a population of 1.4 million. According to these official figures, widely publicized at the time, one in eight Kikuyu adult males were held in British prisons and camps in December 1954.

Over the whole course of the Emergency, the reality was even worse. The daily average figure takes no account of the throughput of these prisons and camps: many other individuals passed through the system who were not counted among the 71,346, and others still spent periods incarcerated illegally in the many Home Guard posts, chiefs' camps and screening centres that littered Kikuyuland. The numbers were never properly recorded for these places, but a conservative estimate is that at least one in four Kikuyu adult males were imprisoned or detained by the British colonial administration at some time between 1952 and 1958.

The Kenya administration had long been fond of incarceration as a form of punishment. Back in 1938 the daily average prison population in neighbouring Tanganyika had been only 54 per 100,000, and in Uganda 114 per 100,000, while in Kenya the figure was 145 per 100,000.[48] Measured in these terms, Kenya then imprisoned a larger proportion of its population than any other colony in the British empire. During the Emergency, the number of 'prison graduates' would rise to unprecedented levels (see tables 7.v and 7.vi, pp. 000–000, for a comparison of prison populations and a breakdown of daily average numbers of Mau Mau detainees and convicts).

As the Emergency began, Kenya's prisons held 9954 convicts, and the detention camps only 2475. This population climbed steadily until Operation Anvil, in May 1954, when additional detention camps were built to hold the dramatic influx of new detainees. When Anvil was being planned, Baring asked London for approval of the expansion of the camps and for regulations that would allow prisoners to be made to undertake heavy labour. Even though he was aware that this would place Britain in breach of international conventions on forced labour, Lyttelton gave his consent, telling Baring to be sure to emphasize the place of work in the 'rehabilitation' of Mau Mau detainees.[49] The language of the psycho docs was crucial in legitimating this draconian system in benevolent terms.

Those Kikuyu arrested in Nairobi during Operation Anvil hugely swelled the detainee population, and by the end of 1954 it reached its peak. After that, the numbers held in the system slowly reduced, reaching 59,419 in December 1955, 40,521 in December 1956, and 19,575 by December 1957. Releases from the camps depended upon the inmates making confessions and recanting their Mau Mau affiliations. The intention was to first break the spirit of prisoners, and then to encourage them to move through a process of 'rehabilitation' that began with a confession of their wrongdoing. Detainees were 'screened' on arrival, and classified by a coding system that isolated the so-called 'hard-core' Mau Mau from other categories thought to be more amenable to 're-education'. Those inmates thought to be most senior in the Mau Mau movement were classified as Z1, those of less importance Z2 or Y categories. As detainees were by stages rehabilitated, they moved along the 'pipeline', being reclassified as X category, towards their eventual release.[50] But many of them, through acts of resistance and defiance, became 'stuck' in the pipeline. In 1957 the process of release was relaxed in order to accelerate the return of detainees to their homes, but by the end of 1958, 4688 so-called 'hard core' Mau Mau who had refused to confess still remained behind the wire.[51]

The vast majority of those incarcerated under the Emergency Powers were never formally convicted in a court, but were detained because of the suspicion that they supported the Mau Mau movement. Though these detainees were not therefore in a strict sense 'convicts', experience of the prison regime pervaded the consciousness of this entire society, and it is perhaps not surprising that the image of the prison should subsequently have come to play a very prominent role in Kenyan culture. The suffering of confinement is a central theme in the story of the birth of the Kenyan nation, and it is a prominent image in writings, both factual and fictional, on the power and authority of the modern state. Whereas elsewhere in Britain's empire, most notably India, the prison graduates of the struggle to be rid of colonial rule were the political elite of the nationalist cause, in Kenya colonial incarceration was a far more widespread and pervasive experience. It has affected Kenya's national psychology ever since.

More than a dozen narratives of detention during the Mau Mau Emergency have now been published, and all have been produced as part of factual life histories and memoirs. These accounts stress the political character of the authors' incarceration, and present prison as a heroic setting of anti-colonial struggle. Among the best known and most widely cited is the brief account provided by Jomo Kenyatta, Kenya's first president, of his eight-year detention in his book *Suffering Without Bitterness*, and the detailed story of J. M. Kariuki, *Mau Mau Detainee*, which was the first to be published (1963) and which set the benchmark for those to follow.[52] The prison memoirs of Bildad Kaggia (*Roots of*

*Freedom*) and Waruhiu Itote (*Mau Mau General*) give accounts of senior Mau Mau commanders, with an emphasis upon nation-building and the sacrifices to be made through personal suffering.

The writings of Gakaara wa Wanjua (*Mau Mau Author in Detention*), Karigo Muchai (*Hardcore*) and Guco Gikoyo (*We Fought for Freedom*), on the other hand, take a less ideological view of the nation; these foot soldiers of the movement stress instead the brutality and humiliation that characterized their experience of detention.[53] For these men, to be detained was 'to enter a world of constantly threatening violence'. It is this image of the brutality of warders, harsh living conditions and dehumanizing treatment (including sexual assault, most harrowingly recounted in Wambui Waiyaki Otieno's *Mau Mau Daughter*),[54] and not Kenyatta and Kariuki's idealized notion of 'suffering for the nation', that emerges as the strongest theme from these Mau Mau memoirs of detention.

Marshall Clough's study of the Mau Mau memoirs as a genre highlights the sparse yet often chillingly matter-of-fact discussion of violence, deprivation and depersonalization that characterizes these autobiographical accounts. Drawing parallels with political prisoners in Soviet Russia, and echoing Fanon's observation on the totalitarian aspects of colonial conditions, Clough describes the complex of more than fifty British camps scattered throughout the country as resembling 'a Kenyan gulag'.[55]

The parallel is tellingly accurate. The regime of Britain's prisons and detention camps in 1950s Kenya might easily have been modelled on the Soviet example. Violence was both routine and random, but it had a purpose. The regimes practised in different camps, and even within different compounds within camps, reflected the category of the prisoners and their place in the pipeline. 'Reasonable force' was permitted in any circumstance where inmates declined to obey prison regulations, and those who resisted the discipline of the system were harshly treated. The regulations governing the administration of the prisons and the camps stipulated a strict punishment regime, but in practice warders could do much as they liked. In the prisons, corporal punishments and the use of leg-irons had to be documented, but other, lesser forms of punishment did not.[56] In the detention camps, this distinction was less apparent. The vast expansion of the prison service meant that many warders were recruited who had no experience, and little knowledge of the rule book. There was little or no training of detention camp staff, and precious little for prison staff – indeed, so desperate was the manpower shortage in Kenya by 1954 that the prison service was notorious for its willingness to employ anyone who applied, regardless of their character or suitability. The regime within the camps was intended to be harsh, but the poor quality of the staff, a lack of training and lax supervision made matters considerably worse.

Violence was not exceptional but intrinsic to the system, and the use of force to compel obedience was sanctioned at the highest level. The insistence that Mau Mau adherents needed to confess before they could be rehabilitated, emphasized in the pronouncements of the psycho docs Carothers and Leakey, led the prison authorities towards tactics that seemed designed to generate confrontation with the prisoners.

The prisons and camps therefore became sites of struggle. Resistance was apparent in all the camps, but especially among the 'hard-core' category of prisoners and detainees, who most often bound together in unified opposition to the authority of the warders. In their memoirs, Mau Mau activists indicate their consciousness of the importance of continuing the struggle 'behind the wire'. Mau Mau organized their own structures of discipline and control within the camps, in opposition to the institutionalized control of the British. Kikuyu prayers and songs were frequently sung to express defiance and lift morale, and in many of the camps the better educated among the prisoners organized classes for their comrades in everything from basic literacy to politics – this often in competition with the 'official' classes run by the authorities. Within the compounds, prisoners organized their own hierarchies of command, with committees and councils to settle disputes, punish those who transgressed the inmates' own code of conduct, and decide upon tactics in the struggle with the prison authorities. Leaders among the detainees, including men such as Kariuki, viewed themselves as political prisoners and presented their resistance as a demand for the recognition of their rights.[57] It was a claim the British were never prepared to consider.

In this struggle, disputes over food and work most often provoked violent confrontations. Rations issued to prisoners were seldom sufficient even by the minimum standards set by the prison authorities, a fact apparent in the high level of nutrition-related illnesses suffered by prisoners and the general poor health reported from within the camps.[58] The withdrawal of food was frequently used as a punishment for non-cooperation, and refusal to work was the most common form of non-cooperation. In camps of all types detainees were required to undertake some form of work, but it was in the 'hard-core' camps that this work was likely to be heaviest. Work strikes were common and were viewed by the British as the most serious challenge to the authority of the prison regime. Towards the end of the Emergency, camp commandants had the authority to break strikes by whatever means was necessary, but throughout, reductions in rations and beatings were standard 'disciplinary' measures against intransigent inmates.

★

Punishment took many forms affecting the health of prisoners. Many of the camps were situated in remote, low-lying, hot, malaria areas, unfamiliar conditions for the majority of the detainees. Medical provision was rudimentary, and medical supervision often cursory. Poor diet and bad sanitation, coupled with gross overcrowding and the imposition of heavy physical labour, were among the most obvious contributory causes to a high incidence of illness among the detainees. Conditions were at their worst in the later half of 1954, after Anvil, when the expansion of the system had stretched resources beyond their limit. This period saw some of the worst excesses, and the worst outbreaks of disease. The typhoid outbreak at Manyani was probably the most serious.

In May 1954 H. G. Waters, the assistant director of medical services in Kenya, paid a visit to the newly opened Manyani Camp.[59] Manyani had been hurriedly constructed in a corner of the Tsavo National Park, close to the main Mombasa to Nairobi highway and the railway line, to accommodate those arrested in Operation Anvil. At the time of his visit Waters was told that the camp was full to its capacity of 6600 detainees. Waters was concerned by the conditions he found at Manyani, and deeply worried that the disregard of those conditions by the officers commanding the camp might result in a serious outbreak of contagious disease. Manyani's kitchens, in which the detainees cooked their food, were fly-infested and disgracefully filthy. Overflowing latrine buckets were left in piles all over the camp. Waters thought it likely that the water supply was contaminated and gave specific instructions that 'Europeans should filter and boil all drinking water'. The African detainees did not have the opportunity to take such rudimentary precautions. Outside the camp confines, Waters found further unhygienic conditions where excrement was being dumped. No proper arrangements had been made for the disposal of night soil. There was 'a very dangerous threat from typhoid, dysentery and diarrhoea to the camp inmates', wrote Waters to his superiors.[60]

It was another fortnight before Waters' original comments found their way into a more general report on the camps by Colonel W. G. S. Foster, Kenya's Director of Medical Services. Within a few days of Waters' visit to Manyani, the Kenya press had got wind of the story. Rumours were circulating that there were already typhoid victims in the camps. At this point the Kenya government did what they did best during the Emergency – they dissembled: the rumours were flatly denied, and the concerned public were reassured that health provision at the camps was more than adequate for the needs of the inmates.[61]

In private, senior officials were deeply worried. The Commissioner of Prisons demanded additional resources to deal with the critical situation at Manyani and Mackinnon Road, and when Kenya's War Council

met on 4 June 1954, the camps were described as a 'sanitary menace'.[62]
Other than warning the camp staff of the danger, nothing was done. By
then typhoid was already taking a grip at Manyani.

The full extent of the outbreak was not 'discovered' until 9 September
1954 – four full months after Waters' initial expressions of concern.[63]
The whistle-blower was Hugh Stott, a medical adviser to the Labour
Department. Copies of the weekly medical returns from Manyani came
to Stott's office, and he noticed that the sharply rising death rate at the
camp was being attributed to increased cases of malaria. Stott thought
this most unlikely. Aware of the rumours about typhoid, he resolved to
investigate the matter. On arriving at the Manyani camp dispensary, Stott
found that another dead body had been brought in that very morning.
On inspecting the corpse, Stott was immediately suspicious that the dead
man was a typhoid victim, and he swiftly proceeded to the compound
from which the body had been brought.

There he saw with his own eyes the gravity of the situation. The
overcrowding was ghastly, and there were sickly men everywhere. Many
were being made to work, despite their obvious incapacity, but 'some
detainees in the compounds were so ill as to be quite unable to walk by
themselves'.[64] These men were not on the sick list, as they should have
been according to the detention camp regulations, but remained within
the compounds, untreated and ignored. Stott could not disguise his
incredulity at the deliberate neglect of the sick prisoners: he berated the
European staff, but they showed utter contempt for his concern. Enraged,
Stott let rip to his superiors: 'These persons must have been known to
be in this state by the camp officers as I understand that a count is made
twice daily of every person in each compound,' he wrote. He could not
understand how the prison staff could have mistaken the outbreak of
typhoid for malaria, especially when they had been persistently and
severely warned about the dangers of such an outbreak over the previous
four months. It was clear to him that typhoid had been in the camp over
that entire period. In his opinion, while the sanitary conditions were
undeniably deplorable, the ambivalent attitude of the staff was *the* significant factor in the typhoid outbreak.

Confronted by Stott's report, the Kenya government again pre-
varicated. The artful Granville Roberts, in Kenya's Office of Information, blithely suggested to the press that the Manyani outbreak was
merely a reflection of a general increase in typhoid cases in Kenya,
pointing out that detainees might have been admitted to the camp
already suffering from typhoid.[65] Why, then, had the outbreak occurred
at Manyani, and not at other camps? Stott attributed the rapid spread of
the disease to the overcrowded and unsanitary conditions at Manyani.
He reckoned that compounds designed for 600 men were in fact housing

800, and he saw that drinking water and defecating buckets were placed side by side in the huts. Stott was right in both respects. Later investigations came to the conclusion that contaminated water was indeed the most likely cause of the outbreak.

The overcrowding was, in fact, far worse than Stott imagined: in September 1954 Manyani was home to 16,000 detainees, some 10,000 more than it was designed to hold.[66] The colonial administration now took steps to improve sanitation, and also at Langata and Mackinnon Road, where further cases of typhoid were reported. Manyani was placed in quarantine for just over two months, while additional medical staff moved in to deal with the sick.[67] But the camp was reopened more rapidly than good medical practice would have suggested – the government simply needed somewhere to put their rapidly growing mass of detainees. There would be further outbreaks in Manyani, and in other camps too. Contagious disease became an unpleasant but widely accepted feature of life for those incarcerated on the Kenya gulag. By the end of the year a total of 1151 typhoid cases had been reported at Manyani, of which 115 proved fatal.

Though conditions at Manyani in 1954 may have been amongst the worst in any of the camps, the general pattern observed by Hugh Stott in his inspections revealed standards of hygiene and welfare that were well below the minimum requirements of the prison regulations. On a round of inspections of other camps, Stott came to the conclusion that the rules were for the most part simply ignored.[68] Camp commanders ran things much as they pleased, and a general attitude prevailed that detainees should be made to suffer. Discomfort and deprivation were part of the punishment regime. Death and disease were all too often the consequence.

It is difficult to establish a general picture of health among the inmates of the camps. The typhoid epidemic at Manyani was the most dramatic example of how poor conditions impacted on the lives of the detainees; but there was also a high incidence of other contagious diseases. Pulmonary tuberculosis was a grave problem in the works camps, for example. Here, again, overcrowding combined with a harsh regime of physical labour and low levels of nutrition to increase the incidence of the disease. By June 1955 tuberculosis was becoming such a danger in the works camps of Central Province that the decision was taken to release the sufferers, and repatriate them to their homes. This was not motivated by concern for the health of the detainees but by the embarrassment of the administration at the high levels of contagion being reported from the camps. The pace of such repatriations increased through 1956,[69] as the sick rates at the works camps steadily climbed. The Director of Medical Services protested, and in January 1956 sternly warned that sick rates in the Kiambu works camps were already four times those in Embu and double those at Manyani.[70] Having incubated disease in the works camps, where the British admitted that standards of hygiene were even lower than in other types of camp, the sufferers were now sent home to spread it to their relatives.

Throughout 1955 the range of deficiency diseases reported from the camps indicated that nutrition was inadequate. High incidences were reported for dysentery, diarrhoea, pneumonia, and for deficiency diseases including scurvy, kwashiorkor, and pellagra. These conditions indicated serious shortages of vitamins in the diet. Pellagra was the most common, especially in the larger camps. At Embakasi in 1955 additional nutrients had to be added to the rations to counter the 220 cases of pellagra that had occurred. Two months later, there were ninety-five new cases as a result of the additional nutrients being suspended. There were also regular outbreaks at other camps, notably in Fort Hall. The prison authorities noted vitamin A deficiencies among many inmates, but also observed that the improper preparation of the maize consumed by the prisoners might have been a principal cause of pellagra.

More generally, it was apparent that many prisoners received a diet that was far below that to which they were entitled under prison regulations. Many camps were deliberately constructed in remote areas, especially those holding the 'hard-core' Mau Mau prisoners. These camps were difficult to supply, and camp commandants often had to procure foodstuffs locally. They fed prisoners whatever was available, with little regard to the regulations. The pilfering of food by camp warders was also acknowledged as a serious problem in some camps. But everywhere the reduction of food rations was used as a punishment. This was provided for in the prison regulations, and warders and commandants made frequent use of it. For all these reasons, it seems probable that many prisoners and detainees persistently received a diet that was inadequate even by the frugal standards of the regulations.

This prevalence of nutritional diseases, especially pellagra, caught the attention of medical researchers at the London School of Hygiene and Tropical Medicine in 1955. Dr G. R. Wadsworth, the Head of Nutrition at the LSHTM, sought permission to visit the camps, and in the early months of 1956 he was finally allowed to make a short 'fact-finding' trip to Kenya. At Embakasi, Wadsworth emphatically demonstrated that the high incidence of pellagra was the result of incarceration and directly linked to the diet in the camp. The incidence of pellagra was completely absent among newly arrived detainees, but rose dramatically among inmates who had been in Embakasi for six months or more.[71] Maize dominated the diet at Embakasi, as at many other camps. Wadsworth also noted that the incidence of pellagra was far higher among inmates who were engaged in physical labour, and at Embakasi he was able graphically to show this by differentiating between those inmates on 'light camp duties', working in the kitchens and sweeping, as opposed to those on the heavy construction work for which the camp became notorious. Quite simply, those inmates exposed to heavy physical labour were far more susceptible to pellagra. This was yet another testimony to the harshness of the Kenya prison regime.

Wadsworth's academic research received no support from the Kenya government. His report was not widely circulated at the time, and there is no evidence that the Kenya administration took any action over his findings other than to advise prison authorities to ensure that maize was properly cooked before serving to inmates. Wadsworth could be ignored, but other bodies that sought to investigate conditions in the camps were obstructed in more determined ways. It took the International Committee of the Red Cross nearly two years to obtain British permission for a visit to the detention camps in Kenya. When they finally arrived for the first visit, in February 1957, it was on the understanding that they would be 'concerned solely with the conditions of detention' and would not pass any comments on the reasons for the detention camps or the political situation. Their report highlighted all of the sanitary and dietary problems that were by then well known to the Kenyan authorities, again documenting the high incidence of illness related to deficiency diseases, but did so in muted, passive tones that implied no especially harsh criticism of the policies of the Kenya government. What failings there may have been were instead assumed to be problems of 'implementation'. The ICRC did not then publish their reports as a matter of policy, and so their findings were not made public at the time.[72]

A second visit by the ICRC was permitted following the scandal of the murder of inmates at Hola Camp, having been proposed by London in 1959 as a way to help quell the political uproar that had ensued. The ICRC's second report was more thorough, more probing, and far more critical. On this occasion the ICRC delegation asked to know why the detainees were not classified as prisoners of war, pointing out that the lack of this status denied them an important set of statutory rights under the Geneva conventions. Under these conventions, to which Britain was a signatory on behalf of the colonial possessions, internment should be precautionary, temporary and 'not be in any way punitive in character'.[73] Detention in Kenya was unquestionably punitive, and could hardly be said to be 'temporary'. By 1958 some had been in the camps for six years, and there was discussion in Kenya at the time of the ICRC's visit that some detainees might be held 'indefinitely' if local loyalist communities did not want them released. As the ICRC pointed out, these were men who had never stood trial for any offence.

The delegation revealed to the Kenya authorities that they were aware that following the first ICRC visit there had been 'a sharp increase in persecution and bad treatment in reprisal for the complaints they had made to the delegates'.[74] And they were again concerned that detainees might have been intimidated into silence and acquiescence. At the Senya works camp they described 'poker faces, drawn, without the slightest expression, and a few of them looked terrified'. Diet deficiencies and hygiene were again to the fore. In the Kandongu camp they found that 'since 1952, no toilet paper had been available ... In a number of compounds we were unable to find any of the grass which was supposed to take the place of toilet paper.' They found fly-infested latrine buckets and no disinfectant. 'It seems incomprehensible', they continued, 'that the health service officer ... should not have noted this unsatisfactory situation.' Prisoners suffered vitamin deficiencies and were poorly nourished, and the incidence of disease in the camps was once again far higher than in the general population.[75]

Even by 1958 little had changed since the first scandals at Manyani in May 1954. Moreover, in every case the camp commandants were aware of the arrival of the ICRC inspectors. Though some camps had evidently been spruced up for the occasion, the majority of the European officers evidently saw nothing wrong with revealing conditions just as they were.[76] When the Colonial Office received the second ICRC report, it was quietly shelved.

Even if ICRC reports did not have to be made public, the detention camps were a scandal that could not easily be hidden. By 1958 several scandals in the camps had received wide publicity in Britain, each one ventilated by members of the opposition Labour Party. Lennox-Boyd seemed to take it all in his comfortable stride, defending the Kenya administration and pleading that the work in the camps was all for the positive good of the prisoners. This was the cure for 'Mau Mau's disease'.

But the catalogue of official mischief was becoming lengthier and increasingly difficult for even the adept Lennox-Boyd to deflect. The complaints about the camps first began after the expansion of the system to accommodate the Anvil detainees, in 1954. The concern of the churches, earnestly trying to locate their lost teachers and trainee clergy in the chaos of the Langata transit camp, brought the first clear signs that all was not well. The typhoid outbreak at Manyani then brought camp conditions to the attention of a wider audience, but it was not until towards the end of 1955, after the shooting war was largely over, that criticism really came to focus upon the system of detention itself.

The most embarrassing revelations came in 1956 with the publication of a pamphlet entitled 'The Truth About Kenya', sponsored by the Movement for Colonial Freedom.[77] The information supplied in this report was of a detail and intimacy not previously seen in criticisms of government actions in Kenya. Its author was Eileen Fletcher, a Quaker social worker who had been employed from December 1954 as a Rehabilitation Officer in Kenya, working for the Department of Community Development in Athi River and Kisumu camps, amongst others. Fletcher's pamphlet detailed the conditions in the camps, highlighting the indiscriminate nature of the detention orders, the brutality of the treatment meted out to inmates, the gross and unsanitary overcrowding, and the fact that among the detainees were children, including girls as young as twelve years of age. This last revelation, given wide coverage in the daily press, shocked public opinion in Britain. So did her assertion that juvenile girls were incarcerated with 'Mau Mau toughs'; and her claims of flagrant abuses within the camps, backed up by examples from her own experience, greatly tarnished the reputations of the various Christian missions whose members were involved in assisting in the rehabilitation effort.

The substance of Eileen Fletcher's claims was demonstrably correct. However, the response of the Colonial Office was to seek to refute Fletcher's claims and to besmirch her character so as to lessen the credibility of her evidence. Here was yet another critic of Kenya who was 'ill-informed' and 'tired and emotional'. The tactic worked to a certain extent, while at the same time the sensationalist tone of the pamphlet deterred many of those within the missionary societies (who certainly had serious reservations about the camps) from supporting her publicly. Therefore, though Fletcher's whistle-blowing instigated an enquiry, this did not result in any significant change to the administration of the camps, and especially not the 'hard-core' camps, where if anything the prison regime became tougher after 1956 than it had been before.[78]

Complaints from 'insiders' like Fletcher were always potentially damaging. The Kenya administration did its best to refute further challenges from its former staff. When Victor Sluter made accusations of brutality and inhumane conditions at Manyani in 1955, a lengthy investigation was held and a report produced meticulously addressing each of the issues raised in the accusations. Just as with Fletcher, the tactic was to undermine the complainant's character and dismiss each of the charges as unfounded or based on a misapprehension. The scandal of the assaults upon prisoners at the Gathigiriri works camp in Embu, which broke in April 1957, was more difficult to dampen down. This case was taken up by the Labour MP Barbara Castle, who raised questions in parliament in an effort to have the camp staff prosecuted.[79]

The complaints raised by Captain Ernest Law, an ex-soldier who joined the prison service as a warder during the Emergency and was based at Kamiti, received less widespread publicity at the time.[80] Law witnessed brutality in the prison on several occasions, and came into conflict with his colleagues when he objected to prisoners 'being beaten senseless'. He was eventually dismissed from his job, on a spurious allegation of poor health. He returned to Kamiti as an inmate a few months later, when he found himself penniless and waiting to be deported back to England. As a prisoner, Law witnessed further abuses, including prolonged and brutal beatings of prisoners who refused to obey instructions. His account, graphically described from first-hand experience, has the sharp ring of authenticity about it.

Attempted escapes were common. In March 1954 nine prisoners overpowered a guard at Embakasi camp, striking him on the head with a spade. The guard was killed, and the prisoners escaped. Two of the men were recaptured shortly afterwards, and both were then tried for murder and convicted. They were hanged in June 1954.[81] In the same month there was a breakout from Wajir prison, this time three prisoners getting away.[82] In July 1954 a work party of prisoners from Embakasi set upon the driver of the lorry taking them back to the camp and stole weapons from their guards. Thirteen prisoners escaped, but eight were quickly caught. Having seized the weapons from the police, all the men were charged with possession of arms or consorting with terrorists, and so when convicted they hanged.[83] At camps holding hard-core Mau Mau detainees, attempted escapes were a very regular feature of camp life.

Full-scale riots within the camps were a rarity, but in 1957, as the British moved prisoners around in preparation for accelerating the release of those considered to be 'less dangerous', there were a number of incidents involving groups of prisoners who had recently been relocated. The intensity of the violence was also fomented by the growing determination on the part of the British to enforce a rigorous work regime upon the hard-core prisoners. These were brutal and bloody events, as the examples of the riots at Athi River and Manyani camps illustrate.

At the end of March 1957 a group of 'hard-core' Mau Mau prisoners were moved out of Mageta camp to Athi River, in an effort to segregate them from other elements at Mageta.[84] At Athi River camp it was intended to break up this batch of Mageta detainees into 'comparatively small groups', to be scattered in amongst the Athi River detainees, and to be made to work. At Mageta camp these detainees had refused to work, and now did so again at Athi River. Their spokesmen announced to the camp commandant that they were 'political prisoners' and should be treated as such. Two days later, on 3 April, when warders tried to carry out the division in order to prepare the work gangs, the detainees resisted with force. Prison staff were compelled to retreat from the compound under a hail of missiles. In the general melee, a group of prisoners singled out the camp commandant, Harrison, and cornered him. He was savagely stabbed in the chest.

Once the authorities regained control of the compound the next day, the inmates were interrogated to find out who had been responsible for the assault on Harrison. However, it took over one week for anyone among the detainees to give any evidence that might help to identify the assailant. During the interrogations, the camp staff were accused of brutally assaulting several prisoners.[85]

The culprit was eventually identified as Kiraka Kirangi, and he was put on trial for attempted murder. Kirangi was acquitted of this charge but found guilty of the lesser charge of riotous assembly (for which he was sentenced to five years' imprisonment with hard labour); but the more remarkable aspect of Kirangi's trial was the revelations about systematic violence at Athi River against prisoners who refused to cooperate. These incidents were reported by witnesses without any apparent awareness that such behaviour might contravene prison regulations. Violence had by then already become intrinsic to the system.

Manyani camp was the site of a very significant degree of organized resistance by its 'hard-core' Mau Mau detainees throughout the Emergency, but this became more severe from 1957 onwards, as the colonial government tried to reassert their control over the more militant elements within the camps. In August 1957 the decision was taken to break up the groups of detainees in Manyani and reorganize the compounds.[86] Compound 16 was one of those to be reorganized. It contained 212 'hard-core' detainees, housed in five huts. When the warders moved into this compound to carry out the reorganization on the afternoon of 17 August, the detainees refused to comply with the instructions. The camp's special riot squad was sent for, and at 6p.m. they entered Compound 16, wearing their steel helmets and carrying long batons and straw shields. They were accompanied by another group of warders, not assigned to the riot squad, armed with shorter batons, but without helmets or shields.

Under the command of their European officers, the riot squad began to force the detainees into the huts. The first group of detainees resisted this, and the warders found themselves the victims of an organized and apparently coordinated attack. The detainees armed themselves with pieces of timber ripped from the huts, iron bars made from the straightened-out handles of latrine buckets, heavy iron bolts, buckets, lumps of hard rock and hard murram. Some of the pieces of wood brandished by the detainees had barbed wire wrapped around the ends, or nails protruding. Many of the weapons had been prepared in advance and hidden, buried in the floors of the huts. This attack was so fierce that the riot squad and other warders were forced to rapidly retreat from the compound. They left behind two dead colleagues, whilst another seven warders and one European officer were badly injured. It was not until five days later, on 22 August, that the prison authorities were able to regain control.

Eleven detainees from Compound 16 were subsequently charged with murder and came before the Emergency Assize Court in Mombasa. Their resistance continued in the courtroom. Each of the eleven accused first declined to be represented by an advocate, and then they refused to cooperate with the conduct of the trial – refusing to plead, claiming they could not understand the interpreter, and refusing to cross-examine witnesses. In summing up, the exasperated judge described their demeanour as 'truculent ... and generally disrespectful throughout the proceedings'. Five of the eleven were acquitted, on the basis of weak evidence of identification, while the remaining six were found guilty of murder and sentenced to hang.

After 1956 the British public were certainly aware that the campaign in Kenya was a dirty business. The violence in the reserves and Nairobi had peaked, and by then the camps probably reflected the worst of it. Despite an increasingly vociferous lobby of Labour MPs clamouring for an end to the Emergency Powers regulations and the closure of the camps, there was no crisis of political confidence. The crunch did not come until 1959, at the Hola detention camp in northern Kenya. This was to be the decisive event in Kenya's path to independence.

Hola contained a group of 'hard-core' Mau Mau who had persistently mounted resistance against efforts to make them work. The decision was taken to step up the level of force to be used against 'recalcitrant' prisoners of this type, and the camp officers received instructions to compel the prisoners to undertake hard labour. The result was a violent clash between the prisoners and their warders. Willoughby Thompson was the local district officer, and was summoned to the camp in the aftermath of the violence:

> On a piece of flat ground, in front of one of the compounds, I could see figures lying or sitting up, holding their heads and moaning. It was immediately obvious to me that most of those lying down were corpses – they were dead. ... I asked what had happened, and I was told that they had taken Mau Mau detainees out of this compound to do some work, and they had been overcome by the heat, and there had been some sort of fight and squabble. There was a big water-bowser nearby, and they said they had thrown lots of water over these

chaps, and as a result of this they had drowned. Which was a very improbable story.[87]

Improbable or not, it was the story that the Kenya administration initially released and transmitted to London. Baring, who by Thompson's own account of his interview with the Governor knew it to be a lie, repeated the story to London all the same. The culture of impunity had reached the very top.

The truth was altogether more sinister, as Willoughby Thompson had easily discovered; but it would take no fewer than three separate government enquiries to penetrate. When taken out and asked to work, the detainees had refused. The guards had then set upon them with whips and batons. At the finish, eleven detainees lay dead, clubbed to death by their African guards whilst European warders looked on.[88]

After Hola there was no way back. The culpability of the most senior officials in the Kenya administration was apparent both in the regime that had resulted in the violence at Hola and in the facile attempt to cover up the incident. When the House of Commons debated the Hola incident, on 27 July 1959, neither Labour nor Conservative MPs could find any reason to support the actions of the Kenya government. The debate was led by Barbara Castle – a champion of the cause of the victims of Kenya's state-sponsored violence. But the key speech was from a Tory back-bencher, who got to his feet to declaim the immorality of an empire that could permit a prison regime of this kind to exist. He went on to declare that Britain had no right to an empire if it could not show moral leadership of a higher order. That young back-bencher was none other than Enoch Powell – then a rising star of the right, and a man who could normally be relied upon to defend the interests of kith and kin in the empire. If Powell and his like were wavering, then the game of empire really was up in Kenya.

# 8

# Spoils of War: Decolonizing Kenya, Memorializing Mau Mau

By the early months of 1957 the forest armies had been broken, their remnants scattered in the remote mountains. The best-known leaders were by then either hanged, taken captive or presumed dead. The loyalists ruled Kikuyuland with a rod of iron. Kenya's Mau Mau freedom fighters had lost their war against the British. The 'civil disturbance' was coming to an end.

To the imperial power, however, this did not feel like much of a victory. The scandal of the detention camps blew up, slowly at first as the breeze caught word of unsanitary conditions and heavy labour, then a raging storm as the reality of brutality against prisoners was revealed. The reports on Hola made difficult reading, but the Kenya administration managed its usual trick of blaming the junior staff. The Fairn Report, commissioned from London to look at the whole camps system, offered a more honest assessment: mistakes of judgement had been made at the highest level with the introduction of a policy of 'shock treatment' and physical abuse.[1]

This all clouded the future. How was Kenya's police state to be dismantled in Kikuyuland? How could the remaining 1600 or so detainees be released if they were not 'rehabilitated'? Things should return to normal, but in Kenya no one seemed any longer to know what normal was. Margery Perham, who in the 1930s had caught the attraction of the settlers' sunny lives in Kenya, now thought the place to be drenched in 'a pathological atmosphere'.[2] Kenya seemed strangely out of step with everywhere else. Iain MacLeod, who became Secretary of State for the Colonies in the Macmillan government after 1959 election that followed Hola, thought that Kenya was locked into an 'emergency mentality'.[3]

If peace was going to be made in Kenya, then these things had to change. Within a few months of coming into the job, MacLeod, the canny bridge player, had already weighed up his possible moves. Over the seven years since the Emergency had begun in 1952, Britain's world role had been steadily changing, the empire slowly coming to its inevitable end. It was now the task of the Secretary of State for the Colonies to find ways to lessen British commitments. Wars were too costly; and empire wars could be costliest of all. Oliver Lyttelton had been at the helm when Britain got sucked into this mess – though even with hindsight it was difficult to see how he could have avoided it. Even as he signed the orders to detain the first supposed leaders of Kenya's rebellion, the flags were already being lowered in other parts of Britain's empire.

By the time that Lennox-Boyd replaced him, decolonization had been accepted as a necessary step, even in places where that might require deft handling. Malaya, Sudan, Ghana and the West Indies, all places where such a transition required careful footwork, each saw the Union Jack lowered. Even the divided regions of Nigeria moved towards a rapid decolonization as a federal state, though the political settlement merely papered over the cracks of deep internal divisions that would all too soon pull the country apart. The Suez crisis of 1956, reaching its apogee in the very week that Dedan Kimathi was shot and captured on the fringe of the Aberdares forest, proved to be Britain's final fling of the imperial age, a woeful misjudgement that would cost Anthony Eden his reputation and his leadership of the Conservative government. An epoch was ending, and Britain could not stand by and let Kenya retain its old form of colonial domination when other places were moving on to a new, post-imperial relationship.[4] A rash of nationalist conflagrations had by then broken out all over the empire's body politic, and they could no longer be contained either by persuasion or by military might. Lennox-Boyd had run around making and mending to fairly good effect, until Hola and the Central African Federation riots in Nyasaland went up at the same time in 1959 and burned him badly. He gracefully waited until Harold Macmillan's government had won the election of 1959, and then gave up his post.[5]

It was now Iain MacLeod's turn. He would be responsible for devising an exit strategy for the most awkward child still in the imperial fold, Kenya. Prime Minister Harold Macmillan, who took over from Eden after the humiliation of Suez, had compiled a 'balance sheet of empire'. He resolved to be rid of the African colonies as speedily as could be managed. Kenya's emergency had cost a princely £55 million. There were cheaper ways of securing influence in the world.[6]

MacLeod revelled in his role as the progressive new broom to sweep away the old empire. By November 1959 he knew what should be done, though not yet quite how to do it.[7] Kenya needed to 'wipe the slate clean'. The first step was to dismantle the 'legal framework of the Emergency'. This edifice so dominated the place that people could think of nothing else. Bitterness and resentment had to be overcome, and wounds allowed time to heal. The demilitarization of Kikuyuland was already well advanced. The problem was that the system of detention camps festered like an open wound. Having for so long sought to convince the world of the evil disease that was Mau Mau, Kenya's administration found it difficult to conceive of the means by which these sick, depraved monsters could now be released without having accepted 'the cure'; but the scandals were becoming an increasing embarrassment to London. Aside from the Hola tragedy, there had been several other deaths in the camps as a result of 'excessive force'. Six African warders had been imprisoned over recent months, and there had been other cases and enquiries besides. More were pending, and the prospect of another major scandal, implicating senior colonial officials, could not be ruled out.

Though it would be tricky, MacLeod resolved to close as many camps as possible as speedily as could be managed, allowing the 1600 Kikuyu still detained to return to their homes – whether 'cured' or not. Another amnesty, applicable to loyalists and rebels alike, might also be needed to 'clear the air' and remove any chance of further legal cases being mounted to seek redress for past wrongs. This would bring Kenya's pathology to an end.

## Coming Home

As Britain prepared to come home, and the traumatic decade drew to a close, there was a changing of the guard. Baring went in 1959. He had stayed at least two years too long and now, it seemed, it might have been better had he never come at all. He was, with the advantage of hindsight, no longer the right man to manage an emergency. He was not decisive enough, nor sufficiently open to win the full confidence of those around him. The squabble between his legal officers and his senior administrative staff contributed to the culture of impunity among the KPR and the Home Guard, a culture that had even come to infect the Governor's own thinking.

Baring's replacement was Patrick Renison. He relished the job and prided himself on getting along well with African nationalists. They didn't get along so well with him. Renison read Corfield's second-rate report on the causes of the Emergency and let it tarnish his view. In his first public speech he made the gaff of declaring Kenyatta to be 'the leader to darkness and death'. The 'time was not right' for his release, Renison said. The speech was a dreadful mistake, from which the new Governor would never recover.[8] Even MacLeod thought it pompous and silly. The Secretary of State had a hot-line to Kenya through his brother Roddie, a liberal-minded settler, that served him better than anything the Governor could drum up. In the end, Renison would not even get the reflected glory of the handover: Malcolm

Macdonald would come in for the final push to independence, in 1963.

Governors came and went; it was London that now called the shots. The sidelining of Nairobi had been apparent since Lyttelton presented Baring with the new constitution in 1954: no negotiation, no prevarication, and no grumbling about the 'sensibilities of the settlers'; the white highlanders would be listened to no more. MacLeod took all the crucial decisions on Kenya's decolonization between 1959 and 1961. The aim was to broker a deal that would secure a conservative succession. There would be majority African rule, but there would be no place at the table for rebels, or for anyone else whose views were too radical. Asians and whites could participate, too, but their protections under the multi-racial constitution of the 1950s would be phased out. This was a bitter pill that would have to be swallowed.

The white highlanders did pose a possible stumbling block, however. Macmillan feared they might yet scare up enough elderly Tories in the House of Lords, and influence enough stuffy newspaper editors, to cause trouble; but he need not have worried. Even these old guard were by 1960 too embarrassed by Kenya's excesses to trouble themselves. Most thought, like Enoch Powell, who had so eloquently condemned his own government in the debate on Hola, that it was time to let go.

MacLeod took the bridge player's gamble, and presented the white highlanders a *fait accompli* at the first set of talks, at London's Lancaster House, in 1960. Majority rule would come in, with an open franchise. They were promised a fair price for their land, but no other concessions that mattered. The settlers' leaders were outraged. Blundell, who had by then already committed to multi-racialism, took it better than his right-wing compatriots, though they blamed his complicity and double-dealing for their plight. One of them threw a bag of silver coins at his feet, but Kenya's white Judas did not bend to pick them up. Blundell's power-brokering ultimately left him without friends on any side.[9] The Kenya economy briefly plummeted on the news of the transition, but things gradually stabilized again. Those white highlanders who were keen to make a fight of it lobbied hard with their friends, but the bad odour around Hola, and the continuing whiff of other scandals too, hung in the air. The white highlands were no more. Erskine's 'middle-class sluts' would have to put up with black masters, or come home.

Those white farmers who opted to leave could sell up their land under a government-sponsored programme, the Million Acre Scheme. The buyers were wealthier Africans, who could afford it. Around Central Province these buyers were invariably loyalists. Some efforts were made to give poorer Kikuyu land, especially in the Kinangop area, where it was feared that landless radicals might simply seize what they wanted from whites on the eve of independence.[10] The government became very alarmed by the emergence of new movements of landless Kikuyu peasants, the Kiama Kia Muingi and the Kenya Land and Freedom Army, that sprang up at this time, fearing that a second Mau Mau might be under way. Even as detainees were being released from the camps, adherents of both these movements were being arrested and imprisoned.

The outpouring of detainees into Kikuyuland brought a flood of poor migrants, reminiscent of the squatter evictions that had marked the beginnings of Mau Mau's violence. The last to return, and coming in the largest numbers, were those whom the British had considered most dangerous and who took longest to get through the 'pipeline'. In 1956 19,000 were released, and in 1957 nearly 21,000 returned to Central Province; in 1958 the figure was 15,000.

Inevitably, it was not always a happy homecoming. Some had lost land, like the Mau Mau militant Bildad Kaggia who had gone into detention with Kenyatta, or had had property taken by the Home Guard or confiscated in collective punishments.[11] They needed to find work. Everything was now dominated and controlled by loyalists. At Othaya, and in other areas where the war had been fought hard, such as southern Murang'a, the divisions between loyalists and the released detainees ran deep.[12] They feared one another. The released men mostly had restriction orders, so they could not travel far. And they wanted jobs. But the loyalists remained in the driving seat.

Coming home would be a difficult experience for many. Karari Njama found that his wife had been raped by Home Guards in 1955 and had given birth to a child.[13] Josiah Kariuki was moved along the pipeline to the works camp, at the Showground in Nyeri Town, just a few miles from his home in Othaya, in October 1958, where he discovered his mother had died. On 9 December he was taken to Othaya. A police constable lectured him: Kariuki must first report to his chief, then his headman. A further report must be made to the chief's office every Wednesday. Kariuki would be expected to do communal labour when requested and to obey any curfew. With these instructions, he walked out of the gates of the police station as a free man. Well, nearly free: he still lived under an order restricting his movements.[14] Joram Wamweya and Karigo Muchai both returned to unemployment, poverty and misery.[15] Detainees were constantly reminded that they now lived in the shadow of their loyalist enemies. In one of the bitterest observations of the returned detainees, Kariuki observed: 'The whole country seemed to be in detention with the village as the compound and the works camps as the small cells. We are not released from anything.'[16]

Many of the men drifted immediately into politics again, although they were prohibited from doing so. Kariuki recalls attending a large political meeting in Othaya, where the candidates for the Legislative Council were to give speeches, and found that many of his old friends from the camps were already employed as 'marshals' and organizers at the rally.[17]

The government didn't want these men in politics of any kind. African political parties had been banned under the Emergency regulations in June 1953, until the introduction of the Lyttelton Constitution in 1954 opened the door to African and Asian participation in central government through an electoral system. But this reform was closely controlled. From June 1955 political parties were again permitted, but only at district level and with the discretion of colonial officials. No parties at all were permitted to register in the Mau Mau heartlands of Central Province.[18] The aim of these colonial reforms, Ogot has astutely observed, 'was to create a base upon which a collaborative African leadership could emerge and to undermine the support of Mau Mau freedom fighters'.[19]

The Legislative Council elections of 1956 and 1957 were the first test of the colonial capacity to 're-make' African politics beyond Mau Mau. African politicians stood for election to the Legislative Council as individuals, not as members of parties; many of the candidates were 'encouraged' to stand by local colonial officials. In Kikuyuland they were all, by definition, loyalists. Their electorate was selected by a qualified franchise, defined on the basis of income, education and government service. This gave some electors two votes, others three; and in Kikuyuland one had to have a loyalty certificate to be eligible to vote. The three Kikuyu elected representatives on the Legislative Council, Bernard Mate, J. G. Kiano and Jeremiah Nyagah, were expected to look after the interests of the constituency that had voted for them – the loyalists. The rebels were locked out of politics.

However, as MacLeod pushed the Kenya administration to empty the camps, more and more of the most determined rebels returned. It was not surprising that the loyalists got nervous. There were quarrels, threats and one or two incidents during 1958 and 1959, especially in Nyeri and Embu. Chiefs and headmen were given bodyguards. People kept to themselves, loyalists separate from rebels. In the most divided communities, such as Lari and Othaya, they drank in different bars, even bought their goods at different stores. Many loyalists worried that retribution would come when Kenyatta returned, or when the British left. They hoped that neither would happen. The war was over, but for those who came home to Kikuyuland, the struggle continued.

## Kenyatta: 'The Reconciler'

Kenyatta came home by stages. From Lokitaung, in the far, far north close to the Sudan border, he was moved to Lodwar, and then to Maralal, still 180 miles south of Nairobi. It was as if he was being pushed along his own, private pipeline to eventual rehabilitation.

At Maralal his family was allowed to visit and to stay with him. The climate was far more to his liking, and he began to put on weight again – in Lokitaung he had looked thin and unwell. He was allowed the freedom to walk around the small town. 'It is like coming from hell to heaven,' Kenyatta said. Renison allowed the international press to have an audience with the 'leader to darkness and death', hoping that they would debunk his reputation. Nothing of the sort happened. Kenyatta came across as dignified, intelligent, thoughtful and far from bitter about his experience.[20] Renison had got it wrong again.

On the morning of 14 August 1961 Kenyatta arrived home, to Gatundu in Kiambu, wearing his trademark belted leather jacket and looking robustly healthy. By then the Emergency had officially come to an end and Corfield's report on the origins of Mau Mau had been released to the public. The white highlanders were delighted to read confirmation that Kenyatta was the leader of Mau Mau; they were now horrified to see him released from custody. Kenyatta spent the next week ensconced with his family. He then picked up the reins of his political career once again, and began a whirl of meetings and discussions.[21]

Kenyatta had two political parties to choose from. Both wanted him as leader. He rejected the Kenya African Democratic Union (KADU), and joined the Kenya African National Union (KANU), but not before asking a few searching questions. KANU was Kenyatta's natural home. The party was a rebirth of the old KAU, with additional strong support from the Luo of the Lake region; but Kenyatta, having once been burned by his previous affiliations, had no wish to join a party that might again succumb to the influence of Mau Mau's hooligans. He needed reassurance that the men of KANU would hold firm against irresponsible influences. The party Kenyatta agreed to lead was to be moderate, and essentially conservative in its politics. The old constitutional nationalist had not changed very much.

But as KANU approached the elections of May 1963 that would take Kenya to independence later that year with Kenyatta as its head, it was by no means a party exclusively for loyalists. Many former rebels were KANU members. Some of these stood as parliamentary candidates for the party, and some were even given junior ministries in the first government that Kenyatta formed after winning the election. Waruhiu Itote, Bildad Kaggia and Fred Kubai would all be acknowledged in this way. Some KANU branches were dominated by ex-detainees, notably in Nyeri. The inclusion of these people was reconciliation, of a kind; but the cadre of colleagues that Kenyatta assembled around himself at the top of the party remained steadfastly moderate, and anti-Mau Mau, for several years to come. Men such as J. G. Kiano and Njeroge Mungai represented the loyalist faction, while older allies, such as James Gichuru and Mbiyu Koinange, came from the same constitutional nationalist tradition as did Kenyatta himself.

KANU's runaway victory in the national elections of 1963 swept Kenyatta into power as Kenya's first president. MacLeod's aim, of handing over to reliable, conservative allies had been achieved. The constitutional nationalists ruled independent Kenya. As the British packed their bags, they prided themselves that so difficult an imperial disengagement had been so smoothly achieved.

The problems that remained were now Kenyatta's to worry about. KANU's leaders had stressed the need for party unity to win the election. Rebels and loyalists alike had been dissuaded from challenging the candidacy of their opponents within the party. This had sometimes been difficult, and it would not get any easier now that the British had gone, for the wounds of the civil war went deeper.

Kenyatta had once been called *Muigwathania* – The Reconciler. It had been the name of the KCA new-sheet he had edited in the 1920s. He needed all those skills in the early years of independence to hold the ring as loyalists and rebels circled around one another within KANU, and within the government. He often spoke of the need to 'forgive and forget', and 'to bury the past'. He acknowledged the part the freedom fighters had played in the struggle, but he never once made any public statement that conceded to them any rights or any genuine compensation. Mau Mau was a thing best forgotten.

This was Kenyatta's way of handling the divisions of the past. Shortly after independence, as a gesture to peace and forgiveness, Kenyatta attended a ceremony at Nyeri to 'welcome' back those still living in the Mount Kenya forests. The football stadium in Nyeri Town was crammed with 30,000 people. Many had come hoping that they would find their relatives, still alive after all. Nearly a thousand rebels walked out of the forest that day, to shake Kenyatta by the hand and rejoin their families in an independent Kenya.

These men thought of themselves as victors, and did not feel defeated. They had refused to come out of the forests until the colonialists had gone; and they now expected to be rewarded for their victory – with land, and property, and the freedom they had fought for. Kenyatta's views were less transparent. As he mingled with them, posing to have photographs taken, he appeared pensive and uncomfortable. When he spoke, his words betrayed the fear in his mind. Looking at the remnants of Mau Mau's rag-tag army, Kenyatta told the crowd: 'What they have done in the past is forgotten. These people in the forest have been hunted like animals just because of politics. Now they are back with us. Now we have got our freedom. . . . Is it not what we have struggled for? Now you must help the government, because it is not a European or Asian who is ruling you but an African government.'[22] These were not his people. They had no political legitimacy, no right to speak for anyone but themselves. Kenyatta would never reward them, for he did not believe they should be rewarded. But he feared their dissenting voices.

At a rally a few months earlier, Kenyatta had been asked about Mau Mau. His answer had been unequivocal: 'We shall not allow hooligans to rule Kenya,' he had replied. 'Mau Mau was a disease which has been eradicated and must never be remembered again,' he would later write.[23] In Kenyatta's Kenya there would be a deafening silence about Mau Mau.

## Monuments, Museums, Movies

The Kenyan nation celebrates its independence each year, on 12 December. Uhuru Day is for national affirmation. 'We all fought for freedom' was its message when Kenyatta was president. The public memories of detention camps, of massacres, of punishments, and of dispossession were suppressed. National unity was the message. But the fact that Kenyatta had to keep reminding Kenyans again and again *not* to talk about Mau Mau was in itself pregnant with meaning. A thin veneer hid the truth: that just below the surface of public life, Mau Mau was being talked about all the time.

Old comrades from the war did what old comrades from wars do: they formed old comrades' associations. There were dozens of Mau Mau associations throughout Kikuyuland in the 1960s, and many of them are still going strong. A few wasted away as their members died, but others came into life, prompted by renewed interest in the history of Kenya's struggles as the country returned to political pluralism in the 1990s. By 2001 there were reckoned to be as many as thirty different Mau Mau groups.[24] Among their members are not just the surviving fighters themselves, but their families, including the sons and daughters of men who died in the forest. To these people, memorializing Mau Mau matters in lots of ways.

In Nyeri town the struggle for remembrance has never ebbed. Sitting on the side of a long, curving ridge, Nyeri looks toward the Aberdares. Behind the town, rising up into the cloud that so often cloaks these hills, is Mount Kenya. It is an imposing setting. The town has sprawled along the ridge since the 1950s, a straggle of wooden and wattle-and-daub buildings, their corrugated-tin roofs glinting between the trees and rolling greenery. The centre of town has none of this charm. It is scruffy, run-down, and displays all the signs and smells of poverty and decay. It was wealthier in the 1950s, and more sedate: a farming town, supplying the local agricultural community with their needs. But Nyeri has been overwhelmed since then by the sheer press of humanity. The central area is busier now, every square foot of pavement occupied by vendors selling second-hand clothes and plastic crockery, or vegetables and fruit. The town has a ragged, faded, half-finished feel about it: everything is happening here, but nothing quite works as well as it should. Nyeri distils the essence of rural Africa.

Block and concrete buildings line the main highway into the town, many of the older ones built during the Emergency as offices for the colonial staff who poured into Nyeri to fight Mau Mau. All around, there are memories of the Emergency. But one dominates all the others. As you drive into town, you come to the traffic island in the highway where the road turns towards the old market, and there it is. It resembles the war memorials of Europe. The tall, thick, tapering concrete obelisk is set on a dais, with steps up from the road. Its original inscription was in honour of the loyalists and soldiers of Nyeri who died in the struggle to defeat Mau Mau; but in more recent times the rebels have repossessed the past here, seizing this little symbolic space for themselves. The obelisk is now Nyeri's monument to the freedom fighters.

As Kenya celebrates the nation's freedom on Uhuru Day, each December, veterans gather at the obelisk to commemorate their war, in February, on Kimathi Day. To those who were in the forests, the anniversary of Dedan Kimathi's execution carries more meaning than the anniversary of the country's independence. It also carries a shrill message: Kenya has thrown off colonialism, but those who went to the forest still wait for their grievances to be addressed. The rebels lost the war, and the loyalists won the peace. The struggle continues.

Back down the hill from the monument, Nyeri has another site of remembrance. The little dirt road turning back along the ridge leads past a modern development of flats to a ramshackle bar and lodging house. The corrugated-tin buildings are painted in garish blue, yellow and red. Through the small gate there is a warren of rooms, most of them laid with tables and chairs. This is a large bar, with a dance floor and a raised stage. Local bands perform on a Saturday night. There's a barbecue to one side, where the goat meat is roasted: drinking the local Tusker beer can make you hungry. There is even a pool room, with three tables, frayed and worn to be sure, but still functional. On a weekend this is one of Nyeri's hottest spots.

Back in the courtyard a set of rickety wooden steps leads up to another door and another room. This is not part of the bar. Above the door a painted sign tells the visitor that this is Nyeri's Peace Museum. The small, oblong room is crammed with tables, along the walls and in the centre, each loaded with artefacts: an old typewriter, said to be the same

as the one used in the Aberdares by Kimathi's scribe Njama; some old
identity papers from the 1950s; tax receipts; loyalty certificates; copies
of documents declaring collective punishments in Nyeri, and others
announcing rewards for information 'leading to the capture of terrorists';
copies of entries in the land registry, and newspaper cuttings about Home
Guards and captives. There is even a tattered copy of Henderson's book
about Kimathi. Stuck to the walls are photographs, many of them
downloaded and printed from archive web sites. It can be difficult to
recognize the grey and grainy scene, yet the captions provide clues. Most
of the pictures are portraits of Nyeri men who fought in the war – there
are Mau Mau fighters, usually photographed after capture, looking tired,
hungry and bitter; and there are loyalist chiefs and headmen, regaled in
traditional dress and looking fierce and determined, or smiling to the
camera in smart khaki suits, only the short pants giving away any sense
of subordination. Rebels and loyalists are mixed together on these walls.
One people, divided in struggle.

This little museum, started by a small group of elderly Christians, is
intended as a memorial to the war, though not to any particular side in
the struggle. The organizing committee comprises loyalists and rebels,
now brought together by a shared church affiliation; and by shared
memories. The museum contains no items of war – no guns, no pangas,
nothing at all to do with violence. Most of those who visit the museum
are children, brought there on school trips to learn about their nation's
past. It has been a success, and there are plans to open a similar museum
at Lari. The message is peace and reconciliation. To achieve that, the
forest fighters must be acknowledged, not ignored. In its quiet little way,
this is a deeply subversive place.

The photographs and the text for the captions stuck to the walls of
Nyeri's Peace Museum have mostly been obtained through the cooperation of staff from Kenya's National Archives in Nairobi. They are very
used to Kenyans coming to look for information about the war. The
reading room of the National Archive, its tall windows opening onto
the square in front of the Hilton Hotel, is packed every day with Kenyans
searching for their past, looking to fill the silence with noise. They can
order books from the library and they can read the surviving files from
the colonial period. There is plenty here that can tell the story.

Those who come to the National Archive can also see films about
Mau Mau. Every Saturday morning the Archive stages a film show. Most
of the films are educational and many of them are historical. It is a
popular occasion. Parties of schoolchildren come, and so do many
university students. Some of the films are originals of those made by the
colonial government, others video copies pirated more recently.

Films dealing with Mau Mau are by far the most popular. The

documentaries are avidly taken in, but for entertainment there is nothing to beat the feature films. Astonishingly, there were three movies made about Mau Mau while the war was still going on.[25] More surprising still, these were not salvoes in the propaganda war but high-quality independent productions, made by the major studios and starring leading actors of the day – Rock Hudson, Victor Mature and Dirk Bogarde all played white highlanders, battling against Sidney Poitier, Orlando Martins and Earl Cameron on the rebel side. These 'jungle adventures' were popular in the 1950s. Now, half a century later, with footage of Nairobi's streets in the Emergency, of fortified Home Guard posts, and of Mau Mau prisoners, chained and carrying out heavy labour, these films give Kenyans a vivid representation of their war.

Inevitably, stereotypes shape the plots of each movie. In *Simba* (Rank, 1955) it is British paternalism – the roughnecks amongst the settlers are dismissed, but the 'good' Brits still know 'their Africans'. In *Safari* (MGM, 1956) Victor Mature plays a white hunter who sets out to kill the Mau Mau. There is no explanation of the rebellion here: only violence. 'Not a minute passes', wrote one critic in the 1950s, 'without someone being minced with a bush knife, blown up by dynamite, buried in a landslide, pounded under a waterfall, trampled by a rhino, or cut in half by a sten-gun.'[26]

The third film, *Something of Value* (Columbia, 1957), based on Ruark's novel of the same name, is more interesting. Published in 1955, Ruark's book enjoyed best-selling popularity with the US public, being chosen as a Book of the Month club selection and emerging as the sixth-best-selling novel in the USA in 1955, with sales of 93,757. Columbia Pictures reportedly paid £300,000 for the film rights,[27] and then recruited the American director Richard Brooks to make the movie. Fresh from his success with *Blackboard Jungle*, he rewrote Ruark's plot and turned the film into a tale that reflected America's civil rights struggle: Brooks was 'looking at some American crisis and its resolution, not at an African one'.[28] He replaced Ruark's unremitting portrayal of African savagery with a 'reap what you sow' narrative, implying that the white highlanders got what they deserved. It's a message that has some appeal to Kenyan audiences.

But *Simba*, *Safari* and *Something of Value* are not historical documentaries. There is no balance, no effort to explain or understand, just fast action and a good story. Not even the earnest *Something of Value* can get to grips with the struggle between loyalists and rebels. Here, once again, is Mau Mau as psychosis, as evil infection and 'impulsive savagery', living on in celluloid long after everyone has given up reading the likes of Leakey and Carothers, or even Ruark and Majdalany. These movies help us to understand why the 'received wisdom' of the Mau Mau war is as it is. In Nyeri, the generation who lived through the Emergency know that the reality was far more complex; but maybe the youngsters who watch these Mau Mau movies are losing that message; and that is why the Mau Mau associations, Kimathi Day and the Peace Museum matter so much. All these things are still part of Mau Mau's daily discourse.

The same elders who set up the Nyeri Peace Museum have established a Peace Garden in the smaller town of Othaya, a few miles into the hills from Nyeri. In the garden they have planted indigenous trees that represent peace and reconciliation. To create this place of tranquillity and reflection they have chosen one of the battlefields of the war, a place, quite literally, where the bones were laid.

The garden is situated on the slope below the old site of the Othaya police post, attacked by Mau Mau in 1953 in a bold attempt to release the prisoners held there. The attackers were beaten back and fled under a hail of machine-gun fire and grenades. More than a dozen were killed. Afterwards, the police threw their bodies into a mass grave and left it unmarked. Rebels got no dignity, even in death. But the people of Othaya need no stone or cross to know the place. They honoured those who lay there, and thirty years later the local Mau Mau association raised some money and began construction of a Memorial Hall on the site. Dedan Kimathi had told his followers that some day there would be such monuments all over Kenya to commemorate the great deeds of the forest fighters. When they were digging out the foundations for the building, they found the bones. They put them to one side, planning to have the remains properly reburied in consecrated ground.

But then something strange happened. A politician sent men with a lorry. They gathered up the bones and took them away. No one in Othaya knows where the bones were taken, though they like to speculate that this is yet another sign of the fear that Kenya's moderate leaders have of the power of Mau Mau's memory. Even in death, they say, the bones of the fighters haunt the living who betray their memory.[29]

The bones are long gone, and the Othaya Memorial Hall is still unfinished. The money ran out, or someone ran away with it. But the Peace Garden is there, a fragile symbol of healing and of reconciliation, but also an acknowledgement of the many lives lost on both sides.

## Mathenge's Return

Among the forest leaders who remain unaccounted for, it is Stanley Mathenge, Kimathi's rival for leadership in the forests, who has attracted the most attention. Mathenge was never captured and, despite repeated rumours that he had been killed, at the end of the war the British believed he had retreated to the forests beyond Meru, on the far north side of Mount Kenya. It was said that a pseudo-gang had chased Mathenge and the last of his men into Kenya's vast Northern Province. Some tall tales were told of forest fighters turning up in Maralal, and in the semi-arid deserts beyond; but after 1957 no more was heard of Stanley Mathenge for many years.

Then, nearly thirty years later, in April 1986, the Kenya press carried the news that Mathenge had been found. He was living in a small village, in southern Ethiopia. The journalist who claimed to have tracked him down reported that other freedom fighters lived in the same area, maybe a hundred of them, the remnants of the band that had accompanied Mathenge into exile. Mathenge was by then seventy-two years old. He had married an Ethiopian woman, and there were children. Mathenge sent greetings to his wife in Nyeri, whom he had not seen since 1952, but declared that he did not want to return to Kenya as the things he had fought for had not been achieved. The report ended by asking whether 'the lost hero would ever return to the motherland'.[30]

Was this story to be taken at face value? Or was it a clever way of raising issues of dissent and of silence about Kenya's past? The same questions arose again in 2002, when Mathenge's life in southern Ethiopia was featured in the Kenya press for the second time. The newspapers ran the story over several months, until eventually, in 2003, Mathenge returned, brought home at the expense of a Kenyan newspaper. On arrival in Nairobi the frail old man appeared startled and desperately uncertain of his surroundings. He was treated as a celebrity, with a car and driver, and an elaborate team of minders guarded him at a good hotel on the hill just above Uhuru Park. People wanted to shake the hero by the hand, and to acknowledge his part in the struggle for independence. His wife and other family members were brought to see him. Then the doubts began to be aired: was this *really* Mathenge? His appearance was not convincing when compared to old photographs, and he seemed not to remember things. Why was he so tongue-tied? and why did he not seem to speak Kikuyu? The intrigue and speculation ran for weeks, until, finally, he was declared a fraud. This was not Stanley Mathenge at all, just a cruel scam that played upon the lust of the Kenyan public to know about the freedom fighters and their struggle.

At the time the Mathenge story resurfaced there was much else besides in the Kenyan press about Mau Mau. A British lawyer was setting out to take a case to court on behalf of the Mau Mau veterans, to ask for reparations from the British. If British officers had committed war crimes during the Emergency, should they not be prosecuted now? In Africa's age of atonement, born after 1994 out of the ending of apartheid and Rwanda's genocide, Kenya would have its turn to set right the wrongs of the past. There was talk of staging a Truth and Reconciliation Commission, following the example of South Africa, to deal with all of the many crimes that had been perpetrated by the agents of the State, both under colonialism and since. In the early months of 2004 the Kenya government gave its backing to such a commission, one part of which would be dedicated to crimes from the colonial period. Wrapped up within these discussions there was considerable speculation about Kimathi's final resting place – what had the British done with his body? Why was there no grave? Where could Kenyans go to commemorate their national hero?

When gathering material for their short play *The Trial of Dedan Kimathi*, Ngugi wa Thiong'o and Miceru Mugo visited Nyeri to speak to those who had known him. It was 1974. It had been seventeen years since the execution. Local people were proud to show the rebel hero's birthplace, the spot in the ditch along the forest edge where he had been shot, and to tell of how his deranged, elderly mother had once been allowed to visit her son in Nyeri prison. Yet when Ngugi asked about Kimathi's death, about the execution itself, the response was hostile and bitter: 'Kimathi will never die,' an old woman defiantly shouted, 'but of course if you people have killed him, go and show us his grave.'[31]

The quest for Kimathi's grave, the search to find his bones, became an obsession for many who wished to celebrate the freedom fighter's achievements. It is not that Kenyans disbelieved he was hanged: rather, they recognized that the denial of mourning, the lack of a place to visit to honour the dead, was part of the conduct of the war. The lack of commemoration is a kind of punishment, and it is a punishment that has continued long after colonialism's end. The anxiety about this symbolizes the national unease that the Mau Mau war has not yet found closure. To locate Kimathi's body, and to give him a proper burial, would satisfy that need to have 'somewhere to go' – a place to mark the suffering of the struggle.

Of course, in the 1950s this is precisely what the British did *not* want. Graves might too easily have become places of pilgrimage, symbols of continued resistance. The dangers were all too clear to Winston Churchill when, in 1953, he instructed Oliver Lyttelton, that 'care should be taken to avoid the simultaneous execution of any large numbers of persons who might be sentenced to death by these courts'. Churchill was warning Lyttelton not to make rebels into martyrs.[32]

So the British did not return the bodies of the hanged Mau Mau convicts to their families. Instead, they removed them from the gallows and took them to the grounds of Kamiti prison. There, the bodies were laid to rest in unmarked graves, all the dead from the hangman's grisly work that morning laid down together. That is where Kimathi has been all these years: at rest alongside all the others – the 1090 gallows victims of Britain's dirty war.

The catalyst for the swirl of public debate about Mau Mau, which was first swept up during 2002 was the general election of December that year, in which Kenyans voted in a new government. Kenyatta had died in 1978, but his party, KANU, continued to rule the country. Finally, after forty years in government, KANU had been voted out of office. With the new government, attitudes to the memory of Mau Mau changed. The order that had remained in place since 1952 banning Mau Mau as an illegal organization was at last rescinded, and it was announced that the government would inaugurate a proper search for Kimathi's remains and that he would be given a proper burial. The new government intended to set aside an area in Uhuru Park, in the centre of Nairobi, for the creation of a national site of commemoration. Kimathi would be laid to rest in Heroes' Acre.

Elsewhere in central Kenya the steady haul of human bones keeps surfacing. There are unmarked graves from the Mau Mau war all over Kikuyuland. Some of them hold the remains of rebels and suspects, killed by the security forces. Other graves hold the remains of people executed by Mau Mau. Some sites have long been known about, like the one at Othaya; others have been rediscovered only as the bones come up. Several burial grounds have been quietly protected over the years, including two in Kiambu, close to Nairobi. In these places local people have prevented any development on the land. A recent attempt to build on one site, close to Dagoretti, caused a public outcry. The land itself is inscribed with memories of Mau Mau.

Should the bones from all these many sites of conflict be brought to Heroes' Acre? and if they are, can the rebels be sorted from the loyalists? Should remains of loyalists be buried in Heroes' Acre, alongside Kimathi? It is a controversy that will have to be addressed. The divisions these questions expose are still deeply felt. Those who survived the Lari massacre, for example, have little sympathy for the idea that Mau Mau fighters should be honoured, let alone compensated for their losses. For Gacheri Wakahangare, the widow of ex-Chief Luka, who was herself maimed in the Lari attack and still grieves for the two children she saw butchered before her eyes, the very thought of compensation for the Mau Mau fighters only rubs salt in the wounds. 'Who will compensate us?' she asks. 'They killed our children.'[33]

Those still seeking emotional closure stand on both sides of the war. The dead have not been properly buried, the graves are unmarked, and the horrors of what happened are largely unresolved for rebels and loyalists alike. Heroes' Acre, that little slice of Uhuru Park set aside as a memorial to the war, presents an opportunity to deepen these divisions, or to try to heal them. The advocates of Heroes' Acre want to create a memorial to the 'freedom fighters', most obviously those who led the fight in the forest;

but what about all of those others buried at Kamiti, in the unmarked pits reserved for the unclaimed bodies of the hanged? They surely belong in Heroes' Acre too. And what about the loyalist dead, left to rot in shallow graves after Mau Mau's assassins had done their work? If the loyalist dead were to join the freedom fighters in Heroes' Acre, then Kenya might really begin to take some steps toward reconciliation and recognition.

The National Museum of Kenya is the place to find bones. There they have collections of all kinds of skeletal remains, covering everything from dinosaurs to the earliest examples of human life. Among the collections they hold is one that is more recent in age. It is a set of some 475 human skeletons. Not all the skeletons are complete. Some have limbs missing, and others lack the skull. The card index that accompanies this collection describes the bones in scientific terms, and includes records of any damage to the bones, and especially of any signs of the injuries that may have caused death. Most of the skeletons here died violently: the records show many head injuries and broken bones.

At the front of the box holding the cards that record the facts about each skeleton, is a simple explanatory note about the origins of the collection. It reads:

> The skeletons of this collection are the remains of Africans (mostly of the Kikuyu tribe) who were killed during the great emergency of 1952–1960. They were uncovered and exhumed by the police and were then used as evidence against the Mau Mau by Her Majesty's Police. This collection was generously donated to Dr Leakey by Dr Morris Rogoff, then the Chief Police Pathologist.

These 475 skeletons are the bodies exhumed from graves during the Emergency. They include the victims of Mau Mau courts in Nairobi, dug up during Operation Anvil, and the many loyalists who were murdered in Mau Mau assaults. They come from all over Kikuyuland. The collection is a grisly reminder of how bitterly this war was fought. Although the identity of a skeleton was often known, the remains were held by the police pathologist while prosecution was still pending. As evidence was gathered, some of the murders relating to these skeletons came to trial; but after the cases were heard, no one bothered to ask the relatives to collect the remains. Instead, they were kept by the pathologist until he, finally, gave them to Louis Leakey at the museum.

That is where they still sit: in boxes, on the shelves of the National Museum. It is time to bury these skeletons, each of them a victim of Kenya's struggle for independence. Heroes' Acre would seem as good a place as any.

# Appendix: Tables

**Table 1.i: Kenya's population by race, selected years, 1905–63**

| Year | White pop. (no of farms) | African pop. | Asian pop. |
|------|--------------------------|--------------|------------|
| 1905/06 | 1,813 | | |
| 1911 | 3,175 | | 9,241 |
| 1914 | 5,438 | | |
| 1921 | 9,651 (1,346) | 2,493,600 | 22,822 |
| 1926 | 12,529 (1,809) | | |
| 1931 | 16,812 (2,106) | 2,969,000 | 39,644 |
| 1936 | 18,269 (1,807) | | |
| 1938 | 20,894 (1,890) | 3,280,774 | |
| 1948 | 29,700 (2,200) | 5,321,000 | 97,700 |
| 1953 | 42,200 | | 131,000 |
| 1956 | 54,000 | | 149,000 |
| 1958 | 59,000 | | 161,000 |
| 1960 | 61,000 | | 169,000 |
| 1963 | 53,000 | 8,600,000 | 180,000 |

Sources: Kennedy, *Islands of White*, 197; Anderson & Throup, 24; Parker, 3–6; Low & Smith, OHEA iii, 576–7

**Table 2.i: Nyeri Christmas Eve attacks, December 1952: the convictions**

| Name | Trial | Date | Judge | Charge | Sentence |
|---|---|---|---|---|---|
| Wabichi Waruhu | CC 101/53 | May 53 | Cram | Murder | Hang |
| James Gichu Kamongurua | CC 101/53 | May 53 | Cram | Murder | Hang |
| Kiiro Githombe | CC 127/53 | June 53 | Cram | Murder | Conviction quashed on appeal |
| | CC 23/54 | Apr 54 | Law | Murder | Hang |
| Kanji Gitemi | CC 127/53 | June 53 | Cram | Murder | Conviction quashed on appeal |
| | CC 23/54 | Apr 54 | Law | Murder | Hang |
| Wahome Githiari | CC 127/53 | June 53 | Cram | Murder | Conviction quashed on appeal |
| | CC 23/54 | Apr 54 | Law | Murder | Hang |
| Nderito Wambogo | CC 127/53 | June 53 | Cram | Murder | Conviction quashed on appeal |
| | CC 23/54 | Apr 54 | Law | Murder | Hang, commute, detained at Governor's pleasure |
| Wanjohi Kamongurua | CC 29/53 | Aug 53 | Salter | Murder | Hang |
| Benjamin Ndirangu | CC 29/53 | Aug 53 | Salter | Murder | Hang |
| Samson Gachura | CC 29/53 | Aug 53 | Salter | Murder | Hang |
| Mukunya Kerisio | CC 29/53 | Aug 53 | Salter | Murder | Hang |
| Kiboi Wachira | CC 270/54 | June 54 | Holmes | Murder | Hang, commute, life imprisonment |
| Kimani Waithaka | CC 270/54 | June 54 | Holmes | Murder | Hang, commute, life imprisonment |
| Kabatha Wakaria | CC 191/55 | Nov 55 | Seton | Murder | Hang |

## Table 3.i: Murders of European settlers: the accused and their sentences

| Victim | Trial | Date | Judge | The accused | Sentence |
|---|---|---|---|---|---|
| **Phase One** | | | | | |
| Meiklejohn (22 Nov 52) | CC 34/52 | Mar 53 | Bourke | Waweru Gitau | Acquit |
| | | | | Watuso Githuri | Hang |
| | | | | Samuel Gachoka | Hang |
| Fergusson Bingley } (1 Jan 53) | CC 95/53 | May 53 | Mayers | Thuku Muchire | Hang |
| | | | | Muchendu Mogo | Hang |
| | | | | Wambogo Maina | Hang |
| | | | | Ngungire Njora | Hang |
| | | | | Nderito Wambogo | Hang |
| Rucks (24 Jan 53) | CC 55/53 | Apr 53 | Bourke | Nderito Kikaria | Hang |
| | | | | Mbogo Githathi | Hang |
| | | | | Githai Kiama | Hang |
| | | | | Kangethe Kihara | Hang |
| | | | | Macharia Magondu | Hang |
| | | | | Ndirangu Kariuki | Hang |
| | | | | Burugu Kungu | Hang |
| | | | | Thuo Bura | Hang* |
| | | | | Gatheru Mbogo | Hang* |
| | | | | Njehia Bura | Hang* |
| | | | | Njathi Mwangi | Acquit |
| | | | | Masai Ndukai | Acquit |
| Gibson (7 Feb 53) | CC 130/53 | May 53 | Cram | Augustino Kiiru Mwaniki | Hang |
| Griffith-Williams (18 Apr 53) | CC 244/53 | Feb 54 | Connell | Kibeti Mwaniki | Hang |
| | | | | Barasa Kibeti | Hang |
| Meloncelli (Apr 53) | CC 39/54 | Feb 54 | Mayers | Waikumbi Gathogo | Hang |
| MacDougall (21 Jul 53) | CC 249/53 | Nov 53 | Mayers | Njomo Ichuge | Hang |
| | | | | Kururi Wanjo | Hang |
| | | | | Kiahara Ndirangu | Hang |
| | | | | Kanyoi Njeroge | Hang |
| | | | | Kangema Kihara | Acquit |
| | | | | Muremi Thagui | Hang |
| **Phase Two** | | | | | |
| Kowalski (10 Mar 54) | CC 487/54 | Aug 54 | Holmes | Kagwamba Kihanda | Hang |
| | | | | Kigoi Nyamo | |
| Bruxnor-Randall (x2) (14 Mar 54) | CC 330/54 | Aug 54 | ? | Njuguna Kimani | Convictions quashed on appeal |
| | | | | Mungai Kiarie | |
| | | | | Mathumba Jnjau | |
| | | | | Ngotho Njuguna | |
| Stephens (3 April 1954) | CC 173/54 | May 54 | Corrie | Gachuhe Kamoni | Hang |

**Table 3.i—*cont.***

| Victim | Trial | Date | Judge | The accused | Sentence |
|---|---|---|---|---|---|
| Critchley (5 June 54) | CC 352/54 | Aug 54 | Cram | Wanjiri d/o Mathai | Hang† |
| | | | | Wanjiri d/o Johana | Hang† |
| Leakey | CC 614/54 | Nov 54 | de Lestang | Gititi Kahutu (Gen Kaleba) | Hang |
| | | | | Wahome Muthigani | Hang |
| | | | | Mwangi Maimba | Hang |
| Shotton (27 Dec 54) | CC 33/55 | Mar 55 | Holmes | Kimani Kagere | Hang |
| | | | | Wanganga James | Acquit |
| | | | | Kamau Kabecha | Hang |
| | | | | Waweru Nganga | Hang |
| | | | | Gitau Muturi | Hang |
| Twohey & Danby (20 Apr 55) | CC 111/55 | Jun 55 | de Lestang | Njenga Ngote (Gen Njeke) | Hang |
| | | | | Ikere Gichungu | Hang |
| | | | | Titus Chege Muchiri | Hang |
| | | | | Mwangi Kamau | Hang |
| | | | | Wanjiro d/o Waikero | Hang† |
| | | | | Waimatha d/o Wakumbi | Hang† |
| | | | | Ndungu Ngenga | Hang |
| | | | | Githuku Nganga | Hang |
| | | | | Kibe Munene | Hang |
| | | | | Kimondo Kimani | Hang |
| | | | | Ngugi Kahinde | Hang |
| | | | | M'ritha M'mugambi | Hang |

* judged to have been under 18 years of age at time of crime. Sentence automatically commuted to detention at the Governor's pleasure.
† clemency, and sentenced to imprisonment for life, on order of Governor.

## Table 4.i: The Lari hanged

*(i) Sentenced on 13 May 1953 for murders in Charles Ikenya's homestead (CC 86/1953), and hanged at Githunguri on 14 October 1953*

Amos Manjare Muchai
Ngugi Kinyanjui
Njehiah Muchuna
Wilson Ngure Gachango
Jacob Boro Munia
Mwaura Karimu
Njeroge Kimana
Kimani Waweru
Justo Mugweru Njehia
Douglas Muchai Manjare
Mwangi Kamau:
Njuguna Waiganjo

*(ii) Sentenced on 8 June 1953 for murders at Samson Kariuki's homestead (CC 93/1953), and hanged at Githunguri on 22 October 1953*

Muranja Iguru
Mugunyi Gachanja
Warui Njeroge
Chege Kamau
Njoroge Gichimo
Mburo Koigi
Thondeka Mwathi
Muranja Iguru
Gatimu Karega
Kamau Kinyariru
Gomba Kamanga
Njonge Nyamuni

*(iii) Sentenced on 22 July 1953 for murders at Nganga's homestead (CC 9/1953), and hanged at Githunguri on 22 October 1953*

Waititu Kimani

*(iv) Sentenced on 15 September 1953 for murders in Kie Kirambe's homestead (CC 67/1953), and hanged at Githunguri on 31 October 1953*

Joram Kangethe Njuguna

*(v) Sentenced on 24 June 1953 for murders in Charles Ikenya's homestead (CC 94/1953), and hanged at Githunguri on 7 November 1953*

Muya Micho
Makume Garuia
Kagai Kinuthia
Mbogo Gichango
Makuni Waihenya

*(vi) Sentenced on 21 September 1953 for murders in Kie Kirembe's homestead (CC 90/1953), and hanged at Githunguri on 7 November 1953*

Gichaga Njuguna

*(vii) Sentenced on 25 September 1953 for murders at Machune Kiranga's homestead (CC 89/1953), and hanged at Githunguri on 10 November 1953*

Heman Rimi Githua
Ndegwa Njeroge

*(viii) Sentenced on 14 August 1953 for murders at Isaac Kagoru's homestead (CC 21/1953), and hanged at Githunguri on 14 November 1953*

Gachanja Waiganjo
Mwangi Njuna
Kimani Wainaina
Chege Njehia
Mbugwa Chege

*(ix) Sentenced on 20 August 1953 for murders at Mbogwa Mumya's homestead (CC 32/1953), and hanged at Githunguri on 18 November 1953*

Ndutumu Nganga

*(x) Sentenced on 12 August 1953 for murders at Kie Kirembe's homestead (CC 11/1953), and hanged at Githunguri on 5 December 1953*

Karugi Njuguna
Mugo Gategwa
Kierko Mugani
Gategwa Mugo
Makuru Mjuguna

*(xi) Sentenced on 10 July 1953 for murders at Charles Ikenya's homestead (CC 7/1953), and hanged at Githunguri on 25 February 1954*

Njehia Njuguna

*(xii) Sentenced on 25 July 1953 for murders at Plot Morson (CC 10/1953), and hanged at Nairobi on 27 February 1954*

Thairu Muhoro
Njoroge Gutu
Thiongo Njau

*(xiii) Sentenced on 22 December 1953 for murders at Luka Wakahangare's homestead (CC 70/1953), and hanged at Nairobi on 21–3 June 1953*

Samwel Gichha Mwaura
Kuria Gichimbe
Kahuya Kinyenge
Kituru Kanyowe
Kishogu Njoroge
Murege Gaitura
Muturi Thiongo
Mwai Mukura
Mungai Nyengenyi

Wanguku Karuga
Kamau Jones Ruitha
Mucheru Karanja
Mbote Kamau
Kigotho Njeroge
Chaure Kagwi
Kanene Kimera
Karanja Mwangi
Kairo Iharo
Mwangi Mbugwa
Muiru Mugiria
Nganga Kihuno
Ngure Njeroge

## Table 5.i: African population in Nairobi, by origin

|                        | 1953  | 1954  | 1955 | 1956 | 1957 | 1958 | 1959 |
|------------------------|-------|-------|------|------|------|------|------|
| **Nyanza**             | 27.5% | 35.2% | 37%  | 39%  | 38%  | 37%  | 38%  |
| **Kikuyu (Embu, Meru)**| 46.5% | 26.3% | 27%  | 22%  | 25%  | 26%  | 28%  |
| **Kamba**              | 18.6% | 27.8% | 25%  | 28%  | 27%  | 27%  | 25%  |
| **Others (Kenya)**     | 4.2%  | 6.4%  | 7%   | 7%   | 6%   | 6%   | 5%   |
| **Non-Kenyan**         | 3.2%  | 4.3%  | 4%   | 4%   | 4%   | 4%   | 4%   |

## Table 5.ii: Closure of shops in Pumwani, 1954[i]

|                   | Prior to 11 June '54 | After 11 June '54 |
|-------------------|----------------------|-------------------|
| **General retail**| 90                   | 36                |
| **Vegetable**     | 22                   | 5                 |
| **Restaurants**   | 10                   | 4                 |
| **Butchers**      | 5                    | 6                 |
| **Tailors**       | 20                   | 2                 |
| **Shoe repair**   | 9                    | 2                 |
| **Hat**           | 2                    | 1                 |
| **Bicycle repair**| 6                    | —                 |
| **Barbers**       | 10                   | —                 |
| **Carpenters**    | 12                   | —                 |
| **Totals**        | 186                  | 56                |

[i] *African Affairs Annual Report, 1954*, appendix G

**Table 7.i: Convictions for Mau Mau offences, October 1952 to March 1958**

| | Executed | Commuted | Appeal allowed | Certified Insane | Died in prison | Total |
|---|---|---|---|---|---|---|
| 1 **Murder** | 337 | 27 | 90 | I | 5 | 460 |
| 2 **Murder + consort** | 6 | – | I | – | – | 7 |
| 3 **Murder + ammo** | I | – | – | – | – | I |
| 4 **Murder + arms + ammo** | I | – | – | – | – | I |
| 5 **Murder + arms + consort** | I | – | – | – | – | I |
| 6 **Arms** | 206 | 56 | 13 | – | I | 276 |
| 7 **Ammo/explos** | 95 | 56 | 17 | I | I | 170 |
| 8 **Oath admin** | 54 | 8 | 20 | – | – | 82 |
| 9 **Further terror** | 8 | – | – | – | – | 8 |
| 10 **Consort** | 207 | 58 | 14 | – | – | 279 |
| 11 **Demand supply** | 2 | I | I | – | – | 4 |
| 12 **Arms + ammo** | 99 | 18 | 4 | – | – | 121 |
| 13 **Arms + consort** | 46 | 2 | – | – | – | 48 |
| 14 **Ammo + consort** | 17 | 11 | – | – | – | 28 |
| 15 **Arms + ammo + consort** | 9 | I | – | – | – | 10 |
| 16 **Consort + further terror** | I | – | – | – | – | I |
| 17 **Oath + consort** | – | 2 | – | – | – | 2 |
| **Totals** | 1090 | 240 | 160 | 2 | 7 | 1499 |

Note: This table is based upon returns in PRO CO 822/1256, covering the period October 1952 to the end of June 1957. Additional figures, reported in correspondence in the same file, have been added covering the period from July 1957 to March 1958, when the last executions of Mau Mau offenders took place. Of the 21 men convicted after June 1957, 8 were executed in 1957, and 8 in 1958. All of these executed men had been convicted of murder. Four men had their murder convictions commuted in 1957, and a further person convicted of murder had his appeal allowed in 1958.

It should also be noted that this table includes convictions from all courts, and includes Supreme Court hearings (mostly before April 1953) and Special Emergency Assize Courts (commencing from April 1953).

**Table 7.ii: Capital punishment convictions in Kenya, October 1952 to October 1959**

| Outcome | Mau Mau other offences | Mau Mau murder cases | Mau Mau totals | non-Mau Mau murders |
|---|---|---|---|---|
| Executed | 744 | 346 | 1090 | 100 |
| Commuted | 213 | 27 | 240 | 106 |
| Appeal allowed | 69 | 91 | 160 | 36 |
| Certified insane | 1 | 1 | 2 | 5 |
| Died in prison | 2 | 5 | 7 | – |
| Totals | 1029 | 470 | 1499 | 247 |

Source: 'Capital Punishment', PRO CO 822/1256

**Table 7.iii: Monthly returns of Special Emergency Assize Courts, March 1954 to December 1956**

| Date | Cases | Persons tried | Acquittals | Convictions | Cases pending (persons) |
|---|---|---|---|---|---|
| 13 Mar '54 | 398 | 948 | 354 | 401 | 81 (193) |
| 2 Apr '54 | 440 | 1056 | 404 | 472 | 78 (182) |
| 7 May '54 | 501 | 1150 | 461 | 543 | 75 (148) |
| 4 June '54 | 561 | 1308 | 525 | 638 | 62 (147) |
| 2 July '54 | 623 | 1416 | 596 | 749 | 43 (73) |
| 6 Aug '54 | 729 | 1622 | 680 | 855 | 42 (87) |
| 3 Sept '54 | 773 | 1718 | 738 | 916 | 29 (64) |
| 1 Oct '54 | 821 | 1820 | 782 | 987 | 27 (51) |
| 5 Nov '54 | 861 | 1885 | 802 | 1049 | 20 (33) |
| 3 Dec '54 | 911 | 2021 | 829 | 1113 | 28 (79) |
| 1 Jan '55 | | | | | |
| 18 Feb '55 | 977 | 2140 | 893 | 1217 | 17 (30) |
| 4 Mar '55 | 988 | 2163 | 900 | 1227 | 16 (36) |
| 1 Apr '55 | 1006 | 2212 | 918 | 1260 | 12 (34) |
| 1 May '55 | | | | | |
| 24 Jun '55 | 1062 | 2310 | 939 | 1360 | 9 (15) |
| 1 July '55 | 1066 | 2321 | 940 | 1363 | 9 (18) |
| 5 Aug '55 | 1091 | 2378 | 946 | 1397 | 14 (35) |
| 2 Sept '55 | 1098 | 2398 | 959 | 1429 | 5 (10) |
| 7 Oct '55 | 1109 | 2413 | 961 | 1441 | 6 (11) |
| 4 Nov '55 | 1121 | 2444 | 966 | 1452 | 9 (26) |
| 2 Dec '55 | 1128 | 2456 | 974 | 1470 | 7 (12) |
| 6 Jan '56 | 1142 | 2480 | 981 | 1492 | 6 (7) |
| 3 Feb '56 | 1155 | 2497 | 985 | 1500 | 7 (12) |
| 2 Mar '56 | 1161 | 2512 | 986 | 1505 | 10 (21) |
| 6 Apr '56 | 1164 | 2519 | 990 | 1522 | 4 (7) |
| 4 May '56 | 1175 | 2540 | 1004 | 1529 | 5 (7) |
| 1 Jun '56 | 1184 | 2556 | 1012 | 1535 | 6 (9) |
| 6 July '56 | 1189 | 2572 | 1023 | 1542 | 3 (7) |

**Table 7.iii—*cont.***

| Date | Cases | Persons tried | Acquittals | Convictions | Cases pending (persons) |
|---|---|---|---|---|---|
| 3 Aug '56 | 1192 | 2575 | 1024 | 1550 | 1 (1) |
| 7 Sep '56 | 1202 | 2599 | 1028 | 1557 | 6 (14) |
| 5 Oct '56 | 1206 | 2604 | 1028 | 1570 | 5 (6) |
| 2 Nov '56 | 1210 | 2608 | 1033 | 1572 | 3 (3) |
| 29 Dec '56 | 1211 | 2609 | 1033 | 1574 | 2 (2) |

Sources: 'Emergency Assize Returns', KNA DC/KSM/1/15/122; 'Emergency Assize Returns 1954', KNA DC/KSM/1/15/286; 'Capital cases – speeding up, 1954–55', KNA CS/1/16/17

**Table 7.iv: Selected collective punishments in Kirinyaga, 1952–6**

| Date of punishment | Area | Reason for punishment | Type of punishment |
|---|---|---|---|
| 23 December 1952 | Kariti, Kiine, Ndia | Murder | 50% of livestock siezed in a 2 mile radius: 43 cattle and 250 sheep/goats taken |
| 20 May 1953 | Kimathi, Mwerua, Ndia | Murder | 50% of livestock siezed in a 1 mile radius |
| 20 May 1953 | Kimathi, Mwerua, Ndia | Local non-cooperation | 50% of livestock siezed in the entire sublocation |
| 21 May 1953 | Uthakahuno, Mwerua Ndia | Murder, non-cooperation | 100% of livestock siezed in the entire sublocation |
| 29 June 1953 | Baragwi, Gichugu | 12 murders | 146 cattle siezed from Mau Mau suspects |
| 7 August 1953 | Kariki, Inoi, Ndia | Local non-cooperation | 25% of livestock siezed in the sublocation |
| 11 August 1953 | Kagumop, Mutira, Ndia | Murder, non-cooperation | Market closed for 3 months |
| 15 August 1953 | Gitumbi, Inoi, Ndia | Local non-cooperation | Market closed for 3 months |
| 10 September 1953 | Kaguya and Kirunda, Inoi, Ndia | 5 murders, local non-coperation | 100% livestock siezed in 2 sublocations: 733 cattle, 845 goats, 1237 sheep from 254 owners, 12 bicycles |
| 6 February 1954 | Kianjege, Kiine, Ndia | local non-cooperation | Market closed for 3 months |
| 4 October 1954 | Kibirigwe, Kiine, Ndia | Murder, non-cooperation | 100% livestock siezed: 100 cattle, 361 goats |
| 9 March 1956 | Gatihi, Kiine, Ndia | Assisting May May | Siezed 168 animals from 28 villagers |
| 14 March 1956 | Kamiuru, Mutira, Ndia | Local non-cooperation | Large number of cattle taken from villagers |

Source: Alfonso Peter Castro and Kreg Ettenger, 'Counterinsurgency and socioeconomic change: The Mau Mau war in Kirinyaga, Kenya', *Research in Economic Anthropology*, 15 (1994), 76

**Table 7.v: Comparative prison populations, East and Central Africa, 1938**

|  | Population | Daily average in confinement | Daily average per 100,000 pop. |
|---|---|---|---|
| **Kenya** | 3,261,522 | 4,724 | 145.0 |
| **Uganda** | 3,711,494 | 4,225 | 113.9 |
| **Tanganyika** | 5,182,289 | 2,818 | 54.4 |
| **Somaliland** | 344,000 | 155 | 45.6 |
| **Zanzibar** | 235,428 | 159 | 66.3 |
| **Nyasaland** | 1,639,329 | 773 | 47.1 |
| **N. Rhodesia** | 1,376,938 | 923 | 66.9 |

**Table 7.vi: Daily average number of Mau Mau detainees and convicts, December 1954 to August 1959**

|  |  | Convicts | Detainees | Total |
|---|---|---|---|---|
| 1954 | December | 17,932 | 53,414 | 71,346 |
| 1955 | March | 17,366 | 52,767 | 70,133 |
|  | June | 15,921 | 50,776 | 66,697 |
|  | September | 15,501 | 48,078 | 63,579 |
|  | December | 13,996 | 45,423 | 59,419 |
| 1956 | March | 12,178 | 43,481 | 55,659 |
|  | June | 10,936 | 41,438 | 52,374 |
|  | September | 9,154 | 37,370 | 46,524 |
|  | December | 8,106 | 32,415 | 40,521 |
| 1957 | March | 7,119 | 27,247 | 34,366 |
|  | June | 5,669 | 23,663 | 29,332 |
|  | September | 4,854 | 20,061 | 24,915 |
|  | December | 4,345 | 15,190 | 19,535 |
| 1958 | March | 3,851 | 11,285 | 15,136 |
|  | June | 3,349 | 8,354 | 11,703 |
|  | September | 1,468 | 6,228 | 7,696 |
|  | December | 281 | 4,407 | 4,688 |
| 1959 | March | 248 | 1,524 | 1,772 |
|  | June | 136 | 1,275 | 1,411 |
|  | August | 148 | 1,158 | 1,306 |

Note: These are total daily averages by month.
Source: KNA AH/6/4–9

# Notes

In the endnotes that follow the full reference of each secondary source has been given when that work is first cited. Subsequent citations have been abbreviated. With primary sources, the full reference to the document has been given each time, but the reference to the archive where the document is held has been abbreviated.

The archive materials form the crucial body of primary evidence upon which the book is based. The most important of these are the trial documents. These are part of the collection held at the Kenya National Archive, in Nairobi. The trial papers appear in two series, the first from the High Court (RR), the second from the Ministry of Legal Affairs (MLA). These papers have been cited with the archive reference number, but I have also included the criminal case number of each trial. The archive files vary in the depth of material held on each case. Where the record is fullest, the files contain records of the committal proceedings (where such a hearing took place, but only for cases heard up to May 1953), police investigation papers, statements made by the accused and by other witnesses (signed and verified by either a magistrate or a senior police officer), a transcript of the trial, including the judge's summing up and final judgment and the statements of the assessors, the details of any appeal to the High Court of East Africa or to the Privy Council, and any papers supporting the appeal, such as statements of character for the convict. A record of prison admission, a medical statement, and a formal record of execution are to be found in all but a handful of the files. The files relating to the criminal cases have been augmented by a wide range of other sources from the Kenya National Archive, and also by materials from archives in Britain, notably the Public Records Office and Rhodes House Library, Oxford.

*Abbreviations used in archival references*
KNA  Kenya National Archives, Nairobi
    AB  Prisons Department
    AG  Attorney General
    AH  Ministry of Defence
    AP  Prisons Department
    BV  Ministry of Agriculture
    CC  Criminal Case
    CS  Chief Secretary
    DC/FH  District Commissioner, Fort Hall (Murang'a)
    DC/KBU  District Commissioner, Kiambu
    DC/KSM  District Commissioner, Kisumu
    DC/LAIK  District Commissioner, Laikipia
    DC/NAI  District Commissioner, Naivasha
    DC/NKU  District Commissioner, Nakuru
    DC/NYI  District Commissioner, Nyeri (North Nanyuki and South)

DC/NYK  District Commissioner, Nanyuki
GO  Governor's Office
MAA  Member for African Affairs
MAC  Murumbi Papers
MfP  Police Department
MLA  Ministry of Legal Affairs
Nbi  Nairobi Extra-Provincial District
PC/CP  Provincial Commissioner, Central Province
RN  Nairobi Extra-Provincial District
RR  High Court
TA  Tel Aviv deposit (a collection of migrated archives)
VQ  Provincial Commissioner, Central Province
PRO  Public Records Office, London
  CAB  Cabinet Papers
  CO  Colonial Office
  WO  War Office
RH  Rhodes House Library, Oxford
*EAS  East African Standard*

## Prologue

1   Elspeth Huxley, *No Easy Way* (Nairobi, 1957), 191, in fact borrowed the phrase from Gerald Hanley's *The Year of the Lion* (London, 1956).
2   Robert Ruark, *Something of Value* (London, 1955), Foreword.
3   Karen Blixen, *Out of Africa* (London, 1937).
4   Graham Greene, *Ways of Escape* (London, 1980), 188.
5   Frederick Cooper, *Africa since 1940: The Past of the Present* (Cambridge, 2002).
6   Robert F. Holland, *European Decolonization 1918–1981: An Introductory Survey* (Basingstoke, 1985).
7   Benjamin Stora, *Algérie coloniale* (Paris, 1991); David Birmingham and Phyllis Martin (eds.), *History of Central Africa: The Contemporary Years since 1960* (London & New York, 1998), chs. 6 and 9; Terence Ranger, *Peasant Consciousness and Guerrilla War in Zimbabwe* (London, 1985); William Beinart, *Twentieth-century South Africa* (Oxford, 1994), pt II; and Robert F. Holland (ed.), *Emergencies and Disorder in the European Empires after 1945* (London, 1994).
8   Richard J. Evans, *Rituals of Retribution: Capital Punishment in Germany, 1600–1987* (Oxford, 1996); Daniel Arasse, *The Guillotine and the Terror* (London, 1989).
9   Peter Linebaugh, *The London Hanged: Crime and Civil Society in the Eighteenth Century* (London, 1991); V. A. C. Gatrell, *The Hanging Tree: Execution and the English People 1770–1868* (Oxford, 1994).
10  The figures quoted here are drawn from the official returns of the courts, records of which are to be found in the following files in the Kenya National Archive [KNA]: 'Emergency Assize returns', KNA DC/KSM/1/15/122; 'Emergency Assize Returns 1954', KNA DC/KSM/1/15/286; and 'Capital cases – speeding up of process, 1954–55', KNA CS/1/16/17.

## Chapter 1. The Hidden History of an Anti-Colonial Rebellion

1   John Lonsdale, 'Kenyatta's trials: the breaking and making of an African nationalist', in P. Coss (ed.), *The Moral World of the Law* (Cambridge, 2000), 196–239.

2   Carl G. Rosberg & John Nottingham, *The Myth of Mau Mau: Nationalism in Colonial Kenya* (Stanford, 1966).

3   Wunyabari Maloba, *Mau Mau and Kenya: An analysis of a Peasant Revolt* (Bloomington & Indianapolis, 1993); Robert B. Edgerton, *Mau Mau: An African Crucible* (London, 1990).

4   John Lonsdale, 'The moral economy of Mau Mau: wealth, poverty and civic virtue in Kikuyu political thought', in Bruce Berman and John Lonsdale, *Unhappy Valley: Conflict in Kenya and Africa: Book Two – Violence and Ethnicity* (London, 1992), 315–468.

5   The phrase is from David Throup, *Economic and Social Origins of Mau Mau, 1945–1953* (Oxford, 1987).

6   The following account of the Koinange family draws upon Marshall S. Clough, *Fighting Two Sides: Kenyan Chiefs and Politicians 1918–1940* (Niwot CO, 1990); Marshall S. Clough, 'Koinange wa Mbiyu: mediator and patriot', in Benjamin E. Kipkorir (ed.), *Biographical Essays on Imperialism and Collaboration in Colonial Kenya* (Nairobi, 1980), 57–86; and Jeff Koinange, *Koinange-wa-Mbiyu: Mau Mau's Misunderstood Leader* (Lewes, 2000).

7   Lonsdale, 'Moral economy', *passim*.

8   Rosberg & Nottingham, *Myth*, 49.

9   Rosberg & Nottingham, *Myth*, 49.

10  *Papers Relating to Native Disturbances in Nairobi (March 1922), Cmd 1691* (London, 1922).

11  Cited from interviews with persons present at the incident, Rosberg & Nottingham, *Myth*, 51–2.

12  Rosberg & Nottingham, *Myth*, 98–9.

13  Rosberg & Nottingham, *Myth*, 117.

14  Summarized from David M. Anderson, *Colonial Crimes: Race, Gender & Justice in Colonial Kenya* (Oxford, in press), ch. 5, drawing upon David P. Sandgren, *Christianity and the Kikuyu: Religious Divisions and Social Conflict* (New York, Bern, Frankfurt & Paris, 1989).

15  David M. Anderson, *Eroding the Commons: Politics of Ecology in Baringo, Kenya, 1895–1963* (Oxford, 2002), 126–35. For the published evidence, *Kenya Land Commission: Evidence and Memoranda, vol. i* (Nairobi, 1934).

16  *Report of the Kenya Land Commission [Cmd 4556]* (London, 1934).

17  *Kenya Land Commission: Evidence and Memoranda, i*, 630–5.

18  Clough, 'Koinange wa Mbiyu', 79–81.

19  Blixen, *Out of Africa*, 9–10.

20  Roger M. A. van Zwanenberg, *Colonial Capitalism and Labour in Kenya, 1919–1939* (Nairobi, 1975), ch. 8 for a comprehensive history of squatting.

21  Elspeth Huxley, *Nine Faces of Kenya* (London, 1990), 88, from Huxley's *White Man's Country: Lord Delamere and the Making of Kenya*, vol. 1 (London, 1935).

22  Tabitha Kanogo, *Squatters and the Roots of Mau Mau* (London, 1987), ch. 1.

23  David M. Anderson, 'Registration and rough justice: labour law in Kenya, 1895–1939', in Paul Craven & Douglas Hay (eds.), *Masters, Servants and Magistrates in Britain and the Empire, 1562–1955* (Chapel Hill, 2004).

24  Kanogo, *Squatters*, ch. 3.

25  Van Zwanenberg, *Colonial Capitalism*, 225–9, on the *githaka* debate.

26  Anthony Clayton & Donald C. Savage, *Government and Labour in Kenya, 1895–1963* (London, 1974), 130.

27  David M. Anderson & David W. Throup, 'Africans and agricultural production in colonial Kenya: the myth of the war as a watershed', *Journal of African History*, 26 (1985), 327–46.

28  The Residents Native Labour Ordinance of 1937, but not approved by the Colonial Office until 1940.

29  David W. Throup, 'The origins of Mau Mau', *African Affairs*, 84 (1985), 414.

30  Throup, 'Origins of Mau Mau', 413–4.

31  Frank Furedi, *The Mau Mau War in Perspective* (London, 1989), 50–2.

32  My account of Olenguruone draws upon: Throup, *Economic and Social Origins*, 121–39; Furedi, *War*, 80–3; Kanogo, *Squatters*, 105–24; and Rosberg & Nottingham, *Myth*, 248–59.

33  Jeremy Murray-Brown, *Kenyatta* (New York, 1973); Koinange, *Koinange-wa-Mbiyu*, 74.

34  John Spencer, *KAU: Kenya Africa Union* (London 1985), 179–82, 205.

35  N. Humphrey, 'The relationship of population to the land in South Nyeri', PRO CO 852/662/19936/2, subsequently published as *The Kikuyu Lands: The Relation of Population to the Land in South Nyeri* (Nairobi, 1945).

36  Throup, *Economic and Social Origins*, 140.

37  Thurston, *Swynnerton*, 75.

38  Throup, *Economic and Social Origins*, 140.

39  Throup, *Economic and Social Origins*, 157.

40  Throup, *Economic and Social Origins*, 156.

41  John Spencer, *KAU: Kenya African Union* (London, 1985), 175–6.

42  Throup, *Economic and Social Origins*, 157.

43  Throup, *Economic and Social Origins*, 159.

44  Both examples are cited in Throup, *Economic and Social Origins*, 161.

45  Blixen, *Out of Africa*, 11.

46  Throup, *Economic and Social Origins*, 171.

47  Rosberg & Nottingham, *Myth*, 191.

48  David Hyde, 'The Nairobi General Strike: from protest to insurgency', in Andrew Burton (ed.), *The Urban Experience in Eastern Africa c.1750–2000* (Nairobi, 2002), 242.

49  Frank Furedi, 'The African crowd in Nairobi', *Journal of African History*, 14 (1973).

50  Berman & Lonsdale, *Unhappy Valley*, 428.

51  Spencer, *KAU*, 167–8, 176.

52  Rosberg & Nottingham, *Myth*, 240; Spencer, *KAU*, 227–8.

53  Supt. of African Locations to Nairobi Police, 28 October 1947, KNA MAA/8/22.

54  Furedi, 'African crowd', 282.

55  Spencer, *KAU*, 227–8.

56 Spencer, *KAU*, 227–30.

57 On oathing, see Rosberg & Nottingham, *Myth*, 259–62.

58 Spencer, *KAU*, 208–9.

59 Spencer, *KAU*, 230–4.

60 Bildad Kaggia, *Roots of Freedom* (Nairobi, 1975), 109.

61 Spencer, *KAU*, 172–3.

62 Rosberg & Nottingham, *Myth*, 241.

63 Hyde, 'The Nairobi General Strike', 240–8.

64 Kaggia, *Roots of Freedom*, 79.

65 Rosberg & Nottingham, *Myth*, 271.

66 Rosberg & Nottingham, *Myth*, 271–4, based upon interviews conducted with the key actors during the early 1960s.

67 This draws upon John Lonsdale 'Moral economy', in Berman & Lonsdale (eds.), *Unhappy Valley*, vol. 2, 315–504.

68 Kaggia, *Roots of Freedom* (Nairobi, 1975), 114; Lapping, *End of Empire*, 411, and 420 for Kubai's personal confirmation. Spencer, *KAU*, 230, is more coy on this point.

69 F. D. Corfield, *Historical Survey of the Origins and Growth of Mau Mau* [Corfield Report] Cmnd 1030 (London, 1960), 64–162, quote from 65. The published version of Corfield's report omitted passages relating to intelligence gathering. This fuller version is available in 'Corfield Report (secret)', KNA GO/3/2/72. Further material on the report's compilation, including the author's own summary, can be found in the Corfield Papers, Rhodes House, Oxford [RH] Mss. Afr s. 1675.

70 Spencer, *KAU*, 249, citing interviews with Beauttah and John Mungai.

71 Lapping, *End of Empire*, 410.

72 Corfield, *Historical Survey*, 77, and Spencer, *KAU*, ch. 3.

73 Corfield, *Historical Survey*, 84–6, 90–2.

74 Corfield, *Historical Survey*, 106.

75 Rosberg & Nottingham, *Myth*, 268.

76 Corfield, *Historical Survey*, 108, 116.

77 Rosberg & Nottingham, *Myth*, 273–4.

78 Corfield, *Historical Survey*, 124–5.

79 Corfield, *Historical Survey*, 90–3, 105.

80 Louis Leakey, *By the Evidence: Memoirs 1932–51* (New York & London, 1974); Mary Leakey, *Disclosing the Past: An Autobiography* (New York, 1984); Sonia Cole, *Leakey's Luck: the Life of Louis Seymour Bazette Leakey 1903–1972* (New York, 1975); Bruce Berman and John Lonsdale, 'Louis Leakey's Mau Mau: a story in the politics of knowledge', *History & Anthropology*, 5, ii (1991); Carolyn Martin Shaw, *Colonial Inscriptions: Race, Sex and Class in Kenya* (Minneapolis, 1995), 95–117.

81 Corfield, *Historical Survey*, 134–6.

82 Compiled from 'Catalogue of assaults on government servants in 1952', 40–43, PRO CO 822/437, and Corfield, *Historical Survey*, 136–7, 146–8.

83 'CID: Memorandum on Mau Mau intimidation, 9 September 1952', PRO CO 822/438; Corfield, *Historical Survey*, 141, 156.

84 CC 317/1952 'Kamau Ndirangu & Githuka Kagwe', at Nairobi, 10 April 1953, KNA MLA 1/464.

85 CC 17/1953 'Kiragi Wathia', at Nairobi, 6 February 1953, KNA MLA 1/465.

86 CC 43/1953 'Muchugu Kago', at Nairobi, February 1953, KNA MLA 1/469.

87 For example, CC 6/1953 'Njuguna Kagari', at Nairobi, January 1953, KNA MLA 1/473, the case of the murder of a headman in Thomson's Falls during September 1952, where the appeal of the accused was allowed because of errors made by the police in filing the prosecution.

88 CC 40/1953 'Karaya Njonji & three others', at Nairobi, 23 April 1953, KNA MLA 1/471.

89 This account is compiled from CC 188/1953 'Thuku Njeabuni', at Nairobi, 29 June 1953, KNA RR 11/12.

90 CC 324/1952 'Nderitu Thega & 6 others', at Nakuru, 29 June 1953, KNA MLA 1/472.

91 Throup, *Economic and Social Origins*, 33–63.

92 Corfield, *Historical Survey*, 141–3, and fuller details in 'Corfield Report (secret)', KNA GO/3/2/72.

93 Corfield, *Historical Survey*, 144–5.

94 The letter is quoted in Corfield, *Historical Survey*, 151–2.

95 For the papers, PRO CO 822/437/1. Whyatt and Davies were joined at the Colonial Office meeting by Leakey, who happened then to be in London: Berman & Lonsdale, 'Louis Leakey's Mau Mau', 143–4.

96 Corfield, *Historical Survey*, 154.

97 Corfield, *Historical Survey*, 157.

98 Photographs of hamstrung and mutilated cattle appeared in the press and were widely circulated at the time. For examples, see Fred Majdalany, *State of Emergency: The Full Story of Mau Mau* (London, 1962), facing 97.

## Chapter 2. Burying the Past

1 Quote from CinC ME, Public Records Office, Kew [PRO] CO WO 286/215.

2 'Chiefs' Character Book', Kenya National Archives [KNA] DC/KBU/11/1, entry for 1952, by District Commissioner Kennaway.

3 All details of Waruhiu's murder are taken from the trial papers, in KNA MLA 1/468, CC32/1953, at Nairobi, 'Gathuku Migwe & Waweru Kamundia'.

4 Rosberg & Nottingham, *Myth*, remains the best study of the origins and the rebellion.

5 Agnes Leakey Hofmeyr, *Beyond Violence: A True Story of Hurt, Hate and Hope* (Nairobi, 1990), 71.

6 Louis S. B. Leakey, *Mau Mau and the Kikuyu* (London, 1952); Louis S. B. Leakey, *Defeating Mau Mau* (London, 1954); Berman & Lonsdale, 'Louis Leakey's Mau Mau', 143–204.

7 'Waruhiu Memorial Fund', KNA AB/8/30.

8 Swann (DC/Kiambu) to Member for Law & Order, 18 May 1953, KNA MLA 1/468.

9 Corfield, *Historical Survey*, 158.

10 See Justice Rudd's summing-up, and the subsequent views of Court of Appeal for East Africa, all in KNA MLA 1/468.

11 Rosberg & Nottingham, *Myth*, 263–4; Koinange, *Koinange-wa-Mbiyu*, 70–1, 77–84.

12 Koinange, *Koinange-wa-Mbiyu*, 84–5; Spencer, *KAU*, 234.

13 Charles Douglas-Home, *Evelyn Baring: The Last Pro-Consul* (London, 1978).

14 'Proclamation of the State of Emergency', PRO CO 822/443.

15 Maloba, *Mau Mau and Kenya*, 76.

16 Baring to Lyttelton, 17 October 1952, PRO CO 822/444.

17 Douglas-Home, *Evelyn Baring*, 230.

18 Koinange, *Koinange-wa-Mbiyu*, 95–7.

19 Rosberg & Nottingham, *Myth*, 83–4.

20 Rawson Macharia, *The Truth About the Trial of Jomo Kenyatta*, 286. These details came to light in the later trial of Macharia, see KNA RR 9/21–30 for the papers. The essential facts are summarized in John Lonsdale, 'Kenyatta's trial', 196–239.

21 Douglas-Home, *Evelyn Baring*, 274.

22 The revelations first caught public attention in July 1985, with the broadcast of the Kenya programme in the ITV documentary series *End of Empire*. See the book that accompanied the series, Brian Lapping, *The End of Empire* (London, 1985). This account draws heavily upon John Lonsdale, 'Kenyatta's trials', 196–239.

23 Peter Evans, *Law and Disorder* (London, 1956), 53–9, gives a vivid account.

24 The 8-volume trial transcript is in KNA RR 9/5–12.

25 Lonsdale, 'Kenyatta's trials', quoting from the trial transcript.

26 See Kaggia's biography, *Roots of Freedom* (Nairobi, 1975), and Kubai's contributions to Lapping's *End of Empire*.

27 On oathing, see Rosberg & Nottingham, *Myth*, 259–62.

28 Lonsdale, 'Kenyatta's trials'.

29 Rosberg & Nottingham, *Myth*, 94; Randall Heather, 'Intelligence and Counterinsurgency in Kenya, 1952–56' (PhD thesis, University of Cambridge, 1993), 39.

30 Baring to Lyttelton, 2 March 1953, PRO CO 822/440.

31 Draft memorandum by 'MHC' to Governor, late 1952, Blundell Papers, RH MSS Afr. s. 746.

32 David Percox, 'Mau Mau and the arming of the state', in E. S. Atieno Odhiambo & John Lonsdale (eds.), *Mau Mau and Nationhood: Arms, Authority and Narration* (London, Nairobi and Athens OH, 2003), 130; Majdalany, *State of Emergency*, 107.

33 David Throup, 'Crime, politics and the police in colonial Kenya, 1939–63', in David Anderson and David Killingray (eds.), *Policing and Decolonization: Nationalism, Politics and the Police 1917–65* (Manchester, 1991), 144.

34 Baring to Lyttelton, 25 & 27 November 1952, PRO CO 822/439, for the official account. The incident was reported in *The Times*, 25 November 1952, and also in the *Daily Mirror*, 24 and 26 November 1952, where James Cameron's coverage was sharply critical of the security forces.

35 Heather, 'Intelligence', 38.

36 Martin Gilbert, *Never Despair: Winston Churchill 1945–1965* (London, 1988), 834.

37 Lyttelton to Baring, 4 December 1952, PRO CO 822/439.

38 Donald L. Barnett and Karari Njama, *Mau Mau from Within: Autobiography and Analysis of Kenya's Peasant Revolt* (London, 1966), 71; Frank Furedi, *Mau Mau War in Perspective* (London, 1989), 118–20.

39 Heather, 'Intelligence', 41.

40 For an example, Derek Peterson, 'Writing in revolution: independent school-ing and Mau Mau in Nyeri', in Odhiambo & Lonsdale (eds.), *Mau Mau and Nationhood*, 76–96.

41 Peterson, 'Writing in revolution', 89.

42 From the evidence of Wamangi Wahome, CC 101/1953 'Wabichi Waruhu & James Gichu Kamongurua', 25 May 1953, KNA MLA 1/479.

43 Trial transcript, and record of committal proceedings, CC 101/1953 'Wabichi Waruhu & 4 others', 25 May 1953, KNA MLA 1/479.

44 CC 127/1953 'Kiiro Githambi & 3 others', 11 June 1953, KNA MLA 1/480, and CC 23/1954, Kiiro Githambi & 3 others', 6 April 1954, KNA MLA 1/776.

45 CC 29/1953 'Wajohi Kahungarua & 3 others', 22 August 1953, KNA MLA 1/516; CC 270/1954 'Kiboi Wachira & Kimani Waithaka', 18 June 1954, KNA MLA 1/885; and CC 191/1955 'Kabatha Wakaria', 11 November 1955, KNA MLA 1/1303.

46 CC 101/1953 'Wabichi Waruhu & 4 others', judgment, 25 May 1953, KNA MLA 1/479.

47 CC 101/1953, KNA MLA 1/479.

48 Appeal Court Judgment, Criminal Appeals Nos. 306, 307, 308 and 309 of 1953, 28 September 1953, KNA MLA 1/516.

49 CC 23/1954, Justice Law, judgment 23 April 1954, and Judgment, Criminal Appeals Nos. 288, 289 & 290 of 1954, 22 May 1954.

50 Trial transcript and judgment, CC 29/1953, Acting Justice Salter, 22 August 1953, KNA MLA 1/516.

51 CC 270/1954, Justice Holmes, judgment 18 June 1954, KNA MLA 1/885.

52 CC 191/1955, 11 November 1955, KNA MLA 1/1303.

53 Statement of accused on conviction, Acting Justice Salter, judgment 22 August 1953, KNA MLA 1/516.

### Chapter 3. 'Parasites in Paradise'

1 Henry Seaton, *Lion in the Morning* (London, 1963), 12.

2 *Correspondence relating to the Flogging of Natives by Certain Europeans at Nairobi*, Cd 3256 (1907), and additional papers in PRO CO 533/28, CO 533/29, CO 533/30 and CO 533/31.

3 Anderson, *Colonial Crimes*, ch. 2.

4 David M. Anderson, 'Master and servant in colonial Kenya, 1895–1939', *Journal of African History*, 41, iii (2000), 435–70.

5 Elspeth Huxley, *White Man's Country*; Ed Paice, *Lost Lion of Empire* (London, 2001).

6 Margery Perham, *East African Journey: Kenya and Tanganyika 1929–30* (London, 1976), 190.

8 For discussion of the growth, and the employment patterns discussed below, Mary Parker, *Political and Social Aspects of the Development of Municipal Government in Kenya with Special Reference to Nairobi* (London, 1949), 5–8.

9    Dane Kennedy, *Islands of White: Settler Society and Culture in Kenya and Southern Rhodesia, 1890–1939* (Durham NC, 1987), 44.

10    Sir H. C. Belfield, 'Report of a visit to the Uasin Gishu plateau', 10 April 1913, PRO CO 533/116.

11    Figures quotes come from Kennedy, *Islands*, appendices.

12    Roger van Zwanenberg, *Colonial Capitalism and Labour in Kenya 1919–1939* (Nairobi, 1975).

13    Kennedy, *Islands*, 46–7.

14    M. P. K. Sorrenson, *The Origins of European Settlement in Kenya* (Nairobi, 1968).

15    Paul Mosley, *The Settler Economies: Studies in the Economic History of Kenya and Southern Rhodesia 1900–1963* (Cambridge, 1983), 17.

16    Mosley, *Settler Economies*, 44–52, 96–100.

17    All the figures come from David M. Anderson & David Throup, 'The agrarian economy of Central Province, Kenya, 1918–1939', in Ian Brown (ed.), *The Economies of Africa and Asia in the Inter-War Depression* (London, 1989), 8–28.

18    Michael Blundell, *So Rough a Wind* (London, 1964).

19    Dane Kennedy, *Islands*, 8.

20    Alison Smith, 'The immigrant communities: The Europeans', in D. A. Low and Alison Smith (eds.), *Oxford History of East Africa* (Oxford, 1976), vol. iii, 458.

21    *Daily Mail*, 21 October 1952; *Daily Mirror*, 25 October 1952. These articles are discussed in Joanna Lewis, 'Daddy wouldn't buy me a Mau Mau: the British popular press and the demoralization of empire', in Odhiambo and Lonsdale, *Mau Mau and Nationhood*, 227–50.

22    For analysis of the US press, Shaw, *Colonial Inscriptions*, (1995), 170–8.

23    Corfield, *Historical Survey*, 316.

24    Guy Campbell, *The Charging Buffalo: A History of the Kenya Regiment, 1937–1963* (London, 1986).

25    Anthony Clayton, *Counter-insurgency in Kenya 1952–60* (Nairobi, 1976), 18–19.

26    Erskine to Lady Erskine, 3 June 1953, quoted in Clayton, *Counter-insurgency*, 11.

27    Baring to Lyttelton, 'Secret Report', 15 October 1952, PRO CO 822/449.

28    A brief account of the attack appears in Majdalany, *State of Emergency*, 11.

29    Edgerton, *Mau Mau*, 57.

30    Heather, 'Intelligence', 37; Majdalany, *State of Emergency*, 111–12.

31    Majdalany, *State of Emergency*, 112–13.

32    Heather, 'Intelligence', 38–9.

33    *Daily Mirror*, 12 December 1952.

34    For discussion of this, and other articles by Cameron, see Lewis, 'Daddy wouldn't buy me a Mau Mau', 237–240.

35    CC 95/1953 'Thuku Muchire & four others', KNA MLA 1/470.

36    Majdalany, *State of Emergency*, 118.

37    The interview was re-broadcast in 1998, as part of the *Empire Warriors* series, made by Pier Productions for BBC Radio 4.

38    Heather, 'Intelligence', 56.

39    Committal proceedings, CC 571/1953 Nyeri, before Magistrate H. Kennedy, 13 April 1953, statement of Reginald Morice, KNA MLA 1/1/478.

40    *EAS*, 27 April 1953.

41    'European is murdered', *EAS*, 20 April 1953.

42    'European dies after shot', *EAS*, 1 June 1953.

43    *EAS*, 25, 26 and 27 June 1953.

44    *EAS*, 18 June 1953; RR 11/21.

45    Mary Gillett, *Tribute to Pioneers: Mary Gillett's Index of Many of the Pioneers of East Africa* (privately published, 1986); *East African Standard*, 10 July 1953.

46    Barnett & Njama, *Mau Mau From Within*, 277.

47    The details that follow come from the trial papers, CC5/1953 'Nderitu Gikaria & 11 others', KNA MLA 1/467.

48    For example, *Illustrated London News*, 7 February 1953.

49    Blundell, *Wind*, 123–4.

50    Blundell, *Wind*, 126–7.

51    A note of the cases can be found in KNA AP/1/905. Both trials were heard before Justice Windham. In CC 248/1952, Mweiga Kirika and Njau Mwahia were sentenced to death, and in CC 250/1952 Wainaina Kibige and Gitau Ronana were sent to the gallows. All four men were originally from Kiambu.

52    Shaylor (Registrar) to Supreme Court Criminal Clerk, 5 December 1953, 'Annual returns of capital punishments', KNA AP/1/905.

53    The cases are listed in KNA AP/1/905, where the condemned men are named as: From CC 276/1952, Wangome Wambogo and Mutugi Bororo; from CC 282/1952, Huria Mbaka, Githi Kimutwe and Kangeta Muriithi; and from CC284/1952, Ngomia Kachuru, Kiama Mithumo, Munyororo Muthoga and Gachanja Girui.

54    This was CC 312/1952. The condemned men were: Mwangi Kamweru, Mathenge Ndegwa, Kamau Mugicho, Kagemi Kimani, Chacha Kamwera, Gichui Waroe, Gaturi Kaguru, Kabui Wamiru, Kinyua Machaia, Muharuro Machaia and Karari Waweru. See KNA AP/1/905.

55    See, for example, Michael Blundell's comments, *Wind*, 114–28.

56    Blundell, *Wind*, 128.

57    The following discussion draws upon the four sets of trial papers: For the Meiklejohn case, CC 34/1953 'Samuel Njehia Gachoka + two others', KNA MLA 1/466; for the Ruck case, CC 55/1953 'Ndirito Gikaria + 11 others', KNA MLA 1/467; for the Fergusson and Bingley case, CC 95/1953 'Thuku Muchire + 4 others', KNA MLA 1/470; and for the Gibson trial, CC 130/1953 'Augustino Kiiru Mwaniki', KNA MLA 1/478.

58    CC 34/1953 'Samuel Njehia Gachoka + two others', KNA MLA 1/466.

59    CC 55/1953 'Ndirito Gikaria + 11 others', KNA MLA 1/467.

60    'Judgment', Justice Paget Bourke, 24 April 1953, trial transcript CC 55/1953, p. 106–7, KNA MLA 1/467.

61    I am grateful to Victor Lal for references to this debate. The matter is covered fully in his forthcoming study, *The East African Asians and the Mau Mau Rebellion*.

62    Criminal Appeals Nos. 109–115, 150, 151 and 181 of 1953, Judgment, 23 June 1953, KNA MLA 1/467.

63    *EAS*, 19 June 1953.

64  *EAS*, 15 and 17 July 1953.

65  The account that follows is reconstructed from CC 95/1953 'Thuku Muchire + 4 others', KNA MLA 1/470, especially the trial transcript, Justice Mayers to Governor, 20 June 1953, and District Commissioner/Naivasha to Provincial Commissioner/Rift Valley, 24 June 1953.

66  *EAS*, 19 June and 15 July 1953.

67  CC 130/1953 'Augustino Kiiru Mwaniki', KNA MLA 1/478. The case was heard before Acting Justice A. L. Cram.

68  *EAS*, 16 July 1953.

69  For the papers on this case, CC 249/1953 'Njomo Ichuga + 5 others', KNA MLA 1/651. The committal proceedings are also lodged on this file, from original case CC 221/1953. Resident Magistrate Nyeri.

70  Justice Henry Mayers to Baring, 20 November 1953, KNA MLA 1/651.

71  Blundell, *Wind*, 152–3.

72  Frank Kitson, *Gangs and Counter-gangs* (London, 1960), 52.

73  For the Carnelly incident, Peter Hewitt, *Kenya Cowboy: A Police Officer's Account of the Mau Mau Emergency* (London, 1999), 137–50.

74  Edgerton, *Mau Mau*, 154.

75  Kitson, *Gangs*, describes many such interactions.

76  Kitson, *Gangs*, 36–7.

77  CC 487/1954 'Kagwamba Kihanda & Kigoi Nyamu', KNA MLA 1/978.

78  Judgement, Justice Corrie, 18 May 1954, CC 173/1954 'Gachuhe Kamoni', KNA MLA 1/807.

79  Emergency Assize CC 352/1954 'Wanjiro d/o Mathai & Wangui d/o Johana', KNA MLA 1/930, before Justice Cram.

80  CC 111/1955 'Njenga Ngote, alias General Njeke + 11 others', KNA MLA 1/1254. Kitson, *Gangs and Counter-gangs*, 172–4, gives an account of the capture of the gang.

81  CC 330/1954 'Njuguna Kimani + 3 others', KNA MLA 1/905.

82  The following comments are taken from the Judgment in the consolidated Criminal Appeal 549–552/1954, 19 August 1954, heard at Mombasa before Justices Worley, Jenkins and Briggs.

83  The quote is from the leader article of the *EAS*, 26 October 1954, and is cited in John Lonsdale, 'The Prayers of Waiyaki: political uses of the Kikuyu past', in David M. Anderson and Douglas H. Johnson (eds.), *Revealing Prophets: Prophecy in Eastern African History* (London, 1995), 279.

84  For accounts of the murder, see Stanley Kinga, 'Why we buried Leakey alive', *Daily Nation*, 10 May 1991; Wachanga, *Swords of Kirinyaga*, 43; and T. Colchester, 'Note on the association between the death of Chief Waiyaki (1893) and the Leakey sacrifice', 16 March 1966, Colchester Papers, Rhodes House Mss. Afr. s.742(3).

85  Hofmeyr, *Beyond Violence*, 74–6.

86  'Special Branch Flash Report – interrogation of Kaleba', 28 October 1954, KNA DC/NYK.3/12/34. For the statements made at the trial, CC 614/1954 'Gititi Kahutu (aka General Kaleba), Wahome Muthigani, Mwangi Maimba, & Wachuka d/o Samweli', KNA MLA 1/1101. All four were convicted, the first three being hanged on 6 January 1955, the female convict being detained at the governor's pleasure.

## Chapter 4. Death at Lari

1   Fiona D. Mackenzie, *Land, Ecology and Resistance in Kenya 1880–1952* (Portsmouth NH & Edinburgh, 1998), 170–207.

2   Rosberg & Nottingham, *Myth*, 290.

3   Baring to Lyttelton, 10 January 1953, PRO CO 822/468.

4   The following account is reconstructed from evidence given at the Lari trials, details of which are given in the next section.

5   Government press release, 27 March 1953, quoted in Edgerton, *Mau Mau*, 80.

6   Gladys W. Kiriga, 'A historical study in social conflict among the Kikuyu of Lari' (MA dissertation in History, Kenyatta University College, 1990), 109–10; Stephen Corradini, *Chief Luka and the Lari Massacre: Contrary Notions of Kikuyu Land Tenure and the Mau Mau War* (African Studies Program Text, University of Wisconsin-Madison, 2000), 21.

7   All the Lari trails will be cited by the case number and archive number only. Fuller details of each trial are listed in the appendix. CC 70/53, MLA 1/645 and RR 11/25–7.

8   CC 5/53 MLA 1/481; CC 7/53 MLA 1/484; CC 86/53 MLA 1/476; CC 94/53 1/483.

9   'Mothers see children murdered', *EAS*, 28 March 1953. Ione Leigh, *In the Shadow of the Mau Mau* (London, 1954), retells Mujiri's story.

10  CC 11/53 MLA 1/492 and MLA 1/518; CC 67/53 MLA 1/520; CC 90/53 MLA 1/532.

11  CC 11/53 MLA 1/492 and MLA 1/518; CC 67/53 MLA 1/520; CC 90/53 MLA 1/532.

12  CC 31/53 RR 11/5.

13  CC 9/53 MLA 1/488.

14  CC 32/53 MLA 1/499 and RR 11/6.

15  CC 21/53 MLA 1/496.

16  CC 10/53 MLA 1/489 and MLA 1/541.

17  Baring to Lyttelton, 7 April 1953, PRO CO 822/734; Clayton, *Counter-insurgency*, 23.

18  Kiriga, 'Social conflict', chapter 3.

19  Kiriga, 'Social conflict', 125–6.

20  The lack of coordination and proper security planning had been noted and reported to London: Robertson to Harding, 12 January 1953, PRO CO 822/468.

21  Peter Evans, *Law and Disorder: Scenes of Life in Kenya* (London, 1956), 170–1.

22  Evans, *Law and Disorder*, 170–1.

23  Evans, *Law and Disorder*, 187–8.

24  Kiriga, 'Social conflict', 132–5.

25  See the evidence of Dennis Kearney, the Assistant Inspector of Police at Uplands, in CC 70/1953 'Njeroge Munyoke & 82 others', trial transcript, p. 149, KNA RR 11/25. Kearney was seconded to the police from the Kenya Regiment. He spoke Kikuyu and Swahili, and worked closely with Frank Kitson in 'special operations' in Kiambu. See Kitson, *Gangs*, 23, and 18 for a photograph.

26  It took police more than five days to gather up the bodies. CC 165/1953 'Chege Mwaura & 51 others', trial transcript, pp. 2–11, KNA RR 11/31, for a description of the chaos in the mortuary.

27  Karigo Muchai, *The Hardcore: The Story of Karigo Muchai* (Richmond BC, 1973), 23–4, and for context, Marshall Clough, *Mau Mau Memoirs: History, Memory and Politics* (Boulder CO, 1998), 156–7.

28  *EAS*, 5 April 1953.

29  Clough, *Memoirs*, 130.

30  For the Naivasha attack: Muchai, *Hardcore*, 15–22; Wachanga, *Swords*, 57–9; Itote, *General*, 81–5; Majdalany, *State of Emergency*, 143–7; Rosberg & Nottingham, *Myth*, 287–91, for the claim that the Lari and Naivasha attacks were coordinated.

31  *EAS*, 4 April 1953.

32  Evans, *Law and Disorder*, 174.

33  Kitson, *Gangs*, 31.

34  CC 70/1953 RR 11/25, p. 142–4.

35  Terence Gavaghan, *Of Lions and Dung-Beetles: A Man in the Middle of Colonial Administration in Kenya* (Ilfracombe, 1999), 187.

36  CC 70/1953 RR 11/25, p. 142–4.

37  CC 70/1953 RR 11/25, pp. 147–9.

38  'Kenya Farm Survey Records 1905–1922' (copied from the registers of the Land Survey Department, and in possession of the author).

39  Lydekker to Senior Commissioner, Kikuyu, 2 February 1927, KNA PC/CP.9/24/12.

40  Northcote to Senior Commissioner, Nairobi, 28 May 1915, KNA PC/CP.9/24/12.

41  DO, Dagoretti to DC, Kiambu, 6 October 1927, KNA PC/CP.9/24/12.

42  Lydekker to Senior Commissioner, Kikuyu, 1 February 1927 and 11 October 1927, KNA PC/CP.9/24/12.

43  Sworn affidavit of Nganga Githanga, 20 September 1927, attested by Lydekker.

44  For example, sworn affidavit of Chege Gathu, 20 September 1927, before Lydekker, KNA PC/CP.9/24/12.

45  Sworn affidavits of Ndirango Thuo, 20 September 1927, and Mukora Kimunyi, 21 September 1927, both attested before Lydekker, KNA PC/CP.9/24/12.

46  Sworn affidavit of Luka Wakahangare, 1 February 1927, attested before Lydekker, and accompanying list of Tigoni *githakas* and resident households, KNA PC/CP.9/24/12.

47  Sworn affidavit of Wachuiri Kabatha, 25 March 1926, KNA PC/CP.9/24/12.

48  Lambert (Ag. Colonial Secretary) to Chief Native Commissioner, 20 August 1927, KNA PC/CP.9/24/12.

49  Vidal (DC, Kiambu) to Senior Commissioner, Central Province, 22 May 1928, KNA PC/CP.9/24/12.

50  Sidney Fazan was later made CBE in 1934, and CMG in 1946.

51  S. H. Fazan, 'The Tribal System of Land Tenure – with special reference to the Kikuyu', prepared for the Commission on Closer Union (May 1929).

52  *Report of Committee on Native Land Tenure in Kikuyu Province* (Nairobi, 1929), 'Minority Report', S. H. Fazan, 53.

53  S. H. Fazan to PC, Nyeri, 19 May 1930, KNA PC/CP.9/24/12.

54  *Report of the Kenya Land Commission* (London, 1934), 115–8.

55  For the petitions, see: Koinange and Philip Karanja to Secretary of State for the Colonies, 5 November 1935; Chief Koinange and George Ndegwa, representing the Joint Kikuyu Associations, to Secretary of State for the Colonies, 29 April 1936, KNA PC/CP.9/24/12, these amplifying a letter first sent on 13 October 1934 in protest against the Land Commission's findings.

56  For the original document: 'Resolutions of a baraza of the Kikuyu Loyal Patriots Association', at CMS Kiambaa, 13 May 1936, KNA PC/CP.9/24/2.

57  La Fontaine to Chief Secretary, 2 June 1936, and 'Notes of a meeting with Kiambu elders', 27 May 1936, both in 'Settlement of Kiambu Natives', KNA PC/CP.9/24/2.

58  E. B. Hosking to Chief Secretary, 27 October 1937, KNA PC/CP.9/24/2.

59  Fazan to La Fontaine, 6 June 1936, 'Additions to the Kikuyu Reserve as recommended by the Land Commission', KNA PC/CP.9/24/2.

60  And for subsequent reiteration of these points, 'Extract from the minutes of a meeting of the Kiambu LNCs, 24 October 1936', KNA PC/CP.9/24/2.

61  See Luka's comments to the LNC, 7 September 1938, KNA PC/CP.9/24/3.

62  J. Hopkins to PC, Central Province, 26 November 1935, KNA PC/CP.9/24/7.

63  'Settlement of Rightholders', 17 February 1941, KNA BV/19/145.

64  After further negotiations, their right to claim land at Lari was left open until the end of 1951. See Chief Native Commissioner to PC, 11 June 1951, KNA PC/CP.9/24/9.

65  J. Hopkins to PC, Central Province, 3 October 1935, KNA PC/CP.9/24/7.

66  For the problems involved, see T. Gavaghan, 'Muguga settlement and accommodation of claimants', 25 October 1950, KNA PC/CP.9/24/3.

67  Chief Philip James Karanja to PC, 8 January 1936, KNA PC/CP.9/24/7.

68  J. Hopkins to PC, Central Province, 3 October 1935, KNA PC/CP.9/24/7.

69  A battered and frayed copy of Coutts' 'Report on Ndeiya Settlement' of 23 October 1943 survives in KNA DC/KBU/4/10.

70  'Settlement of Kiambu Natives, 1938–53', KNA PC/CP.9/24/3 for examples.

71  Their representations are to be found in the archive files. Marius Ng'ang'a Karatu was interviewed by John Nottingham in 1963, Rosberg & Nottingham, *Myth*, 287–9.

72  Kennaway to John Mbugwa, 22 March 1950, and reply, 18 March 1950, KNA PC/CP.9/24/9.

73  Marius Nganaga Karatu to Governor, 20 June 1936, KNA PC/CP.9/24/7.

74  Kennaway (DC/Kiambu) to PC, 2 May 1949, and Chief Secretary to PC, 27 May 1949, KNA PC/CP.9/24/8.

75  Lambert to PC, 31 July 1943, KNA DC/KBU/4/10.

76  Kennaway to PC, 9 June 1949, KNA PC/CP.9/24/8.

77  Louden (DC/Kiambu) to Luka, 15 September 1949, KNA PC/CP.9/24/8.

78  Lyttelton, *Memoirs*, 380.

79  For example, minutes by Rogers, 23 April and 4 May 1953, PRO CO 822/734.

80  Blundell, *Wind*, 139–41, urged the need for reform upon Lyttelton when the two met in London during March, before and after Lari.

81 Baring to Lyttelton, 4 April 1953, PRO CO 822/734.

82 Minute by Roberts-Wray, 31 March 1953, PRO CO 822/734.

83 Baring to Lyttelton, 11 May 1953, PRO CO 822/734.

84 Nihill to Roberts-Wray, 20 May 1953, PRO CO 822/734.

85 Lyttelton to Baring, 28 May 1953, and reply 10 June 1953, and minutes, PRO CO 822/702.

86 'The Emergency (Emergency Assizes) Regulations, 1953', Government Notice 931, 12 June 1953, *Kenya Official Gazette, Supplement 45*. An amendment, under Government Notice 998, 20 June 1953, gave the police authority to hold prisoners awaiting trial. Baring to Lyttelton, 22 June 1953, PRO CO 822/734.

87 Minute by Roberts-Wray, 2 July 1953, PRO CO 822/734.

88 Minute by Roberts-Wray, 16 July 1953, PRO CO 822/734.

89 PRO CO 822/735.

90 Baring to Lyttelton, 7 April 1953, PRO CO 822/734.

91 'Minutes of meeting at Attorney General's Chambers', 7 April 1953, KNA DC/KSM/1/15/106; Baring to Lyttelton, 16 April 1953, PRO CO 822/734.

92 Bethwell Alan Ogot, *Historical Dictionary of Kenya* (Metuchen NJ & London, 1981), 21–2.

93 Argwings-Kodhek to Registrar, 27 August 1953, KNA DC/KSM/1/15/106.

94 See Acting Solicitor General to Registrar, 14 October 1953, and reply, 16 October 1953, KNA DC/KSM/1/15/106.

95 CC 9/1953 'Waititu Kanini & Nduati Kamau', Judgment, 22 July 1953, KNA MLA 1/488.

96 CC 9/1953 'Waititu Kanini & Nduati Kamau', trial transcript, 'Statement of Waititu Kanini', attested by A. L. Cram, KNA MLA 1/488.

97 CC 32/1953 'Ndutumi Nganga & Kinyonyo Mondo', trial transcript, and statements, 13 April 1953, KNA RR 11/6.

98 'Deposition of Ndutumi Nganga', 13 April 1953, attested by A. L. Cram, KNA RR 11/6.

99 CC 93/1953 'Muranja Iguro & 72 others', trial transcript, evidence of John Baker, 68–71, and Muranja Iguro, 72–3, KNA MLA 1/534.

100 I am grateful to Ben Knighton for assistance.

101 For an example of Kearney's role, see CC 9/1953 'Waititu Kanini & Nduati Kamau', trial transcript and judgment, 22 July 1953, KNA MLA 1.488.

102 CC 86/1953 'Amos Manjare + 25 others', KNA MLA 1/476.

103 CC 86/1953 'Amos Manjare + 25 others', Judgment, Salter, KNA MLA 1/476.

104 CC 94/1953 'Muya Micho and 25 others', Judgment, Mayers, 24 June 1953, KNA MLA 1/483.

105 CC 5/1953 'Gatenjwa Kinyanjui', Criminal Appeal No. 226 of 1953, 14 September 1953, KNA MLA 1/481.

106 CC 7/1953 'Njehia Njuguna', Judgment, Salter, 10 July 1953, KNA MLA 1/484.

107 The following details are taken from Machune's testimony to the court, CC 165/1953 'Chege Mwaura & 51 others', trial transcript, pp. 34–183, KNA RR 11/31, and Harley's summing up, KNA RR 11/37.

108 CC 165/1953 'Chege Mwaura & 51 others', trial transcript, testimony of

Duncan Mahinda, pp. 395–411, KNA RR 11/32, and evidence of witnesses, pp. 725–55, KNA RR 11/34.

109   Evidence of Vernon Smith, Chief Inspector CID, Nairobi, CC 165/1953 'Chege Mwaura & 51 others', trial transcript, pp. 419–23, KNA RR 11/33.

110   Questioning of Mwangi, CC 165/1953 'Chege Mwaura & 51 others', trial transcript, pp. 831–43, KNA RR 11/35.

111   CC 165/1953 'Chege Mwaura & 51 others', Judgment, KNA RR 11/37. Of the four remaining prisoners, two were discharged during the trial because of illness, one because he was to be charged with another offence, and the last because of a confusion of identity with another prisoner. Of the 48 convicts, four were found to be juveniles. The others were sentenced to hang.

112   'Lari massacre appeal', *The Times*, 2 December 1953.

113   PRO CO 822/702.

114   Deputy Governor to Lyttelton, 8 December 1953, PRO CO 822/702.

115   Whyatt to Pritchard (Sec to Governor), 4 March 1954, PRO CO 822/783; Acting Governor to Lyttelton, 30 March 1954, PRO CO 822/783.

116   Interview, Nyeri Town, July 2002.

117   Criminal Appeals Nos 2–4, 6–8, 10, 12–14, 16–17, 20–28 of 1954, Judgment, 3 March 1954, Justices Nihill, Worley and Briggs, KNA MLA 1/645.

118   CC 70/1953 'Njoroge Munyuko & 82 others', trial transcript, pp. 56–7, KNA RR 11/25.

119   CC 14/1954 'Mwangi Kubai, Muthoni Machaia & Muthoni Njeroge', KNA RR 11/55.

120   Three persons stood trial, but all were acquitted. CC 14/1954 'Mwangi Kubai, Muthoni Macharia & Muthoni Njeroge', judge's notes 18 March 1954 (Corrie), KNA RR 11/55.

121   Minutes by Rogers, 23 April 1953, PRO CO 822/734.

122   Whyatt to Roberts-Wray, 26 November 1953, PRO CO 822/702.

123   'Kenya massacre trial', *The Times*, 22 December 1953.

124   CC 70/1953 'Njoroge Munyuko & 82 others', Judgment, 22 December 1953, KNA MLA 1/645.

125   CC 70/1953 'Njoroge Munyuko & 82 others', Judgment, p. 24, 22 December 1953, KNA MLA 1/645.

126   See comments in the *Mombasa Times*, 10 October 1953, reflecting a cautious approach to legal change, and *The Citizen*, 10 October 1953, a far right-wing settler newspaper.

127   CC 10/1953 'Thairu Muhoro + 2 others', Criminal Appeals 251, 252 and 253/1953, KNA MLA 1/489.

128   '12 guitwo tondu wa Kuuragana', KNA AHC/9/113, and Government of Kenya Press Release no. 600, 15 October 1953, PRO CO 822/702.

129   See figures reported in 'Condemned prisoners, 1954–57', KNA AH/14/20.

130   Baring to Lyttelton, 19 June 1954, PRO CO 822/783.

131   For example, see Nowrojee's complaints to Justice de Lestang of Home Guard attacks on defence witnesses in CC 93/1953 'Muranja Iguru & 72 others', trial transcript, pp. 237–8, KNA MLA 1/534.

132   'Money still flows for Lari fund', *Mombasa Times*, 9 October 1953; Kiriga, 'Social conflict', 178–84.

133 Majdalany, *State of Emergency*, 230.
134 Throup, 'Kenya police', in Anderson & Killingray, *Policing and Decolonisation*.
135 Clayton, *Counter-insurgency*, 6.
136 Edgerton, *Mau Mau*, 8.
137 Clayton, *Counter-insurgency*, 6–7.

## Chapter 5. Struggles in the City

 1  The phrase is from Ngugi wa Thiongo's fictional account of the strike, *Weep Not, Child* (Oxford, 1987), 56–7.
 2  Dave Hyde, 'The Nairobi General Strike (1950): from protest to insurgency', in Andrew Burton (ed.), *The Urban Experience in Eastern Africa, c.1750–2000* (Nairobi, 2000), 235–53, quoting Patrick O'Donovan in the *Observer*, 21 May 1950.
 3  Robert Ruark, *Something of Value* (London, 1955), 192–6; Anja Kervanto Nevanlinna, *Interpreting Nairobi: The Cultural Study of Built Forms* (Helsinki, 1996).
 4  James Smart, *A Jubilee History of Nairobi* (Nairobi, 1950).
 5  L. W. Thornton White, L. Silberman & P. R. Anderson, *Nairobi: Master Plan for a Colonial Capital. A Report Prepared for the Municipal Council of Nairobi* (HMSO: London, 1948).
 6  W. Robert Moore, 'Britain tackles the East African bush', *National Geographic Magazine*, 48 (March, 1950), 313.
 7  Andrew Hake, *African Metropolis: Nairobi's Self-Help City* (Brighton, 1977).
 8  Mary Parker, *Political and Social Aspects of the Development of Municipal Government in Kenya, with special reference to Nairobi* (HMSO: London, 1948), appendix 1.
 9  *Report of the Committee on African Wages [Carpenter Report]* (Nairobi, 1954), 186.
10  Throup, *Economic and Social Origins*, 188.
11  *Carpenter Report, passim.*
12  Figures from Carol Dickerman, 'Africans in Nairobi during the Emergency: social and economic changes, 1952–1960' (MA dissertation, University of Wisconsin-Masdison, 1978), 75, n. 5.
13  K. McVicar, 'Twilight of an African Slum: Pumwani and the evolution of African settlement in Nairobi' (PhD thesis, UCLA, 1968).
14  Terry Hirst and Davindar Lamba, *The Struggle for Nairobi* (Nairobi, 1994), 61.
15  Hake, *African Metropolis*, 48–50; Thornton White et al., *Master Plan*, 36.
16  Hake, *African Metropolis*, 45, 129–46.
17  'Report on the Housing of Africans in Nairobi, with suggestions for improvements', authored jointly by the Senior Medical Officer and Municipal Native Affairs Officer (Tom Askwith) and tabled before the Native Affairs Committee of NCC on 30 April 1941. See, Lewis, *Empire State-Building*, 138–41.
18  Stren, 'The evolution of housing policy', 64.
19  Thornton White et al., *Master Plan*, 18.
20  Stren, 'The evolution of housing policy', 71.
21  Parker, *Political and Social Aspects*, 158.
22  Thornton White et al., *Master Plan*, 18, 36.

23 Claire Robertson, *Trouble Showed the Way: Women, Men and Trade in the Nairobi Area, 1890–1990* (Bloomington & Indianapolis, 1997).

24 'Housing in British African Territories, 1952' (summary of the Housing Research Conference, Pretoria, November 1952), PRO CO 822/588.

25 Luise White, *The Comforts of Home: Prostitution in Colonial Nairobi* (Chicago, 1990).

26 Throup, *Economic and Social Origins*, 172–96.

27 Throup, *Economic and Social Origins*, 176–7.

28 *African Affairs Annual Report, 1954*, 176.

29 DC Nairobi to Rylands, 3 December 1953, TA KNA Nbi/PC/ Arch/Adm/15/1.

30 Nairobi Extra-Provincial District Annual Report, 1954, p. 174.

31 Throup, *Economic and Social Origins*, 274; Rosberg & Nottingham, *Myth*, 265–6. The quotation is from the trial transcript, cited in Corfield, *Historical Survey*, 89.

32 Rosberg & Nottingham, *Myth*, 268.

33 Majdalany, *State of Emergency*, 113–14.

34 See KNA RR 11/43 for examples.

35 Baring wrote to Lyttelton, 29 October 1953, describing Mau Mau's urban committee structure in detail, PRO CO 822/692.

36 Erskine to Harding, 23 July 1953, PRO CO 822/693, and 4 August 1953, PRO WO 216/855.

37 Heather, 'Intelligence', 130.

38 'Report on the removal of Kikuyu/Embu/Meru from Kaloleni', 20 October 1953, TA KNA papers, NBI/PC/Arch/Adm/15/50.

39 Yusuf Nzibo, 'A history of the Swahili-speaking community of Nairobi, 1895–1963' (doctoral thesis, University of Nairobi, 1986), 99–105; Dickerman, 'Africans in Nairobi'.

40 'Precis of Intelligence Appreciation', 9 January 1954, Rhodes House, Blundell Papers Box 36/2.

41 Small (DC/Nairobi) 'Photographs on identity cards', 5 November 1954, TA KNA Nbi/PC/Arch/Adm/15/1.

42 Small, 'Housing in Bahati, November 1953', TA KNA Nbi/PC/Arch/ Adm/15/1.

43 Heather, 'Intelligence', 205.

44 Corfield, *Historical Survey*, 225–30.

45 Baring to Lyttelton, 29 October 1953, PRO CO 822/692.

46 CC 174/1953 'Ndegwa Kamau & Hiram Karagu Wangoro', Corrie to Governor, 2 February 1954, KNA MLA 1/619.

47 CC 2/1954 'Gathu Gutuchi', trial transcript, KNA RR 11/44.

48 The thieves were later caught. CC 45/1953 'Karioki Kamau & 3 others', KNA RR 11/16.

49 CC 143/1954 'Muchai Kikara', trial transcript, KNA MLA 1/755; CC 445/1954 'Kuria Nganga & Muturi Njeroge', trial transcript, KNA MLA 1/983.

50 CC 453/1954 'Muthine Kibe', trial transcript, KNA MLA 1/966.

51 CC 68/1954 'Kanyi Ngunyi & Mathenge Wambugu', Holmes to Baring, 1 March 1954, KNA MLA 1/714.

52 CC 35/1954 'Ndungu Kamau', trial transcript, KNA RR 11/8; CC 113/1953 'Wakianda Gachunga', trial transcript, KNA MLA 1/548.

53 CC 69/1953 'Karanja Hinga', trial transcript, KNA MLA 1/509.

54 CC 23/1953 'Zakayo Mwaura Maina', trial transcript, KNA MLA 1.498.

55 CC 44/1953 'Munene Muimbu', trial transcript, KNA MLA 1/504, and KNA RR 11/15.

56 T. F. C. Bewes, *Kikuyu Conflict: Mau Mau and the Christian Witness* (London, 1953), 63.

57 Criminal Appeal 132/1954, judgement, KNA MLA 1/703.

58 CC 70/1954 'Nganga Kiriba', Rudd to Governor, 15 March 1954, KNA MLA 1/726; Nzibo, 'Swahili-speaking Nairobi', 99–103.

59 CC 155/1953 'Chege Mwangi', Holmes to Baring, 21 October 1953 KNA MLA 1/576.

60 CC 58/1954 'Njehia Kimani', Rudd to Baring, 2 February 1954, KNA MLA 1/671.

61 CC 41/1954 'Muthumba Ngombe', Law to Baring, February 1954, KNA MLA 1/692.

62 CC 1/1954 'M'Miragwi M'Mwithia, M'Murairi Karegwa & 6 others', KNA MLA 1/749.

63 For example, CC 61/1953 'Chege Muchege', trial transcript, KNA MLA 1/562; and CC 117/1954 'Mburu Wanyoike', Corrie to Baring, 18 December 1954, KNA MLA 1/813.

64 CC 243/1953 'Henry Karioki Njoroge', trial transcript, KNA MLA 1/668.

65 For information on Karkar, see CC 11/1954 'Nguro Bibiyo', trial transcript, KNA RR 11/51.

66 Heather, 'Intelligence', 207–8.

67 CC 110/1954 'Kamau Njerogi & Mathew Mwangi Kariuki', judgement, Corrie, 12 May 1954, KNA MLA 1/891.

68 CC 12/1954 'Charles Kareiithi Muthumo', trial transcript, KNA RR 11/53.

69 'Note on Crime in Nairobi, July to December 1953', printed report for Nairobi Police, copy held by KNA Library, Nairobi.

70 Mathu, *Urban Guerrilla*, 20.

71 Percox, 'British campaign in Kenya', 69–70, based upon Erskine's 'Situation reports' in PRO WO 216/860 and PRO WO 216/861.

72 Heather, 'Intelligence', 185.

73 For the minutes of the relevant planning meetings, see 'Operation Anvil', PRO WO 276/187.

74 This account draws upon Heather, 'Intelligence and counter-insurgency', 173–7, and the following key documents: General Erskine 'Kenya emergency', 2 May 1955, PRO WO 236/18; 'Operation Anvil: Outline Plan by Joint Commanders, 22 February 1954', PRO WO 276/214; and, various papers, PRO WO 276/187 and PRO CO 822/796.

75 Mathu, *Urban Guerrilla*, 27.

76 Tom Mboya, *The Kenya Question: An African Answer* (London, 1956), 19. The passage is repeated, with additional comments, in Tom Mboya, *Freedom and After* (London, 1963), 37–9.

77 'Directives to investigating teams', 9 April 1954, PRO CO 822/976.

78 Caroline Elkins, 'Detention and rehabilitation during the Mau Mau Emer-

gency: the crisis of late-colonial Kenya' (PhD thesis, Harvard University, 2000), 144–5.

79    Crawford to Lyttelton, 11 May 1954, PRO CO 822/796.

80    Figures were reported in the *EAS* for 26 April, 28 April and 16 May 1954. See also, Acting Governor to Lyttelton, 11 May 1954, PRO CO 822/796.

81    Elizabeth Jackson and E. P. Wilkinson (Women's Welfare sub-Committee) to Nairobi African Affairs Officer, 8 January 1957, TA KNA Nbi/PC/Arch/Lab/27/23/I.

82    The figures were announced by the Office of Information, and reported in *The Times*, 27 April 1954.

83    Kitson, *Gangs*, 81.

84    Dickerman, 'Africans in Nairobi', 22.

85    Justin Willis, *Potent Brews: A Social History of Alcohol in East Africa 1850–1999* (Oxford, 2002), 183.

86    Acting Governor to Lyttelton, 11 May 1954, PRO CO 822/798.

87    Michell to Rylands, 7 May 1954, TA KNA Nbi/PC/Arch/Adm/15/1/(P).

88    Dickerman, 'Africans in Nairobi', ch. 4.

89    General Secretary, NCCK to Crawford, 28 June 1954, KNA AH/5/31.

90    Memo from Peter Bostock on Dedan Kihato, 8 October 1954, and additional papers in KNA AH/5/31.

91    Secretary for Defence to Commissioner for Prisons, 12 August 1954, KNA AH/5/31.

92    Minute by Baring, 4 September 1954, KNA AH/5/31.

93    'Kenya government criticised', *The Times*, 10 January 1955; minute by Bunce, 20 January 1955, on David Steele's comments, PRO CO 822/796.

94    In response to the criticism, an 'Anvil Information Centre' was established to assist in tracing lost relatives, but its records proved to be incomplete: Labour Commissioner to Secretary for Labour, 14 June 1954, KNA MAA/7/755.

95    Major Richard Corner to Norman Harris (MLC), 20 September 1955, TA KNA Nbi/PC/Arch/Adm/15/51.

96    Michell to Henfrey (Oi/c MacKinnon Road), 10 May 1954, TA KNA Nbi/PC/Arch/Adm/15/1/(P).

97    Michell to Secretary for African Affairs, 9 August 1954, TA KNA Nbi/PC/Arch/St/1/1/29.

98    Bhandari (Advocate) to DC Pumwani, 12 July 1954, TA KNA Nbi/PC/Arch/15/5.

99    Amalemba to DC Nairobi, 14 May 1954, TA KNA Nbi/PC/Arch/Adm/15/51.

100   Government Workers, Starehe African Quarters to Mr Payet (Secretary, Starehe Village Committee), 5 March 1954, TA KNA PC/Nbi/Arch/Hou/1/1.

101   Anonymous letter to Rylands, 27 March 1954, TA KNA Nbi/PC/Arch/St/1/1/9/(p); Arthur Ochwada to Rylands, September 1954, TA KNA Nbi/PC/Arch/Adm/15/51.

102   Hook (Traffic Superintendent) to Rylands, 23 October 1954, TA KNA Nbi/PC/Arch/Adm/51/15.

103   Security Officer, Block Hotels to Rylands (Oi/cNbi) 2 September 1954, TA KNA Nbi/PC/Arch/Adm/15/51.

104 Minutes of the Nairobi Emergency Committee, for example meeting 164, 27 March 1957, KNA RN/14/113.

105 Mathu, *Urban Guerrilla*, pp. 26–32 for a personal account; Heather, 'Intelligence', 176–7 for the broader context; Itote, *Mau Mau in Action*, for a photograph of Chotara, 86–7.

106 Kitson, *Gangs*, 117–8; Heather, 'Intelligence', 202.

107 Mathu, *Urban Guerrilla*, p. 54.

108 Heather, 'Intelligence', 202, n. 99.

109 Mathu, *Urban Guerrilla*, 50–1.

110 *EAS*, 18 and 20 September 1954, and *The Times*, 20 September 1954; 'Report on Lukenia Raid, 17 September 1954', KNA War Council/1/2.

111 CC 593/54, 22 November 1954, 'Njogu Njeroge + 7 others', evidence of Hamilton-Paxon, KNA MLA 1/1110.

112 CC 593/1954, 18 December 1954, evidence of Hamilton-Paxon, KNA MLA 1/1129.

113 This description draws upon the case papers from the seven trials arising from the battle, cited below. Accounts of the battle can be found in Itote, *Mau Mau in Action*, 86–7; Heather, 'Intelligence', 202, n. 99; Kitson, *Gangs*, 123; and Hewitt, *Kenya Cowboy*, 285, though all give inaccurate figures.

114 *EAS*, 29 October 1954.

115 CC 593/1954, 22 November 1954, trial transcript, KNA MLA 1/1110; CC 593/1954 at Thika, 18 December 1954, trial transcript, KNA MLA 1/1129.

116 CC 595/1954, KNA MLA 1/1116; Itote, *Mau Mau in Action*, 86.

117 CC 595/1954, evidence of Nyagi Nyaga, KNA MLA 1/1116.

118 Mathu, *Urban Guerrilla*, 56–61.

119 *EAS*, 20 September 1954.

120 CC 597/1954, 'Judgment', Rudd, KNA MLA 1/1112.

121 All those named appeared in the same trial, CC 598/1954, KNA MLA 1/1120.

122 CC 598/1954, evidence of Karanja Kihara, KNA MLA 1/1120.

123 CC 597/1954, evidence of Kirongochi Nyaga, KNA MLA 1/1112.

124 CC 594/1954, Rudd to Governor, 18 December 1954, KNA MLA 1/1129.

125 CC 597/1954, Rudd to Governor, 16 December 1954, KNA MLA 1/1112.

126 CC 593/1954, Rudd to Governor, 22 November 1954, KNA MLA 1/1110.

127 CC 594/1954, KNA MLA 1/1129,

128 David M. Anderson, 'The battle of Dandora swamp: reconstructing the Mau Mau Land and Freedom Army, October 1954', in Odhiambo and Lonsdale (eds.), *Mau Mau and Nationhood*, 155–75.

129 The quote is from Clough, *Memoirs*, 163. For the success of Anvil, Majdalany, *State of Emergency*, 206–7.

130 Majdalany, *State of Emergency*, 224.

131 'Closer control of Nairobi: administrative measures to curb Mau Mau', Press Handout No. 581, 26 May 1955, KNA DC/FH/3/13/18.

132 'Nairobi Extra-Provincial Emergency Committee minutes, July–August 1954', PRO WO 276/64.

133 Nzibo, 'Swahili-speaking community', 101.

134 CC 497/1954 'Kareri Mbue', MacDuff to Governor, 21 August 1954, KNA MLA 1/1012; and CC 520/1954 'Frederick Mukiri Gichuho', De Lestang

to Governor, 9 September 1954, KNA MLA 1/1028. Both were convicted and hanged.

135  'Training Pamphlet for the operational element of Special Branch, 1954', PRO WO 276/231, outlines the structures established for intelligence gathering.

136  CC 201/1954, 'Kamiti Njeroge', trial transcript, KNA MLA 1/834.

137  CC 345/1954 'Njeroge Muthoro', Justice Holmes to Governor, 22 June 1954, KNA MLA 1/894.

138  CC 405/1954 'Kirau Gauma', Beechgaad to Governor, 21 July 1954, KNA MLA 1/916.

139  CC 29/1955 'Gathuku Kinyanjui', Judgment, de Lestang, 12 February 1955, KNA MLA 1/1178.

140  'Incident at the sweepers lhandies, Shauri Moyo, 19 January 1955', TA KNA Nbi/PC/Arch/15/51.

141  'Housing in the British Africa Territories', PRO CO 822/588.

142  DC/Nbi to Dir PWD, 26 April 1954, TA KNA Nbi/PC/Arch/Adm/15/1.

143  Atkinson to Rogers, 4 January 1953, and 'Housing in British African Territories, 1952', both in PRO CO 822/588.

144  Emil Rado and Judith Wells, 'The building industry in Kenya', in John Hutton (ed.), *Urban Challenge in East Africa* (Nairobi, 1971), 200–24.

145  'Records of the Commission of Enquiry, vols 1–10, 1955–56', KNA RN/1/136 to RN/1/146.

146  Summarized from *Rose Commission Report*, 3–6.

147  *Rose Commission Report*, 13–25.

148  Examples from *Rose Commission Report*, 12–13, 26–33, 36–8, 42–4.

149  *Rose Commission Report*, 47–9.

## Chapter 6. General China's War

1  For Itote's life story, see his autobiographies, *Mau Mau General* (Nairobi, 1967); his second book, *Mau Mau in Action* (Nairobi, 1979); B. A. Ogot, *Historical Dictionary of Kenya* (London, 1981), 80–81; and Marshall Clough, *Memoirs*, 72–5.

2  Itote, *General*, 43.

3  Itote, *General*, 50.

4  Itote, *General*, 41.

5  CC 34/1954 'Kefa Manyoni & Karwe Kagume', trial transcript, KNA MLA 1/735.

6  Ian Henderson, with Philip Goodhart, *The Hunt for Kimathi* (London, 1958), 36–8.

7  Majdalany, *State of Emergency*, 194–6.

8  'Interrogation of General China', dated 26 January 1954, in author's possession, courtesy of Professor John Lonsdale.

9  CC 35/1954 'Waruhiu Itote', KNA MLA 1/677.

10  CC 82/1954 'Karani Karanja', Law to Baring, 25 February 1954, KNA MLA 1/720.

11  J. C. Carothers, *The Psychology of Mau Mau* (Nairobi, 1954).

12  Kanogo, *Squatters*, 139; Njama and Barnett, *Mau Mau from Within*, 129; Buijtenhuis, *Essays on Mau Mau*, 36–9.

13  Baring to Lyttelton, 2 March 1953, PRO CO 822/440.

14  CC 153/1954 'Muchange Macharia', trial papers, KNA MLA 1/1250.

15  CC 658/1954 'Njau Thorongo & three others', Hooper to Governor, 21 December 1954, KNA MLA 1/1132.

16  Corfield, *Historical Survey*, 236.

17  Joram Wamweya, *Freedom Fighters* (Nairobi, 1971), 74.

18  Ngugi wa Thiong'o, *Petals of Blood* (London, 1977); Ngugi wa Thiong'o, *A Grain of Wheat* (London, 1967).

19  *EAS*, 29 August 1952, 27.

20  M. Tamarkin, 'The Loyalists in Nakuru during the Mau Mau revolt and its aftermath 1953–63', *Asian & African Studies* (Tel Aviv), 12 (1978), 247–61.

21  'Kikuyu ministers sign six pint anti-Mau Mau pledge', *EAS*, 22 August 1952, 7.

22  Chief Native Commissioner to PC/Central Province, 24 November 1952, KNA VQ/1/30.

23  Hughes (DC/Nyeri) to Superintendent of Police, 1 December 1952, KNA VQ/1/30.

24  Monthly Intelligence Report, Kiambu District, December 1952, KNA VQ/1/30.

25  Monthly Intelligence Report, Kiambu District, December 1952, KNA VQ/1/30.

26  Figure from KNA MAA/7/761.

27  For examples: T. F. C. Bewes, *Kikuyu Conflict* (London, 1953); Anthony Lavers, *The Kikuyu Who Fight Mau Mau* (Nairobi, 1955); K. N. Phillips, *From Mau Mau to Christ* (Stirling Tract, 1958); E. M. Wiseman, *Kikuyu Martyrs* (London, 1953).

28  Donald Barnett, 'Mau Mau: The structural integration and disintegration of the Aberdare guerrilla forces' (PhD thesis, University of California at Los Angeles, 1963), 71–3.

29  Clough, *Memoirs*, 73.

30  Edgerton, *Mau Mau*, 112.

31  Clough, *Memoirs*, 135–42.

32  *Kenya Calling*, no. 76, 29 January 1955.

33  Edgerton, *Mau Mau*, 115–6.

34  Cora Ann Presley, *Kikuyu Women, the Mau Mau Rebellion, and Social Change in Kenya* (Boulder, 1992); Luise White, 'Separating the men from the boys: constructions of gender, sexuality and terrorism in Central Kenya, 1939–59', *International Journal of African Historical Studies*, 23 (1990), 1–25.

35  Barnett and Njama, *Mau Mau from Within*, 221–2, 226–7.

36  Henderson, *Hunt*, 97–115.

37  Heather, 'Intelligence', 95–6.

38  Heather, 'Intelligence', 111–14.

39  Barnett, 'Mau Mau', 103–4, 114, 126–7, 134.

40  Njama & Barnett, *Mau Mau From Within*, for Njama's own story.

41  Peterson, 'Writing in revolution', 76–95.

42  H. Kahinga Wachanga, *The Swords of Kirinyaga* (Nairobi, 1975).

43  Kitson, *Gangs*, for Kago's activities.

44  CC 331/1954 'Joshua Douglas', KNA MLA 1/989. General Gatunga was hanged on 16 August 1954.

45  For example, CC 74/1953 'Waingatu Ruga', KNA MLA 1/551.

46  CC 118/1953 'Muchiri Gathothwa & Ndambini Kiamburi', KNA MLA 1/586.

47  CC 199/1953 'Mungai Kihika', judgment, 27 January 1954, KNA MLA 1/572.

48  Hughes to PC/Central Province, 15 December 1952, and subsequent letters, KNA VQ/1/30.

49  M. P. K. Sorrenson, *Land Reform in the Kikuyu Country* (London, 1967), 103–4, from *Proclamation Rules and Regulations*.

50  Njama & Barnett, *Mau Mau from Within*, 177–8; interviews at Othaya, July 2002.

51  Sorrenson, *Land Reform*, 109.

52  Greet Kershaw, *Mau Mau From Below* (Oxford, 1997), 251–7.

53  E. N. Wanyoike, *An African Pastor* (Nairobi, 1974), 200.

54  *EAS*, 9 April 1953.

55  CC 38/1953 'Karanja Waichonge, Kabogo Kangethe & Miugai Gathura', KNA RR 11/10.

56  'Organisation and strengthening of Home Guard', 3 April 1953, KNA VQ/1/30.

57  See papers in KNA VQ/1/30.

58  O'Hagan to Chief Native Commissioner, 20 March 1953, KNA VQ/1/30.

59  Swann (DC/Meru) to O'Hagan, 13 May 1953, KNA VQ/1/30.

60  Editorial, *Baraza*, 11 April 1953.

61  Erskine to CIGS, 7 July 1953, PRO WO 216/855; Clayton, *Counter-insurgency*, 37–42.

62  The full text, dated 23 June 1953, is in Pro CO 822/474.

63  Erskine to Lady Erskine, 28 November 1953.

64  Luke Wilkins, 'Control and command: the imposition of discipline an the fight against Mau Mau, 1953–54' (MA dissertation, SOAS, London, 1998).

65  Reported in all British dailies on 1 December 1953.

66  *Parliamentary Debates, House of Commons*, 26 January 1954.

67  Clayton, *Counter-insurgency*, 41–2.

68  Potter to Hugh Fraser (MP), 18 April 1953, Pro CO 822/474.

69  Interview, May 1997.

70  Erskine to Harding, June 1953, PRO CO 822/693.

71  The quotes are from Erskine to Lady Erskine, 17 January and 3 June 1954, cited in Clayton, *Counter-insurgency*, 11.

72  Erskine to Lady Erskine, 29 June 1953, cited in Clayton, *Counter-insurgency*, 7.

73  Leigh, *Shadow*, 173.

74  Clayton, *Counter-insurgency*, 43.

75  *The Times*, 8 August 1953.

76  'Interrogation of General China', 26 January 1954, and Barnett, 'Mau Mau', 115.

77  Erskine to Harding, 7 July 1953, PRO WO 216/855.

78  Barnett, 'Mau Mau', 124.

79  Erskine, 'Kenya Emergency', 2 May 1955, para. 24, PRO WO 236/18.

80  Erskine to Harding, 23 July 1953, PRO CO 822/693.

81  'Future Police Establishment', Government House, 27 July 1953, KNA MFP/7/10/4.

82  Sidney Fazan, *History of the Loyalists* (Nairobi, 1958), 35–7, though he exaggerates all the figures.

83  Fazan, *Loyalists*, 37.

84  Anthony Lavers, *The Kikuyu Who fight Mau Mau* (Nairobi, 1955), 24–6. The frontispiece carries Njiri's photograph.

85  Fazan, *Loyalists*, 38–9.

86  Fazan, *Loyalists*, 52.

87  CC 169/1953 'Mwangi Kara & 19 others', KNA MLA 1/752; Fazan, *Loyalists*, 51, says 40 rebels were killed.

88  CC 9/1954 'Kiambati Murithe & 2 others', KNA MLA 1/769.

89  Kitson, *Gangs*; Fazan, *Loyalists*, 62–3.

90  Three men hanged: CC 247/1954 'Mungai Mutiri & 2 others', KNA MLA 1/858.

91  CC 391/1954 'M'Muthami M'Mwiritha & 5 others', judgment, 16 September 1954, KNA MLA 1/1036.

92  Heather, 'Intelligence', 157–8.

93  Blundell, *Wind*, 130.

94  Erskine, 'Kenya Emergency', 2 May 1955, para. 75–7, PRO WO 236/18.

95  Heather, 'Intelligence', 209.

96  Heather, 'Intelligence', 235, fn. 27.

97  'Statistical Handout', 12 April 1955, PRO WO 236/18.

98  Erskine, 'Kenya Emergency', 2 May 1955, para. 11, PRO WO 236/18.

99  CC 531.1954 'Kimani Githinji & 2 others', KNA MLA 1/1045; CC 126/1955 'Muchiri Mwehe', KNA MLA 1/1273.

100  O'Rorke to Hugh Fraser, 'Notes on Kenya Police', March 1954, PRO CO 1037/36.

101  Fazan, *Loyalists*, 71.

102  'Secretariat: Emergency Measures, 1954', KNA MAA/8/171.

103  Sorrenson, *Land Reform*, 104.

104  *Legislative Council Debates*, vol. LXV, 16 June 1955, 1675–92.

105  Sorrenson, *Land Reform*, 105–6.

106  Baring to Lyttelton, 15 February 1954, PRO CO 822/774; 'Prosecution of surrendered terrorists', 28 July 1954, PRO CO 822/496.

107  'A Short History of Operation Wedgwood', April 1954, PRO CO 822/744; G. W. Croker, 'Mau Mau', *Journal of the Royal United Services Institute*, vol. C (Feb–Nov 1955), 47–53; Itote, *General*, 155–9.

108  Barnett and Njama, *Mau Mau From Within*, 348–56.

109  Fazan, *Loyalists*, 63.

110  Barnett and Njama, *Mau Mau From Within*, 348–56.

111  *The Times*, 5 March 1954.

112  Gribble to Young, 7 December 1954, Young Papers, Rhodes House, File 3, 31–2.

113  Fazan, *Loyalists*, 63.

114  Crawford to Lyttelton, 30 March & 11 April 1954, PRO CO 822/774.

115  Edgerton, *Mau Mau*, 90.

116  Fazan, *Loyalists*, and Majdalany, *State of Emergency*, blame Gatamuki, but the archival record points toward the KAR as villains of the piece.

117  CC 91/1954 'Miano Ngemwe', statement of accused, 25 march 1954, KNA MLA 1/766.

118  Clough, *Memoirs*, 73–4.

119  Recounted in Blundell, *Wind*, 183–5.

120  Heather, 'Intelligence', 154–6.

121  'Meeting with African representatives', 17 March 1954, PRO CO 822/822.

122  Ruark, *Something of Value*, 386.

123  Antony Smith, *High Street Africa* (London, 1961), 134.

124  Blundell, *Wind*, 171.

125  Quotes taken from Lennox-Boyd's statement to the Commons in response to the motion of censure after the Hola camp deaths.

126  Elkins, 'Detention and rehabilitation', 137–9.

127  H. E. Lambert, *Kikuyu Social and Political Institutions* (London, 1956).

128  Berman and Lonsdale, 'Louis Leakey's Mau Mau', 143–204.

129  Leakey, *Mau Mau and the Kikuyu*; Leakey, *Defeating Mau Mau*.

130  Jock McCulloch, *Colonial Psychiatry and 'The African Mind'* (Cambridge, 1985).

131  Lonsdale, 'Mau Maus of the mind', 410–11.

132  Heather, 'Intelligence', 189–90.

133  Kitson, *Gangs*, 72–95.

134  Hewitt, *Kenya Cowboy*, 237–58.

135  Details of his life can be gathered from Njama and Narnett, *Mau Mau from Within*, Tabitha Kanogo, *Dedan Kimathi* (Nairobi, 1996), and Henderson & Goodhart, *Hunt*.

136  Henderson & Goodhart, *Hunt*.

## Chapter 7. Crimes of Punishment

1  'Privy Council Petition, Dedan Kimathi Wachiuri', and related papers, KNA MAC/KEN/73/11.

2  Based on original correspondence from the Consolata Archive, Rome, generously copied by Dr Christiani Pugliese.

3  Christopher Hibbert, *The Roots of Evil: A Social History of Crime and Punishment* (London, 1963), 373–9, 393–6.

4  Robert Holland (ed.), *Emergencies and Disorder in the European Empires after 1945* (London, 1994).

5  J. Talbott, *The War without a Name: France in Algeria 1954–62* (London, 1981); Benjamin Stora, 'Algeria: the war without a name', in Holland (ed.), *Emergencies*, 208–16; Benjamin Stora, *Histoire de la guerre d'Algérie (1954–62)* (Paris, 1993); Alistair Horne, *A Savage War of Peace: Algeria 1954–62* (London, 1977).

6  P. Aussaresses, *Services speciaux: Algérie, 1955–57* (Paris, 2001) repeated the admissions in print, provoking a heated debate in the pages of *Le Monde* during May 2001.

7  Martin S. Alexander, Martin Evans & J. F. V. Keiger (eds.), *The Algerian War*

*and the French Army, 1954–62: Experiences, Images, Testimonies* (Basingstoke, 2002).

8   Alistair Horne, 'The French Army and the Algerian War 1954–62', in Ronald Haycock (ed.), *Regular Armies and Counter-insurgency* (London, 1979), 79.

9   Bruce Berman, 'Bureaucracy and incumbent violence: colonial administration and the origins of the Mau Mau emergency', *British Journal of Political Science*, 6 (1976), and *Control and Crisis in Colonial Kenya: The Dialectic of Domination* (London, 1990).

10  Alfonso Peter Castro and Kreg Ettenger, 'Counter-insurgency and socio-economic change: the Mau Mau war in Kirinyaga, Kenya', *Research in Economic Anthropology*, 15 (1994), 63–101.

11  Sorrenson, *Land Reform*, 110–11.

12  *EAS*, 20 October 1955.

13  Sorrenson, *Land Reform*, describes the process in detail for Nyeri, Murang'a and Kiambu.

14  CC 472/1954 'Kangethe Kangau and Gibson Mwangi', KNA MLA 1/982.

15  CC 105/1955 'Kariuki Hungu', Goudie to Baring, 21 May 1955, KNA MLA 1/1237.

16  CC 131/1955 'Muhia Kamau & 5 others', KNA MLA 1/1299.

17  CC 121/1955 'Indiru Mutua – alias General Russia', KNA MLA 1/1258.

18  CC 6/1956 'Gathitu Kiondu', KNA MLA 1/1360.

19  CC 583/1954 'Githinji Njaguna and Mwangi Mweru', trial transcript and statements, and CA 988 & 989/1954, Judgement, 23 December 1954, KNA MLA 1/1098.

20  The following is taken from the full transcript of the trial papers: CC 240/1954 'Murui Wamai & 5 others', KNA MLA 1/1179.

21  Clayton, *Counter-insurgency.*

22  Edgerton, *Mau Mau*, 155, quoting an anonymous interview from July 1962.

23  MacPherson to Young, 23 December 1954; Young to Baring, 22 November, 14 December and 28 December 1954, all Young papers, Rhodes House.

24  Young to Baring, 14 December 1954, Young Papers, Rhodes House.

25  Erskine to Redman, 29 December 1954, PRO WO 216/879.

26  A detailed precise of the relevant documents appears in PRO CO 822/1293. There are further materials in Young's own papers, at Rhodes House, Oxford.

27  The quotes are from Anne Perkins, *Red Queen: The Authorized Biography of Barbara Castle* (London, 2003), 137–9. On Lennox-Boyd, see Philip Murphy, *Alan Lennox-Boyd; A Biography* (London, 1999).

28  Erskine to Harding, 5 January 1955, PRO WO 216/879.

29  Heather, 'Intelligence', 227–8.

30  Baring to Lennox-Boyd, 9 January 1955, PRO CO 822/775.

31  'Text of Governor's Speech at Nyeri, 18 January 1955', KNA (TA) Nbi/PC/Arch/Adm/15/1.

32  Part I of the Holmes Enquiry is in PRO CO 822/787, and Part II in KNA MAA/7/121; Windley to Lennox-Boyd, 25 March 1955, PRO CO 822/787; Nihill and O'Connor to Lennox-Boyd, 11 October 1955, PRO CO 822/785.

33  The phrases are from Perkins, *Red Queen*, 138.

34  Charles Chenevix Trench, *Men Who Ruled Kenya: The Kenya Administration 1892–1963* (London, 1993), 259.

35   Oliver Lyttelton, *The Memoirs of Lord Chandos* (London, 1962).

36   Majdalany, *State of Emergency*, 227–9.

37   Leigh, *Shadow*, 171–2.

38   Leigh, *Shadow*, 172.

39   Evans, *Law and Disorder*, 275–6.

40   Governor's Deputy to Colonial Office, 16 December 1952, PRO CO 822/439.

41   Bewes to Baring, 28 January 1953, PRO CO 822/471.

42   Bewes, *Kikuyu*, 56.

43   The papers on this case are in PRO CO 822/471.

44   Evans, *Law and Disorder*.

45   Clayton, *Counter-insurgency*, 44–5.

46   CC 289/1954 'Wambugu Karanja', Law to O'Connor, 17 January 1955, and related papers from September 1954, KNA MLA 1/1042.

47   Antony Smith, *High Street Africa* (London, 1961), 133–41.

48   David M. Anderson and Daniel Branch, 'Death and disease in the Kenya prison' (unpublished paper, University of Cambridge, February 2004), calculated from Prison Department Annual Reports.

49   Lyttelton to Baring, 5 February 1954, PRO CAB 129/65.

50   'Annexure to Resettle Committee Report', PRO CO 822/801.

51   'Monthly Reports, December 1954–December 1958', KNA AH 6/8, and 'Monthly Reports, January–August 1959'. Elkins, 'Detention and rehabilitation', 151–2.

52   Jomo Kenyatta, *Suffering Without Bitterness: The Founding of the Kenya Nation* (Nairobi, 1968); Josiah Mwangi Kariuki, *Mau Mau Detainee: The Account of a Kenya African of his Experience in Detention Camps 1953–1960* (Oxford, 1963).

53   Gakaara wa Wanjau, *Mau Mau Author in Detention* (Nairobi, 1988); Karigo Muchai, *The Hardcore* (Richmond, BC, 1973); Gucu Gikoyo, *We Fought for Freedom* (Nairobi, 1979).

54   Wambui Waiyaki Otieno, *Mau Mau's Daughter: A Life History* (Boulder, 1998), 77–86.

55   Clough, *Memoirs*, 205.

56   Daniel Branch, 'Cruel and unusual punishment: violence and control in the Kenyan penal system, 1930–1952' (MA dissertation, SOAS, London, 2002).

57   Kariuki, *Detainee*.

58   Ian Enslin, 'Health, violence and rehabilitation: conditions in detention camps in Kenya 1952–60' (MA dissertation, Birkbeck College, London, 1996).

59   The following account is based upon Enslin, 'Health', 6–8, and additional material from PRO CO 822/801.

60   H. G. Waters, 'Public Health Report, Manyani Camp, 9 May 1954', PRO CO 822/801.

61   Kenya Office of Information, Press Release No. 568, 'Medical arrangements at Detention Camps', 10 May 1954.

62   Lewis to Minister of Defence, 'Emergency expenditure: Sanitation, Mackinnon Road & Manyani', 21 May 1954, KNA AH 9/5/16; War Council Secretariat, 'Hygiene of Mackinnon Road & Manyani Detention Camps', 4 June 1954, KNA AH 9/4/6.

63 Enslin, 'Health, violence and rehabilitation', 7–8.

64 H. Stott, 'Typhoid outbreak at Manyani', 14 September 1954, PRO CO822/801.

65 Granville Roberts, 'Typhoid at Manyani', 29 September 1954, PRO CO 822/801/35.

66 War Council Brief, 'Numbers of detainees', 15 October 1954, PRO CO 822/801/35.

67 See Elkins, 'Detention and rehabilitation', 160, for a first-hand account.

68 See Stott to Lewis, 'Central Province Works Camps', 4 September 1954, KNA AH 9/19/22, and Stott 'Report on health and hygiene in Emergency Camps', 9 November 1954, KNA AH 9/13/43.

69 Elkins, 'Detention and rehabilitation', 171.

70 'Work Camps, Kiambu district', 19 January 1956, KNA AH 9/25/187.

71 Dr G. R. Wadsworth, 'Report of visit to Kenya', Kenya Box, London School of Hygiene and Tropical Medicine archive.

72 'General Report on the Mission of the ICRC to Kenya', PRO CO 822/1258.

73 Enslin, 'Health', 12–13, citing correspondence between the ICRC and London, in PRO CO 822/1258.

74 See papers in 'Second Mission of ICRC to Kenya, 1959', PRO CO 822/1258.

75 These examples are quoted in Enslin, 'Health', 12–13.

76 'Second Mission of ICRC to Kenya, 1959', PRO CO 822/1258.

77 *The Truth About Kenya – An Eyewitness Account by Eileen Fletcher*, Conference of British Mission Societies [BCMS], A/T 2/5, box 278, Archives of the School of Oriental & African Studies [SOAS].

78 Joshua Ubaldi, 'Mau Mau detention camps and rehabilitation in Kenya, 1952–59: Eileen Fletcher and the moral conscience of Empire' (BA dissertation, University College London, 1999).

79 'Enquiry into allegations of brutality at Gathigiriri Works Camp (1957)', KNA Library, and related papers in KNA AB/18/1.

80 Peter Benenson (ed.), *Gangrene* (London, 1959), 97–126.

81 CC 181/1954 'Muya Gatura & Wainaina Mureithi', KNA MLA 1/823.

82 CC 93/1954 'Kamuyu Ndegwa & 2 others', KNA MLA 1/920.

83 CC 507/1954 'Mambo Ndwgwa & 7 others', KNA MLA 1/1041.

84 This account draws upon CC 182/1957 'Kiraka Kirangi' KNA RR 11/97.

85 CC 1358/1957 Committal Proceedings, 'Cyril R. Harrison & 2 others', KNA RR 11/101.

86 CC 27/1957 'Kibugi Ruibiri & 10 others', KNA RR 11/95.

87 Willoughby Thompson, interview, June 1999.

88 Govt of the UK, *Documents Relating to the Death of Eleven Mau Mau Detainees at Hola Camp in Kenya*. PP, Cmd 778 (London, 1959); Govt of the UK, *Further Documents Relating to the Death of Eleven Mau Mau Detainees at Hola Camp in Kenya*. PP, Cmd 816 (London, 1959); Govt of the UK, *Record of Proceedings and Evidence in the Enquiry into the Deaths of Eleven Mau Mau Detainees at Hola Camp in Kenya*. PP, Cmd 795 (London, 1959).

## Chapter 8. Spoils of War

1 *Report of the Committee on Emergency Detention Camps [Fairn Report]* (Nairobi,

1959), also printed as a Special Supplement to the *Kenya Gazette*, 1 September 1959.

2   Quoted in Clayton, *Counter-insurgency*, 51.

3   MacLeod, 'Colonial Policy Committee, Kenya: Proposed Amnesty', PRO CO 822/1337.

4   John Darwin, *Britain and Decolonisation: The Retreat from Empire in the Post-War World* (London, 1988).

5   Murphy, *Lennox-Boyd*; and for the context, Philip Murphy, *Party Politics and Decolonization: The Conservative Party and British Colonial Policy in Tropical Africa 1951–1964* (Oxford, 1995).

6   A. N. Porter & A. J. Stockwell, *British Imperial Policy and Decolonization 1938–64*, vol. 2, 33–8.

7   Drawn predominantly from 'Colonial Policy Committee, Kenya: Proposed Amnesty', PRO CO 822/1337, and various papers, 'Cessation of Emergency' PRO CO 822/1230.

8   Keith Kyle, *The Politics of the Independence of Kenya* (Basingstoke, 1999), 113–5.

9   Interview, Michael Blundell, Nairobi, February 1982.

10   Gary Wasserman, *The Politics of Decolonization: Kenya Europeans and the Land Issues 1960–65* (Cambridge, 1976).

11   Kaggia, *Roots*, 179.

12   David Mukara Ng'ang'a, 'Mau Mau, loyalists and politics in Murang'a, 1952–70', *Kenya Historical Review*, 5 (1977).

13   Njama & Barnett, *Mau Mau from Within*, 128.

14   Kariuki, *Detainee*, 142–3.

15   Wamweya, *Freedom Fighter*, 198; Muchai, *Hardcore*, 85.

16   Kariuki, *Detainee*, 145.

17   Kariuki, *Detainee*, 163–4.

18   See Wasserman, *Decolonization*, 15, for British policy.

19   B. A. Ogot, 'The decisive years, 1956–63', in B. A. Ogot and W. R. Ochieng' (eds.), *Decolonization and Independence in Kenya 1940–93* (London, Nairobi, Athens OH, 1995), 48.

20   'With Mzee at Maralal', *Drum Magazine* (November 1970), reprinted in Jim Bailey (ed.), *Kenya: The National Epic* (Nairobi, 1993), 104–7.

21   'Mzee returns!', *Drum Magazine* (May, 1968), reprinted in Bailey (ed.), *Kenya*, 128–30.

22   The quote is from an article in *Drum Magazine* (March 1964), reprinted in Bailey (ed.), *Kenya*, 149.

23   Kenyatta, *Suffering*, 189.

24   Joseph Kariuki, 'Mau Mau associations in the 1990s', in Herve Maupeu (ed.), *L'Afrique Orientale Annuaire 2002* (Paris, 2003), 375.

25   David M. Anderson, 'Mau Mau at the movies: contemporary representations of an anti-colonial war', *South African Historical Journal*, 48 (May 2003), 1–17.

26   *Evening Standard*, 6 April 1956.

27   *New York Times Book Review*, 24 April 1955, section 7:1.

28   Cameron, *Africa on Film*, 122.

29   Interviews with Paul Thuku, Munyi Mutahi, Ngugi Gathecha and Kimunyi, Nyeri, July 2001.

30  'The lost hero – General Mathenge', *Drum Magazine* (April 1986), reprinted in Bailey, *Kenya*, 74.
31  Ngugi wa Thiong'o & Micere Mugo, *The Trial of Dedan Kimathi* (Nairobi, 1976), preface.
32  Martin Gilbert, *Never Despair: Winston S. Churchill 1945–1965* (London, 1988), 834.
33  Interview, Lari, May 2000.

# Glossary

**Anake a forti**  the 40 Group, the name given to the most prominent criminal gang in Nairobi in the mid-1940s
**askari**  soldier or policeman
**baraza**  public meeting
**batuni**  a platoon, and also the name given to one of the strongest Mau Mau oaths
**boma**  enclosure
**gikunia**  the hooded informants used to identify Mau Mau suspects in Operation Anvil, in the detention camps, and at confessional *barazas*
**githaka (ithaka)**  land which belongs to a person or *mbari*
**githathi**  sacred stones used in Kikuyu rituals
**itungati**  Mau Mau forest fighters
**karing'a**  meaning pure, the name given to those who supported the continuation of female circumcision
**kiama**  a council
**kipande**  registration document, carried by all male Africans
**kirori**  a thumb-print, the name given to those who sighed the order issued by the missions outlawing female circumcision
**komerera**  bandits, the name given to Mau Mau groups who operated independently, raiding into the Kikuyu Reserves
**mbari**  name for a descent group which owns its land jointly and individually. The word is also used for the land itself.
**Muhimu**  the central committee who organised Mau Mau from Nairobi, later extending into the Kikuyu Reserves
**Muhoi (ahoi)**  someone who uses land, but is not a member of the descent group who hold rights in the land
**Ngai**  God
**Nyimbo**  songs
**panga**  large and heavy-bladed knife, used in farm work
**safari**  a journey
**shamba**  Swahili term for a cultivated garden
**Tai-tai**  nickname for the African clerks and other office workers in Nairobi who wore European-style clothing

# Chronology

| | |
|---|---|
| **18 June 1895** | British proclaim a Protectorate over East Africa |
| **1896–1901** | Great East African railway constructed from Mombasa to Lake Victoria (Nyanza), opening up East African trade |

| 1902 | First white settlers arrive to take up land in Kenya's central highlands |
| 1907 | Kenya's Legislative Council is formed, with white settler members |

## 1920s

| 1920 | East African Protectorate becomes Kenya Colony |
| December 1920 | Young Kikuyu Association formed |
| March 1922 | Arrest of Harry Thuku leads to shooting of African supporters in Nairobi |
| July 1923 | White Paper on Indians in Kenya issues ruling on African paramountcy in colonial policy, known as the 'Devonshire declaration'. This ruling denies Indians the right to hold land in the White Highlands |
| 1923 | British territory of Southern Rhodesia becomes self-governing under a white settler government |
| 1926 | Kikuyu Central Association [KCA] founded |
| 1928 | Jomo Kenyatta becomes editor of KCA newsletter, *Muigwathania* |
| 1929 | Kenyatta leaves Kenya to represent KCA in London |

## 1930s

| 1930 | Crisis over female circumcision promotes creation of independent schools movement among Kikuyu |
| 1932 | Kenya Land Commissioners visit Kenya and take evidence on African land requirements |
| May 1934 | Report of Kenya Land Commission published, denying and nullifying virtually all Kikuyu land claims against European expropriation |
| 1939 | Peter Mbiyu Koinange returns from USA |

## 1940s

| 1941 | KCA banned as part of wartime clamp-down on dissent |
| February 1942 | Fall of Singapore to Japanese leads to great increase in demand for agricultural produce from Kenya |
| September 1944 | Sir Philip Mitchell becomes Governor of Kenya |
| October 1944 | Kenya Africa Study Union formed, later to be renamed as the Kenya African Union (KAU) |
| | Oxford-educated Eluid Mathu becomes the first African Member of Kenya's Legislative Council |
| 1944 | Kikuyu at Olenguruone resettlement scheme take oath of unity to defy government imposition of controls |
| | Land crisis emerging in Central province, with beginnings of government terracing campaign in the Kikuyu countryside |
| 1945 | Restrictions begin to be imposed on cattle-holding by squatters on European-owned farms in Rift Valley, and first Kikuyu repatriations begin |

| | |
|---|---|
| **December 1945** | Proposal for constitutional change in Kenya are rejected by African political leaders as doing too little to advance African representation |
| **1946** | First squatter resistance to repatriation, with strikes and arson attacks against white farms |
| **September 1946** | Jomo Kenyatta returns to Kenya from London |
| **February 1947** | Kenyatta and Koinange visit Olenguruone |
| | A further constitutional reform again disappoints Africans, leading Eluid Mathu to campaign for the introduction of more rapid political change giving Africans greater political freedom |
| **June 1947** | Kenyatta becomes President of KAU |
| **July 1947** | Violent opposition to government cattle-dipping campaign in Nyeri |
| **August 1947** | 'Women's revolt' against terracing in Murang'a |
| **September 1947** | Strike at Uplands Bacon Factory in Kiambu, leading to a riot and the shooting of African strikers |
| **Late 1947** | *Muhimu* activities in Nairobi becoming apparent, within context of increased criminality, led by the 40 Group |
| **1948** | National Party wins South African general election and begins to implement policy of *apartheid* |
| **April 1948** | Kenya's Legislative Council has an unofficial majority, with four nominated African members but no elections for Africans |
| **1949** | Moderate leaders of KAU in Kiambu seek to co-opt the radical leaders of Nairobi's *Muhimu* |
| **November 1949** | Evictions of Kikuyu from Olenguruone |

## 1950

| | |
|---|---|
| **1950** | Mass oathing begins throughout central Kenya, led by *Muhimu* activists |
| **1950** | First *apartheid* laws passed in South Africa |
| **February 1950** | Attempts to assassinate two moderate African leaders in Nairobi, Mbotela and Gikoyo, for which crimes the radical *Muhimu* leader and trade unionist Fred Kubai is arrested |
| **May 1950** | Nairobi General Strike |
| **July 1950** | District officers in Nyeri report threats against lives of African chiefs |
| **August 1950** | Mau Mau movement is outlawed |

## 1951

| | |
|---|---|
| **February 1951** | Kubai released, and *Muhimu* oathing campaign stepped up |
| **February 1951** | KAU moderates call for a common roll and elections, but this is rejected by Governor Mitchell |
| **June 1951** | Radicals seize control of KAU in Nairobi |
| **25 October 1951** | General election in Britain brings Conservative Party back to government, with Winston Churchill as Prime Minister |

| | |
|---|---|
| **November 1951** | Violent resistance to government inoculations of cattle in Murang'a |
| **1951** | Kwame Nkrumah's Convention People's Party wins general election in Gold Coast, and he goes onto become first Prime Minister |

# 1952

| | |
|---|---|
| **1952** | Pass Laws introduced in South Africa, forcing all non-whites to carry identification cards |
| **1952** | Kenya's Legislative Council enlarged, with six nominated African members, and one African nominated to the Executive Council, but still no elections |
| **February 1952** | Royal Visit to Kenya of Princess Elizabeth, who receives news of the death of her father, King George VI, whilst at Treetops, in the Aberdares forest |
| **January/February 1952** | Arson attacks against white farmers in Nanyuki, and against government chiefs in Nyeri |
| **April 1952** | First full administrative report on Mau Mau, compiled by Director of Intelligence & Security |
| **May 1952** | Mau Mau assassinations of 'loyal' Africans begin. 59 will be murdered over the next six months |
| **21 June 1952** | Reports of militants administering a 'killing oath' to followers in Nyeri and Kiambu |
| **July/August 1952** | Anti-Mau Mau 'cleansing' ceremonies in Kiambu and Murang'a |
| | Legislative Council debate on law and order – settlers demand firm government action against Mau Mau |
| **August 1952** | Warahiu Itote (General China) goes to forest |
| **21 September 1952** | Sir Evelyn Baring arrives to take up duty as Governor |
| **7 October 1952** | The government's 'tower of strength', Paramount Chief Waruhiu, murdered near Nairobi |
| **20/21 October 1952** | Emergency declared by Governor Baring |
| | First British battalion arrives, Lancashire Fusiliers |
| | Six battalions of the King's African Rifles based in Kenya (Kenya 3rd, 5th, 7th and 23rd; Uganda 4th; Tanganyika 6th) |
| | Operation Jock Scott – roundup of Mau Mau suspects. More than 80 African political activists arrested |
| **22 October 1952** | Chief Nderi murdered in Murang'a |
| **28 October 1952** | Two MPs from the opposition Labour Party, Fenner Brockway and Lionel Hale, arrive in Kenya at invitation of the KAU |
| **29 October 1952** | Oliver Lyttelton, Secretary of State for the Colonies in Churchill's Conservative government, arrives to consult with Governor Baring |
| **November 1952** | Large scale 'repatriation' of Kikuyu squatters from Rift Valley farms |
| **11 November 1952** | The two Kikuyu independent school's organisations, K.I.S.A. and K.K.E.A. are declared illegal, and their assets and seized. 34 independent Kikuyu schools are closed by government |

| | |
|---|---|
| **12 November 1952** | First white settler murdered by Mau Mau |
| **17 November 1952** | Kenyatta trial begins at Kapenguria |
| **26 November 1952** | Tom Mbotela murdered in Nairobi |
| **24 December 1952** | Christmas Eve attacks upon Christian Kikuyu loyalists in Nyeri |

## 1953

| | |
|---|---|
| **1953** | South African government brings in emergency legislature to deal with African passive resistance |
| **January 1953** | Government begins to build up Home Guard |
| **January–June 1953** | Mau Mau offensive against white settler farms |
| **24 January 1953** | Ruck murders. Settlers march on Government House |
| **26 March 1953** | Lari massacre, and retaliation |
| | Mau Mau raid on Naivasha police post |
| **March–August 1953** | Mau Mau offensive against Home Guard and Loyalists in the Reserves |
| **April 1953** | Additional legislation introduced under the Emergency Powers regulations, intensifying collective punishments and extending capital punishment |
| **7 April 1953** | Two further British battalions arrive, Devons and Buffs, bringing total to nine military battalions in all |
| **8 April 1953** | Kenyatta trial at Kapenguria ends |
| **End April** | Lari trials begin |
| **8 May 1953** | Unsuccessful Mau Mau raid on Othaya police post |
| **June 1953** | Special Emergency Assize Courts begin to hear Mau Mau Cases |
| **7 June 1953** | General George Erskine arrives in Kenya |
| | Frederick Crawford arrives in Nairobi to take up post as Deputy Governor |
| **8 June 1953** | KAU formally banned |
| **July 1953** | Erskine mounts offensive against forest armies. Dedan Kimathi identified as 'most wanted' rebel leader |
| **1 August 1953** | Black Watch battalion arrives to replace Lancashire Fusiliers |
| **24 August 1953** | First surrender offer to Mau Mau fighters |
| **29 September 1953** | Inniskillings and Northumberland Fusiliers arrive, bringing number of battalions to 11 |
| **October 1953** | First Lari convicts are hanged at Githunguri |
| **21 November 1953** | Ambrose Ofafa murdered in Nairobi |
| **27 November 1953** | Royal Bucks arrive to replace Buffs, and King's Own Yorkshire Light Infantry arrive, bringing battalions to campaign maximum of 12 |
| **December 1953** | Swynnerton Plan for development of African agriculture |

## 1954

| | |
|---|---|
| **January 1954** | Parliamentary delegation visit Kenya from UK |
| **15 January 1954** | General China captured in Murang'a |
| **February 1954** | Devons leave, reducing battalions to 11. |
| | Carpenter Report published (African wages) |
| | Surrender negotiations begin with China |
| **March 1954** | Lyttelton Constitution announced |
| | War Council created |
| | Arthur Young arrives as Commissioner of Police |
| | Surrender negotiations collapse |
| **2 April 1954** | Black Watch leave, reducing battalions to 10 |
| **24 April–21 May 1954** | Operation Anvil |
| **June 1954** | Gloucestershire Regiment and King's Shropshire Light Infantry arrive, and Inniskillings leave, taking number of battalions back to 11 |
| | Villagization begins in Kikuyu Reserves |
| **August 1954** | Northumberland Fusiliers and 4th KAR (Uganda) leave, reducing military to 9 battalions |
| **November 1954** | King's Own Yorkshire Infantry leave, reducing battalions to 8 |
| | Lennox-Boyd replaces Lyttelton as Secretary of State for the Colonies |
| **10 December 1954** | Cram's judgment in Ruthagathi case |
| **14 December 1954** | Young resigns as Commissioner of Police |

## 1955

| | |
|---|---|
| **18 January 1955** | Surrender offer made, and amnesty declared saving security forces from prosecution |
| **5 April 1955** | Churchill resigns as Prime Minister, to be succeeded by Antony Eden |
| **April 1955** | 6th KAR (Tanganyika) leave, bringing number of battalions down to 7 |
| **26 May 1955** | Conservatives win general election |
| **May 1955** | General Lathbury arrives to take over from Erskine |
| | Gloucestershire and Royal Bucks depart, leaving only 4 battalions of the KAR and 1 battalion of the King's Shropshire Light Infantry in Kenya |
| **June 1955** | Government lifts ban on local African political organisations |
| **10 July 1955** | Surrender offer ends, and pseudo-operations in forests intensify |
| **November 1955** | Barbara Castle (Labour Party) visits Kenya and publicises accusations about torture of Mau Mau suspects |
| **1955** | State of Emergency declared by French government in Algeria |

# 1956

| | |
|---|---|
| **1956** | Sudan gains independence from Britain |
| **February 1956** | British parliament debates the abolition of hanging |
| **May 1956** | Eileen Fletcher's accusations of torture and ill-treatment of detainees published in London |
| **August 1956** | Registration of African voters for Legislative Council elections begins, but restricted to Loyalists in Central Province |
| **21 October 1956** | Dedan Kimathi captured |
| **29 October 1956** | Suez crises explodes with Israeli invasion. French and British forces attack on Canal Zone two days later |
| **17 November 1956** | British Army units withdrawn from forest operations against Mau Mau |
| **27 November 1956** | Dedan Kimathi's trial, at Nyeri |

# 1957

| | |
|---|---|
| **1957** | Gold Coast achieves independence from Britain as Ghana |
| **9 January 1957** | Eden resigns as Prime Minister, to be replaced by Harold Macmillan |
| **18 February** | Dedan Kimathi hanged |
| **March** | First African elections for Legislative Council, with limited franchise (property, education and loyalty certificates) |
| **31 August 1957** | Malayan Federation gains independence from Britain |

# 1958

| | |
|---|---|
| **1958** | Lennox-Boyd Constitution increases Legislative Council substantially, to include elected African members |
| | Last hangings of Mau Mau convicts |

# 1959

| | |
|---|---|
| **3 March 1959** | Murder of 11 detainees at Hola Camp |
| **27 July 1959** | House of Commons debate on Hola Camp |
| **1 September 1959** | Fairn report published, admitting British use of excessive force in the emergency detention camps |
| **1959** | Sir Patrick Renison replaces Evelyn Baring as governor of Kenya |
| **1959** | Macmillan wins general election, and in Cabinet reshuffle Iain Macleod replaces Lennox-Boyd as Secretary of State for the Colonies |

# 1960

| | |
|---|---|
| **12 January 1960** | Emergency in Kenya ended |
| **3 February 1960** | Harold Macmillan's 'Wind of Change' speech in Cape Town |
| **1960** | Nigeria and Somalia achieve independence from Britain |
| **1960** | Congo achieves independence from Belgium, followed by violence |

| | |
|---|---|
| **1960** | First Kenyan constitutional conference in London, at Lancaster House, leads to further increase in size of Legislative Council giving Africans an effective majority |
| **1960** | Kenya African National Union [KANU] formed, with alliance of Kikuyu and Luo politicians |
| **1960** | Kenya African Democratic Union [KADU] formed, with alliance of Kalenjin, Maasai and liberal European and other minority political groupings |

## 1961

| | |
|---|---|
| **1961** | *Apartheid* South Africa becomes a republic and leaves the British Commonwealth |
| **1961** | Tanganyika gains independence from Britain |
| **14 August 1961** | Kenyatta is released from detention and returns to Gatundu, Kiambu |

## 1962

| | |
|---|---|
| **1962** | French agree to Algerian independence at Evian Peace talks |
| **1962** | Uganda becomes independent |
| **14 February–6 April 1962** | Second Kenya constitutional conference in London |
| **15 June 1962** | General China (Waruhiu Itote) released from prison |
| **18 November 1962** | Malcolm Macdonald appointed as Kenya's final colonial Governor |

## 1963

| | |
|---|---|
| **8 April 1963** | New constitution proclaimed, paving way for independence elections |
| **18-25 May 1963** | General elections, on a common franchise, with a sweeping KANU victory |
| **1 June 1963** | Jomo Kenyatta invested as Kenya's first Prime Minister |
| **25 September–19 October 1963** | Third and final Kenyan constitutional conference in London |
| **18 October 1963** | Harold Macmillan resigns as Prime Minister, to be replaced by Sir Alex Douglas-Home |
| **12 December 1963** | Kenya achieves independence from Britain, under presidency of Jomo Kenyatta |

# Acknowledgements

The research for this book began in the mid-1990s, when I first located the legal papers for the Mau Mau trials in the Kenya National Archive, Nairobi. I was initially so overwhelmed by the sheer quantity of material, and by the richness of the many stories of human tragedy that these historical papers revealed, that I imagined writing several books cataloguing the deeper local histories of the struggle. This ambition soon gave way to the practical realization that an informed and candid general history of the Mau Mau war had not yet been written. As it dawned upon me that these unique materials might provide a distinctive and revealing pathway through the story of the end of empire in Kenya, this book gradually took its present shape.

In six public lectures delivered in October and November 2002, as Evans-Pritchard Visiting Lecturer at All Souls College, Oxford, I then rehearsed my ideas before an attentive and probing audience. The questions that followed those lectures sharpened my awareness of the strengths and weaknesses of my approach, and went a considerable way towards improving the final draft of the book. I must express my sincere gratitude to the electors of the Evans-Pritchard Lectureship, and to the Warden and Fellows of All Souls College, for the opportunity this provided for deeper reflection on the project, and for the tremendous impetus it gave to my writing.

This book could not have been written without the assistance of a great many people. The most important of these are undoubtedly Musila Musembi, the Director of the Kenya National Archives, and his Reading Room staff. They have collectively been unfailingly helpful to me over many years. A historical truffle-hunter by nature, preferring to dip into archives to see what tasty morsels I can unearth, for this project I had to become a sludge-gulper – working my way systematically through a catalogue of over a thousand case files. This suited neither my temperament nor my inclinations. The archive staff sensed my discomfort and did their best to ease my burdens. I was allowed to order files by the box, rather than be limited to six at a time. This greatly speeded up the process of gathering the data and allowed me to more easily cross-reference separate trial papers relating to common events. At a later stage on the project, by then familiar with the character of the story I was reconstructing, archives staff drew my attention to several important files that I might otherwise have overlooked. I am well aware that this is a higher standard of service than any jobbing historian deserves, and it is a debt I am only too happy to acknowledge.

Henry Mutoru and Godfrey Muriuki were always helpful and welcoming colleagues at the University of Nairobi. The British Institute in Eastern Africa (BIEA) provided a base for my many research visits. The BIEA's director, Paul Lane, and three consecutive assistant directors, Justin Willis, Shane Doyle and Andrew Burton, were all hospitable companions. Thanks must also be extended to John Lonsdale, Ed Steinhart, Richard Waller, Andrew Burton, Joyce Kannan, Mike Jennings, Chloe Campbell, Dave Hyde and Daniel Branch, friends and colleagues all, the latter six sometime-students, who listened to my ill-formed ideas and thoughts and had the tolerance to endure the barrage and the patience to offer constructive comments. John Lonsdale, with typical generosity, provided numerous sources that I would otherwise have missed and was always prompt to respond to my many calls for help. Derek Peterson generously shared data on Christian communities in Nyeri; Greet Kershaw made available to me her field-notes from her time in Kiambu at the end of the 1950s; and Daniel Branch located additional materials in Kenya during the final phase of writing up the research. Sultan Somjee introduced me to war veterans in Nyeri, and was also instrumental in my meeting survivors from Lari. Andrew Burton and Justin Willis provided assistance with translating pieces of the *shenzi kabisa* Kiswahili from police reports and court records, and Ben Knighton helped with advice on Kikuyu words. Paul Lane joined me in exploring the materials at the National Museum. Two scholars working under the BIEA's Graduate Training Scheme contributed important elements to the project: Gabrielle Lynch meticulously logged the somewhat gruesome materials from the National Museum in Nairobi; and Kathleen Gotts catalogued the newspaper sources on Lari. And I must thank Ed Paice. Ed's enthusiasm for the history of Africa miraculously survived my stumbling efforts to teach him more than twenty years ago, and he is now a firm friend and a distinguished historical author. It was Ed who first convinced me that *Histories of the Hanged* could be written, and his encouragement has been a boon at times when I felt myself to be losing my way.

At an early stage of this project, my work was supported by a seed grant from the Research Fund of SOAS, London, where I was then employed, and then by a research award from the British Academy for archival studies in Kenya and in the UK. The Evans-Pritchard Visiting

Lectureship at All Souls College was of huge benefit in the final phase of writing this book. I must also express my gratitude to the Rhodes Professor of Race Relations, William Beinart, and the members of the African Studies Committee at the University of Oxford, for funding a last (and somewhat nervy) research visit to Nairobi in June 2003. Since October 2002, it has been my privilege to be based at St Antony's College and to work amongst an intellectually lively and immensely supportive group of Africanist colleagues in the University of Oxford. I can only hope that this book lives up to the high standards of scholarship and authorship that they would rightly expect.

St Antony's College, Oxford
December 2003

# Index